IM PRESS

Павел Ильин:
Две жизни — один мир

Составитель и редактор Элла Каган

Бостон · **2021** · Boston

Pavel Ilyin:
Two Lives, One World

Compiled and Edited by Ella Kagan

БОСТОН · **2021** · BOSTON

PAVEL ILYIN: Two Lives, One World

Compiled and Edited by Ella Kagan
Translated by Mary Cochran, Julia LaVilla-Nosova, Irina Kuzes,
Irina Holms, Irina Loring, Liza Evseeva

ПАВЕЛ ИЛЬИН: Две жизни — один мир

Составитель и редактор: Элла Каган
Перевод: Мэри Кокран, Юлия ЛаВилла-Носова, Ирина Кузес,
Ирина Холмс, Инна Лоринг, Лиза Евсеева

ISBN 978-1950319473

Library of Congress Control Number: 2021943377

Published by M•GRAPHICS | BOSTON, MA
✉ mgraphics.books@gmail.com
🖥 mgraphics-books.com

Book Design by M•GRAPHICS © 2021
Cover Design by Ella Shaikind © 2021

Printed in the United States of America

Content/Содержание

PAVEL ILYIN

Two Lives, One World

PREFACE

LEARNING FROM PAVEL ILYIN

by Blair A. Ruble
Distinguished Fellow, Woodrow Wilson Center
Washington, D.C.

I don't remember how we found out about one another but I very much remember the first time I met Pavel Ilyin. I worked for the Social Science Research Council in New York during the late 1980s. The Council was located on the seventeenth floor of the most southerly skyscraper in Midtown Manhattan and 39th Street and Third Avenue. All of downtown Manhattan stretched out from my window from the Empire State Building to the World Trade Center and beyond. The view was a marvel, especially for an urbanist.

Pavel came to visit on one of his first trips to New York. As he walked into my office his eyes grew larger and larger. He then began his own narration explaining the urban machine that stretched out before us. Pavel could explain all the fine details about life in New York even though he had never seen the view we now both were examining. I understood at that moment that I might never meet another human being who understood the urban condition as well as Pavel.

We remained in close touch, became colleagues when I moved to Washington to become Director of the Kennan Institute where he was a scholar, and became close friends thereafter. We frequently collaborated on projects and always found ways of sharing our love of cities with one another. Every once in a while, he would review something I had written and I always knew I would learn from his reaction something new about my own work.

Pavel was for me the ideal scholar and intellectual. Always honest and curious about the world around him Pavel maintained the highest standards of intellectual integrity. He was more than a friend; he was a role model.

During the late 1990s and early 2000s I had the privilege of co-editing a volume on turn-of-the-century Moscow with Pavel and Ella. The resulting *Moskva rubezha XIX i XX stoletii: Vzglyad v proshloe izdaleka* collected eight essays by six authors, appearing in Moscow in 2004. I always sensed that this enterprise was an opportunity for them to set down their thoughts about Moscow with the complete freedom of scholars completely free of life's obstructions imposed by institutional constraints. I loved the process as it liberated me to write and publish a comparison of Moscow and New York around 1900; something I had wanted to do ever since that meeting with Pavel overlooking downtown Manhattan. I always felt this volume — and Pavel's contributions to it — reveal something of the scholar Pavel would have become had life not gotten in the way.

Pavel's essay on the cultural geography of turn-of-the-century Moscow is a masterful innovative work that calls on readers to reconsider everything they think they know about culture in that city. He begins by arguing that, as with all aspects of human existence, culture has its own spatial distribution. The character of a particular city is reflected in and, in turns, shapes that distribution. Where and how theaters are located, for example, are different in Moscow and New York and, as important, in Moscow of a century ago and the Moscow we know today. Appreciating those differences helps us understand Moscow and the art that emanated from it.

As Pavel notes, Moscow was not always a theatrical center. During the middle years of the nineteenth century Moscow had only two professional theaters — The Bolshoi featuring opera and ballet and the Malyi for dramatic theater. Just a few decades later, the city was chock-a-block full of amateur and professional theaters; and the artists of all sorts who made theater possible. This transformation, as he reveals, reflected profound changes in every aspect of Moscow life at a time when it was among the fastest growing cities in the world.

In telling the story of Moscow's theatrical life Pavel reveals profound insights into the merchants who built and sponsored theater, the middle-class audiences who attended them, the actors and writers and directors who shaped what went on stage, the backstage workers who enabled them to do so, and so forth and so on. By the end of Pavel's essay, the reader has a complete view of how Moscow at the time actually worked.

Similarly, Pavel writes about how music and cinema developed, providing important insights into how technology was changing the arts and the city simultaneously. He contrasts the privately sponsored Moscow scene with the state-sponsored cultural life of St. Petersburg; thereby distinguishing these very different yet very Russian cities from one another.

In preparing this essay, Pavel devoted considerable research effort to what he called the "geography of addresses." It is at this moment that the urban geographer takes over much as it did when he stood at my window overlooking Manhattan. His careful work—which presages his subsequent work on town names for the Holocaust Museum—opens up a fresh view of how Moscow fit together. He identifies an expansion of Moscow's cultural zone which similarly tells an important story about how the city developed at this important moment in its history. He concluding section looking at suburban Moscow demonstrates how city and region were merging into a single urban organism.

Pavel's chapter was a discovery for me, as were his other contributions to our volume. Beyond the judiciously collected data, Pavel's analysis revealed a completely new Moscow from that which I knew from other writing and my own work. He revealed the importance of the small—a specific street address—for the large—Moscow and its region—for trying to understand urban processes.

Pavel and I did not formally collaborate after the publication of this particular volume. Nonetheless, his intellectual impact on my own way of understanding cities continued to grow. Watching his work move into new areas and having the pleasure of speaking with him about that work and my own continued to profoundly shape how I have come to think of cities. Most important, Pavel taught me that a city is a verb not a noun. It constantly changes and evolves rather than settles into an object.

Looking back at my initial meeting with Pavel in New York I better appreciate how much of a visionary Pavel truly was. We met at a time when New York was beset by a crack cocaine epidemic, when the city seemed to be hurtling to its own destruction. Pavel had ridden on decrepit subway trains to meet with me; as had I coming to work. The streets were in disrepair and nothing appeared well kept or well-functioning the closer to the ground one came.

Up on the seventeenth floor, Pavel showed me how to set those daily challenges aside for just a moment and to think of New York as an integrated urban machine that was full of dynamism. He made me believe that New York would storm back to national and global prominence. A decade or so later the city was at the top of the world once more; just as Pavel told me it would be as he stood out looking at the sun glisten off the Empire State Building.

INTRODUCTION

Ella Kagan

The book "Pavel Ilyin: Two Lives, One World" is a collection of selected works by my late husband Pavel Ilyin (1936–2015). Only those texts that Pavel merited as his achievement were included in this book. The reader is going to find a variety of pieces from different times as well as different genres.

Pavel Ilyin was a geographer, a historian of the Holocaust, an expert in Russian urban culture and, at the same time, the author of a popular long-running radio show for children. Over the course of his life, he had worked actively for a total of nearly 60 years, first half of it in Russia, and then in the USA.

Pavel graduated from College of Geography at the Moscow State University; he completed his postgraduate studies and defended his PhD at the Institute of Geography of the Academy of Sciences in Moscow where he went on to work. He combined his academic work with long-term engagement with the national radio network for children where he wrote a series of broadcasts featuring geography riddles. Papers reporting results of Pavel's research were published in both the USSR and America long before he landed in the USA.

In 1982, our family applied for emigration visas. When our request was denied American colleagues sent a letter of appeal to the Soviet government demanding that Pavel Ilyin and his family be allowed to leave immediately. The letter was approved at a session of the American Association of Geographers and signed by leading scholars (see full text in the Appendix).

Finally, Pavel and family arrived in America in 1987, and our second life began. Soon upon arrival, Pavel was awarded a grant from the Kennan Institute, a major International center for East-European and Russian studies, in Washington, D.C. The family followed Pavel to the capital.

On arriving in the USA, Pavel devoted his research to toponymy of the USSR and the Russian Empire, that is, the study of place names that embraced history, geography, linguistics, and architecture among other fields of study. Pavel focused on historical approach to geography, or historical toponymy. The results of his study were reported in the paper "Renaming of Soviet Cities after Exceptional People: A Historical Perspective of Toponymy." The paper was a success and got translated into Russian. It appeared in a variety of publications. In another paper, "Toponymic Pogrom in the Ukraine," he demonstrated, taking Ukraine as an example, how the USSR conducted campaigns of massive politically based place renaming at different junctions of Soviet history. Both papers are included in Part I.

For the greater part of his American life, Pavel worked at the United States Holocaust Memorial Museum where he researched geographic aspects of the catastrophe of European Jewry. He considered that project to be one of the greatest importance in his life. He studied changes in names of countries, their boundaries, and misinformation about those changes. His studies examined territories of all European countries occupied by Germany in WW2. In his years with the Holocaust Museum, Pavel amassed a unique collection of historical maps that reflected those changes. The collection is now kept in the Museum's library.

For a Jewish man, it was a sacred mission. He used to say: "If I were a rich man, I would be paying for the honor of doing this kind of work." The results of his studies in Holocaust geography are also presented in Part I of the book.

Pavel was a third generation Moscovite and loved Moscow, the city where he had lived for the first 50 years of his life. He knew this city backward, with its history, geography, lore and architecture, and walking old Moscow lanes, gateways and shortcuts was his favorite pastime. Pavel never stopped reading and collecting books about Moscow, from scholarly treatises to memoirs of Moscovites from varying social circles.

His many years of interest, vast layman knowledge and systematic studies resulted in the book "Moscow at the Turn of the 20th Century: Glance into the Past from Afar." The book has two editors: Pavel Ilyin and Blair Ruble. In Part II of the book, one can find Pavel's chapter, "Cultural Geography of Moscow in the Late Nineteenth, Early Twentieth Centuries". The book's Introduction and Conclusion are written jointly by the two editors.

Pavel's father, Mikhail Ilyin (Myron Turkreltaub, 1901–1967) was a well-known journalist and a popular author of literature for children. In April 1958, he started a series of children's broadcasts at the national radio network that featured a ship's boy named Zakhar Zagadkin, or Zakhar the Riddleman (see Part III). It contained geographic riddles for young listeners to solve and send back the answers. In those pre-computer years, a lot of time and effort went into identifying sources for the scripts and processing the mail. Pavel helped his father at all stages of work since his time in college. The broadcast grew to become very popular with the audience: the authors would get back over a thousand replies at a time. See Part III for the description of some episodes, the texts of Pavel's presentations at conferences devoted to the series, and letters from former listeners.

When his father passed, Pavel continued the series on his own, no matter where his regular place of work was at the time. Neither the father nor the son allowed their names to appear in the credits so that the children could believe in the reality of the leads, ship's boy Zakhar the Riddleman and his friend, the ship's cook. The series ran for 24 years before it was closed. I will be telling the story of its closure in my own memoir in Part V.

Pavel was a true patriot of America, in the best sense of the word. He wrote: "From the moment I arrived, I knew this was my kind of country... I became a US resident in November 1987, a US citizen, in May 1993, and I felt I was fully an American in September 2001...I love America and I've never betrayed this feeling."

Pavel was awed by the sight of a chorus of US Congressmen singing "God Bless America" on Capitol steps after the explosion of World Trade Center towers on September 11, 2001 in New York. As a man of two cultures, he wanted to unite the two. Pavel chose three most popular American songs, "This Land is My Land", "America the Beautiful", and "God Bless America", and told his readers about the authors of their music and lyrics. Most importantly, he translated the songs into Russian and the resulting verses go well with the tunes. Pavel's essay on these three songs, their texts in Russian translation and his own recollections of this work in progress are to be found in Part IV.

Part V contains personal recollections of Pavel by his friends, colleagues, and family members.

This book has been made possible owing to the efforts of many people. First, I'd like to express my most sincere gratitude to the two people who gave me wealth of advice and support, in words and deeds, over all the years of work on the book, Igor Krupnik and Blair Ruble. I doubt I could have completed this project without their help.

I'd also like to thank our friends and colleagues who, while living in different cities and countries, have each contributed, in their own ways, to my work on the book. Those are Vladimir Frumkin, Robert Gohstand, Gregory Ioffe, Pavel Polian, and Svetlana Vasilyeva.

I am most grateful to everyone who contributed their own recollections of Pavel Ilyin. My daughter, Nadya Ilyin Bartol, and her husband, Timothy Bartol, have accompanied me at every step of this long and strenuous path. The publication of this lovely book, so dear to my heart, was greatly assisted by its translators Marie Cochran, Julia LaVilla, Irina Holmes, Irina Kuzes, Liza Evsikova.

Thank you to all of you!

Ella Kagan

PART I

Cities and Their Destinies
(Historical Toponymy)

RENAMING OF SOVIET CITIES AFTER EXCEPTIONAL PEOPLE: A HISTORICAL PERSPECTIVE ON TOPONYMY

Pavel Ilyin

Abstract: A senior urban geographer examines historical trends in the renaming of urban places bearing people's names in the former USSR, from the Bolshevik Revolution to the formal end of its existence in December 1991. Particular attention is devoted to waves of renamings (a) to honor political and military leaders during the 1920s and 1930s; (b) to erase the legacy of Stalin; honor native writers, composers, and poets; and boost fraternal relations within the socialist block in the 1950s; and (c) to eliminate unwanted vestiges of the communist past during the period from the late 1980s to the present.

INTRODUCTION

Western observers, witnessing the constant change of place names in the then-USSR, dubbed the practice the "Soviet Name Game." [1] This activity is correctly termed a game — and a political game at that — in as much as, like any other game, there are certain rules which, however, were subject to constant change throughout Soviet history.

From its inception, the Soviet regime politicized geographical names — the names of cities, streets, industrial enterprises, and other features — even the names of mountains and islands. The politicization of toponymy was an integral component in a broader politicization of Soviet society as a whole. However, since various aspects of the policy were in constant flux, the practice of naming and renaming geographic features in the Soviet Union also remained in a state of change.

This article concerns itself with namings and renamings of cities in honor of various personages, i.e., that bear (or bore) the names of persons and have attained (or once attained) city status. In other words, what is under consideration here are the names given to Soviet cities for memorial or commemorative reasons, that is to honor exceptional people (Murzayev, 1974, p. 22).

It should be noted here that "exceptional personality" is a historically dynamic concept. The modern and historical names of many cities are drawn from personalities from the past who sometimes no longer are familiar to the current generation. Others are viewed as "exceptional," but exceptionally bad—some former Party leaders, for instance. At the time of the name change, however, they were considered exceptional by the leadership and their names given to cities whose fate was controlled by that leadership. The present paper therefore will not address the propriety of the appearance on the map of one name or another, no matter how disagreeable to some. Rather the simple fact of its appearance (or disappearance) at successive rounds of the name game will be noted.

One of the chief goals of renaming cities in Soviet times was immortalizing the names of communist leaders and persons in their favor and the eliminating from the map those names displeasing to the regime. There were several waves of fashion in renamings. The fashion in vogue at any particular time could reflect the personal passions of the regime in power, the relation of the powers of the moment to certain political movements (for example: terrorism as a form of revolutionary combat), to the culture of the peoples of the Soviet Union, tendencies toward greater or lesser decentralization of power, etc.

Various figures of the political past and present, cultural and historical figures, scientists, and others could be in or out of favor at a particular time. Choices were evaluated according to then-current political views. The political winds blowing across the Soviet landscape shifted several times during the 75 years of Soviet rule, each change accompanied by a reassessment of history, as reflected in educational and propagandistic materials.

METHODOLOGY

Despite the dynamism in the rules of the name game, one rule remained constant: the pretension that certain events and phenomena of the past never occurred. This was, of course, a general trend in Soviet policy, not restricted to toponymy. This policy of silence made it difficult to consult Soviet sources in the course of the research leading to this article. At times the author almost imagined himself as a detective, searching out that which was hidden and discovering the lies, filling in lacunae, cross-checking sources, and, most importantly, attempting to understand the motives of the "player" at every stage of the game. As appropriate, the author will identify the main sources documenting a name change and present examples of main sources of information regarding renamings.[2] It is well known that handbooks in the series SSSR. *Administrativno-territorial'noye deleniye soyuznykh respublik* contain much information on changes in the names of cities (including comments on the year and sometimes even the exact date of the change). The same source also contains both an "Index of Newly Given Names" and an "Index of Previous Names" which, at first glance, would seem impressively comprehensive. It even encompasses the renaming of Sankt-Peterburg and Novyy Margelan under the Tsars. In these two lists, as in the present work, there is much detail on renamings of the Soviet period. However, it should be added, much also has not been elaborated, either as a result of past censorship, or, it seems to the author, because of carelessness on the part of the editors.

Nonetheless, such sources make satisfactory references, especially when it is possible, as in this study, to compare editions from various years (SSSR, 1960, 1961, 1965, 1983, 1987). However, the main source for references on renamings after 1917 was the Index and Gazetteer prepared by Chauncy Harris (1970)—the most comprehensive list of cities in the USSR showing all city names and the dates of their naming.

None of the sources above addresses the matter of for whom these cities were renamed. This is where encyclopedic references come into play. And indeed, Soviet encyclopedic sources contain articles on renamed cities that register the date and in whose honor the city was renamed. But these sources are far from complete, primarily due to that same political censorship mentioned above: those facts which were undesirable for the regime were made to disappear, leading to distortions and major omissions constituting half-truths.

Here, for example, is a citation from *Geograficheskiy entsiklopedicheskiy slovar'* (1983, p. 478): "Chapayevsk (until 1929, Ivashchenkovo), a city... in Kuybyshev Oblast." The current Chapayevsk indeed carried the name Ivashchenkovo previously, but only until 1918, after which, until 1929, it was called Trotsk, after Lev Trotsky. [3] Such omissions and manipulations of history, practiced in the former Soviet Union for decades, make it unwise to rely heavily upon Soviet sources as a dependable guide to renamings in the USSR. But, armed with the knowledge of how politically fickle the source is, the information nonetheless can be quite a valuable research tool.

Acquiring knowledge that a city has been renamed is but half the battle. One must also establish for whom the city was named. In many cases this is obvious. However, one example of the process of verifying a renaming should suffice to illustrate how complex the problem can be. Harris (1970, p. 404) indicates that the city of Leninsk [4] in Uzbekistan (Andizhan Oblast) was listed in the 1926 census as Assake and, until 1938, as Zelensk. However there is nothing in the available Soviet sources to show that Assake-Leninsk was once Zelensk. From this the author suspected strongly that Zelensk came from a surname, perhaps Zelenskiy, and that the bearer of that surname was a Party functionary filling an important post in Central Asia. He no doubt was repressed in 1937–1938, at the time of the "Great Terror," probably killed, and later posthumously rehabilitated. In fact, the author, turning to *Sovetskiy entsiklopedicheskiy slovar'* (1987), found on page 458 an article on I. A. Zelenskiy, Secretary of the Central Asian Bureau of the VKP(b) Central Committee from 1924–1931, who died in 1938.

Mention of the "name game" naturally was forbidden in the former Soviet Union. But it was possible to publish material on the subject in the free Russian press of the West. A book that may be among the first to deal with the matter is Andrey and Tat'yana Fesenko's *Russkiy yazyk pri sovetakh* (1955), which contains a chapter on ethnic and geographical themes. This book is of great interest because it is one of the first attempts at viewing Soviet "newspeak" in a wide range of variations, including those on the map. In the former Soviet Union, this problem was widely discussed only in the period of *perestroyka* and *glasnost'*.

The material presented in this paper can in no way be considered all-inclusive with respect to both historical and modern names, the latter still changing quite rapidly. Certainly greater familiarity with and access to sources published during the Soviet years will give rise to additional discoveries. However, the current situation — with new, independent states — will make material on new renamings difficult to obtain in any standardized form.

AFTERMATH OF THE REVOLUTION

Soviet toponymic policy always was founded on immortalizing the names of revolutionaries and activists of the Communist Party and Soviet state. The renamings began one year after the revolution — in

1918. It is very significant that among those commemorated on the map was the leader of the Bolshevik Revolution — V. I. Lenin. The village of Taldom in Moscow Guberniya was incorporated as a city and named Leninsk in his honor. [5] In 1923, Gatchina, near Petrograd, was named Trotsk in honor of the second captain of the revolution, L. D. Trotsky. [6] These and similar renamings, supposedly were spontaneously demanded by the residents of the respective towns. Such spontaneous demands are feasible in that revolutionary time, particularly from local Party leaders, but it is hard to imagine that they could have been carried out without the approval of Lenin and Trotsky themselves.

Such renamings in honor of living persons were an exceptional and illuminating practice of that period. In the first years after the Revolution, cities were named in honor of those who had died in the Revolution and Civil War much more frequently. The names of famous Bolsheviks (M. S. Uritskiy and V. Volodarskiy) made their way onto the map, [7] as well the names of lesser-known personae. [8] As a rule, cities were given the surnames of those in whose honor they were named, but in the Caucasus, where the first name traditionally is used to describe a famous person, such a name could be assigned to a city. Thus, when the Nagorno-Karabakh Autonomous Oblast was formed in 1923, its regional center, the village of Khankendy, was incorporated as a city and renamed Stepanakert in honor of the Bolshevik Stepan Shaumyan. [9]

One renaming of this period was of a purely political nature. In 1922, the leader of the Estonian communist party, V. Kingisepp, was executed and the old Russian town of Yamburg, which at that time was on the border of the independent Estonian republic, was renamed in his honor. Thus, the main route from capitalist Estonia into Soviet Russia was through this city, named for an Estonian communist. [10]

In 1921, the village of Romanovskiy Khutor in the North Caucasus was renamed Kropotkin (with concurrent incorporation of the village as a city). This renaming was in memory of the famous anarchist P. A. Kropotkin. Anarchism was a revolutionary movement differing with Bolshevism, but in those years the Bolsheviks still acknowledged the contributions of other revolutionary parties to the battle with Tsarism. Another example of such a renaming is the change of Orlov in Vyatka Guberniya to Khalturin, in honor of Stepan Khalturin, the 19th century revolutionary and terrorist. Later, under Stalin, only marxists were declared to be bearers of the torch of emancipation, and all other revolutionary movements were declared enemies of the working class. Under such conditions, with the corresponding changes in the rules of the toponymic games, such renamings as those of Kropotkin and Khalturin became impossible. [11]

In 1920, the Bolshevik "god" Karl Marx (Russian spelling Marks) found his place on the map. The city of Yekaterinienshtadt (also known as Baronsk, Saratov Gubernia) was renamed Marksshtadt. [12] Any comprehensive description of the name game during this period must include the renaming, in 1918, of Nikolayevsk, Saratov Guberniya, to Pugachev, in honor of the leader of the 18th century peasant revolt Yemel'yan Pugachev.

In the course of 1918–1923, 14 cities were renamed (including two named for living persons). But during the same period the names of other persons were removed from the map — those of the royal family and of Tsarist generals. This latter group of cities included the former Nikolayevsk and Yekaterinienshtat in Saratov gubernia, as noted above, as well as Yelizavepol', where the authorities of what was then independent Azerbaijan reinstated the old name of Gandzha or Gyandzha (1918). [13] The next name to disappear was Yekaterinodar (Krasnodar from 1920), Konstantinograd (Krasnograd from 1922). A short time later Yekaterinburg was renamed (Sverdlovsk from 1924), Aleksandropol' (Leninakan from 1924), Yekaterinoslav (Dnepro-petrovsk from 1926), [14] and Novonikolayevsk (Novosibirsk from 1926). [15]

All three cities bearing the names of Tsarist-era generals were renamed after the Bolshevik victory. The first "victim" was Przheval'sk on lake Issyk-Kul' in Kyrgyzstan, named in honor of the renowned adventurer N. M. Przheval'skiy. Przheval'skiy held a general's rank, and thus was regarded as an enemy by the new "bosses." His contributions to science were of no interest to anyone in that period. So, in 1921 Przheval'sk was reassigned its old name of Karakol. [16] Skobelev (formerly Novyy Margelan) became Fergana (1924) and Perovsk (formerly Ak-Mechet') became Kzyl-Orda (1925). [17] As can be seen, except for the two cities that reverted back to their former names (Karakol and Gyandzha), only one city was given a politically neutral name — Fergana, which was named after the place in which the city stands.

One unusual instance is to be found in the renamings of these years — a change motivated by the similarity in sound of a place name to a *persona non grata* of the Soviet authorities. The city of Kerensk stood at the meeting of the Kerenka and Vad rivers in Penza Guberniya and was named after the Kerenka river. The city had borne that name since the 17th century, but it so reminded the Bolsheviks of the premier of the Provisional government that they recently had overthrown (A. F. Kerenskiy) that the city was renamed. Now it embodies the name of the other river — Vadinsk. [18]

THE QUICK AND THE DEAD: THE QUICK

The death of Lenin in 1924 marked the beginning of a new period in the process of renaming cities. Petrograd was renamed Leningrad immediately after Lenin's death. Soon thereafter Ul'yanovsk appeared (the former and current Simbirsk), Leninakan (formerly Aleksandropol'), Leninsk in Turkmenistan (formerly Chardzhuy or Novyy Chardzhuy) in 1924 [19] and Leninsk-Kuznetskiy (formerly Kol'chugino, in the Kuzbas) — in 1925. But, in yet one more paradox of the Soviet name game, in 1927 Leninsk in Turkmenistan became Chardzhuy again, [20] and in 1929, Leninsk near Moscow once again became Taldom. [21] The author has been unable to find any reason for the removal of Lenin's name at that time, and cannot make any reasonable conclusions on the matter. [22] This is especially interesting in view of Leninabad appearing on the map in the same period (1936, formerly and now Khodzhent, or Khudzhand), Leninsk in Uzbekistan (1938, formerly Zelensk, and before that and now Assake), and Leninogorsk in eastern Kazakhstan (1941, formerly Ridder). [23] However, the practice that sets this period apart is the naming of cities after living people.

First to arrive on the map was the General Secretary of the VKP(b) Central Committee, I. V. Stalin; the Chairman of the Communist International Executive Committee, G. E. Zinov'yev; and the Chairman of the Council of People's Commissars of the USSR A. I. Rykov; as well as Chairman of the Central Executive Committee of Ukraine, G. I. Petrovskiy. Stalin was the champion in this game, with his name appearing on the map three times in the course of five years — Stalino (1924, formerly Yuzovka, now Donetsk), Stalingrad (1925, formerly Tsaritsyn, now Volgograd), and Stalinabad (1929, formerly Dyushambe, now Dushanbe). The other leaders were honored with Zinov'yevsk (1924, formerly Yelizavetgrad, currently Kirovograd), Rykovo (1928, formerly and now again Yenakiyevo in the Donbas) and Dnepropetrovsk as mentioned above.

A photograph survives that depicts the celebration of Stalin's 50th birthday on December 21, 1929 in the Kremlin. The celebrant is shown along with his closest helpers: G. K. Ordzhonikidze, K. E. Voroshilov, V. V. Kuybyshev, M. I. Kalinin, L. M. Kaganovich, and S. M. Kirov. This "magnificent seven" of Bolshevik leaders received 29 cities in their name, some of them before, some after their deaths.

After Stalin had established his primacy in the Party and country, he started to award his sycophants with city renamings (and more, of course, but that is outside the scope of this piece). Aides who witnessed cities assume their surnames included K. E. Voroshilov — four cities, [24] L. M. Kaganovich — two cities, [25] M. I. Kalinin — two cities, [26] G. K. Ordzhonikidze — two cities, [27] A. I. Mikoyan — one city, [28] and V. M. Molotov — three cities. [29] S. M. Budennyy, hero of the Civil War, also had a city named in his honor. [30] Stalin did not neglect himself in the process. Another three cities appeared on the map bearing his name during the early 1930s. [31]

Since he did not occupy any government posts at the time, Stalin could not sign any government resolutions. This led to some absurdities in the Soviet name game. When the USSR Central Executive Committee changed the name of Tver' to Kalinin the resolution was signed by none other than… the Chairman of the USSR Central Executive Committee, M. Kalinin! [32]

The people who seized power in 1917 felt the need to find symbols bolstering the legitimacy of their rule. A name on the map was a powerful symbol, as well as a means for ensuring a place in history. Furthermore, as time passed the notion that many of these renamings were carried out "at the demand of the workers" became more believable, as the leadership continued to be isolated from daily reality. They bore the names of cities like ribbons on their chests, which in truth they were — awards for loyalty to the regime. Cities were even named for the local party leaders. Kabakovsk, the former Nadezhdinsk in the northern Urals, was renamed in 1935 in honor of I. D. Kabakov, First Secretary of the Ural Party Committee. Mirzoyan, the former Auliye-Ata in southern Kazakhstan, was renamed in 1936, in honor of L. I. Mirzoyan, leader of the Kazakhstan party organization. Makharadze, the former Ozurgeti, in 1934, and Mikha Tskhakaya (from 1977, Tskhakaya), the former Senaki in Georgia, 1935, were named in honor of local Bolshevik leaders F. I. Makharadze and M. G. Tskhakaya. [33]

The desire to immortalize one's name on the map was particularly strong among Party leaders in Ukraine. Dnepropetrovsk was followed by Postyshevo in the Donbas, formerly Grishino (Fesenko, 1955, p. 75), Chubarovka in Zaporozhye Oblast, formerly Pologi (Harris, 1970, p. 420), *Poselok imeni tovarishcha Khatayevicha* ("The Comrade Khatayevich Commemorative Town") in Dnepropetrovsk Oblast, formerly Sinel'nikovo (Harris, 1970, p. 393), and Kosiorovo in Lugansk

Oblast (Harris, 1970, p. 429). These were named for P. P. Postyshev, V. Ya. Chubar', M. M. Khatayevich, and S. Vi Kosior, all Ukrainian leaders. These population centers (except for Kosiorovo) were incorporated as cities in 1938, but the author is not certain under what name they were incorporated, those presented above, or the current names of Krasnoarmeysk, Pologi, and Sinel'nikovo, respectively. This also is true regarding the town of Zelensk in Uzbekistan, mentioned earlier in this article (formerly Assake), later known as the city of Leninsk.

Four writers also were awarded with cities, all for loyal service to the regime. The best known of these events was the renaming, in 1932, of Nizhniy Novgorod to Gor'kiy. But the "great writer of the proletariat" was not the first literary figure to be so honored. The first was the court poet of the Kremlin, Dem'yan Bednyy, a friend of Stalin. In 1925, the city of Spassk in Penza Oblast was renamed Bednodem'yanovsk. [34] The Cossack village (stanitsa) of Ust'-Medveditskaya on the Don (Rostov Oblast) was renamed Serafimovich for the same reason, this time in honor of the writer A. S. Serafimovich (1933). Later the name of the Kazakh akyn (people's poet) Dzhambul appeared on the map. It should be noted that the literary works of Dem'yan Bednyy, Serafimovich, and Dzhambul have now sunken into obscurity.

The horticulturalist I. V. Michurin, whose works were declared the model of "materialist" science, also was rewarded with a city. In 1932, the city of Kozlov in Tambov Oblast was renamed Michurinsk. [35]

In all, over the years 1918–1940, names of 29 persons still living were assigned to urban settlements. [36] But the playing field of the Soviet name game soon became tinged with blood, and the names of 12 of these people appeared on the map only to disappear once again, a phenomenon that served in the 1930s as a sign of their arrest and subsequent execution. First to go was the name of Trotsky, in 1929. [37] Trotsk, the former Gatchina, was renamed Krasnogvardeysk. [38] In 1934, Zinov'yevsk was renamed Kirovo (from 1939, Kirovograd), and Rykovo was given its old name of Yenakiyevo.

In the period of 1937–1939 the names of Kabakov, Mirzoyan, Postyshev, Chubar', Khatayevich, Kosior, and Zelenskiy disappeared from the map. [39] The name of Batalpashinsk, the center of the Cherkessk Autonomous Oblast at the time, changed three times during the period 1936–1939, first receiving the name Sulimov, after Chairman of the RSFSR Council of People Commissars D. Ye. Sulimov, then Yezhovo-Cherkessk in honor of the People's Commissar of Internal Affairs N. I. Yezhov, through whom Stalin carried out the bloody terror of 1937–1938, and finally, after the all-powerful head of the NKVD had suffered the fate of his many victims, his city became plain old Cherkessk.

THE QUICK AND THE DEAD: THE DEAD

Revolutionaries who died or were killed were not bypassed in the renaming process. The renamings carried out in their honor can be divided into two groups: those performed several years after their death (natural or otherwise), and those done immediately after their passing. In the first group are renamings in honor of Ya. M. Sverdlov, who died in 1918 (Yekaterinburg became Sverdlovsk in 1924) [40] and F. E. Dzerzhinskiy (death in 1926, first city named after the secret police chief in 1929— Dzerzhinsk, formerly the town of Rastya-pino near Nizhniy Novgorod). [41]

Six cities on the map of the former Soviet Union were named for the Bolshevik Artem, who died in 1921. They are all located in mining areas. Artem (F. A. Sergeyev) was in a leadership position in the Don-bas, then led a mining union. The first city named after him appeared in 1924, when Bakhmut in the Donbas was renamed Artemovsk. In 1938–1939, four more cities were named for this now-forgotten Communist, with another so named after the war. [42]

Three cities with religious names were renamed near Moscow in the 1930s. Two of them received the names of deceased Bolsheviks: Sergiyev became Zagorsk, in honor of V. M. Zagorskiy, [43] and Bogoro-dsk became Noginsk, in memory of V. P. Nogin. [44]

A number of cities were named after heroes who perished in the Civil War. Nearly all the well-known participants of the Civil War later were declared "enemies of the people," but several of them, particularly those who were lucky enough (if it can be called luck) to die early, were "canonized." First to appear on the map was Chapayev, replacing Trotsky as the name of the former Ivashchenkovo, then came G. I. Kotovskiy, [45] and the hero who was not a hero— N. A. Shchors. That is to say there really was a man named Shchors who participated in the Civil War on the Bolshevik side, but his actions cannot be construed as heroic. Shchors's heroic biography was composed at Stalin's behest, who referred to him as "the Ukrainian Chapayev." [46] The city of Snovsk (Chernigov Oblast) was named after Shchors in 1935.

The popularization of these three canonized figures brought about the making of films about them. Chapayev was a particularly popular film and truly was well made. The film was based on the novel of the same name by D.A. Furmanov, a former commissar in Chapayev's division. In 1941, Sereda in Ivanovo Oblast was renamed Furmanov.

Some other small cities received the names of dead revolutionaries. [47] In 1941, Mysovsk in the Trans-Baykal was renamed Babushkin in honor of the Bolshevik I.V. Babushkin, shot there in 1906.

Finally, in 1931 the city of Pokrovsk, then a capital of Volga German ASSR, was renamed Engels (Russian spelling Engel's) after Friedrich Engels.

Several cities received the names of Party and government leaders in the 1920s "right on the tail" of the leader's death. Such was the case in the death of Lenin, M.V. Frunze, [48] and A.D. Tsyurupa, [49] and in the 1930s in the cases of S.M. Kirov, V.V. Kuybyshev, and G.K. Ordzhonikidze.

Kirov was assassinated on December 1, 1934, and Zinov'yevsk immediately was renamed Kirovo in his honor [50]; it now is called Kirovograd. Vyatka was renamed Kirov, and Khibinogorsk on the Kola Peninsula became Kirovsk. In 1935, Karaklis in Armenia became Kirovakan, Gandzha in Azerbaijan Kirovabad, [51] Kalata in Sverdlovsk Oblast Kirovgrad. A year later the town of Pesochnaya in Kaluga Oblast was incorporated as yet another city of Kirov. [52]

After Kuybyshev's death in 1935, three cites were named for him: two on the Volga — Samara and Spassk-Tatarskiy, and one in West Siberia — Kainsk. One more city with his name appeared in Amur Oblast: Kuybyshevka-Vostochnaya (formerly Aleksandrovka). [53]

Ordzhonikidze died in 1937 (it was a suicide, though the fact was not revealed at the time). Two cities were added to the two already bearing his name: Ordzhonikidze in the Donbas (formerly and currently Yenakiyevo, and at one time Rykovo) and Sergo (formerly Kadiyevka, now Stakhanov), which was named for Ordzhonikidze's party pseudonym.

Another group of renamings performed "fresh on the trail" were those in honor of fliers. The fame of Soviet fliers in long flights, Arctic research, as well as in the Spanish Civil War was widely publicized in the 1930s. They helped create an illusion of the tremendous success of socialism and distracted people from the actual situation in the country. Fliers were elevated to the rank of national heroes, and cities were named after them upon their deaths. In 1938, immediately after his death in an air crash, the city of Orenburg was named Chkalov in honor of Valeriy Chkalov, commander of the first aircraft to fly non-stop from Moscow across the North Pole to America. Three other cities were to receive the names of fliers who perished in the 1930s: Osipenko (formerly Berdyansk on the Sea of Azov), in honor of Polina Osipenko, a participant of a flight from Moscow to the Far East, Babushkin (formerly Losinoostrovskaya near Moscow), in honor of arctic flier Mikhail Babushkin, and Serov (once again losing the name of Nadezhdinsk) in honor of Spanish Civil War participant Anatoliy Serov. [54]

The author has only been able to discover four cities renamed before the war that were not directly political. These are Pushkin near Leningrad, named in honor of the Russian poet Alexander Pushkin, [55] Fort Shevchenko on the Mangyshlak Peninsula, in honor of the Ukrainian poet Taras Shevchenko, [56] Karpinsk in the northern Urals, in honor of geologist and president of the USSR Academy of Sciences A. N. Karpinskiy, [57] and Sabirabad in Azerbaijan, named in honor of the Azeri poet Sabir. [58]

The 1930s marked the apex (or, conversely, nadir) of Soviet renamings for various leaders. There is a proposed name change that was not, in the end, enacted. In the period of 1937–1938 there were letters from workers (probably "inspired" letters) demanding that Moscow be renamed Stalinodar (Stalinodar means "gift of Stalin," as Yekaterinodar is "gift of Katherine"). In one of the surviving letters the writer notes: "...I am firmly convinced that all people on the planet in our age and all people in ages to come will look upon this decision to rename Moscow as Stalinodar with joy and satisfaction." The matter was considered at the Extraordinary XVII Session of the All-Russia Congress of Soviets, the TsK VKP(b) Politburo, and the Presidiums of the USSR and RSFSR Supreme Soviets. However, Stalin apparently rejected the proposal and Moscow remained Moscow (*Izvestiya TsK KPSS*, 1990, No. 12, pp. 126–127).

THE WAR YEARS AND AFTER

The Nazi German attack on the Soviet Union in June of 1941 brought a lull in the name game, but not for long. As early as 1942 the city of Dzharkent in Kazakhstan (Taldy-Kurgan Oblast) was renamed Panfilov, in honor of General I. V. Panfilov, who died in battle defending Moscow. The game of the cities thus began again, albeit at a more modest pace. There were only 12 renamings after individuals in the war years. The concomitant process of removing offensive names continued. Several renamings in 1943–1944 were carried out to remove Ordzhonikidze from the map: Ordzhonikidzegrad became Bezhitsa again, [59] Sergo was given its old name of Kadiyevka, the capital of North Ossetia was given the neutral name of Dzaudzhikau. [60] As to the city of Ordzhonikidze in Donetsk Oblast (which was then named Stalinskaya), "the Bolsheviks prefer to return to the old name of "Yenakiyevo," that of one of the owners of a large number of mines, than return it to the name of that member of the Politburo" (Fesenko, 1955, pp. 75–76). [61]

Voroshilov and Kaganovich each "lost" a city in 1943 for reasons that are not clear: Stavropol' appeared once again on the map of the North Caucasus and Popasnaya in the Donbas. The reason Mikoyan lost his city is, however, abundantly clear: the Karachay Autonomous Oblast was dissolved in 1944, its residents exiled from their homeland and all Karachay place names changed. On top of all this, part of the territory of the oblast was given to Georgia. The former Oblast center, Mikoyan-Shakhar, ended up in Georgia, and was named Klukhori. [62] Finally, the city of Slutsk near Leningrad was given back its historic name of Pavlovsk (1944). [63]

Thus, for various reasons, the names of Bolsheviks were removed from eight cities. Only four cities received new names in honor of individuals. Two renamed cities in Ukraine were of a political or patriotic nature. In both of these cases a new portion was added to the traditional name — Pereyaslav-Khmel'nitskiy (1943, in honor of the 16th century hetman Bogdan Khmel'nitskiy) [64] and Korsun'-Shevchenkovskiy (1944, in honor of Taras Shevchenko).

Two cities were renamed after dead heroes during the war years. One is Dzharkent-Panfilov, already mentioned above, the other Likhvin in Tula Oblast, which was named Chekalin in honor of the partisan Aleksandr Chekalin (1944). After the war, in the campaign of renamings in the Eastern Prussian territory annexed by the Soviets, six cities were named for Heroes of the Soviet Union who perished in battles on that territory. These cities are Chernyakhovsk (formerly Insterburg), Gusev (formerly Gumbinnen), Gur'yevsk (formerly Noyhausen), Ladushkin (formerly Lyudvigsort), Mamonovo (formerly Hailgenbail) and Nesterov (formerly Stallipönen). [65]

In the course of another campaign, on the territory of the Karelian isthmus taken by the Soviets from Finland, Uuras was renamed Vysotsk (1948). [66] In all, there were very few renamings in honor of heroes of the War of 1941–1945 when one considers the tremendous propaganda value attached to the war, officially known as the "Great Patriotic War." [67]

There was an interruption during the war of the practice of naming cities after living persons. Now one had to die in order to "receive" a city. The younger generation of leaders such as N. S. Khrushchev, G. M. Malenkov, and L. P. Beria did not have cities renamed for them under Stalin. [68] But a totalitarian regime always allows exceptions to its own rules, and the name Khrushchev did finally make its way to the map. But this was some time later, under Khrushchev. [69]

After the war, cities were once again named for the ruling elite. Another Kaliningrad appeared after Kalinin's death (1946, formerly Königsberg), Shcherbakov, after the death of A. S. Shcherbakov (1946, formerly and currently Rybinsk, Yaroslavl' Oblast), Zhdanov, after the death of A. A. Zhdanov (1948, formerly and currently Mariupol', Donetsk Oblast), and Mir-Bashir, after the death of the Azerbaijani leader Mir Bashir Kasumov (1949, formerly the town of Terter, which now has regained its old name).

After World War II, the Soviet Union annexed the southern part of Sakhalin Island and the Kurile Islands. The Japanese place names of these areas were changed to Russian in 1946. Four cities in southern Sakhalin were renamed for figures from Russian history: Chekhov (formerly Noda) in honor of the writer A. P. Chekhov, who spent time on Sakhalin Island in the late 19th century [70]; Nevel'sk (formerly Khonto) in honor of navigator G. I. Nevel'skoy, who discovered the strait dividing Sakhalin from the mainland; Makarov' (formerly Siritoru), in honor of Admiral S. O. Makarov, who died in the Russo-Japanese war of 1904, and Korsakov (formerly Otomari) in honor of the governor-general of East Siberia M. S. Korsakov. [71]

Sometimes renamings were associated with anniversaries. Thus, on the hundredth anniversary of the birthday of literary critic V. G. Belinskiy his native city of Chembar in Penza Oblast was renamed Belinskiy (1948); a year earlier, in honor of the birthday of the "Father of Russian Aviation," N. G. Zhukovskiy, the town where the Central Aero-Hydrodynamic Institute (TsAGI), founded by him, is located was incorporated as a city and given the name of Zhukovskiy (Moscow Oblast). Cities were named for two other Russian scientists, Oranienbaum near Leningrad to Lomonosov [72] and Ranenburg in Lipetsk Oblast to Chaplygin, [73] cannot be called strictly commemorative. These were openly declared replacements of German place names with Russian names. These renamings completed the sweep of "German" names from the map of the Soviet Union, a process that had started with the beginning of the First World War in 1914, when Sankt-Peterburg was Russified to Petrograd. [74]

The first years after the war found the names of two other figures from the past appearing on the map: General Bagration, hero of the wars with Napoleon, when the city of Preussisch Eylau in what was formerly East Prussia, was renamed to Bagrationovsk, 1946; [75] and P.N. Nesterov, military pilot and a pioneer of acrobatic flying, when the city of Zholkva in L'vov Oblast was renamed Nesterov, 1951. [76]

THE KHRUSHCHEV ERA

Within one year of the death of Stalin (1953), the first political re-naming already had been carried out: the city of Dzaudzhikau was renamed Ordzhonikidze. [77] This was a clearly antistalinist act, and one of the signs of the upcoming denunciation of the cult of Stalin by Khrushchev.

In 1957, the name game took an unexpected turn. Khrushchev came out the winner in his battle with opponents in the CPSU Po-litburo—the so-called "Anti-Party group" of Molotov, Malenkov, and Kaganovich. The names of some members of this group— Molotov, Kaganovich, and Voroshilov (who was also included in the group, al-though not announced at the time), were on the map of the USSR. It was clearly a situation Khrushchev could no longer tolerate. So a res-olution was made forbidding the naming of cities and other objects of that scale after living persons. [78] Thus the names of the "anti-Party group" were removed from the map "for legal reasons." Molo-tov became Perm' once again, one of the cities of Molotovsk was given back the name Nolinsk; the other, newer city was given the name of Severodvinsk. Voroshilovgrad became Lugansk once more and the city of Voroshilov was renamed Ussuriysk. [79] Kaganovich became Novo-Kashirsk. [80]

Along with those described above, all the other population centers named for Molotov, Voroshilov, Kaganovich, as well as Mikoyan and Budennyy, were renamed. Eventually there was not a single popula-tion center named for a living person... with the exception of the town of Khrushchev. Can one imagine a person willing to be responsible for changing the name of a town bearing the name of the CPSU First Secretary without orders from above? Those orders took some time in coming. What is more, in 1961 this town was actually incorporated as a city. [81] But in the following year an order did come down, and Khrushchev's name disappeared from the map with the city named in his honor becoming Kremges (from Kremenchugskaya GES, a hydro-electric power plant). [82]

Three other cities regained their historical names in 1957. Chkalov went back to being Orenburg, Shcherbakov became Rybinsk, and Osipenko became Berdyansk.

The exposure of Stalin's crimes initiated by Khrushchev at the XXth Party Congress in 1956 reached its apogee at the XXIst, in 1961. This Congress had a direct effect on toponymy. After this Congress, all the objects named for Stalin were renamed, including cities. Some cities got back their old names: Stalinsk became Novokuznetsk, Staliniri became Tskhinvali and, with a slight variation in the spelling—Stalinabad became Dushanbe (until 1925, it was Dyushambe). Other cities received new names: Stalingrad—Volgograd, Stalino—Donetsk, and Stalinogorsk—Novomoskovsk. [83]

Thus, during the rule of Khrushchev, 17 cities named after individuals were renamed. But as one set of cities lost its new names, others lost the old names. The practice of renaming cities after various persons continued, but the professions of those so honored changed. The number of revolutionaries and activists of the Communist Regime of the USSR so honored decreased during the period. The few renamings that did fit the traditional mold were the incorporation, in 1955, of the town of Novaya Pis'myanka, in Tataria, to the city of Leninogorsk, and the renaming of Mariyampole in Lithuania to Kapsukas (in honor of one of the leaders of the Lithuanian Communist Party V. S. Mitskyavichyus-Kapsukas); the change in 1959, of Nor-Bayazet in Armenia to Kamo, in honor of the Armenian Bolshevik S. A. Ter-Petrosyan, known by his party pseudonym of Kamo; and the renaming in 1962 of the town of Balanda in Saratov Oblast to Kalininsk and its incorporation. A new layer of names, however—leaders of foreign communist parties—was introduced.

The foreign contingent was sparsely represented on the map prior to this: one city each for Marx and Engels—and nothing more. The new renamings reflected the policy of "friendship and unity of the international communist movement." Cities were given the names of deceased communist leaders. The first, in July of 1964, was French Communist leader Maurice Thorez, [84] followed one month later by his Italian colleague Palmiro Togliatti. The city of Stavropol' on the Volga (Samara Oblast) was named Togliatti (Russian spelling Tol'yatti). It was in this very city that Italian capitalists (from Fiat) were building a large automobile factory. But the city in which the factory stood was named for a communist.

In 1963, the town of Vakhrushevo in Lugansk Oblast [85] was incorporated as a city. It was renamed in honor of Minister of the Coal Industry V. V. Vakhrushev — the only instance in the history of renaming cities in the USSR in which one was named after an industrialist.

Eight names were named for writers, two in Russia and for Russian authors (the town of Lopasnya in Moscow Oblast to the city of Chekhov in 1954, in commemoration of the 50th anniversary of the author's death, and the naming of a new city in Stavropol' Kray as Lermontovskiy in honor of M. Yu. Lermontov. [86] The others were in other union republics and in honor of writers of those republics with one exception, an exception typical of the Soviet name game.

The following appeared on the map: Navoi in Uzbekistan (formerly the town of Kermine, 1958), Fizuli in Azerbaijan (formerly Karyagino, 1959), Abay in Kazakhstan (Karaganda Oblast, formerly the town of Churubay-Nura, 1961), Ivano-Frankovsk in Ukraine (formerly Stanislav, 1962), Abovyan in Armenia (formerly the village of Elar, 1963), [87] and Shevchenko in Kazakhstan (formerly Aktau, 1964).

The last renaming mentioned is deserving of additional attention. Taras Shevchenko was a Ukrainian poet, but lived part of his life on the Mangyshlak Peninsula in Kazakhstan, where he was exiled by the Tsar's government. When the exploitation of the natural resources of this peninsula began in the 1960s, it was decided to name the main city there after the poet. The name of a Ukrainian poet given to a city in Kazakhstan was supposed to symbolize the friendship of the peoples of the USSR. In carrying out this renaming the authorities did not take note of another city on the peninsula already bearing the exiled poet's name — Fort Shevchenko. Or perhaps they did note, but chose to ignore this fact. After all, Shevchenko was to be a large city, not like the little burg of Fort Shevchenko! And so, for a quarter century the name of one man was on two cities on one peninsula. [88]

It goes without saying that the decision to change Aktau to Shevchenko was made, as they say in Russia, "at the very top." Also decided at the summit was renaming of Stanislav, done on the orders of Khrushchev (Imya, 1989, p. 83–84).

The first and only composer whose name was to appear on the map of cities was P. I. Tchaikovsky. In 1962, when a settlement of workers building the Votkinsk Hydroelectric Plant in Perm' Oblast achieved the status of city, the composer's name (in Russian spelling, Chaykovskiy) was given the new city.

The physical map of the world is covered with the names of those who made discoveries and contributed research on the planet, but there are few cities named in their honor. In Tsarist Russia, there were two cities named for discoverers, Przheval'sk, already discussed above, and Khabarovsk. [89] There were a few more of these renamings in the Soviet period. In addition to Nevel'sk and Makarov, already mentioned in connection with Sakhalin, there were Arsen'yev in Primorskiy Kray (1952, formerly the town of Semenovka), named for V. K. Arsen'yev, a traveler and researcher in the Far East; Dokuchayevsk in Donetsk Oblast (until 1954, the town of Yelenovskiye Kar'yery), named for the great soil scientist V. V. Dokuchaeyev; and Shelekhov (Shelikhov) in Irkutsk Oblast (a city since 1962), named for 18th century merchant G. I. Shelikhov (Shelekhov), who founded the first Russian settlements in North America, and two cities named for geologists — Karpinsk (see above) and Gubkin in Belgorod Oblast. [90]

A number of cities were named after historic persons. In 1954, to commemorate the 300th anniversary of the Ukraine's consolidation with Russia, Pereyaslav-Khmel'nitskiy was joined on the map by Khmel'nitskiy (formerly Proskurov). Other names appearing on the map in this period included: Salavat, Biruni (Beruni), and Yermak. [91] As can be seen, the overall number of cities named for writers, scientists, explorers, and other "apolitical" figures was on the increase.

THE BREZHNEV PERIOD

Khrushchev was driven from power in 1964, and L. I. Brezhnev became First Secretary (later his title become General Secretary) of the CPSU Central Committee. The period of Brezhnev's rule over the Party, along with those of A. V. Andropov and K. U. Chernenko, was dubbed the "Period of Stagnation" under the rule of M. S. Gorbachev. It was a relatively quiet period in the name game. There were no mass renamings of cities and the overall number of renamings was relatively small. There were, however, some changes in the "rules of the game." The overall tendency changed, and the names of political figures began once again to appear on cities more often than writers, scientists, and other non-political figures.

The Brezhnev administration definitely chose to tone down the condemnation of Stalin seen under Khrushchev. It did not go so far as to attempt the full rehabilitation of Stalin, and Volgograd did not return to being Stalingrad, [92] but this policy was, nonetheless, reflected in names: a tendency arose to return to cities the names of Stalin's cronies, removed under Khrushchev, after the death of those cronies. Thus, after the death of Voroshilov, Lugansk once again became Voroshilovgrad (1970, and since then, Lugansk again) and after Budennyy's death Prikumsk was again renamed Budennovsk (1973).

Who knows, perhaps if Molotov had died earlier than 1987, already in the time of Gorbachev, his name would once again have illuminated the map where Perm' earlier had been.

Meanwhile the cult of Lenin carried on full tilt, and its influence on toponymy continued, with several cities named for him in this period. For some reason there was a spate of cities being renamed for his patronymic — Il'yich — as well as his real surname of Ul'yanov. Ul'yanovo appeared in Uzbekistan (1974, Dzhizak Oblast, formerly the town of Obruchevo), and three Il'yichevsk's — one near Odessa (1973), one in Uzbekistan (Andizhan Oblast, 1980), [93] and one in Azerbaijan (Nakhichevan ASSR, 1981; until 1964, Norashen). In addition to these, a town in Azerbaijan, Port-Il'yich, was incorporated as a city (1971).

There was, as a matter of fact, another new city of Leninsk, in addition to the two already existing at that time. [94] But there were very few people in the country who knew of this Leninsk, since it was a city that grew up next to the manned missile launch site in Baykonur, Kazakhstan and was kept secret until very recent times. [95]

As in the preceding period, many new names appeared on the map in the union republics of the USSR. But if there was a tendency shown under Khrushchev for naming places after writers and other cultural figures, under Brezhnev cities were most often named for local Party and government figures: the cities of Stuchka in Latvia (until 1967, poselok imeni Petra Stuchki), Akhunbabayev in Uzbekistan (Andizhan Oblast; until 1975, the town of Sufikishlak), Gafurov in Tajikistan (Leninabad Oblast; until 1978, the city of Sovetabad); and in 1982 the town of Gegechkori (formerly Martvili) in Georgia was incorporated as a city. [96] Two cities were named Narimanov — after revolutionary and government figure Nariman Narimanov: one in Uzbekistan (Tashkent Oblast, until 1981, Bakhtemir) and one in Astrakhan' Oblast (until 1984, the town of Nizhnevolzhsk). [97]

The naming of cities for foreign communists continued. The Romanian communist leader Gheorghe Gheorghiu-Dej died in 1965, and the city of Liski in Voronezh Oblast was immediately renamed Gheorghiu-Dej (Russian spelling — Georgiu-Dezh), [98] thus continuing the trend started a year before for naming cities after such personages soon after their death. Then the toponymic authorities seemed to suddenly recall that there were other very worthy candidates for renaming, who died before the tendency for such renamings had come into fashion. The city of Melekess in Ul'yanovsk Oblast was renamed Dimitrovgrad after the Bulgarian leader Georgi Dimitrov (1972), [99] and Zmiyev in Khar'kov Oblast was renamed to Gottwald (Russian spelling Gotval'd) in honor of the leader of communist Czechoslovakia, Klement Gottwald (1976). [100]

A "toponymic monster" made its appearance on the Soviet map in 1965: Karlolibknekhtovsk in Donetsk Oblast, growing into a city from poselok imeni Karla Libknekhta ("Karl Liebknecht Commemorative Town"). [101] There were only four cities appearing on the map in this period with the names of writers. One of the cities is of special note. In 1967, the city of Lusavan in Armenia was renamed Charentsavan in honor of the Armenian poet Yegishe Charents, who died in the years of the "great terror" and was posthumously rehabilitated. The name game had taken another zig-zag. [102]

The city of Mayakovskiy in Georgia was incorporated in 1981. Bagdadi, the village where the Russian poet V. V. Mayakovskiy was born, had already been renamed Mayakovskiy back in 1940. This was an understandable renaming. After all, Mayakovskiy was born in Bagdadi, became a famous poet, visited Georgia repeatedly and dedicated verses to the country. Similarly, the Tajik state poet Mirzo Tursun-Zade died in 1978, and the city of Regar in Tajikistan was immediately changed to Tursunzade. But the appearance, in 1966, of a city of Pushkino in Azerbaijan is another matter. This renaming was another manifestation of the mythological friendship between the peoples of the USSR: Pushkin never visited Azerbaijan and never wrote verses about it.

Three cities were named for scientists. In 1967, the town of Bindyuzhskiy in Tataria was incorporated as a city and renamed Mendeleyevsk in honor of the great Russian chemist D. I. Mendeleyev. In 1983, the town of Kurchatov was incorporated as a city. This city near the Kursk Nuclear Power Plant was named for Academician I. V. Kurchatov, the first scientific leader of the Soviet nuclear program. Another Kurchatov came to light under Brezhnev, similar to Baykonur's Leninsk, a secret city near the Semipalatinsk nuclear test range in Kazakhstan.

The world's first cosmonaut, Yuriy Gagarin, died in a plane crash in 1968. The people did sincerely love the cosmonauts, particularly Gagarin, and the successful Soviet space program played the same role for the regime as fliers had in the 1930s— helping to disguise the failures of socialism. When Gagarin died, his native city of Gzhatsk in Smolensk Oblast was renamed Gagarin. [103]

In a decree of the USSR Presidium of the Supreme Soviet dated September 11, 1957, among the persons who could have cities renamed in their honor were "heroes of labor. " But heroes of labor did not get cities, with one exception. The most famous worker of the 1930s was

Aleksey Stakhanov who, in 1935, purportedly set a record for output in coal mining. Stakhanov was praised as a hero, and his name given to the movement of leading industrial producers (the "Stakhanov movement" or the "Stakhanovets"), but no cities were named for him at that time. Those who could have cities named for them in life were, as a rule, only high-ranking Party and government leaders. It is true that in 1938, the town of Otdykh near Moscow was named Stakhanovo in his honor (Harris, 1970, p. 444), but when it came time for the town to become a city, it was renamed Zhukovskiy. Stakhanov got his city only after his death, in 1978, when Kadiyevka in Lugansk Oblast was renamed Stakhanov.

The last ostentatious renamings of the Period of Stagnation were carried out after the deaths of Brezhnev, Andropov, D. A. Ustinov, and Chernenko. Their names were given to Naberezhnyye Chelny in Tataria (renamed Brezhnev in 1982), Rybinsk, renamed once again (named Andropov in 1984), Izhevsk (renamed Ustinov in 1984), and Sharypovo in Krasnoyarsk Kray (renamed Chernenko in 1985). The decisions for these renamings were made in the Politburo of the CPSU Central Committee and were issued as resolutions of the CPSU Central Committee, the Presidium of the USSR Supreme Soviet, and the USSR Council of Ministers.

GORBACHEV, *PERESTROYKA*, AND BEYOND [104]

After Chernenko's death in 1985, M. S. Gorbachev became General Secretary of the CPSU Central Committee. Soon the winds of change were blowing — *perestroyka* had begun. Of course, this was also to have its effect on geographical names: there was a movement in the country for returning historical names to cities. So the process of the preceding years was thrown into reverse. Figures from the Period of Stagnation who were the last to "receive" their cities were also the first to "lose" them. Thus, in 1987, Ustinov disappeared from the map, followed by Brezhnev and Chernenko the next year. [105] The desire of the residents to return the old names to their cities coincided with a less than total love for those figures on the part of the current leadership of the country. But a game is a game, and when the question came to returning the historical name of Rybinsk to Andropov (Andropov, after all, had been Gorbachev's political godfather), this presented a problem. But even here a solution was found. In contrast to other "reverse renamings," [106] the resolution on renaming the city of Andropov to Rybinsk was written without any reference to the name of the renamed city! [107]

Glasnost' progressed even faster than *perestroyka*. As *glasnost'* increased, a movement arose favoring the total removal of the names of the old communist leadership from the map. The first direct demand to "remove such-and-such figure from the map" was directed against one of the most despised figures of the Stalin period— Zhdanov. [108] In January 1989, Soviet authorities finally decided to rename cities and all other objects bearing his name. [109]

One by one, the turn of all the other communist "holy ones" came. Kirovabad disappeared in 1989 (now, as of old, it is Gyandzha), Voroshilovgrad was renamed the following year (regaining its name of Lugansk), then Kalinin (Tver'), Ordzhonikidze in North Ossetia (Vladikavkaz), and Gor'kiy (Nizhniy Novgorod). [110]

For the first time in the entire course of Soviet history, the authorities had to contend with the opinion of the populace. But the name of the communist "god," Lenin, was still untouched on the map. Finally, in November of 1990, an article appeared in *Trud* (November 11, 1990) that may be said to have heralded the first signs of a change— "Leninakan has been given back its old name of Gyumri." [111] However *Trud* published a correction less than two weeks later (November 24, 1990). Nonetheless, Leninakan was the first city to lose its Leninist name in the process of *perestroyka*. [112]

In early 1991, Kuybyshev became Samara once more, [113] followed by Frunze [114] and Leninabad. [115] A number of other cities lost the names of communist leaders, but the main battle raged around the "cradle of the revolution"—Leningrad.

The Party bureaucracy was actively opposed to renamings from the start of the process of *perestroyka*, frequently blocking proposals for returning old names to cities. Sometimes the orders for changing the names of cities were accompanied by orders that the names of streets and other objects should remain unchanged. But nowhere was there such a struggle with supporters of the communist system as in the renaming of Leningrad. [116] The battle over the name of this city was widely and thoroughly described in the press, including the Western press. Even Gorbachev himself, then President of the USSR, was among the proposal's opponents. But the voters made themselves heard, and in the referendum of June 11, 1991, 54 percent of Leningraders voted to return the city the name given her by her founder, Peter the Great: Sankt-Peterburg. But the opinion of the city's populace was not final, and only in September, after the collapse of the August coup, was the Resolution of the Presidium of the RSFSR Supreme Soviet issued on restoration of the city's historical name.

In that same September of 1991, Sverdlovsk regained the historic name of Yekaterinburg and Zagorsk became Sergiyev Posad once more. Shevchenko in Kazakhstan was given back its name of Aktau at this time also. [117]

In all, according to this author's data, from 1987–1991 there were 39 renamings of cities on the territory of the former USSR named after various personages, with most cities regaining their historical names. [118] It is entirely possible that there are more renamings about which the author has no information.

In December 1991 the Soviet Union ceased to exist. Now new, independent governments are turning to address the toponymic inheritance left by their communist predecessors. Many cities, particularly in Russia and Ukraine, continue to bear names given them by former communist masters. So the herculean labor of the cartographers is not yet at an end.

AFTERWORD

In as much as no "game" is complete without its "champions," a listing of those cities that have changed names more times (four) than any others appear to be in order. They are:

Yenakiyevo — Rykovo — Yenakiyevo — Ordzhonikidze — Yenakiyevo
Lugansk — Voroshilovgrad — Lugansk — Voroshilovgrad — Lugansk
Vladikavkaz — Ordzhonikidze — Dzaudzhikau — Ordzhonikidze —
    Vladikavkaz
Rybinsk — Shcherbakov — Rybinsk — Andropov — Rybinsk.

Actually, there is one other city that should be added to this group, which the author predicts will become the all-time record-holder for the former Soviet Union: that is the city named for Stalin's Marshal Budennyy. Its first name was Svyatoy Krest, then Prikumsk, then Budennovsk, then Prikumsk, and finally Budennovsk again. I have no doubt that there will be another renaming, it just a matter of when and to what. It could be that as I write these lines a Russian cartographer is entering a new name on the map. The name game, now "post-Soviet," continues.

REFERENCES

Asankulova, S. "Imya dlya goroda" (A Name for a City), *Izvestiya*, October 17, 1989.

Bol'shaya Sovetskaya entsiklopediya (Great Soviet Encyclopedia), 2nd ed., Vols 1–51. Moscow: Sovetskaya Entsiklopediya, 1950–1958.

Bol'shaya Sovetskaya entsiklopediya (Great Soviet Encyclopedia), 3rd ed. Vols. 1–50. Moscow: Sovetskaya Entsiklopediya, 1970–1978.

Bol'shoy entsiklopedicheskiy slovar' (Large Encyclopedic Dictionary), Vols 1 and 2. Moscow: Sovetskaya Entsiklopediya, 1991.

Chernov, A. "Gorod pod psevdonimom. Poka" (A City with a Pseudonym. For Now), *Moscow News*, May 12, 1991.

Dobbs, Michael. "Andropov Succumbs Again, by Popular Demand," *Washington Post*, March 4, 1989.

Fesenko, A. P.. "Shchorsa vy znayete?" (Do You Really Know Shchors?), *Voprosy istorii*, 12:169–173, 1989.

Fesenko, Andrey and Tat'yana Fesenko. *Russkiy yazyk pri sovetakh* (The Russian Language Under the Soviets). New York, 1955.

"The Game of the Name," *The Economist*, June 8, 1991.

Geograficheskiy entsiklopedicheskiy slovar'. Geograficheskiye nazvaniya (The Geographical Encyclopedic Dictionary. Geographical Names). Moscow: Sovetskaya Entsiklopediya, 1983.

Gorbanevskiy, Mikhail. "Toponimicheskiy bespredel" (Toponymic Free-for-All), *Posev*, 1991, No. 5, pp. 100–108.

Harris, Chauncy D. "Index and Gazetteer," *Soviet Geography: Review and Translation* (special issue), 11, 5, May 1970.

"Imya na karte" (A Name on the Map), interview with V. P. Neroznak and M. V. Gorbanevskiy, *Kommunist*, 5:82–85, 1989.

Ivina, Natal'ya. "'Zachem nam otrechen'ya'? Razmyshleniya nad pis'mami" ('Why the Renunciation'? Thoughts on Some Letters), *Literaturnaya gazeta*, September 28, 1988.

Karyakin, Yuriy. "'Zhdanovskaya zhidkost' ili protiv ochernitel'stva" ('Zhdanov Juice', or Going Against the Blackball), *Ogonyok*, 19:25–27, 1988.

Lushin, Yuriy. "Kosmodrom i lyudi" (The Cosmodrome and Its People). *Ogonyok*, 13:3–5, 1991.

Maslennikov, B. *Morskaya karta rasskazyvayet* (Tales from the Maritime Chart), 2nd ed. Moscow: Voyenizdat, 1986.

Murzayev, E. M. *Ocherki toponimiki* (Toponymic Issues). Moscow: Mysl', 1974.

Nikonov, V. A. *Vvedeniye v toponimiku* (Introduction to Toponymy). Moscow: Nauka, 1965.

Nikonov, V. A. *Kratkiy toponimicheskiy slovar'* (Short Toponymic Dictionary). Moscow: Mysl', 1966.

Sankt-Peterburg. Petrograd. Leningrad. Entsiklopedicheskiy spravoch-nik (St. Petersburg. Petrograd. Leningrad. Encyclopedic Handbook). Moscow: Bol'shaya Rossiyskaya Entsiklopediya, 1992.

Sovetskiy entsiklopedicheskiy slovar' (Soviet Encyclopedic Dictionary), 4th ed. Moscow: Sovetskaya Entsiklopediya, 1987.

SSSR. Administrativno-territorial'noye deleniye soyuznykh respublik na I aprelya 1960 goda (USSR, Administrative-Territorial Division of Union Republics on April 1, 1960). Moscow, 1960.

SSSR. Administrativno-territorial'noye deleniye soyuznykh respublik. Dopol-neniye k spravochniku vypuska 1960 goda (USSR, Administrative-Territorial Division of Union Republics. Appendix to the 1960 Hand-book). Moscow, 1961.

SSSR. Administrativno-territorial'noye deleniye soyuznykh respublik. Yanvar' 1965 goda (USSR, Administrative-Territorial Division of Union Repub-lics. January 1965). Moscow, 1965.

SSSR. Administrativno-territorial'noye deleniye soyuznykh respublik na 1 yanvarya 1983 goda (USSR, Administrative-Territorial Division of Union Republics on January 1, 1983). Moscow, 1983.

SSSR. Administrativno-territorial'noye deleniye soyuznykh respublik na 1 yanvarya 1987 goda (USSR, Administrative-Territorial Division of Union Republics on January 1, 1987). Moscow, 1987.

Tarkhov, S. A. "From Karlo-Libknekhtovsk and New York to Propoysk and Rastyapino? How Place Names are Changing in the Former USSR," *Post-Soviet Geography*, 33, 7:454–462, September 1992.

Tumarkin, Nina. "The End of the Soviet Name Game?," *Boston Globe*, No-vember 16, 1988.

NOTES:

[1] See, for example, coverage in *The Boston Globe* (Tumarkin, 1988), *Washington Post* (Dobbs, 1989) (the author of this article refers to the "great Soviet name-changing game"), and *The Economist* (The Game, 1991).

[2] In order not to load down the article with citations, the author has not listed them in cases where the source is widely available: e.g., the third edition of the *Great Soviet Encyclopedia* (Bol'shaya, 1971–1978) and Soviet and geographic encyclopedic dictionaries (*Sovets-kiy*, 1987; *Geograficheskiy*, 1983). Unless otherwise noted, dates in parentheses indicate the year in which a city was named or renamed. Reference to administrative divisions for the early Soviet years is to the "old" system based on guberniyas and, for the rest of the period under study, to the "new" system based on oblasts that was in place until the dissolution of the USSR.

[3] The same disinformation also is found in other sources — for instance, in *Sovetskiy entsiklopedicheskiy slovar'* (Sovetskiy, 1987, p. 1485). It is not even corrected in the last editon of the dictionary, published in 1991 under the new title of *Bol'shoy entsiklopedicheskiy slovar'* (Bol'shoy, 1991, Vol. 2, p. 625).

[4] Not the current name, as revealed later in the paper — *Ed.*

[5] One year later another village, Prishib (now in Volgograd Oblast) acquired the name of Leninsk. But this Leninsk was not incorporated as a city until 1963.

[6] There already was another Trotsk on the map at the time — the former settlement (*sloboda*) of Ivashchenkovo (Samara Guberniya). But it was not a city at the time.

[7] The city of Poshekhon'ye-Volodarsk appeared on the map in 1918, formerly it was called Poshekhon'ye (Yaroslavl' Guberniya). Uritsk, the former Ligovo in Petrograd Guberniya, was a city from 1925, and since 1935 was incorporated within the city limits of Leningrad (See Sankt-Peterburg, 1992, p. 631).

[8] In 1918, Pavlovsk, near Petrograd, was renamed Slutsk in honor of the revolutionary V. K. Slutskaya, Porech'ye (Smolensk Guberniya) to Demidov, after Ya. Ye. Demidov, chairman of the local Communist Party committee, and Romanovo-Borisoglebsk (Yaroslavl' Guberniya) became Tutayev — after the Red Army soldier I. P. Tutayev. In 1919, Askhabad was named Poltoratsk in honor of one of the Soviet leaders of Turkestan, P. G. Poltoratskiy (in 1927 it regained its old name in a slightly different form, the one familiar to us today — Ashkhabad).

[9] Stepan Shaumyan's given name showed up on the map again in 1924, in Armenia, when the village of Dzhalal-Ogly was renamed Stepanavan (a city since 1938). Another city in the Caucasus given a first name is Makhachkala (formerly Petrovsk-Port), "Fort Makhach." The title was given it in 1922, in memory of Dagestani revolutionary Magomed Ali Dakhadayev (Makhach is a shortened form of Magomed, see Nikonov, 1966, p. 261). Another city in Dagestan named in this period (1922) is Buynaksk, the former Temir-Khan-Shura, which, however, was named for the surname of local Bolshevik U. Buynakskiy.

[10] After the Soviet Union annexed Estonia, the name of the first leader of Estonian communists appeared on the Estonian map as well. In 1952 the city of Kuressaare on the island of Saaremaa was renamed Kingisepp. In the years of *perestroyka* it was one of the first cities to be given back its former name. So far there have been no reports of a change in name for the Russian Kingisepp.

[11] Names already given in these cases, however, were not removed. Instead, the biographies of the persons themselves were "revised." In V. A. Nikonov's *Kratkiy toponimicheskiy slovar'* (1966), for example,

it is stated that Romanovskiy Khutor was renamed for the revolutionary and geographer P. A. Kropotkin (p. 217). Although this description is not false — Kropotkin was in fact an accomplished geographer — the city was not named in his honor for his studies of the Quaternary period of the Earth. One cannot hold the author (Nikonov — a noted scientist and authority in the field of onomastics) responsible for such inaccuracies, which are plentiful in the dictionary. Rather than inaccuracy or reticence on his part, the author, like all other authors of that period of publication in the Soviet Union, had a secret co-author in the person of the censor.

There is another example of such "semi-truth." The same dictionary states that S. Khalturin was a "workerrevolutionary" (Nikonov, 1966, p. 450). Khalturin was actually a worker, and one of the first revolutionaries among the working class. However, he is notable in the history of the Russian revolution movement rather for organizing the attempted assassination of Alexander II and other terrorist acts. Stalinist historians, however, rejected terrorism as a valid method of revolutionary conflict. One result of this was the division of Khalturin's biography into two parts — an approved, non-terrorist portion, and an unsanctioned portion when he became a terrorist.

[12] This city appeared in the 19th century, when Katherine II settled the Lower Volga region with German colonists. After the Revolution it was on the territory of the Volga German ASSR. In the early days of the war with Nazi Germany, all the Germans were deported from the Volga, their republic annulled, and all German place names replaced with Russian. During this period the name for the city of Marksshtadt lost its second part and became simply Marks.

[13] The city was to lose and once again gain its traditional name in the future. For the latest renaming, see *Soviet Geography*, February 1990, pp. 147–148.

[14] Yekaterinoslav, named for Katherine the Great at its founding, lost its "royal" name three times. The first time under Pavel I when it was renamed to Novorossiysk, the second time during the Civil War when Ukraine was controlled by S. Petlyura and was called Sicheslav in honor of the Zaporozh'ye Cossacks (Fesenko, 1955, p. 74), and a third time under the Bolsheviks. The last name originated from the name Petrovskiy and the Dnieper River, by which the city stands.

[15] This marked the end of renamings of cities with royal names and a number of cities kept their regal monikers. These include Pavlograd, Aleksandriya, Nikolayevsk-na-Amure, and some others. It is true that one more such city was renamed when, in 1948, Mariupol' became Zhdanov, but that was because Zhdanov was born in that city. (Now Zhdanov has reverted back to Mariupol', and Sverdlovsk has become Yekaterinburg once again.)

[16] The city was named Przheval'sk again in 1939, during one of the periodic turnarounds in Soviet historiographic policy toward Russia's past. Now, in independent Kyrgyzstan, reversion back to Karakol is being considered (see Tarkhov, 1992, p. 461).

[17] Kzyl-Orda, in Kazakh, means Red Capital, and was the capital of Kazakhstan at the time.

[18] Information from Ye. Orlovskiy and K. Yankov (see Gorbanevskiy, 1991, p. 105). In the 1920s Kerensk-Vadinsk was reduced in status from a city to a rural settlement along with other cities that had lost their economic significance.

[19] According to several sources (for example, Harris, p. 385), Leninsk-Turkmenskiy.

[20] From 1940—Chardzhou.

[21] The fact that Lenin's name was taken from, as well as given to cities was until recently a forbidden subject in the former Soviet Union.

[22] For a short period in the 1930s, the city of Peterhof near Leningrad was named Leninsk (Harris, 1970, p. 419). From 1944 it became Petrodvorets.

[23] One more Leninogorsk appeared in 1955 in Tataria (formerly Novaya Pis'myanka).

[24] Voroshilovsk in the Donbas (1931, formerly Alchevsk, now Kommunarsk), Voroshilovgrad (1935, formerly and currently Lugansk), Voroshilov (1935, formerly Nikol'sk-Ussuriyskiy, now Ussuriysk), and one more Voroshilovsk in the North Caucasus (1935, formerly and currently Stavropol').

[25] One city was named for Kaganovich in 1935—Ternovsk in Moscow Oblast (the city of Kaganovich, later Novokashirsk, now incorporated into Kashira). But this leader, and the others mentioned, had towns and other population centers named after them, as well as other industrial and agricultural features, educational institutions, streets, squares and other objects. For example, Popasnaya railroad station in the Donbas was renamed to *Stantsiya imeni L.M. Kaganovicha* ("L.M. Kaganovich Commemorative Station"). In 1938, the town near the station was named *gorod imeni L.M. Kaganovicha* ("L.M. Kaganovich Commemorative city"). Such Soviet names as *"poselok imeni..."* ("Commemorative town") are not all that rare. There are *poselok imeni V.I. Lenina, poselok imeni M.I. Kalinina, poselok imeni Kirova*, and others (SSSR, 1987), although there is no logical explanation why Lenin and Kalinin have initials, and Kirov not. Another, even more awkward, name is *poselok imeni 26 Bakinskikh Komissarov* ("26 Baku Commissars Commemorative town") (*Ibid.*). Later *g. im L.M. Kaganovicha* (as the name was abbreviated), reverted back to Popasnaya. It is interesting to note in passing that even the form *"gorod imeni"* had a rural counterpart *"selo imeni,"*

such as in *selo imeni Sverdlova* ("Sverdlov Commemorative village") in the Ukraine: Sverdlovsk (Lugansk Oblast) was named this until it became a city (*SSSR*, 1983, p. 684)

[26] Kalinin (1931, formerly and now again Tver') and the city of Kaliningrad, incorporated in 1938 near Moscow (formerly the town of Kalininskiy and before that Podlipki). Only much later, after Kalinin's death, was another "Kaliningrad" so named (see below). Then there appeared Kalininabad in Tajikistan (1956), Kalininsk in Saratov Oblast (1962), and Kalinino in Armenia (incorporated in 1983, now Tashir).

[27] Ordzhonikidze (1931, formerly and currently Vladikavkaz) and Ordzhonikidzegrad (1935, before and later Bezhitsa, now incorporated into Bryansk).

[28] The center of the Karachay Autonomous Oblast was named for Mikoyan in 1929 as Mikoyan-Shakhar (in Karachay "City of Mikoyan," now Karachayevsk).

[29] Molotov "received" his first city after the others, in 1938, when the town of Sudostroy in the delta of the Northern Dvina was incorporated and named Molotovsk (now Severodvinsk). Then, in 1940, he was "given" two cities at once: Molotov (formerly and currently Perm'), and a second Molotovsk in Kirov oblast (formerly and currently Nolinsk).

[30] Budennovsk (1935), formerly Prikumsk; until 1920 it was known as Svyatoy Krest (Holy Cross).

[31] Stalinsk (1932, formerly and currently Novokuznetsk), Stalinogorsk (1934, formerly Bobriki, now Novomoskovsk in Tula Oblast), and the center of the South Ossetian Autonomous Oblast Staliniri (1934, formerly and currently Tskhinvali).

[32] The text of the resolution was published in Izvestiya on November 23, 1931 (See Ivina, 1988).

[33] Now these Georgian cities have regained their old names.

[34] Can any person, even one who speaks Russian with total fluency, pronounce this name without getting tripped up? This is not the only product of "nomination" by these governmental pundits of the Russian language. Later came such gems as Ivano-Frankovsk and Karlolibknekhtovsk.

[35] Michurin lived and worked in Kozlov.

[36] But not at one time. Sometimes they even traded places as the name of one and the same city.

[37] In 1929, Trotskiy was exiled from the USSR and his name removed from the map. But he was not immediately executed: "Stalin's hand" only reached him in 1940 in Mexico.

[38] At the time, the town of Trotsk in Samara Oblast (formerly Ivashchenkovo) was incorporated as a city, but received a different name, Chapayevsk, in honor of Civil War hero V.I. Chapayev. In 1944, Krasnogvardeysk regained its old name of Gatchina.

[39]   Kabakovsk was Nadezhdinsk once again for a time; Mirzoyan, formerly Auliye-Ata, was named Dzhambul, in honor of the Kazakh
poet who glorified in verse the Party, Stalin, and the "batyr" (Turkic folk hero) Yezhov; Postyshev, formerly Grishino, now Krasnoarmeysk; Chubarovka and *poselok imeni tovarishcha Khatayevicha*
now bear their old names of Pologi and Sinel'nikovo; and the town
of Kosiorovo now is Stanichno-Luganskoye. Zelensk was renamed
Leninsk at the time.

[40]   In 1991, Sverdlovsk once again became Yekaterinburg. But there is
another Sverdlovsk still on the map, in Lugansk Oblast (incorporated in 1938).

[41]   A second Dzerzhinsk appeared later, in Minsk oblast (1932, formerly Koydanovo), Dneprodzerzhinsk (1935, formerly Kamenskoye), yet
another Dzerzhinsk, this one in Donetsk Oblast (1938, formerly the
town of Shcherbinovka), and Dzerzhinskiy in Moscow Oblast (incorporated in 1981). All of them continue to bear these names. It is unlikely that the Dzerzhinsk near Nizhniy Novgorod will resume its former name — Rastyapino means "bungler" (see Tarkhov, 1992, p. 459).

[42]   In 1938, Artem in the Primorskiy Kray, Artemovskiy (formerly the
town of Yegorshino) in Sverdlovsk Oblast, and Artemovo in Donetsk Oblast (thus in one oblast we find an Artemovsk and an Artemovo); in 1939 Artemovsk in Krasnoyarsk Kray (formerly the town
of Ol'khovskiy); in 1961 one more Artemovsk, this one in Lugansk
Oblast. Thus, the number of cities named after Artem are as many
as those named after Stalin. It should be added here that Artemovo
started out as *poselok imeni Artema,* then became *gorod imeni Artema (SSSR,* 1960), and finally Artemovo *(SSSR,* 1965).

[43]   Until its renaming, the city bore the name of Sergiy Radonezhskiy,
founder of the Troitse-Sergiyevskiy monastery, at first as Sergiyev
Posad, then, from 1919, as the city of Sergiyev. It was renamed Sergiyev Posad in 1991.

[44]   The third renaming of the city — initially Voskresensk, now Istra.

[45]   Kotovsk, formerly Birzula in the Moldavian ASSR (1935, a city
since 1938). After the annexation of Bessarabia in 1940, the former Moldavian ASSR was split in two, with one part forming with
the greater part of Bessarabia the Moldavian SSR and the other
becoming part of Odessa Oblast. Kotovsk ended up on the Odessa
portion of the territory and Moldavia was without a city of Kotovsk for a quarter century. Although in that same year the town
of Gancheshty in the Bessarabian portion of Moldavia was given
the name Kotovskoye, it was only in 1965 that Kotovskoye was incorporated as Kotovsk. Now the Moldavian Kotovsk bears its old
name, but in a Moldavian spelling — Khynchesht'. In 1940 a city
of Kotovsk appeared in Russia. The name was given to a newly
formed city separated from the territory of Tambov.

[46]   For an account of the posthumous promotion of Shchors, see A. P. Fesenko "Do You Really Know Shchors?" (1989).

[47]   Konakovo in Tver' Oblast, named after a local worker and revolutionary P. P. Konakov (1930, a city from 1937), formerly Kuznetsovo; Tsulukidze in Georgia in honor of the Georgian revolutionary A. G. Tsulukidze (1936, formerly and currently Khoni); Khanlar in Azerbaijan, in honor of the Azeri revolutionary Khanlar Safaraliyev (1938, formerly Yelenendorf); one more city in Azerbaijan, Kazi-Magomed, in honor of another local revolutionary, Kazi Magomed Agasiyev (see *Bol'shaya*, 2nd ed., Vol. 1, 1950, p. 289; until 1938, the town of Adzhikabul); Skovorodino in Amur Oblast, in honor of the first chairman of the local soviet A. Skovorodin (1938, formerly Rukhlovo, see Nikonov, 1966, p. 385); Roshal' in Moscow Oblast, in honor of October Revolution participant S. G. Roshal' (incorporated in 1940).

[48]   Pishpek, the capital of Kyrgyzstan, was named Frunze in 1926. In another paradox of the Soviet name game, the name was given to a Kirghiz city, even though there is no letter "f" in the Kirghiz language and, as a rule, all consonants are followed by vowels. Thus residents of Kirghiziya pronounced the name concocted for their city in Moscow as "Boronso" or "Purunze" (Asankulova, 1989). The city now bears its old name, but in a slightly different spelling — Bishkek.

[49]   The city of Aleshki in Kherson Oblast was renamed Tsyurupinsk in 1928.

[50]   Zinov'yev was accused of organizing the murder of Kirov.

[51]   In 1936 Kirovabad in Azerbaijan received a namesake, the town of Kirovabad in Tajikistan, which in 1953 was incorporated as a city, but in 1963 was renamed Pyandzh. The Azeri Kirovabad lost its "Kirov" name only in the *perestroyka* period, in 1989, when it assumed its former name, Guandzhe (Gandzha).

[52]   Another four cities named after Kirov appeared later: Kirovsk in Leningrad Oblast (1953, formerly the town of Nevdubstroy, then *imeni Kirova*), Kirovo-Chepetsk (the city of Kirov on the river Cheptsa, formerly the town Kirovo-Chepetskiy) in Kirov Oblast (1955), Kirovskoye in Donetsk Oblast, and yet one more (the third) Kirovsk in Lugansk Oblast created out of the northern part of the city of Kadiyevka in 1962 (Harris, 1970, p. 400).

[53]   There now are no cities on the Volga left bearing the name of Kuybyshev; they were renamed in 1991 (the name for Kuybyshevka-Vostochnaya in the Far East was changed in 1957, perhaps because it sounded odd. It is now named Belogorsk).

[54]   Only one of these names remains on the map — Serov. Orenburg and Berdyansk were given back their historic names in 1957 and Babushkin were incorporated into Moscow in 1960. There are, however, still cities on the map named after Chkalov. While he was still alive, in 1937, the village of Vasilevo on the Volga, where he was born,

was renamed Chkalovsk (a city since 1955). Another Chkalovsk appeared in 1956 in Tajikistan.

[55] The city of Detskoye Selo (until 1918, Tsarskoye Selo) was renamed Pushkin in 1937, for the centennial of the poet's death.

[56] The former Fort Aleksandrovskiy (in Shevchenko's time — Novopetrovskoye Ukrepleniye). It was renamed Fort Shevchenko in 1939. It also was referred to in the 1930s as Fort Uritskiy (Harris, 1970, p. 390).

[57] Incorporated in 1941 from the towns of Bogoslovskiy and Ugol'nyy.

[58] Incorporated as a city in 1935.

[59] After the war, Bezhitsa was incorporated into Bryansk.

[60] From the Ossetian personal name plus "kau," or village (Nikonov, 1966, p. 311).

[61] Yenakiyevo thus was renamed four times in the space of 16 years.

[62] In 1957 Karachay autonomy was restored and the Cherkess Autonomous Oblast was changed to Karachay-Cherkess, with the addition of Karachay territory located in Georgia. This was the point at which the city of Klukhori (formerly Mikoyan-Shakhar) was renamed Karachayevsk.

[63] At this time the historic name of Gatchina was returned to Krasnogvardeysk, formerly Trotsk.

[64] In 1654, Bogdan Khmel'nitskiy declared the unity of Russia and Ukraine, taking an oath of fealty to the Moscow Tsar. When Ukraine became an independent state, Cossack's meeting in June 1992 in Pereyaslav-Khmel'nitskiy with their hetman, Vyacheslav Chernovil, renounced this oath (*Moscow News*, June 28, 1992). However, the city's name remains unchanged.

[65] Named for general I. D. Chernyakhovskiy, I. S. Gusev, S. S. Gur'-yev, I. M. Ladushkin, N. V. Mamonov and S. N. Nesterov, respectively.

[66] Named for machine-gunner K. D. Vysotskiy, Hero of the Soviet Union, who died in the Soviet-Finland War of 1939–1940 (Maslennikov, 1986, p. 65, 270).

[67] In all the years since 1946, only the following cities were renamed for war heroes — Vatutino in Ukraine's Cherkassy Oblast (1952), for general I. F. Vatutin; Gorodovikovsk in Kalmykia (1971, formerly the town of Bashanta), for general O. I. Gorodovikov; Kuznetsovsk in Rovno Oblast (1984), named for intelligence agent N. I. Kuznetsov; and Shopokov in Kyrgyzstan (until 1985, the town of Krasnooktyabr'skiy, see *SSSR*, 1987, p. 667), named for D. Shopokov, a member of Panfilov's Division. It is interesting to attempt to speculate regarding what the qualifications were for participants in the war to be "decorated" with a city. Major General Panfilov's division distinguished itself in the defense of Moscow; Generals of the Army Vatutin and Chernyakhovskiy commanded fronts and died in battle. The names of these three military leaders were widely

publicized during the war. Agent Kuznetsov became famous after the war. As to Colonel General Gorodovikov, of the many other warriors of greater and lesser glory, his name appeared on the map of Kalmykia for the simple reason that he was a Kalmyk. The same is true of Shopokov, a Kirghiz. The others seem to have appeared on the map by chance.

[68] There was only the town of Beriya in Armenia.

[69] Khrushchev's name was given to a builders' settlement at the Kremenchug Hydroelectric Plant on the Dnepr (Kirovograd Oblast). For its further history, see below.

[70] In fact, Chekhov visited the northern part of the island and was never in southern Sakhalin.

[71] Renaming Otomari Korsakov was actually a restoration of an old name, predating the seizure of southern Sakhalin by Japan in the war of 1904–1905. Korsakovskiy Post stood where the city now stands. When the Japanese annexed the island, they changed all the Russian names to Japanese. Such renamings on conquered territory have occurred throughout human history. The Soviets, as can be seen, are no exception. But in this instance an interesting dilemma resulted. On the one hand, it would have been good to restore the old Russian name, but, on the other hand, it would not have been desirable to rename the city after a tsarist governor-general. So, a version was created in which it was named for the Russian hydrographer V. A. Rimskiy-Korsakov (see, for example, *Bol'shaya*, 2nd ed., Vol. 23, 1953, p. 69). Only later was the truth restored (*Geograficheskiy*, 1986, p. 227; *Sovetskiy*, 1987, p. 635).

[72] In honor of Russian 18th century scientist, M. V. Lomonosov.

[73] In honor of Soviet aerodynamic engineer, Academician S. A. Chaplygin.

[74] This sweep took on the appearance of a campaign in the years of the Second World War, when the second half of Marksshtadt disappeared and Peterhof became Petrodvorets, Shliiselburg became Petrokrepost', and Bal'tser in the former Volga German ASSR became Krasnoarmeysk. A complete listing of the German place names swept from the map during this campaign is beyond the scope of the present article.

[75] General Bagration distinguished himself in battle near Preussisch Eylau in 1807.

[76] P. N. Nesterov died during WWI in a dogfight over this region, becoming the first ever to ram his opponent in air combat.

[77] As always happens in such situations, this either is an apparent popular initiative or at least is accompanied by the appearance of approval for such a decision. Here, for example, is that was in the North Ossetian newspapers on the change in name of the republic's capital in 1931: "The workers approve of the state proclamation on

renaming Vladikavkaz to Ordzhonikidze. Lengthy applause, becoming an ovation... says it all." In 1944: "The renaming of the city of Ordzhonikidze to Dzaudzhikau... is in the cultural and economic interests of the Ossetian people. Stalin's personal concern for the present and future welfare of the Ossetian people shows through this action." And in 1954: "The workers of North Ossetia are overjoyed and deeply gratified regarding the proclamation on renaming the city of Dzaudzhikau to Ordzhonikidze, an action that fulfills their wishes and desires" (Imya, 1989, p. 83). The city currently is named Vladikavkaz.

[78] "To establish that in future the awarding of names...can only be carried out posthumously..." (from the September 11, 1957, Decree of the Presidium of the USSR Supreme Soviet, as cited by Nikonov, 1965, p. 175).

[79] For reasons unknown to this author, one of these cities bearing Voroshilov's name, Voroshilovsk in Lugansk Oblast (the former Alchevsk) kept its new name until 1961, becoming Kommunarsk.

[80] Later incorporated into Kashira. The city of Budennovsk was renamed Prikumsk at this time also. Its original name, Svyatoy Krest (Holy Cross) was of course totally unacceptable for the Soviet authorities.

[81] According to sources which the author has discovered, Khrushchev's name was removed from the map by guile. The town of Khrushchev was incorporated into the neighboring city of Novogeorgiyevsk, and the city formed from their union was given a third name — Kremges. But in the SSSR (1961) he unexpectedly discovered that the sequence of the incorporation occurred somewhat diffrently than earlier anticipated: On March 17, 1961, the city of Novogeorgiyevsk was in fact incorporated into the newly incorporated city of Khrushchev (p. 62).

[82] Eventually Kremges was changed to the better-sounding Svetlovodsk.

[83] The old names of these cities were unacceptable for Soviet toponymy. Yuzovka (Stalino) was named for an English entrepreneur, John Hughes (Russian spelling Yuz), who owned the factories around which the city grew. Bobriki (Stalinogorsk) was a village previously, and named after its owner, Count Bobrinskiy. The former name of Stalingrad, Tsaritsyn, was associated with some former Tsaritsa in people's minds, when in fact the name comes from the Turkic *sar su* "yellow water" or *sarshin* "yellowish," turned by Russian settlers to the more familiar sounding Tsaritsyn (Nikonov, 1966, p. 127, 296, 88).

[84] The name of Thorez was assigned to the city of Chistyakovo in Donetsk Oblast (Russian spelling Torez).

[85] The former town was named *poselok Shakhty No. 5-bis* (Harris, 1970, p. 131).

[86] Lermontovskiy was later changed to Lermontov.

[87] These cities were named for the Uzbek poet Alisher Navoi, Azeri poet Mukhammed Fizuli, Kazakh poet Abay Kunanbayev, Ukrainian writer Ivan Franko, and Armenian poet and educator Khachatur Abovyan, respectively.

[88] The city of Shevchenko is gone now, too, having regained its original name of Aktau.

[89] Khabarovsk was named in honor of 17th century Russian Cossack Yerofey Khabarov, who made several expeditions to the Amur River area.

[90] The town of Gubkin in Belgorod Oblast, an iron mining center on the Kursk Magnetic Anomaly deposits, was incorporated as a city in 1955. It was named for the geologist who had studied these deposits, I. M. Gubkin (until 1939 it was the town of Korobkovo).

[91] Salavat in Bashkiria (1954), was named in honor of Salavat Yulayev, a Bashkir who was a confederate of Pugachev; Biruni (Beruni) in Karakalpakia (city from 1962; until 1957, the town of Shabbaz), in honor of Biruni (Beruni), a Central Asian scientist of the 10–11th century; Yermak in Kazakhstan (Pavlodar Oblast, 1961), in honor of Yermak Timofeyevich, whose expeditions in the 16th century marked the beginning of Russia's acquisition of Siberia.

[92] Discussions of preparations for such a resolution occasionally arose during the Brezhnev period.

[93] Thus, it came to be that there were two cities in this oblast named for Lenin — Leninsk and Il'yichevsk.

[94] In Volgograd and Andizhan oblasts.

[95] The city is located in Kzyl-Orda Oblast near the Tyura-Tam railroad station. The existence of secret cities is characteristic of Soviet geography. The principles for their naming were various. Some were named for the nearest large city with the addition of a post-office box number (for instance Arzamas-16, Tomsk-7, Chelyabinsk-65, Krasnoyarsk-26 and others), others took the name of the place nearest to their physical location (Plesetsk in Arkhangel'sk Oblast); and a third group were given new names (such as Stepnogorsk in Kazakhstan). Leninsk passed through various stages. It was first named Tashkent-50, then Zvezdograd, and, finally, Leninsk (*Izvestiya*, October 3, 1991). There is an amusing anecdote regarding the secrecy of this place published in *Ogonyok*. A specialist who worked at Baykonur recalls finding a map of Kazakhstan in an American military magazine in the 1960s with Tyura-Tam on it in English, and next to it in parentheses "Russian Canaveral" (Lushin, 1991, p. 3).

[96] Named for one of the founders of the Latvian Communist Party, P. Stuchka, the Uzbek government figure Yu. Akhunbabayev, the Tajik party leader B. G. Gafurov, and the Georgian Bolshevik A. A. Gegechkori, respectively. In addition to these, in 1976 the

city of Bautino appeared in Kazakhstan, on the Mangyshlak Peninsula, named after A. G. Bautin, who died in the Civil War (Maslennikov, 1986, p. 34).

[97] It is interesting to note that, although nearly all of Nariman Narimanov's activities were in Azerbaijan, there were no cities named for him there, only a town, Narimanabad. But the leadership of this republic can certainly not be accused of negligence regarding keeping alive the memory of Communists: 1966 saw a city of Zhdanovsk here (the second city to so honor Zhdanov in the USSR), and the city of Kasum-Ismailov, named for another local revolutionary. Also, in 1978, a city of Babek appeared in 1978, in the Nakhichevan ASSR, named for the instigator of a revolt in Azerbaijan and Western Iran in the 10th century.

[98] Since 1991 the name has reverted to Liski.

[99] But several years earlier, in 1965, *poselok imeni Dimitrova* in Donetsk Oblast was incorporated as a city named Dimitrov (Harris, 1970, p. 388). Did the legislators in Moscow know about this? Or was it a moment that called for a loud pronouncement of Soviet-Bulgarian friendship?

[100] Since 1990 the city reassumed the name of Zmiyev.

[101] German revolutionary Karl Liebknecht (Russian spelling Karl Libknekht) was killed with another leader of the German socialists, Rosa Luxemburg (Russian spelling Roza Lyuksemburg) in 1919. There was also a town named after Rosa Luxemburg on the map — the former Yekaterinofel'd in Georgia. But it was renamed Bolnisi and incorporated as a city under this thoroughly Georgian name, leaving Rosa Luxemburg without a city.

[102] In fact, it turned out more like a ziglet than a zig-zag. Charents was the only rehabilited person for whom a city was renamed. None of the others repressed by Stalin were given cities, even those whose names were on the map in the 1930s. There were streets named for them, but not cities, which were too obvious to the public eye. It was, however, safe to return cities to Voroshilov and Budennyy who "lost" them under Khrushchev, whom the new leaders appeared to have disliked, unlike their generally positive feelings toward Stalin.

[103] One more city of Gagarin appeared in 1974 in Uzbekistan (the former town of Yerzhar, Dzhizak Oblast). It remains to be explained just what relation there was between the cosmonaut and this city named for him.

[104] For an expanded account of this recent round of renamings (including republics and oblast-level administrative units), see Tarkhov (1992).

[105] As a result, the cities regained their old names: Izhevsk (Ustinov), Naberezhnyye Chelny (Brezhnev), and Sharypovo (Chernenko).

[106] Here, for example, is a quote from a TASS report of December 1988: "The CPSU Central Committee, Presidium of the USSR Supreme Soviet, and the USSR Council of Ministers have resolved to remove (author's italics) the names of Leonid Brezhnev and Konstantin Chernenko from the titles of all enterprises, administrative regions, educational institutions, and all other organizations" (*Novoye russkoye slovo*, December 30, 1988).

[107] In the official report published in *Pravda* it is worded as follows: "Paragraph 2 of the CPSU Central Committee, Presidium of the USSR Supreme Soviet, and the USSR Council of Ministers No. 204 of February 23, 1984, regarding renaming of the city of Rybinsk in Yaroslavl' Oblast, is cancelled" (*Pravda*, March 4, 1989).

[108] The May 1988 article, "'Zhdanov Juice,' or Going Against the Blackball," by Yu. Karyakin (1988), received a particularly large public response.

[109] Among the cities renamed were Zhdanov and Zhdanovsk (the latter in Azerbaijan), which now bear the names Mariupol' and Beylangan.

[110] The fate of these cities' names was the subject of general attention, leaving less fanfare for renaming in the Baltic republics, Moldova, and Georgia, where all names of communists were removed from the map: in 1988 Kingisepp in Estonia returned to being Kuressaare; in 1989 Kapsukas in Lithuania got back its old name of Mariyampole (Marijampole) and four cities in Georgia were renamed in one decree, all bearing the names of communists (Mayakovskiy's name survived, but within a year after the decree was once again Bagdadi); in 1990 Stuchka in Latvia was renamed Ayzkraukle (Ajzkraukle), and Kotovsk in Moldova became Khynchesht'. In addition, Gotval'd in the Ukraine was once again Zmiyev.

[111] Until its renaming as Aleksandropol' in 1837, the city was named Gumri (Nikonov, 1966, p. 231).

[112] There are two spellings of this city name extant: Kumayri and Gyumri. But the exact year of the renaming remains in question. Even those whose duty it is to register all changes on the geographical map do not claim certainty of the date. For example, in the first volume of the *Bol'shoy entsiklopedicheskiy slovar'* (p. 863), we find that Leninakan was renamed in 1990 to Kumayri, and in the second volume (p. 764) that it was renamed in 1991 to Gyumri.

[113] The name of the other Kuybyshev, in Tatarstan, also was changed. But with the weakening of central authority, republics (and even some national enclaves in the Russian Federation), began to establish their own rules. Formerly, this Tatar Kuybyshev was named Spassk-Tatarskiy, but the Tatar government, given its nationalistic policy, could not return the old name. Instead, it was renamed Bulgur — in honor of the Volga Bulgars, ancestors of modern Tatars.

[114]   Frunze was renamed Bishkek.

[115]   Leninabad regained its old name but, judging by the press, as with Gyumri-Kumayri, two spellings are used: Khodzhent (as the city was officially known before), and Khudzhand (the city's name since at least the 7th century) (see Nikonov, 1966, p. 231).

[116]   Aleksandr S. Solzhenitsyn proposed two variants of new names for the city: Nevograd (the City on the Neva) and Svyato-Petrograd (a Russian form of Sankt-Peterburg, i.e., the City of Saint Peter) (see Chernov, 1991). By the time of the referendum on the name change, however, the new name proposed was the city's original name, Sankt-Peterburg.

[117]   The following cities also were renamed in the course of 1991: Georgiu-Dezh (now Liski again), Il'yichevsk, Kasum-Ismailov, Mir-Bashir and Pushkino in Azerbaijan (now named Sherur, Geranboy, Terter, and Bilyasuvar, respectively), Kalinino in Armenia (now Tashir), and Leninsk and Il'yichevsk in Uzbekistan (now Asake and Karasu).

[118]   Lost in the cloud of "reverse" renaming was the renaming of Nikol'skiy in Kazakhstan (Dzhezkazgan Oblast) to Satpayev, in honor of the famous Kazakh geologist K. I. Satpayev (1990), as part of the de-Russification of placenames in Kazakhstan.

POST-SOVIET NAME GAMES

Pavel Ilyin

It seems very appropriate that this speech about the post-Soviet name game should open the morning session on the first of April. It is hard to imagine anything more ridiculous than this combination of words: "the city of St. Petersburg of the Leningrad oblast"...

In 1988 the Boston Globe published an article by the historian Nina Tumarkin, entitled "The End of the Soviet Name Game?" (with question-mark). Today, six years later, I can say that the Soviet game may have ended, but the post-Soviet game is going on everywhere. Perestroika in the former Soviet Union, and the formation of new states in its place, has led to a huge number of place name changes from country names to street names. The major motives for renaming are the drive to eliminate communist attributes, the resurgence of nationalism and the tendency to return to objects their historical names. The methods used to assign names in various parts of the former Soviet Union vary, but politics plays a powerful role throughout the region. Examples of this are the preservation of the Leningrad, Sverdlovsk and Leninabad oblasts, when their capitals have returned to being St. Petersburg, Yekaterinburg and Khodzhent.

The current games started in 1989, before the Soviet Union disintegrated. We all know the name of the Estonian capital: Tallinn. In Estonian, Tallinn is spelled with two "N's" at the end. In Russian it is spelled with one. In 1989, the Estonian government demanded that the Russian spelling of the Estonian capital be changed to have two "N's" at the end, the same way as it is in Estonian. This happened during the period when the people of Estonia, as well as of the neighboring countries, Latvia and Lithuania, were fighting for their independence. The Gorbachev government refused to give them independence, but satisfied their demand for a change in spelling. The basic message was: "Damn you, we will write your capital in whatever way you want, but you are not going to see your independence." All his resistance was in vain Estonia became free anyway, and the Russian spelling disappeared.

The next phenomenon the declaration of independence or sovereignty by one after another of the former union and autonomous republics was later named the "parade of sovereignties". Some of those republics received new names. More precisely, these names existed earlier in the languages of peoples of these republics. Byelorussia was always called Belarus in Belorussian; Moldavia was always called Moldova in Moldavian; Kirgizia was always called Kyrgyzstan in Kirgizian. Now, however, in a naive attempt to prove themselves self-confident, the governments of these countries demanded that the whole world call them by these names and not by any other without any consideration for the historic and linguistic traditions of other peoples. Official Russia accepted this demand because of political considerations.

Now, imagine a map in which the countries are called Polska, Deutschland, Ellas, Magyarorsag, Chzhun-Go, Nippon. These are only few examples. The country which its own residents call Deutschland has many other names: Allemagne in French, Niemcye in Polish, Germaniya in Russian, Nimetchina in Ukrainian, Germany in English, Saksa in Finnish, Vokietuja in Litianian — as many names as there are languages in the world. The country, however, does not feel offended by that. Even in the former Soviet Union itself, Sakartvelo is quite unruffled about being called Gruzia in Russian and Georgia in English. The same can be said about Lietuva which is called Litva in Russian and Lithuania in English, or Armenia whose "native" name is Ayastan.

It is not surprising that many Russian cultural activists have raised their voices against the new names. In one of his speeches devoted to Pushkin, academician D. S. Likhachev mentioned Moldavia and stressed that he called the country Moldavia, and not Moldova, because he was speaking Russian. Kyrgyzstan looks and sounds really awkward in Russian. This combination of letters and sounds is not possible in the language. Nevertheless, the new names were officially accepted in Russian and started to spread around in the vernacular.

Following the demand to change country names, a new demand was voiced: to change the pronunciation and spelling of city names. Special laws, defining Russian spelling and pronunciation of city names, were issued in Turkmenia, Kazakhstan, Moldavia: Ashgabat instead of Ashkhabad, and Almaty instead of Alma-Ata, etc.

I have to mention that some people understand how ludicrous the demands of their leaders are. A friend of mine went on a business trip to Lvov, to meet with several local economists. They were speaking Russian, but out of respect my friend kept calling the city Lviv. Every time they would correct him: " No, not Lviv, Lvov. We are speaking Russian". I will return to Ukraine later, but at this moment I would like to talk a little bit longer about the renaming of cities in other republics.

Up till now I have only been talking about changes in spellings of city and country names. In their law, the Kazakhstan Supreme Soviet referred to this process as the "reorganization of Russian spelling of city names". We should not equate mere changes in spelling and pronunciation (Ashkhabad | Ashgabad), with renamings. In Kazakhstan for example, during the de-Russification some cities got the spelling of their name changed (examples are Alma-Ata — Almaty, Chimkent — Shimkent), while others got new names. For example, Shevchenko regained its old names: Aktay. However, the renaming of the city of Gur'yev into Aterau is not a restoration of history, but, on the contrary, the destruction of it. The motives here are nationalistic. Gur'yev was named after its founder, a Russian fisherman Mikhail Gur'yev. At the same time Leninogorsk is still on the map, as well as the second Leninogorsk, in Tataria.

There is a city in Kirgizia that used to be called Rybach'ye. The locals call it Balykchi, Kirgizian translation of the Russian name. The city was renamed into Issyk-Kul' (afte the lake) in 1989. This name, however, is only used as an official name. Its population still calls it Rybach'ye or Balykchi. The second city on the Issyk-Kul' lake, Przheval'sk, got its old name, Karakol, back for the second time in 1992. At the same time, many streets still carry names of communists. Dzerzhinsky Street in Bishkek was renamed to Erkindik Boulevard only partially around the location of the US Embassy. By the way Erkindik means "freedom"!

The toponymic situation in Zakavkazie is very complicated. The Armenian-Azeri war for Nagorny Karabakh is six years old. During these years in Armenia all geographic names which had Turkish linguistic roots were renamed. In Azerbaijan the reverse occurred: all names with Armenian roots were changed: for example, Vartashen is now Ogus, Getakshen is Gabelya. Also, in Armenia all cities named after communists were renamed, except for the city of Stepanavan. This city was named after the Bolshevik Stepan Shaumyan. Another city named after Shaumian is the capital of Nagorny Karabakh, Stepanakert. Azeri authorities announced the return of its old name, Hankedi, but neither Nagorny Karabakh nor Armenia, accepted this renaming. Thus, Armenia still has both Stapanakert and Stepanavan on the map.

Armenians experienced a certain difficulty with Kirovakan. The old name, Karaklis, could not be used because of its Turkic roots. For two years they were thinking of a new name and finally, last year the city was renamed into Vanadzor.

I still have an issue of Isvestia from June 16, 1992 with two articles about South Osetia. The article presenting the situation from the Georgian point of view called the capital of South Ossetia, Tskhinvali. The article presenting the situation from the Ossetian side called the same city, Tskhinval. The same city was mentioned under two different names on the same page of a newspaper.

Of course, this reflects a very complicated, often tragic, process going on in different regions of the former Soviet Union. The policy of de-Russification which is being implemented by many governments is understandable. However, many of the actions of the governments of the newly independent states actually repeat the old actions of Moscow, although from a different point of view. This is not surprising. First, the leaders of the states grew up during the communist rule. Second, many of these leaders used to have prominent positions in the leaderships of local Communist parties. The former First Secretary of the Central Committee of the Turkmenian Communist Party, now the president of independent Turkmenistan, Sapamurad Niyazov, has surpassed everybody. The following entities are named after him: Karakum canal (formerly named after Lenin), the former Lenin region and Lenin Street in the capital, central streets of the oblast centers, the Academy of Agricultural Sciences, several industrial enterprises, kolhozes, sovhozes, and many more. Three regions (etraps, in Turkmenian) are also named after the president: Niyazovskiy, named after S. Niyazov, and named after Sapamurad Turkmenbashi.

The last name needs to be discussed in greater detail. "Sapamurad Turkmenbashi" means "Chief of all the Turkmens". This name was officially given to Niyazov. A suggestion was raised to build a new, contemporary, city in Turmenistan and to name it "Sapamurad Turkmenbashi". It is known, however, that building a city is a long business, so in December 1993, the city of Krasnovodsk was renamed into the city of Turkmenbashi. The newspaper "Novoe Russkoye Slovo" published an article titled, "The country named after the president".

Some illuminating conflicts arise between anti-Communist and nationalist interests. Bolshevik leaders are still honored with the names of Dnepropetrovsk (formerly Yekaterinoslav) and Kirovograd (formerly Yelizavetgrad) in Ukraine. Returning their old names to them would mean doing honor to Russian tsarinas Katherine the Second and Elizabeth, both hated by Ukrainian nationalists.

In the former Soviet Union, during the name game there have been created not only new country names but also new geographic region names. Looking through the Russian papers, all of us have noticed that the world "Baltia" has been substituted for "Pribaltica". Can anybody explain why Baltia is better than Pribaltica? I have only one explanation for this phenomenon. The Russian language is currently being subjected to a very strong American influence. According to the American geographic and geopolitical tradition, Lithuania, Latvia and Estonia are called the Baltic States: Baltiyskiye Strany, which is Baltia.

Here is another example of American influence. There are two different terms in Russian geographic tradition: Central Asia and Middle Asia. According to the Geographic Encyclopedic Dictionary, Middle Asia is "the part of the Asian territory of the USSR stretching from the Caspian Sea, in the West, to the China border, in the East; and from the Aral-Irtysh divide, in the North, to the Iran and Afghanistan borders in the South. Very often this term is used only for the territory which includes Uzbekistan, Kirgizia, Tadzhikistan and Turkmenia". In contrast, Central Asia is a natural region which encompasses the continental portions of China and Mongolia. However, in American tradition, Central Asia comprises what the ex-members of the Soviet Union call Middle Asia and Kazakhstan. Today, the countries of that region are calling themselves Central Asia in Russian, and the Russian newspapers repeat this definition after them. I have to say that by no means is this the fault of the English language or of the United States.

Unfortunately, I do not have enough time to tell you about other manifestations of the name game. So, I will limit myself to the freshest news. Two weeks ago, the Associated Press reported from Moscow that "The Russian name game, the decades-old practice of changing place names every political season, is taking a new spin. Russian-language television and radio programs broadcast the dropping of a pronunciation they had been using since the breakup of the Soviet Union in 1991. Under the new policy, the former Soviet republic of Belarus once again will be referred to as Byelorussia, Moldova becomes Moldavia and Kyrgyzstan becomes Kirgizia. The Kazakh capital will be called Alma-Ata instead of Almaty, and the Russian Federation republics of Tatarstan and Bashkorstan will again be Tataria and Bashkiria..."

What is the appropriate reaction to this decision?

The Associated Press quotes a representative of the Academy of Russian language: "No language can dictate to the Russian language its own pronunciation and spelling rules for proper names..." In other words, Russian officials used linguistic arguments to support the change in policy. However, it is very obvious that the change had political ramifications.

I suspect, though, that in their usual fashion the Russian politicians failed to think through all the details. The names Bashkorstan and Tatarstan are included in the Constitution of the Russian Federation accepted just three months ago.

I have good reason to finish with the same words I did three years ago on Miami: the name game continues. Here is another fresh piece of information. One of the streets of the city Baranovochi in the Brest oblast has gotten back the communist name which it had recently lost: "the Street of 50-year anniversary of Komsomol". Everything is possible in the so-called "newly independent states".

Political Maps Issued During World War II: A Review

Pavel Ilyin

In this paper, I will offer a review of some maps published during the Second World War in Germany, Italy, the Soviet Union, the United States, and other countries, and discuss questions of the accuracy of maps and the degree to which they are reliable for researchers. This is rather an introduction to such an extensive subject: I would like to show the importance of this kind of research, first for studying how the events of the war were reflected on maps, and second for understanding the different approaches to the political geography of Europe at the time of the war, or, in other words, to politics and cartography.

The map research presented is mainly based on the collections of the Library of Congress; at the registry of Holocaust Survivors at the United States Holocaust Museum, we have a big collection of maps mostly photocopied from that library. It includes maps from 26 countries in 18 languages. In addition, I have used maps on DVD issued by National Geographic Society and studied atlases from my own small collection of old American publications. The oldest one in my collection is issued in 1830, but that was long before the wars of the 20th century.

Now I would like to ask a question. When did the First World War end for cartographers? Not on November 11, 1918, the date of the Armistice, which we now celebrate as Veterans Day, and not after the signing of the Versailles Treaty in 1919, or after changes to the map of Europe during the next several years. For cartographers, the First World War ended on January 13, 1935. That day a small parcel of prewar Germany, later known as Saarland, which had been ruled by France during the fifteen years following the end of the war, transferred to Germany after a referendum was held on which country the province should belong to.

Accordingly, for cartographers the Second World War started almost one and a half years before September 1, 1939-on March 13,

1938, when Hitler announced in Linz the legislation on the Anschluss of Austria into the German Reich.

The Munich agreement then followed: Germany, and afterwards Hungary and Poland annexed various pieces of Czechoslovakia, some large, some small. That was just the beginning; during the war, state boundaries in Europe changed some 40 times.

A couple more questions. In what country was Auschwitz, the main Nazi extermination camp? In Poland? No, it was located in Germany, in the Prussian province of Upper Silesia. And in what country did Białystok belong, let us say in 1940? It belonged to the Soviet Union and bore the Russian name Belostok.

When exploring the political geography of Europe, we need to use the maps published in different countries. Figuring out where events really took place is tricky when different maps tell different stories. Let us look at several especially interesting examples of such stories.

The Viennese publishing house of Freytag and Berndt has been printing maps for about a hundred years. It is very interesting to trace a country, or a continent, through its changes during several decades using their maps.

This is a map of Europe based on one published by Freytag and Berndt in 1942 (*see Appendix 3, Map 1*).

The war is in full swing. Eight countries that existed before the war have disappeared from the map: Czechoslovakia, Poland, Free City of Danzig, the three Baltic states (Estonia, Latvia and Lithuania), Yugoslavia, and Luxembourg. Two new countries have appeared — Slovakia and Croatia. Germany has new boundaries as the Greater Germany; ten other countries have new boundaries as well. We see six new administrative areas: The Protectorate of Bohemia and Moravia and Bialystok Gebiet within Greater Germany; the Reichskommissariats Ostland and Ukraine on the territory of the Soviet Union under German civil administration; Serbia under German military administration; and Montenegro under Italian administration. Only three countries involved in the war remained as they were in 1937—The Netherlands, Denmark, and Norway. Many changes on the map made some sense for the aggressors: Germany and Hungary got back some lands lost after the First World War; Bulgaria regained territories had ceded to neighboring countries following the Second Balkan War. Albania expanded to lands with Albanian populations.

The changes occurred so fast that publishers could not keep up. As a result, they used overprinting and depicted approximate borders instead of the actual ones. Sometimes they had to use newspapers as sources, as acknowledged in the margins of a map of Germany, issued by the General Staff of the Red Army.

First, I would like to demonstrate fragments of a map of Germany (Deutsches Reich) published before the war. (*Maps 2 and 3 — Germany before WWII*).

You can see here, outside German territory, boundaries of lands lost by the country after the First World War — A kind of cartographic revenge.

Here are two fragments of maps of Germany published by Ravenstein (*Map 4 — Germany after Munich Agreement*). The first one was published in 1938, after the Munich.

The map reflects the depiction of Austria. We see old Austrian names, such as a word "Österreich" and the names of provinces Ober- and Nieder-Österreich (Upper and Lower Austria). At the same time, we see overprinted the word "Ostmark"; Nazi renamed Österreich ("Eastern State") Ostmark ("Eastern March"). Another particularity of the map — the overprinting of the new boundaries of Czechoslovakia over the name of the country, as well of the name of the annexed territory: Sudeten Gau.

The second map was published a year later, after the final partition of Czechoslovakia.

Notice that new boundaries are overprinted in place of Czechoslovakia. The first part of the former country's name is crossed out, and the name of the newly born Slovakia starts with a dash.

Second: Ober and Nieder Österreich (Upper and Lower Austria) are no more: we see names Ober and Nieder Donau (Upper and Lower Danube) for these two former provinces, which are now Reichsgaues.

So, the former Austria is now Ostmark. But not for long. In 1942, the term was officially replaced by "Alpen-Donau-Reichsgaue" or "Donau und Alpenreichsgaue" (Alpine and Danubian Territories) (*Map 5 — New names of occupied countries*).

The partition of Czechoslovakia began with the tearing away of the Sudetenland. This is a fragment of what may be the first German map with the new German-Czechoslovakian boundaries of 1938 (*Map 6 — Czechoslovakia in 1938–1939*).

The joy of Nazi cartographers was so big that they made a new boundary line in the legend even much thicker than on the map.

This is fragment of another German map showing the partition of Czechoslovakia between Germany, Hungary, Poland, and Slovakia in 1938–1939 by using different colors.

In March 1939 Bohemia and Moravia were integrated into Germany as a protectorate. Slovakia was proclaimed as an independent state, which is currently referred to as the first Slovakian Republic. But this independence was so limited by Germany that on first maps, even German ones, we see Slovakia depicted as part of Germany — also as a protectorate.

Let us compare fragments of two German maps of France:
1940: Alsace and Lorraine in France (*Map 7*).
1942: Alsace and Lorraine in Germany (*Map 8*).
French map of the same period in1942 is showing Alsace and Lorraine in France! This is definitely not mistake, other lands annexed by Germany — Belgian Eupen and Malmedy, and Luxembourg — are shown within the boundaries of Greater Germany. We talked about cartographical revenge, and here I believe we can talk about cartographical resistance.

On the greater area of pre-1939 Ukraine the Nazis organized the so-called Reichksommissariat Ukraine under German civil administration (*Map 9 — Ukraine, occupied by Germany*).
This is a schematic map of the Reichskommissariat showing its division into Generalbezirks or administrative districts.
This map, titled Reichksommissariat Ukraine, was published by Freytag and Berndt.
This map (*Map 10—Transnistria, 1941*)is especially valuable because it shows the boundaries of Transnistria. In 1941, Romania took back its lands that had been ceded to the Soviet Union in 1940 (Bessarabia and North Bukovina), and gained the territory between the Dniester and Southern Bug Rivers, named Transnistria, with Odessa as its capital city. Interestingly, while this territory was annexed by Romania, it is shown on almost all German maps as Soviet territory occupied by Romania. This is a puzzle for me.

MAPS PUBLISHED IN DIFFERENT COUNTRIES

How much can a researcher trust a map? Let us explore.
Until September 1, 1939, when Poland was invaded by Germany and Soviet Union, one could rely on maps to be true.
After September 1, 1939, the maps published in Germany, Italy, and their allied countries continued to show the actual situation on the European continent. This is quite understandable since the

boundaries in Europe were changing with Germany's and Italy's blessings. Just note, however, that Germany used geographical maps for propaganda, as in the title of this ordinary map: "The New Order on the East." (*Map11— Italy and Albania, 1941*)

And another remark: the zero meridian on some Italian maps is not centered on Greenwich, but Rome!

The Soviet Union

We can also trust Soviet maps, at that time an ally of Germany. (*Map 12 — Belorussia, 1938*). Please note that Polish territory occupied by Germany is labeled on Soviet maps as "Sphere of State Interests of Germany." Everything changed after June 22, 1941, when the war between Soviet Union and Germany began. All boundaries in the maps published in the USSR returned to their pre-Munich state, with one exception, the boundaries of the Soviet Union!

Take a look at this Soviet map (*Map 13 — Poland after 1942*), published after June 22, 1941: you can see the Soviet boundaries drawn after September 1939, while all others as prior to Munich. I remember when I was seven or eight during the war, I could not understand why Poland had a small strange enclave north of Belostok. I did not know that this territory around Suwalki was a part of East Prussia at the time.

The United States

And what about American maps? This is the most interesting question. I must tell the truth, I understand nothing. Let us look on the following examples.

Collier's Atlas of 1941. The atlas opens with the Rand McNally map of Europe. Poland is shown divided between Germany and USSR.

Collier's Atlas of 1940 Poland is not divided between Germany and the USSR!

You can see the boundaries of Romania with Hungary and Bulgaria as after August 1940, but Romanian-Soviet one as before June 1940. And Poland is not shown divided between Germany and the USSR! The partition of Yugoslavia is not shown either.

Let us look at maps of that American geographical idol, National Geographic.

May 1940. Everything is all right. Poland divided, Wilno in Lithuania.

September 1941. The next maps of Europe were issued in 1942 and 1943-again without some exist boundaries.

Here are the National Geographic maps published in 1944 of Germany (in July) and the USSR (in December). Europe on these maps looks different. On the map of Germany (*Map 14— Germany, 1944*), all boundaries are as of September 1, 1939; on the map of the USSR (*Map 15—Germany, 1944*), Soviet boundaries are noted on the map as being "according to Russian treaties and claims as of October 1, 1944."

Sometimes the political correctness of that period seems bizarre. Hammond published three small maps on the same sheet (*Map 16— Poland, Baltic Republics, Hungary and Slovakia*).

Two of those maps depict the Baltic Soviet Republics and Poland with its prewar boundaries! On the map of the Soviet Baltic Republics Wilno (Vilnius) is indicated as the capital of the Lithuanian Soviet Socialist Republic; on the map of Poland it is the capital of the Polish Województwo Wileńskie! Geographical fiction.

Here are some more examples demonstrating that we have to be critical when using maps published in different countries.

Let us compare two maps of **Lithuania**, both issued before the war. Lithuania on those maps appears differently. On the map published in Lithuania (*Map 17—Lithuania before war, published in Lithuania*) we see the boundaries of Lithuania of as 1918, after the country proclaimed its independence. In 1920 Poland occupied and in 1922 formally annexed a substantial part of Lithuanian state, an action that Lithuania never recognized. A new actual boundary created by that action is referred to as an "administrative line" (or on some other maps as a "demarcation line") line. Accordingly, the lost lands are shown as "occupied by Poland," and all place names on this territory are the Lithuanian ones. On a map published in Poland (Map 18— Lithuania before war, published by Poland) the "demarcation line" is shown as a real state border.

Another example—the entire world considered **Bessarabia** to be a part of Romania. The Soviet Union considered Bessarabia as its territory illegitimately occupied by Romania. As a result, all Soviet maps published before 1940 showed this territory as shaded (*Map 19—Ukraine and Bessarabia before 1940, published by Soviet Union*).

CONCLUSION

In conclusion, I would like to say a few words about the practical importance of knowing the real boundary changes for Holocaust studies. In 1941, Yugoslavia was divided between six administrations: Albania, Bulgaria, Croatia, Germany, Hungary, and Italy. Each of those dealt with the "Jewish Question" somewhat differently. Under German rule the local Serbian authorities were the first in occupied Europe who proclaimed their territory "Judenfrei." Bulgarian policy against Jews was rather contradictory; one could say Bulgarian authorities sacrificed Macedonian and Thracian Jews to the Nazis to save Bulgarian Jews. Croatia established concentration camps for Jews, Serbs and Gypsies just several days after proclaiming independence. Italy not only made an effort to save its own Jews but also provided refuge to the Croatian Jews who were escaping from northern Croatia occupied by Germany to the southern area occupied by Italy. Albania is the only country in Europe where the Jewish population after the war was higher than before. Of course, Albania was under Italian rule, but Albanians themselves and their government were not enemies of the Jews. In Hungary the Jews of Bačka (Bacska), as well as of Transylvania, south Slovakia, and Ruthenia were considered "Hungarian Jews" by the Hungarian government and until German occupation of the country in 1944 felt relatively safe.

And a couple more words concerning postwar Europe. Some prewar boundaries were restored in the aftermath of 1945, but nevertheless by 1947, 11 countries had different borders than they had prior to the war and four prewar countries vanished completely as independent states. But that is another story.

THE POGROM ON THE MAP:

How The Soviet Regime Rewrote History By Changing Ukrainian Place Names

Pavel Ilyin

HIS NATIVE SHTETL

Professor Isaak Mayergoyz (1908–1975) was a prominent Soviet urban geographer and lecturer at the Moscow State University. Short and stocky, with a thick mane of silver hair, he was memorable, and although his classes were not included in my academic major (economic geography of the USSR), I noticed him whenever I happened to pass him in the hallway. Which was not that often, as his classes were on a different floor.

I first heard him speak after my graduation (I graduated in 1960), at a meeting of the Moscow Geographical Society, which was held in the lecture hall of the Moscow Society of Naturalists in the MSU's old building, as the Geographical Society then had no space of its own. Over time, hearing him speak or meeting him in an official or unofficial context, I came to greatly admire the depth and breadth of his thinking, his talent as a presenter, and his accessibility. Always surrounded by young people, he was never arrogant or overbearing but kind and patient, a compelling speaker one always wanted to keep listening to.

My next encounter with Professor Mayergoyz happened in 1985, ten years after his death, when his students decided to publish his collected works and needed someone to type up the text.[1] At that time, my family and I had already joined the ranks of refuseniks: we had applied to emigrate to Israel back in 1982, were denied permission, and as a result had lost virtually all our sources of income — a common punishment for would-be emigrants in those years. Thankfully,

---

[1] This means on a typewriter, as computers were then unavailable to ordinary Soviet citizens — *Translator's note.*

our friends periodically found various paying projects for us. Among them was Pavel Polian, who asked us to type up the first of Professor Mayergoyz's books. My wife, Mikhaella (Ella) Kagan, an urban developer by training, did most of the work, and I also did my part. That book, *The Territorial Structure of the Economy,* came out in 1986; another volume, *The Geography of Cities,* was published in 1987, after we had left the country. We kept our role in these publications a secret because at that time mentioning it could get people in trouble, and not only ourselves but also those who gave us this work. I am glad to be able finally to publicly thank Pavel Polian — along with other friends, such as Emma Vaynberg, Zhanna Zayontchkovskaya, Boris Ivanov and Inga Kantsebovskaya — for their courageous and generous help during our difficult years.

Although I knew that Professor Mayergoyz had been born in a shtetl (a small Jewish town or village) of Janów, or Yanov,[2] in the Ukraine, its exact location proved elusive: some sources place it in the Vinnytskaya *oblast* (region) in central and northern Ukraine, others in the historic region of Podolia. Of course, both are technically correct, since today's administrative region of Vinnytskaya *oblast* was once part of the Russian Imperial province (*gubernia*) of Podolia. As I was writing this article, I came across a third version, which claims that the former Podolian shtetl of Janów is now the town of Ivanpol in the Zhytomyrsky district. That, however, has to be an error, because Ivanpol's previous name was Januszpol, not Janów, and the city of Zhytomyr that gives its name to the district is located in yet another historic region, Volhynia (which straddles several countries, including Western Ukraine), and not in Podolia. I suspect that the error stems from the fact that Professor Mayergoyz graduated from a teachers' college in Zhytomyr and later taught in the area.

No, our Janów must be that village near Vinnytsia. Next, I turned to the map — and was surprised to discover that there was no Janów anywhere on the map of the Ukraine. No such place was listed in my administrative directory of Soviet Ukraine published in 1987. Guessing that the village must have been renamed, I was lucky to discover, at the Library of Congress, a Ukrainian edition of the same directory from 1946, which confirmed that the village of Janów is known today as Ivanov.

---

[2] Because virtually every place name mentioned in this article has variant spellings (Russian vs. Ukrainian vs. Polish, etc.), an effort has been made, when rendering them into English, to preserve the spelling that best reflects the historical context being discussed — *Translator's note.*

The Ukrainian edition proved to be a lucky find indeed. As I have since learned, Ukrainian directories, unlike their Russian counterparts, listed all population centers under both their old and new names. The 1946 directory, which covered the years of 1941–1946, showed that during that period, around 3,000 population centers were renamed, including several towns and villages originally named Janów. The pace of change varied, slowing down during the Nazi occupation and resuming on a mass scale in 1944 and especially 1946, after the restoration of the Soviet power in the Ukraine.[3]

This gave me the idea to write about changing toponyms in Soviet Ukraine at the end of World War II and in its immediate aftermath — starting with the history of the *shtetl* of Janów, a.k.a. the village of Ivanov.

JANÓW BEFORE THE SOVIET REVOLUTION

The old folks remember Janów, not Ivanov. The old Janów, known for its boisterous market days, taverns and numerous shops.

Online blog of Janów native
Leonid Reznik[4]

It is easy to find a place on a map, even one that has been renamed, if its location is known. Thirty kilometers above the city of Vinnytsia, the South Bug river veers south and is joined by the Snivoda river. There, in the bend of the Bug and the mouth of the Snivoda, stood the "settlement of Janów," mentioned in a 1552 chronicle describing the Vinnytsia castle. Other sources trace it even farther back, to the 14th-15th centuries. The name clearly derives from a Polish man named Jan, probably its founder or first landowner. The settlement was then part of the Grand Duchy of Lithuania, specifically the Podolian *voivodeship* (governorate). In 1566, it passed into the newly formed Bratslav *voivodeship*. That administrative act gave rise to a new geo-

---

[3] I should add that the same renaming fervor that overtook Professor Mayergoyz's birthplace also affected him personally. In 1950, at the height of Stalin's anti-Semitic campaign against "cosmopolitanism", the publishing house specializing in geography books published his book Kiev — replacing his own, unmistakably Jewish name with a bland pseudonym "I. Marchenko".

[4] http://leonid-70.narod.ru /text/Doc12.htm.

graphic region, the Bratslav (Breslov), whose inhabitants firmly believed that Bratslav and Podolia were separate and distinct entities. Three years later, the Union of Lublin created a Polish-Lithuanian Commonwealth, and both the Podolian and Bratslav voivodeships passed under the Kingdom of Poland. As did Janów, now counted as part of the Pikowski *volost* (district).

Local lore maintains that originally Janów was located on the right shore of the Bug and was re-founded later on the left shore, closer to the mouth of the Snivoda. (In fact, there is still an area on the right shore known as Janowka.) The new location offered the greater safety of rivers and woods, but more importantly, proximity to the busy trade route from Vinnytsia to Khmilnyk. Whereas the aforementioned chronicle lists Janów as possessing 16 households, that number tripled within a quarter-century, and on March 1, 1578 the Polish King Stefan Bàtory granted it the status of township. The royal charter, issued to then-landlord Gniewosz Strijevski, empowered him to "found a town within his estate of Janów in the Bratslav *voivodeship*." This included the right to build castles for the protection of the villagers, who in turn were enjoined to "drink, sell, buy, and pay taxes on their goods" and to "have within their homes sundry shops and taverns serving mead, beer, vodka and other drink", as well as to "hold a market day each week on Friday" — a tradition that continued for 400 years and only recently was changed to Saturday. The original inhabitants of Janów made their living by farming, raising cattle, fishing and woodcraft. The upgrade in status transformed Janów into a place of commerce and skilled trades. Around this time, the first Jews came to settle in the town, which eventually came to be known as a shtetl.

A *shtetl* is commonly known as a kind of settlement, in between a village and a town, possessing a mostly Jewish population and a distinctive culture and way of life. Within the Pale of Settlement, the shtetl became synonymous with Jewish life and worldview. Why did Jews settle in shtetls? The reasons lie in social, economic and legal circumstances: like larger cities, shtetls attracted Jewish merchants and artisans by their right to hold fairs and market days, which were a prerequisite to commerce. In turn, the landowners, interested in the economic development of their estates, granted certain privileges to Jews, such as the right to build homes in designated areas, to have a separate cemetery, a synagogue, their communal self-government, etc.

Though legend holds that in olden times the rivers ran deeper and the woods grew thicker, neither could shield Janów from the depreda-

73

tions of the Crimean Tatars, which regularly raided the Podolia and Bratslav regions. Janów found itself penned in between two roads used by the Tatar cavalry in their raids into the Ukraine and Poland: The Black Way (Czarny Szlak) ran along the left shore of the Bug, along the Dnieper watershed, while the Chumatsky Way ran along the right shore, along the Dniester watershed. When we add to this the periodic anti-feudal uprisings by the peasants and townsfolk, it becomes clear why Gniewosz Strijevski wanted to build a castle — albeit a smallish one, judging by contemporary sources, which refer to it as a "little castle".

In the beginning of the 17th century, the Pikowski and neighboring volosts became the arena of conflict between two magnates: Jan Tyczkiewicz and Jan (Ivan) Ostrojski, known to history under an affectionate diminutive of Janusz. The rivals ended their conflict by dividing their lands, with the Pikowski volost falling to Janusz Ostrojski. Upon assuming control of Janów, the new landlord renamed it Januszpol, or the Town of Janusz. This first administrative name change was short-lived, and the town itself disappeared from written records for a while; perhaps it was sacked by the Tatars. In any event, an authoritative map of the Ukraine from 1648, printed by Guillaume Levasseur de Beauplan, a French-Polish military engineer and cartographer, shows a "New Town of Ivanov," and other contemporary documents refer to a New Janów. The Podolia and Bratslav regions were annexed by Turkey in 1672 but reverted to Rzeczpospolita (Poland) in 1699.

Janów sat on private land that changed owners several times, until it came to be owned by the Kholonevsky family, kin to the Polish King Jan Sobieski and the source of future counts of the Austrian and Russian empires. At the end of the 17th century their holdings in Janów included over 300 households and up to 2,000 serfs. At the beginning of the next century the Kholonevskys made Janów their residence. In 1750 king August III confirmed Janów's township charter. The Kholonevskys built a new castle, founded a Bernardine (Cistercian) convent, built the Church of the Immaculate Conception and a town hall with a clock tower. Janów enjoyed a period of intensive growth as a commercial and skilled-trade center. Janów's textiles and shoes were much in demand, and members of the shoemakers' guild adopted a distinctive green dress.

The artisans and merchants — most if not all of them probably were Jews — lived in the center of town, near the castle. In 1765, the number of Jews in Janów and neighboring villages was 795; the rest of the inhabitants were Ukrainians or, to a lesser extent, Poles.

A "suburb" of Janów, known as Słobódka Janowska, grew up across the Snivoda; it survives today as the village of Słobódka.

In 1793, during the second partition of Poland, Janów — along with the rest of the Bratslav region — became part of the Russian empire. The voivodeships were reconstituted as the Podolian and Bratslav viceroyalties (*namestnichestvo*), and in 1797, as the Podolia gubernia with its seat in the city of Kamenets-Podolsk. The Bratslav region ceased to exist, and the town of Bratslav dwindled in importance, eventually becoming the village it is today. Janów's administrative transformations continued: it was made part of the Litinsky parish (uyezd) and then, in 1882, of the Vinnytsky parish. Which made sense, since Janów did not lie on a direct route to Litin, the parish center, and to reach the parish center one had to cross the neighboring Vinnytsky parish.

At the beginning of the 19th century, two print shops operated in the town, though not at the same time: one was Jewish (Hassidic), the other Christian. The latter printed books by Polish authors as well as by Old Rite Orthodox schismatics (*raskolniki*, or Old Believers): I was surprised to learn that in the middle of the century, over ten thousand Old Believers — a group more commonly associated with Siberia — lived in the Podolia *gubernia*. In 1864, the town had two churches: The Orthodox church of St. Nicholas, with a parish of 1,617 souls (the parish, originally Eastern-Rite Catholic, became Orthodox after its annexation by Russia), and a Roman Catholic church — the aforementioned Church of the Immaculate Conception — with 1,010 souls. The sources do not mention any synagogues or the size of their congregation, noting only the overall number of Jews in the *gubernia* and highlighting those population centers that housed "Jewish societies." These include our Janów: the 1847 census mentions a "Jewish society" of 1,798 people.

After 1861, a monument to the Russian emperor Aleksandr II (no longer extant, of course) was erected in Janów, and two schools were established, one of them a girls' school. And an 1882 source lists "[u]p to 2,000 inhabitants, half of them Jews. 410 households. A Catholic church, 2 Orthodox churches of stone, 2 synagogues, a beer brewery and a winery, 4 grain mills, 26 markets, 44 shops; 362 artisans, including a notable shoemakers' guild. 4,938 acres under cultivation."

The discrepancy between the 1847 and 1882 records is interesting: how likely is it that the Jewish population would have fallen so drastically in the absence of war or pogrom? I believe the reason lies not only in the flawed census-taking methods but also in the fact that the earlier census may have included the neighboring villages in the count.

In the 19th century the birthplace of Professor Mayergoyz was not the only Janów in the Western gubernias: the magisterial Russian-language Brockhaus and Efron encyclopedia lists at least three other towns of the same name. And Lippincott's *Gazetteer of the World* for 1866, 1873 and 1883 has an entry for "Ivanov, Ianov, or Janów", the name of several market-towns in Russia, with the most important of them being in the Podolia gubernia on the Bug River, 14 miles north-east of Litin.

Leonid Reznik, citing "archival sources," paints the following picture:

> A mail route runs through the town. The central part of town is taken up by Jewish homes. In the center is the market square with a rectangular remnant of the town hall converted into a hotel. The square is bounded on the west side by the Kholonevsky castle and a Roman Catholic church. The neighborhood located on the high bank of the Snivoda river is known as King's Hill: a folk legend claims that during a Polish-Turkish war, a Polish king encamped there with his army...
>
> Janów's artisans are still organized into three main guilds: the shoemakers, the potters, and the pig butchers. These guilds are like castes that avoid mingling with outsiders and maintain a distinctive style of dress... Besides these artisans, most of the Orthodox inhabitants are peasant farmers.
>
> There are around 3,000 Orthodox, 400 Catholics, and many more Jews... in 1887, there were 2,220 Jews, one synagogue and two Jewish prayer houses.

The 1897 census listed 5,545 total inhabitants, including 2,088 Jews. In the beginning of the 20th century, the town had a local bank and a post office. The work of local artisans continued to be in high demand: Brockhaus and Efron note that at local fairs, about three thousand rubles' worth of embroidered shirts were sold, a significant sum at the time. In 1900, a narrow-gauge railroad line Berdichev-Kalinovka passed through Janów. A portion of the line ran through Count Kholonevsky's land. The count gave his consent on condition that a station would be named after him. The railroad agreed, and to this day the local train station is called Kholonevskaya.

The Kholonevsky name is prominent in Janów, and deservedly so, as the family actively invested in its development. In the beginning of the 20th century Andrey Kholonevsky had close to 6,000 acres under cultivation, using mechanical planters, harvesters, balers, cultivators, and even a Case tractor from America. When a spark from the tractor caused a large fire, the Count funded the construction of new, tin-roofed homes to replace those lost in the fire and paid compensation to the families to cover their other losses. In 1905 he, with the help of the village council, built a bridge across the Bug to replace the existing ferry.

Around the time when Professor Mayergoyz was born, Janów regularly hosted a large fair. Twice a month, on Fridays, buyers and sellers from towns and villages far and near came to the fair. Sources described the Market and Horse Squares jammed with up to four hundred horse-drawn wagons; up to 150 cattle and countless smaller animals and poultry were offered for sale on any given market day. For two days, business was brisk and taverns were filled with people, especially the famous Blue Danube tavern. Then things quieted down until the next market day.

JANÓW AFTER THE REVOLUTION

The front line of World War I never reached Janów. In 1917, an independent Ukrainian People's Republic was proclaimed, but Janów, like the Ukraine generally, saw several regime changes in quick succession; armed forces loyal to various Ukrainian governments, to Nestor Makhno, or to a variety of warlords came and went. Several Jewish pogroms took place; Professor Mayergoyz probably remembered them. The worst pogrom lasted three days, July 15–17, 1919, and claimed 300 Jewish lives. A Jewish self-defense force was formed in the town but was unable to protect the residents from the thugs. A contemporary source lists Janów as one of the places most affected by pogroms. In 1920, the Polish Army forces took Janów, followed by the Red Army a few weeks later.

In 1922–23, the administrative system of gubernias and uyezds was replaced with *okrugs* and *raions*. Janów became part of the Pikovsky *raion* of the Vinnitsky *okrug* within the Ukrainian Soviet Socialist Republic. The shtetl ceased to exist as a category, and Janów officially became a village, even though everyone (including official documents) continued to refer to it as a shtetl. For example, documents issued by the Janów village council were signed by the "Chair of the village council, the shtetl of Janów."

The years of the Lenin's New Economic Policy in the 1920s were a time of relative prosperity for Janów. Its inhabitants resumed their skilled crafts, commerce and farming. A government-owned machine tractor station was set up, as well as the first farming co-ops (*selkhozartel*) — first, a Ukrainian one, then a short-lived Polish one. Jewish residents were also encouraged to farm, and a Jewish farming co-op was formed. The records of the local Communist Party branch of the Pikovsky *raion* paint an interesting picture of the life of Janów. The largest "industrial enterprise" was a 12 horse-power water-powered grain mill (previously owned by Count Kholonevsky) with a staff of three; there were two other similarly-sized businesses: a tannery and a sugar beet factory. This was typical in a *shtetl* — as was the fact that all the workers, as well as all the shopkeepers, were Jews: I did not find a single non-Jewish name on the lists of artisans and merchants.

In 1929, the population was 6,481, including 4,570 Ukrainians, 240 Poles, 47 Russians, 5 Belarussians and 1,619 Jews. A second, exclusively Jewish village council was established, which oversaw 2,301 residents in 1931 — a number that probably includes not only Janów's own Jews but also those from the surrounding areas. Despite the official anti-religious propaganda, the churches and prayer houses and the synagogue continued to operate, and Jewish children attended their own school.

At that time Professor Mayergoyz, like many of his compatriots, left home forever. Those who stayed behind fell victim to the "Great Break" that replaced the New Economic Policy, bringing *dekulakization* (the destruction of the wealthy peasantry) and *collectivization* (the forced consolidation of farmland and labor into collective farms). Another collective farm, a *kolkhoz* named after Kliment Voroshilov, was set up alongside the original co-op. Like their peers across the Ukraine and in other farming and cattle-raising areas, the peasants resisted these policies, slaughtering their livestock rather than turn it over to the *kolkhoz*. Disaster struck in 1932, when all food and seed grain were confiscated and none at all remained for the people. The terrible winter of 1933 saw incidents of cannibalism; some records put famine-related deaths in Janów at three hundred. The *Holodomor* (Government-induced famine) broke the spirit of resistance, and in 1935 the level of collectivization in Janów reached the official goal of 100%.

In 1932, the Vinnitsky *okrug* became part of the newly formed Vinnitskaya *oblast*. The intermediate entities, the *raions*, were consolidated, and Janów was assigned to the Kalinovsky *raion*, where it remains today. Life in the town slowly became more settled. In 1936, a new railroad line Kiev-Kamenets-Podolsky was extended to run through the town. Although the material conditions improved, all religious institutions and the Jewish village council and school were closed. The Great Terror left its mark on the town. And then came the year 1941.

The Germans occupied Janów exactly a month after the start of the war, on July 22, 1941. Few people were able to evacuate. At first, the town was placed under German military rule, but at the end of October it was transferred under German civilian administration and assigned the following "address": *Janów, Rayon und Kreisgebiet Kalinowka, Generalbezirk Shitomir, Reichskommissariat Ukraine.*

Dark days began for the Jews of Janów: they were ordered to wear a six-pointed star (to which, later, a yellow circle was added) and forced to perform hard labor, often without pay. As everywhere in the Ukraine, they were robbed and beaten by German-appointed Ukrainian policemen and eager anti-Semitic civilians.

And in the beginning of 1942, the Janów ghetto was established. In March, a group of young Jewish men and women was brought in from Pikov. They worked felling timber in the nearby woods, and in May they were force-marched to Kalinovka. The Janów ghetto was short-lived: on May 30, 814 Jews were shot there. Not all victims met their death quietly: Leib Yanovsky, a frail, elderly tailor, called a gendarme over, snatched a razor blade from his pocket and slashed the enemy across the back of his neck, killing him. Another 194 Jews perished in two mass killings on June 6 and 11, bringing the total death toll among Janów's Jews to 1,008.

Leonid Reznik remembers:

> My grandfather and grandmother, along with seven other family members who had not managed to flee, were herded into the ghetto together with the rest of the shtetl's Jews and shot on May 30, 1942 in a ditch in the center of town... In 1945, immediately after the end of the war, my sister traveled to Vinnitsa and visited the mass grave containing the remains of her family members, along with the rest of Janów's Jews. The mass grave was marked with a small, modest monument. The place was as quiet as a ghost town.

On March 9, 1944 Janów was liberated by the Soviet forces of the 1st Ukrainian Front. All its Jews had been destroyed but the village remained, although it could no longer be called a *shtetl*. Its new official name, Ivanov, made the break with the past complete.

Today's Ivanov is home to 5,400 people, most of them farmers, raising wheat, sugar beets and cattle. The village has the typical village amenities: grain mills, repair shops for farm equipment, retail and service outlets. There are two other enterprises, perhaps less typical: a granite quarry and a gravel pit.

The notable buildings of the village have seen a lot of drastic changes. The castle was confiscated in 1920 to house a state buying agency that purchased farm produce (*zagotkontora*); three years later, it became a juvenile penal colony, and shortly before the war, an orphanage for children whose parents had been arrested in the purges. From 1963 to the present, the caste has been home to a boarding school. The town hall was destroyed during the war. The Kholonevsky train station is still in service. St. Nicholas' church was pulled down in 1935, and its bricks repurposed to build a school; 70 years later, a new St. Nicholas' church was built. The Catholic church was used as a club before being converted to a sports school. Today it is back in service as a church, but the red star was never removed from its façade.

The one building that is no longer there is the synagogue: after World War II, there were no Jews left in Ivanov and there are none today, except once a year, on May 30, when family members of Jews executed by the Nazis return to gather before the monument that marks their mass grave.

A TOPONYMIC POGROM

The Russian writer Vladimir Soloukhin, in a 1957 travelogue, consults the map to learn who lived in Vladimirskaya *oblast* in olden times. Yet if we were to query the map of the Ukraine, it would tell us little…

In 1918, the Central Council (Central Rada) of the newly independent Ukrainian People's Republic renamed the city of Yekaterinoslav as Sicheslav, after the previous experiment in Ukrainian independence, the Zaporozhian Sich of the 16th-18th centuries. The name changes continued apace after the Ukraine became a Soviet republic, as indeed they did all across the Soviet Union. Historical names of cities, towns, villages and hamlets disappeared from the map, to be replaced with names commemorating — in Russian or Ukrainian — the Soviet regime and its symbols: the youth league Komsomol, the revolutionary month of October, the Red Army and May Day. A sizeable number of places were renamed after Communist Party and Soviet leaders.

Even so, the name changes of 1943–1946 stand out — first, because of their sheer mass, and second, because they show a sort of "proletarian nationalism", a concerted effort to "Ukrainize" the map. I have already mentioned the 1946 directory that recorded over 3,000 official (i.e., forced) name changes during those years. This toponymic reform, which deserves a separate essay, was not necessarily all bad — in some instances, it corrected historical anomalies, such as a village named Village or a hamlet named Hamlet. But now I would like to look at the fate of those names that have historical significance, i.e., those that reflect the ethnic diversity of pre-war Ukraine.

In today's Ukrainian discourse, one hears of "toponymic genocide" committed by the Soviet regime in giving Soviet names to Ukrainian places. Yet even a cursory look at a map shows that, while Soviet toponyms stand out, their density is not that high. Evidently, the "Sovietization" of the map was not aimed at supplanting everything Ukrainian. In contrast, the concerted replacement of German, Polish, Jewish, Hungarian, Romanian, Tatar and other "foreign" names with Ukrainian names suggests a xenophobic intent that may be understood as a sort of "toponymic pogrom."

Prior to it, the map of the Ukraine included 9 places named Janów and 33 places named Janowka, in addition to over a hundred other toponyms actually or possibly derived from the Polish name of Jan. These included not only places that sat on Polish lands annexed to the Ukraine during the 1939 partition of Poland but also places that had been part of the Soviet Union from its inception and had inherited their names from Rzeczpospolita and subsequently from the Russian Empire. The birthplace of Professor Mayergoyz was one of them.

Most of these Jan-derived names were replaced with those derived from the Russian/Ukrainian equivalent, Ivan: half of them became Ivanovka while the rest took on the more varied forms of Ivanov, Ivankovka, Ivankovichi, etc. Only three of the original names escaped the massacre of the 1943–46: a Janiszevka in Odesskaya *oblast*, a Januszevka in Kharkovskaya *oblast*, and a village adjoining the Janów railroad station in Kievskaya *oblast*. This last Janów fell victim to another disaster: the Chernobyl nuclear power plant was built nearby, attached to the city of Pripyat; after the Chernobyl disaster, Janów was razed and buried as part of the cleanup and is now officially off the books as being uninhabited. The Januszevka in Kharkovskaya oblast did not survive, either; only the Janiszevka in Odesskaya oblast remains, a lone survivor out of a group of a hundred and ten.

The second most common group of toponyms on the map of the Ukraine were names derived from the Polish name of Józef: 20 villages named Józefovka, five Józefpols, a Józefin, a Józefovo, etc.: forty-eight in total. Not one of the names remains today, and forty-three of the places bear the name of Osipovka, derived from the Russian equivalent, Osip. Today's city of Donetsk was originally named Yuzovka, though that name was not derived from the similar-sounding Polish "Józef" but (even worse, from a xenophobe's standpoint) from the name of its founder, British businessman John Hughes.

The same fate befell other foreign names on the map, which spanned an entire alphabet of proper names, including Adam, Barbara, Cecilia, Hermann, Isabella, Leonard, Raphael, Sigmund, Vincent, etc. Most of these were Polish and German; less common were Czech, Hungarian, Romanian and Bulgarian names. There were also names hailing from faraway lands, carried here like exotic seeds on a stray wind: the French André, the Swedish Gustav, the Georgian Irakli. I counted 220 place names derived from foreign proper names (not counting Jan and Józef). They are all gone, even Aristarkhovka, named after the impeccably Orthodox saint Aristarch but doomed by the foreign sound of its name.

And this is not even counting Jewish names, which would have seemed worse than foreign names to the anti-Semitic officials of that time: Meyerovka, Taubovka, Leibovka, Hertzevo, Berkov.

Under the rubric of place names derived from foreign places, the old map contained a hamlet named Amerika in the Lvovskaya *oblast* and a Novo-Amerika in the Nikolayevskaya *oblast,* as well as a Kitai (China), two Manchurias, two Shveytsarias (Switzerland), an Alsace, a Baden, an Alt-Nassau, a Bosniachina. All have been renamed. The rulers of the new, Soviet Ukraine even erased names derived from sister Soviet republics, such as the hamlets of Litva (Lithuania), Moldova and Novaya Moldavia.

Most of the place names derived from ethnonyms (names of people groups) were also erased. These were, if anything, even more revealing of the rich and varied history of the Ukraine, the home and transit point to many ethnic groups. The Poles were in the lead, with over forty place names derived from "Lyakh", the Ukrainian word for "Pole": Lyakhi, Lyakhov, Lyakhovtsy, etc. The Tatars were next, with 29 place names: Tatary, Tatarintsy, Tatarovka, etc. There were villages and hamlets named after the Germans, Prussians and Swabians; there was a hamlet Yevreyskaya Dolina (Jewish Dale); there were villages named after the Lithuanians, the Czechs, the Bulgarians, the Hungarians, the Turks, the French, the Greeks, the Italians, the Gypsies, the Persians. None remain today.

A separate subgroup of names denoted ethnic groups living together in neighboring villages: Ukrainskaya Dolina and Czechskaya Dolina, Slobodzea Moldavskaya and Slobodzea Ukrainskaya, Novoselki Russkiye and Novoselki Czechskiye, Ulyaniki Polskiye and Ulianiki Ukrain-skiye, etc. All are gone. Which is understandable, in a way: if the authorities had renamed Czechskaya Dolina but left Ukrainskaya Dolina alone, some inquiring mind might guess that the existence of Ukrain-skaya Dolina meant that there once had been some other kind of Do-lina. So, these neighboring pairs became simply Dolina and Dolina II.

There were also villages named after foreign cities: settlers often named their new homes after their native towns. Most of these were German, since German colonists played a prominent role in the set-tling of the Ukraine, especially in the Novorossiya region in the south. The old map was adorned with Lesnye Berlintsy and Vorobyevo-Berlin, Heidelberg and Stary Danzig, Kassel, Munchen and Novo-Munchen, and no fewer than three Strassburgs. To these can be added Dalekiy Rim (Rome), Zurichtal, Varshava (Warsaw), etc. All of them fell victim to the purge of 1946. A village of New York in the Donbass region mi-raculously escaped the purge but was renamed a few years later.

Could it be that there were simply too many foreign toponyms? Let us briefly leave the Ukraine and look over to the South Ural region in Chelyabinskaya *oblast*, in Russia. I recall traveling there in my college days, in 1957: after passing a Bulgarian-sounding Varna, we reached a French-sounding Fère-Champenoise, the administrative center of the Nagaybaksky *raion*, the next day. The same area of Russia is also home to the villages of Paris, Kassel, Arcy, Berlin, Leipzig, Borodino, Tarutino, and others, named after battles won by the Russian army and fleet.

The old map of the Ukraine also contained a Borodino and a Taru-tino, in South Bessarabia. There were, as well, a Leipzig and a Berlin, a Paris and a Fère-Champenoise (Old and New). When South Bessara-bia was first colonized, in the early 19th century, these villages were named after the battles of the war against Napoleon. But they ap-pear only on old maps — except one, Artsys, named after the 1814 bat-tle on Arcis-sur-Aube. There was a city of Orenburg in Russia, in the Ural, and a hamlet of Orenburg in the Ukraine, in Dniepropetrovskaya *oblast*. The Russian Orenburg was renamed Chkalov three years be-fore the German invasion; its Ukrainian namesake followed suit in the 1940s. However, while the Russian Orenburg regained its historical name in 1957, its Ukrainian counterpart was forgotten.

A few words on other foreign toponyms, beginning, again, with German names. Many Ukrainian place names ended in -berg, from the German word "mountain" (e.g., Gayberg), -burg ("town", as in Yam-burg), -stadt and -stedt ("city", as in Liebenstadt, Hochstedt), -tal ("dole", as in Kleinliebental), -*wald* and -*walden* ("vale", as in Unter-walden), -*feld* ("field", as in Dornfeld), -*stein* ("stone", as in Blumen-stein), -*heim* ("home", as in Gnagenheim), -*dorf* ("village", as in Lust-dorf, the famous suburb of Odessa, which became Tchernomorka). There were many names beginning in *Neu-* or its Russified equivalents of *Noy-* or *Nay-* ("new", as in Naydorf), and many others. None of them have survived!

Alongside villages and hamlets, there were also "colonies" — reminders of the time of German colonization. The name "colony" was part of the toponyms of the village of Kolonia Dubrovka, the hamlet of Kolonia Melnitsa (Grain Mill), etc. These are also gone: the colony as a category was abolished and the names were changed.

Polish names are another discrete group. Whereas German names were clearly "foreign" (even those going back to the 19th century), Polish names are arguably native to the region, because Ukrainian lands, over several different periods (some of them quite prolonged), were part of a Polish state. This is reflected in the toponyms. For example, I found 24 names derived from the Polish *wojt* (a type of local official), e.g., Wojtow, Wojtowka, Wojtowiczy, as well as six names derived from *soltys* (village elder), such as Soltysy, Soltystwo, etc. There were also names derived from *szlachta* (nobility), *ksiądz* (priest), *pan* (landowner), etc. All of them are gone.

The same is true of Turkic names, also native to the region. Before World War II, there were ten place names beginning with *ak-*, the Turkic root meaning "white", as in Akmangit or Akkerman, the latter meaning "white fortress"; there were such names as Yurtuk, Urzuf, Hajji-Hurda, Cheremurza, Kairakliya, Ajigol, etc.; they were all changed.

The renaming fever claimed the names with religious connotations tied to other faiths beyond mainstream Orthodox Christianity: Mechet' (mosque), Baptisty, Massony (Freemasons), or names of heretical sects within the Orthodox faith, such as Skoptsy or Molokans. Equally undesirable were names reminiscent of prior attempts at the reunification of the Catholic and Orthodox churches, or "unia" (union).

Most of the renamed places were villages or hamlets; only a handful were towns or cities, and only two of those had original names of "foreign" origin: Kamenka-Strumiłowa in Lvovskaya *oblast* (a Polish name), renamed Kamianka-Buzka in 1944, and Sevlyush in Zakarpatye (a phonetic transcription of Romanian "Seleuşu Mare"), now Vinohradiv.

Jewish names deserve a special mention. Perhaps we should have started with them: since no Jews remained in the Ukraine at the end of the Nazi occupation, Jewish place names were the first to be erased from the map. Ukrainian Jews spoke Yiddish, which shares many words with German: for example, in both languages *dorf* means "village", and *feld* means "field". Therefore, such toponyms as Neudorf or Neufeld might be either Jewish or German, and it is difficult to determine their provenance without knowing their history.

In the first half of the 19th century, the Russian government initiated and encouraged the colonization of recently annexed lands around the Black Sea, including by Jewish settlers. Between 1807 and 1860, 38 Jewish colonies were established in the Khersonskaya and Yekaterinoslavskaya *gubernias* in Novorossiya. Only four of them — Seidemenukha (from "sde menukha", הדש החונמ = "quiet field"), Yefingar (from "yofi" and "nagar", יפוי רהנ = "beautiful river"), Nagartav ("nagar tov", רהנ בוט = "good river") and Izrailevka — were given names derived from Hebrew; the government quickly put a stop to this practice.

The next phase of Jewish agricultural settlement in Southern Ukraine took place in Soviet times: over 120 villages were established in 1924–1938, and many were given Yiddish names: Lenindorf and other -*dorfs* (e.g., Ratndorf, Freidorf); Blumenfeld and other -*felds* (e.g., Reutfeld, Frunzenfeld); villages called Grosser, Neuvelt, Freiland, Freileben, Emet, Sholem Aleichem... Around that time, Big Seidemenukha became Kalinindorf, and Little Seidemenukha became Sterndorf. These toponyms proved short-lived; the Nazis, after murdering all the Jews who had not fled, gave German names to their villages: Kalinindorf became Gross Ingulez, Stalindorf became Friesendorf, probably in order to remove the memory of Soviet leaders for whom these villages were named. Although I have no information on the other villages, how likely is it that a Judendorf would have survived in Reichskommissariat Ukraine?

Nor did these names survive in the Soviet Socialist Republic of Ukraine; the liberation of its territory from Nazi occupation completed the "final solution to the Jewish question" on the map of the Ukraine. Most of the Jewish place names were erased (modern anti-Semites would say "wiped out") in 1944, and the rest, in 1946. The village of Ozetovka was renamed, to remove the memory of OZET, the Society for the Settlement of Jewish Toilers on the Land. The only two to survive, whether through an oversight or for other, unknown reasons, were the Kalinindorf station on the Odesskaya railroad line and the village of Little Seidemenukha, which got its name back in 1944. (In one instance, the cartographers displayed uncanny political foresight, renaming the villages of Weismanovka and Mendeldorf in advance of the fateful 1948 session of the Soviet Academy of Agricultural Sciences that denounced traditional — i.e., Western — genetics, and with it the works of August Weismann and Gregor Mendel.)

A similar dynamic existed in the Crimea. New Jewish settlements in the Crimea in the 1920s were initially given Hebrew names — a practice that was quickly squashed by the Soviet regime once it was established in the area. Yiddish toponyms were allowed but, once again, not for long. In this way, the Soviet regime took the same stance on the "Jewish question" as the Czarist regime had done previously.

After the fall of the Soviet Union, some of the results of the toponymic purges described above began to be reversed. Among the first original place names to be restored in newly independent Ukraine were German-derived Berlin and Germanovka, Polish-derived Lyakhovtsy, Wojtowka, Szlachtentsy and Uniev, Tatar-derived Urzuf, Hungarian-derived Ugorskoye, Czech-derived Tudorovici, French-derived Surété, and two of the names beginning in "Jan-": Janoszy and Jangelovka.

* * *

Today's Ivanov, formerly Janów, is proud of its native sons, among whom are writers Stefan Witwicki, Oleg Chornoguz and Vitaly Berezinsky, and other prominent figures. Professor Isaak Mayergoyz deserves to be counted among them.

A Shift in The Main Functions of Urban Settlements and Its Impact on the Dynamics of Urban Population Dispersion

Pavel Ilyin

Dynamics of population dispersion in the USSR is characterized by constant growth of the large cities' share (population in excess of 100 000 residents) in the urban population and the population of a country as a whole. However, the development of individual cities is not consistent — different cities performing different functions are distinguished by their high dynamism at different times. In addition, among the multiple functions of cities, there are some functions that play a leading role and, consequently, draw other functions to a city, stimulate development and growth of cities, and exert influence on the whole picture of urban population dispersion. Shifts in such leading functions are related to societal development patterns as a whole.

Study of the dynamics of large Soviet cities' population during the inter-census periods has revealed that one can single out two stages of the large cities network development: the first stage in which the leading role belonged to an industrial function, and the second (current) stage in which the leading role has moved on to an administrative function (this function implies serving as a capital of a Soviet republic, a capital of an autonomous republic, or as an administrative center of an oblast or a krai).

The baseline is set by the first national census that registered the urban population at the end of the recovery period in December of 1926. The beginning of industrialization in the USSR was accompanied by a tremendous growth of urban population. From 1926 through 1939, the number of large cities had increased from 31 to 84. Moreover, 28 of them had increased by three times or more — among them were five that had grown practically from scratch (Novokuznetsk,

Karaganda, Magnitogorsk, Murmansk, Dzerzhinsk), and seven of them had grown by more than five times (Prokopyevsk — which had grown tenfold, Gorlovka, Krivoy Rog, Kemerovo, Zaporozhye, Zhdanov, Bryansk).

Not a single one of those aforementioned 12 cities at its inception was an administrative center, and neither were many other cities. Industrialization first and foremost demanded the development of coal and metallurgical bases. This is precisely why coal-mining and metallurgical cities grew at the highest pace — 16 of the aforementioned 28.

Administrative units of the USSR at that period of time were undergoing two stages of development: firstly, their enlargement at a time when the cities, which, by virtue of their industrial capacity and their economic and geographic location, were able to govern vast territories and become centers of large krais and oblasts; secondly, their breaking into smaller localities, which process continued into the post Second World War years. Additionally, there emerged a large number of the centers of various national subdivisions. However, administrative status was, as a rule, not playing a significant role as a driving force of urban development (with the exception of a few national centers.) Moreover, industrial development led to a situation in which many of dynamic cities of that time became oblast centers (Karaganda, Donetsk, Murmansk, Voroshilovgrad, Zaporozhye, Kemerovo, Bryansk, etc.).

It could be assumed that 1959 was a turning point in the mechanism that was driving urban development. This turning point had to do with scientific and technical revolution. At that point, the dynamism of administrative centers soared, while the growth of purely industry-based cities — especially coal-mining and metallurgical cities — slowed down and, in some cases, even came to a halt. Thus, among the large cities of the 1970s which had experienced insignificant growth as compared to 1959 — by less than 20% (there are 18 cities of this kind, excluding Moscow and Leningrad which were ranked first and second among all cities of the country based on their overall population growth) — there is not a single administrative center. Seven cities with a population of more than 100 000 in 1959 (all of them were coal-mining towns) had become less populous.[1] This was unprecedented for peaceful times. Moreover, 11 out of the 25 cities whose population had increased insignificantly or decreased were

---

[1] *Results of the All-Union Census*, 1970, v.1, Moscow, 1972.

among the most dynamically growing in the course of industrialization and during the war.

The same trends persisted in the 70s. Among the 17 large cities recorded by the 1979 census, the populations of which had increased only by 10 percent[2] as compared to 1970, there is only one oblast-level center (Karaganda). Among the five cities with a population of 100 000 that had become less populous, there are no administrative centers either. All of them are purely industrial cities. The largest of the "non-administrative" cities, Krivoy Rog, is ranked 31st among the list of cities in the country.[3]

The predominant development of administrative centers brought about a clearly pronounced monocentric nature of urban population dispersion in the USSR: the populations of nearly two thirds of the so-called "second" cities comprised less than 30 per cent of the populations in the corresponding administrative centers.[4] Based on the data of the 1979 Census, there were only two oblasts — Vologoda Oblast and Kemerovo Oblast — in which the "second cities" (Cherepovets and Novokuznetsk) were more populous than the oblast centers.

There are, of course, not only administrative cities that developed at a fairly quick pace. Moreover, six of the most dynamic large cities that had grown twofold in the 1970–1979 period happen to be non-administrative. These cities are Naberezhnye Chelny, Tolyatti, Nizhnekamsk and Staryi Oskol — the seats of the largest industrial enterprises in the nation; Surgut and Nizhnevartovsk — centers of the new developing regions that are based on extraction industry (for example, in this case, based on oil industry in Western Siberia; development of such centers may even lead to their transformation into oblast centers, as it happened with Shevchenko in Mangyshlak.) However, among the 14 centers which had grown by more than one and a half times we find 10 oblast centers (including the aforementioned Shevchenko) and four satellites of cities with more than a million-size population.[5]

---

[2] Due to the overall decrease in the urban population growth, the criterion for designating cities as localities with "high" and "low" dynamism became less stringent.

[3] *On the Preliminary Results of the 1979 All-Union Census. Report by the USSR Central Statistical Directorate.* Pravda, April 4, 1979.

[4] В.В. Покшишевский. *Проблема «второго» города.* In the book «Проблемы урбанизации и расселения». Moscow, 1976.

[5] Zelenograd and Odintsovov (satellites of Moscow), Kolpino (satellite of Leningrad), and Sumgayit (satellite of Baku).

One could say that non-administrative cities are growing "piecemeal" and "on a selective basis," while the administrative cities are growing "unanimously." Whereas in 1959 there were only 33 administrative centers among the 118 cities in the RSFSR, Ukraine, Belorussia and Kazakhstan (or 28 per cent) with a population of less than 100,000 — today only six of the current 121 administrative centers of these republics (just five per cent) have not become large cities.

As a side comment, one should point out that considering cities with more 100,000 residents to be large, most likely, does not apply to all times. If the notion of "large cities" were to incorporate not only quantitative, but also qualitative content defined by the role the cities play in the geographical organization of societal life — by their place in the hierarchy of cities — then for earlier historical times, it would be legitimate to consider cities with smaller populations as large (while for the modern times those would be cities with population larger than 200,000 people.) The following data is curious in that regard: Of the 34 cities that had 151,000 to 200,000 residents in 1970, 20 administrative centers had grown to larger than 200,000 residents by 1979, as compared to only eight of the remaining 14 cities.

One could quote even more statistical data evidencing a clear-cut trend of predominant growth of administrative centers in the network of large cities in the USSR for the past two decades. However, what we have already mentioned above is sufficient to support this statement. It is more important to try to answer the following question: what reasons have made and continue to make administrative functions so dominant that they stimulate development of other functions and attract more residents?

The answer to this question, apparently, resides in two different spheres: the general logic of the urbanization process on the one hand, and the internal properties of individual cities, on the other hand. In the period of industrialization, urbanization depended heavily on the development of material production.[6] Consequently, industrial function played a key role in the development of the network of large cities. This status quo undergoes a profound change with the conditions of scientific and technical revolution. The role of resources-related factors in the geography of the national economy decreases,[7] while the importance of governance, information, sci-

---

[6] А.С. Ахиезер, А.В. Кочетков. *Урбанизация и интенсификация производства в СССР.* В кн. «Ресурсы, среда, расселение». Moscow, 1972.

[7] А.А. Минц. *Прогнозная гипотеза развития народного хозяйства Европейской части СССР.* В кн. «Ресурсы, среда, расселение». Moscow, 1974, pp. 30–33.

ence, culture, social infrastructure, etc. increases. The criteria for assessing a particular territory by organizations that plan the national economy, as well as by the population in general, change.[8] In accordance to the demands and conditions of the scientific and technical revolution, the direct role of material production in the progress of urbanization decreases, which, in particular, is manifested in the loss of industrial function's leading role in the development of the network of large cities (however, for some cities, its significance may persist, as has been shown above.)

This is a kind of an external side of the process as relates to actual cities. From the internal perspective, administrative centers ended up being better prepared for the modern shift in manufacturing forces, which is characterized by the intellectualization of labor and an increase in the scale and magnitude of intellectual production,[9] as well as in requirements which scientific and technical revolution imposes on the geographic distribution of many spheres of activity, including the dispersion of advanced industries.

What can we say about internal properties that have contributed to this process? E. E. Leiserovich lists the high concentration of large cultural and social services institutions, the availability of higher education and scientific establishments, and the presence of public, government, and economic institutions as advantages of oblast, krai and republican (Autonomous Soviet Socialist Republics) centers as advantages.[10] Capitals of the Soviet republics have even more of these advantages. The latter one is the primary factor in this regard: the status of these cities leads to the concentration of public, government, and economic institutions. The administrative centers constitute complex and multifunctional cities with a large diversity of urban environments that is so important for the development of an identity.[11]

---

[8] С. Ахиезер, П. М. Ильин. *Задачи разработки социальных оценок территории в условиях научно-технической революции.* Vol. 1, Geographic Series of Izvestia of the USSR Academy of Sciences, 1975.

[9] С. Ахиезер. *Научно-техническая революция и некоторые социальные проблемы производства и управления.* Moscow, 1974, p. 102.

[10] Е. Е. Лейзерович. *Особенности развития областных, краевых и республиканских (АССР) центров в СССР.* Vol. 2 of the Moscow State University Gazette, Geography, 1972.

[11] Я. О. Яницкий. *Урбанизация и некоторые проблемы общественного развития.* В кн. «Урбанизация и формирование систем расселения». Moscow, 1978.

Under the conditions of the scientific and technical revolution, the urbanization and intensification of production process, "lead to significant shifts — primarily, in the outperforming growth rate of centers of manufacturing, storage, processing, and information broadcasting and of the development of governance centers... The higher the rate of societal development is, the higher is the role of governance and information production hubs.[12] Administrative centers belong to the realm of such hubs in the USSR.[13]

It should be expected that the leading role of the administrative function in the development of the network of large cities in the USSR will continue to grow in the modern stages of urbanization.

---

[12] С. Ахиезер, А. В. Кочетков. *Урбанизация и интенсификация производства в СССР*. В кн. «Проблемы современной урбанизации». Moscow, 1972, p. 82.

[13] In other countries administrative function may not play such a significant role. Read about the differences between the USSR and the USA in this regard in М. В. Гохман, П. М. Ильин, Ю. Г. Липец. *Значение фокусов роста в региональном развитии*. Vol. 6, Geographic Series of Izvestia of the Academy of Sciences, 1979.

THE SIGNIFICANCE OF GROWTH POLES
IN REGIONAL DEVELOPMENT

V. M. Gokhman; P. M. Ilyin; Yu. G. Lipets

(Institute of Geography, Moscow)

Abstract: A comparative analysis of the factors underlying growth-pole development in the USSR, the United States and India stressed the significance of the administrative factor in the USSR in recent years, the limited role played by that factor in the United States, and the multi factor aspect of growth centers in a developing country in India. With respect to spatial planning in the Soviet Union, a flexible policy of polarized growth is advocated. Such a strategy, which would call for continuous shifts in polarized development such as the latest propulsive industries are introduced into new growth points, is designed to limit the growth of extra-large urbanized areas and to help preserve an equilibrium in ecological systems.

Problems of economic growth and closely related aspects of socioeconomic development have assumed significance for all countries. Since most of them contain territories with a pronounced spatial differentiation of natural and socio-economic conditions, territorial aspects of development have assumed as much importance as general economic or sectoral aspects. They play a particularly significant role in such large countries as the USSR, the United States and India, although the territorial aspects should not be ignored in any country, regardless of size.

The economic growth concept is associated with absolute and relative (per capita) increases in some of the basic economic indicators, such as income, industrial and agricultural output, etc. The concept of socioeconomic development is much broader and includes a number of parameters that cannot be measured by the usual economic indicators and call for a system of social indicators. Such a system would include various kinds of nonmaterial production (public health, education, science and culture) and measures to protect the social and natural environment. The concepts of growth and development are not linked by a single-valued positive relationship, as reflected, for example, in the character of the impact of the growth of production and of consumption on the environment.

Some of the territorial problems of socioeconomic development involve regional balance, the overcoming of regional disparities, the revival of previously lagging regions and the development of new regions. Of interest in this connection is a determination of the regularities of spatial development based on analysis of the experience of various countries. Such an approach may help us understand the mechanisms of sectoral and territorial concentration of production and of population as an inherent factor in industrialization and urbanization.

The mechanism of concentration of economic activity is most evident not in continuous space but in discrete space, in the form of localized growth nodes or poles. The significance of spatial aspects of a concentration and its expression in polarized, rather than uniform, development of a territory was recognized as early as the 19th century by many geographers and economists (for example, J. H. Von Thunen, J. G. Kohl and L. Lalanne).

In the USSR, spatial aspects of development have been the focus of attention on the part of scientific and planning-administrative circles since the very first years of existence of the Soviet state. The early work on regionalization of the USSR made the point that "regionalization is not a technique for achieving decentralization, but, on the contrary, a key method for concentrating forces, attention, purpose, management and organization in Soviet development" (Rayonirovanye SSSR, 1926, p. 11).

The early GOELRO plan (for the electrification of Russia) and the first five-year plans, aside from stressing the significance of some of the older base centers and industrial regions, pointed up the role of new growth centers and poles, as reflected in the creation of the Urals-Kusnetsk development project and a number of giant industrial plants and the transition to the creation of territorial production complexes. This approach enabled N. N. Kolosovskiy, an active participant in the early plans, to formulate a rigorous territorial production complex theory back in the 1940s (Kolosovskiy, 1947).

Economic practice in the USSR has convincingly demonstrated the fundamental significance of polarized economic growth and its importance for the regulation of regional development with a view to optimization. But this has also required a theoretical conceptualization.

POLARIZED GROWTH CONCEPTS

The use of new mathematical techniques and linear algebra and programming, in conjunction with computers, made it possible to re-formulate some key propositions in the theory of spatial and regional development. In the USSR, this was reflected mainly in further per-fecting of territorial production complex theory and its practical ap-plication, especially in regions of pioneering development. In West-ern spatial economics, an effort to consider the growing role of spatial and regional aspects of development and the growing regional con-flict of scientific-technical revolution and the general crisis of cap-italism led, in particular, to the formulation of growth pole theory, which served as the core of concentration for a number of philosophi-cal and methodological approaches to problems in spatial economics and in economic geography. Growth pole theory, which was initially proposed by Perroux (1950, 1955), based on Leontief's input-output models, formalized the multiplier effects associated with the growth of production in certain industries. The input-output principle used in the Leontief model suggested that the growth of certain economic activities in a given center (the growth pole) might foster growth in the entire regional economy. It was suggested that decision makers might use growth pole theory in selecting suitable centers for invest-ment, especially governmental and other public investment designed to spur development in backward, underdeveloped or depressed re-gions, i.e., for at least a partial resolution of the social problems fac-ing the governments of capitalist countries. The choice of growth cen-ters was also expected to foster indirect economic measures, such as tax incentives and other benefits for attracting private capital.

Over the next decades, growth pole theory was frequently dis-cussed in the scientific literature, leading to the gradual accumulation of a veritable library of articles and books concerned with criticism, further development and possible applications of the theory. The most serious criticism that has been made, in our view, involves the fact that the methodological basis of the theory — and input-output model — is static and not very suitable for a conceptual framework that seeks to explain economic dynamics (Lasuen, 1969). Moreover, the theory had nothing to say about the origin of the propulsive in-dustries in the first growth point. It was also noted that the theory did not lend itself to quantification of the dominance of the growth center (Blaug, 1964), that it discounted the importance of innovation diffu-sion and that it could not be easily related to other theories in geography and in spatial economics. In an effort to interconnect the various lines of investigation in spatial development, D. Todd suggested that regional problems be categorized in three basic groups (Todd, 1973).

The first would include empirical regional studies, the typology of regions, the use of descriptive models (such as coefficients of localization and shift-share analysis), analysis of regional differentiation (for example, in the concepts of central place theory) and the construction of regionalization schemes (for example, the delimitation of polarized regions, as in Boudeville, 1966). The two other groups distinguished by Todd would be theoretical in character. One of them would be purely economic and would include attempts to use dynamic models such as the balanced growth models of the Harrod-Domar and Hartman-Seckler types or Hirschman's model of unbalanced growth.

Perroux's polarization concept was placed by Todd in the third group, together with theories regarding the export base, innovation diffusion and industrial complex analysis. These topics are probably closest to economic regionalization, unbalanced growth theory and the analysis of the location and integration of production.

In our view, a general theory of polarized development, even though imperfect and partly contradictory, can serve as a useful methodological tool in the forecasting and planning of regional development. However, lest it prove disappointing in practical application (see, for example, Darkoh, 1977), it would be well to cast such a theory in broader historical-geographic and spatial-economic terms. Moreover, it would have to be interlinked with improved models of the intersectional balance and the territorial production complex.

For refinement and quantification of the propulsive industries and the multiplier effects, industries would have to be broken down in terms of their spatial impact into at least four groups: local, regional, national and international (Tinbergen, 1963). Further refinement would have to be in keeping with the system of territorial production complex models, which consider the interconnected impact of industries on the entire territory (Modelirovaniye..., 1976). Such systems of models were initially constructed for a socialist economy based on the likelihood of labor shortages, but there are now also modifications for developing countries, with their labor surplus and need for coordinated development of large and small industries (Kuz'min, Lipets, 1974). Such models provide a sounder framework for tracing the impact of growth centers and systems of centers, especially in regions of new pioneering development.

However, such an evolution of polarized growth theory, while strengthening its applicability and economic soundness, still does not save it (or, for that matter, many of the other modern economic theories) from a major methodological shortcoming. The growth poles, by being considered solely in industrial-economic terms, are not being treated sufficiently as social entities, thus ignoring the overall trends of development of the system of centers and the factors that accounted for the growth of these centers in the past (and such an analysis is essential in view of the "ultrastability" of urban systems; see, for example, Steiss, 1975).

In the traditional terminology, growth pole theory represents an important sphere of application of historical-geographic analysis, without which, in our view, the theory (and especially its applications) would rest on a rather shaky foundation.

Our brief analysis was designed to point up the need for a differentiated functional-genetic approach to the behavior of growth poles in an overall system of urban centers. We don't agree with those critics who, together with the shortcomings and limitations of the work of Perroux and his followers, also reject the very existence of distinctive polarized development patterns, which assume different forms in socialist, lions developed capitalist and developing countries. The study of historical regularities of polarized development also strikes us as an essential for general economic and social forecasting for a more rational location of productive forces, and for the forecasting of systems of settlement.

The polarization of growth (or development) reflects the dual character of processes of societal development. "The development of leading centers and of their periphery does not constitute two interacting processes, but two aspects of the same process. The leading centers require the development of the periphery just as the periphery requires the development of the leading centers... It must be borne in mind, however, that these aspects if the development of society are far from equivalent or symmetrical. The determining aspect is the development of the leading centers, their organizing and directing role, since that is where the growth points are" (Akhiyezer, 1974, pp. 178–179). What we have, therefore, is an objective inevitability of polarization in the course of formation and development of growth centers, including geographical growth centers.

THE ROLE OF ADMINISTRATIVE STATUS
AS A FACTOR IN POLARIZED GROWTH IN THE USSR

In view of the universality of polarization, it may be of interest to trace the relative weight of factors that foster the conversion of a given center into a growth pole. The structure of such factors is usually reflected in genetic classifications of urban centers. For our purposes we made use of a typology that distinguished the following types of centers: administrative, transport-distribution, mining, and industrial centers and small centers with a favorable transport-geographic situation (which are potential growth centers, especially in newly developed regions or rapidly developing regions). (Another classification, devised by A. Mitra [1967] for Indian centers, distinguishes the following types: (1) mining and plantation; (2) craft industry; (3) manufacturing; (4) trade; (5) transport.)

A study of the dynamics of growth poles should be based on quantitative indicators. The simplest and most generally available measure is the change of population of cities (or agglomerations) that function as growth centers.

By combining a functional typology with the quantitative analysis of population of all the centers in a system of cites, we can study the dynamics of growth poles retrospectively. We used as our basis the relative growth of population, which (despite the usefulness of absolute growth) is a better indicator of trends of development.

Since the weight of one percent of growth will vary with the scale of the examined magnitude, we had to introduce a lower population limit for the growth poles. Many studies have used a population of 20,000 or so as a lower limit. However, for a microsystem as a whole we selected a limit of 100,000 population (it should be noted that we used a lower limit for the earlier stages of development).

A crucial factor in determining which cities are likely to become growth poles and, in particular, which ones are likely to display the highest rates of population growth and expansion of tributary areas is the administrative-political status of cities. It appears that the role of administrative centers as growth poles will greatly depend on the extent to which not only political-administrative, but also economic-management functions are concentrated in the hands of the state, i.e., the extent to which the state has an impact on country's economic life.

Using the USSR and the United States as examples, we can show the great extent to which administrative centers will differ in their roles as growth poles and the way in which these differences will affect the growth rates of cities with different administrative status and functions both through space and through time. (The retrospective analysis was based on census results and vital statistics for the respective years.)

Since cities of different types functioned as growth poles in the USSR during various periods, it may be useful to start with a periodization of this phenomenon. The best approach would be to use census data and to group the intercensal periods into historically significant epochs. In the case of Russia, however, this procedure is complicated by the fact that both World War I and the Civil War intervened between the first two census years of 1897 and 1926. We therefore used as our initial study period that time that elapsed between the 1897 census and World War I.

That initial period may be viewed as one of accelerated development of capitalism in Russia. We examined the cities that had at least 50,000 population at the beginning of the war. The country's industrial development was then based on existing large cities. However, capitalism also had need for new centers, especially in view of the vast size of underdeveloped regions in Russia. Out of the 10 cities with the highest rates of population growth, eight wars were in Siberia and the Far East; they were of two types: transport-distribution centers and potential growth poles with a favorable transport-geographic situation. Their development was undoubtedly affected by the construction of the Trans-Siberian Railroad, which greatly facilitated economic linkages with European Russia.

Among the centers of this group was Novorossiysk, the Black Sea port with a favorable transport-geographic situation.

All these centers grew by three times or more. The same high rate of growth was also observed in Ivanovo, which had developed in the heart of an old region of craft industries and manufactures. This rapid growth in an old industrial region can be explained by the fact that its leading activity (textiles) was based on an old technology. No such rapid rate of growth would have been conceivable in the traditional regions of charcoal-based iron smelting since the advanced technology in the iron and steel industry at that time had already shifted to coke. In the Southern coal and steel region (the Donets Basin, where the coke-based iron and steel industry was then developing), three growth poles showed a rate of population increase of twice or more between 1897 and World War I.

In general, administrative status did not play a significant role at that time, except for centers in densely settled outlying regions like Transcaucasia and Central Asia. In European Russia, high growth rates were characteristic of centers with favorable transport-geographic situations irrespective of administrative status.

The Great October Socialist Revolution led to a change in socioeconomic system and to a fundamental reorganization of the economy. The reconstruction of the economy after World War I and the Civil War was followed by a period of industrialization accompanied by a tremendous growth in urban population. Rapid growth was recorded by old industrial centers; at the same time many new growth centers also arose. Out of the cities with a population of 100,000 or more in 1939, 28 had grown by three times or more over the 1926 level; of these, five had arisen virtually from scratch, and seven others had grown by five times or more. None of these 12 cities was an administrative center, and there were also few administrative centers among the others. The early industrialization called mainly for coal and steel development, and therefore it was the coal and steel cities that recorded the most rapid growth (16 out of 28). Accordingly, most of the dynamic growth centers were concentrated in three regions: The South (10 cities), the Urals (five) and he Kuznetsk Basin (four with Novosibirsk).

The administrative division of the USSR passed through two stages during that period. The first stage was one of consolidation, in which large krays and oblasts were headed by cities that, by virtue of industrial potential and economic-geographic situation, were capable of administering large territories. The second stage was one of breaking up the original large units, and it continued through the war period and into the early postwar period. In addition, there were many centers of ethnic entities. However, administrative status as such, though becoming more significant as a moving force of urban growth, still did not play a determining role (except for some of the ethnic centers). Moreover, it was mainly industrial development that ultimately led many of the dynamic growth poles to become oblast capitals.

The Great Patriotic War of 1941–1945 led to a slowdown of urban development in the west and more rapid urban growth in the eastern regions, a trend that was fostered by the evacuation of industry from regions threatened by enemy invasion. Urban growth in the war years and early postwar period can be judged from the results of the 1959 census: of the 25 most dynamic 100,000 population cities of the 1939–59 period, not one was situated in territory that had been occupied during the war, and 15 were in the Urals and Siberia.

The year 1959 can be taken as a turning point in the mechanisms that fostered centers of growth, a turning point associated with the scientific and technical revolution. The new trend was marked by a declining role of purely industrial cities, especially coal and steel centers, and by the increasing significance of administrative status. Among the cities of 100,000 or more in the 1970 census that had grown by less than 20 percent during the intercensal period (there were 18 such cities, not counting Moscow and Leningrad, which recorded the greatest absolute growth of population), there was not a single oblast capital; and seven of the cities of 100,000 or more in 1959 (all of them coal-mining centers) actually lost population. It should be noted that 11 of these 25 cities of low population growth or actual decline had been among the most dynamic cities during the period of industrialization and the war.

The trend continued in the 1970s. Among the 17 large cities in 1979 whose population rose by less than 10 percent from 1970, there was only one oblast capital (Karaganda). Nor were there any administrative centers among the five 100,000 population cities that lost population during the 1970–79 period; all of them were purely industrial cities. The largest of these non-administrative cities, Krivoy Rog, ranked 31 in the 1979 census.

The highest rates of growth are now being recorded by cities of the following types: administrative centers (capitals of union and autonomous republics, krays and oblasts); newly created industrial centers that are the focus of national priority projects (Togliatti, Naberezhnyye Chelny, Volgodonsk [centers, respectively, of automotive-chemicals, truck manufacturing and nuclear reactor manufacturing]); cities next to large hydroelectric stations, where cheap power and large construction facilities foster the development of major industrial undertakings; and cities that serve as bridgeheads for the penetration of new regions of pioneering development. (Some of these growth poles are of a mixed type. For example, Bratsk, one of the most dynamic cities, is both a city associated with a major hydro station and a bridgehead for penetration into new areas of East Siberia.) In some cases, bases for pioneering development may turn into oblast capitals (as in the case of Shevchenko [the center for oil and gas development on the Mangyshlak Peninsula on the north-east shore of the Caspian Sea]). In general, however, non-administrative cities appear to be growing on a selective basis, while administrative cities are growing "across the board." In 1959, 33 of the 118 administrative capitals in the RSFSR, Ukraine, Belorussia and Kazakhstan (or 28 percent) had populations of less than 100,000; in 1979, only six out of 121 (or 5 percent) fell into that category.

The predominant development of administrative centers has led to a pronounced mono centrism in the system of urban settlement in the USSR: almost two-thirds of the second-ranking cities in major civil divisions have populations less than 30 percent of those of the administrative capitals (Pokshishevskiy, 1976). Only in two oblasts (Vologda and Kemerovo) do the so-called second cities (Cherepovets and Novokuznetsk) actually exceed the oblast capital in population.

What were the factors that made administrative capitals so attractive for all forms of human activity, including industry? Ye. Ye. Leyzerovich (1971) has pointed to the concentration of large service establishments, higher education and scientific research, public, governmental and economic institutions in the capitals of oblasts, krays and ASSR. (All these attractions are present to an even greater extent in the capitals of union republics.) In our view, the determining factor is the presence of public, governmental and economic institutions.

In principle, any central place can be assumed to be a potential growth pole. However, appropriate conditions are required for its actual conversion into a growth center. Under the conditions of the scientific and technical revolution, when the impact of the resource factor on industrial location has been weakening (Privalovskaya, 1974) and the significance of administration, information, science, education, social infrastructure, etc., has become enhanced, virtually all the administrative centers of the USSR have become growth points. ("The higher the rates of development of society, the greater becomes the role of the centers of the administration and of the generation of information" [Akhiyezer, Kochetkov, 1972, p. 82].) It is in these administrative centers that the urban environment achieves the greatest diversity needed for the development of the personality (Yanitskiy, 1978), which determines progress in all forms of human activity, including production. On a territorial level, this process helps to perfect the network of large cities in the USSR (for more detailed discussion of the significance of administrative status for the growth of large cities, see Il'yin, 1978).

THE SMALL ROLE OF ADMINISTRATIVE STATUS IN THE UNITED STATES

A different picture can be observed in the United States. In the first place, it should be noted that the 25 largest urban agglomerations, aside from Washington, include only three state capitals — Boston, Atlanta and Denver, with the last two at the end of the list. This alone suggests that administrative status does not play a significant role as a factor in the growth of American cities and does little enhance their roles as growth points. This is further borne out by the fact that only in 13 states is the state capital also the largest city and principal economic center. In most cases, this is actually explained by the city's favorable economic-geographic situation rather than by its political-administrative functions.

Let us now look at the data on the most rapidly growing cities of the United States in various periods from 1900 to 1970. These periods were so selected that their limits were census years and that they corresponded roughly to the periods examined for the USSR.

In the period 1900–1930, out of the 25 cities with the highest rates of growth of three times or more (we took cities of 100,000 or more as of of 1930 since urban agglomerations were not yet being defined at that time), only two were state capitals; the set did not even include Washington at that time. An analysis of leading functions suggests that 10 were centers of extractive industry and primary processing, mainly oil; nine benefitted from a favorable seaboard location and important port functions, and seven had what were then the propulsive industries (mainly automotive and associated activities).

In 1930–40, a period marked by the greatest economic crisis in the history of capitalism and a sharp increase in government intervention in economic life (Franklin D. Roosevelt's New Deal), the 25 urban agglomerations displaying the highest rates of growth included Washington and five state capitals (all in the South and the West). There were no industrial centers in the list, and the number of centers of extractive industry and their rates of growth declined sharply.

In 1940–60, as the rates of growth of the economy and of population rose slightly as a result of the war boom and the postwar destruction in other combatant countries, the list of the 25 urban agglomerations with the most rapid growth included six state capitals, of which only two (Phoenix and Sacramento) also figured in the preceding list. In at least three of these state capitals, the high rate of growth was not due mainly to administrative functions.

Finally, in 1960–70, the 25 most active growth points included Washington and four state capitals, with one state capital (Phoenix) the third time in a row. The list was dominated by diversified economic centers of varying rank and large suburban and resort agglomerations. The role of administrative status remained small.

In other words, in the 20th century at least, the role of the administrative factor was noticeable in the United States only at the national level (Washington), with virtually no impact in the largest and economically most developed states.

The most active growth points in all the study periods were in the younger and actively developing regions of the West and the Southwest, and in the more recent periods also in the once economically and socially lagging Southeast. In the 1900–1930 period, give of the 25 leading growth points were in the North, six in the Southeast, eight in the Southwest and six in the West. In 1930–40, nine were in the Southeast, seven in the Southwest and eight in the West (leaving Washington, which we included neither in the North nor in the Southeast). The situation remained virtually the same in 1940–60, with one in the North, six in the Southeast, 11 in the Southwest, and seven in the West.

Finally, in 1960–70, there were two in the North, nine in the Southeast, three in the Southwest, and 10 in the West.

Incomplete data since the 1970 census suggest an intensification of an earlier tendency for a partial "blurring" of the urban growth pattern, with a slowdown in the development of most of the larger cities and an acceleration of growth in areas outside the urban agglomeration. This has led to a diffused settlement pattern without the formation of large nodal points. Examples would be some of the agglomerations in California (especially Anaheim-Santa Ana-Garden Grove) and in Florida.

A comparison of the dynamics of growth points and the succession of factors in Russia (USSR) and the United States suggests certain differences deriving mainly from the change in sociopolitical system in the USSR after the October Revolution, the increasing significance of central planning and the growing role of administrative functions. The last factor is characteristic not only of the USSR, but of other European socialist countries, for example Poland. At the same time, the vast territory of the USSR and the United States and the space-time differentiation in the development of their territory suggest some similarities in growth factors of urban centers, especially those endowed with favorable transport-geographic situations and centers of extractive industry. But that similarity is fairly limited since the new centers in Siberia are arising in previously undeveloped territory and the growth centers in the southeast of the United States are developing in the "old slave-owning South."

FACTORS IN THE DYNAMICS OF GROWTH POINTS
IN A DEVELOPING COUNTRY
(WITH PARTICULAR REFERENCE TO INDIA)

In using the functional-genetic approach to the analysis of growth centers in developing countries, attention must be given from the very start to the date of formulation and the history of development of urban places, the traditions of the urban mode of life, the size and the physical-economic differentiation of the given country. The factors will evidently be different for countries where cities arose only in the 18th and 19th centuries or even the beginning of the 20th century and for such a country as India.

A number of studies have shown that centers with predominantly service functions make up the largest number of towns in India (Sdasyuk, 1975), but three-fourths of them are small, slowly growing towns. At the same time, all the state capitals, with their concentration of administrative functions, are distinguished by higher rates of growth. However, the very highest rates are characteristic of industrial centers with a predominance of manufacturing industry (for details, see Mitra, 1967).

The tendency for large cities to be formed in India, starting at the beginning of the 20th century, has given rise to an entire system of such cities (Sdasyuk, 1971). The data for these cities have been processed by principal components analysis (for the methodology, initial data base and interpretation of factor loadings, see Goryacheva, Lipets, 1976; Goryacheva, 1976). On the basis of 1961 census data, 41 variables were examined for 103 cities and urban agglomerations, reflecting nine basic groupings: population size and rates of growth (3 variables); migration (2), natural increase (4), structure of employment (10), density (3), level of crowding and availability of housing (6), quality of life (6), level of modernization of industry (2), accessibility of the city or relative location (4).

Calculations yielded 13 factor components that explained 80 percent of the overall variation of the 41 characteristics. The degree to which each of the characteristics was reflected was quite high: it ranged from 64 percent (the variable for urban growth 1905–1961) to 93 percent (with six variables reflected by more than 90 percent).

A comparison with similar investigations for European countries (Medvedkova) pointed up the multifactor nature of Indian city growth. The number of independent factors reflecting conditions for growth in India turned out to be much higher (13 compared with three or four factors for Poland and East Germany), reflecting the long history of India, the established traditions of urban living and a high density of settlement in the principal population nodes.

The generalized factors that were thus obtained can be interpreted as reflecting the inertia of growth processes in old industrial centers, the growth of new centers, modernization of industry, the filling in of empty spaces in the network of cities, growth of the service sector and enhancement of migration streams from overpopulated rural areas (with differences in the attractiveness of cities for migrant from rural areas and from other towns), quality of urban life and housing, and so forth. Factor analysis revealed a relatively minor role for purely transport specialization and an association of a high level of employment in agriculture with mining specialization.

Historical-geographic analysis makes it possible to identify changes in the forms of polarization in economic-geographic space. Point-like growth points in the form of separate cities make way (especially in large mining districts and in the hinterlands of million-size cities) for agglomerated forms in which groups of adjoining cities are closely linked by daily journals to work, technological linkages and information flows. Rapidly growing agglomerations, in turn, give rise to "ribbon shapes" in the form of megalopolises, corridors and zones. It is not always easy in such entities to identify a particular growth point because of uneven development in various parts and because of the intricate functional linkages within such entities.

A typical example of growth areas in the USSR would be the territorial production complexes of West and East Siberia, where propulsive industries have been introduced in a planned fashion into centers of varying rank, including entirely new settlements favorably situated with respect to resources, hydroelectric power and transport lines. In such cases, the problem of growth points becomes a more general problem of regional development, with would have to become the methodological basis in proceeding from national plans to their territorial aspects and down to the level of individual cities.

Any planning over a sufficiently long term should make use of a strategy of changing priorities in the selection and use of growth points. It is always desirable to locate the latest types of industry, which are the ones endowed with propulsive qualities, in new growth points in an effort to prevent possible negative consequences of polarized growth.

Among these consequences might be: (1) an inertia of growth in previously formed centers; (2) aggravation of an imbalance in economic regional development; (3) the generation of social problems, especially in ethnic areas and has outlying territories. It must also be remembered, as V. V. Pokshishevskiy (1978) has pointed out, that "social aspects will increasingly replace economic factors in determining patterns of settlement" (p. 83).

Such a sequence of priorities and carefully thought-out channeling of investments at various stages of the development of growth points and regional systems of settlement would be the most effective policy designed to limit the growth of extra-large urbanized areas. A constant shifting of the spatial accent in polarized growth is also essential for preserving an equilibrium in ecological-economic systems, which are inevitably subject to serious disruption if growth remains focused continuously in the same set of centers.

This shifting sequence of development is justified on several objective grounds inherent in scientific and technical progress, which manifests itself in the continual creation of new industries and reduction in transport costs, differences in the inertia of sectoral and territorial structures, and changes in the structure and volume of consumption.

On the territorial level, it would be reflected in changes in such an integrated variable as the economic-geographic situation of growth points of various scale. The economic-geographic situation and its dynamics determine in many ways the forms of development of growth points at various historical stages in socioeconomic development.

BIBLIOGRAPHY

Akhiyezer, A. S. *Nauchno-tekhnicheskaya revolyutsiya i nekotoryye sotsial'-nyye problemy proizvodstva i upravleniya* [The Scientific-Technical Revolution and Some Social Problems of Production and Management]. Moscow: Nauka, 1974.

Akhiyezer, A. S., Kochetkov, A. V. "Urbanization and the intensification of production in the USSR," in: *Problemy sovremennoy urbanizatsii* [Problems of Contemporary Urbanization].

Blaug, M. "A case of the emperor's clothes: Perroux's theories of economic domination," *Kyklos*, 1964.

Boudeville, J. P. *Problems of Regional Economic Planning*. Edinburgh, 1966.

Darkoh, M. "Growth poles and growth centers with special reference to developing countries; a critique," *The Journal of Thopical Geography (Malaysia)*, Vol. 44, 1977.

Goryacheva, A.M. "Factor analysis of the growth of India's largest cities and the differentiation of economic functions," *Izv. AN SSSR*, ser. geogr., 1976, No. 3 [Soviet Geography, June 1977].

Goryacheva, A.M., Lipets. Yu.G. "Interrelation of factors of growth in the system of Indian cities," in: *Urbanization in Developing Countries* (S. Manzoor Alam and V.V. Pokshishevskiy, eds.). Hyderabad, 1976.

Il'yin, P.M. "The significance of administrative functions for city growth in the USSR," in: *Urbanizatsiya i formirovaniye sistem rasseleniya* [Urbanization and the Formation of Settlement Systems]. Moscow Branch, Geographical Society USSR, 1978.

Kolosovskiy, N.N. "The territorial-production combination (complex) in Soviet economic geography." *Voprosy geografii*, No. 6, 1947 [Journal of Regional Science, 3, 1961, pp. 1–25].

Kuz'min, S.A., and Yu.G. Lipets. "Use of territorial production complex models in optimizing interaction between large and small industries in developing countries," in: *Ekonomiko-geograficheskiye problemy TPK Sibiri* [Economic-Geographic Problems of Territorial Production Complexes in Siberia], Vol. 6. Novosibirsk, 1974.

Lasuen, J.R. "On growth poles," *Urban Studies*, Vol. 4, 1969.

Leyzerovich, Ye.Ye. "Characteristics of development of Oblast, Kray and ASSR capitals in the USSR," *Vestnik MGU*, geogr., 1971, No. 2.

Medvedkova, O.L. "A parametrization of macrosystems of cities based on the procedures of geoinformation systems," *International Geography '76*. Vol. 7: Geography of Population. Moscow, 1976.

Mitra, A. *Internal Migration and Urbanization*. Delhi: Office of Registrar General, 1967.

Modelirovaniye formirovaniya territorialo-proizvodstvennykh kompleksov [Modeling of the Formation of Territorial Production Complexes]. Novosibirsk, 1976.

Perroux, F. "Economic space, theory and application," *Quarterly J. of Economics*, Vol. 64, 1950.

Perroux, F. "Note sur la notion des poles de croissance," *Economie Appliquee*, 1955, 1 and 2. (Paris)

Pokshishevskiy, V.V. "The problem of the second-ranking city," in: *Problemy urbanizatsii i rasseleniya* [Problems of Urbanization and Settlement]. Moscow: Mysl', 1976.

Pokshishevskiy, V.V. "Population and Geography: Theoretical Essays", in: *Naseleniye i geografiya: teoreticheskiye ocherkti*. Moscow: Mysl', 1978.

Privalovskaya, G.A. "The physical factor in the system of conditions of industrial location in the USSR," *Voprosy geografii*, Vol. 95, 1974.

Rayonirovaniye SSSR [Regionalization of the USSR], a collection of papers on regionalization from 1917 to 1925. K.D. Yegorov, Ed. Moscow-Leningrad: Planovoye khozyaystvo, 1926.

Sdasyuk, G. V. "Urbanization and spatial structure of the Indian economy," in: *Economic and Socio-Cultural Dimensions of Regionalization.* Census Cent. Monograph No. 7, 1971.

Sdasyuk, G. V. *Indiya: Geografiya khozyaystva* [India: Geography of the Economy]. Moscow: Mysl', 1975.

Steiss, P. Models for the Analysis and Planning of Urban Systems. Lexington, Mass.: *Lexington Books*, 1975.

Tinbergen, J. "The spatial dispersion of production: a hypothesis," *Schweiz. Zeitschrift fur Volkswirt. and Statistik,* Vol. 97, 1963, No. 4.

Todd, D. The Development Pole Concept and Its Application to Regional Analysis in: *Appraisal of the State of the Art.* London School of Economics. Discussion Paper, 1973, No. 47.

Yanitskiy, O. N. "Urbanization and some problems of social development," in: *Urbanizatsiya i formirovaniye sistem rasseleniya.* Moscow Branch, Geographical Society USSR, 1978.

Significance of Administrative Functions for Urban Growth in the USSR

Pavel Ilyin

The network of large cities and urban agglomerations could be considered, in a first approximation, as a backbone of the national economy's territorial structure (Lappo, 1978). It has formed and developed unevenly in terms of territory as well as in terms of time: each historical era has put to the forefront its own centers of growth. Such unevenness has to do, in particular, with the fact that each period is characterized by its own main urban functions; they "serve as flagships" for other functions and stimulate development of those other functions.

Administrative function is one of those urban functions which becomes key under certain circumstances. This has always been a typical characteristic of cities — starting from the time of their inception. However, its significance for urban development has changed. Without elaborating on its earlier stages, let's try to trace the influence of administrative status[1] on population dynamics in large cities, the centers of growth, in comparison with other factors, using the inter-census periods data for the past 80 years.[2]

Due to a world war and a civil war between the first two censuses in 1897 and 1926, for our purposes, we will consider the time between 1897 and World War I as an initial period which may be viewed as a time of rapid development of capitalism in Russia. The corresponding industrial development relied on the established urban centers. However, capitalism also needed new centers — a condition that was especially important in view of the expanse of the underdeveloped lands in Russia. Of the ten most dynamic cities whose population had reached 50,000 residents by the onset of the WWI, eight were in Sibe-

---

[1] This term implies the status of guberniya and oblast cities before the revolution and the status of capital cities in autonomous republics or oblast and krai centers after 1926.

[2] The term "large city" implies cities with the population of 50,000 for the pre-revolutionary period; subsequently, it had to be over 100,000 residents.

ria and the Far East: Chelyabinsk, Omsk, Novonikolayevsk, Barnaul, Krasnoyarsk, Chita, Khabarovsk, and Vladivostok). Their development had been definitely prompted by the Trans-Siberian Railroad.

All of these cities had grown threefold and more. The same rate of growth had been observed in Novorossiysk due to its favorable transport and geographical location, as well as in Ivanovo which had grown in the middle of a region with a high density of old homecraft industries and textile mills. The rapid development of this center in the midst of a well-established old industrial area can be explained by the fact that its leading industry was based on old technology (textile industry.) This city could not have grown in traditional areas of charcoal industry since the advanced technologies of the time were based on coke metallurgy. At the same time, three centers of growth in the Southern coal and metallurgy area had expanded twofold and more (Ekaterinoslav, Lugansk, Aleksandrovsk).

Even though many of the aforementioned cities (as well as the ones that immediately follow them in the list of the most dynamic centers) in prerevolutionary Russia were centers of gubernias or oblasts, one can assert that, as a rule, administrative status was not playing a leading role in urban development at the time. Among the exceptions, one should mention centers of densely-populated peripheral regions, such as Tiflis and Tashkent.

The industrialization of the USSR—accompanied by a tremendous rise in urban population—began after the reconstruction of the national economy which had been devastated by WWI and the Civil War. The cities grew rapidly: the old industrial centers were growing fast; a large number of new centers of growth emerged; and the number of those new centers was incomparable to the prerevolutionary numbers, both in terms of magnitude and in terms of growth rate. Thus, 28 of the "100,000 residents cities" had grown by more than three times from 1926 to 1939, while five of them started from practically nothing (Novokuznetsk, Karaganda, Magnitogorsk, Murmansk, Dzerzhinsk); and the other seven had grown by more than five times (Prokopyevsk—by ten times, Gorlovka, Krivoi Rog, Kemerovo, Zaporozhye, Zhdanov, and Bryansk).

None of these 12 cities was initially developing as an administrative center, and there are also few administrative centers among other cities. Industrialization demanded first and foremost the development of coal and metallurgical bases, and this is why coal-mining and metallurgy towns were the fastest-growing—they amounted to 16 out of 28. Correspondingly, the majority of the most dynamic centers of growth were concentrated in three regions: South (10 cities), Urals (5 cities), Kuzbass (4 cities — including Novosibirsk).

During that period of time, the administrative division in the USSR was going through two stages: first, there was a process of agglomeration whereby the cities, which, by virtue of their industrial capacity and economic and geographic location, were able to govern vast territories and gain control of large krais and oblasts; then, second, there was a process of breaking down into smaller regions, which continued during the war and the years immediately after the war (*Great Patriotic War—translator's note*). However, as a rule, the administrative status was not a significant driving force (with the exception of some of the national centers).

Moreover, it was exactly the industrial development that had caused many of the most dynamic centers of that period to become oblast centers (e.g., Karaganda, Donetsk — in 1932; Murmansk, Voroshilovgrad, Zaporozhye — in 1938–1939; and Kemerovo, Bryansk — in 1943–1944). Thus, a key role at the time belonged to the industrial function.

The Great Patriotic War of 1941–1945 caused the slowing down of urban development in the west of the country and the speeding up of urban development in the east which had been facilitated by the evacuation of industries from the areas that were subjected to enemy attacks. Among the 25 most dynamic large cities in 1939–1959 there was not a single one located on occupied territory; 15 of them were located in the Urals and Siberia.[3]

The year 1959 could be taken as a watershed year in the mechanisms that drove the development of the centers of growth. The role of purely industrial, especially, coal and metallurgy cities, declined drastically while the importance of administrative centers was growing. Thus, in 1970, there were no administrative centers among the large cities which had grown insignificantly — by less than 20 per cent (there were 18 of them);[4] the population of seven cities which had over 100,000 residents in 1959 (all of them were coal-mining centers) had grown smaller. This had never happened in peaceful times before. Moreover, 11 of these 25 cities whose population had decreased or grew insignificantly were among the "leaders" in the times of in-

---

[3] Seven cities in the western regions which on the eve of the Great Patriotic War had more than or close to 100,000 residents did not even have time to regain their population by 1959 (Leningrad, Vitebsk, Smolensk, Kerch, Novorossyisk, Konstantinovka, Kremenchug).

[4] Excluding Moscow and Leningrad, which were ranked first and second among all cities of the country in terms of absolute population growth.

dustrialization and during the war (among the cities whose population declined were Prokopyevsk, Kiselevsk, Kopeisk, and Cheremhovo). At the same time, only five administrative centers with less than 800,000 residents had grown by less than by 30 per cent. The same trend of predominant growth of administrative centers continued into the 1970s (USSR. Administrative and Territorial Division..., 1977).

What factors have made the administrative functions so important, stimulating the development of other functions, including the industrial factors? E.E. Leiserovich (1971) identified the following advantages of oblast, krai, and republican (ASSR) centers: concentration of large cultural and social services institutions; concentration of higher educational and academic establishments; and concentration of public, state, and economic institutions.[5] Putting aside the order in which these factors should be listed, we will point out that their role in the formation of the support backbone for the territorial structure of the national economy will continue growing in conjunction with the scientific and technical revolution.

A.S. Ahieser and A.V. Kochetkov (1972, p.82) point out that the process of urbanization and intensification of production "brings about significant shifts which primarily constitute the outperforming development of centers of manufacturing, centers of storage and processing, centers of information broadcasting, centers **of governance**... The higher the rates of societal development are, the more prominent is the role of centers of governance and information production" (*the bold is mine—P.I.*) Such are the administrative centers in the USSR.

Under the conditions of scientific and technical revolution, when the influence of natural resources on the geographic distribution of industries grows weaker (Privalovskaya, 1974) and when the importance of governance, information production, science, labor, and social structure, etc. increases, practically all administrative centers become centers of growth.

Naturally, other cities may be developing—and fairly rapidly developing—too. First and foremost, these are the cities which accommodate the largest (in terms of their significance for the national economy) enterprises—for example, Toliatti, Naberezhnye Chelny, Volgodonsk, etc.); these are cities that grow around the largest hydropower stations where the presence of low-cost energy and powerful construction bases facilitates the development of large-scale industry; and these are cities that serve as "bridgeheads" for the develop-

---

[5] Capitals of the Soviet Republics have even more advantages of this kind.

ment of new regions.[6] However, one could say that the "non-administrative" cities are developing "randomly"; whereas the administrative centers are growing almost without exception. While 31 administrative centers (at the oblast, krai, and ASSR level) in 1959 out of 112 cities, in the RSFSR, Ukraine and Kazakhstan (or about 28% of the cities) had less than 100,000 residents, now only six of the current administrative 115 centers of these republics (or 5%) are short of becoming large cities. Three of them are clearly moving toward the 100,000 residents' threshold (Uzhgorod, Taldy-Kurgan, and Dzhezkazgan).[7]

Let's point out that, apparently, one should not always consider cities with a population of more than 100,000 as large cities. As it appears to be customary to consider cities with a population of more than 50,000 to be large cities by the early 20th century standards, in modern times they would be cities with 200,000 residents. In this regard, it is worth pointing out the following curious data: among the 33 cities with 151,000 to 200,000 residents in 1970, there were 19 administrative centers. By 1977 all of 19 had crossed the threshold of 200,000 residents. Only six of the remaining 14 were able to accomplish the same results.

The prevailing development of administrative centers has led to a clearly pronounced monocentric nature of Soviet urban dispersion systems (Pokshishevsky, 1976). It is worth pointing out that in three of those four oblasts where currently the population of the second most important city is higher than the first, the absolute increase in population of the oblast center (not to mention its relative increase) has been higher in recent years than that of the "second" city: Kemerovo is gradually catching up with Novokuzntesk, Dzhezkazgan is approaching Balhash).[8] For now, only Cherepovets continues to be (in absolute and relative terms) ahead of Vologda. We say "for now" because it is possible, based on experiences with other "second" cities, to consider this phenomenon as temporary (unless Cherepovets receives back its administrative status of 1918–1927 when it was the center of Cherepovets gubernia).[9]

---

[6] Some centers of growth belong to the mixed type. For example, one of the most dynamic modern cities, Bratsk, that is developing near the largest hydropower station on the Angara river, concurrently serves as a base for further development of the regions in Eastern Siberia.

[7] The remaining three urban centers are Kyzyl, Elista, and a very "young" Arkalyk.

[8] Arkalyk has beaten Derzhavinsk only several years ago (USSR. Administrative-Territorial Division..., 1974).

[9] There are four more cases when the second city would beat the first city in terms of its absolute population growth. These cities are Toliatti, Naberezhnye Chelny,

Let's summarize some of the conclusions. The criteria for assessment of various localities by the organizations, which engage in planning of the national economy distribution and population dispersion, are undergoing transformation in view the conditions of today's scientific and technological revolution (in the course of which the role of the centers of governance and information production is growing and the progress in all spheres of activities is becoming more and more dependent on the level of individual personality development) (Ahieser, Ilyin, 1975). The predominant and wide-spread growth of urban administrative centers (and agglomerations thereof) is a consequence of all of these processes.

BIBLIOGRAPHY:

Ахиезер А. С., Ильин П. М. *Задачи разработки социальных оценок территории в условиях научно-технической революции.* Issue 1, geographic series of the Izvestia of the USSR Academy of Science.

Ахиезер А. С., Кочетков А. В. *Урбанизация и интенсификация производства в СССР.* Issues of Modern Urbanization. Moscow, 1972.

Лаппо Г. М. *Опорный каркас территориальной структуры народного хозяйства,* в сб. "Территориальная организация производительных сил СССР". Moscow, 1972.

Лейзерович Е. Е. *Особенности развития областных, краевых и республиканских (АССР) центров в СССР.* Moscow State University Vestnik, geography, 1972, issue 2.

Покшишевский В. В. *Проблема "второго" города.* В сб. "Проблемы урбанизации и расселения". Moscow, 1972.

Приваловская Г. А. *Природный фактор в системе условий размещения промышленного производства в СССР.* Voprosy Geographii, col. 95, Moscow, 1975.

СССР. Административно-территориальное деление союзных республик на 1 января 1975 г. (USSR. Administrative and Territorial Division of Soviet Republics as of January 1, 1975), Moscow, 1974.

СССР. Административно-территориальное деление союзных республик на 1 января 1977 г. (USSR. Administrative and Territorial Division of Soviet Republics as of January 1, 1975), Moscow, 1977.

Harris Ch. D. *Cities of the Soviet Union,* Chicago, 1970.

Sevastopol, and Kremenchug. The first two clearly represent the transient nature of such a phenomenon — even more so than in the case with Cherepovets: there are hardly any reasons to assume that these cities will take over Kuibyshev and Kazan, respectively, in population.

THE SOCIAL EVALUATION OF A TERRITORY
UNDER CONDITIONS OF THE SCIENTIFIC-TECHNICAL
REVOLUTION

A. S. Akhiyezer
(Institute of the International Workers Movement)
P. M. Ilyin
(Institute of Geography)

Abstract: The present practice of economic and technological evaluation of a territory for development purposes is found to be inadequate because the evaluation made by Soviet planning and design agencies does not always coincide with the perception of particular places by individual citizens. As a result, the outflow from rural areas has been particularly heavy in areas where agricultural labor is especially short, and the predominant direction of interregional migration has been southward rather than to the east, where it is most needed. It is therefore suggested that spatial planning is based on a social evaluation of territory that would eliminate the present conflicts in perception and bring the interests of society more into line with the interests of individual citizens. Social evaluation is based on two value indicators: (1) the uniqueness of the creative process localized in a particular place, tending to make that place attractive; (2) accessibility of the place from surrounding areas. One possible approach to measuring the social attractiveness of a place is the extent to which individuals strive to establish direct contact (visits, direct dealings) or indirect contacts (eliciting of information) with that place.

E valuation problems have been taking up an increasing part of geographic research in recent years. Work has been done on the economic evaluation of natural resources and physical living conditions, the technological evaluation of natural complexes, spatial differences in the need for services, etc. (Lopatina, Mints et al., 1970; Mints, 1972; Lopatina, Nazarevskiy, 1972; Mukhina, 1973; Kovalev, 1973).

The growing number and diversity of evaluations now confronts geographers with the problem of systematizing these evaluations and establishing relationships between them. The point is that the increasing variety of evaluations enhances the likelihood of conflicting results in the solution of any spatial problem based on different forms of evaluation of a territory. Such a danger can be avoided by establishing logical relationships between different evaluations, a hierarchy of evaluations and a systematic sequence. This would provide a scientific basis for the appropriate choice of evaluations under a particular set of conditions, which is extremely important if the evaluative approach is to be fostered in geography.

In the present paper we will be examining some aspects of the problem of a social evaluation of a territory under socialism and its specific features under the conditions of the scientific-technical revolution (an analysis of the concept of "territory" was made by Mints and Petryakova, 1973). Such an evaluation is closely linked to changes in the function of place (Mints, Preobrazhenskiy, 1970).

Any human activity always includes a preference for sonic places within a territory over others. A value judgment with regard to any place derives from the fact that people associate different needs, different potentialities and different degrees of effectiveness of their activity with various places within a territory. "Value arises on the basis of the contradictory character of human activity as an unrealized potential that calls for realization" (Drobnitskiy, 1966). The evaluation of a territory thus derives from man's evaluation of his own capacity for achieving a particular purpose al appropriate points in space. The multiplicity of forms of human activity accounts for a multiplicity of forms of evaluations of a territory.

The objective needs of society and their relationship to objective spatially localized conditions for production and other forms of human activity give rise to a system of social orientation in space. The entire territory is visualized by man as a distinctive polarized cultural field with foci of attraction and repulsion (Akhiyezer, 1972). This value judgment with respect to a territory is social in character because it represents an aspect of human activity. Any evaluation of a territory calls for establishing a certain substantive content of the territory and the historical sequence of functions of place, as defined by a set of conditions that are localized at a given point within the territory and are essential for the purpose of a particular human activity. A social evaluation of a territory would, moreover, include the purpose, the need or the spatial problem that man has set for himself as well as the practical means for achieving that purpose at the given place. The need for achieving practical goals requires that we remove any contradictions between evaluations by critically re-examining the evaluations themselves. Such an approach would render the evaluations more dynamic and stimulate a growing complexity of evaluations in the process of development of production, in the process of increasing complexity of social goals and needs.

The basic historical evaluations of a territory depend on the overall evolution of the leading goals of society. In the Soviet Union, the principal goal of all economic activity is the development of the human personality. Under the conditions of the communist form of society, the development of the "creative gifts of man" becomes a goal in itself (see Marx and Engels, *Soch.* [Works], in Russian, Vol. 46, Part 1, p. 476). The achievement of that basic social goal requires the resolution of various intermediate tasks, each of which is associated with a particular type of evaluation of a territory. Let us briefly examine the hierarchical levels of these types.

The satisfaction of any social need that involves the choice of place calls for the evaluation of territory from the point of view of the presence of the substantive conditions required for resolving a given problem at each of a set of places. The evaluation of territory according to this criterion includes both physical conditions and natural resources, the presence of engineering structures and the totality of embodied past labor, i.e., the entire complex of natural and technogenic properties On which the possibility and the efficiency of construction and operation of the desired object depend. This type of evaluation, which focuses both on relevant elements of the environment and on the results of past human activity may be termed a natural-technological evaluation even though it, too, is basically social in character. In geography, the significance of this type of evaluation has been evident in efforts to identify and map the infinite diversity of natural resources as well as the substantive results of human activity. This type of evaluation includes the technological evaluation of natural complexes, agricultural productivity evaluations, medical-biological evaluations, etc.

However, the evaluation of territory cannot be restricted to the natural requisites for resolving particular economic problems. Society always disposes of limited resources, so that the evaluation of territory from the point of view of natural potential must be supplemented by an evaluation based on the criterion of the minimum cost of realizing that potential. (Mints [1972] drew attention to a persistent habit among some geographers to stress the environmental and engineering aspects of resource use at the expense of socio-economic aspects.) The natural-technological evaluation thus becomes an essential condition and a methodological step toward a higher level of evaluation that also considers the socio-economic need for economizing resources and social labor in achieving a certain level of satisfaction of the entire set of social needs. The cost-minimization approach to satisfying particular needs was used by A. Ye. Probst (1972) in his "law of extractive industry" and in a number of other economic location studies.

With the growth and increasing structural complexity of the Soviet economy, the problem of economic evaluation also becomes far more complex and assumes new forms. An example is the technique for an economic evaluation of natural resources that has been worked out for regular economic planning and design calculations by the Central Economic-Mathematical Institute and representatives of other agencies, including the Institute of Geography (A. A. Mints). In that technique, the criterion for evaluating any type of natural resource is the "aggregate economic benefit produced by that resource" and "the most complex expression of that aggregate economic benefit is the contribution made by the particular resource to the criterion of optimality of the state economic plan" (*Ekonomicheskiye problemy*, 1973).

The problem of minimizing costs is thus converted into the subordinate problem of maximizing the benefit of outlays, which is achieved not through minimal, but through optimal expenditures; we thus have the problem of evaluating territory from the point of view of achieving maximum national-economic benefit.

However, although an economic evaluation, like all preceding levels in the hierarchy of evaluations, remains essential, it is still inadequate under the conditions of developed socialism, under the conditions of scientific-technical progress, when the operation of the production process depends increasingly on the worker's ability to make effective decisions and on the level of development of his personality, education 'and skills. The 24th party congress [1971] called for the creation of conditions that would foster the comprehensive development of the abilities and creative activity of Soviet people, of all working people, i.e., the development of the principal productive force of society (*Materialy XXIV s'yezda KPSS* [Proceedings of the 24th Party Congress], Moscow, 1971, p. 41). Under these circumstances, the criterion for evaluating the activity of each economic sector, of each establishment, must more fully reflect the broad cultural and social needs of man and of society. This brings us to the social evaluation of territory properly speaking. In accordance with the fundamental principles of historical materialism, the essential aspect of such an evaluation is economic relations, taken in the broad diversity of their interaction.

An analysis of territory based on the extent to which it favors the development of the personality shows that each sphere of human activity, whether machine-tool making, ballet or summer recreation, has its particular geography, which reflects substantial differences from place to place and thus the particular significance of each place for the development of the personality. For every sphere of activity there are localized centers that yield optimal results and foster the best achievements. Moreover, different spheres of activity are not independent of one another. A territory thus produces zones in which the creative potential of a set of activities reaches a maximum integral effect. The highest rating based on that criterion is obtained by the most highly urbanized territories, where the basic creative potential of society is concentrated.

The leading evaluation of a territory subordinates all the preceding types of evaluation to itself. The higher the value of a territory for the integral development of the personality, the more likely it is to be a source of economic efficiency, production skill and labor productivity. Within such a territory, greater significance is assumed by savings of resources, which, however, should not be viewed in absolute terms, but within the overall framework of development of the personality. At the same time, there is an increasing need for mobilizing all available resources for achieving the same end. Shifts in the social needs of society may result in a reordering of the hierarchy of evaluations, i.e., convert a latent, subordinate evaluation into a leading evaluation, or a long-term evaluation into an element of everyday life. This process is recorded in party and government directives, in scientific research, and in the mass consciousness of people. It reflects the further development of the social needs of socialist society and the perfection of its ability to resolve ever more complex problems, including spatial problems.

A particular evaluation of territory cannot serve simultaneously as the driving force of all strata of society, of each social group or of each person. Evaluations of territory taking shape in the minds of millions of workers, on whom the socio-economic development of society ultimately depends, may differ, and quite significantly at that, from evaluations made by planning agencies and design institutes. Plenty of examples of such differences in perception might be cited.

For example, the migration of rural population in the USSR has been distinguished by a trend that adversely affects the development of agriculture: people tend to move to the cities precisely from those rural areas where farm labor is short (Perevedentsev, 1974). A great deal has been written about the fact that existing patterns of southward migration run precisely contrary to the task of opening up the natural resources of the eastern regions. We are evidently dealing here with a conflict between the desire of people to live and work in a particular set of places, i.e., a system of territorial evaluations perceived by large numbers of people, and the evaluations that have been incorporated into the state economic plan. Such conflicts arise whenever planners ignore "the extraordinary multiplicity of motives and modes of behavior that ultimately account for the redistribution of the population through migration" (Pokshishevskiy, 1973).

The ignoring of that motivation often makes it impossible to control migration processes and yields results contrary to those intended. For example, planners do not always succeed in gradually eliminating certain satellite settlements by resettling the inhabitants in larger centers; the population of such places sometimes not only does not decline, but continues to increase (*Puti razvitiya...*, 1967). Efforts to concentrate the rural population of the Allay Mountains in a few population centers often tends to reduce the efficacy of land use and fosters rural out-migration (Ginzburg, 1968). Many other examples could be cited.

The perception of places by the broad masses has a wide range of consequences. It includes, for example, the attitude toward housing. Tomsen (1970) found that Moscow housing situated farther than 15 minutes from the nearest subway station was rated by residents at 17 percent. The system of values of city dwellers constitutes in principle the point of departure for the entire system of city services. "The wide range of professional social and personal interests of man accounts both for the system of distribution and the types of buildings of service establishments" (Orlov, 1973).

Efforts to preserve an outdated motivation are also contrary to the requirements of socio-economic progress. It has been suggested, for example, that a "human scale" might be found in towns with predominantly single-story dwellings and predominantly pedestrian traffic (Zhemchuzhnikova, 1969). Such a "localized microcosm," which was associated by Marx with an agricultural commune (Marx and Engels,

Soch. [Works], Vol. 19, p. 405), conflicts with the need of socialist society to stimulate man's striving toward higher values, no matter where they might be localized.

Thus, under the conditions of the scientific-technical revolution, when the efficacy of outside influences on human activity tends to decline (Faynburg, 1969), differences in the evaluation of a particular territory may have a strong negative impact on the resolution of national economic problems. This negative tendency can be eliminated by solving two problems that are closely interrelated. First, there is a need for elaborating a soundly based hierarchy of evaluations of territory reflecting the needs of society, identifying the leading evaluation and harmonizing the entire hierarchy on the basis of that leading evaluation. Second, there is a practical need for introducing such a progressive hierarchy of evaluations into the consciousness of the broad masses. This calls for the study of techniques for instilling motivations and for controlling the development of such motivations.

Once a soundly based system of evaluations has been developed, socialist society acquires the theoretical requisite for eliminating conflicts in evaluations. This can be achieved by instilling the soundly based evaluations in all of society, in all its strata and institutions. But this cannot be realized simply by propagandizing the findings of scientific research. It requires the creation of conditions that will stimulate man to make a higher evaluation of a particular territory. Places that are considered socially valuable by planning and design agencies on the basis of scientific research must, in fact, be rendered valuable so as to attract population. This cannot be achieved simply by economic means (payments of various wage increments, etc.). With the development of Soviet society, greater value is being placed on the quality of life. Moreover, under the conditions of the scientific-technical revolution, the value of places with a high cultural potential is also greatly enhanced.

The social evaluation of territory tends to rise as the social homogeneity of a set of places declines and the spatial diversity of human activities increases. The evaluation of a particular place by certain population groups will tend to rise if an industrial establishment or institution in that place assumes a leading role in its sphere of activity, say, in a given sector of the national economy. The most advanced industrial plants offering prospects of growth for skilled labor, the best schools and institutions of higher learning, the best theaters, etc., all tend to foster the development of higher forms of human activity. As a result, such places promote the comprehensive development of the personality, and the objective value of such places for man rises. These processes also lead to a changing perception of places on the part of the broad masses. The development of unique creative activity, which has always been a powerful driving force, thus becomes an increasingly important requisite for resolving any complex national economic problem. "Priority is assumed by enhancement of the social significance of a place, by an increase in its 'yield,' i.e., by the transition from functions that are less significant and efficient for society at the given moment to more significant and efficient functions" (Mints, Preobrazhenskiy, 1970).

A second key aspect of raising the value of territory is enhancement of accessibility. An individual is obviously limited in his ability to visit various places or in obtaining information from them. Any input of time and money for reaching one particular point in space tends to reduce the ability of reaching other points so that any act of developing means of transport or communications is the result of a desire to enable society to develop places that arc of the greatest social significance and to enhance their functions, and thus a desire to further increase the value of territory.

The real social significance of territory thus becomes a function, first, of the uniqueness of the creative process localized in a place and, second, of its accessibility from surrounding areas. These two aspects are closely interrelated. The development of one creates conditions stimulating the other. However, there are situations where the parallel development of both aspects may not be harmonious. Despite the great absolute growth of urban transportation in the city of Gor'kiy, for example, the travel time to the city center increased from 1914 to 1964, and its accessibility for city residents declined (Kagan, 1970). In other words, we have here a case of uneven growth of the two aspects that make up the value of such an important place as the center of a city.

A socialist society, in controlling both the development of populated places, centers of production, science and culture, and the allocation of investment, is endowed with means of influencing the perception of territory by the broad masses and the structure of motivation in the interest of all of society by modifying the function of places, enhancing their diversity and level, and increasing the accessibility of places that are judged most significant from the point of view of individual citizens and of society as a whole.

Further development of the concept of a value hierarchy of territory will require the elaboration of quantitative indicators. Several approaches are possible. The social value of a place, for example, might be measured by the number of people who are striving, directly or indirectly, to have dealings with that place. Indirect contact involves mainly an effort to obtain information through various channels of communication. Direct contact involves an ability to reach that place and to have direct dealings with people engaged there in a particular form of activity. Such an evaluation of a place might be obtained by measuring, first, the flow of information originating in the study point either in printed form or over radio and telephone channels and, second, the rate of arrivals of people per unit of time. Such measures might be further improved by considering the degree to which the desire for direct or indirect contact with the study place is not being satisfied (because of the limited capacity of communications channels, limitations of employment opportunities, limitations of university admissions, restrictions of an administrative nature and other causes). Further work on a system of social value indicators may ultimately lead to the compilation of special-purpose evaluative maps.

In this paper we made only a preliminary attempt to deal with the problem of a social evaluation of territory under the conditions of the scientific and technical revolution. It is a complex and many-sided problem at the boundary between geography and sociology, a problem in social geography. It may be difficult at this time to delimit the problem between the two disciplines, and actually there is no need for such a delimitation. But there is no doubt that it falls within the sphere of interests of the geographical sciences to establish the social significance of territory at various hierarchical levels, to investigate the accessibility of territory from the point of view of socially significant parameters, to study the use of territory in its social aspect, to develop measures of social evaluation and to map such evaluations.

BIBLIOGRAPHY

Akhiyezer, A. S. "The working class and urbanization under the conditions of the scientific-technical revolution," in *Urbanizatsiya, nauchno-tekhnicheskaya revolyuisiya i rabochiy klass* [Urbanization, the Scientific-Technical Revolution and the Working Class]. Moscow, 1972.

Ginzberg, N. S. "Comment," in *Materialy Vtorogo mezhvedomstvennogo soveshchaniya po geografii naseleniya* [Proceedings of the Second Interagency Conference on Population Geography], Part I. Moscow, 1968.

Drobnitskiy, O. G. "Some aspects of the problem of values," in *Problema tsennostey v filosofii* [The Problem of Values in Philosophy]. Leningrad, 1966.

Zhenichuzlinikova, N. I. "The future of small towns in areas of intensive industrial development," in *Nauchnyye prognozy razvitiya formirovaniya sovetskikh gorodov na baze sotsial'nogo i nauchno-tekhnicheskogo progressa* [Scientific Forecasts of the Development and Formation of Soviet Cities on the Basis of Social and Scientific-Technical Progress], Vol. 3. Moscow, 1969.

Kagan, M. I. "Urbanization, spatial mobility and [social] mobility," in *Urbanizatsiya i rabochiy klass v usloviyakh nauchno-tekhnicheskoy revolvutsiy* [Urbanization and the Working Class Under Conditions of the Scientific-Technical Revolution]. Moscow, 1970.

Kovalev, S. A. "On the geographic study of the service sector," *Vestnik MGU, ser. geogr.*, 1973, No. 6 [Soviet Geography, December 1974].

Lopatina, Ye. B., A. A. Mints, L. I. Mukhina, O. R. Nazarevskiy, V. S. Preobrazhenskiy. "The present state and future tasks of work on the theory and method of evaluating physical conditions and natural resources," *Izw. AN SSSR, ser. geogr.*, 1970, No. 4 [Soviet Geography, March 1971].

Lopatina, Ye. B., O. R. Nazarcvskiy. *Otsenka prirodnykh usloviy zhizni naseleniya* [Evaluation of Physical Conditions of Human Life]. Moscow: Nauka, 1972.

Mints, A. A. *Eknomicheskaya otsenka yestestvennykh resursov* [Economic Evaluation of Natural Resources]. Moscow: Mysl', 1972.

Mints, A. A., T. I. Petryakova. "The use of territory as an economic-geographic problem," *Izv. AN SSSR, ser. geogr.*, 1973, No. 4 [Soviet Geography, February 1974].

Mints, A. A., V. S. Preobrazhenskiy. "The function of place and its changes," *lzv. AN SSSR, ser. geogr.*, 1970, No. 6 [Soviet Geography, May 1972].

Mukhina, L. I. *Printsipy i melody tekhnologicheskoy otsenki prirodnykh kompleskov* [Principles and Methods for the Technological Evaluation of Natural Complexes]. Moscow: Nauka, 1973.

Orlov, M. O. "Forecasts of the development of networks and types of buildings of retailing and service establishments," in *Perspektivy razvitiya sovetskogo gradostroiterstva* [Prospects of Development of Soviet Urban Planning], Moscow, 1973.

Perevedenstev, V. "For all and for everyone; a sociologist's notes," *Nash sovremennik,* 1974, No. 1.

Pokshishevskiy, V. V. "Population migration as a social phenomenon and the tasks of statistical study," in *Statistika migratsii naseleniya* [Statistics of Population Migration]. Moscow: Statistika, 1973.

Probst, A. Ye. *Razmeshcheniye sotsialisticheskoy promyshlennosti (teoreticheskiye ocherki)* [Location of Socialist Industry (Theoretical Essays)]. Moscow: Ekonomizdat, 1962.

Puti razvitiya malykh i srednikh gorodov tsentral'nykh ekonomicheskikh rayonov SSSR [Lines of Development of Small and Middle-Size Towns in the Central Economic Regions of the USSR]. Moscow: Nauka, 1967.

Tomsen, A. "Problems of the efficacy of investment in urban construction," *Planovoye khozyaystvo,* 1970, No. I.

Faynburg, Z. I. "Prospects of the scientific-technical revolution and the development of the personality," *Voprosy filosofii,* 1960, No. 2.

Ekonomicheskiye problemy optimizatsii prirodopol'zovaniya [Economic Problems of Optimizing Resource Use]. Moscow: Nauka, 1973.

PART II

Cultural Geography of Moscow

Introduction

Pavel Ilyin and Blair A. Ruble

Все дороги ведут в Москву
(All roads lead to Moscow)
Russian saying

Moscow marked its 850th anniversary in 1997. This date brought with it an opportunity to rethink the city's history, while pausing to consider the significance of individual stages in its development, and its fate as a whole.

Moscow has long been the hub of Russia. Even when St. Petersburg was Russia's capital, one noted Russian historian assuredly remarked, "…Moscow will forever be true capital of Russia. It is the hub of realm, of all movements of trade and industry and civic consciousness… He who has been to Moscow knows Russia."[1] We add to this a comment from a foreigner who visited Russia in the late-nineteenth century: "Moscow is always, for the inhabitants of Greater Russia, the mother city, Moskva mátushka."[2]

The turn from the nineteenth to the twentieth centuries was among the most important phases in Russia's history. A free-market economy flourished. The country, although slowly and with fits and starts, moved along a path towards democracy. Russian art experienced its "Silver Age".

However, in October 1917, catastrophe struck: the Bolsheviks seized power in Russia. For many years the Communist regime was silent about the economic successes of this capitalist period. Political progress in pre-revolutionary Russia was denied. Its turn-of-the-century art was declared decadent and the architectural achievements of the period were not considered valuable enough to preserve. [3]

This silence and distortion of events of the last decades leading up to the October Revolution of 1917 were based on an official doctrine that can be summarized roughly as follows: Russia was in a shambles when the October Revolution occurred. The Bolsheviks rescued the country from collapse with a new society which promoted Russia's economic and political development. As the 1935 decree on a general reconstruction plan for Moscow stated: "Moscow developed spontaneously in the course of centuries, inevitably reflecting the barbarous nature of Russian capitalism even in its best years."

However, Russia was actually a relatively developed country at the turn of the twentieth century. Moscow, as Russia's second largest city after St. Petersburg, played a prominent role not only in domestic, but in European affairs as well. The significance of the political and economic changes in Russia prior to the Bolshevik Revolution was understood by historians long before the erosion of official doctrine permitted discussion even in specialized publications.

The "rehabilitation" of late-nineteenth-and early-twentieth-century Moscow began thirty years ago. Research dedicated to the cultural figures, literary movements, and architectural style of the time slowly began to appear in print. [4] However, the role played by the Russian bourgeoisie in the country's economy, civic affairs, and cultural and social life remained suppressed. It was popular in those days to write of the unrealized plans of the Moscow City Duma, "forgetting" how that very same Duma's activities had been cut short by the Bolsheviks.

The situation changed during Gorbachev's perestroika and glasnost period. After the Communist regime fell, interest in the late-nineteenth and early-twentieth centuries became particularly intense. The renewed attention is traceable to Russia's return to capitalist development.

A number of western scholars similarly began to explore Moscow's pre-revolutionary life, including James Bater, Joseph Bradley, William Chase, Bill Gleason, Timothy Colton, Robert Gohstand, Laura Engelstein, David Hoffman, Robert Johnson, Diane Koenker, Thomas Owen, Alfred Rieber, Jo Ann Ruckman, Albert Schmidt, and Robert Thurston. [5]

Scholars' choice of the turn of the century for further investigation was not a matter of chance. The old Moscow of today has been clearly shaped by that period, a time of both horizontal and vertical growth. The city moved outward into new territories and upward, with new construction materials allowing the move from small buildings to multistoried urban structures. This was also the time when new industrial enterprises and civic, cultural, and educational institutions appeared.

The contributors to this book represent various fields in the social sciences: geography, political science, urban studies, architectural history, literature criticism, and art history. They are united by their interest in one of the greatest cities in the world and its development at the turn of the twentieth century. The authors consider the city's life from several points of view and perspectives: its history; its role in the world in comparison to other cities of comparable function, size, and level of economic development; its cultural life; its appearance; and other aspects of an everchanging and constantly growing urban organism.

The volume stresses the description of the Fin de Siecle Moscow urban environment from the geographical point of view with an emphasis on its spatial aspects. This geographical approach to the study is demonstrated beginning with the first chapter (by Pavel Ilyin and Mikaella Kagan) which presents three aspects of Moscow at the turn of the century: the place of Moscow in Russia's economic and cultural life, the territorial structure of the city, and its spatial diversity. This chapter's specific task is to give the reader a foundation for better understanding the remaining chapters of the book.

If the Earth's surface was homogenous, then the science of geography would not be necessary. However, fortunately for scholars (and likewise for travelers), our planet is heterogeneous. The comparison of the different areas on Earth has been one of humankind's favorite pursuits since ancient times. The second chapter by Blair A. Ruble presents a comparative analysis of the development of New York and Moscow at the turn of the twentieth century. While both of these cities were not their countries' capitals at that time, both were very rapidly developing. Of course, the differences between the industrial and economic development of the United States and Russia were enormous, which governed the larger differences between the two cities to a great extent.

It is clear that comparison of distinct cities needs to pay the most attention to the cities' macro-features. Meanwhile, more detailed examination of a city's characteristics is required for its spatial diversity study. The third chapter by Robert Gohstand maps, examines, and explains one of this essential characteristics of Moscow — the relative values of land in the city in the beginning of the twentieth century. The chapter includes a map, published for the first time, of land values in Moscow at that time.

Moscow's cultural geography during this period is examined by Pavel Ilyin. He shows how while on the one hand cultural institutions are drawn to certain area of the city, on the other hand the various types of cultural enterprises have their own specific and inherent rules for location.

At the turn of the twentieth century, architects and entrepreneurs in Moscow collaborated in the development of a new urban habitat. Large apartment buildings built in innovative architectural styles began to dominate certain key areas in the city, and served to indicate the formation of a new social and economic order based on private capital in Russia. The location and design of these buildings, which still define much of contemporary Moscow, are investigated by William C. Brumfield in the fifth chapter.

Moscow's image and appearance at this time found expression in many literary and artistic works. This theme is touched upon twice in the book. Robert Whittaker considers the role Moscow plays in the thoughts and actions of Anton Chekhov's characters. Chekhov set many of his works in Moscow. Several of his characters viewed Moscow as an idealized city, almost like a secular Mecca (as in The Three Sisters, for example). Katya Rosenzweig looks at Moscow through the eyes of its avantgarde artists — Malevich, Kandinsky, and Lentulov, whose efforts are directed at showing the city's atmosphere, mood, and spirit.

The victory of the Bolshevik revolution in 1917 brought about a change in Russia's social system. The chapter by Mikaella Kagan examines the function of place in Moscow with the change of power. The physical seizure of ideologically dominant points around the city was of paramount importance for the new authorities. Bolsheviks did their best to destroy the old ideological focus points of the city, and replace them with new ones. The paradoxical conclusion is that for all the outward appearance of change, the intrinsic functions of place remained quite stable. This also occurred with cultural, residential, and other functions of place in the city — the function of place remained while the content of the activity changed.

The volume's final chapter by Pavel Ilyin and Blair A. Ruble quickly brings the reader up to the present, comparing today's Russian hub with that of almost a century ago. Ilyin and Ruble thus provide some context for the reader, helping those familiar with today's city better understand the city of the past.

Together, the volume's contributors strive to enhance today's appreciation of the life, appearance, and problems of Moscow at the turn of the past century. Success will advance an awareness of the city's profound role in Russia's next century as well.

NOTES

[1] Nikolai Mikhailovich Karamzin. "Zapiski o moskovskikh dostopami-atnostiakh," in N. M. Karamzin. *Zapiski starogo moskovskogo zhitelia* (Moscow: Moskovskii rabochii, 1986), 321 (translated by Vladimir Talmy).

[2] Georg Brandes. *Impressions of Russia*, trans. Samuel C. Eastman (1889; reprint, New York: Thomas Y. Crowell Company, 1966), 13.

[3] Examples of the "silence," or at least paucity of comments on this period of Moscow's life, may be found in the second edition of the Great Soviet Encyclopedia. For instance, only one of fifty illustrations in the article on Moscow shows an edifice built at the turn of the century, and only because it housed the Central Museum of V. I. Lenin. See *Bol'shaia Sovetskaia Entsiklopediia. Vtoroe izdanie, vol. 28* (Moscow, 1954), 361–86.

[4] Among the first objective works on art and architecture of the period were the books: Grigorii Sternin. *Khudozhestvennaia zhizn' Rossii na rubezhe XIX–XX vekov* (Moscow: Iskusstvo, 1970); Ievgeniia Borisova and Tat'iana Kazhdan, *Russkaia arkhitektura kontsa XIX—nachala XX veka* (Moscow: Nauka, 1971); Dmitrii Sarab'ianov, *Russkaia zhivopis' kontsa 1900-kh—nachala 1910-kh godov. Ocherki* (Moscow, 1971); Ievgeniia Kirichenko, Fedor *Shekhtel* (Moscow: Stroiizdat, 1973).

[5] James H. Bater. "The Industrialization of Moscow and St. Petersburg," and "Modernization and the Municipality: Moscow and St. Petersburg on the Eve of the Great War," in *Studies in Russian Historical Geography*, James H. Bater and R. A. French, eds. (London-New York: Academic Press, 1983): Vol. 2, 279–303 and 305–27; Joseph Bradley, *Muzhik and Muscovite: Urbanization in Late Imperial Russia* (Berkeley: University of California Press, 1985); William J. Chase, *Workers, Society, and the Soviet State. Labor and Life in Moscow*, 1918–1929 (Urbana and Chicago: University of Illinois Press, 1987); William Gleason, "Public Health, Politics, and Cities in *Late Imperial Russia*," *Journal of Urban History* 16, no. 4 (August 1990), 341–65; Timothy J. Colton, *Moscow. Governing the Socialist Metropolis* (Cambridge: Harvard University Press, 1995); Robert Gohstand, *The Internal Geography of Trade in Moscow from the Mid-Nineteenth Century to the First World War*, Ph.D. dissertation (Department of Geography, University of California, Berkeley, 1973); Laura Engelstein, Moscow, 1905. *Working-Class Organization and Political Conflict* (Stanford: Stanford University Press, 1982); David L. Hoffman, *Peasant Metropolis: Social Identities in Moscow, 1929–1941* (Ithaca: Cornell University Press, 1994); Robert E. Johnson, *Peasant and Proletarian: The Working Class of Moscow in the Late-Nineteenth Century* (New Brunswick, N.J.: Rutgers University Press, 1979); Diane Koenker, *Moscow Workers and the*

1917 Revolution (Princeton, N.J.: Princeton University Press, 1981); Thomas C. Owen, *Capitalism and Politics in Russia: A Social History of the Moscow Merchants. 1855–1905* (New York: Cambridge University Press, 1981); Alfred J. Rieber, *Merchants and Entrepreneurs in Imperial Russia* (Chapel Hill: University of North Carolina Press, 1982); Jo Ann Ruckman, *The Moscow Business Elite: A Social and Cultural Portrait of Two Generations. 1840–1905* (DeKalb, Ill.: Northern Illinois University Press, 1984); Albert J. Schmidt, *The Architecture and Planning of Classical Moscow: A Cultural History* (Philadelphia, Pa.: American Philosophical Society Press, 1989); and, Robert W. Thurston, *Liberal City, Conservative State: Moscow and Russia's Urban Crisis, 1906–1914* (New York: Oxford University Press, 1987).

CULTURAL GEOGRAPHY OF MOSCOW

Pavel Ilyin

> *Moscow gave rise to a new Russian art: the art of the large city, young, modern and fresh.*
> Boris Pasternak [1]

I define cultural geography in the context of the present article as the geography of human activity in the realm of the arts, literature, etc. — activity in the creation and distribution of those products of the human intellect which are, if one can use such a phrase, non-technical achievements of creativity.

As any type of human activity, culture has its own territorial differentiation, in other words its own geography. Turning to the map of any country, we see that cultural activity is not evenly distributed across its surface, but concentrated in cultural foci. Each such focus has its cultural venue. For example, when one speaks of a "Broadway theater" it is not some particular theater at a specific address, but a theater in a very specific region of New York with very specific characteristics.

The geography of culture is not, however, limited to the study of how cultural establishments are displaced. In my opinion it includes the study of those places where culture is produced and presented; where cultural figures a) produce cultural objects, b) distribute the same, and c) exchange information. In other words, cultural geography studies places from the perspective of their cultural functions. The greater the intensity of creative activity, the greater the interest it holds.

The cultural differentiation of city space has long been an object of study, along with its social, ethnic, and other areas of differentiation. An example of a work most closely akin to this is D. S. Likhachev's *On the Intellectual Topography of St. Petersburg in the First Quarter of the*

20th Century, [2] in which the author speaks of differences between various culturally active zones in St. Petersburg in that period. However, what I have termed "cultural geography," he calls "intellectual topography." I prefer the term "geography" because topography is limited to description of a place or region, while geographical studies include the relationships between phenomena as well. Also, it is not proper to speak of a "country's topography." [3]

There is one interesting peculiarity of the geography of culture — the independence of intellectual activity from material forms. The geography of industry, for example, is in fact a geography of factories, mines, etc. The geography of agriculture considers farms, fields, plantations; that of transportation focuses on roads and transportation terminals. But the geography of culture is a geography of the activity of individual creative personalities, collectives, and groups.

Thus, we consider theaters, clubs, picture galleries, libraries, bookstores, magazine editorial offices, and other cultural establishments; as well as those places where writers, artists, actors, and the like, live, work, gather, interact, and spend their free time. In other words, all activity which results in the creation of culture and the enriching interchange which helps culture develop.

As a rule, no poet, writer, artist, or composer needs a collective to create. They work alone, yet they do need a creative atmosphere. This atmosphere arises in the process of socializing with others living a creative life and stimulates all participants. They need to socialize with one another, but also with those who admire their work — the "consumers" of their creative activity. The same applies to representatives of "collective" arts, such as actors, who find that solely socializing with theater colleagues is not enough. It is important for people in the arts to live in a cultural environment. This is what gives rise to the concentration of addresses for those circulating in this milieu. The houses in which socializing occurs are clustered, until they form a kind of "thicket" in which "places of activity" are concentrated and people gather to converse and meet in an atmosphere conducive to creative openness. [4]

The geographic disposition of residences—"geography of addresses," is also of interest. We note that the space occupied by "cultural addresses" is narrower than that of the city as a whole. In our view, this is caused by two factors. First, there are areas of social differentiation in the city, and culturally active people belong to some, but not all, social classes. Thus, they are not to be found in all regions of the city. Secondly, those active in culture must live where areas of cultural activity and socialization are within reach. Both of these require-ments are met by Moscow's central region, within the borders of the Garden Ring, in what is now known as "Old Moscow."

The time under consideration in this article is the brief period of "normal" capitalist development in the city which ended with the collapse of Russian society in 1917. The cultural development of this period was based on the rich spiritual traditions of Moscow's aristo-crats. The so-called "Silver Age" of Russian art is connected, in the main, with Moscow and St. Petersburg. The cultural geography of this "Silver Age" was naturally founded on the geography of the preced-ing period and formed the basis, in turn, for cultural geography of the succeeding, Soviet period. It suffices to say that in the late-1980s, more than half of the professional theaters of Moscow were located in buildings that had housed entertainment establishments during the turn of the century.

Let us take a quick look around the cultural map of Moscow at the turn of the century (*see Appendix 4, Map 1*).

The mid-nineteenth century saw the formation of a powerful cul-tural center which developed along the axis of Theater Square (with the two imperial theaters, Bol'shoi and Malyi), Okhotnyi Riad (the No-blemen's Assembly), and Mokhovaia Street (the University, the Mane-zh, [5] and the Rumiantsev Museum). Most cultural establishments in Moscow in the late-nineteenth and early-twentieth centuries were lo-cated in the sector which developed along this axis between Petro-vka and Bol'shaia Nikitskaia streets, with its "backbone" on Tverskaia: theaters, concert halls, art galleries, clubs, and cafes where actors, po-ets, and writers gathered.

Nearly all of cultural life was restricted to the area of Belyi Gorod. Only in rare cases did cultural activities take beyond the Boulevard Ring, and mainly along Tverskaia Street. But development was not limited to radials running from the Theater Square — Okhotnyi Riad — Mokhovaia axis. The axis was continued on Volkhonka Street, starting with the building of the Fine Arts Museum at its point of origin, and developing largely as a line of visual arts.

Outside this zone, the density of cultural establishments, had de-creased. Of note are the Stroganov Applied Arts School on Rozhdest-venka; Lubianskaia Square, surrounded on various sides by the German Club on Sofiika [6] and the Polytechnic Museum; Lazarev Institute on Armianskii Lane; and the Painting, Sculpture and Architecture School and Turgenev Library near Miasnitskie Gate Square of Belyi Gorod.

Notable for its lack of cultural institutions was the merchant region of Zamoskvorech'e. The first theater was built here only in 1916. But, as in natural deserts, there were oases here. One such oasis housed a great cultural pearl of Moscow — the Tretiakov Brothers gallery.

Cultural establishments are notable in their absence from the city's "city" Kitai-Gorod. The authors of the guidebook *Po Moskve* ("Around Moscow") call Nikol'skaia Street the "street of enlightenment of Old Moscow" and even devote a special tour to it. [7] But in the time we are considering, all that remained of culture on Nikol'skaia was the Synodal Press. The focus of Kitai-Gorod functions had shifted.

The cultural activity of Muscovites extended beyond the city limits, but here too there was a concentration in specific zones. Thus the early-twentieth century saw a sharp concentration of these establishments in the dacha settlements along the Severnaia Railroad and to an even greater degree along the Riazanskaia Railroad.

We will consider below the distribution of various types of creative activity within Moscow city limits at the turn of the century. It is of course not possible to touch on all that occurred in this period in Moscow. The reader should understand that addresses of cultural life in Moscow were a hundred times greater than those discussed. If, however, the reader gets an idea of the cultural richness of Moscow and its geography at this time the author will consider his task accomplished.

THEATERS

Entertainment has always been very popular in Russia; and, in the time period we are considering, the most popular form of entertainment was the theater. An American researcher on the Russian theater wrote that in Russia the theater is not "a relief from life... To the Russians, the theater is rather a microcosmos, a concentration and the explanation of life. If life cannot be explained, at least its inexplicability can be faced..." [8]

There were only two professional theaters in Moscow in the mid-nineteenth century: the Bol'shoi (Great) Theater (theater of opera and ballet) and the Malyi (Small) Theater (of drama). At the time there was a government monopoly on the dramatic arts, and theaters could only be imperial. However, these two theaters were not able to meet the demands of the educated populace of Moscow for the performing arts, despite the highly professional level of both Moscow imperial theaters. This was especially true in light of the overall increase in Moscow's population, with a proportional increase in potential theatergoers. This was not just a matter of the limited repertoire; the companies of these theaters could not accommodate all those who wanted to have their moment on stage. In fact, not even every professional actor, even some quite good ones, could join the theater company.

So, lovers of the performing arts sought out various ways to start theater collectives and organizations which were not subject to government control. One of these forms of organizations was the serf theater, where serfs put on performances for the entertainment of landlords and their guests. The theaters of Count Sheremetev at his estates of Ostankino and Kuskovo outside Moscow and that of Prince Iusupov in Arkhangel'skoe are well-known chapters in eighteenth- and nineteenth-century Russian theatrical history. Succeeding these were theaters in the houses of aristocratic families in Moscow itself. Their place in the city's geography was determined by the location of the city estates in Moscow. Since the distribution of aristocratic houses was fairly widespread, the theaters were scattered around the city rather broadly. Thus, one of the most famous of such theaters was located on Znamenka Street, and another, that of Prince Iusupov, was located on Bol'shoi Khariton'evskii Lane.

The emancipation of serfs brought an end to the age of the serf theater. It was replaced by productions put on by amateur actors and held in private homes. Carnivals and similar light entertainment associated with family celebrations, Christmas, or the like, were in fact a common practice in noble estates starting in the eighteenth century. When the bourgeoisie class developed in the nineteenth century, they started to make their way into merchant estates. The founders of many of the Moscow merchant families were poorly educated people; they were often self-made men in the realms of business and finance. Their heirs, on the other hand, were brought up in a more cultural environment and their interests went beyond the door of the factory or office. It is no mere chance that this class produced so many notable patrons of the arts in the second half of the nineteenth century, a turning point in Russian social relations.

"Moscow," recalled the renowned Moscow journalist Vlas Doroshevich, "was full of amateur troupes. There was no public, everyone was an actor." [9] For the most part these productions left nothing more behind than pleasant memories for the participants. However, the world-renowned theater personality K. S. Stanislavsky began his acting career on a stage in his home amateur theater. [10]

The popularity of amateur home theater, and the aspirations toward wider creative associations by dilettantes, led to the most productive venue of the Moscow stage of that time — theater lovers started to create theater groups disguised as amateur troupes. One form these groups took were the various theater societies, usually called *kruzhki* (circles). These circles performed in private homes and their geographical distribution was much more limited than that of the serf theaters of earlier days. In the days of serfdom, the actor was actually the property of the theater's owner, and thus lived in his house or nearby. The spectators were part of the same gentry as the owner, people for whom getting to any part of Moscow to take in a show presented no problems.

The new theater groups were another matter altogether. Their participants and spectators were drawn mainly from the middle class, or to be more precise, from the Moscow intelligentsia (students, professors, teachers, civil servants, doctors, lawyers, etc.). This class was undergoing intensive growth in tandem with the rapid growth of the city in the capitalist period. The theaters -were concentrated in the Belyi Gorod and Zemlianoi Gorod, between Volkhonka-Ostozhenka and the Maroseika-Pokrovka streets.

One of these theater groups was concealed under the name "Moscow Artists Circle of the Russian Actors Society." This circle, active from the 1860s to the 1880s, rented the first floor of the former Golitsyn's palace on Theater Square (bought in the 1840s by the merchant Bronnikov), refurbishing it as a theater with a large auditorium.[11] Thus the entire northern portion of Theater Square, first established as a square only for the two imperial theaters, was now surrounded by theaters.

As a rule, the theatrical acting circles were social organizations, but sometimes camouflaged the presence of a commercial company. Thus the actress Anna Brenko was able to establish on Tverskaia Street a theater, which was Moscow's first professional commercial theater. This theater became known as the Pushkin Theater from its proximity to the Pushkin Monument on Tverskoi Boulevard.[12]

Paradoxically, the Brenko's Theater closed when the owner went bankrupt in 1882, a historic year for the Moscow theater. It was in this year that the government monopoly on theaters was lifted. Private theaters began to appear immediately, along with new theater buildings. It was the start of a theater "boom" of sorts.

This would be a good point to discuss the social and spatial role played by the Theater Square. The Square was planned by the architect O. I. Bove in 1817–1824, and was specifically designed as a theater area, receiving the name Theater Square in 1829. [13] Together with the Noblemen's Assembly around the corner at Okhotnyi Riad and Bol'shaia Dmitrovka (known for its magnificent Hall of Columns), this square served as a powerful civic center forming a nidus for the subsequent territorial development of the Moscow theater.

As early as 1882, immediately after the removal of the state monopoly on theater, the Golitsyn's house on Theater Square was openly refurbished as a theater, and named the Novyi (New) Theater, in contrast with the old Bol'shoi and Malyi. Starting in 1913, the first studio of the Moscow Art Theater began productions here.

The 1880s and 1890s saw the opening of the G. G. Solodovnikov's Theater on Bol'shaia Dmitrovka (in its best years it was home to the Mamontov private opera), the establishment of a theater in the Lianozov house in Kamergerskii lane, and the construction of theaters by the entrepreneurs F. A. Korsh and G. Paradiz. Finally, in 1902, and due to the patronage of S. T. Morozov, the Lianozov's Theater building was reconstructed for the Moscow Art Theater.

All of these theaters were located in a relatively small space near the main cultural axis and main street of the city, Tverskaia. But the Bol'shoi Theater was the only Moscow theater which formed a center of the urban composition for its area, in this case Theater Square.

Another characteristic of theater in Moscow was the large number of professional theaters located in buildings not originally built as theaters. The Solodovnikov Theater was outwardly indistinguishable from its former role as an apartment building. At the Moscow Art Theater the architect F. Shekhtel placed a high relief piece of a sculptor A. Golubkina at the entrance to make the building seem more "theatrical." (Plans to redesign the entire facade remained unrealized.) It is also notable that even the older imperial Malyi Theater had a front on the Neglinnyi Proezd side (now Neglinnaia Street) which was similar to many other facades of the city. This theater had been reconstructed from a private home belonging to the merchant V. V. Vargin which, though having a concert hall (Vargin was a great lover of music), was not originally intended to be a public building. [14]

Only two buildings were designed and built as theaters at the end of the nineteenth century: Korsh's (1885) and Paradiz's (1887). Both of these buildings were certainly distinctive architectural landmarks of their era, but did not have any role to play in the organization of the civic space around them. They were built in spaces available in the densely built-up center of Moscow. No new theater buildings were constructed after this. The first theater to appear in Zamoskvorech'e on the eve of the Revolution (the P. P. Stryiskii's Theater on Bol'shaia Ordynka Street, 1915) and the later famous A. Ia. Tairov's Kamernyi Theater on Tverskoi Boulevard (1916) were both housed in refurbished buildings.

The troupes performing in the theaters named above, which formed the basis of the Moscow theater district, were as a rule serious, professional groups and the public in attendance was analogous. But a large city demands a variety of entertainment genres.

There was a continuation of the Tverskaia Street theater district with a cluster of light entertainment theaters in the area of Triumfal'naia Square, where it ran across Garden Ring: the Zon Theater, the Alkazar Variety Theater, and the Evropeiskii (European) Theater. One of the popular recreation areas for Muscovites was a garden which originally was called the Chicago Garden, [15] but after its 1897–98 reconstruction named the Aquarium. There was a theater building in this garden which mainly presented light pieces.

This tangle of amusement theaters, intended for a wide audience, was located at the "contact points" of areas where different classes of society inhabited: the more intellectual audiences came from the Garden Ring area and the pettier bourgeoisie from beyond the ring.

A very popular form of art for all social classes of the late-nineteenth and early-twentieth century was the circus. The first stone circus building in Moscow went up in 1868 on Vozdvizhenka, but the circus could not hold out there for very long since the "local crowd" gravitated to the more serious theatrical and musical genres. Thus, it was not by chance that later circus buildings were also erected at the "contact points" between social zones: the Solomonskii's Circus (1880) on Tsvetnoi Boulevard and the Nikitin Brothers' Circus (1911) on the Garden Ring near Triumfal'naia Square, mentioned above as an "amusement center."

The Hermitage Garden theaters were located beyond the borders of the theater district, but the Hermitage changed over time. In the early years, 1878–1893, it was located beyond the Garden Ring on Bozhedomka Street. The head of this Hermitage was Mikhail Lentovskii, a great figure in the Moscow theater, called a "mage" and "wizard" by the Moscow public. [16] The fairy tales, entertainment revues, operettas, and carnivals presented there were very popular with Muscovites, but the garden still closed and its wooden structures did not long survive. Why did the owners not maintain the facilities? Perhaps their decision was influenced by the remoteness from the main cultural zones of Moscow? In any case, when the new garden appeared under the same name in 1894 it was much closer to the center, in Karetnyi Riad, and not prone to suffer the fate of the "Old Hermitage."

Another fact clearly demonstrates the striving by theaters to concentrate around the main cultural center. Serious groups took whatever spaces were available in the cultural center to start work. The Mamontov Private Opera started to offer performances on Prechistenskii Boulevard, the Zimin Opera appeared in the Aquarium Garden Theater, and the Art Theater spent its first four seasons in the Hermitage Garden in Karetnyi Riad. But they moved to the theatrical "core" of Moscow at the first possible opportunity. Mamontov leased the Solodovnikov Theater, Zimin the Novyi Theater on Theater Square,[17] and Art Theater took over the former Lianozov Theater in Kamergerskii Lane.

The reader has already encountered a description of Moscow's "depths" in this article: Khitrov Market, surprisingly was part of Moscow's theatrical geography as well. At the time nearly all scripts for plays in Moscow were either copied out by hand or lithographed. This lithography work was carried out in the theatrical library on Tverskaia, producing scripts for the individual roles for the theaters. The copying work, however, was carried out in a filthy flophouse in Khitrov Market. Here the copyists, cast out of life by circumstances, shared a large room with a group of beggars. This was a tormenting work, and the pay was almost nothing.[18]

While the theater was entertainment for the educated class, the other social classes were satisfied with more accessible forms of entertainment, which fulfilled the role of theater, but at a different level. One example of this was the balagan, or buffoon's booth. These booths had a geographic distribution of their own, offering a simpler alternative in entertainment outside the main cultural zone of Moscow, mainly in areas of popular celebration, the largest of which at the turn of the century was Devich'e Pole.

MUSIC

Moscow has always had a rich musical life. It seems social and territorial geographic distinctions appeared in music more than the other arts. Serious music is the most abstract of the arts, requiring greater preparation than other artistic forms both on the part of the performers and listener. The type of music, the type of listener, and the type of facilities differed in various parts of the city.

The Noblemen's Assembly and its remarkable Hall of Columns was a center of Moscow's musical life for a long time before the creation of the Moscow Conservatory. Nikolai Rubinshtein was the driving force behind the Conservatory's opening, its first director and the conductor of its first evening concerts. [19] Founded in 1866 on Vozdvizhenka, the Conservatory moved to Bol'shaia Nikitskaia in the 1890s. [20] From this time forward the Conservatory, with its two performance halls, Bol'shoi and Malyi, became the center of classical music in Moscow. Both Western European and Russian symphonic music were played and operas were performed here as well.

The principal listeners at the Conservatory's halls were upper- and middle-class intellectuals. In addition to paid concerts, the musicians forming the Moscow Chapter of the Russian Music Society performed open concerts for the public in the Hall of Columns of the Noblemen's Assembly and the Manezh. The Moscow Philharmonic Society, Moscow Choral Society, Amateur Russian Music circles, the Artists Circle, and other musicians' organizations gave concerts as well. Concerts of Russian and foreign music, "Musical Exhibitions," were held in the Synodal Choir College located on Bol'shaia Nikitskaia, next to the Conservatory.

As we shall see, concert activity also gravitated toward Moscow's main cultural zone. One can add that private operas, first the Mamontov's, then that of Zimin and other musical groups, offered performances and concerts in this same area of the city.

The same city sector was home to several private music schools and colleges. The Gnesin Sisters' college was a notable cultural point. The sisters first organized the college in their apartment in Gagarin Lane on Arbat, renting a small mansion for themselves and the college a few years later on another Arbat lane called Sobach'ia Ploshchadka. [21]

Music remained an indispensable part of the life of all layers of society, forming part of both large festivals and everyday events. But popular music for the city's petty bourgeoisie took other forms. Choirs, including Russian folk choirs and Gypsy choirs, became popular at the end of the nineteenth century. This type of music was accessible for a very wide portion of the public. Large audiences attended choir concerts.

The urban romance became a popular genre. Romances were often sung in middle class homes to the accompaniment of a piano, or in the poorer houses with a guitar.

The working-class outskirts and poor neighborhoods had their own musical life. People in these neighborhoods sang Russian folk songs to the accompaniment of concertinas and guitars.

FILM

The new art form of cinematography came to Moscow on the eve of the twentieth century. The first film was shown in 1896 in the Hermitage Garden. After this a temporary cinema was established on Devich'e Pole.[22] The first cinemas appeared in 1903–1904, and by 1913 there were sixty-seven cinemas in Moscow.[23] Their pattern of distribution differed from that of theaters, with the choice of place explained by differences between theater and cinema.

The process of preparing a performance and its place of presentation coincide in theater. At any particular moment the performance can only be seen in one specific place, generally the theater where it was prepared. In cinema, the process of creating and exhibiting a film occur in different places. One film, reproduced at the studio, can then be shown anywhere the requisite equipment is to be found.

Theater is intended for a public prepared for viewing a dramatic presentation. In this respect it is intended for a public which is elite to a degree (not for naught is the term "theater-going public" used). The film, as an art form, is intended for the general public. Due to this, the distribution of cinemas around the city was wider than that of theaters. However, cinemas too conformed to certain principles: cinemas were located on main city streets, with a tendency to be close to transportation hubs such as the intersections of Moscow's main streets with the Boulevard and Garden rings.

The first cinemas were established in residences with areas converted for use as viewing rooms.[24] Subsequently, special buildings were built for cinemas: the Khudozhestvennyi on Arbat Square, the Kolizei (Coliseum) on Chistoprudnyi Boulevard, the Forum on Sadovaia-Sukharevskaia. Like theater buildings, some old houses went through major renovations to emerge as cinemas. These included an old house on Triumfal'naia Square for the Khadzhenkov's cinema (A. A. Khadzhenkov founded the first Moscow's film studio), and another on Sretenka, for the Uran Cinema. A cinema was also established in the Metropole Hotel Building.

An accompanist played the piano on a stage in front of the screen for the silent films of that time. There was a spacious foyer where an orchestra played and a dance floor for film viewers waiting for the next showing. Symphonic concerts were even held. It became a tradition to come to the cinema early and have a light meal or a drink in the buffet.

It is interesting to note that the architecture of cinemas was in many ways a continuation of theater architecture. An example of this is the Kolizei Cinema built in 1912–14 by the architect R. I. Klein. The cinema entryway was executed in the classical style, which seemed appropriate to theater buildings; there was a balcony and boxes in the auditorium. Cinema buildings, as well as their viewing rooms and foyers, were often decorated with marble and crystal chandeliers. These decorations also recalled the style of theater buildings. [25]

MUSEUMS

There were several remarkable museums in turn-of-the-century Moscow. Their distribution in the city layout had a certain regularity based on the ownership of this or that particular museum.

In central Moscow, its cultural core, were the state museums — Rumiantsev and the History Museums. The Rumiantsev Museum was originally the collection of Count N. P. Rumiantsev, brought in 1861 from St. Petersburg and placed in one of Moscow's best locations, the Pashkov's building. The Museum continually expanded its collections thanks to private donations. It consisted of three basic parts — the ethnographic museum, the picture gallery, and the library.

The History Museum evolved somewhat differently. It was conceived as a central museum of Russian history, and those most directly responsible for founding it were count A. S. Uvarov and I. E. Zabelin, who were both noted historians and archaeologists. [26] The Museum was founded as part of a wave of renewed interest in Russian society for its history, and it was placed in that most central of all central locations — Red Square, where the architect V. O. Shervud designed a neo-Russian style building to accommodate it.

The idea of creating a history museum was born during the Moscow Polytechnic Exhibition of 1872, at the Varvarskie Gate of the Kitai-Gorod wall. Another museum was born of this exhibition, the Polytechnic Museum, also known at the time as the Museum of Applied Knowledge. But these two museums were placed in different parts of the city, the History Museum in Red Square, the city's historical center, and the Polytechnic Museum beyond the Kitai-Gorod wall at the Il'inskiie Gate, near the city's business center.

Another public museum appeared in the city's center in the 1880s, again riding the wave of interest in Russian history. There was an exhibition of folk crafts from Moscow Gubernia in 1882. This exhibition gave rise to the Moscow Crafts Museum, also located in the city's cultural zone — on Leont'evskii Lane. Like other museums of this time, the Crafts Museum building was built in neo-Russian style.

Thus, all of Moscow's public museums were built in the city's main cultural zone. It is of interest to note, though, that unlike the theaters, individual buildings were custom built for the museums.

This tradition of building new museums in the cultural core of Moscow continued throughout the late-nineteenth and early-twentieth centuries. The Museum of Fine Arts was built on Volkhonka, initially due to the efforts of Moscow University professor I. V. Tsvetaev. Another museum was established as an offshoot of this "hotbed" of culture, the Zoological Museum on Bol'shaia Nikitskaia, next to the Old University building.

Interestingly, the architect Klein chose a classical style for the fine arts museum, a style common for the museums of the time throughout Europe (London, Budapest, etc.). [27]

Thus, in the time under study, Moscow was home to a concentration of a number of museums of great cultural significance. (To this must be added what is undoubtedly Moscow's oldest museum — the Kremlin Armory.) The main fields covered by these museums are: history, ethnography, technology, crafts, and art (found in the Fine Arts Museum), in addition to the one representative of the natural sciences, the Zoological Museum.

The representational arts are almost absent in this group of museums, with the exception of the Rumiantsev Museum's Picture Gallery. [28] This is due to the fact that the organizers of these museums were more concerned with ideological, pragmatic, scientific, or scholarly goals. Collecting art objects in Moscow was almost wholly the realm of private persons. In this respect Moscow differed markedly from St. Petersburg, which had already long been home to the imperial Hermitage collection.

It is not surprising that private collectors in Moscow, Russia's ancient capital, showed an interest in Russian art before those in the new capital of St. Petersburg. The growth of the merchant class gave rise to a sharp upswing in collecting artwork. Many in this class were driven by patriotic feelings for the city of Moscow, collecting art and local antiques. Naturally for some this urge was driven by trying to catch up with the aristocracy, for others it was merely a desire to decorate their homes. However, for others collecting became a central part of their lives and some eventually created nationally and internationally renowned museums.

Naturally, when we are speaking of Moscow museums, the name of textile manufacturer Pavel Tretiakov, creator of the largest collection of Russian paintings, springs to mind. In addition, Petr Shchukin collected works of medieval Russian art and folk crafts and his brother, Sergei Shchukin, was known for his collection of contemporary European paintings. He was one of the few people, not only in Russia, but in France as well, who recognized the merits of the Impressionists, post-Impressionists, and their followers.

The significance of many of Moscow collectors lies not only in their remarkable collections. Many of them, including the Tretiakovs, Shchukins, Mamontovs, Morozovs, Riabushinskiis, Botkins, and others, were patrons of the arts. They supported artists by buying their works and expanding their own collections in the process.

Private museums began as home collections. In the course of time, when the patrons recognized their social significance, they opened them for public viewing. The collectors commissioned the construction of special buildings to house their collections from renowned artists and architects. The main entrance of the Tretiakov Gallery was designed by Victor Vasnetsov, who also built the Tsvetkov Gallery building on Prechistenskaia Embankment. Petr Shchukin Museum of the Applied Arts was built in the neo-Russian style by the architect B. V. Freidenberg. Shchukin purchased a plot for construction of his museum on Malaia Gruzinskaia Street. Over the years, some museum owners contributed their holdings to the city of Moscow.

Thus, the geography of private museums depended on where their owners lived. As a rule, they lived where their social status dictated — outside Moscow's cultural center. A notable exception to this was Sergei Shchukin's gallery, which first was located on the periphery of Moscow's cultural center and then, after construction of the Fine Arts Museum practically next door, found itself right in Moscow's cultural center. This can, of course, be considered a mere matter of chance. However, it cannot be regarded as exclusively accidental, as the house was formerly the mansion of Prince Shcherbatov. Sergei Shchukin's father, the wealthy industrialist Ivan Shchukin, purchased the home. We can see in this purchase the desire of the Moscow merchant class to drive the aristocrats not only out of the upper echelons of political and economic power, but out of the more prestigious residential districts of the city as well.

The Theater Museum built by Aleksei Bakhrushin holds a special place among those museums established by the Moscow merchants. This member of one of the richest Moscow families had a passion for the theater and collected programs, portraits of thespians, costumes, set designs, documents, objects relating to famous actors, and other theater memorabilia throughout his life. Bakhrushin founded the Theater Museum in his home in Zamoskvorech'e in 1894, turning it over to the Academy of Sciences in 1913.

THE GEOGRAPHY OF "ADDRESSES"

Moscow's cultural life was not limited to its cultural institutions — theaters, concert halls, museums, etc. It was also to be found in the homes where writers, artists, actors, and musicians lived and gathered, in the salons where exhibitions were held, and in the cafes where actors and poets congregated. The geography of these places is the geography of "addresses," wider than that of cultural institutions alone, though the two were closely connected. Concentrations of culture were to be found in the residencies of cultural figures and the places where they gathered (*see Appendix 4, Map 2*).

One example of such a nest of culture was 21 Miasnitskaia Street, across from the Main Post Office. This house, formerly belonging to General Yushkov[29] was home to the Moscow School of Painting, Sculpture, and Architecture. Many famous artists were teachers and students of this college (with some both studying and teaching): A. K. Savrasov, I. I. Levitan, A. E. Arkhipov, K. A. Korovin, M. V. Nesterov, V. A. Serov, R. R. Fal'k, and many others. In the early-twentieth century, apartment buildings were built on land belonging to the college and many teachers lived in these apartments, with a dormitory being built in the College's courtyard to house the students. The College continually held art shows with discussions continuing (or beginning) in the artists' apartments. Artists were not the only ones to be encountered at this address. The future great poet and writer Boris Pasternak spent his childhood in the College building, in his father L. O. Pasternak's apartment, a teacher in the College. Pasternak writes in his memoirs of the rich spiritual life and associations he was fortunate enough to experience in those years. [30]

Another noted cultural center at the turn of the century on Miasnitskaia Street was the mansion on the corner of Furkasovskii Lane. It was home from 1896–1899 to the Moscow Society of Architects. Architectural, artistic, and technical exhibits were shown here for two years. Then for one year the Literary and Artistic Circle met in the house.

Both the Society of Architects and the Literary and Artistic Circle were really clubs where Moscow's creative intelligentsia gathered. There were many such gathering places as the Actors Circle, places where like-thinking artists would meet. These creative clubs changed addresses more than once. For instance, the Literary and Artists Circle started out on Vozdvizhenka, then moved to Miasnitskaia, then Tverskaia, finally ending up on Bol'shaia Dmitrovka. But all the "migrations" of this and other circles and societies still never took them outside the borders of Moscow's cultural zone.

The Literary and Artistic Circle serves as a good illustration of how closely interconnected the interests of the Moscow intelligentsia were: the directors of the board of this circle were the poet Valerii Briusov, the singer Leonid Sobinov, and the actor Aleksandr Sumbatov-Iuzhin. As one contemporary recalled: "...although there were several different circles... for those interested in the theater and literature, professors' circles and others, all of them were in close contact and one encountered the same people at all of them." [31]

The geography of Moscow literary life in the late-nineteenth century and early-twentieth centuries (and indeed its musical, theatrical and other lives) could be the subject of a separate study in and of itself. We will only note here that the representatives of various literary schools had their favorite spots. For instance, the Symbolists gathered around the *Skorpion* publishing house and the editorial offices of the magazine *Vesy* (Scales), located in the Metropole Hotel building on Theater Square. They liked to gather over "a dram of spirits" in the cafe on Tverskoi Boulevard. [32] The Futurists opened their cafe-cabaret, *Rozovyi Fonar'* (Pink Lantern) in Mamonovskii Lane on Tverskaia. [33] And of course the literati of all schools were familiar with the Great Auditorium of the Polytechnic Museum, where literary evenings and debates were often held.

The actors liked to meet in the Shcherbakov's Inn on Kuznetskii Lane between Neglinnyi Proezd and Petrovka, and, after that inn closed, in the Livorno Restaurant or Welde's German restaurant which was behind the Bol'shoi Theater. [34] Nikolai Tarasov, one of the financial backers of the Art Theater, and the actor Nikita Baliev, created something like an Art Theater club near the Church of Christ the Savior. This club later developed into the cabaret theater *Letuchaia Mysh'* (The Bat). [35]

Moscow's Bohemian community met in establishments located either right in the center of Moscow in the Slavic Bazaar (*Slavianskii Bazar*) Restaurant, the Great Moscow (*Bol'shoi Moskovskii*) Inn, Maxim Cabaret, and several others), or outside the city, at the Krynkin's Restaurant on the Sparrow Hills (with its magnificent view of Moscow) and the famous Iar, a "pleasure palace" renowned for its Gypsies, both choirs and soloists, that was located on the Petersburg Highway at Petrovskii Park. [36] Once every year the Hermitage Restaurant on Trubnaia Square turned bohemian. Usually, it was frequented by wealthy merchants, but on the day the Moscow University was founded, St. Tatiana's day (the 12th of January according to the Julian Calendar then in use in Russia), the Hermitage became a center for the celebration which followed the official anniversary ceremony. One can understand the nature of these celebrations from what Chekhov noted about one such occasion: "That year everything was drunk down except the Moscow River, and it was only saved by being frozen at the time." [37]

One cannot discuss places where Muscovites socialized and spent time without mentioning the baths. For the Muscovite, the bath was always more than just a place to wash up. Baths offered their customers a whole range of services: barber shops, cosmetic and medical facilities, pools, buffets. But their main function was, like that of the ancient Roman thermae, as distinctive places to meet and socialize with people of like mind.

There were sixty baths in Moscow. [38] They were located in all the city's regions, and some of the older baths are still operating today. Most of the bath buildings were built in the late-nineteenth century — often replacing older baths which had occupied the same space. This-turn-of-the-century "bath boom" was brought about by technical progress in the form of electricity and water mains. The building for the most famous Moscow baths — the Sandunovskie, [39] known by Muscovites as *Sanduny*, went up in 1896. This bath even had its own electric station (the second in the city) and water main. [40] Top craftsmen worked on the building, and Carrara marble was brought in from Italy for its decoration. The changing room of the Sandunovskie Baths was a "club for a most variegated society, with each person finding his circle of acquaintans; and all this with a bar offering every drink imaginable, from kvas (Russian weak beer made from bread) to champagne..." [41] Entrepreneurs, actors, and writers came to swim in the Sanduny's pool. An owner of a music publishing house P. I. Iurgenson even opened up a successful music store on the premises.

Part of the building of the Sandunovskie Baths was occupied by comfortable apartments. The apartment on the first floor with windows facing the Zvonarnyi Lane was rented by A. P. Chekhov, a great afficionado of *Sanduny*, after his wedding.[42] The geography of the residences poses special interest. In order to show this more clearly, I would like to use material prepared by N. Shestakova. In her book *Po teatral'noi Moskve* (In the Theater Moscow) she lists all the residences of four members of Moscow's theater elite (except for short periods spent in hotels): the playwright and writer, Anton Pavlovich Chekhov; one of the founders and heads of the Art Theater, Vladimir Ivanovich Nemirovich-Danchenko; an actor from the same theater, Vasilii Ivanovich Kachalov; and the playwright and actor, and later head of the Malyi Theater, Aleksandr Ivanovich Sumbatov-Iuzhin[43] (*see Apendix 3, Map 2*). As we shall see, for the most part these remarkable people lived in the city's center and the northwestern sector of the Garden Ring, i.e., in the residence zone of the Moscow intelligentsia, noted many other times in this study.

However, several of the addresses shown are outside Moscow's main culture zone. None of these four men were born in Moscow and came to the city as young people, thus their first addresses may be considered simply a matter of chance, though one cannot call them entirely random. Chekhov first lived in the notorious Grachevka (later Trubnaia Street), in Malyi Golovin Lane on Sretenka, and on Bol'shaia Iakimanka in the Zamoskvorech'e (C1 to C6 on the map). In those years he was just starting out as a writer and changed his residence frequently, living wherever his means allowed. However, he still tried to live not too far from the city's center: from the Moscow University where he studied medicine, the university clinics on Rozhdestvenka, and Ekaterininskaia Hospital near Petrovskie Gate Square on the Boulevard Ring where he had medical practice, and from the editorial offices of magazines to which he contributed. Only later, when he was a famous author, could he rent a house on Sadovaia-Kurdrinskaia (C7 on the map). This is how the author himself described what most attracted him to his new residence: "...a clean place, quiet, and close to everything..." We will look into this "close to everything" remark in the light of Moscow's layout. Even in those years when Chekhov lived in his estate Melikhovo south of Moscow he usually stayed in the Great Moscow Hotel on Voskresenskaia Square — in the very heart of the city.

Sumbatov-Iuzhin and Kachalov's first addresses were also not in best of neighborhoods, which may be explained by their limited resources as young actors. But Sumbatov-Iuzhin's first Moscow apartment was nonetheless close to the Malyi Theater, and Kachalov's first apartment was close to the Hermitage Garden in Karetnyi Riad, where the Art Theater was performing at the time.

Nemirovich-Danchenko lived his entire Moscow life in the center of Moscow. Here all the places of his activities were found, especially the Philharmonic College and Art Theater.

Many of Moscow's creative intelligentsia (actors, artists, writers, scientists) lived in one section of the city, which was often called the "aristocratic realm" or the "nest of gentry." "One vaguely felt," recalled the writer Andrei Belyi, son of a Moscow University professor, "that out there an ocean encircled and enclosed 'our' area: Arbat, Povarskaia, Sobach'ia Ploshchadka, Tolstovskii, Novinskii, Smolenskii, Prechistenka..." [44]

"We all lived in those parts," recalls the writer, Boris Zaitsev. [45] That is correct, of course, but not entirely. It is symbolically true enough, but there were quite a few exceptions, of which we have already discussed several, and will discuss others further on.

I now would like to discuss several more remarkable residences on the map of Moscow. The list must certainly include Zinaida Morozova's house on Spiridonovka and that of Stepan Riabushinskii on the corner of that same Spiridonovka and Malaia Nikitskaia. The actual owner of Morozova's house was her husband, the prominent patron of the arts, Savva Morozov. After his death the house was bought by the renowned art collector Mikhail Riabushinskii. His brother Stepan Riabushinskii acquired a unique collection of icons in his home. But it is not merely the value of the collections themselves, but the cultural interchange which went on between guests visiting the houses' hospitable owners.

Both of these homes on Spiridonovka are products of the architectural genius of Fedor Shekhtel. A building's architectural and artistic merits do not, however, necessarily coincide with its significance on the cultural map. One regular gathering of authors and others were the "literary Wednesdays," held by the writer Nikolai Teleshov, which were frequented by Leonid Andreev, Ivan Bunin, Maksim Gorky, Vladimir Korolenko, Aleksandr Kuprin, as well as other writers, along with actors, musicians and artists. [46] Teleshov moved several times in his long life (to Chistye Prudy, Zemlianoi Val, Chistye Prudy again, and finally Pokrovskii Boulevard). His "Wednesdays" moved with him. Not one of the houses in which Teleshov lived was notable for its architectural features, but each was undoubtedly a high-point on the city's cultural map. Every time the "Wednesdays" moved; the city's cultural geography changed.

For some reason Wednesday was a popular day in Moscow. In addition to Teleshov's "Wednesdays" there were also "Wednesdays" held by V. E. Shimrovin on Bol'shaia Molchanovka, where up to a hundred artists and art lovers gathered. [47] There were also "Wednesdays" held by the poet Valerii Briusov on 1-ia Meshchanskaia Street. [48]

We have repeatedly stressed that almost all of Moscow's cultural life carried on in a relatively limited section of the city's territory. However, we also spoke of the cultural enclaves and oases which existed beyond these borders. They also had a place in the geography of "addresses." Certain residential addresses stand out on the map as gathering places of artists and literati, and the owners of these homes played a key role in the development of culture. Two late-nineteenth-century examples of such homes were located close to one another near Krasnye Gate Square on the Garden Ring. These were Savva Mamontov's house, which was "a sanctuary for all talented painters, sculptors, actors, musicians, singers and dancers," [49] and the home of the industrialists, the Alekseevs. In this home, productions by the Alekseev Dramatic Circle took place, directed by the son of the hosts — Stanislavsky. In the early-twentieth century there was the house of the Nosovs, a family of merchants, on Vvedenskaia Square. The lady of the house, Ievfimia Pavlovna (maiden name Riabushinskaia) turned it into an art salon. Another such home was the "Black Swan" dacha in Petrovskii Park, owned by the famous art patron Nikolai Riabushinskii, publisher of the journal *Zolotoe Runo* (Golden Horn).

Many artists lived or had their studios beyond the Garden Ring. This is possibly due to the low real estate prices in that region and the artists' need for a large space for their studios. The studios of Valentin Serov and Konstantin Korovin were at one time located next to one another on Dolgorukovskaia Street. The sculptors Sergei Konenkov and Stepan Erzia had studios near Butyrskaia Zastava Square. Konenkov later rented a studio on Presnia. Viktor Vasnetsov built himself a home in a quiet area of the Meshchanskie Streets region. [50]

Personalities from the arts experimented with their residences, seeking the ideal home. Petr Il'ich Tchaikovsky, whose life was deeply connected with Moscow, came to love living in the picturesque suburbs of Klin on the Petersburg road. He tried to settle in Moscow for one winter late in his life, and he rented an apartment on Ostozhenka, but he was bothered by the constant visits of strangers. He hung a sign on his door which read: "Not at Home. Please Do Not Ring." Unfortunately, the composer had failed to take the Moscow urban environment into account. Every passing schoolboy reading this notice regarded it as a personal invitation to ring the bell as hard and long as he could and immediately hide himself. [51] Eventually Tchaikovsky left the country and moved to Italy. He later settled once again at his estate near Klin.

However, all could not afford such luxury. The composer Karl Metner, for instance, preferred to live and work out of town all year. But in the end, as his niece recalls, he was forced to take an apartment in Moscow. He gave private lessons and held a job at a music publishing house, both of which demanded that he remained in the city. He did, however, live at the edge of Moscow, in a quiet alleyway near the Novodevichii Convent. [52]

Students could not be as particular in their choices. The composer R.M. Glier recalls how his friend from the conservatory asked for his help in harmony classes, offering him a place to stay in his home on the St. Petersburg Highway beyond Tverskaia Zastava Square in payment. This house was hardly an ideal home for a musician, located as it was next to a hippodrome and on the road leading to the restaurants and night clubs of Petrovskii Park. But with the modest means at Glier's disposal he jumped at the offer. [53]

EXPANSION OF MOSCOW'S CULTURAL ZONE

Progressive members of the intelligentsia sought ways to spread culture to the city's masses. Stanislavsky organized performances by a group from the Art Theater in a factory of which he was part owner. When the area used for shows was needed to expand production space the theater started to distribute tickets to its shows among the factory workers.

Liberal members of the Moscow City Duma found an alternative manner for spreading culture — setting up cultural and educational establishments similar to clubs for the working class and neighborhoods and other residential areas of the poorly educated public.

The Moscow Duma was known for its liberal tendencies and actions. For example, the Moscow budget, in contrast to that of St. Petersburg, set aside considerable funds for education, city beautification, and the development of cultural establishments for the masses. So, it is no surprise that the Moscow Duma took the initiative on building cultural and educational buildings for the masses. Development of these people's clubs was furthered by offerings from Moscow merchants.

These people's clubs usually had a library, an auditorium, and sometimes a Sunday school. There were ten such facilities in Moscow at the beginning of the twentieth century and all were located in bourgeois or working-class neighborhoods. The Sergievskii (or Novo-slobodskii), and Vvedenskii peoples clubs had theaters. Noted figures in Russian culture often took part in the activities of these clubs.

Institutes of higher education also formed foci of culture in the city's peripheral territory. Several institutes were located in buildings which the city purchased from members of old aristocratic families. The Konstantinovskii Surveying Institute, which prepared specialists in land improvement, geodesy, and topography, occupied the Demidov's home in Gorokhovskii Lane on Staraia Basmanaia Street. The Imperial Technical Academy was located in the Slobodksoi Palace in Lefortovo, and the suburban estate of Petrovsko-Razumovskoe was given to the Agricultural and Forestry Academy. The location of institutions of higher learning (and sometime secondary schools as well) [54] in the city's best buildings demonstrates Russian society's attitude toward education. [55]

With the twentieth century, new demands appeared for highly qualified specialists in the country's growing economy. Two new institutes appeared, the Railway Engineering Institute was built near Sushchevskii Kamer-Kollezhskii Val in northern Moscow, and the Commercial Institute became the first institute of higher education in the Zamoskvorech'e. [56] New buildings were being constructed at this time for housing these new institutes.

The clinical buildings of the Moscow University medical school were built in 1880, on Devich'e Pole (Bol'shaia Tsaritsynskaia, now Bol'shaia Pirogovskaia Street) in southwest Moscow. In the early-twentieth century the same region was home to the buildings of the Higher Women's Courses, Russia's first institute of higher education for women.

Finally, the last cultural enclave of pre-Revolutionary Moscow made its appearance in 1912 with the construction of the Moscow City People's University on Miusskaia Square. This institution was intended for persons who lacked a systematic education and was established on the initiative and with the support of Moscow philanthropist A. L. Shaniavskii. Shaniavskii himself did not live to see his university opened. The university which bore his name was opened in 1908, and expanded rather haphazardly at first into several facilities in central Moscow.

The takeover of Miusskaia Square is a good example of the planning activities of the Moscow Duma. This area, a large vacant space at the end of the last century, was turned into a spacious square with a public garden in the center, along with several streets and lanes. Miusskaia Square's buildings consisted primarily of educational institutions.[57] Built here, in addition to the Shaniavskii University, were two of the so-called city academic buildings, each home to several vocational schools. Following the law of concentration, here too were built the Physical Research Institute of the Moscow Science Society and the Moscow Archaeological Institute. Miusskaia Square came to occupy a prominent spot-on Moscow's cultural map.

Beyond the built-up portion of Moscow lay its rest and recreation areas. From the late-nineteenth century into the first years of the twentieth the lower classes held its celebrations on Devich'e Pole. The celebrations continued to be held there until 1911, when they were moved to Presnenskaia Zastava Square on Kamer-Kollezhskii rampart. Medical institutions by then were occupying a large part of Devich'e Pole and could not operate among the noise and dust of the celebrations.[58]

Khodynskoe Pole was another area in Moscow were large fairs and celebrations took place. A hippodrome was built here and further down the Petersburg Highway[59] was an area where various exhibits were shown.[60] Two great events held on Khodynskoe Pole at the end of the late-nineteenth century stand out, though one is famous and the other notorious: The All-Russia Trade and Industry Exhibit of 1882, and the tragedy at the coronation festivities for the last Russian Emperor, Nicholas II.[61]

Rest and recreation areas for the more noble and intellectual Muscovites of the time included Sokol'niki, the Sparrow Hills, and Petrovskii Park. Petrovskii Park was known for its restaurants — Iar, Strel'na, and El Dorado. During the warm months of the year, shows were performed in the park at its summer theater.[62]

The park was laid out at the beginning of the nineteenth century near the Petrovskii Travel Palace, an example of how powerful and distinctive an influence transport can have on a location's value. The palace was built in the late-eighteenth century by the famous Moscow architect Matvei Kazakov for the Empress Catherine the Great. It was here that she made her last stop before entering the old capital.[63] The pompous structure could not help but attract the attention of all travelers on their way to Moscow from the direction of St. Petersburg. It was a building one could love or hate, but never ignore. In this regard it is interesting to note two nearly identical impressions of this building, the first by the French aristocrat the Marquis de Custine, describing it during his travels through Russia in 1839, as "the very real Petrov Palace, a heavy castle... in bizarre taste," and an American who traveled from St. Petersburg to Moscow some fifteen years later, "the very real and clumsy castle... in the oddest taste." [64] Nonetheless, as we can see, both of them took note of the palace in their travel notes. Those who later traveled from St. Petersburg to Moscow on the train did not, as a rule, even see this palace. There is not a word about it in the writings of the American traveler J. B. Bouton, or G. Brandes, though the latter mentions the Iar Restaurant and its Gypsies in his book. [65] But he made his way to Iar on the Petersburg Highway from the south, from Moscow, and went only as far as the restaurant, not going on to the palace.

The quaint tradition of stopping off at the Petrovskii Palace before a ceremonial entry into Moscow remained with the royal family even into the time of railroads. There was a special rail branch line built to transfer the Tsar's train from the Nikolaevskaia Railroad to Brest Station, near the Petrovskii Palace. The branch was called just that—the Tsar's Branch Line. [66]

There is one more place beyond the Petrovskii Park which, against all odds, became a place of high culture for a time. This was Dr. F. A. Usol'tsev's psychiatric clinic, where the terminally ill artist Mikhail Vrubel' was sent. It was here, commissioned by the owner of the journal *Zolotoe Runo* Nikolai Riabushinskii, that he worked on a portrait of the poet Valerii Briusov, a portrait which never was completed. [67]

THE MOSCOW ENVIRONS (PODMOSKOV'E)

Moscow's cultural life did not end at the city limits. There are at least two reasons for this. The first is that through all the centuries preceding the time under study, the bearers of Russian cultural heritage were the landed aristocrats, owners of lands and holdings. It is therefore completely natural that many cultural figures coming from these circles or connected therewith inherited country homes, lived and performed their creative work in the suburbs, and visited their friends and colleagues in the country.

The second reason for these "cultural enclaves" outside the city was the seasonal rhythm of Moscow life as a whole and in particular its cultural life. The summer geography of cultural life differed from that of the winter season. The academic year in the secondary schools and institutions of higher education ended in the summer. The theater and concert season was over. Society life froze in Moscow during this time. Muscovites left for their estates and those lacking an estate rented dachas. [68]

This did not, however, mean that cultural life ground to a halt, it simply moved to other locations. There were performances in the summer theaters of the city itself, for instance the theater at Petrovskii Park. There were also concerts in the parks. The summer symphonic concerts in Sokol'niki were very popular. But the bulk of cultural life moved out to the country estates and dacha settlements (see *Appendix 4, Map 3*). Some estates were open year-round, others only for the brief summer season. Many of these estates were gathering places for musicians, artists, writers, and those who admired their work. These were places where culture was created.

I will introduce several examples of such estates in the Moscow suburbs.

One of the most noted artistic locations in the Moscow suburbs was Abramtsevo. This was the estate of Savva Mamontov, a great supporter of the development of the arts in his time. Those who gathered in Abramtsevo included artists such as the Vasnetsov brothers, Repin, Nesterov, Vrubel, Polenov, Serov, the sculptor Antakol'skii, the singer Shaliapin, the actress Iermolova, and others. At the estate were a pottery and woodcarving shop, plays and operas were performed, and literary discussions held. The salon which formed around Mamontov became known as the Mamontov or Abramtsevo artistic circle. Unfortunately, Abramtsevo dropped out of the cultural scene in 1900 when Mamontov went bankrupt. [69]

Melikhovo, to the south of Moscow, is associated with Chekhov in Russian cultural history. Here he worked in a country hospital and it was also here that he wrote many of his stories and most of his significant plays. He was also visited by Giliarovskii, Levitan, Nemirovich-Danchenko, and others.

A whole batch of such country estates which left a bright trail in cultural history were clustered near Klin, northwest of Moscow on the St. Petersburg Road. Many figures from the arts and sciences of Moscow and St. Petersburg met at the Dem'ianovo country estate, property of the sociologist and philosopher V. I. Taneev. Some, like the owner's brother, the composer S. I. Taneev, and the chemist I. D. Kablukov, came to visit the owners. Others, among them the biologist K. A. Timiriazev, the Gnesin sisters, and the artist Apollinarii Vasnetsov rented dachas at the estate and lived there for many years. [70] P. I. Tchaikovsky lived in the area for many years, first in Maidanovo, later in

Frolovskoe, and finally, toward the end of his life, in a estate on the outskirts of Klin where a museum was later created.

Two estates were located closely to one another in Klin Uezd: Shakhmatovo, where the poet Alexander Blok spent his childhood and youth, and Boblovo, property of the famous Russian scientist D. I. Mendeleev. The poet's frequent visits to Boblovo ended with him marrying the estate's owner's daughter.

Not far from Tarasovkaia station on the Severnaia Railroad was Liubimovka, the estate of K. S. Stanislavsky's family. It was the place where he made his debut as an actor, [71] and later discussed the creation of the Art Theater with V. I. Nemirovich-Danchenko. In time this estate became a kind of outpost of the Moscow Art Theater.

In the early-twentieth century an interest in the study of country estates appeared in Russia. Some owners of estates preserved them as museums, such as Ostaf'evo and Muranovo, both estates closely linked with Russian culture. But the owners of some country estates seemed to breathe new life into them. Such an estate was Serednikovo, associated with Mikhail Lermontov when the property belonged to its last owner, Vera Ivanovna Firsanova. Shaliapin visited Serednikovo several times, as did Rachmaninoff and many other cultural figures. The area surrounding it became a popular spot for the dachas of the Moscow intelligencia. [72]

With the precipitous growth of the capitalist urban intelligentsia, a group which lacked estates of their own, Muscovites started renting dachas en masse. The first of such dachas went up close to Moscow, in Sokol'niki, Petrovsko-Razumovskoie, Petrovskii Park, Pokrovsko-Streshnevo, Liublino, and Bogorodskoe. For the local residents, renting out their house to city dwellers for the summer became a considerable source of income, sometimes the main income for the household. Enterprising businessmen began building houses near the rail lines, later selling special plots of land for building dachas. [73] Dachas (summer homes) were built along all the rail lines leaving Moscow, but the greatest concentration of dachas was along the older lines: the Nikolaevskaia (going to St. Petersburg), Severnaia (to Yaroslavl'), Aleksandrovskaia (to Brest-Litovsk), and Riazanskaia. Of course, the age of the rail line was not the sole factor influencing the density of dacha construction. Building was also affected by the appearance of the site: picturesque and pristine or heavily-built up (for example the Nizhegorodskaia line, one of the first in Moscow, which passed through industrial workers' towns).

The artist Konstantin Korovin recalled the dachas near Moscow in the early years of the twentieth century this way:

> "Moscow's surroundings were beautiful. They gradually filled up with dachas, and these wooden dwellings took on a poetic look in the summer... Tomilino on the Riazanskaia Railroad was very pleasant. There, in wide open spaces, in the woods, near the river, they built dachas. And what dachas they were! They were made of pine, with decorative carvings and all manner of embellishment... The terrace went down into the garden, which was full of lilac and jasmine. These dachas were like some kind of new toys peeking out of the forest. The dacha smelled of pine, and the aromas of flowers and hay drifted in from the forest and the garden..." [74]

Moscow's cultural life was transplanted to these dachas each year during the summer. The dacha settlements usually had their center, located near at the rail station, containing a public park with an open-air dance floor, small stores and stands, often a restaurant and even a theater. [75] (Later cinemas appeared as well.) The Moscow and St. Petersburg troupes would tour the summer theaters. Well-known actors would appear, as well as young actors just making their debut. The most well-known of these theaters was in Malakhovka on the Riazanskaia Railroad. [76]

I would like to discuss several other areas which played an important role in cultural history.

In Pushkino on the Severnaia Railroad the first season of the Moscow Art Theater prepared to open in the summer of 1898. Rehearsals took place in a barn, remodeled for this purpose (fig. 4.6), and the actors lived in dachas close by. [77] In 1905 this trial was repeated through the creation of the Studio of the Art Theater, directed by Vsevolod Meierkhold. "Pushkino once again became the center of a new art." [78]

Many cultural figures were attracted by the picturesque Zvenigorod Uezd area to the west of Moscow. This region became known as Russia's, or Moscow's, "little Switzerland," and Tchaikovsky, Chekhov, Levitan, S. I. Taneev, and others spent many of their summers here. The writer V. A. Giliarovskii called Kraskovo on the Riazanskaia Railroad home. Here he was visited by Chekhov, Kuprin, Shaliapin and others.

The architect Fedor Shekhtel had his dacha in Kuntsevo, and it was here that Vladimir Maiakovsky spent the summer of 1913. [79] There were many artists, architects, and men of letters among the guests.

Moscow's intelligentsia would often be neighbors for the summer. This gave rise to a kind of cultural "dacha community". The poet Pasternak recalls what an important role in his life socializing with the composer Skriabin played when their families lived next door to one another in the summer of 1903 near Malyi Yaroslavets on the Brianskaia (Kievskaia) Railroad. [80]

There are many more examples. In one way or another cultural figures continued their creative activity and maintained their creative community outside Moscow's borders in Podmoskov'e.

The geography of Moscow culture also extended to a number of places outside Moscow Gubernia. The bank of the Oka River near Tarusa in Kaluga Gubernia was known for its beauty. The "discoverer" of Tarusa was the artist Vasilii Polenov, who settled near the city in the 1890s. He established a museum and art center in his estate and had a constant stream of visiting artists, musicians, writers, and scholars. At the turn of the century this city became a popular place for Moscow's intelligentsia to build and rent dachas. The founder of the Fine Arts Museum, I. V. Tsvetaev, had a dacha here for many years. His daughter, a poetess Marina Tsvetaeva, spent her childhood and youth in Tarusa. But the Tarusa area was the special favorite of the artists. [81]

A similar role in the development of Russian culture was played by Princess M. K. Tenisheva's estate in Talashkino. Even though the estate was actually located in the neighboring Smolensk Gubernia, it was really an enclave of Moscow culture (and in fact of St. Petersburg culture also). Talashkino was a gathering place of artists and of many of the participants in the Abramtsevo circle — Vrubel, Korovin, S. Maliutin, Nesterov, Repin, and other figures of Moscow and Petersburg culture.

Finally, the geography of Moscow's culture beyond Moscow itself and Moscow Gubernia would not be complete without mentioning Yasnaia Poliana, where Lev Tolstoy spent many years of his life. Iasnaia Poliana was a magnet not only for Muscovites, but for the cultural people of the entire educated world.

CONCLUSION

In conclusion, I would like to note the following. First, the geography of the Moscow intelligentsia's addresses as a whole is close to the geography of theaters, museums, institutes of higher learning, and other cultural institutions. The participants both within and outside the walls of these institutes were both generators of culture and as well as its consumers. A unified cultural field existed in Moscow.

Secondly, the tempo of cultural development at the turn of the twentieth century was so intense that, despite the social cataclysms, the main centers of culture in Moscow at the end of the century are the same as they were in the early century, and the greater part of them remain concentrated in the same part of central Moscow as in the time of this study.

NOTES

[1] Boris Pasternak. "Liudi i polozheniia," in *Izbrannoe v dvukh tomakh*, Tom 2 (Moscow: Khudozhestvennaia literatura, 1985), 230.

[2] Dmitrii Likhachev. *Zametki i nabliudenia. Iz zapisnykh knizhek raznykh let* (Leningrad: Sovetskii pisatel', 1989), 39–48.

[3] The question of concepts and terminology is clearly one of the most difficult issues in science. Traditionally, cultural geography is considered a subfield of human geography, "focused upon the patterns and interactions of human culture, both material and non-material, in relation to the natural environment. Today the term 'cultural geography' covers a diverse range of studies with only tenuous links to a common tradition" [*The Dictionary of Human Geography*, R. J. Johnston, Derek Gregory and David M. Smith, eds., Third edition (Oxford, UK; Cambridge, Mass.: Blackwell Publishers, 1994), 11This is partly due to the numerous meanings of the concept "culture" in language.

[4] Likhachev. *Zametki i nabliudenia*, 48.

[5] The Manezh grandiose building was used for celebrations, symphony concerts, and exhibitions.

[6] With the beginning of the First World War, the German Club was renamed the Slavic Club, see *Moskva. Entsiklopediia* (Moscow: Sovetskaia Entsiklopediia, 1980), 454.

[7] *Po Moskve. Progulki po Moskve i ee khudozhestvennym i prosvetitel'nym uchrezhdeniiam*, N. A. Geineke, N. S. Ielagin, Ie. A. Iefimova, I. I. Shits, eds. (1917; reprint, Moscow: Iso-brazitel'noe iskusstvo, 1991), 192–208.

[8] Oliver M. Sayler. *The Russian Theatre* (New York: Brentano's Publishers, 1922), 7–8.

[9] Vlas Doroshevich. *Izbrannye stranitsy* (Moscow: Moskovskii rabochii, 1986), 267.

[10] The Moscow merchant K. S. Alekseev, who later became known to the cultural world as Stanislavsky, first used the pseudonym while performing in the amateur theater, Sekretarev's; see Nataliia Shestakova, *Progulki po teatral'noi Moskve* (Moscow: Soiuz teatral'nykh

deiatelei RSFSR, 1989), 151. This theater was popular in the second half of the nineteenth century and was located in the lane between Vozdvizhenka and Bol'shaia Nikitskaia. The Nemchinov Theater on Povarskaia was another of Moscow's popular amateur theaters.

[11] A. V. Anisimov. *Teatry Moskvy. Vremia i arkhitektura* (Moscow: Moskovskii rabochii, 1984), 37.

[12] For a description of this theater see Yurii Aikhenval'd, *Aleksandr Ivanovich Sumbatov-Iuzhin* (Moscow: Iskusstvo, 1987), 65–78. Vladimir Giliarovskii dedicated a very sympathetic essay to Anna Brenko, see Vladimir Giliarovskii, *Sochineniia v chetyrekh tomakh*, Tom 1 (Moskva: Isdatel'stvo "Pravda", 1989), 316–324.

[13] Moskva. *Entsiklopediia*, 556.

[14] Across from the Malyi Theater on Neglinnyi Proezd (at the corner of Sofiika) was the Imperial Theater College (in reality the Malyi Theater's school), which was also located in a formerly residential building; see Shestakova, *Progulki po teatral'noi Moskve*, 53–62.

[15] The name "Chicago" was very popular at this time due to the famous World Columbian Exposition, which took place in Chicago in 1893.

[16] On Lentovskii and his *Hermitage* see Giliarovskii, *Sochineniia*, Tom 1, 330–334.

[17] Zimin Opera was performed in the Solodovnikov's Theater starting in 1908.

[18] See Giliarovskii. *Sochineniia*, Tom 1, 344–359. Also recounted is how Giliarovskii brought actors from the Art Theater, who were preparing to present Maxim Gorky *The Lower Depths*, to the building where copyists were working. The "scenery" the artist V. A. Simov viewed in that visit was reproduced to the last detail on the stage.

[19] It is of interest that Nikolai Rubinshtein's brother, Anton Rubinshtein, was the founder and first director of the St. Petersburg Conservatory. The brothers were from a Moscow merchant family.

[20] As with many other theater buildings, the Conservatory's building had previously been a residence.

[21] This historic mansion, one of Moscow's cultural landmarks, was destroyed, along with all of Sobach'ia Ploshchadka, for the construction of the New Arbat in the 1960s.

[22] Moskva. *Entsiklopediia*, 301.

[23] Moskva. *Entsiklopediia*, 302.

[24] For a description of the cinema on Ielokhovskaia, one of Moscow's first, see the memoirs of Nikolai Anoshchenko, a veteran of the Moscow cinema: Nikolai Anoshchenko, "Iz vospominanii," in *Minuvshee. Istoricheskii al'manakh. 10* (Moscow-St. Petersburg: Athenium-Feniks): 343–393.

[25] It was no matter of chance that the Kolizei building was used afterward on several occasions as a theater. Now it is the home of the Sovremennik Theater.

[26] Ievgeniia Kirichenko. *Istoriheskii muzei* (Moscow: Moskovskii rabochii, 1964), 22.

[27] This tradition has been carried on, an example being the National Gallery in Washington, D.C.

[28] The History Museum was also used for art exhibits.

[29] The building's construction is attributed to the architect Bazhenov.

[30] Boris Pasternak. "Liudi i polozheniia," 226–29.

[31] K. M. Iel'tsova. "Sny nezdeshnie," in *Kniga o Vladimire Solov'eve* (Moscow: Sovetskii pisatel', 1991), 120–21

[32] O. Tochenyi. "Valerii Iakovlevich Briusov", in *Russkie pisateli v Moskve* (Moscow: Moskovskii rabochii, 1973), 766. Pasternak wrote: "Although the summer coffee house on Tverskoi Boulevard did not have a name, it was always called the Café Grec," see Boris Pasternak, "Okhrannaia gramota," in *Izbrannoe v dvukh tomakh*, vol. 2 (Moscow: Khudozhestvennaia literatura, 1985), 153. To which can be added that it was not just the symbolists who enjoyed sitting in the *Café Grec*.

[33] The café did not operate for long. It was closed by the police after the scandal arising from a poetry reading by Vladimir Maiakovsky, who had a penchant for shocking the public. See Il'ia Shneider, *Zapiski starogo moskvicha* (Moscow: Sovetskaia Rossiia, 1970), 104–06.

[34] Giliarovskii. *Sochineniia*, Tom 4, 342–45.

[35] The club-cabaret of the Art Theater opened in 1908 in the basement of the Pertsov building near the church of Christ the Survivor. However, in this very year the spring flood from the Moscow River flowed into the basement, and *Letuchaia Mysh'* moved to a different basement — in Miliutinskii Lane on Miasnitskaia. Finally, in 1915 the cabaret moved to its third and final basement location in the Nirnzee building in Bol'shoi Gnezdnikovskii Lane on Tverskaia.

[36] On meeting places of Moscow's bohemians see S. Abarbarchuk, "Gde sobiralas' bogema. Chast' vtoraia. Moskva," *Novoe russkoe slovo*, 13 November 1992.

[37] A. P. Chekhov. *Polnoe sobranie sochinenii i pisem v 30-i tomakh. Sochineniia v 18-i tomakh, Tom 16* (Moscow: Nauka, 1979), 141 (translated by Christopher Gait). The celebration of St. Tatiana's Day became more decorous toward the end of the nineteenth century, after Leo Tolstoy's call for the day to be celebrated as a day of enlightenment, not a romp of bumpkins. See Nikolai Teleshov, *Zapiski pisatelia. Vospominaniia i rasskazy o proshlom* (Moscow: Moskovskii rabochii, 1980), 242.

[38] Giliarovskii. *Sochineniia*, Tom 4, 283.

[39] The Sandunovskie Baths were named for the actor Sila Sandunov, who constructed the first baths at this location on the banks of Neglinnaia River in the mid-eighteenth century.

[40] Anatolii Rubinov. "Bil'iard v Turetskom zale", *Novoe russkoe slovo*, 15 Feb. 1996.

[41] Giliarovskii. *Sochineniia*, Tom 4, 291–92.

[42] Iurii Fedosiuk. *Moskva v kol'tse Sadovykh* (Moscow: Moskovskii rabochii, 1991), 205.

[43] Shestakova. *Po teatral'noi Moskve*, 232–33.

[44] Andrei Belyi. "Staryi Arbat (Iz knigi 'Nachalo veka')," in Andrei Belyi, *Staryi Arbat. Povesti* (Moscow: Moskovskii rabochii, 1989), 43 (translated by Vladimir Talmy). Sobach'ia Ploshchadka (now does not exist) and Tolstovskii (Bol'shoi Tolstovskii, now Karmanitskii) are lanes on the Arbat; Novinskii and Smolenskii are boulevards on the Garden Ring.

[45] Boris Zaitsev. "Dalekoe," in *Sochineniia v trekh tomakh*, (Moscow: Khudozhestvennaia literatura; TERRA, 1993), 3:362.

[46] Teleshov. *Zapiski pisatelia*, 32–58

[47] Giliarovskii. *Sochineniia*, Tom 4, 127–132.

[48] Raised in a middle-class Moscow merchant family, Briusov spent the first thirty-two years of his life in his father's house on Tsvetnoi Boulevard. After this he lived in his own home, but stayed in his accustomed region. For a description of his "Wednesdays" see Bronislava Pogorelova, "Valerii Briusov i ego okruzhenie," in *Vospominaniia o serebrianom veke*, Vadim Kreyd, comp. (Moscow: Respublika, 1993), 34–35.

[49] Constantin Stanislavsky. *My Life in Art,* trans. J. J. Robbins (Boston: Little, Brown, and Company, 1924), 141.

[50] For a description of this home built in the neo-Russian style see Vsevolod Vasnetsov. *Stranitsy proshlogo. Vospominaniia o khudozhnikakh brat'iakh Vasnetsovykh* (Leningrad: Khudozhnik RSFSR, 1976), 91–102.

[51] N. D. Kashkin. *Vospominaniia o P. I. Chaikovskom* (Moscow: Muzgiz, 1954), 176.

[52] V. K. Tarasova. "Stranitsy iz zhizni N. K. Metnera," in *N. K. Metner. Vospominaniia. Stat'i*. Materialy (Moscow: Sovetskii kompozitor, 1981), 46.

[53] R. M. Glier. *Stat'i i vospominaniia* (Moscow: Muzyka, 1975), 80.

[54] The Academy of Applied Commercial Sciences, for instance, was located in the former palace of the Durasovs on Pokrovskii Boulevard, the Second Moscow Academic Gymnasium was housed in the Musin-Pushkin palace at Razguliai Square, the Fourth Gymnasium in the Apraksin home near Pokrovskie Gate, the L. I. Polivanov's Gymnasium, the best in Moscow, was located in an old noble estate on Prechistenka, etc.

[55] The other social institutions established in former palaces of the Moscow aristocracy were hospitals.

[56] The location of the Commerce Institute in this region was no matter of chance. The Zamoskvorech'e was the primary residence of the "consumer" of its "production."

[57] A. V. Rogachev. *Okrainy Staroi Moskvy. Ekskursii dlia moskvichei* (Moscow: MIROS, 1993), 34–47.

[58] Rogachev. *Okrainy Staroi Moskvy*, 78.

[59] The highway was renamed Petrograd Highway in 1914, when St. Petersburg was renamed Petrograd. It later became the Leningrad Highway, and has remained so to the present, although Leningrad has been renamed St. Petersburg.

[60] It is shown as just this on plans of Moscow from that time: "Exhibit area."

[61] Some 1,400 people were crushed to death and 1,300 injured during the public celebration of the coronation of Nicholas II.

[62] The theater is long gone, but its memory remains in the names of the streets in Theater Alley.

[63] There is a tendency in Russia to associate everything beginning in "Petr-" with Peter the Great. But this palace was named for its proximity to the village of Petrovskoe. The village was also not associated with the first Russian emperor. It was the property of the Vysoko-Petrovskii Monastery, which in turn was named for Peter, Moscow's first Metropolitan.

[64] See Astolphe Custine. the Marquise de, *Journey for Our Time*, Phillos Penn Kohler, ed. and trans. (Washington, D.C.: Regnery Gateway, 1987), 264, and "A Trip from St. Petersburg to Constantinople", *National Magazine*, 5, no. 3 (September 1854): 214. The author of the present essay, though in agreement with Custine in many regards, and impressed by his perception and understanding of Russia, cannot agree with him (or that of the anonymous American) in this view.

[65] John Bell Bouton. *Roundabout to Moscow. An Epicurean Journey* (New York: D. Appleton and Company, 1887); Georg Brandes. *Impressions of Russia*, trans. Samuel C. Eastman (1889; reprint, New York: Thomas Y. Crowell Company, 1966), 123.

[66] Rogachev. *Okrainy Staroi Moskvy*, 145.

[67] Briusov recounts his visit to the ailing artist in the sketch "Posledniaia rabota Vrubelia," see Valerii Briusov, *Iz moei zhizni. Avtobiograficheskaia i memuarnaia proza* (Moscow: Terra, 1994), 16–25.

[68] I can recall how my father told me that before the First World War his family gave up their city apartment for the summer and moved to a dacha, returning to another apartment for each winter. This was a common practice for Moscow's middle-income families at the time.

[69] Abramtsevo has long been a museum, but one work created there has gone on to live a life of its own. It was at Abramtsevo that the artist Sergei Maliutin made a sketch of the first matryoshka doll, fashioned after a Japanese toy.

[70] A. Vasnetsov's son wrote very warmly of Dem'ianovo and his permanent and temporary visitors. See Vsevolod Vasnetsov, *Stranitsy proshlogo,* 45–76.

[71] Stanislavsky. *My Life in Art*, 56–62.

[72] There was even a special stop for dacha trains, called Firsanovka.

[73] Several suburban Moscow stations bear the names of those entrepreneurs who bought land nearby for dachas: Perlovskaia, Zagorianskaia, Nemchinovka.

[74] Konstantin Korovin. *Shaliapin. Vstrechi i sovmestnaia zhizn'* (Moscow: Moskovskii rabochii, 1993), 186 (translated by Christopher Gait).

[75] An essay on dachas in Podmoskov'e (Mariia Nashchokina. "Gosti s"ezzhalis' na dachu...," *Podmoskov'e. Pamiatniki otechestva,* no. 31, 1994: 80) names twelve settlements which had theaters, and the list ends with "et al."

[76] The facade of the theater at Malakhovka, which was built in 1912 to replace the one which burnt down, was taken from a sketch by Shaliapin, see Ia.M. Belitskii. *Okrest Moskvy* (Moscow: Legprombytizdat, 1960), 108.

[77] Stanislavsky. *My Life in Art*, 300–01.

[78] V. Verigina. "Po dorogam iskanii," in *Vstrechi s Meierkhol'dom. Sbornik vospominanii* (Moscow: VTO, 1967), 32. The studio unfortunately did not last for long. Its existence came to a sudden end with the revolutionary events of 1905.

[79] L. Rakhmanova. "Vladimir Vladimirovich Maiakovsky," in *Russkie pisateli v Moskve* (Moscow: Moskovskii rabohii, 1973), 791.

[80] Boris Pasternak. "Liudi i polozheniia," 231–33.

[81] Another popular dacha area for Muscovites on the Oka was outside the city Aleksin in Tula Gubernia.

Moscow Then and Now

Pavel Ilyin and Blair A. Ruble

> *A city is like a person: if we don't establish a genuine relationship with it, it remains a name, an external form that soon fades from our minds. To create this relationship, we must be able to observe the city and understand its peculiar personality, its 'I', its spirit, its identity, the circumstances of its life as they evolved through space and time.*
>
> Ivan Klíma [1]

What is Moscow's "I," its spirit, its identity? What is most remarkable about the contributions to this volume is that they echo so many themes one hears about Moscow today even though the city is in many ways a totally different place. Moscow is a city of contrasts, of great wealth and great poverty; it is a rough and tumble place without the superficial elegance of more "aristocratic" cities such as St. Petersburg; it is as much a metaphysical experience as a city.

This is a book about Moscow at the turn of the nineteenth and twentieth centuries published on the eve of the new, twenty-first century. Many events have occurred in the intervening time which have influenced all aspects of life in Russia and its capital: the Revolution and the Bolshevik terror unleashed by Lenin, the Civil War and NEP, industrialization and collectivization, Stalin's "Great Terror" and World War II, the Khrushchev thaw and the Brezhnev stagnation, Gorbachev perestroika, the decline and fall of the Communist empire. As political and economic regimes came and went, the city changed, as did its population and material environment. The very content of life changed. The change of regimes in 1917 was meaningful for Russia as a whole, but more so for the city of Moscow, which once again became the nation's capital. [2]

Post-Soviet Moscow is quickly emerging as Russia's dominant economic and financial center. Moscow "inside the Garden Ring" is coming to resemble the West more than the rest of Russia, as international and homegrown capital renovate the city's historic center for their own use. The swaggering capitalism of a century ago is no longer unimaginable — one need only walk down a brash central Moscow street to see that combination of confidence and aggressive tastelessness that so caught the eye of foreign visitors at the dawn of the century. To paraphrase the observations of Scottish geographer MacKenzie Wallace, Moscow still offends the Protestant mind.

When looking at the "before" and "after" of old and new Moscow we strive not to forget the "in-between" which connects the two — how the city became what it is today. We attempt to answer the following questions: is Moscow really a different city now? What is the truly "Moscow" element in the city's character which drives its development? You, the reader, already understand the key to Moscow's character. Moscow is all about leadership. Moscow was born to lead.

TERRITORY AND POPULATION

Moscow's territory in 1913 was 177 square kilometers or 68 square miles. Beginning in 1917, Moscow's official limits expanded several times, and the city's current limits, after the last expansion in 1984, are 994 square kilometers or 384 square miles: 5.6 times larger than it was at the turn of the century. Interestingly enough, population growth nearly kept pace with territorial growth, increasing five-fold from 1.8 to 9.0 million persons. The population and dimensions of a large city alone do not suffice to describe it in our days. According to several experts the population of Moscow agglomeration is greater than 20 million persons, with a territory covering nearly the entire Moscow Oblast. [3]

Since there was a fivefold numerical increase in the city's population, the number of native Muscovites, (i.e. descendants of the city's pre-Revolutionary residents), would normally be expected to increase proportionally, constituting at least one-fifth of the current population. However Moscow's population suffered tremendous losses in the Soviet period. This is more than numbers alone. The reduction in numbers that followed the Revolution of 1917 took some nine years to be compensated. Thousands of Moscow's aristocrats, merchants, bourgeoisie, clergy, and intelligentsia fell victim to the Civil War and Bolshevik terror. Many more fortunate people from the same groups emigrated or were exiled abroad. But this was only the beginning. Next came the terrible Stalin years. While Moscow's population far outstripped other cities of the USSR, it was far "ahead" of them in the number of victims it produced for the communist regime as well. Moscow's population grew due to the stream of migrants from other cities and from the countryside. These people had to assimilate the lifestyle and mindset of a large city. As a result of all this the number of native Muscovites is a mere 200–300,000-some 3 percent of the city's total population. [4]

Moscow was always a multiethnic city. Nonetheless, Russian ethnicity dominates, with some 95 percent of the population at the start of the century and 90 percent at its end. [5]

Moscow at the turn of the century was marked by a great tolerance for people of other lands and faiths, yet it was precisely this period, in 1891–92, that the Jews were driven from Moscow. [6] One other incident of note: when war was declared on Germany in 1914, a wave of chauvinism swept Russia, and many German-owned enterprises in Moscow were destroyed.

The xenophobia already widespread in Russia intensified in Soviet times, particularly during the Stalin years. In those days merely being seen speaking with a foreigner without official permission could be sufficient grounds for being shipped off to the camps. Such restrictions on freedom were gradually reduced under Khrushchev. Moscow became a host to international youth, film, and music festivals; scientific conferences; sport competitions; etc. However unofficial associations with foreigners were still risky. Now that the Soviet Union is gone, the old fear of associating with foreigners is virtually gone as well. Moscow is Russia's most international city, with thousands of foreign residents and the greatest concentration of jobs associated with foreign investments in the country. However traditional xenophobic sentiments have led some Muscovites to blame "outsiders" for their problems.

INDUSTRY

In the early years of the century Moscow was on par with St. Petersburg as one of the leading industrial centers of the Russian Empire. The city's dominance of the textile industry was undisputed. At the same there was time in Moscow a great amount of growth in machine-building, at a rate of development which surpassed that of the textiles industry.

Beginning in the late 1920s, in the years of so-called "socialist" industrialization, the rate of Moscow's industrial growth (in absolute figures) was unmatched by any other city of the Soviet Union. Moscow became an industrial center of unparalleled capacity. The city became a leading producer of automobiles, machine tools, and a key center of the military-industrial complex.

Numbers do not, however, tell the whole story. The most advanced production technologies were to be found in Moscow and the cities in the Moscow agglomeration, spreading from there to cities and enterprises throughout the country.

Moscow's industrial base was founded on old industrial sites. Many of the buildings housing modern industrial enterprises date to the early-twentieth century. In some places even the machine tools date from the same period.

Industry, as so many other things, has found the Moscow of late-twentieth-century Russia unprepared. This is particularly true of the textile industry. This industry lost its leadership role near the century's start, continuing to run on inertia into the 1920s, then artificially kept alive in Soviet Moscow, with the resulting in the industry becoming hopelessly out of date. In addition, many other branches of industry in contemporary Moscow are in a state of decline.

BEYOND INDUSTRY

Industry dominated the Moscow scene for a long time. However universal laws of social development eventually applied even in the Soviet Union. The number of industrial workers in Moscow, the USSR's first city, gave way to an increasing number of non-industrial workers, particularly in science, education, and the service industries.

Pre-Soviet Moscow shared St. Petersburg's preeminence as Russia's trade and finance center, even outpacing St. Petersburg in the volume of bank deposits and transactions in certain types of bonds. [7] This function was maintained and increased in Soviet times: as the city was the administration and command center of a totalitarian government, it became the center for the distribution of material and financial resources throughout the country. After the fall of that system, Moscow continues to be Russia's leading administrative and financial center. One-third of the nation's commercial banks are located in the capital [8] and up to 80 percent of all financial operations for the country are conducted in Moscow. [9]

This "capital character" was a decisive influence on Moscow throughout the Soviet period. Now, as the free market develops and production falls off, the role of control in all sectors of the economy is becoming increasingly important. Today Moscow is first and foremost a capital — a city of bureaucrats and white-collar workers.

SCIENCE AND EDUCATION

Moscow occupied second place in early-twentieth-century Russia as a center of science and education. Moscow University played a leading role in Moscow, functioning not only as an educational institution, but also as a point of concentration for most scientific activity in Moscow. Overall, however, St. Petersburg with its Academy of Sciences and University held the lead in science. The 1930s saw the Academy of Sciences move to Moscow from the former capital. It was in this period that Moscow became Russia's greatest scientific center, a function it maintains to this day, with the largest concentration of scientific researchers and highly qualified workers.

The military-industrial complex plays a special role in Moscow. Approximately 40 percent of Russian scientific research and design organizations engaged in defense work are located in Moscow. In addition, more than half of Moscow's scientific research institutes are in the defense sector. [10]

Moscow plays even more of a dominant role in Russia's higher education than it does in science. There are high quality educational institutions in many places. However, few institutions found outside of the capital possess the prestige of their counterparts in Moscow.

CULTURE

At the turn of the twentieth century, Moscow was, along with St. Petersburg, a center of the "Silver Age" of Russian art. After the Revolution, "culture and spirituality was demonized" and the "Silver Age went into emigration." [11] This demonizing wreaked havoc on Moscow's culture. But the news of Moscow's cultural demise was premature. In spite of the ideological pressure and the censorship thinking people still remained and more continued to appear. More of them made their appearance in Moscow than anywhere else. The most productive creative atmosphere in Russia was to be found here, and more than one generation of creative intellectuals was nurtured in this environment.

It was no matter of chance that many in Moscow were acquainted with the free underground culture. Many writers, both famous and obscure, wrote "for their desk drawer," often without the hope of ever seeing their work in print. Avant-garde artists organized shows to which the authorities responded with bulldozers. Scientific seminars and screenings of western films were held in private homes. The solo song performed by the songwriter, (usually accompanying him or herself on the guitar), thrived in Moscow, a cool breeze for the many people not utterly crushed by the official ideology. Moscow produced most of the authors of both Samizdat and Samizdat. Although many of the elite of Moscow's intelligentsia emigrated abroad in the 1970s-1990s, [12] Moscow remains Russia's most progressive cultural center.

Due to its unique cultural atmosphere and the high social status given to creative people, Moscow has always enjoyed an intellectual life more intensive than that of other cities. Many fledgling writers, poets, artists, and musicians made their start in Moscow. Here their talent was recognized and sustained by the Moscow public, and many of them went on to greater recognition in the world at large.

SPATIAL STRUCTURE, APPEARANCE, AND BUILDING

The spatial structure of a city is the most stable of its civil engineering elements. The radial-concentric street structure that formed in medieval Moscow is still prevalent in the city's planning structure. All Moscow development projects in the Soviet period were founded on developing new rings, an idea which was partially implemented. The picture becomes more complex when we consider the radii.

In Moscow, as in many other European cities, the street system that has evolved throughout its history is in conflict with modern demands for city transportation. [13] The "eternal question" of our time comes down to: what is more important, a street's transportation throughput or the architectural and historical significance of its layout? The former won out in Moscow, with new radial streets cutting into the city's living tissue: New Arbat and Novokirovskii Prospect (now Academician Sakharov Prospect).

A good deal of Moscow's buildings date to the nineteenth century and early-twentieth century. The bulk of buildings are of course from Soviet times, particularly the construction boom in residential buildings from the Khrushchev era. There were difficulties in renting apartments in Moscow during the capitalist industrialization period. There were also areas of slums. However today it is hard to imagine the housing conditions most Muscovites faced from 1920–1960. Some 8 percent of Muscovites still live in communal apartments, [14] an "invention" of the Communist regime.

Moscow's historic buildings have always been in jeopardy. Many buildings were torn down at the turn of the century when space was needed in the city's center for apartment buildings. The 1935 "Stalin" plan for city reconstruction entailed removal of many entire blocks of old buildings; but this plan was disrupted by the War. [15] Construction was started on New Arbat under Khrushchev. Under Brezhnev the zone within the Garden Ring was officially declared a preservation district. In reality, however, the Brezhnev period damaged historic buildings on a massive scale, with high-rise apartments for the nomenclatura quietly replacing them in the Arbat and Spiridonovka areas. The new Moscow authorities are unfortunately continuing the same policy of replacing historic buildings with modern high-rises, this time with new motivation — pleasing investors. [16]

Overall, however, Moscow's central area has not changed as radically as it may seem at first glance. Many fragments of old Moscow remain: the streets Kuznetskii Most, Sretenka, Prechistenka, Krivokolennyi lane, Bol'shaia Ordynka in Zamoskvorech'e, and a number of other streets and lanes. Go from Red Square to the Garden Ring along Il'inka and Maroseika-Pokrovka and you encounter only a couple of buildings that went up after 1917.

Moscow's skyline changed radically. The city's old skyline was peppered with the spires of belfries and onion domes of churches. After construction of the first Moscow's "skyscraper," the ten-story Nirnzee building in 1912, construction of ever larger buildings was inevitable. With normal development, the city's skyline should have added new heights. However, the Bolsheviks chose a different path, which began by pulling the old skyline down. In the end, almost all that remained of the old city skyline was the Kremlin and Pashkov House. Nearly all the other dominant buildings had been torn down or refurbished beyond recognition. An attempt was made to restore the old skyline with the construction of skyscrapers with tall spires in the 1950s. This attempt marked something of a return to old "Russian roots." Later Moscow architects turned to the West, producing such buildings as the "Rossiia" and "Inturist" Hotels, the new CPSU Central Committee building, and the buildings along New Arbat. One could hardly accuse their designers of good taste.

Moscow really demonstrated its urban development leadership through the boldness of its experiments. New planning and urban development techniques were tried out in Moscow: the microregion, free planning, taller apartment buildings, and other projects. Moscow was a city where the rebirth of the old city center was carried out with much more intensity than any other major Russian metropolitan area.

There are, of course, major differences between the city's current engineering infrastructure and that of the past. The Moscow City Duma really only took the first steps toward city improvement: laying out waterlines, sanitation, paving roads, lighting streets, etc. The days of horse-drawn carriages in Moscow are a faded memory, replaced by modern transportation. The trolley has been joined by the bus, the trolleybus, and Russia's first subway.

MOSCOW – THE LEADER

Has Moscow become a different city? Yes and no.

Moscow entered the twentieth century as a leader of capitalist development in Russia. After the October revolution, Moscow became the center of the communist world. Following the collapse of communism and the resurgence of capitalism in Russia after seventy years of communist rule, Moscow is once again playing the leading role in Russia.

In fact, Moscow has a long history of leadership, and has preserved its leadership role independently of the political and economic regime. Even when the capital was St. Petersburg, "in several ways Moscow continued to play a dominant role in the country. Thus it was Moscow that set the tone for social opinion. Peter the Great had to deal with this, as did all the czars who came after him." [17]

Social opinion lost its meaning to the "powers that be" of the Soviet period, but Moscow's role in Russia continued to grow at an unprecedented pace. The development of the Soviet Union as a whole depended largely on that of Moscow. Greatly disparate interests drew masses of people into Moscow. The prestigious schools were located in Moscow, as well as the best places to work in administration, production, and cultural enterprises. The Moscow lifestyle surpassed Russia's prevailing deficit conditions.

The magnetic attraction of Moscow motivated those outside the city to perform. A good example of this was the provincial leadership who sought positions in Moscow to improve their careers. To show that they were capable of moving in the higher circles of power these leaders would show off their prowess by improving their own cities and locales. [18]

After the totalitarian regime's collapse, Moscow remained a leader, this time taking the leading role in Russia's democratization and capitalist economic reforms.

It can be said that, as before, Moscow today represents a great magnet, attracting people with the variety and availability of its activities and the opportunity to participate in its unique experiments. No other city in Russia can offer people such diversity.

Leadership is Moscow's chief characteristic. This being said, it must be kept in mind that there is a tendency to idealize a leader. Just as its human counterparts, Moscow—the leading city—has dark as well as light aspects. The leader both attracts and repels. Moscow attracts people with its cultural environment and broad choices, its festive atmosphere, and hospitality. But Moscow also has a less attractive side: high crime, run-down neighborhoods, and xenophobia. In today's Moscow, demonstrative opulence is cheek by jowl with many people living in poverty and semi-starvation. Through it all, most people say with the Chekhov heroine: "To Moscow! To Moscow! To Moscow!"

Moscow is what it has always been: the hub of Russia.

NOTES

[1] Ivan Klima. "The Spirit of Prague," in *The Spirit of Prague and Other Essays* (New York: Granta Books, 1994), 39.

[2] As Soviet propaganda put it: "capital of the world's first socialist country."

[3] This is analogous to estimates used for the population and territory of any large American city (SMA).

[4] A. I. Alekseev et al. *Moskvovedenie. Geografiia Moskvy i Moskovskoi oblasti* (Moscow, Ekopros, 1994), 79.

[5] In the early-twentieth century this included the Ukrainians, who were not considered a separate nationality in the Russian Empire and thus not counted separately. Sources: "Statisticheskii portret Moskvy na 1910 god," in Moskovskii arkhiv. Istoriko-kraevedcheskii al'manakh. Vypusk I (Moscow, Mosgorarkhiv, 1996), 169; Alekseev, Moskvovedenie, 90.

[6] This was ordered by Alexander III's administration and zealously carried out by Moscow's Governor General Grand Duke Sergei Aleksandrovich. Anti-Jewish laws are a shameful part of the Russian Empire's laws at the turn of the century. There was nothing like this remaining in any other country of the world. Yet even the Moscow City Duma, Russia's most liberal body, dared not voice its opposition.

177

[7] See Boris Anan'ich. *Bankirskie doma v Rossii 1860–1914 gg. Ocherki istorii chastnogo predprinimatel'stva* (Leningrad: Nauka, 1991), 153–54.

[8] Alekseev. *Moskvovedenie*, 125.

[9] Alekseev. *Moskvovedenie*, 123.

[10] Alekseev. *Moskvovedenie*, 113.

[11] Vadim Kreyd. "Vstrechi s serebrianym vekom," in *Vospominaniia o serebrianom veke*, Vadim Kreyd, ed. (Moscow: Respublika, 1993), 6–7.

[12] Some voluntarily, some driven out by the authorities.

[13] This problem is not exclusively to be found in old European cities, but in their younger North American counterparts such as New York, Washington, D.C., and others.

[14] A. V. Rogachev. *Moskva. Gorod-chelovek-priroda* (Moscow: MIROS, 1994), 45.

[15] One of history's paradoxes: the War saved Moscow.

[16] See A. Komech. "'Rekonstruktsiia' Moskvy prodolzhaetsia," *Novyi mir, no. 1*, (1997): 244–47. "I often shudder at the thought: what would have happened to Rome, Prague or Vilnius if they had fallen into the hands of those who determined Moscow's fate?" the author wrote in his letter to the editor.

[17] Sergei Bakhrushin. *Trudy po istochnikovedeniiu, istoriografii i istorii Rossii epokhi feodalizma* (Moscow: Nauka, 1987), 165.

[18] Blair A. Ruble. *Leningrad. Shaping a Soviet City* (Berkeley: University of California Press, 1990).

PART III

Who is Zakhar Zagadkin?

Sailing The Radio Waves

by *Pavel Polian*

EXPLORING OUR COUNTRY

Perhaps the first long-running Soviet children's radio show was the popular "Captains' Club", first aired on December 31, 1945. The second, an educational children's show called "Exploring Our Country", was released in April 1958. It was followed, in December 1963, by the last series of this kind called "KOAPP", which stands for "The Committee For The Protection Of Nature", which focused on environmental issues and bionics.

"Exploring Our Country" was a geography game show, featuring a former midshipman named Zahkar the Riddleman ("Zakhar Zagadkin") and his friend, ship's cook Tony Galley ("Anton Kambuzov"), owner of Jacquot the parrot. They were creations of Pavel Ilyin's father, Mikhail Ilyich Ilyin (1901–1967), a talented journalist with a special gift for geography and a wide knowledge of the Soviet Union and the world. His first books on geography — *From The Black Sea To The Caspian,* which he wrote, and *The Soviet Land: Essays And Stories On The Latest Discoveries In The Geography Of The USSR,* which he co-authored and edited, — came out in 1948 and 1950, respectively.

These were the dark years of repressions and anti-Semitism, when his adopted last name of Ilyin proved to be a brilliant piece of protective camouflage. There is a family legend (undoubtedly based in fact) that explains how his Jewish name of Tirkeltaub became a Russian-sounding "Ilyin."

Unlike Vladimir Lenin, who used the same moniker of "Ilyin" as an alias in his early revolutionary days, Mikhail Tirkeltaub did not set out to change his name. During the Russian civil war,[1] where he fought on the side of the Red forces, he served in a hospital train whose director gave up trying to pronounce "Tirkeltaub" and started to call him instead by his patronymic (*Ilyich*), or rather its peasant variant (*Ilyin*).

---

[1] https://en.wikipedia.org/wiki/Russian_Civil_War

In 1928, Comrade Tirkeltaub put himself down as Ilyin when registering for a Soviet passport, and so both his children — Pavel and his sister Yulia — were born with the last name of Ilyin.

In April 1958, during Khruschev's thaw,[2] the trio of Zahkar the Riddleman, Tony Galley and Mikhail Ilyin first took to the radio waves. The first two years they ranged all over the globe but from 1960 on their horizon shrunk to one-sixth of its former size — namely, to the borders of the USSR.

In 1959, the leading Soviet children's publisher released the *Memoirs Of Zahkar the Riddleman, Midshipman,* and in 1963, the *Incredible Yet True Geographical Adventures Of Zahkar the Riddleman On One-Sixth Of The Earth's Landmass, As Told By Himself, With Notes By Future Scientist Thomas Answeroff* ("Foma Otgadkin"). In 1965 both books came out in one volume titled *Memoirs And Incredible Adventures Of Zahkar the Riddleman.* This was just the beginning: Zahkar the Riddleman books went through 14 editions totaling over 600,000 copies, in eight languages, in the USSR, Poland, Czechoslovakia and China.

The radio show gave rise to another spin-off: the Moscow planetarium created a popular lecture on the travels of Zahkar the Riddleman, complete with slides, which was then published in print format and sold to the public.

The radio show aired at 6 pm every other Thursday and ran for 20 minutes. Its theme music was a popular children's song. Tony Galley the Cook opened each show in the familiar deep voice of the great Soviet actor Leonid Bronevoy by chanting the last words of the song, before giving his iconic lead-in: "Greetings, my friends!" — followed by Zahkar the Riddleman and his stories and puzzles.

Here is one of these novellas, entitled "Why I Never Became The Owner Of Jacquot The Parrot":

> At dawn I ran up on deck and beheld a stunning sight. As far as the eye could see, the sea was covered with olive-green grass. A light breeze stirred the grassy thickets, broken in places by ribbons of dark-blue water. Without a doubt, we were sailing through a giant meadow! I was admiring the rare sight when I was struck by a sudden fear: what if the ship's keel became entangled in the countless stalks? We could be stuck in this strange sea meadow for a long time...
>
> I went down to the galley where the Cook was making pancakes on the stove to go with our morning coffee and shared my concern.

---

[2] https://en.wikipedia.org/wiki/Khrushchev_Thaw

The Cook smirked. "You're not the first to be taken aback by this sight, Zakhar," he said, handing me a steaming cup of coffee. "In fourteen hundred and ninety-two a famous mariner was no less surprised to see these emerald-green meadows. His sailors were spooked by the strange sound the ships made when they tore through the meadow and, like you, feared that the ships would get caught in the floating tangle.

"But all ended well. The famous mariner made it out of here, and the future showed that these plants do not hinder navigation. So have no fear: we won't get stuck, either. Have some hot coffee, Zakhar, and forget your concerns. In fact, we face another, more serious danger: the sea we're sailing through has no shores!"

"No shores? How is this possible? All seas have shores..."

"All other seas do but not this one. History knows of no sailor who has ever come ashore here. If Midshipman Zakhar manages to see the shores, even far off on the horizon, that will be a great discovery in the annals of geography! Which I, though a mere ship's cook, will celebrate by giving you my parrot!"

Who could turn down the chance to make a great discovery, and get the gray parrot Jacquot, everyone's favorite, into the bargain? Surely not Midshipman Zakhar! I spent all my free time up on deck, patiently waiting for the shoreline of this sea meadow to appear on the horizon. I did not care whether it would be rocky or sandy, high or low, populated or deserted; I had to see it — because there could be no sea without shores!

Alas, my vigils were in vain. We crossed this sea from east to west, and I found, to my chagrin, that indeed it had no eastern or western shore. On our return voyage we crossed it from north to south, but saw no northern or southern shore, either.

So I never became the owner of Jacquot the parrot.

The listeners were expected to send in their answer — which was, of course, "Sargasso Sea."

After telling his story, Zakhar (voiced by the actor Lev Durov) would take his leave and call out to the cook: "Mr Galley, your watch!" The Cook would come on and ask a couple of simpler questions. The two divided their audience by age: Zakhar's stories were aimed at older schoolchildren while the Cook's puzzles targeted the younger age group.

Here is one example:

In our last show, Tony Galley asked our young geographers to find the shortest route from Amur to the Dnieper. Although everyone knows these names as belonging to two great rivers, many of you, know-

183

ing the Cook's wily ways, guessed that this was a trick question, and found the railroad station "Amur" in the city of Dniepropetrovsk, located almost on the bank of the river Dnieper.

Another one of the Cook's specialties was the geographical dictation: a short passage of several sentences comprised of words that were also geographical names found on the maps of the USSR. These were also tricky, in that a place name could be made up of two or more words appearing together in the sentence, or it could be made up of parts of words. Here is an approximate translation of one that contains, in the original, no less than thirty-two place names:

The Midshipman, the Cook and I lived in a beautiful house on the bank of a river. It was morning. Zakhar went into the woods to look for berries. The Cook and I went to a remote lake. There, Anthony and I caught six hares.

Finally, the Cook read out the answers to the questions from the previous show and gave the names of the best responders. The theme music came on again, and the show ended.

The questions and puzzles were designed to intrigue the young listeners and get them interested in a more in-depth study of geography. They were intentionally pitched to a level of difficulty that went beyond the curriculum of a Soviet geography class. To find answers, boys and girls had to go to the library and consult encyclopedias, maps and atlases, all the while learning the skills of working with sources and systematic study habits in general. One former listener — Galina Kopytova, who provided the above dictation example — recalled that these habits helped her later in her college studies, and that in answering these questions she began compiling her own index of Soviet toponyms.

PAVEL POLIAN FROM 8TH GRADE

For my part, I was in love with the Great Soviet World Atlas, second only to the Naval Atlas in splendor, since both featured an index at the end listing all the geographical names appearing on their maps.

The radio game show was open to schoolchildren of all grades, but over half the participants were in seventh and eighth grades, because their school curriculum focused on the geography of the USSR. Geography teachers also followed these shows, and some of them used elements of the game in their lesson plans.

As Pavel Ilyin would later note, many kids first joined the game because hearing the results of dictations reviewed on the air sparked their sense of competition, but by solving Zakhar's puzzles they expanded their knowledge of geography. Mikhail Ilyin was well-versed in child psychology and knew that, to maintain their interest, they needed a way of interacting with the characters and with one another. That is why he came up with the game format, diplomas and log books. Children willingly joined and participated in the game; many thought Zakhar and the Cook were real and shared their thoughts and dreams with them.

Each show brought over a thousand letters with answers, not including group letters from approximately 150 school clubs and geographical societies. Nearly two thirds of the radio "travelers" lived in villages or small towns. But since not every listener was bold enough to write to Zakhar and Tony, the overall audience of "Exploring Our Country" was surely much larger than that.

Those who wrote in and entered the game were assigned individual scorecards, where the hosts kept a tally of the points earned by their answers. Periodically (usually once a month) the kids received their own "logs," printed on A5-sized cards emblazoned with the game show's colorful logo and signed "Your seafaring friend, Zakhar." The logs recorded the listener's score in the game.

I experienced the game show from both sides, not only as a participant but also as staff, because Pavel Ilyin soon asked me to help him screen the mail and score the cards while he typed the letters to the kids. I enjoyed the work, as well as the pay, little though it was, since every little bit helped to round out my meager intern's salary.

At the end of each annual, numbered "round," 500 or 600 most knowledgeable "travelers" received diplomas printed with their names on thick paper, and the best of the winners also received prizes — geography books signed by Tony and Zakhar. Overall, around 13,000 or 14,000 students received awards during the show's run. Another reward was to hear one's name read out by the Cook as the author of the best answer to the previous show's questions.

The show did not air in the summer, but Zakhar and the Cook ran special contests on such topics as "The Geography Of My Region," "The Rivers Of My Region," "How I Spent The Summer", etc. The kids sent in entire notebooks and albums filled with descriptions of their summer travels, complete with maps, sketches and photos; the best ones also earned prizes.

Many schoolchildren who first became interested in geography thanks to Zakhar the Riddleman went on to enroll in geography programs at universities and teachers' colleges. Some became geography teachers, formed geography clubs in their schools, and re-entered their favorite game with their students. And some former "travelers" earned their graduate degrees and became university professors and heads of geography departments. These veterans were sometimes invited on to the show: I recall one show in which I took part along with Nico Berouchishvili, future chair of the department of physical geography at the University of Tbilisi.

GALYA KOPYTOVA FROM IRKUTSK

Of course, not all young geography buffs, even among those who did well on the show or were obsessed with travel, went on to become professional geographers. But all — as can be seen from letters sent by friends of Zakhar and the Cook's after they grew up — preserved the most wonderful memories of this game of travel tales, so educational and magical.

Here is one such memory, found on the Internet. Galina Germanovna Kopytova from Irkutsk, one of the faithful followers and successful participants in the game show, has titled her articulate and well-illustrated account — "Exploring Our Country."

I first began listening to the show in 1971 and at first kept it to myself: I solved the dictations with the help of my beloved geography atlases but was too shy to write to the show. I don't know how I ever overcame my bashfulness, but my letter was answered — by Zahkar the Riddleman himself!

This happened in the early 1972... And from that point on I never missed a show. When I had school in the afternoon, I had to ask someone to write the questions down (this was before tape recorders, let alone more modern means of recording). The questions were always interesting and challenging. To answer them, one had to spend hours in libraries and reading rooms, but the effort was worth it: the results were always fun and exciting. My knowledge of geography grew, and the subject itself became an object of desire... By the way, my geography teacher at school was also wonderful! This obsession later influenced my choice of career...

But back to the show. [...] We were supposed to mail in our answers to Zahkar the Riddleman's questions and our solutions to the dictation question. In return, we periodically got back pages of our log book containing our score and information on upcoming shows. Sometimes they even mentioned our name on the show – that was cool!

A whole school year's worth of shows was called a "round." At the end of each round, we got a "diploma." Getting one was more exciting than receiving an award in front of the whole school... I took part in five rounds and earned five diplomas.

During the summer vacation after my last two years of school, they ran contests "Summer-74" and "Summer-75", which also involved performing certain geographical tasks. Winners earned wonderful books as prizes.

In 1976, I finished school and, after enrolling in the geography program at the University of Leningrad, sent a letter to my radio friends, Zahkar the Riddleman and Tony Galley... and received the last page of my log book in response.

Pavel Ilyin (or rather, Zakhar!) wrote back:

Dear Galya, greetings! My congratulations upon your admission to the geography program. The Cook has already read out his best wishes on the air, and I am recording mine now in your log book... Thank you for your kind words about our show.

I am sending the diploma you earned in the 17th round of our game show – your fifth and final diploma. I also have not forgotten the prizes I owe you from Summer-74 and Summer-75: I will send them soon. My best wishes on your future successes.

Your seafaring friend,
Zahkar the Riddleman.

A little later Galya received the books "owed" to her by Zakhar.

The show ran for almost a quarter-century: nine years under Ilyin Sr. and sixteen years under Ilyin Jr. Over 400 episodes in total aired between 1958–1982.

A final note: eventually, Pavel Ilyin himself, with his wife and daughter Nadya, a young musician, set out on a journey, but this time they were bound far away from the USSR. In June 1982, at the tail end of Leonid Brezhnev's reign, they applied for permission to emigrate to the United States, whereupon the radio show was immediately shut down.

Travels In My Wonderful Homeland:
A Geographic Radio Game
for Soviet Schoolchildren

Pavel M. Ilyin

Moscow, USSR

Since April 1958, schoolchildren of the Soviet Union have been tuning in to a popular geographic radio shows featuring Zakhar the Riddleman and his friend the Cook, Tony Galley, on Moscow radio. There have been about 300 such shows in the past 18 years. Those two characters were created by children's author Mikhail Ilyich Ilyin (1901–1967). He wrote all of the Zakhar the Riddleman shows in the first nine years of the series existence. From late 1967 onward, all scripts have been written by the speaker of this presentation.

Zakhar the Riddleman was instantly popular with the children. A young man and an inquisitive traveler, he often finds himself caught up in "stories" that he records in his traveler's log. Every story is a geography riddle told in an enticing way.

In early broadcasts, Zakhar described his travels on every continent and ocean of the Earth: at that time, he "served as" a ship's boy in merchant marine. In 1960, "Travels in My Wonderful Homeland" was launched as a competition game for best knowledge of geography of the Soviet Union where a school year housed one round of the game. "Traveling" with the characters of the game on a biweekly basis, young radio listeners get acquainted with administrative, economic and physical geography of the USSR.

Every broadcast runs for 20 minutes and consists of a problem story by Zakhar the Riddleman and one or two riddles from the Cook. Every other show, the cook announces the answers and names the best problem-solvers. The stories by Zakhar the Riddleman are targeting higher-grade schoolers, and the Cook's riddles are for younger students. To give you a better idea of devices used for content delivery, here are examples of three such problems stories.

Zakhar and the Cook are going by train from the Crimea to the Caucasus. The Ship's Boy is so sure the train will go on land around the Azov Sea that he makes a bet with the Cook. But, to his great surprise, the train is running across sea waves! This is just the gist of it, but the whole story of Zakhar's argument with the Cook and their remarkable train ride takes about ten minutes. The story has clues to lead the listeners to the solution. What it doesn't say is that there is a railway ferry across the Kerch Strait (Zakhar was not aware of it).

Another story takes place in the north of European USSR. Zakhar tells about a conversation he had with a hydrologist he met on the train. The hydrologist told him how he had lost a team member on an expedition. They were walking along a small river, he on its right bank, and his mate on the left one. The river forked into two sleeves, which did not meet again! Each of the hydrologists came in time to a big river, but it was not the same river! That's another ten-minute piece, an example of the Pizhma river bifurcation into the Mezen Pizhma and the Pechora Pizhma, where schoolchildren get acquainted with river bifurcation phenomenon.

Tony Galley asked his young audience to find the shortest way from the Amur to the Dnepr. But knowing the Cook's tricky nature, many guessed there had to be a trick to this request. They eventually found a railway station, the Amur, the Far East river's namesake, right at the Dnepr's bank, in the city of Dnepropetrovsk.

From time to time, the Cook offers dictations where all words are actually geographic names that can be found on the map of the USSR. Deciphering those geographic dictations does not require as much learning as solving Zakhar's problems does. Many children get attracted to the game owing to the competitive nature of dictation deciphering; later, they go on to try solving Zakhar's problems and develop a broader geographic outlook.

Every show generates a feedback, around a thousand letters with solutions. Students of all grades, from elementary through high, take part in the radio game. Half of the audience are students from the seventh and eighth grades where geography of the USSR is taught. Apart from those, letters with solutions come from more than 150 school geography clubs and societies that number thousands of schoolchildren. About two-thirds of "radio travelers" live in rural developments and small towns, while the total number of children, who are listening to the show 'Travels in My Wonderful Homeland', and absorbing new geographic knowledge, must be much greater.

Game participants must work hard as what they get in class is not sufficient for a winning solution to problems posed by Zakhar and the Cook. They spend hours pouring over maps, searching atlases, reference books and encyclopedias, as evidenced by excerpts from books and references to sources that provide the answers. Many answers are accompanied by self-made maps, drawings and diagrams. Moreover, the kids suggest their own puzzles: "radio travelers" have composed most of the Cook's dictations themselves or prompted topics for many of those as well as for some of Zakhar's stories.

Every game participant has an individual file where his or her results are recorded as a score. From time to time, they are sent "traveler's reports", issued on forms with the game's logo and signed personally by Zakhar the Riddleman, to inform them of their "track records". After each round is completed, about 500 to 600 "radio travelers" are awarded diplomas, also printed specifically for the show, and the best of the best get prizes (books on geography). The total number of schoolchildren, awarded for achievements in the game, is approaching ten thousand.

Zakhar and the Cook also conduct special competitions, usually during vacation time, such as "My Native Land", "Rivers of My Native Land", "Geographic Names in My Native Land", "How I Spent My Summer", etc.The show receives notebooks and albums describing summer trips, with drawings and snapshots. The winners also receive awards.

Mikhail Ilyin had great insights into child psychology; he realized that, in order to keep up their interest, children needed direct communication with the characters of the show and with one another. Hence the show format as a game, and diplomas for the winners, and travel logs. Children take to the game easily and willingly. Many believe in actual existence of Zakhar and the Cook: they invite them home, and share with them their thoughts about life and dreams of the future.

In numerous letters from teachers, parents and the children themselves, the show "Travels in My Wonderful Homeland" is said to help with learning, promote interest in geography of the USSR, nurture willingness to learn more about their homeland, teach map and book reading skills, and encourage consistent effort. Many teachers use information from the show in class. Numerous school children, first exposed to travels with Zakhar the Riddleman, have chosen a geography major at universities and teachers' colleges. There are PhD doctors in geography among former "radio travelers". Others have become geography teachers, and have created similar geography clubs in their schools where they have resumed the game with their students.

Needless to say, it's not that every former geography fan, even if a winning one, becomes a professional geographer. Yet, judging by letters from former friends of Zakhar and the Cook, who have grown up, they cherish their best memories of this, in their own words, "fabulous game". A former schoolgirl from the town of Mirny in Yakutia who had chosen a different professional career, wrote: "I'll carry these most wonderful memories of childhood into my adult life".

About a hundred inquisitive stories that were broadcast between 1958 and 1965 were also published in a book. Mikhail Ilyin's book about Zakhar the Riddleman was published in the USSR, Poland, Czechoslovakia, and China. It withstood 14 editions in 8 languages, for a total of over 600,000 copies. A popular presentation with slides, based on Zakhar the Riddleman book, was developed and produced.

LETTERS OF PARTICIPANTS

ALEXANDER GAVRILOV

In the late sixties, I lived in Kratovo Township outside of Moscow and attended Railway School No.2. While the place was a stone throw from Moscow, it seemed, the difference in educational standards was enormous. I realized it in full when my parents and I moved to "real" Moscow. There was a lot of catching up to do in nearly all subjects, with the exception of one subject only, namely, geography, where I was quite on the level (in good shape). My success in geography was due to the radiogame "Travels in My Wonderful Country", a pet project of my geography teacher, Valentina Gittenberg.

She taped broadcasts by Zakhar Zagadkin (Zakhar the Riddleman) and Cook Anton Kambuzov (Tony Galley) on an ancient "Dniepr" taperecorder and met with us, students from different grades, twice a week after classes for fascinating sessions of riddle guessing. Those were not easy riddles. One had to do some digging at the library, and we were lucky in that there was an excellent library in the nearby Zhukovsky, a town of aviation designers. I can still remember a huge "Atlas of the USSR" mounted on a separate desk. It was eventually thumbed through to pages full of holes, all in search of answers to questions posed by the Riddleman and his colleagues.

Radiotravels presented to us by Mrs.Gittenberg opened the doors to the big world for students of Kratovo Railway School No. 2, which can hardly be overestimated.

MASHA GUSEV ABOUT ZAKHAR ZAGADKIN

When I was little I read a lot. I read more than I really lived. Hence, most of my childhood knowledge of geography came from the stories and quizzes of Zakhar Zagadkin. There was no doubt in my mind that he was a real person, observant and inquisitive, with a good sense of maritime humor. And all of his stories were rich in content, lively, and motivated the listener to learn more about our planet — as much as it was possible at the time, within the realities of the USSR.

What is the Gulf Stream and a tsunami? How to sail in the Sargasso Sea, and why the moon causes the ebb and flow of the tides? I, having read and listened, was theoretically ready to travel around the world.

My children read with great enthusiasm the last — with a green cover (my own childhood copy) 1964 edition of Zakhar Zagadkin. And we all joyfully quizzed those around us on geographic literacy and all kinds of natural disasters.

What can I say? This sort of book is not published now. Everything is either abridged to the size of a "read and forget" file, a kind of disposable plastic fiction, or served with partisanship or some other ugly seasoning. It is not interesting to read books on geography nowadays, gentlemen.

LERA FREIDLIN

I have two children, and I am already a grandmother. I still remember the broadcast of the journeys and adventures of Zakhar Zagadkin. I listened to this program with my children, and we all enjoyed it a lot. It was our favorite radio game. We had a large geographic map hanging on our wall. Children used it when they were solving the puzzles of Zakhar, and they mailed their answers to the broadcast studio. We all learned how to read the map. In America this skill helped me to drive around when there was no GPS yet. My children fell in love with natural sciences and as adults they have chosen specialties related to nature. They love traveling across America and to other countries, and they have taught their own children to enjoy it too.

KRUKOV'S RECOLLECTION

When I was growing up my parents worked all the time and my grandmother mostly raised me. She always had the radio on, so whether I wanted to or not, I listened to all the programs. One I especially liked was unforgettable voyages with Zakhar Zagadkin! When it came on my grandmother and I would turn up the volume, get comfortable, and hit the road!

I really liked geography and still remember many geographic names. I had no problem with the subject at school, made good grades, and it was all thanks to Zakhar Zagadkin. My friend and class-mate Vladimir and I exchanged geographic riddles even during other classes. It was very thrilling!

As a father, recalling my school years, I tried to convey an appreciation for geography and for our vast Motherland to my own children.

PART IV

Word

THIS LAND IS MY LAND, AMERICA THE BEAUTIFUL, GOD BLESS AMERICA:
AMERICA'S THREE PATRIOTIC SONGS [1]

Pavel Ilyin

I n the last years of our life in Russia, even before my family had applied for permission to emigrate, I had stopped referring to the Soviet Union as "us." Yet when we finally came to America (after a five-year period spent in limbo as refuseniks while the Soviet government withheld that permission), I could not, at first, refer to America as "us." Not for the same reasons: in the Soviet Union I refused to identify with the regime under which I was forced to live; but here... From the moment of our arrival I knew that this was my country but still I felt constrained somehow; perhaps I did not yet feel sufficiently American.

Then came September 11th, the day of America's great tragedy and its great unity. "United We Stand" was the rallying cry of those days. That was when I noticed, to my surprise, that I had begun to say "us." I became an American resident in November 1987, an American citizen in May 1993, but I fully felt myself an American in September 2001.

I love America and have never wavered in this feeling. There were three patriotic American songs that kept playing in my head, so much so that I decided to translate their lyrics into Russian and to learn more about the authors of the songs, the genesis of their lyrics and melodies, their origin. That was how these essays that I am now offering to the reader first came together. I am grateful to Semyon Reznik, Aleksander Sinelnikov, Inna Talmy and Vladimir Frumkin whose comments helped me improve my text, as well as to Irina Khomutova who helped me with my translations.

---

[1] Published in the Russian literary journal *Time and Place*. See Ilyin, Pavel. "Three Songs." *Time and Place, 3 (20)*. New York, 2011: 113–136.

GOD BLESS AMERICA

On September 11, 2001, as the World Trade Center collapsed before the eyes of the entire world, TV audiences also saw a different, uplifting image: members of Congress standing on the steps of the Capitol, singing God Bless America! The first line of the song was everywhere the very next day: "God Bless America" appeared on bumper stickers, in storefronts, on buildings, on fences. The greatest catastrophe in the nation's history brought Americans together, and one of the symbols of their unity (together with the American flag) was this song written by a Jewish emigrant from Tolochin, a shtetl in Belarus (then part of the Russian empire).

Israel Isidor "Izya" Beilin entered the United States through Ellis Island in 1893, aged five. The only memory he retained of his prior life was lying on a blanket by the side of a road, watching his house burn to the ground in an anti-Jewish pogrom. In America, the Beilins settled in New York City, on the Lower East Side, a neighborhood that was then filled with Jewish immigrants from Russia. Young Izya began to work for pay at the age of eight, which was normal for an immigrant boy at the time. He worked all kinds of jobs: as a newsboy, a sailor, a guide for a blind street singer and eventually as a singer himself. He began as a street singer but then was hired as a "singing waiter" at a saloon in Chinatown. Here, in 1907, he wrote the lyrics for a tune composed by the saloon's pianist. When the sheet music for the song was published, it contained a spelling error, listing the author of the lyrics as I. Berlin instead of I. Beilin. At that point he decided to change his first name to match his new surname.

Soon Irving Berlin (the name is accented on the second syllable, like the capital of Germany) began writing music for his songs in addition to the lyrics. Sometime later, famous American composer Jerome Kern (1885–1945) said that Irving Berlin "has no place in American music — he is American music."

In 1938, with a new, large-scale war threatening Europe, Irving Berlin felt obligated to create a patriotic song that was peaceful, not warlike. He ran into difficulties: "[p]atriotism was harder to put to music than love and longing."[2] Then he was approached by Kate Smith (1909–1986), "America's Songbird," a hugely popular singer who was preparing to perform in a radio show celebrating the 20th anniversary

---

[2] Furstinger, Nancy. *Say It With Music: The Story of Irving Berlin*. Greensboro: Morgan Reynolds, 2003, p. 63.

of Armistice Day commemorating the end of WWI (renamed Veterans' Day in 1954) and needed a song right away. And Berlin remembered a song he had written in 1918 for the finale of a musical revue but had set aside, deeming it too bombastic. The song was God Bless America. (Young Izya had often heard the words that became the song's title from his mother who lived in a poor neighborhood in Manhattan. This brings to mind my fellow Russian immigrants, especially the elderly, who might complain about their health, the work of various social services agencies, about life in general, but as soon as their innermost feelings are involved, one hears: "God bless America!") He took the song, updated it by changing a few lines to match the needs of the time, and gave it to the singer. It was a song whose time had come.[3]

Berlin wrote two verses but we — we Americans who love our country, whether we are old-timers or "new Americans" — usually sing only one of them. Like many other lay people (I am not talking about experts) I had no idea that the song contained another verse, which came first, until I had come across it in Caroline Kennedy's "Patriot's Handbook."[4] That verse helped me understand what the author had meant when he used the word "bless" and, therefore, what he had meant by his title.

All my fellow "new Americans" know the meaning of the word "to bless," and the title of the song is usually translated literally into Russian using the Russian equivalent of "to bless". Yet the English word also may carry other meanings. I became aware of a disconnect between the conventional translation and the song's message right after September 11 when one heard and saw these words everywhere. I sensed a disconnect between the concept of "blessing" and the immediately following line: "*Stand behind her/And guide her...*" I finally understood this line, and with it the title of the song, after reading the first verse (as some will recall, Berlin had released the song in anticipation of a global catastrophe):

---

[3] One of the changes he made to the song reflects the changes that had occurred in American English usage since the time of its creation. As Berlin later remembered, the song originally had contained the lines "*Stand behind her/And guide her/To the right/With a light/From above.*" In 1918, "to the right" did not carry a political connotation but meant something like "in the right direction." By 1938, the political connotation was there, and Berlin replaced these words with "Through the night." *See* Furia, Philip. *Irving Berlin: A life in Song.* New York: Schirmer Books, 1998, p. 193. These words are sometimes printed in a contracted form: "Thru the night".

[4] *A Patriot's Handbook: Songs, Poems, Stories, and Speeches Celebrating the Land We Love.* Selected and introduced by Caroline Kennedy. New York: Hyperion, 2003, p. 577.

> While the storm clouds gather
> Far across the sea,
> Let us swear allegiance
> To a land that's free;
> Let us all be grateful
> For a land so fair,
> As we raise our voices
> In a solemn prayer.[5]

Now, reading the note of alarm in this first verse that I had not known before, I came to understand the meaning of that core line of the song: "God keep America safe! "

Below is my Russian translation side by side with the original:[6]

I kept the words *God bless America* in English. Everyone knows them; these words evoke indifference in some people, hatred in others, but most say them as a prayer. There is a Russian saying: "you can't cut words out of a song," and that is true here. Truly, *God bless America!*

God Bless America	**Боже, храни Америку**
God bless America,	God bless America,
Land that I love.	Мою любовь.
Stand behind her and guide her	Поддержи ее, и веди ее,
Through the night with a light from above.	Освещая ей путь вновь и вновь, —
From the mountains	Через горы,
To the prairies,	Через прерии,
To the oceans	Под небесным
White with foam.	Шатром.
God bless America,	God bless America,
My home, sweet home,	Мой дом, милый дом,
God bless America,	God bless America,
My home, sweet home.	Мой дом, милый дом.
Irving Berlin	*© 2011 Pavel Ilyin (transl.)*

---

[5] I am indebted to my friend Vladimir Frumkin who helped me translate this verse into Russian.

[6] My sincere thanks to my friends Blair Ruble, Irina Khomutova and Vadim Scheglov. Our conversations helped me understand the meaning of bless in the title of I. Berlin's song.

Kate Smith introduced *God Bless America* on her radio show by calling it one of the most beautiful compositions, a song that will never die. As one of the countless books written about Irving Berlin says, the song—as performed by her—spread like wildfire: people sang it in schools and in churches, in theaters and sports stadiums—in short, everywhere. Both political parties, the Democrats as well as the Republicans, made it their theme song during the presidential elections of 1940. There was serious talk of making it the national anthem: Francis Scott Key's *Star-Spangled Banner*, which had been adopted as the national anthem in 1931, was considered by many to be too clunky and difficult to perform and therefore not really suited to be the national anthem. Berlin opposed this, in part, because his song is a prayer.[7]

Not everyone liked *God Bless America*. Church preachers found its religious spirit and patriotism too ostentatious; many were offended that the song had been written by a foreigner; and the KKK called for its boycott merely because Irving Berlin was a Jew.

God Bless America is not simply a song that inspires the living; it is also one of those great songs that can lend dignity to death. On July 8, 2002 President George W. Bush awarded Captain Humbert "Rocky" Versace a Medal of Honor, which was given posthumously to the Captain's family. Captain Versace was the first American POW to receive this high honor. In 1963, he had been captured in Vietnam, survived two years of severe torture and was executed by firing squad on September 26, 1965. The last time his fellow prisoners heard Rocky's voice, he was singing *God Bless America* at the top of his lungs.[8]

The time passed, and as the musical styles Irving Berlin worked with—the ragtime, the swing—gave way to new rhythms, Berlin's popularity, like that of his contemporaries, began to decline. But it was this music and these words that were needed on the day of a national tragedy. It was *God Bless America*, which had first been heard sixty-three days prior, that helped lift the nation's spirit. Kate Smith's words had been prophetic: this song will live forever.

It should be added that, in token of gratitude to the country that had accepted him, Irving Berlin donated his entire royalty stream from *God Bless America* to the Boy Scouts of America and Girl Scouts of America, which continue to receive these payments.

---

[7] "Patriotic Music." *New Grove Dictionary of American Music.* Vol. 3. New York: McMillan, 1986, p. 488.

[8] Sorokin, Ellen. "Bush Awards Medal of Honor to POW." *Washington Times,* 9 July 2002: A3.

THIS LAND IS YOUR LAND

In July 1912, during a presidential election, the family of Charles Guthrie, resident of Okemah, Oklahoma, welcomed a baby boy, naming him Woodrow Wilson in honor of one of the presidential candidates. The candidate would go on to become President while the boy would grow up to be a great American musician and folk singer, Woody Guthrie (full name: Woodrow Wilson Guthrie, 1912–1967).

Okemah, a nondescript Midwestern town (both before and since then), had become an oil boom town and was going through a brief period of prosperity. In his autobiography, Woody called it one of the "singiest, square dancingest, drinkingest, yellingest, preachingest, walkingest, talkingest, laughingest, cryingest, shootingest, fist fightingest, bleedingest, gamblingest, gun, club and razor carryingest" towns.[9] But life in that town was not kind to the boy: he experienced the tragic death of a beloved sister, his father's bankruptcy, his mother's severe illness, a fire that burned down their home. To support the family, Woody was willing to take on any work so long as it paid. He even played a harmonica for change. At sixteen he quit school, and at nineteen, leaving the once again depressed Okemah behind, he headed to neighboring Texas. He learned to play the guitar and began writing songs. He played and sang anywhere he could make some money: in saloons, at parties, on the street, but his life continued to be hard.

Meanwhile, the Great Plains were hit by one of the greatest natural disasters in United States history: a terrible drought that turned the country's main wheat-producing zone into a "Dust Bowl." The drought dried up the plowed-up topsoil whose particles rose upward with the slightest breeze, gathering into black clouds of dust that covered the ground and blocked out the sky. The drought lasted throughout the 1930s, coinciding with the Great Depression, and the impoverished population fled the long-settled lands: 2.5 million people left the Great Plains.[10]

One of them was Woody Guthrie.[11] Riding freight trains, hitchhiking, walking working odd jobs, Woody — like many other refugees —

---

[9] Klein, Joe. *Woody Guthrie: A Life*. New York: Dell, 1981 (reprinted 1990), p. 160.

[10] The phenomenon of the magnitude of the Dust Bowl could not fail to find resonance in literature, music, graphic arts, and the cinema. Among the many works depicting it are John Steinbeck's *Grapes of Wrath* and Woody Guthrie's own *Dust Bowl Ballads*.

[11] Drought as a natural, meteorological phenomenon is beyond man's power to control. Yet the catastrophe of the 1930s was man-made. Farmers plowed up the fertile prairie lands, stripping them of everything they could, with no thought

headed for California. He settled in Los Angeles, where he got a job with a radio station. His songs were popular, his life was looking up, but as his biographer notes, Woody was never comfortable with success or with being in one place for too long.[12] And so in 1940 he headed to New York City across the entire country, from the West Coast to the East.

In New York, Woody joined the extreme Left, became close to the radical intellectuals, worked for the Daily Worker, the newspaper of the Communist Party USA. He was active in the anti-war and civil rights movements. Among his close friends and fellow performers was Pete Seeger (1919–2014), another prominent folk singer and one-time member of the Communist Party USA. "I ain't a Communist necessarily, but I've been in the red all my life," as Woody would later say about himself.

Woody Guthrie settled in Manhattan, on 43rd Street and 6th Avenue. Here, on February 23, 1940 he completed his most famous song: *This Land Is Your Land*.[13] Woody based its melody on the old Baptist hymn *Oh, My Loving Brother* (a song that had become popular after being recorded by the Carter family under the title *When The World's On Fire*). Woody often used well-known tunes in his songs and never objected to others using his own tunes.

Woody wrote *This Land Is Your Land* in response to Irving Berlin's *God Bless America:* he was tired of constantly hearing this song on the radio; Kate Smith's performance irritated him; he found the lyrics too complacent. This can be seen in his manuscript of the song, where he crossed out the original last line of each verse: *God blessed America for us.* Here, unlike in *God Bless America*, the word "bless" carries a connotation of sanctification. But how is his song less "complacent" than Berlin's?

---

for the future. And the future took the form of the Dust Bowl. Soviet propaganda cited the dust storms in the US as an example of "predatory misuse of land under capitalism" — omitting to mention that after the most catastrophic year of 1935, America woke up. Since then, improved land use rules and new farming methods have prevented a recurrence of this natural disaster, although severe droughts have visited the Great Plains more than once.

[12] Arevalo, Jorge. "Woody Guthrie's Biography." *Woody Guthrie*. Woody Guthrie Publications. New York: Mt. Kisko. Viewed Apr. 29, 2017. **http://www.woodyguthrie.org/biography/biography4.htm**.

[13] This address and date appear on the manuscript of the song posted on the website of the Department of Arts and Sciences of the Washington University in St. Louis, MO at **http://web.archive.org/web/19970814121656/; http://www.artsci.wustl.edu/~davida/pics/woody/this_land.gif**. Viewed on Apr. 29, 2017.

This Land Is Your Land | ## Эта земля — твоя

This land is your land,
    this land is my land,
From California
    to New York Island,
From the redwood forest
    to the Gulf Stream Waters,
This land was made for you and me.

As I was walking
    that ribbon of highway,
I saw above me
    that endless skyway,
I saw below me
    that golden valley
This land was made for you and me.

I've roamed and rambled,
    and followed my foot steps
To the sparkling sands of
    her diamond desert,
While all around me
    a voice was chanting:
This land was made for you and me.

When the sun came shining,
    and I was strolling
And the wheat fields waving
    and the dust clouds rolling.
As the fog was lifting,
    a voice was chanting:
This land was made for you and me.

Nobody living
    can ever stop me,
As I go walking
    that freedom highway.
Nobody living
    can make me turn back.
This land was made for you and me.

Woody Guthrie

Эта земля твоя,
    эта земля моя,
От Калифорнии
    и до Нью-Йорка,
От рощ секвойи
    до струй Гольфстрима, —
Здесь все вокруг для нас с тобой.

Люблю шагать я,
    направив стопы
По уходящим
    Ввысь горным склонам,
По уходяшим
    вниз каньонам, —
Здесь все вокруг для нас с тобой.

Когда брожу я
    под небом синим
Среди алмазных
    песков пустыни,
То где б я ни был,
    я слышу голос:
«Здесь все вокруг для нас с тобой».

Восходит солнце,
    и свежий ветер
Листву колышет,
    день будет светел,
Туман уходит,
    и слышен голос:
«Здесь все вокруг для нас с тобой».

Остановить нас
    никто не сможет,
Преодолеем
    мы все невзгоды,
И не свернуть нас
    с пути свободы, —
Здесь все вокруг для нас с тобой.

© 2011 Pavel Ilyin (transl.)

When I translated the song into Russian, I used the five verses that are commonly performed (the first four of them are heard most often). Not many people know that the song contains two more verses:

> As I was walking, I saw a sign there,
> And on the sign it said "No Trespassing."
> But on the other side it didn't say anything:
> That side was made for you and me.

(The early versions of the song had "Private Property" instead of "No Trespassing".)

And:

> In the squares of the city, in the shadow of the steeple,
> By the relief office I seen my people;
> As they stood there hungry, and I stood there asking,
> Is this land made for you and me?[14]

In these verses, Woody contrasts the beauty of American land with the inequality among Americans. When these verses are included, the song becomes a protest against the injustices of life, but the verses are seldom remembered, and even Woody himself did not always sing them. Without them, This Land Is Your Land became one of the most patriotic American songs able to lay claim to being the American national anthem.

Woody often changed his domicile. He moved to Greenwich Village, the "nest" of New York radicals; to Oregon; back to California and then back to New York, this time to Coney Island. His nomadic soul gave him no rest, but then he developed a serious illness, the same that had carried away his mother many years ago. He spent the last years of his life in a hospital...

Besides his protest songs, Woody Guthrie also wrote children's songs, novels, biographies and essays. But This Land Is Your Land is the most famous part of his legacy. It has spread all over the globe, taking on a local flavor in many places. In Canada, the song is sung with the line From the Arctic Circle/To the Great Lake Waters; in Great Britain, From the coast of Cornwall/To the Scottish Highlands. There

---

[14] Both verses exist in different (albeit similar in meaning) versions; Woody himself performed them differently. I chose the version given in the *Patriot's Handbook* by Caroline Kennedy, pp. 646–647 (*see* n. 3 above).

are local versions in the American Virgin Islands and in the Bahamas, in Ireland, Israel and Namibia. The song is sung not only in English but also in Welsh and Swedish, in Hebrew and even in Esperanto.[15]

This song is also played as part of the soundtrack for many films and TV and radio shows, often with variant lyrics: for example, Put your hand in my hand... or This song is my song...[16] And in 2004, the digital entertainment website JibJab ran a spoof video in which the presidential candidates George W. Bush and John Kerry sang the song; both agreed that This land is your land,/This land is my land, but each claimed that This land will surely vote for me![17]

In conclusion, let us hear from three of Woody Guthrie's contemporaries.

John Steinbeck: *"Woody is just Woody. Thousands of people do not know he has any other name. He is just a voice and a guitar. He sings the songs of a people and I suspect that he is, in a way, that people. Harsh voiced and nasal, his guitar hanging like a tire iron on a rusty rim, there is nothing sweet about Woody, and there is nothing sweet about the songs he sings. But there is something more important for those who will listen. There is the will of the people to endure and fight against oppression. I think we call this the American spirit."*

Bob Dylan: *"Woody Guthrie was my first idol/he was the last idol/because he was the first idol."*

Pete Seeger: *"Shall I tell you what I think of Woody? He's a genius."*

One can agree or disagree with Woody Guthrie's politics but it is hard to argue with Pete Seeger's assessment of him.

---

[15] Wikipedia Contributors. "This Land Is Your Land." *Wikipedia, The Free Encyclopedia*. Wikipedia, The Free Encyclopedia. 28 Mar 2017. **http://en.wikipedia.org/wiki/This_Land_Is_Your_Land**. Viewed on Apr 29, 2017.

[16] *This Song Is My Song*, performed by Woody's son Arlo Guthrie (b. 1947) on a popular radio show. Arlo became a popular folk singer in his own right. *See* New Grove Dictionary of American Music, vol. 2, p. 299. Arlo's children—a son and three daughters—also became musicians and singers. Arlo's grandson (Woody's great-grandson) Krishna, the fourth generation of the singing Guthries, continues their musical line.

[17] "This Land." JibJab Originals. *JibJab* JibJab Bros. Studios. 9 July 2004. **http://sendables.jibjab.com/originals/this_land** (video). Viewed on Apr 29, 2017

AMERICA THE BEAUTIFUL

How does a song come into being? A composer writes music to existing lyrics, a poet writes the words to an existing tune... Or, sometimes, the composer and poet may join and work together as a creative duet. This song, however, is different: the poet who wrote the lyrics did not know about the tune, written long ago; and the composer of that tune had died without ever reading the words that would make his music famous.

Let me begin from afar. In 1805, an expedition led by Captain Zebulon Pike (1779–1813) discovered a mountain in the Front Range of the Rocky Mountains in Colorado, which later was named Pike's Peak after the expedition's leader.[18] Sometime later, the apostrophe dropped out of the summit's name, which is now known as Pikes Peak.[19] Pike never reached the top due to inclement weather; that summit would remain unconquered for another fifteen years. In 1859, gold was discovered in the area, and a gold rush ensued. Gold seekers rushed in to seek the yellow metal, their slogan: "Pike's Peak or Bust!" And although no gold was found in the mountain itself, its name ended up on the front pages of major American newspapers.[20] Yet the gold rush was not what made Pikes Peak famous: that was an English teacher, Katharine Lee Bates (1859–1929).

Katharine Lee Bates lived all her life in Massachusetts. She was born in Falmouth, on the southern shore of Cape Cod, in a traditional Puritan family.[21] When she was twelve, her family moved to Granville near Wellesley, a suburb of Boston.[22] At seventeen, Katharine enrolled

---

[18] Elevation 4302 m, or 14,114 ft.

[19] The vanishing apostrophe in Pikes Peak, originally a possessive, is not a unique phenomenon. So, for example, the town of Harpers Ferry on the Potomac river was originally called Harper's Ferry (in memory of the town's founder, Robert Harper, who ran a ferry there). The same is true of the Pennsylvania towns of Pottsville and Pottstown, named after their founder John Pott, a German settler.

[20] The Pikes Peak gold rush has left traces elsewhere in Colorado: the cities of Denver and Boulder grew out of mining settlements.

[21] Katharine (Katie) did not know her father, who died a month after she was born. *See* Sherr, Lynn. *America the Beautiful: The Stirring True Story Behind Our Nation's Favorite Song.* New York: Public Affairs, 2001. 15. Print. (The only other book about a song I am aware of is Rosen, Jody. *White Christmas: The Story of an American Song.* New York: Scribner, 2002 about Irving Berlin's song *The White Christmas.*

[22] Granville (now Wellesley Hills) is a neighborhood in the town of Wellesley, Mass. The latter, when Katharine attended high school there, was part of the town of Needham. Today, both these towns are part of Greater Boston.

in Wellesley College, graduating in 1881 at the age of 21.[23] She worked as a schoolteacher, and in 1885 she began teaching English literature at Wellesley.[24] And always and everywhere, she wrote poetry.

And so, in June 1893, the Wellesley professor and poet Katharine Lee Bates, 33, took a train from Boston to Colorado. That summer, the president of Colorado College in Colorado Springs invited a group of leading educators from the East to join his summer faculty in order to bring his students of the West "in contact with the brightest minds and most progressive spirits of the country."[25] Katharine Lee Bates was part of this group; she would teach two classes over the three-week summer semester.

Bates had taken other long-distance trips, going east, across the ocean — to Europe and the Middle East. This was her first trip out west. And it was this trip that gave us *America The Beautiful*. Bates made a fateful (as it turned out) stop in Chicago, where a World's Fair celebrating the 400th anniversary of Columbus' discovery of America, was in progress. It was a showcase of the achievements and potentialities of human reason — the achievements of today and possibilities of the future. Fantastic illuminations, an 80-meter (264-ft) wheel built by an American engineer named George Washington Ferris,[26] other technological marvels... But the part that made the greatest impression on Bates was the "White City" — the main exhibition with its pavilions, pools and canals, and especially its centerpiece: fourteen buildings, built by leading American architects in the neoclassical style and finished with a stucco-like exterior that practically glowed with a white, alabaster-like light that made an indelible impression. "A thing of beauty," wrote Bates in her diary.[27]

Katharine's continued journey took her across Kansas; wheat fields floated past. It was July 4, Independence Day, and looking at the sights in her window, Bates felt ever more in love with America...

The train brought Katharine to Colorado Springs, a city founded twenty-two years previously at the foot of Pikes Peak. The visiting professors taught their summer classes and spent their free time tour-

---

[23] Wellesley College, a women's liberal arts college and the most prominent women's college in the US, was founded in 1875, a year before Bates enrolled there.

[24] Katharine Lee Bates worked at Wellesley for over 40 years until her retirement in 1926.

[25] Sherr at 30.

[26] These types of carnival rides continue to be known today as the Ferris Wheel.

[27] Sherr at 29.

ing the area. Her departure was drawing near when the turn of Pikes Peak finally came: Katharine Lee Bates and her colleagues set out to go up on the mountain.

By that time, a cog railway had been built to effortlessly carry tourists up to the summit of Pikes Peak. But the railway was not working that day, and the travelers hired a horse-drawn wagon similar to those used by the pioneers to conquer the Wild West, with the traditional slogan "Pikes Peak or Bust!" — especially appropriate here — emblazoned on it. The cart was pulled by horses at first but halfway through the ascent they were replaced with sturdy mules. The ascent took several hours, and Bates felt very tired. But when the Great Plains, endless as the sea, opened before her eyes, she was filled with boundless joy. She seemed to behold the whole great country spread out before her, with white cities shining, wheat stalks swaying in the wind, and people living happily...[28] And so the first line of a poem came to her: *O beautiful...*

When she came back to her hotel room, Bates wrote down that line and the lines that followed. That day, July 22, 1893, was born the poem that would become a great song.

The poem, which the author named *America*, was first printed on July 4, 1895 in the popular Boston weekly *The Congregationalist*: the editors held back the poem for several months in order to publish it on Independence Day. The second printing was in November 1904, in the *Boston Evening Transcript*, then the most influential daily in New England; Katharine Lee Bates gave them a revised version of *America*. But the poet continued working on the poem, and in 1911 she published the final version, under the new and final title, in her new book, *America the Beautiful and Other Poems*.

The text of America the Beautiful clearly reflects the author's emotional and visual impressions from her journey to Colorado: here are "alabaster cities gleaming" (the White City) and "amber waves of grain" (the Kansas prairie), "purple mountain majesties" (the Rockies) and the view from Pikes Peak over the boundless expanse of America — "from sea to shining sea."[29]

---

[28] The next day Katharine's mother received a telegram from her daughter: "Greetings from Pikes Peak glorious dizzy wish you were here." Sherr at 37.

[29] The phrase "from sea to shining sea" became an idiom and has been used countless times in literature, the arts and the media. See, e.g., Martin, Gary. "From sea to shining sea." *The Phrase Finder.* **http://www.phrases.org.uk/meanings/from-sea-to-shining-sea.html**. Viewed on Apr 29, 2017.

America the Beautiful	Ты прекрасна, Америка!
O beautiful for spacious skies, For amber waves of grain, For purple mountain majesties Above the fruited plain! America! America! God shed His grace on thee, And crown thy good with brotherhood, From sea to shining sea!	Прекрасна небесами ты И золотом хлебов; Величьем гор прекрасна ты Над зеленью садов! Америка! Америка! Бог милостив к тебе, И братства свет здесь светит всем На всей твоей земле!
O beautiful for pilgrim feet Whose stern, impassion'd stress A thoroughfare for freedom beat Across the wilderness! America! America! God mend thine ev'ry flaw, Confirm thy soul in self-control, Thy liberty in law!	Прекрасна пилигримов ты Наследством на земле Пути свободы – их следы – Проложены везде! Америка! Америка! Тебя Бог укрепит, Свободы ниспошлет закон, И душу закалит!
O beautiful for heroes proved In liberating strife, Who more than self their country loved, And mercy more than life! America! America! May God thy gold refine Till all success be nobleness, And ev'ry gain divine!	Прекрасна героизмом тех, Кто жизни не щадя, Боролся за свободу всех, Страну свою любя! Америка! Америка! Тебя Бог вдохновит, Он благородство даст тебе, Со славой породнит!
O beautiful for patriot dream That sees beyond the years Thine alabaster cities gleam Undimmed by human tears! America! America! God shed His grace on thee And crown thy good with brotherhood From sea to shining sea!	Прекрасна ты мечтами тех, Кто видел сквозь года, Как будет счастлив человек В лазурных городах! Америка! Америка! Бог милостив к тебе, И братства свет здесь светит всем На всей твоей земле!
Katharine Lee Bates	*© 2011 Pavel Ilyin (transl.)*

In my Russian translation, I tried to reproduce the expressiveness of the original, occasionally sacrificing the literal meaning in order to achieve the poetic effect.

Coming back to the story of the song: as soon as Katharine Lee Bates' poem appeared in print, people began to sing it — to any available music. Composer Silas G. Pratt (1846–1916) was the first to set it to music. But no one knew that the music for *America the Beautiful, Music* with a capital "M," already existed. It had been written by composer Samuel Ward and was called *Materna*.

Samuel Augustus Ward (1848–1903) was an organist and choir director at an Episcopal church in Newark, New Jersey. One beautiful summer day (a day that was beautiful both literally and figuratively) he went with his friend, choirmaster Henry Martin, to the Coney Island amusement park. The park was accessible by horse carriage and by train but the two friends chose to go over by steamboat. We do not know how they spent their day at the wonderful park with its magnificent beach, but there is little doubt that they headed home in excellent spirits.

"Harry," said Sam suddenly to his companion, "if I had something to write on, I'd put down a tune that has just come to me." Harry dug through his pockets in search of a scrap of paper but could not find any. So he took off a starched linen cuff and handed it to Sam. And Sam drew a staff and wrote down the tune that was playing in his head: the tune that would become *America the Beautiful*.

This story may well be apocryphal. But as Lynn Sherr has noted, who's to say that an amusement park and an ocean are any less inspirational than a World's Fair and a mountain?[30] I agree completely.

Sam Ward was then thirty-three — the same age as Katharine Lee Bates during her ascent of Pikes Peak.

Of course, *America* would not come into existence for another eleven years. The music Ward wrote on the cuff was intended for an old religious hymn *O Mother Dear Jerusalem* which, in the composer's opinion, needed new music. Ward called it *Materna*.[31] In 1888 *Materna* spread beyond the walls of the church in Newark when it was printed in the weekly *Parish Chorus*. It turned out to be the best and most enduring part of the composer's oeuvre.

---

[30] Sherr at 48.
[31] Possibly from the Spanish term for "maternal."

Samuel Ward died in 1903.[32] He never met Katharine Lee Bates, and he did not live to witness the triumph of his *Materna*. The words and the music came together a year after the composer's death, in November 1904, brought together by Dr. Clarence Barbour (1869–1937), the pastor of Lake Avenue Baptist church in Rochester, New York and his wife, an accomplished musician. They were familiar with *Materna*, which was regularly printed in church hymnals, and pastor Barbour read the poem in *Boston Evening Transcript*. The couple felt that the words and the tune were perfect together.[33]

Lake Avenue Church became the first place in America where *America the Beautiful* was sung to the music of *Materna*. Later, in 1910, Barbour published the words and music in his collection of religious hymns. *America the Beautiful* spread all over the country. It was included in poetry collections, textbooks and elementary school readers. Soldiers heading over to Europe to fight in 1918 carried this song in a songbook specially printed for them and sang it on the march and on the last day of the war. *America the Beautiful*, wrote George M. Kohan, the "father of American musical comedy" (1878–1942), was what they were fighting for and what they brought home.[34]

Not everyone thought *Materna* the best tune for *America the Beautiful*; it had to compete against tunes of other composers.[35] This rivalry reached its peak in late 1926—early 1927, when the National Federation of Music Clubs announced a contest for a new and better tune for the song. 961 tunes were sent in by authors seeking fame and money. But the $500 prize[36] was never awarded: the judges deemed none of the entries received worthy of becoming the music for *America the Beautiful.* *Materna* had won.

Katharine Lee Bates never expressed a preference for one tune over another and refrained from criticism. It seemed fit, she said, that the choice of music should be made by the singers rather than the writer.

---

[32] The obituary published in the Newark Daily Advertiser called Ward "one of the best known musical men in the State." Sherr at 59.

[33] Sherr at 58. At the end of his life, Dr. Clarence Barbour was elected president of an Ivy League school, Brown University in Providence, Rhode Island. Wikipedia Contributors. "Clarence Barbour." *Wikipedia, The Free Encyclopedia.* Wikipedia, The Free Encyclopedia. 6 Feb 2017. http://en.wikipedia.org/wiki/Clarence_Barbour. Viewed on Apr 29, 2017.

[34] Sherr at 66

[35] Lynn Sherr has reproduced photographs of several sheet music versions of the song in her book. See Sherr at 64, 65, 67.

[36] Over $6000 in today's dollars. See http://www.dollartimes.com/calculators/inflation.htm.

But she firmly (though politely) rejected all attempts to suggest changes to the text, "so that we may not have as many texts as we already have tunes."[37]

However, she did not object when the poem was translated into other languages or changed to adapt to other countries: there were versions of the song sung in Australia, Germany, India, Canada, Mexico and the Philippines.[38] "If they can use it and like it that is all right," said Bates.

Professor Katharine Lee Bates ran her English department, wrote books and articles in her field, published collections of poetry and travel essays, wrote children's books, edited various publications.[39] She also received and answered letters. Her correspondents sent her reactions and suggested changes to the song, many asked for her advice and, of course, asked for her autographs. She never turned anyone down. "I have been working like a beaver," said Bates about herself.[40] So voluminous was her correspondence that she had to devote an entire cupboard in her house to storing it.

It strikes me as a historical curiosity that the United States were without an official state anthem as recently as the beginning of the 20th century.[41] The issue was raised repeatedly, and in 1912 a bill to make Francis Scott Key's (1779–1843) *Star-Spangled Banner* the national anthem. But the debate was inconclusive, while outside the Capitol there was a growing clamoring to make *America the Beautiful*, which was then at the height of its popularity, the national anthem. Back in 1904, the *Boston Evening Transcript* had introduced Katharine Lee Bates' poem as "the American national hymn,"[42] and in 1908 a Chicago lawyer wrote to President Theodore Roosevelt that "a poem of such remarkable beauty and strength" as *America the Beautiful* should be considered for "adoption as the National Air." Such voices grew and multiplied, and in 1926 the National Hymn Society called upon Congress to adopt *America the Beautiful* as the national anthem.

---

[37] *Ibid.*

[38] *Ibid.*

[39] A list of books authored or edited by Katharine Lee Bates contains around fifty titles. See, e.g., Wikipedia Contributors. "Katharine Lee Bates." *Wikipedia, The Free Encyclopedia.* Wikipedia, The Free Encyclopedia. 22 Apr 2017. http://en.wikipedia.org/wiki/Katharine_Lee_Bates. Viewed on Apr 29, 2017

[40] Sherr at 66.

[41] As my Russian readers know, the same Russian word, гимн, is used to translate both the English terms "anthem" and "hymn."

[42] For a photo of the newspaper column, see Sherr at 58.

To use a sports metaphor, the song had "made it to the finals," becoming the only remaining rival to the *Star-Spangled Banner*.

Sports fans know that the top team does not always win. The debate in Congress reignited in 1930, and in April of the next year President Herbert Hoover signed into law the bill making the *Star-Spangled Banner* the national anthem of the United States.

But the supporters of the Bates-Ward song feel that they have only lost a battle, not the war. In 1985, a bill to replace the *Star-Spangled Banner* with *America the Beautiful*, drafted by a Congressman who was a former Marine, was introduced in Congress. Similar bills have been introduced since then. Although there have been no movement in this direction, we should stay tuned.[43]

A street in Katharine Lee Bates' hometown of Falmouth bears her name; a plaque at the entrance to the city announces that the author of *America the Beautiful* was born there; her childhood home has been carefully preserved. In Wellesley and Colorado Springs there are schools named after Bates. The words of her great song are etched in gold on a memorial plaque at the summit of Pikes Peak.[44] Samuel Ward's name is preserved on the wall of the church in Newark where he worked. A park in Colorado Springs is named "America the Beautiful Park." Are there any other parks in America, I wonder, that are named after a song?

2001–2011
Washington

---

[43] For a more in-depth discussion of the Congressional debates on the national anthem see Sherr at 85–89.

[44] Pike was killed in the Battle of York during the War of 1812. Over a dozen other towns and localities have been named after him. I have often driven around the Baltimore Beltway, not knowing that the town of Pikesville, reached by I-140 that crosses it, is a namesake of sorts to Pikes Peak.

"I Know the Clock Keeps Ever Turning"

Pavel Ilyin

> *I know the clock keeps ever turning,*
> *But were to run it longer, then,*
> *I must be certain, every morning,*
> *Of seeing you that day again.*

Puskin, in Onegin's Letter to Tatyana, wrote these magical lines, perhaps the most magical in all of Russian poetry — or at least, among the most magical lines. In any case, what could be more magical? We read these lines aloud, read them to ourselves, skim over them. They sound like music: "I know the clock keeps ever turning, But were to run it longer, then, I must be certain, every morning, Of seeing you that day again."

Meanwhile, these lines are astonishingly illogical. Caught unawares by this sudden, unexpected thought, one stops in disbelief and starts over: "I know the clock keeps ever turning, But were to run it longer, then, I must be certain, every morning, Of seeing you that day again."

Indeed. Consider this. "I know the clock keeps ever turning..." This means I know and am aware that my days are numbered and that there are a limited number of them left to live. But the fact that I do not know that number does not change the fact that limited they are. Then the second line contradicts the first: "But were to run it longer, then..." That is, something can prolong my life, and if something truly can prolong it, then how can my days be numbered?

Nevertheless, let's assume that the will of Providence can be bent. In order to do so, and to make the hours run longer, "I must be certain, every morning, Of seeing you that day again." Here lies another contradiction, and more than one.

If I am sure that I will see you that day again, this will prolong my life. But also, If you have led me to believe that I will see you that day again, then this certainty will prolong my life. In that case, what will, in fact, prolong my life? Certainty that I will see you, or the fact of seeing you again? And if it is certainty alone, then what happens if I do not see you again that day?

Does this make sense? It does. Logical thinking makes sense, but not the poet's lines. Yet again,

> I know the clock keeps ever turning,
> But were to run it longer, then,
> I must be certain, every morning,
> Of seeing you that day again.

My musings do not amount to a hill of beans when compared to this magic. Magic because it is magical and not because it is logical. Magic indeed!

Maryland

Fragments of My Memory

The title of this essay comes from a book I read about at the Library of Congress, many years ago, while conducting researching for my own book about Moscow at the turn of the 20th century. One of my sources referred to a memoir by Pavel Annenkov, the son of a prominent Pushkin scholar, published in St. Petersburg sometime in the 1800s, that had a similar title. Although I never found the actual book, the title has stayed with me. It is even more appropriate now, when my formerly excellent memory has come to be filled with holes that threaten to swallow it up; it is shrinking like Balzac's magic skin.

Some of my fragments come from my sister, Yulia Ilyina (married name: Keda). My baby sister, three years younger than me and, as behooves a youngster, a good deal faster: she has already written her own memoir! I was the first person she shared it with, and while I made a few comments and edits, I also learned some new things — and was reminded of others that I had, incredibly, forgotten! Because her material overlaps with mine, especially as regards our family, I will use and occasionally even quote it here.

The fragmentary nature of this essay is also intentional, in that, like many people, I am loath to disclose every last event and episode, especially when they might upset someone or concern matters that someone else expected to remain private. After all, old Russian intelligentsia used to look down on people who were too eager to overshare.

There's not much to say about my earliest years. I was born on August 24, 1936...

* * *

In May 1980 I changed jobs and went to work for a publishing agency that put out the iconic Great Soviet Encyclopedia,[1] which had by then already had its name shortened simply to "Soviet Encyclopedia." I soon discovered, to my surprise, that the publisher was storing

---

[1] https://en.wikipedia.org/wiki/Great_Soviet_Encyclopedia

the back issues of the *Pravda* and *Izvestiya* newspapers, dating back to 1935! The reason this was surprising was that back issues from before WWII were generally inaccessible to the public, having been either destroyed or locked up in special archives requiring official permission to access. But here they were freely available to the publisher's staff. I recalled some popular newspaper features, e.g., "On this day, 100 years ago", that reprinted selected news items from old Russian newspapers, and decided to check the issue of *Pravda* that came out on my birthday, August 24, 1936. Leafing through the bound stack, I opened it to the right date and saw, on the front page, an announcement that Grigory Zinoviev[2] and Lev Kamenev[3] had been executed, together with a verbatim transcript of their sentence. I have little sympathy for these Old Bolsheviks, especially for Zinoviev, one of the most odious revolutionary leaders, but it was interesting to see what happened on the day of my birth.

* * *

September 10th of this year marks 60 years since I entered the workforce. On that day, September 10, 1952, I started my first job — as a factory worker. I was sixteen, the same age as Sasha is now.

I grew up in a family of Moscow intellectuals. My parents were journalists: my father was a copy editor at *Trud* (Labor), one of the top five Soviet newspapers; my mother worked in agricultural trade press for many years and was a correspondent of the Sovinformburo,[4] the official information agency of the Soviet Union. In later years, she stayed home: there were three of us children in the family, and our parents decided that she should devote her time to raising us. Our family was financially comfortable: Trud printed Father's articles almost every week; he had published two collections of essays; another book was being prepared for publication, and I still remember the thick manuscript on Father's desk...

And then everything fell apart.

It happened late at night on November 1, 1950. The doorbell rang; some men came in, showed us an arrest warrant and took Father away. On his way out, he said to Mother: "Sonya, don't worry, I haven't do-

---

[2] https://en.wikipedia.org/wiki/Grigory_Zinoviev

[3] https://en.wikipedia.org/wiki/Lev_Kamenev

[4] https://en.wikipedia.org/wiki/Soviet_Information_Bureau

ne anything. I'll be back soon..." He came back — five and a half years later.

After Father was taken away, three MGB men stayed behind in our apartment. MGB stands for the Ministry of State Security, the precursor to today's FSB...

* * *

Here's an excerpt from my sister Yulia's memoir about my college admission process.

The year was 1954: Year Four of Father's labor camp sentence. Pavel was finishing 10th grade at night school, and it was time to think about college. Our father had gotten him interested in geography at an early age. In his last couple of years at night school he worked at a factory during the day and also competed in geography contests held by the Moscow State University, winning prizes every time. A factory worker winning university-level contests was so unusual that he was even invited to appear at a children's radio show called "Young Geographers' Club." At the closing ceremony for the last of these contests an MSU professor spoke to Pavel... But we will let him tell about it in his own words:

Professor Yulian Glebovich Saoushkin, head of the MSU department of economic geography of the USSR, handed me my winner's diploma and my prize (some books on geography). He shook my hand and asked:

"What are your plans after high school? I assume you'll apply to our program?"

"Well..." said I. "Actually, I'd like to talk to you about it..."

"Of course. Come see me when this is over," said he warmly.

That's how I found myself back on stage, in front of all the judges (MSU professors and docents) still seated at their table, telling Saoushkin that I would love to join his program, but I was Jewish, and my father was serving time at a labor camp.

Saoushkin, naturally, started talking about the Soviet constitution with its guarantees of non-discrimination, but I interrupted him, saying that while all that was well and good, in practice things were different. And the professor changed his tone.

"In our program we really don't care about that. Even our dean feels the same way. Isn't that right, Anatoly Georgievich?" he ad-

219

dressed a professor sitting beside him, who agreed with him. (As I would later learn, this was the head of the department of biogeography, Professor Voronov.)

"And as regards your father being in a labor camp, well, you've got your factory job, you're more of an independent person [than a minor, where that would count—*translator's note*]. *Go ahead and apply to our program."*

Pavel took his advice and registered for the entrance exam to the MSU geography department, earning slightly fewer points than were required for admission. The admission rules gave the examiners some discretion in admitting a few of the candidates with the same number of points. My brother was one of the chosen few; we didn't ask ourselves why. A little later, but still during the admissions season, he and Mother went to see Mother's cousin, Eva Sinelnikova, an actress at the Obraztsov Puppet Theater who had gotten us tickets to many wonderful puppet shows. Among her other guests was a lady who was one of the MSU examiners for the geography department and who started talking about one talented girl she hadn't been able to admit even though the girl had done great at the exam.

"I argued really hard in her favor," said the lady with regret, "but Professor Voronov had his mind set on some Ilyin boy, and he cast the deciding vote as the chairman of the examining committee."

"That Ilyin boy is sitting right here, with his mother," someone said with a smile.

"How do you know Professor Voronov?" asked the lady. "Are you related?"

"I've never laid eyes on him," said Mother, and told them the whole story.

"Ah, so it was right, then," said the lady, relieved.

That's the kind of stories that used to happen at that time.

PART V

Memoirs of Pavel's Friends and Colleagues

My Pavel

Ella Kagan

Forty-nine years. That's how long we lived together...

Although we were very different in temperament, the life we lived was as conjoined as our joint email address: **pavella.** Though our personalities were independent, they were also intertwined and influenced each other.

Pavel loved life, he loved his family, he loved traveling and collecting books. His friends remember him as a kind, cheerful, easy-going man. He loved gathering around the table and was a warm, welcoming host.

Pavel was always helping someone, in small things and large, even when that entailed some risk to himself. He shared his thoughts generously, be it on improving the road network or on a new book. That was his public, outward-facing side.

His other side, less open or accessible, was his life's work (which transcended his job), his ideas, his principles. There, he was immovable and brooked no compromise.

Pavel always worked hard, taking great pains with his work. He set very high standards for himself and worried he might fall short of them. He worshiped his father and lived in his shadow, comparing himself to his father and not wishing to let his father down, so to speak, by shoddy writing. His father, Mikhail Ilyich Ilyin, was a popular children's author and a man of rare talent, so Pavel's plank was set high. I was aware of this internal dynamic and tried to help Pavel by pointing out the differences in subject matter and style between his father's writings and his own, but my efforts were largely in vain.

To understand what made Pavel what he was, it is necessary to know at least the key events in his life and the environment in which his socialization took place.

THE ILYIN FAMILY

Pavel's parents were unusually formal in their manner, using the formal Russian form of address (the plural "you") even to each other. To me they at first seemed very old school, even aristocratic, even though both turned out to be very warm and welcoming people.

They lived on Pushechnaya street, behind the Children's World department store and not far from the government clubhouse for arts professionals. Their apartment building had been built before the 1917 revolution as a rental property belonging to a Russian Orthodox church. The church supposedly still stands, and although no one can recall when the high wall topped with barbed wire that encloses it today was built, Orthodox superstition left its mark upon the apartment building in the omission of number thirteen: unit number twelve was followed immediately by number fourteen. The apartment building is no more: it was pulled down to make room for yet another office of the KGB, which is spreading like cancer from its seat in Lubyanka square toward the Boulevard Ring.

The Ilyin household consisted of five people: the father and mother (Mikhail Ilyich and Sofia Ilyinichna), Pavel, his younger sister Yulia, and a cousin by the name of Volodya, Sofia Ilyinichna's nephew whom she had taken in after his parents perished in Stalin's repressions. They shared their communal apartment with another family, as well as with Mikhail Ilyich's sister Vera, whom everyone called Verochka.

The five members of the Ilyin household had to make do with two tiny rooms. One of the rooms served as the living room as well as the children's bedroom; the other belonged to the parents and housed the large desk where Mikhail Ilyich did his work. He came from educated, cultured stock: his father (Pavel's grandfather) had graduated from the University of Krákow. The grandfather's university diploma entitled him to residency in Moscow, which at the time was forbidden to Jews unless they were merchants first class, doctors, or university graduates. That is how Pavel's father happened to be born in Moscow.

Mikhail Ilyich worked almost every waking moment, but his desk faced the door to the other room so he could see everything that went on. Taciturn and private, he was nevertheless a very astute man with an excellent sense of humor who was apt to drop a witty remark or — despite his reserved exterior — play a prank or a practical joke; Pavel sometimes helped him set them up. The son inherited the father's love of the unexpected, of mysterious projects, of new places. And yet they were so different that the father jokingly called his son a "punk." Mikhail Ilyich practiced old-fashioned courtesy, doffing his hat to the gossiping women who congregated at the entrance to their apartment building, even though he knew none of their names. Pavel's style was entirely different, unadorned and blunt — dispensing with the formal "you plural" altogether, even when talking to my co-workers with whom I myself was on formal terms. He did not mince words and did not try to sugar-coat his opinions, to his own occasional detriment.

Sofia Ilyinichna was a merchant's daughter who had come alone from the town of Surazh to Moscow as a very young woman. Talkative and hospitable, she was quite unlike her husband in her manner.

Living space was extremely tight: even after they had moved their wardrobe out into the hallway, there was not enough floor space to fit beds for everyone, so one of the boys slept in Verochka's room. Nevertheless, they were always glad to make room for friends when we came by.

Everyone smoked. Despite the window that stayed open, the house always smelled of tobacco: the furniture, the window drapes, the people's clothes. This smell was one of my first impressions when I first walked into their home.

Pavel's parents were journalists. Mikhail Ilyich, in his youth, had written poetry and had belonged to several literary groups, which, however, didn't last long: the 1930s put an end to any freedom of the press or the arts. He became a journalist, writing theater reviews, writing for newspapers, writing educational pieces for children and adults about the different places throughout the country. The work involved a lot of travel, which he enjoyed and taught Pavel to love, too.

Sofia Ilyinichna was of that generation of journalists who carried their portable typewriters with them when they went to interview people. She typed as fast as she spoke, chain-smoking but never making any typos.

Theirs was a peaceful and secure life, but it all fell apart when WWII began. The family was evacuated first to Omsk in Siberia then in Alma-Ata in Kazakhstan. They lived in evacuation for about a year and a half, returning to Moscow in 1943.

THE TRAVAILS OF YOUTH

After the war, things began to go back to normal — until that fateful day that turned the family's life upside down. Pavel recalls:

We lived fairly well. The Trud newspaper printed Father's articles nearly every week; he published two books of essays; another book was almost ready to print, the thick manuscript lay on his desk, I still remember what it looked like. And then it all collapsed...

> *This happened late at night on November 1, 1950. The doorbell rang;*
> *people came in with an arrest warrant and led Father away. As he was*
> *walking out, he told Mother: "Sofia, please don't be alarmed, they've got*
> *nothing on me. I'll be back soon..." He came back five and a half years*
> *later.*

The charge on which he was arrested was absurd, having to do with an anarchist group he had joined in his youth; he was forty-nine when he was arrested.

Now the family lived on the brink of starvation. Sofia Ilyinichna couldn't find work anywhere because she was now classified as the wife of an "enemy of the people." She learned to sew to make ends meet. She sold everything that could be sold, including books. Books of poetry were committed to memory before being sold. That was when Pavel learned to love the poetry of the Russian "silver age" of the late 19th—early 20th century, a love he kept for the rest of his life.

When his father was arrested, Pavel was fourteen. In August 1952, he turned sixteen, the legal age, and in September he went to work at a factory, transferring from his regular high school to evening school for working youth to complete his education. An intellectual, college-bound youth with his head filled with poetry was now immersed in a completely different kind of life. Cousin Volodya was enrolled in trade school. Only Yulia, the youngest, continued her regular schooling.

As is often the case, adversity brought the family closer together. During the years his father was away, Pavel became an adult, the man of the house, the breadwinner. All the family members supported each other. With his mother, Pavel made the rounds of bureaucratic waiting rooms, filing petitions on behalf of his father and sending care packages to him at labor camps. Throughout these difficult years, Pavel managed to remain his usual kind and warm-hearted self at home.

Outside the home, however, he became a different person. He quickly learned to get along with his fellow factory workers and was exposed to the life and problems of a different social class. His neglect of the formal form of address dates from that time, but the changes went deeper than his manners and deportment. His circle of friends now included young men from his evening school — each with his own story of hardship, of course, otherwise they wouldn't have had to work days and study nights. Pavel's outlook changed; he found he could relate to people from different social backgrounds, provided they were people of integrity. These were formative years for Pavel, years of change. The one thing that did not change was his affinity for language and the art of writing.

In times like these, the support of friends becomes more important than ever. The first such friend was Pavel's former schoolmate from his regular school, Alexander (Sasha) Kirillov. Their friendship proved enduring, lasting through all the twists and turns in the friends' lives. Alexander Alexandrovich Kirillov became a world-renowned mathematician and now lives in Philadelphia.

In evening school, Pavel met two remarkable young men: Vadim Scheglov and Eugene (Zhenya) Kokorin. Vadim later became a member of the human rights organization The Christian Committee for the Protection of the Rights of Believers in the USSR. He was a thorn in the regime's side, which could have arrested him at any time but chose to push him out of the country, forcing him to move to America. Sadly, neither Vadim nor Zhenya is still living.

The year was 1954; it was time to think about college. Pavel's love of geography, instilled by his father, had only grown in his absence. Every year, Pavel competed in geography contests held by the Moscow State University and won. For a factory worker to win a university-level contest was very unusual. However, Pavel's path to college was blocked by the fact that his father had been convicted under the infamous Article 58 (treason).

Pavel remembers:

Professor Yulian Glebovich Saoushkin, head of the MSU department of economic geography of the USSR, handed me my winner's diploma and my prize (some books on geography). He shook my hand and asked:

"What are your plans after high school? I assume you'll apply to our program?"

"Well..." said I. "Actually, I'd like to talk to you about it..."

"Of course. Come see me when this is over," said he warmly.

That's how I found myself back on stage, in front of all the judges (MSU professors and docents) still seated at their table, telling Saoushkin that I would love to join his program, but I was Jewish, and my father was serving time at a labor camp.

Saoushkin, naturally, started talking about the Soviet constitution with its guarantees of non-discrimination, but I interrupted him, saying that while all that was well and good, in practice things were different. And the professor changed his tone.

> *"In our program we really don't care about that. Even our dean feels the same way. Isn't that right, Anatoly Georgievich?" he addressed a professor sitting beside him, who agreed with him. (As I would later learn, this was the head of the department of biogeography, Professor Voronov.)*
>
> *"And as regards your father being in a labor camp, well, you've got your factory job, you're more of an independent person [Tr: than a minor, where that would count]. Go ahead and apply to our program."*

Pavel was admitted to the MSU geography department. The exciting life of a college student was now his to experience and enjoy.

Mikhail Ilyich came back in 1956. Oddly, he had survived labor camp thanks to a tumor that was diagnosed and removed by the camp surgeon, himself a camp inmate, who gave him a medical exemption from hard labor. Mikhail Ilyich was transferred to work at the camp office, where he earned the good graces of the camp's director not only by his good work but also by giving the director his tobacco ration.

The Ilyin family archives contain two photos of Mikhail Ilyich, one taken right after his release from camp, the other taken ten years later. In the second photo, he looks much younger. The passport he was issued upon his release bore the code ZK, which stood for "convict." The line for the first and last name read: "Ilyin, Mikhail Ilyich, alias Tirkeltaub, Myron Ilyich." The family jokingly called him "alias" for a long time afterwards.

It was in those years after his release that Mikhail Ilyin created Midshipman Zahkar the Riddleman ("Zakhar Zagadkin") and ship's cook Tony Galley ("Anton Kambuzov"). Only a man of his unbounded imagination could have created these characters, which populated radio shows for twenty-four years and continue to live in books and on the Internet.

After Mikhail Ilyich passed away, Pavel took over his radio show and ran it until the summer of 1982. The show was shut down immediately after the KGB came to search our home. But that is a different story.

WHEN WE WERE YOUNG...

In 1960, Pavel and I — both recent college graduates — both found ourselves working at Giprogor, an urban planning agency. We were placed in the same workshop and occasionally worked on the same projects together. These were happy years; we were young and full of hope. A few years later, we got married.

1967 was a difficult year for our family. Our daughter, Nadya — her full name is Nadezhda, meaning "hope" in Russian — was born in June; Pavel's father passed away in October. There is an old Jewish saying that as one soul leaves a family, another enters. I don't know if that's a universal truth but that's the way it happened in our family.

As a father, Pavel was charmingly tender: the word "no" was not part of his relationship with Nadya. He saw his main job as passing down his own knowledge to his daughter. When Nadya was three, Pavel put a big map of the country up on the wall, and that was the beginning of his "homeschooling" project. He talked to her about history, taught her to work with maps and many other things besides. His daughter inherited a "travel gene" from her dad.

The same thing happened when our granddaughters were born. Pavel adored them and, naturally, began teaching them all kinds of things — always in a light-hearted, playful way. For example, when the oldest, Sasha, was learning about the structure of the universe, Grandpa Pavel showed up holding a globe in his hands and began walking in circles around the table while spinning the globe. But the main thing he taught them was how to travel: they prepared by reading guidebooks and other materials, they prepared maps, they took travel notes and made sketches. Each was given a beautiful album for her travel notebook.

Each time the girls went somewhere, we received priceless information afterwards. For example, in Italy the youngest, Margot, wrote down the flavor of ice cream she ate each day. And in New Zealand, Sasha, the oldest, drew pictures of exotic birds that do not live in America. Grandpa's "travel gene" was successfully passed down to the next generation.

But let us return to GIPROGOR. Time passed, and the charming novelty of urban planning wore off. Pavel enrolled in the post-graduate program of the Institute of Geography of the Academy of Sciences (IGAN), successfully defended his dissertation and stayed on at IGAN as an employee. His department was headed by Aleksey Aleksandrovich Mintz, a young and talented scientist who was beginning to shift their work from conventional, descriptive regional studies to issue-centric research.

Pavel had wide-ranging interests, from theoretical geography to geographic puzzles in his radio shows to poetry. His Giprogor colleagues were understanding and supportive of this "double life" because many of them were also multi-talented people with their own outside interests. In contrast, his academic colleagues felt that Science demanded total devotion, total commitment; many looked down on other pursuits as unbecoming a serious scientist.

But Pavel cared little about people's opinions. He was always pursuing other projects that interested him, alongside his assigned work. He would write his papers first and then try to find others who might also be interested in his topic.

The writing process didn't come easily to him; the beginning stage of each letter, essay, book was always a struggle. I remember talking through his thoughts about a new piece, discussing, occasionally debating. Our minds worked differently: whereas Pavel always started with examples and particulars, I asked him to articulate his thesis first. Nevertheless, we always arrived at a reasonable solution. We helped each other, published joint works and often attended the same conferences.

Pavel left IGAN for the geography desk of a publishing house that specialized in encyclopedias and dictionaries. Words were his passion, and editorial work suited him well. At the same time, he continued his scientific work, writing and publishing and giving presentations. His interests began to shift toward social issues, both in science and in society.

THE STORM CLOUDS GATHER...

Pavel was fortunate in his places of employment, which offered a relatively liberal environment; but the overall political situation in the country was grim. Though Pavel was never actively involved in political dissent, he was close to dissident circles. As a KGB man would later say to him: "For a good man, Pavel Mikhailovich, you sure keep bad company." I don't remember a single loyal fan of the regime among his friends; they all had their causes: religious rights, political activism, etc.

When our Jewish peers began to emigrate, we realized that it was time we did the same. We did not want to keep living under that regime and especially did not want to raise our daughter there.

Right around that time, in summer 1982, the KGB came to search our home. They searched the homes of eight of our friends on the same day. We knew that the reason for their visit was the "bad company" we kept.

It was a nasty experience, which confirmed us in our decision to leave the country. The KGB rummaged through everything, interrogated everyone (including our daughter, who had turned fifteen a month earlier), carted away several sacks of papers and our typewriter. They also took Pavel away to the Lefortovo prison. They let him go soon afterwards but did not leave him alone.

There was a sort of mystical symmetry in this: Pavel had been fourteen when Mikhail Ilyich was arrested; our daughter was fifteen when Pavel was arrested.

Soon after the house search, we overcame a mountain of bureaucratic hurdles and filed our application to emigrate. It is hard to explain the sense of moral relief this gave us. We felt a sort of mental freedom — which was ironic, as we now had less physical freedom because we were now under surveillance.

Pavel continued to work but was transferred to a different department and demoted, as a punishment for wanting to emigrate. We were not surprised when our application was denied, and quickly found our natural place in the growing crowd of refuseniks, among which were many of our friends.

Pavel continued to write, although the nature of his writings changed. He was known not only as a good writer but also as a good editor, so now he helped his friends with letters and petitions in support of someone who was being persecuted by the authorities, or in protest against some outrage committed by the regime. The KGB began to come for him at work and haul him in for their little "chats"; they threatened and pressured him, trying to turn him into an informer. They failed...

Together with our friends, we kept busy — writing letters, staging hunger strikes and demonstrations against the regime, sending care packages to those of our number who were in prison or labor camp.

At the initiative of Robert Gohstand, Pavel's American colleague and friend, the American Association of Geographers (AAG) in March 1987 adopted the following resolution[1] of support of Pavel Ilyin and his family:

> "*Whereas, Pavel Mikhailovich Il'in* [sic] and *Mikaella Isaakovna Kagan,* who are professional colleagues of the members of this Association, desire to emigrate with their family, but have been repeatedly denied permission to do so,
>
> *Be it resolved,* that the members of *the Association of American Geographers...* strongly urges [sic]... *that the Il'in family be granted the right of emigration without further delay.*"

---

[1] *See* Apendix IV

Finally, after a five-year wait, we received our permission to emigrate in May 1987 and flew out of Moscow in July.

BETWEEN MOSCOW AND BOSTON

We had a layover in Vienna, Austria, where we were met by polite airport staff and smiling representatives of our American sponsoring agency, the Hebrew Immigrant Aid Society (HIAS). We were taken to a room where we saw a photocopier — open and available for all to use. Only hours prior, we had left a country where all copy machines were kept under lock and key and required official written permission to make each copy. This was the first thing that stunned us in the West, though not the last.

Vienna is a city of true beauty. We loved walking around it. And yet, on our walks we soon saw that not everything was quite rosy in this earthly paradise. Armed guards were posted at the entrance to the synagogue; there were more armed guards outside HIAS, as well as some sort of security scanners in the lobby. HIAS had reasons for their vigilance: we were told that right before our arrival, there had been instances of attacks on Jews in the streets. The storied Vienna Central Cemetery, which houses the remains of heads of Austrian governments and prominent cultural figures, also has a Jewish section. We found it to be so overgrown with weeds that it was difficult to make our way between the grave sites; we had to tear away the brush to see the names on the gravestones.

In Vienna we had a disagreement with HIAS, which refused to cover the shipment costs of one of the boxes in our very modest luggage. The box contained Pavel's collection of almost three hundred figurines of sailors, which Pavel had spent most of his life collecting in honor of the protagonists of his radio show, Midshipman Zahkar the Riddleman and Cook Tony Galley. Pavel intended to gift the collection to Robert Gohstand, who had served in the U.S. Navy in his youth and had seen his collection and liked it. With Robert's help, the collection was finally shipped to the U.S. and took its place upon the shelves of Robert's office at the California State University, Northridge. Sadly, the 1994 major earthquake that damaged the university building did not spare the sailors; Robert had to hunt around afterwards for their broken-off arms, legs and heads.

OUR SECOND LIFE

It was like jumping off with a parachute into the unknown. Picture two fifty-year-old academics with not very marketable qualifications entering their new life with ninety dollars and one suitcase per person; that's all we were allowed to take out of the Soviet Union. Our daughter and my mother traveled with us.

We were stunned and deeply touched by the reception provided by our local Jewish community for new immigrants. All the things we needed to get started were donated to us. Our sponsors, Valery and Etya Godyak (our friends from Moscow and fellow *refuseniks* who had left before us) also helped us. We gratefully accepted it all but were keenly aware that this largesse was bound to run out soon, and we must look for employment. Years later we learned that the Jewish resettlement agency that handled our case considered us the least promising couple out of that year's intake in terms of the likelihood of achieving financial independence.

Pavel applied for jobs at multiple universities, largely to no avail. He did get invited to speak at the Harvard University's Russian Center. He offered to speak on the subject he was working on: urbanization in the USSR. They gladly accepted, because while everyone was interested in the USSR, no one understood what was going on there. Pavel gave his talk and was asked what impact *perestroika* was having on the country's urban development; no impact, said Pavel. (This was before the 1991 law on the privatization of state enterprises, which led to actual changes.) Harvard's left-leaning professors were disappointed: this was not the rosy picture they were expecting. But even had Pavel been aware of their expectations, he would have given them the same answer. They did not invite him back.

Around that time something happened that was to have far-reaching consequences for our family. Pavel came across a newspaper article that talked about how places in Russia were being renamed (unfortunately, I can recall neither the name of the newspaper nor the name of the author). This was a topic that had long attracted Pavel and one he was well-versed in — unlike the author, who was clearly new to the subject and had made several errors. Pavel wrote to him, offering detailed corrections. The author did not respond, but this gave Pavel an impetus for a new project.

He contacted the Kennan Institute for Russian studies and went to New York to meet with its then-director, Blair Ruble, who received him warmly and advised him to apply for a grant. The new wave of

Russian immigration was just beginning, and Pavel was its first, exotic representative. One problem that arose was submitting copies of Pavel's publications over the past several years, but refuseniks were not allowed to publish. Somehow Blair Ruble found a way around this, and Pavel received his grant, allowing him to work for a year. That was a wonderful year for him.

However, it passed, and it was time to look for another job. Fortunately, the Washington Processing Center was hiring. This was an organization that processed applications filed by people from the former Soviet Union seeking to immigrate to the United States. He was hired, thanks to our friend Yelena Raben who worked there and gave his resume to her boss. His job was to verify the places of birth and residence listed in the applications. It was necessary because everything in the former Soviet space was being renamed, from cities and towns to entire countries (the former Soviet republics). This job supported us for several years.

THE BOOK

Time passed. In due course, Pavel decided to participate in the 1998 annual AAG conference as part of a session on Moscow, Russia. The panelists and their reviewers all came from different fields, and each had his own angle and approach to the issues. The result was an interesting, composite picture of that super-complex city.

Blair Ruble attended the session and told Pavel afterwards that the presentations should be collected and published as a book. Pavel thought that Blair was just being nice, but Blair was serious. The book came out: *Moscow At The Turn Of The XX Century: A Glance Into The Past From Afar*, Pavel Ilyin and Blair Ruble, eds.. Moscow, Russia, 2004. It includes chapters by each of the editors and others written jointly by both. Other contributors include Robert Gohstand, William K. Broomfield, Robert Whittaker, Katya Korotkina-Rosenzweig, and Mikaella Kagan.

The work took many years to complete, pausing several times for extended periods for one reason or another. But Pavel was never in a rush when he was working. This was work that he loved, and he enjoyed the process. He began by relentlessly pursuing sources of information. Once he knew what he was going to say, he began the painstaking work of wordsmithing. Finding illustrations was the next step. Pavel had no wish to deal with Russia on the issue of copyright to pictures; accordingly, he decided to limit himself to picture postcards made before the Russian revolution. He went around to picture post-card fairs, wrote to colleagues in Moscow and Germany. Finding his illustrations took him about two years.

The book was Pavel's brainchild. He loved the city of Moscow and knew it intimately in all its particulars, down to the humblest court-yards and alleyways. At times I felt that he was as reluctant to part from the manuscript as a child is reluctant to let go of a favorite toy.

Pavel loved books and collected them all his life, finding money to buy them even when money was tight. In the end, he had amassed a peerless collection of materials about Moscow that included over a thousand titles.

He had a tentative deal with a major publisher in Chicago. But over a period of year, public interest in Russia went down, and the publisher decided that they no longer needed a book about Moscow. Now the book, originally made for publication in English, had to be re-done in Russian. The editor in Pavel rose to the challenge, and he threw himself into the work with gusto.

In 2001 we visited Moscow, where Pavel finally signed a contract with a Russian publisher, Rosspen, which brought the book out in 2004.

THE FUN AND GAMES OF POLITICAL TOPONYMY

Of course, during those years Pavel did not limit himself to Moscow. The renaming of cities, streets, natural objects that was underway in Russia was achieving epidemic proportions. Pavel enjoyed watching these political games from afar and, as usual, slowly and methodically collected information on this rewriting of maps. Eventually, he put together a presentation and gave it at the next annual AAG conference in 1992. The presentation was well received, but the manifest absurdity of playing politics with toponyms produced an unexpected reaction in the audience: never in my long life, neither before nor after that, did I witness an academic gathering where the learned audience guffawed and giggled quite so much.

When we came home, Pavel found on his desk a letter from the Post-Soviet Geography magazine inviting him to submit his presentation to them as an article for publication. In 1993, they printed his article *Renaming Soviet Cities after Exceptional People: A Historical Perspective on Toponymy*.

The article was later reprinted several times, reaching as far as Japan. Pavel had had other works published in French, Polish, Finnish and other languages but he had never thought of publishing in Japan.

HOLY WORK

In 1995 Pavel left WPC, and in 1996 he started work at the U.S. Holocaust Memorial Museum. His article on the renaming of cities had a lot to do with it: a colleague of his, Vadim Altskan, took his article to the Holocaust Museum just as they were beginning to build a database of places where the Holocaust took place. They needed someone who specialized in toponymy.

Pavel, for his part, saw this as holy work for a Jewish man. He often said: "If I were rich, I would pay them to let me do this work."

Besides the database, Pavel worked on several other projects at the Museum. He edited their publications from the geographical standpoint. A special part of his job was responding to inquiries from colleagues and others looking for their relatives and friends. Often, it was hard to find the places where the individual was last known to reside. Pavel rejoiced each time he was able to help someone, bring together long-lost Jewish souls.

Pavel published new works on Holocaust-related issues, e.g., *The Pogrom On The Map: How The Soviet Regime Rewrote History By Changing Ukrainian Place Names.* Unfortunately, his presentations on toponymy given at conferences in New Orleans (2003), Boston (2008), Bad Arolsen (Germany, 2013), Vilnius (Lithuania, 2013), and Tbilisi (Georgia, 2013) were never published.

Pavel's work required maps of Central and Eastern Europe. Pavel loved maps and collected antique maps. His collection includes the famous *Madaba* map — a copy of the oldest extant map of the Middle East and Israel that forms part of the mosaic floor of a Byzantine church in Madaba, Jordan.

Most of his work with maps took place at the Library of Congress' Geography and Maps Reading Room. In the beginning, he had to dig through boxes of maps that had not been catalogued. He determined the date and country of publication and other information required to create a catalog description of each map. After Pavel passed away, his colleagues had the collection of 39 maps that he assembled for the Holocaust Museum formally designated to Museum Library as *Pavel Ilyin's Collection Of Published Road And Tourist Maps.*

THE ARTISTRY OF LANGUAGE

All his life, regardless of what he was doing — whether radio shows for children or scientific — Pavel paid careful attention to words. He loved poetry and could recite it for hours from memory. He got that from his family: his father in his youth had published poetry; his mother read to the children out of those same poetry books that were later sold to help keep food on the table. Nevertheless, he published only one essay about poetry — the poem in verse *Eugene Onegin* by the revered Russian poet Alexander Pushkin — exploring one of the verses that has been part of Russian lore for the past three hundred years:

> *My span on earth is all but taken,*
> *But lest too soon I join the dead,*
> *I need to know when I awaken,*
> *I'll see you in the day ahead...*[2]

It took Pavel a long time to feel at home in America — a feeling that finally came to him after 9/11. Living in two different languages and cultures at the same time, he tried to bring them together by choosing three popular American songs — *This Land Is Your Land, America The Beautiful,* and *God Bless America* — and translating them into Russian so they could be sung to their original music. The process of translation was long and painstakingly precise. He tested each word against multiple sources, asked endless questions of his professional translator friends, before settling on a word that suited him. He introduced his Russian readers to the authors of these songs, as well as their best-known performers. He visited many of the places associated with these people. He wanted to get a sense of who these people were who created the songs that have retained their popularity for such a long time. This essay, the last major work Pavel wrote, was published in a New York-based Russian-language magazine *Vremya i mesto (Time and Place), issue 4 (20), 2011.*

In the last few year of his life Pavel continued to speak at Holocaust-themed conferences, translate materials on topics that interested him, and wrote several book reviews.

His close friend Igor Krupnik has called Pavel a "master of words" — as good and affectionate a description as anyone has come up with.

Pavel passed away on March 12, 2015.

---

[2] Ильин П. «Я знаю: век уж мой измерен...». – *Новый журнал,* Кн. 207, Нью-Йорк, 1997. English text quoted from Pushkin, Alexander. *Eugene Onegin.* Translated by James E. Falen, Oxford World's Classics, 1998.

My Father

Nadya Ilyin Bartol

A s we say in Russian, my dad was "born in a shirt." He survived 5 cancers, random broken bones, a dislocated shoulder, potentially deadly car accidents, and the KGB. Or one could say that he had a guardian angel. Born in 1936, he was 5 when WWII started in Russia, 14 when his father was taken by the soviets, and 20 when his father returned. And he was 42 when we applied to emigrate — and the KGB came for him instead of his father. But they returned him, only to take him again later. They thought he was a softie and would inform on his friends. A polite man, he did not tell them to get lost but he did try to explain that he would not be an informer. Eventually we came to believe that from their point of view, he was not important enough and probably too much trouble to imprison permanently. So, he always returned — but these visits took their toll.

When his father was taken he had to quit regular school, get a job in a factory, and go to school at night. Ironically, he was accepted into Moscow University — unusual for a Jew — because his working in a factory qualified him as a proletarian... Somehow the admissions board missed the fact that he was a son of an "enemy of the state". He did well. He must have been what we call today an "auditory learner" since he made it all the way through the university without studying. Just listening to the lectures earned him the equivalent of a B average.

His father was a journalist. In the US, I think he would have been called a travel writer and theater critic. When Dad was little they traveled all over the Soviet Union on my grandfather's business trips. Years later my dad became a geographer and continued the travels his father started. When he came to the States he kept traveling whenever he could and started collecting refrigerator magnets from all those places. Wherever I went he only wanted one thing — a magnet, but the magnet had to be immediately recognizable of the place.

He picked up more than travels from his father. My grandfather wrote a famous radio geography quiz show and Dad took over that job after his father's death. He wrote the show for years until it was shut down because we applied to emigrate. Every time I came back from the Far East I told him that I felt like his main character — arriving a couple of hours after I left while being on a plane for hours, or, even better, arriving before departing.

I learned to read maps shortly after learning to read. I knew everything about the huge map of the Soviet Union that hung above my parents' pullout couch. When we traveled Dad told me about the places themselves while mom explained how the cities and the buildings were designed. They both transferred their passion for travel to me and I passed it on to my girls, somewhat to my husband's chagrin. The girls have gotten used to asking "where are we going next" at the end of each vacation.

He got his love of travel and books from his father and of the theater and arts from his mother. He knew so much that his coworkers called him Diderot Dolombertovich, after the two French enlightenment figures who reinvented (published the first French) "Encyclopedia". He really had an encyclopedic mind. He taught me Russian medieval history — 9th through 16th century with all the names, genealogy, and the dates — by telling stories while mushroom hunting. Please note this was feudal Russia before it became an absolute monarchy so there were lots of principalities, but he knew them all.

My parents applied to leave in 1982 and we emigrated in 1987, one of the first in the last wave of soviet Jewish emigration. During our refusenik years we benefited tremendously from the support of the American Jewish community and of American politicians who were relentless in their resolve to get us all out of there. Dad's and Mom's colleagues managed to put them onto some list of scientists that Americans pulled out every time the soviets needed more wheat or something like that. Eventually that worked.

When my family came to Lynn Massachusetts, they were dubbed the most hopeless among the then-present immigrant population. Two 51-year old PhDs with geography and urban planning degrees plus a daughter with a music degree. I am happy to report we surprised them all. While it was not easy, Dad's first job was as a fellow with the Kennan Institute for Russian Studies. Once his grant ended he worked as a contractor providing geographical consulting for the State Department that was at the time (the early 90's) furiously processing Soviet immigrants. And then his friend got him into "the museum."

Over the next 20 years he became one of the foremost world experts on the geography of the Holocaust. He leaned to phonetically read and transcribe all the Eastern European languages including Hungarian, became a regular in the Library of Congress, and began creating complex maps of which country controlled what territory in the first half of the 20th century in those countries of Central and Eastern Europe that were occupied by Germany. When he went to Jerusalem and visited Yad Vashem he was treated like a celebrity. He found maps in the Library of Congress that they did not know they had, and he told them what they were. He said that if he were rich he would have paid the museum to let him do this work — he loved it so much.

Our house in Moscow was always full of people. Mom made a tray of food at a time because "who knows who may stop by". She cooked and he made vodka. Well, he did not really make it — he infused it with a top-secret spice mix that he inherited from his father. He perfected his process over the years and I have the latest recipe. But I have only made it a couple of times and I have to warn everyone that you will now be subjected to years of experimentation. Because I have to perfect it to the quality of product that he made.

When his granddaughters were born, he became "Didi". In Russian, Deda is grandpa but that is too close to Daddy. So, Sasha called him Didi. The name stuck and thus Margot used it too when she came along. His response was that he really did not care what they called him. As long as they loved him. And he became a favorite horse/donkey, board game partner, and teacher of things about the world. When Sasha started learning about the solar system he brought over a globe and started walking around it to demonstrate the concept of an orbit. And he did the usual trick with the light to show how eclipse happens. He taught Margot about constellations — something I myself never absorbed from him for some reason.

Didi gave us all a sense of wonder, a love of different places and cultures, and a love of books. His library is amazingly vast and comprehensive. His friends are numerous as we see here today. And we will all miss his infectious laugh...

March 15th, 2015

Sasha and Pasha

Aleksandre Kirillov

CHILDHOOD

There were once in Moscow two boys: Sasha and Pasha. Both were born in 1936, both were evacuated during WWII and came back to Moscow toward the end of the war.

Sasha started school in the fall of 1944. At the time, boys and girls in Russia attended separate schools. Many schools had been closed during the war, and the closest boys' school to his house, No. 239, was in Kolokolnikov Lane near Trubnaya Square. The school was filled beyond capacity: it had ten first-grade classes.

Pasha, who had health problems, started school third grade, in Sasha's class, in 1947. That's how they met, although they didn't become friends right away.

In fourth grade it emerged that there were three best students in their class: Sasha, Pasha and Kamil Abyanov. This Kamil, who lived in the slums in Trubnaya Square populated by displaced Tatar people, held sway in their class because he was three years older the rest of the boys, having lost both legs in an accident where he was run over by a tram, and much stronger. For some reason, he came to respect Pasha and protected him to the end of school.

Around 6th grade Sasha and Pasha developed new interests alongside their usual boyhood pursuits: math for Sasha and geography for Pasha. Following the example of a beloved Soviet children's author, Lev Kassil, they also invented their own country and located it in Antarctica, with embassies in the nearest countries.

Their school offered a seven-year program of study, and in 1951 the boys graduated from 7th grade, marking the end of childhood. By that time they were close friends and spent a lot of time together.

Pasha lived in a three-room apartment, small but separate, with his parents, his sister Yulia, his adopted brother Vladimir (Vovka) — both siblings were three years younger than he was — and Auntie Vera. Sasha shared a 20-meter room in a communal apartment with his parents and his own sister Yulia. Given their housing situation, the boys spent their time either walking around Moscow or at Pasha's place.

ADOLESCENCE

The war was over, and people were returning from evacuation (though not everyone came back). The authorities decided to expand primary education to ten years and formed two 8th grades at the boys' school: 8A and 8B. Sasha was enrolled in 8A; Pasha's situation, however, was more complicated.

His father, journalist and children's author Mikh. Ilyin (a pseudonym chosen in order to distinguish him from another children's writer, M. Ilyin), was arrested by the KGB — ostensibly for his prior work for a newspaper that had since been deemed to be counterrevolutionary and closed down, but everyone understood that this was part of the anti-Semitic campaign that was gathering steam across the country.

As a result, Pasha had to quit school, go to work for the Moscow metallurgical factory called "Hammer and Sickle", and go to night school at a remedial school for working-class youth in Markhlevsky street. But the boys' friendship did not end there.

In those days, people whose family members had been arrested faced different reactions from those around them. Some cut them off and no longer spoke to them; others pretended that nothing was wrong but kept their distance just in case; but there were also those who empathized and tried to help. Sasha's family was among those, even though his father was employed by the KGB.

Life went on, and our protagonists achieved their first significant victories: in 10th grade, each earned first prize at citywide scholastic competitions, in geography (Pasha) and in math (Sasha). They had one newfangled ballpoint pen between the two of them (the schools were still using dip pens) and used it to write their submissions, since the competitions took place on different days. They kept the pen for a long time afterwards until eventually it broke and was lost.

In 9th grade, in November 1952, the boys went to see the building of the Moscow State University being built on Lenin Hills. But the weather was bad, there was a thick fog, and they could see nothing beyond the fence surrounding the construction site.

Both of them decided to go to MSU after high school, to the geography and mechanics and math departments, respectively — and both of them got in!

Which was relatively easy for Sasha, as he had graduated with a gold medal and was exempt from entrance exams and only had to pass an interview.

It was more difficult for Pasha as a son of an "enemy of the people." But the year was 1954, the Khruschev Thaw was beginning, and his first prize at that city competition combined with the support of one of the MSU professors finally prevailed, and Pasha was admitted.

Now began their student life, happy and intense. Sasha found a large group of student friends, and Pasha also joined it. As busy as they each were, they kept in touch, and the summer after their third year Pasha went to visit Sasha in Kustanay Oblast where Sasha was working as part of the government's campaign of reclaiming virgin lands.[1] Pasha easily found his place among Sasha's mathematician friends and even appeared as a character in a humorous poem "The Virgin Lands Alphabet" included in the 2003 book *We Are Mathematicians From Lenin Hills* commemorating the 70th anniversary of the MSU Department of Mechanics and Math.

ADULTHOOD

The student years flew by, and our friends started their post-graduate studies: Pavel at the Institute of Geography of the USSR Academy of Sciences, and Sasha at the Department of Mechanics and Math. Both defended their dissertations, married and started families and were now seeing each other less often — though with no less pleasure.

Two or three times a year they took trips together exploring different towns and villages. They started out with walking tours of Moscow and its surrounding countryside, then began to use available public transportation, and after Sasha brought back a car from a business trip to France in 1967, that became their means of transportation. Usually Pavel came up with a destination, mapped out an itinerary and navigated while Sasha drove.

In the summer 1986 the friends celebrated their joint century: the sum of their ages had reached 100. They celebrated it with a dayslong expedition to the north of the Moscow Oblast.

---

[1] The Virgin Lands Campaign was Nikita Khruschev's 1953 plan to dramatically boost the Soviet Union's agricultural production, in order to alleviate the food shortages plaguing the Soviet populace, by placing hitherto undeveloped (virgin) land in Siberia, Western Kazakhstan, the northern Caucasus, and along the Volga under cultivation. *See* **https://en.wikipedia.org/wiki/Virgin_Lands_Campaign**

Meanwhile, life in Russia went on, and not always for the best. The détente of the 1970s brought a brief relaxation of domestic tensions. Jewish emigration began (though it was soon paused again). Instead of Communism and the resultant abundance of food and consumer goods, boldly promised by Khrushchev in 1961, Olympic games (though marred by boycotts by many countries) were held in Moscow in 1980, and a Food Programme was adopted in 1982.[2] The same years brought increasing ideological pressures on scientists and technical workers, writers and artists — the classes that, though often reviled today, were at the time the keepers of the few remaining high ideals.

For a long time, Sasha could not imagine life outside Russia. This was especially so because in the 1950s and early 60s, MSU had been a global leader in terms of the number of world-class mathematicians working there, so that those years would later be called the "golden age of Soviet mathematics." The courageous support of the MSU rector Ivan Georgiyevich Petrovsky, combined with the fact that the defense industry depended on modern physics for its continued success, served to shield mathematics from the dire fate of genetics and cybernetics.[3] Nevertheless, he and his peers were feeling an increasing scientific isolation.

After two trips abroad — to Sweden to attend the 1962 International Congress of Mathematicians and to France in 1968 to teach a course at the Henri Poincare Institute — Sasha realized that the people outside Russia were just as human, and the phobia of "capitalist encirclement" ingrained in our Soviet minds was the creation of government propaganda.

The two friends talked a lot about the relationship between the state and the individual. They agreed on many things (for example, that the individual was more important than the state) but not on the issue of emigration.

"You're a Soviet Jew", said Sasha to Pasha. "You've lived here in Russia for half a century; you know and love the language and the culture. You and I, and all our friends, have always been able to distinguish the country from its rulers. You can still achieve so much without leaving the country." But Pasha remained unconvinced. He began

---

[2] The Food Programme was a set of reforms designed to relieve the severe systemic food shortages produced by the centrally planned Soviet economy without abolishing central planning. *See* https://en.wikipedia.org/wiki/Food_Programme

[3] Both genetics and cybernetics were attacked by politically motivated opportunists, denying their scientific validity, and their practitioners lost their jobs and often their lives. *See* https://en.wikipedia.org/wiki/Bourgeois_pseudoscience

to lean toward emigration and eventually applied for permission to move to Israel.

1987

After submitting his application, Pasha spent the next five years as a *refusenik*. Sasha's friend and classmate, Mark Freydlin, was also a *refusenik*, as were many others who applied in 1980. The friends kept in touch but the life of the *refuseniks* changed dramatically, as many experienced reprisals and job loss.

Finally, in 1987, the spirit of *perestroika* percolated down into emigration policy, and Pasha and Mark both received permission to emigrate. It was a bittersweet victory. Freedom awaited (as well as a good job, in Mark's case), but an entire life, an entire network of friends were being left behind. No one knew when the friends would meet again but everyone was sure that it wouldn't be for a long time, and perhaps not in this life.

That same year, Sasha was permitted to attend a conference in Bulgaria. On his first day off he took a bottle of red wine and climbed the Vitosha mountain in order to contemplate life in peace and privacy, as he and Pasha used to do during their travels around Russia. And it came to him that Vitosha, and Bulgaria in general, was a marvelous meeting place for those coming from Moscow and from America.

The idea was so good, it called for a drink. Not having a bottle opener with him, Sasha resorted to the popular method of banging the bottle against a birch tree to knock the cork out. Whether due to faulty execution or an unusually well-seated cork, the neck of the bottle broke off, nearly severing his right thumb. Strangely, this did not perturb Sasha but made him feel that he would soon see Pasha. After bandaging his thumb, Sasha finished the bottle, remembering to raise leisurely toasts to the absent Pasha. On his return to his hotel room, he wrote and sent off a letter to Pasha describing this event. Pasha responded with several letters filled with humorous descriptions of his first impressions of Europe and America. Only later would Sasha learn that this was a difficult time for Pasha, who was having trouble adapting to his new American life.

1988–1990

As far as the outside world was concerned, perestroika began in Russia in 1985. However, it came late to MSU. Its administration, including the department that processed travel papers for assignments abroad, remained the same and continued to behave accordingly.

In 1988, a conference was convened in Denmark on the Kirillov orbit method in representation theory, first introduced in Sasha's dissertation. He was invited to attend the conference and to give a series of lectures at the University of Copenhagen. When Sasha went to the appropriate MSU department for his travel papers, the official in charge told him that he was cleared to submit an application to attend the conference but that the invitation said nothing about giving lectures. Although this was blatantly untrue (Sasha had the invitation in his pocket), he wisely refrained from arguing and received his travel papers.

Once arrived in Denmark, he asked a Danish official if he could extend his stay in Denmark in order to give his series of lectures. Of course he could, said the Danish official and gave him the appropriate document. But when Sasha went with it to the Soviet embassy, the Soviet official sternly asked where he had gotten that document and then began to shout: "Who gave you permission to talk to the Danish bureaucrats! You must leave Denmark at once and return to Moscow!" Sasha showed him his official invitation, told him that his lectures were already scheduled, and explained that his return ticked was dated two weeks from that date. The Soviet official said he would request instructions from Moscow by telex (the precursor to the fax), and that Sasha must come back to the embassy in the morning. This went on for five or six days, and every morning the official greeted him with an angry shout: "What, are you still here?" On day 7 the mysterious telex must have arrived because the official said with a frown that he could stay.

A year later, *perestroika* had advanced to the point that Sasha was permitted to travel to France. That same year, however, he was forbidden to travel to Israel, ostensibly because MSU was an "ideological" institution and Israel was an ideological adversary and a reactionary country.

Finally, in 1990, real changes came. In spring, Sasha was allowed to travel to Israel (in his private capacity and not as an MSU professor), and in the fall, to everyone's surprise, the administration had no objection to a semester-long assignment at the University of Maryland. Mark Freydlin was working there, and Pasha was working for the Holocaust Museum in Washington, DC. In this way, only three years after parting in Moscow, the three friends found themselves once more or less in the same city.

Sasha called Pasha the day he arrived, but they weren't able to get together right away: their two locations were 20 miles apart and unconnected by any public transportation, and neither of them had a car.

LIFE IN AMERICA

I think that the emails we exchanged after the summer of 2013 give the best picture of our relationship.

On 08/07/2013 08:40 PM, Pavel Ilyin wrote:

Greetings, signore!

So, first you weren't writing to me, then I wasn't writing to you, and then I wrote to you, or am writing to you now.

In late May — early June I went to Germany and from there to Georgia. I've been to Tbilisi several times, the last time was in spring 1982 right before we applied to emigrate. It was very nice to see all the old friends (the city of Tbilisi included) and to discover that many here still remember me. Ella and I went there to attend a conference celebrating the 70th birthday of our good friend Rezo Gachechiladze. You've seen him: he was toastmaster at my own 60th birthday party. In the first four days there I gave my lecture at the conference, spoke at the presentation of Rezo's book, said five toasts (including one in English) and gave two interviews, one for TV and one for the evening newspaper.

After all that was over, we were hosted by another old friend of ours who had once been a post-graduate student in Moscow. Some years ago he bought a house with a vineyard in Kakheti and served us wonderful wine in that house. It was a wonderful trip. But as soon as we got back, I found myself booked solid until we left for Maine. Where I am now resting in a state of utter nirvana.

How was your speech at Gelfand's birthday party? I've read a Wikipedia article about him (which mentions you as one of his students; you rate a separate mention, before the "et al."). I am waiting to hear from you about the prevailing mood in Moscow. Of course, I've heard about the situation at the Academy of Sciences. Do you think it can change from worse to less bad?

Say hi to Alex A. for me.

Did you get to see my relatives this time?

We've got lots to talk about. I'll be home on the 20th, and my birthday party is scheduled for the 24th.

Give my love to Louisa if you see her.

P. I.

P. S. If you have time, take a look at this: http://www.youtube.com/watch?v=yZTgv29IXbY —P.

Greetings, signore!

I'm glad that you've had a successful trip and your presentation went well. My laptop has no sound, so I could see your presentation but couldn't hear it. If you didn't look down all the time it would have been brilliant. But it looked good anyway.

Gelfand's party went OK. There were many top-notch mathematicians there and almost no administrators. A quick summary: as you recall, the speaker of the Russian parliament once famously stated that the parliament is not a place for debates. Well, the conference hall of the Russian Academy of Sciences, apparently, is not a place for scientific presentations.

I've walked around Moscow a bit; my legs get tired quickly, and I feel sleepy all the time. I can walk from Chistye Prudy (where we're staying) to the Bolshoy Karetny Lane (where my Institute is), though it does make me tired, but I've made the round trip twice now by different routes.

I missed your sister Yulia's birthday this year, and I didn't get to see Zhenya, either. I did go to see Bob Minlos[4] at his dacha on the Gorky branch of the Kursky road.

I went to the Independent University to attend a conference of young mathematicians. I also went to see the Kovalyovs. Sergey Adamovich isn't feeling well (he's already 84). Now we're getting ready to to the Yugo-Zapadnaya [South-West] metro again, not for a social visit but to collect our pension at a Sberbank branch.

Moscow is still an expensive city. A Metro ride costs 30 rubles ($1.33).

---

4 A Russian mathematician. *See* https://en.wikipedia.org/wiki/Robert_Minlos

I got a raise and am now making 24,000 rubles, plus 7,000 for my degree.

Dinner at a MuMu café [a chain of cafeteria-style restaurants] costs 250–300 rubles. (And beer at the Korston Hotel, the former Orlyonok Hotel, is 400 rubles a pint.) But people manage somehow.

That's all for now, see you soon (on the 24th?)

Sasha

How I Knew And Remember

Vadim Altskan

I am a friend and colleague of Pavel. I met Pavel and Ella in the mid–1990s while working at the Jewish Community Center in Rockville. I was taken by the complexity of their long and rich life they left behind, and at the same time, by their enthusiasm toward a new chapter of their life.

Pavel and Ella represent a famous, sadly famous, group of Soviet Jews known as refuseniks. They were among those people, who dared to express their desire to leave the Soviet Union, but were denied this right, and yet were no longer allowed to continue normal life and work in the USSR.

In fact, the story of Ella and Pavel's personal "exodus" is now a part of the recently opened Jewish Museum and Tolerance Center in Moscow, Russia, which displays a unique historical document from Ella and Pavel's family archive — a so called "exit visa" which they finally received in 1987.

Upon coming to America, Pavel and Ella faced yet another challenge — to find in the new country a place of their own. It was the time when I met Pavel. I was greatly impressed with his encyclopedic knowledge of geography.

It was a fortunate coincidence that I worked at that time at the Museum's Registry of Holocaust survivors, which needed a specialist with expertise in geographical names. And so, good things happen in life sometimes indeed soon, Pavel and I became colleagues. The Museum's staff welcomed Pavel with much appreciation for his skills.

For the next twenty years, Pavel was the Museum's only expert on historical maps and place names, and a unique resource for staff members, interns, scholars, researchers, and survivors and their families and anyone who came his way with question about geography.

There are not too many things in life as confusing as the East European political geography, with its ever-changing borders, place names and variations of spellings in dozen of languages. Pavel was one the few people in the world who had never been confused by such things. In fact, he was a true authority in this field. He knew not only all the places by their names and current geographical borders, but also why, when, and for how long these borders and names existed before they were changed again.

Pavel could answer any of these questions. However, he was a very humble and generous about his expertise. It did not matter to Pavel who asked him a question—a high school student, intern, or distinguished scholar, as long as this person needed Pavel's help. A phrase "I do not know" was never an option for Pavel as an answer. If he could not provide information on the spot, he would give an answer next morning, after checking countless books and maps. While dealing with the stream of geographical requests coming to the Museum, I've got used to referring them to Pavel, often with the remark: "Check with Pavel. If Pavel does not know this place, then this place probably never existed".

For the last two days, the Holocaust Memorial Museum flags have been flown half-staff in memory and honor of Pavel Ilyin. It is my honor to speak here on behalf of the Holocaust Museum, to pass on condolences from the museum's staff, and to give Pavel's family the flag presented by the Museum.

All the museum colleagues I spoke with during the last two days have mentioned Pavel's special open smile, and this is how he will be remembered.

March 15th, 2015

Remembering Pavel Ilyin

Tatyana Runova

I got to know Pavel in the mid-60s of the last century, when he joined the Institute of Geography of the Academy of Sciences of the USSR. Although he had already worked as an economic geographer at Giprogor, a Moscow-based urban planning agency, he joined us as a junior researcher — the standard job title for young scientists. That was the time when our department of economic geography was changing course from its traditional focus on specific country studies to topical research. This shift had been initiated and was being championed by our youthful and talented department head, Aleksey Aleksandrovich Mintz, who was then just beginning to be known in the field. Like any significant change, it was met with predictable opposition from the establishment, comprised of economic geographers who had come to prominence in the 1940–1950s and were behind the "Blue Book" series — over 20 volumes of exhaustive studies in economic geography of all economic regions and republics of the Soviet Union.

After his new policy resulted in the resignation of several dissenters, Aleksey Mintz shored up his position by filling the vacancies with younger scientists who had some prior experience working for scientific or planning organizations, had distinguished themselves in some way and were progressing toward their advanced degrees. With my newly awarded Candidate's degree,[5] I was one of the first to be hired. Soon, our department came to also include Inga Kantzebovskaya, Yuri Pivovarov, Yuri Vedenin, Igor Zorin, Aleksandr Levintov, and others. They all later became prominent scientists (most of them earned their doctorates) and even pioneered new areas of study.

Pavel Ilyin was part of this "draft". He joined the group that was working on practical applications of geography by developing methods of analyzing local physical environments and natural resources. Using his urban planning experience from Giprogor, he took on the analysis of physical environments for purposes of urban planning.

---

[5] https://en.wikipedia.org/wiki/Candidate_of_Sciences

This was a very timely and needed work, because the Soviet Union was actively developing its natural resources, especially in Siberia, and new towns and villages were springing up near their locations. I remember the presentations he gave on this subject at the Geographical Society and at several conferences, presentations that were received with great interest — in part because unlike other, more prominent geographers that used comparative scoring methods of analysis, Pavel analyzed the physical environment in economic terms, in terms of the cost of development. I would like to stress the courage and novelty of this approach, because cost matters were then the preserve of economists, who were barely beginning to broach the issue of natural resources.

Importantly, Pavel used his theoretical and methodological work to develop a detailed map of our country that showed different areas, their physical environments and their cost impact on development. As far as I know, his map was widely used in Giprogor urban planning projects. This work served as a basis for his Candidate's thesis, which he had successfully defended by 1970, and as a point of departure for his subsequent research. It is a great pity that his scientific work was interrupted by emigration, since in his native country he had by then become an authority in his field and might have soon produced further significant achievements.

But there was more to life than science, and Pavel was always interested in all aspects of life. I remember how in 1970 or 1971 our newly rejuvenated department celebrated its first successes, including a prize from the Institute of Geography of the Academy of Sciences for our scientific achievements: we all went on a three-day river cruise together down the Volga river to the city of Uglich. Many of us brought our children. Fun and excitement overflowed, and Pavel Ilyin presided over it as the event organizer. Ella, his wife, "mothered" everyone, making endless sandwiches and handing them out through the deckside window of their cabin to all the hungry souls hanging out on deck around that center of attraction.

Our shared work and our youth helped us all become family friends. I will never forget our trip to Pushkin Hills over the winter school break during the severe winter of 1977–78. Almost a dozen people went, including Genrietta Privalovskaya, V. Avanesova, Pavel and Ella, and myself, including our kids. It was so cold on the train ride to Pskov that everyone slept with their coats and shoes on in their compartments. I remember how we had to literally sprint around Pskov to keep warm on our sightseeing tour, and our dinner at the train station restaurant where Genrietta and I gave our sons, who were in 9th or 10th grade, a small glass of wine to warm them up. The buses to Pushkin Hills were not running because the engines had frozen up — until we got some cash together, and the engines miraculously started. In Pushkin Hills we found unheated hotel rooms, but thankfully the electricity was on, and so our "hostess", Ella, kept the hot tea ready for us in their room, which served as the group's sitting room. That tea was especially welcome, and tea-time was especially cheerful and convivial, after our outings to the surrounding villages of Mikhailovskoye, Trigorskoye and Petrovskoye — on foot, or on skis, or in horse-driven sleighs operated by local drivers, who were still friendly at that time.

And on New Year's Eve, Father Frost (the Russian Santa) came to visit, complete with a bag of presents for everyone: our younger kids squealed in delight and ran clattering up and down the hallways while the older kids peered suspiciously at the house slippers peeking out from under his suit, made from a fur coat turned inside-out. This special treat was brought to us by Pasha, the acknowledged leader of our crowd of women and children. And the trip gained even more luster when the kids learned that the beloved radio personality of Zahkar the Riddleman (Zakhar Zagadkin) was traveling with them! And after the trip, all of us got invited to the Moscow Conservatory to hear his talented daughter Nadya give her first piano recital — with a reception to follow, appropriately, at their hospitable home.

That was our life. Time has passed, many things have changed. New people joined our department, and few people remain who were there during these times I am remembering. As the Russian poet Aleksandr Pushkin said, some are no more, and others, far away. That was and is the way of it. We must be grateful for the goodness and kindness that was. We're grateful to you, Pavel.

A Toast to Pavel Ilyin

Pavel Polian

AUGUST 1974: YOUNG AND NAIVE

In August 1974 I reported to my first post-graduation job placement at the Institute of Geography of the Academy of Sciences (IGAN) as a research intern at the department of economic geography, with a salary of a mere 95 rubles a month. The only person I knew there was the head of the department, Georgy Mikhailovich Lappo. I had met him once or twice before in the home of Isaak Moiseyevich Mayergoyz, my university professor who had also taught him.

At first, I didn't fully appreciate the extent of my good fortune in landing this job. I've had a chance to visit a few dozen Soviet research institutes (certainly not all) and have spoken with people from another few dozen. Based on this unscientific sampling, I will say that our IGAN was the most liberal place of work in the entire Academy of Sciences system and the most respectful of its researchers and their natural freedoms. This was less a function of our flexible work schedule than of the atmosphere that had gradually formed at the Institute and was being carefully nurtured. The freedom and flexibility we enjoyed did not lead to anarchy but produced in us a sense of responsibility, and our productivity was orders of magnitude higher than if we had been required to toil at our desks day in and day out.

I worked at the Institute for 43 years (sic!) under three different directors: Innokenty Petrovich Gerasimov, Vladimir Mikhailovich Kotlyakov and Olga Nikolayevna Solomina. I can say that each of them appreciated our flexible schedule and did their part to protect it. They all were aware that such flexibility not only was fair in itself and attractive to the employees but also that it produced better results for the Institute and for Soviet science.

We had one regular "office day" a week when we came in to meet on current work issues, discuss recent presentations and generally interact with one another. This was amply sufficient. We also came in to attend all-hands staff meetings, scientific presentations on relevant topics, and — of course — to receive our pay, which was distributed in cash twice a month.

Our management justified this to the higher-ups by pointing out that our space was so tight that people were physically unable to do research while crammed together like sardines. All our researchers worked at home or at the public library, which allowed them to spend their time both on work and their personal needs, but they appreciated the trust placed in them by our management and did not abuse it, putting their work responsibilities first. I got so used to working from home that I continued to do so during my time in Germany, when I had a wonderful office at my disposal.

MY DEPARTMENT

When I joined IGAN as a research intern, I had already been immersed in geography, in one way or another, for ten or eleven years: five happy years at university (under Mayergoyz!) plus another five or six years of competing in various geography contests, especially the radio game show "Exploring Our Country." I had won enough of them to begin to feel at home at IGAN right away.

Much time has passed since that August; many memories have been overwritten by later events, but I still recall some of my impressions from that time.

The first people I met were our three lab technicians: Vera Avanesova, Lyuba Obolonkina and Nadya (Nadezhda Pavlovna) Merzlikina. In my research into population issues, I worked especially closely with Nadya, who was reliable, thorough and also kind. I worked with her for years and even decades, with much pleasure and gratitude.

The department I joined included a strong group of colleagues who specialized in environmental management. The group was headed by Aleksey Mintz himself, then — after he passed away in 1973 — by Henrietta Alekseyevna Privalovskaya and Tatyana Grigoryevna Runova, and included Inga Veniaminovna Kantsebovskaya and Tatyana Petryakova.

The group also included Tatyana Nefedova and Ira Volkova, although both of them joined the Institute later. So, too, did Andrey Treyvish, my best friend at the time. Fairly soon, and quite predictably, Andrey became the strongest and most brilliant of our economic geographers.

Our department head, Lappo, continued to nurture the topical research pioneered by A. A. Mintz, but alongside it he began intentionally and carefully to advance his own area of interest: population geography. He recruited prominent scientists such as Grigory Abramovich Goltz or Zhanna Antonovna Zaionchkovskaya.

PASHA ILYIN

Our department's academic secretary, Pasha (Pavel Mikhailovich) Ilyin, worked both in environmental geography and population geography, the two major fields of study in our department. In September 1974 he came back from vacation and immediately marched up to me with one of his disarming, myopic smiles and with his hand extended for a handshake. He was so easy to relate to, right from the start!

Within the first five minutes it emerged that I was talking to a walking legend: Zahkar the Riddleman and Tony Galley, both together, in person! A worthy son of his father and himself a credentialed and experienced geographer, he had taken over his father's radio show.

Within a week I was invited to his warm and welcoming home, which was run by his wife, Ella Kagan. Pavel and Ella had met in the early 1960s at Giprogor, an urban planning agency. While Ella was setting the table in the kitchen, Pasha showed me his Zahkar the Riddleman corner: his father's books, a collection of little striped-shirted sailor figurines made of every possible material and, of course, a whole filing box (if not two) filled with the addresses and scores of the kids who wrote in to Zakhar's game show. There was also the ancient typewriter with round keys on which Zahkar the Riddleman had typed his letters to my own schoolboy self, assisted first by Mikhail Ilyin and then by another Ilyin: Pavel, the same man who now stood beside me, looking at me with a youthful smile.

Lighthearted and fun-loving, he loved to sit and have drinks with his friends, though never to excess. What he enjoyed most was not the drinking itself but the convivial atmosphere, and he was ever ready to put business aside and have a feast. That's why he loved Georgia so much — a culture where (unlike in Russia) feasting is serious business. The venerable Georgian ritual of toasting requires more from its practitioners than a mere gift of gab: it calls for a certain refinement of expression rooted in a centuries-old tradition of public oratory.

Pavel tried to instill his love of ritual at home. He made his own special kind of vodka, which he kept in a special bottle and served chilled in a special way, accompanied by a sort of incantation.

Yet this wasn't what defined him. At his core, he was an intellectual, a man of culture and decency with a special talent for friendship, always willing and prepared to help someone in need even without being asked. Witnessing meanness in others always left him bewildered, although he did not like to judge.

He was a voracious reader (oh the ineffable joys of *samizdat!*) and considered his twin passions — poetry and geography — to be sister disciplines. I, too, share these passions, and they were part of what brought us close.

PASHA'S ROOTS

He was born on August 24, 1936, i.e., he was 38 when me met. His home consisted of two tiny, smoky rooms in a communal apartment in an apartment building that stood on Pushechnaya street and pre-dated the Revolution. The first room served as the children's room as well as the living room; the second belonged to the parents. Both par-ents — Mikhail Ilyich (descended from Krakow intellectuals) and Sofia Ilyinichna (descended from Surozh merchants) — were journalists: the father ran a column in the newspaper *Trud,* as we would say now. Ac-cording to their daughter-in-law, they had old-fashioned, aristocratic manners and used the Russian formal "you plural" even to address each other. Their children included Pavel and his younger sister Yulia as well as their orphaned cousin Volodya whose parents had perished in Sta-lin's repressions. The Ilyins shared the apartment with another family as well as with Vera, Mikhail Ilyich's sister. Cousin Volodya slept in her room for lack of other space.

Mikhail Ilyich spent every waking moment working. Reserved and private, he was also a prankster and daydreamer (an unlikely combina-tion) and liked to involve his son in his inventions, teaching him to love geography and maps along the way, so it's not surprising that Pavel be-gan to win one prize after another at MSU geography contests for pri-mary school students.

During the war the family was evacuated, first to Omsk, then in Alma-Ata. A year and a half later, in 1943, they returned to Moscow, and all seemed well for a while…

In 1944 Pasha went to school; he was a little over 14 on November 1, 1950 when his father was arrested. In 1952, after he turned 16, Pasha transferred to night school and went to work at a factory; he was now the family's sole breadwinner. But geography lived on in his soul, and when he won another contest (a rare case for a night school student!), he was noticed by Professor Saoushkin. "What are your plans after high school, young man?" the professor asked. "I assume you'll apply to our program?" Pasha told him candidly about the black marks on his re-cord: one for being a Jew, another for being the son of an "enemy of the people." To Saoushkin's credit, he ignored these things utterly, and — oh joy! — in 1954 Pasha was admitted to the MSU.

His father came back in 1956. In 1960, after graduation, the son went to work for Giprogor, where he stayed until 1965. Among the planning projects he participated in were those located in three oblasts (Sverdlovskaya, Gorkovskaya and Ryazanskaya); the Mordovskaya autonomous republic; several industrial districts: Orsko-Khalilovsky in Orenburgskaya oblast, Serovo-Ivdelsky in Sverdlovskaya oblast, and Igrim-Beryozovsky in Tyumenskaya oblast; and general plans of the towns of Ryazhsk in Ryazanskaya oblast, Kirzhach in Vladmirskaya oblast, and Ust-Kut in Irkutskaya oblast.

Pasha's work at Giprogor and IGAN involved a fair amount of travel. Of course, the Soviet Union was reluctant to let people go abroad, especially those without a Communist Party membership. But the number of cities within the Soviet Union he was able to visit during his lifetime exceeded three hundred!

In 1965, IGAN's graduate program began accepting applications. Some people he knew at IGAN told him that the department of economic geography was changing its focus and would be needing people with a more practical background like himself. And, miraculously, Pavel Ilyin — a Jew — was admitted despite the Six-Day War!

Now his life was very different: he was around prominent scientists; he was in charge of his own work schedule and his own workload. The department was then headed by Aleksey Aleksandrovich Mintz, a young and talented scientist brimming with new ideas and full of energy for implementing them. Geographers engaged in conventional regional studies found themselves having to switch to topical studies.

Mintz was also Pavel Ilyin's academic advisor. In 1971, Pavel successfully defended his thesis on the economic impact of the environment on urban construction in the USSR.[1]

The life of the department was disrupted by Mintz's death in an airplane crash in Prague in February 1973. This was a tragedy for science and for everyone who worked with him, including Pasha Ilyin, who by then was the department's academic secretary. However, the appointment of G. M. Lappo as the new department head, whose background — like Pavel's — was more practical than academic solidified Pavel's standing in the department.

---

[1] Опыт экономической оценки природных условий градостроительства //Известия Академии наук СССР. Сер. геогр. 1970. № 6. С. 44–54; О географии жилищного хозяйства // География сферы обслуживания. Ред. В. В. Покшишевский. Вопросы географии. Сб. 91. М.: Мысль. 1972. С. 164–175.

The shift in the department's focus coincided with an evolution in Pavel's own interests, i.e., his move toward social geography. Perhaps a further nudge in that direction came from his friendship with the philosopher Aleksandr Samoylovich Akhiyezer; the two of them began to look at ways to analyze social issues in a given territory almost immediately after Pasha had defended his thesis.

Ilyin's stature as a scientist was growing, as evidenced by the invitation he received from V. V. Pokshishev to become a co-editor of a publication of the Moscow branch of the Geographical Society dealing with issues of migrant populations in the USSR. Here, too, Akhiyezer was his co-author: their article in that magazine analyzed the motivational basis of migration.[2]

1976 was a big year in Soviet geography: the country hosted the XXIIIth International Geographic Congress. Our director, Academician Innokentiy Petrovich Gerasimov, chaired the conference organizing committee; Yury Vladimirovich Medvedkov was program chair to the conference. All of us — IGAN staffers — had our jobs, too. For example, G. M. Lappo chaired a workshop on the geography of urbanization, and I was Sancho Panza to his Don Quixote, i.e., the workshop organizer. Pasha Ilyin served as the organizer of the session on Geography in Education, Publishing, and the Dissemination of Geographic Knowledge chaired by V. P. Maksakovsky and L. S. Abramov. Together, Pasha and I organized one of the numerous working groups that were held after the Congress; ours was held in Belarus, and Pasha wrote an excellent travel guide to Belarus for working group members.[3]

Meanwhile, Pasha was still trying to find his place in the field of social geography and urban planning. One of his themes was the impact of municipal administration on growth;[4] another dealt with the growth foci in regional development.[5]

EXPLORING HIS BELOVED SECOND HOMELAND

In June 1982 Pavel Ilyin, his wife Ella and their daughter Nadya, an aspiring musician, applied for permission to undertake a trip far from the Soviet Fatherland — i.e., to emigrate.

---

[2] See *List of Publications*.
[3] Ibid.
[4] Ibid.
[5] Ibid.

For five tough years, from 1982 to 1987, the Ilyins lived as *refuseniks*. They outlived two Communist Party heads, Konstantin Chernenko and Yury Andropov, who died during that time. Thankfully, Pasha was not fired from his job at the publishing house specializing in encyclopedias (a job he got thanks to his friend Sasha Gorkin, then editor of the geography desk, later head of the publishing house) but he was demoted in punishment for seeking to emigrate. And Ella was fired from her job at an urban planning institute. Life was tough, and I was happy when I was able to find paying work for them, even low-level work such as typing up manuscripts. Those were quite sophisticated manuscripts, though: articles by Professor Mayergoyz and poetry by Osip Mandelstam!

The Ilyins received their permission to emigrate under Mikhail Gorbachev, in June 1987.

They emigrated to the United States, settling first in Boston, then permanently in Bethesda, MD. Their Soviet geographer colleagues stayed with them during their ever more frequent visits to America, spent time in their hospitable home and brought back stories about their life and greetings to their friends back in Russia.

In 1991 I, too, found myself in the United States while attending a conference on Osip Mandelstam's work in the New York City. And in 1999 I returned for two back-to-back internships: one in Washington at the Holocaust Museum, another at Princeton University working on Osip Mandelstam's poetry.

It was Pasha who found me a cheap but adequate hotel that allowed me to have breakfast at a hospital cafeteria during certain hours. It was only two or three metro stops from the Holocaust Museum, where Pasha was working at the time—as a geographer unraveling the complicated geography and toponymy of the Holocaust! It was Pasha who led me, as my personal Virgil, through the maze of this excellent (and very American) institution and introduced me to all the right people. Once he arranged for me to be interviewed by Vladimir Frumkin, a friend of his from the Voice of America; I think it was my first radio interview.

I spent several weekends with the Ilyins at their Bethesda home. Pasha and Ella answered my many questions and drove me around, proudly showing off their American "antiquities" (not all that ancient, of course), including a whole big bookstore filled with Russian émigré literature. When my ancient Soviet-era suitcase broke, they bought me a new American suitcase that I used for a long time afterwards.

What the Ilyins experienced in America—ordinary courtesy and kindness—stood in stark contrast to the Soviet Union, where people were treated like dirt. Pasha's enchantment with America grew as he learned more about it and about ordinary Americans: their sense of inner freedom coupled with a sense of responsibility, their relationship with the government — a relationship of equals — and many other things, including their patriotism that was genuine and not imposed from above. The more he traveled across the country, the more he felt himself an American patriot, and his fridge became a repository for souvenir magnets from every state he visited.

Pasha published almost nothing during the 1980s — understandably so: the decade included his years as a *refusenik* back home and the first years of getting settled in his new country. But during that time a new and quite serious research topic was germinating in his mind: toponymy, and specifically the analysis of the practice of geographical renaming in the USSR and the logic behind it. In 1993 and 1994 it erupted into two mighty publications in English and Russian[6] that drew on Pavel Ilyin's greatest strengths as a geographer and researcher: his inquisitiveness and the breadth of his scholarship.

I should also mention some of Pasha's other interests and publications in America, both scientific and personal. One of them is traditional urban geography, expressed in essays or book reviews about Washington, Leningrad and, most importantly, Moscow, such as the book *Moscow At The Turn Of The 20th Century: A Glance Into The Past From Afar*[7] that included four chapters written or co-authored by Pasha. Besides this, he also became an expert in and an advocate for American patriotic songs, publishing a Russian-language article about three such songs in his own Russian translation.[8] But perhaps the most important area was his Holocaust research from the geographic, cartographic and toponymic standpoint. Here he became a real expert, fully justifying the solemnity of his job title as Chief Geographer of the Holocaust Museum in Washington, DC.

Pavel passed away at his Bethesda home on March 12, 2015...

---

[6] Ilyin P. Changing of Cities Names in the CIS as a Reflection of Soviet History // *27th International Geographical Congress. Technical Program*. Abstracts. Washington, 1992. P. 273–274; Ibid. Renaming of Soviet Cities after Exceptional People: A Historical Perspective on Toponymy // *Post–Soviet Geography*. December 1993. P. 631–660

[7] Ильин П., Рубл Б. (отв. Ред.). *Москва рубежа XIX и XX столетий. Взгляд в прошлое издалека*. М.: РОССПЭН, 2004, 302 с.

[8] Ильин П. «Эта земля моя, она прекрасна, Боже, храни ее!» Три патриотические песни Америки //*Время и место* (Нью-Йорк). 2011. Вып. 4 (20). С. 116–137.

Recollection by Nancy
and Tony Allison-Fisher

NANCY:

In 1978, I was a 23-year-old graduate student at the University of London, studying under R. A. (Tony) French. My research was focused on the city of Moscow — specifically, its transportation networks and land use patterns, an eminently geographical theme. When the university granted me travel funds to spend a month doing research in Moscow, Tony French sent me off with a list of professional contacts. Just two years prior, the International Geographical Congress had convened in Moscow. Dr. French and many other British and American geographers had developed ties with their Soviet colleagues, both in academia and at the Institute of Geography of the USSR Academy of Sciences. Pavel Ilyin, a scholar at the Institute, was on my list; dutifully, I contacted him. Immediately, Pavel offered to meet with me, in order to discuss my work and perhaps even advise me. To organize our meeting, he gave me the first of many similar instructions to come: Ride the metro to such-and-such a station, exit onto the platform, stand by the last car — we'll find one another there. I described my appearance: long, dark hair; not very tall; wearing a "Scottish" coat (I didn't yet know how to say "plaid" in Russian). I would have stood out like a sore thumb anyway, but these clues were effective for our initial meeting. We strolled to an elegant little café in central Moscow, where we shared our academic interests. It didn't take long for me to realize that I was sitting in the presence of someone with encyclopedic (not to mention deeply personal) knowledge of Moscow.

I cannot recall at what point we inaugurated our regular walking tours around the city, but it must have soon thereafter — I was only in Moscow for that one month in late 1978. Pavel didn't merely know his way around the city; he was a treasure-trove of information, familiar with every lane, every building, and even the history of the buildings' occupants. My fascination with architectural history is rooted in those walks with Pavel. To my delight, Ella joined us on these strolls. Who isn't immediately enamored of Ella? One snowy Sunday, Pavel and Ella took me to a working church along the Boulevard Ring. The smell of incense, glow of candles, and sounds of chanting affected me in a spiritual way. As we left the church, Pavel gently asked whether I practiced any particular religion. Now, Pavel and Ella already had assumed that I was Jewish (surname, appearance), while I was naively trying to cover this fact. Oh yes, I replied, I was connected to a very ancient religion. "You're Jewish, then," Pavel and Ella said — and added, "So are we." This tribal connection added greatly to what was already a strong intellectual meeting of minds. Eventually, Pavel and Ella invited me to their home, where I met Nadya, Mariam Abramovna, and Ella's father, Isaak. Little did I imagine that my relationship with this extraordinary family would continue until the present day. Although Pavel is no longer among us, he remains in my mind's eye, whether along a narrow Moscow street or in the halls of the U.S. Holocaust Memorial Museum, where his colleagues clearly adored him. I am profoundly grateful to have known Pavel Ilyin.

ANTONY:

My memories begin at a later date, in a different epoch, but also in Moscow. Nancy and I had met in graduate school at the University of Washington in Seattle, where she was earning a PhD in Geography. In January of 1986 I was sent by a Seattle-based Soviet-American fishing company to open their new office in Moscow. I was fluent in Russian and had lived previously in the Soviet Union. By the time I left for Moscow, Nancy and I had become engaged, but she stayed behind to finish her Ph D.

A couple of weeks after arriving in Moscow, I called a telephone number Nancy had given me for her friends Pavel and Ella. It was snowy and muddy in Moscow, and I was lonely and struggling to get our business office running in the face of daunting bureaucratic obstacles and delays. I called from a phone booth on the street, the usual practice to avoid listening in by Soviet security services. Gorbachev had come to power nine months before, and change was in the air, but the familiar rules of living in Soviet Union still held: one had to be careful of endangering Russian friends by contacting them openly.

"I want to see you!" Ella said as soon as I explained who I was and my connection to Nancy. "You must come over to our apartment as soon as possible!" This began a tradition of riding the Metro to the bedraggled but charming historical district of Baumanskoye and having dinner at their place. It became a kind of refuge for me from the official world of being a new American businessman in Moscow. Grandmother Maria Abramovna was there, quietly friendly toward me, and so was teen-age Nadya, a strikingly bright and precocious kid who looked much like her mother. The food Ella made was beyond delicious — far better than I could ever get in the hotel where I was living — and the talk even better. The hours would roll by as we discussed Russian literature, science, and the rapidly evolving political scene of Perestroika. The conversations were bolstered by shots of Pavel's home-brewed Ilynka vodka, which went in superlative combination with zakuski of marinated mushrooms also prepared by Pavel.

On weekends the three of us sometimes took walks around Baumanskoye or ranged further afield to monasteries or tsarist-era estates. Soon I became aware of the massively detailed, integrated encyclopedia that Pavel carried around in his brain. He was never showy about it, but just answered my many inquiries with quietly stated facts, amusing digressions about figures and places, and humorous observations on Russian and Soviet society. I soon learned that his father was a legendary radio personality called "Zakhar Zagadkin" or Zakhar the Riddle-Man, who displayed a similar broad erudition and good-naturedness on his regular show for children. When I asked other Moscow friends of Pavel's generation about this, they fondly remembered listening to Zakhar Zagadkin as kids.

When Pavel turned 50, Ella arranged a raucous birthday party. I arrived at their small, book-filled apartment, and found it packed and noisy. Ilynka flowed freely. Witty, off-color poems were recited by Pavel and others. Songs by banned bards were sung or shouted to the strum and pick of a guitar. It was a joyous, hedonistic tribute to Pavel by a large group of his friends, who were Russian intelligenty and, in some cases, refuseniks like Pavel and Ella. The toasts to Pavel were eloquent, loving, hilarious, and endless.

Nancy and I were married in the US in the summer of 1986. By April of 1987 we had a newborn son and were living in our own apartment on October Square. My company's Moscow office was thriving. By then Gorbachev's reforms had taken hold, and life in Moscow was rapidly shifting. We kept up our visits to Ella and Pavel's apartment, but now they could visit us as well without much trepidation. They were hoping that their time as refuseniks would soon be over. Then, suddenly, they received permission and left for the US. Now we were the ones left behind in Moscow.

We managed to visit them several times in Washington DC over the following years Once, when I was in Washington DC on business, Pavel gave me an unforgettable, excruciatingly vivid "inside tour" of the Holocaust Museum, where he worked identifying obscure geographic locations in Eastern Europe and Russia where Jews had lived before they were slaughtered. Afterward we decamped, at my urging, to a nearby bar for several needed shots of vodka.

Ella and Pavel came to Seattle twice over the years, and once to our island dacha, where Pavel was delighted by a funky, rural Fourth of July parade. It was 2011, and our talk turned, as always, to Russia — now about how it had sadly swung back toward authoritarianism. By then Pavel's health had begun to fade, but his acumen, warm spirit, and sense of humor never did. That was the last time I saw him: a sustaining, happy memory of relaxing and sipping vodka, though no longer Ilynka, in summer weather on an island in Puget Sound, a world away from wintry Moscow where we first met.

My Time With Pasha Ilyin

Revaz Gachechiladze

I 've known Pasha Ilyin since the mid-1970s. That's over 40 years! A long time, but it feels like yesterday.

We met in 1975. He came to Tbilisi, Georgia to attend an event — it may have been a meeting of the Geographical Society or a nation-wide geography conference. I do remember that it was the year before the meeting of the International Geographical Congress in Moscow, and I believe we talked about taking the Georgian delegates sightseeing around Moscow after the Congress.

Although Pasha was six or seven years older than me (40 years ago that meant something; as we got older, we felt more like peers), we "clicked" right away. We had a similar education and similar family backgrounds: both our fathers were writers. We even had similar tastes in literature! I remember well Pasha's excellent writing style and the ease and speed with which he edited my conference paper, correcting my non-native Russian.

In 1979, a Soviet-Indian geographical seminar was held in Moscow. The seminar continued in Tbilisi and included an excursion to the Georgian wine-producing province of Kakheti and then on to the city of Baku in neighboring Azerbaijan. Russian geographers from the Moscow-based Russian geographical society far outnumbered our guests from India. Pasha, cheerful and gregarious, was — as usual — one of the seminar organizers and its informal leader, the soul of the party. Together with another man, he brought an enameled pail filled with the local vintage to our Intourist hotel in the provincial capital of Telavi, and our merry band of geographers used an aluminum mug also supplied by Pasha to toast international peace and cooperation — although our Indian colleagues, who were tea-totalers to a man, abstained.

We passed through the Georgian town of Lagodekhi and crossed into Azerbaijan, stopping for the night in the hospitable town of Nukha (now Shaki). There, we got no wine but were served some excellent tea instead, and Pasha Ilyin summarized our geographical and cultural findings thusly: "Now I know where Europe ends and Asia begins: after Lagodekhi!"

When Pasha and Ella moved to America, with their daughter whom Pasha adored, we lost touch — fortunately, only temporarily. Then came 1991, bringing Georgian independence and freedom: a difficult time at first, but the Iron Curtain was gone, and with it all the bureaucratic Communist Party formalities and restrictions on travel and correspondence. And so we found Pasha again.

When I visited the U.S. in the 1990s, giving lectures and attending conferences, I was more than once welcomed by Pasha and Ella at their cozy home in Bethesda, near Washington, DC, and invited to stay the night, which was very thoughtful of them in those lean times. Pasha was delighted that they were able to see deer around their condominium, and that the deer were not afraid of people.

I did not know the origin of the name "Bethesda". But when, in 1998, fate (in the person of Eduard Shevardnadze, the first president of independent Georgia) sent me to Israel as the first ambassador of Georgia, I found there, in the great city of Jerusalem, the original Bethsaida — the source of the name!

In 2013 I was finally able to lure Pasha and Ella to Tbilisi, to an international conference at which my young colleagues from the geography department, for some odd reason, had decided to celebrate my 70th birthday. They hadn't been there in a long time. Back in the 1980s, Ella had visited Tbilisi and had been appalled at the city's traffic problems. She told her urban planner colleagues, and me, that if urgent measures were not taken, the city would begin to choke in 20–25 years.

Her words proved prophetic! And now, in 2013, she saw her prophecy fulfilled. But we put her and Pasha up at a hotel near the Tbilisi State University, the site of the conference, which greatly simplified the Ilyins' commute.

Pasha showed up leaning on a cane but with his sparkling wit intact, and his presentation on the moving borders in Europe during WWII was received with great enthusiasm by the young geographers.

Pasha and I periodically exchanged health updates. His condition did not seem too grave... but what did we know!

And now he's gone, this big-hearted man, wonderful friend, husband, father and grandfather.

We, his old friends, will miss him greatly.

But we will remember him as a true Man who was good at friendship, writing, humor, who lived a life worthy of a man.

Professor Revaz Gachechiladze, Ph.D. and D. Sc. in Political and Economic Geography, is a Corresponding Member of the Georgian National Academy of Sciences, Ambassador, and former President of the Georgian Geographical Society.

A Geographer's Geographer-Memories
of Pavel Ilyin

Robert Gohstand

My wife Maureen and I first met Pavel and his family in 1984, when I was on a research trip to the Soviet Union. Introduced by a mutual friend.

I was immediately impressed by his friendliness, warmth, and passionate interest in the world around him and in the field of geography. His wife, Ella Kagan, and daughter, Nadya, were equally friendly and lively conversationalists. I found him a kindred spirit in his interest in the historical geography of Moscow and in the study of maps. In subsequent meetings he and Ella (a planner and urban historian) took me on enthusiastic and information-packed tours of Moscow districts. We also shared a certain propensity to collect interesting information and things, and to tinker. Books and maps absorbed us both, and we could not resist new acquisitions. Pavel's command of geographical facts seemed inexhaustible and we spent happy times poring over maps of Moscow. Certainly he contributed markedly to my research on all subjects Russian, but particularly on Moscow.

In those days, I recall that he was an enthusiastic mushroom picker and pickler and was very proud of the final product, which was vigorously salted. To accompany his mushrooms, he would bring out alcoholic infusions of his own secret formulas, some of which required considerable courage to ingest. He also had a marvelous collection of souvenir miniature sailors collected in ports all over the USSR. Since we shared an interest in things maritime, (I was an officer in the U. S. Naval Reserve), I was mightily impressed by this collection of Soviet jack tars. Unfailingly hospitable as the Ilyins were, we spent very pleasant times in their apartment and were introduced to, besides Pavel's concoctions, many examples of Russian and Georgian cuisine.

The Ilyin family was numbered among the so-called "refuseniks," Jewish families who sought, and were denied, the right to emigrate and who suffered loss of position and discrimination as a result. Despite this, the Ilyins were resolutely optimistic and cheerful in the face of adversity.

We parted from them with sadness and hope for a brighter future.

Once back in the States, I made some small contribution to the effort to assist in their departure from the Soviet Union by enlisting the support of the Association of American Geographers, which at its annual meeting passed a resolution of support which I had written. We were delighted when we got the news that the Ilyins were on their way to America via Vienna and Italy.

Despite the difficulties which most new immigrants endure, the Ilyins proceeded to carve out successful new careers. Pavel eventually became a cherished and respected staff member of the Holocaust Museum, where he was the acknowledged expert on maps and places. He authored numerous research papers on place names and locations which helped Holocaust survivors and their descendants identify their home localities. His personal library on various subjects, but particularly on Russia and Moscow, continued to grow and again we had much in common in our bibliographic interests. He also became an ardent American patriot and citizen, driven by his innate belief in the ideals of justice and freedom advanced in the American dream, however imperfect it may have been in reality. He wrote lovingly-researched articles on several American patriotic songs, reflecting his always optimistic view of America's future as an example to the world.

One touching gesture performed by Pavel was his insistence on making a gift of most of his sailor figurine collection to me. Despite my demurrals, most of his little guys took up residence in my university office, where for years they beamed down on visitors from every shelf. They surround me even now as I write in my home office and make Pavel's presence as a fellow sailor hover over me.

Since we lived on opposite coasts, our opportunities to meet were not as frequent as we would have liked, but he and Ella managed some visits to California and Maureen and I to Washington, and he was often on the phone with new ideas for research and to pass the time of day. We also met at geographic conferences, where he could be expected to always take the stage with a new and interesting paper.

Pavel's absence is keenly felt by everyone who knew him, but the memories of his joy in life and in knowing the world will live on and serve as an example to us all.

Pavel, Pasha…

Vladimir Frumkin

They say the older we get, the harder it is to make friends. I have found it to be true. With age, my own narrow circle of close friends has stopped growing. I still meet new people but none of them become intimates, people who understand me so completely they can finish my sentences. Almost none: one new acquaintance did become a close friend.

We met soon after I moved from Oberlin, OH to Washington, DC to work for the Russian service of the Voice of America. I rented a room at a colleague's house located within a ten minutes' walk from the VOA. Another colleague, who lived next door, rented a room to a new immigrant from Moscow who had moved there from Massachusetts to write a paper on geography on a fellowship from the Kennan Institute. Eight or so years prior to that, I myself had received a grant from the Kennan Institute, albeit for a paper that was in a very different field from geography: I was studying the twin phenomena of Soviet pop song and its unofficial, semi-clandestine competitor — the work of "bards", independent singer-songwriters who sang their uncensored songs, accompanying themselves on the guitar. Now I expected this new acquaintance, to all appearances a nice, sociable man, to become a pleasant addition to my "outer circle" and no more than that. But something unexpected happened: some mysterious centripetal force soon carried Pavel Ilyin from the outer circle into the most exclusive inner sanctum of my friendship. Soon he was no longer "Pavel" to me but "Pasha", a companion who was a pleasure to talk to and equally fun to drink a glass with, especially a glass of his own aromatic, home-made "Ilyinka" (he never did tell me his recipe)…

One day Pasha came to see me carrying a bottle of kosher Manisch-ewicz wine instead of his customary Ilyinka. This was early in our acquaintance, in the spring, on the day of Pesach — the Jewish Passover, which I was spending alone because my wife and daughter were in Oberlin, and none of my numerous Jewish colleagues at the Voice of America had thought to invite me over. There came a knock on the door, and there was Pasha on the doorstep with a package in his hands, from which he produced a bottle of Manischewicz, some matzoh, an egg, the traditional apple-nut mixture called charoset, some greens...

"Have you got wine glasses? plates?" asked my surprise visitor. "Look, I even got the maror, the bitter herbs, for it is written: 'on all other nights we eat all different kinds of vegetables, but on this night we eat maror, because the Egyptians made bitter our ancestors' lives in Egypt'..."

Well, what do you know, I thought. Why did I ever doubt him? It turned out that Pasha Ilyin was a fellow Jew, and a knowledgeable one at that, well-versed in the Passover ritual. We toasted our ancestors' deliverance from Egypt with our first glass of Manischewicz and our own recent departure from the Soviet Union — a move that still felt to us like its own kind of miraculous deliverance from captivity — with our second...

Soon Pasha surprised me again, when it emerged that he could keep up a conversation not just about his own field of geography (where he knew masses of interesting stories) but also about literature, music, and poetry, including the sung poetry of bards: Pasha turned out to be a connoisseur of this art form and a discerning critic of the work of its best practitioners. It was clear that he did not approach music and song from a distance, from the outside, as part of the cultural baggage mandatory for every enlightened Soviet intellectual, but as something that was close to his heart, uniquely his own. Soon all became clear: his entire family lived inside this culture: his daughter Nadya, a pianist and graduate of the Moscow Conservatory, was also an amateur singer of bard songs who performed the works of such masters as Bulat Okudzhava,[1] Alexander Galich,[2] etc. Pasha did not play any instruments and never sang (in front of me, at any rate) but his erudition and unerring taste, combined with his editorial talent, inspired me to start sending him my new articles to review prior to publication. He was strict in his critique but his comments were always substantive and helped improve my writing.

I was not surprised when, during his work for the Holocaust Museum, Pavel became friends with the musicologist Bret Werb, who occasionally consulted him, although mostly on issues of geography and ethnography and not on music.

Then, a colleague of Pasha's by the name of Edna asked him if he wanted to take on a side job reading Russian literature aloud to

---

[1] https://en.wikipedia.org/wiki/Bulat_Okudzhava
[2] https://en.wikipedia.org/wiki/Alexander_Galich_(writer)

her father, a prominent American professor of Russian studies who had lost his eyesight as a result of complications of diabetes. For reasons I don't recall, Pasha declined the job and offered it to me. I was stunned to learn the professor's name: Maurice Friedberg, former chair of the Russian department at the University of Illinois at Urbana-Champaign, who had recently retired for health reasons and was moving to Washington to be near his daughter.

I knew Maurice Friedberg. Born in 1929 (like myself), in Krakow, he had fled Nazi-occupied Poland in 1939 to Soviet Russia with his family. In the 1980s, he had twice invited me to his university to give my lectures and concerts. Maurice Friedberg, a man of sparkling wit and boundless energy, brought low by a tragic stroke of fate. I was glad to help my old friend who, deprived of his ability to read that Russian literature that he had taught and written about throughout his whole career, was now in need of a Russian speaker to talk to and to read to him. I met with him twice a week for the next four years, which was all the time my friend had left to live. It was remarkable, I thought, that it was Pavel who brought us back together: Pavel, who had used his geographical knowledge to reunite so many families scattered by WWII, had now, almost by accident, brought together two old friends.

Pavel never returned to Massachusetts, to my great delight. After completing his year at the Kennan Institute, he found a job in Washington and brought his wife and daughter over. Eventually, he even bought a car, although he had no drivers' license, did not know how to drive and now had to learn it. I helped him practice his driving, sitting in the passenger seat and giving him tips on staying in his lane, on when to begin to apply the brakes, how to make a turn, how to parallel park… I can't say that Pavel was a natural: the new skills came hard at first, and Pasha became irritable and nervous while driving. Perhaps this was the first time in his life he was not able to master a new skill with his accustomed speed and ease…

* * *

His first name did not fit him well. Paulus means "small" in Latin. Pavel was small only in his physical appearance; everything else about him was far above average. He was a scientist of stature, a large and brilliant personality—a true Man who will be remembered with love and gratitude by all those fortunate to have known him well.

Pavel Ilyin: A Memory

Grigory Ioffe

avel, Pasha... I cannot bring myself to say "he was": he is — a kind, cheerful, spirited man filled with good will. And then there's Ella. I can't think of them separately, although I started out thinking of them separately because I met each of them at a different time and under different circumstances and was surprised to learn that they were husband and wife. In fact, they complement each other perfectly: Ella brings inspiration and organization to Pasha's action. Over the last 25 years I've grown closer to their amazing family than to my own relatives. Their apartment in Bethesda near Washington, DC is filled with that familiar, nostalgic spirit we know so well, those "kitchen talks" that were the mainstay of the Russian-Jewish intellectual circles of Moscow. But while the talks themselves were important, Pasha and Ella have created an environment of spiritual kinship that transcends them, precisely because it both liberates and comforts one's spirit. In my life I've only twice been privileged to be received in homes that had that accepting, comfortable ambiance — but one of those homes is no more, and yet Pasha and Ella's home is always with me.

It is strange to recall that Pasha and I used to disagree on political or ideological grounds. Pasha used to watch the Fox TV Channel, which I used to consider reactionary — and yet now Fox is the only TV I watch. Pasha kept kosher, he disliked a certain Soviet civic holiday that means a lot to me... There were other differences as well. The older we get, however, and especially the more friends and loved ones we lose, the more we become imbued with certain values that are difficult to put into words. We begin to understand certain things. Pasha's work for the Holocaust Museum on the toponyms of Jewish places in the Ukraine and Belarus, his essay on changing place names, the book on Moscow and St. Petersburg he edited — all these have come to mean even more to me now than they did when Pasha... was... with us. There are some people who function as transmitters of civilization, as its teachers or missionaries, who work constantly to promote a cross-penetration and enrichment of cultures. Most of us

275

don't even manage to pass on to our children those things that made us who we are. Pasha managed to do so, and not only to his and Ella's child, Nadia...

I keep thinking about Pasha's home. Bookshelves made of planks laid on bricks... books, books, endless books... a map of old Moscow, a view of Israel from space, and that magnificent picture of an old Jew that hung in their hallway. I see Pasha in his apron in the kitchen; I see him taking out a bottle of his "Ilyinka" — homemade vodka based on an old family recipe; I see him raising a toast; I see him dozing off. And I see him smiling his happy, welcoming smile — and I smile, too, and my heart soars.

PavElla

Olga Medvedkov

Almost half a century ago in summer of 1972 I made a visit to the Institute of Geography of the Soviet Academy of Science (IGAN as a short Russian Abbreviation) for the grad school interview. It probably was lunchtime, because the department looked pretty much deserted. Besides Professor Minz, with whom I had an appointment, I noticed in the corner a man in his mid thirties, looking at me with curious eyes and smiling very gently. From time to time during my conversation with Professor Minz, this man gave me an encouraging nod that made me feel very welcomed. This man was Pavel Ilyin (everybody called him Pasha), and we became close friends ever since.

I am aware that quite a few colleagues have already written about Pavel as a scholar. I would like to pay my tribute to him as a friend. It is difficult for me to separate Pavel from Ella, his wife, hence PavElla — as they still listed on my IPhone and in my mind and heart. Not only they were partners in life, they were true soul mates till death them apart.

My husband, Yuri Medvedkov, and I spent numerous hours together with Pavel and Ella at the professional meeting, seminars, workshops, but also listening music, having heart-to-heart conversations, and travelling together.

In Russia friendship is almost sacred — you trust your friends with your life. And we have experienced it first hand, while denounced as persona non-grata, when joined an independent peace movement after the Soviet invasion into Afghanistan.

We lost a lot of friends during that period of our life. Some denounced us openly, some looked in opposite direction when my husband and I will show up.

But not PavElla! If anything else, they became only closer to us in the face of real danger. We were at least protected to some degree by foreign journalists coverage; they were not. And yet, they would come frequently to our place that was under the KGB surveillance. It required lots of courage.

The most memorable incident, which I see as it happened yester-day, was when in the very beginning of our political activity Yuri was arrested, under pretense that he was drunk, to prevent his meeting with Swedish peace activists. He found himself in a jail with a bunch of drunkards. It was during summer 1982, and my parents were with our son in our log cabin on Volga River. I was horrified that they would learn about Yuri's arrest from Voice of America or Voice of Liberty, and would have a heart attack. Without any hesitation, Pavel volunteered to travel to comfort my parents.

In his absence the KGB conducted a search of their apartment, and Pavel returned back only to find his home being invaded and violated.

Indeed, friendship is sacred in Russia, and we are truly blessed hav-ing PavElla our close friends.

My Neigbor, Pavel Ilyin

Igor Krupnik

I met Pavel Ilyin — or Pasha, or even Panchik, as my wife and I soon began to call him — in June 1991 at a conference on Russian Jews (or Soviet Jews, as they then were) organized at Stanford University by Igor Kotler and Victor Rashkovsky. I remember Ella's presentation, given in Russian and translated by young Nadya, who looked at Ella with her large round eyes while Pasha sat smiling next to her. A year later, we all got together in Washington, where all of us were living by that time; but we didn't become really close for another three years, when we moved within a ten minutes' walk from them and became, as Pasha liked to joke, the kind of neighbors that have good fences. So we knew each other well for about twenty years.

It was amazing and even unfair on some level. Very quickly we identified so many friends and acquaintances we had in common that it seemed odd that we hadn't met in our prior lives. Pasha and I had graduated from the same geography department (although he had done it fourteen years before I did) and knew many of the same people, colleagues, and even former teachers, and some of my teachers were Pasha's classmates. I knew many people who worked at with him at the Institute of Geography, then at the Encyclopedia, and then were fellow refuseniks with him. Clearly, we had trod similar and often the same paths but somehow had never intersected.

This all changed when we became neighbors. Our wives worked at the same office, we visited each other's homes and had Shabbat together, and our dog Finya could pull us at the end of her leash toward Ella and Pavel's home (and take us home again) with her eyes closed because there was always a carrot waiting for her at their house. But I digress...

When I remember Pasha and our talks and meals, our shared metro rides to work, I want to record the main things about him in that last and relatively happy period of his life. Outside of the last years, when he was ill, he was always working and writing and liked to spend time with people and talk about the past. His was an active life filled with true creativity. That is how I remember him; and some of his qualities have stayed in my memory as permanent, not restricted to specific events or memories.

Pavel Ilyin was a man of devotion. He had his own clear moral code that he never hid or changed. He was loyal to his friends, both old and new; he did not deny his prior life and was not embarrassed by the idealistic and enthusiastic cast of his early professional memories; and he viewed his difficult past with subtle dignity. In that, he was a man of integrity — and also in his candid, unvarnished devotion to writing, to working with and on language — in a word, to the kind of work that goes into a serious text. We talked a lot about the need to work on language, especially when he was working with Blair Ruble on their 2004 book about the history of Moscow. Some of the chapters were originally submitted in Russian, others in English, and Pavel worked on the translations, the originals, and then the illustrations, with a kind of rapturous meticulousness. The book took a tremendous amount of work but it brought him great joy — joy from the work itself and not from all the positive reviews, which Pavel never mentioned.

Reserved and even taciturn, especially in public and with strangers, Pavel was a man of passion. He had few shades of grey, and his intensity was plain to see. Ella often called him "rabid". He was known to stand up and leave, or change the subject, if he disagreed or felt that the conversation was about to cross one of his lines. Surprisingly, we never quarreled over (American) politics, even though we read different newspapers, watched different TV programs and voted for different parties. He was intransigent yet forgiving, especially toward his friends. He had a powerful moral compass and sometimes ironically called himself a Stalinist (referring only to the strength of his convictions), which sounded odd in view of his family history and his own biography.

I think this had to do with his predilection for stability, for a strong tradition of justice, which he identified with America. He loved America with the same kind of passion and could not stand hearing it attacked or made fun of, and would clam up and withdraw when that happened, making it clear that he found the conversation unpleasant. He was equally passionate in identifying with Israel and the Jewish people, which, as I suspect, did not come from his early life in Moscow.

His passion was an emotional corollary to his devotion, and they both coexisted in that integral man. I found him easy to relate to, because we had a lot in common, loved and valued many of the same people, and were in agreement on the main things, despite some of our differences. Yet not everyone found him as easy, and I understand why.

His devotion, his firmness of character, even his intransigence existed side-by-side with another quality: an ability to change and creatively transform himself, something that few people are able to do. I only got to know Pavel in his American life, his third, so to speak, and then toward the end of it, when he was working at the Holocaust Museum, studying the history of toponyms and mapping the places of massacres of Jews during World War II, an emotionally heavy topic. We talked about that, too, although I could see how difficult it was for him. And yet I had no trouble picturing him as a young and gregarious associate at the Institute of Geography in the 1970s, working on urban planning and territorial modeling. I could also see how he had left it all behind and how, despite his passionate love for geography and his training as a geographer, he now enjoyed working on history, urban culture, and later poetry. Since I, too, had left geography for the humanities, we two old renegades got along well.

His love for America and his strong feeling for both its history and its current reality were part of the same ability to creatively remake himself. He had had to do so as a mature adult, well into his fifties, with no prior knowledge of English and without many of the skills required in his new life. And yet he was entirely free from bitterness about the life he had had to leave behind. Although he had left his beloved books back in Moscow, he later bought new copies in America, supplementing them with various American encyclopedias and books on Jewish history, as well as old prints and maps that he found in antique shops. Pavel enthusiastically gave his guests guided tours of Washington, DC and its outlying suburbs, as though he had lived here his whole life. He had found itself here and had adapted successfully, remaining in harmony with himself and his surroundings. This is how we would like to remember him.

Here are his words to us with which he signed his book *Moscow At the Turn of the XXth Century* (2004):

> *To my dear Alla and Igor Krupnik, as a token of my great love and friendship and my sincere thanks — not only for supplying the inspiration behind certain things in this book but also for living within walking distance from us, which allows us to get together for a drink more often than would be possible otherwise. And also in memory of the city in which all of us grew up and which all of us left.*

Our thanks to you, Panchik — for these words, for that book, and for all the good memories...

About Authors

ALEKSANDR S. AKHIYEZER (1929–2007) was a Russian social philosopher and culture critic and a holder of a doctoral degree in philosophy who was known for his socio-cultural approach to Russian history. A. S. Akhiyezer authored over 500 scientific articles and 20 books. He coined a number of new terms that are used today in culture studies and sociology. He introduced a theory of spiral socio-cultural evolution and described the stages of development of a prevailing moral ideal in society. In his early work, he made a significant contribution to the Soviet theory of urbanization.

TONY ALLISON was born and raised in Seattle. His career was primarily in international fisheries, and included living and working in the Soviet Union. He served as CEO for Marine Resources Company International, a joint Russian-American venture, for eleven years. Tony later became a high school history teacher. He resides on Guemes Island, in Washington State, with his wife Nancy.

NANCY FISHER-ALLISON became intrigued by the Soviet Union while reading Soviet Life in her school library. She studied in Leningrad, and spent decades immersed in Russia's culture and geography. Along the way, she met Pavel and Ella — a blessing. Nancy ended up back in a school library — as the librarian. She retired to Guemes Island in Washington State with her husband, Tony Allison.

VADIM ALTSKAN is a historian specializing in East European, Balkan, and Jewish history. He is the Project Director of the International Archival Programs at the U. S. Holocaust Memorial Museum's Institute for the Holocaust Documentation. He directs archival research in the Balkans, Baltics, Caucasus, Central Asia, and East Europe, fulfilling the Museum's mission to preserve evidence of the Holocaust and make historical materials available to scholars and the general public.

NADYA BARTOL, is Managing Director at BCG Platinion, a division of Boston Consulting Group. Nadya has 25 years of cybersecurity technology and management experience across multiple industry and government environments. At BCG, Nadya advises clients in many industries, including financial services, technology, energy, insurance, professional services, and consumer packaged goods on cybersecurity strategy and implementation. Nadya co-authored a number of cybersecurity publications by the National Institute of Standards and Technology (NIST) and led development of several ISO standards on a variety of cybersecurity topics. Nadya holds Masters of Music in Piano Performance, Master of Science in Information Systems, and Master of Business Administration degrees.

VLADIMIR FRUMKIN is a musicologist, journalist and essayist. He holds a post-graduate diploma in musicology from the Leningrad Conservatory. During the Soviet era he pioneered the study of the "bard" movement — the Russian cultural phenomenon of independent, uncensored song, usually sung to an acoustic guitar accompaniment. He himself performed the songs of leading bards such as Bulat Okudzhava, Aleksandr Galich and many others. In 1974, Mr. Frumkin immigrated to the U.S., where he worked at Oberlin College in Ohio and the Russian Summer School at the Norwich University in Vermont. In 1988–2006 he was part of the Voice of America's Russian service in Washington, DC. He is the author of several books on classical music and the bard movement.

REVAZ GACHECHILADZE is a prominent Georgian scholar and diplomat. He graduated from the School of Oriental Studies, Tbilisi State University (TSU), and received his Ph.D. in Human Geography from TSU. He served as the Director of the Institute of Georgia's Neighborhood Studies, TSU and taught at his Alma Mater as well as at Oxford University, UK and at Mount Holyoke College, USA. Gachechiladze authored multiple books and articles. His most well-known publication in English is "The New Georgia: Space, Society, Politics," London, University College of London Press 1995. Gachechiladze has served as Georgia's Ambassador Extraordinary and Plenipotential to Israel, Armenia, the UK, and Slovakia.

ROBERT GOHSTAND is a Professor Emeritus of Geography at California State University, Northridge, where he taught courses in the geography and historical geography of Russia and the Soviet Union, map interpretation, and the history of geography. His research and publications concentrated on the commercial geography of Pre-Revolutionary Russia. Born in China, he is the founder and director of the Old China Hands Archives in the university library. A life-long advocate of the merits and pleasures of reading, he established and endowed the university library's leisure reading room and a biennial lecture series on reading. He remains active in his support of the library and its collections. He is married and resides in Southern California.

VENIAMIN GOKHMAN (1918–1986) was a Soviet geographer who specialized in American studies and was known for his contributions to the discipline of country studies as well as to theoretical geography.

In the late 1950s, V.M. Gokhman helped pioneer a data-based approach to geography. In 1960s and 1970s he was instrumental in the development of theoretical geography in the USSR. Together with his colleagues, he proposed a new paradigm of country studies: topical (rather than descriptive) studies. He stressed the social aspects of economic geography and authored pioneering studies in cultural geography and metageography. V.M. Gokhman helped found the Soviet school of American studies. Although V.M. Gokhman never visited the United States, his works on the country's economic geography were well known there, and Gokhman enjoyed the respect of American geographers.

V.M. Gokhman authored over 150 publications, some of them classified; over 600 encyclopedia entries; and over 80 scholarly articles and book reviews.

GRIGORY IOFFE was born and raised in Moscow, graduated from Moscow State University as a specialist in human geography, worked at the Institute of Geography of the Russian Academy of Sciences; in 1989, emigrated to the USA; since 1990 has been affiliated with Radford University in Virginia; authored and coauthored 10 books devoted to the former Soviet Union.

ELLA (MIKAELLA) KAGAN was born in Moscow, Russia; graduated from the Institute of Civil Engineering; worked for the Moscow-based Urban Planning Institute and for the Institute of Urban Studies, and earned her Ph.D. in urban planning. In 1982, Ella and her entire family applied for emigration from the Soviet Union and were denied exit visa. In 1987, under Gorbachev's liberalization, they were allowed to leave and settled in the United States. Since 1988, Ella has been working for several Jewish Agencies of Greater Washington. In 2003, she founded Shalom Education Center — a Sunday school for children of Jewish immigrants from the former Soviet Union.

ALEXANDRE KIRILLOV is a Soviet and Russian mathematician, known for his works in the field of representation theory and topological groups. He worked at Moscow State University in 1961–1994. Currently, Professor at Department of Mathematics, University of Pennsylvania; Principal researcher at the Institute of Information Transfer Problems, Russian Academy of Sciences; Professor at the Advanced School of Economics (Moscow, Spring 2019). Fellow of American Mathematical Society. Doctor Honoris Causa of the Reims University (France).

IGOR KRUPNIK — ethnographer specializing in Northern nations, curator of Arctic collections at the National Museum of Natural History, Smithsonian Institution (Washington, DC, USA). Born in Moscow

(USSR), graduate of Moscow State University Department of Geography; post-graduate student and, eventually, research member of the Institute of Ethnography, USSR Academy of Sciences. Awarded PhD in History and Biology. Author of many books and catalogues devoted to the cultures of Arctic nations. In the 1980s, took part in the Jewish Cultural movement in Moscow; was scientific secretary of the independent Jewish Historical/Ethnographic Committee (1980–1990).

Yuli G. Lipets (1931–2006) was a Soviet and Russian economic geographer, a holder of a doctoral degree in geography and a specialist in the geography of global development.

Y. G. Lipets was one of the creators of the discipline of topical country studies. A known expert in the geography of the world economy, he also worked on issues in theoretical geography and data-based methods in geography and helped create geographic information systems for territorial management.

Y. G. Lipets was the first Soviet scientist to study the geography of development, a synthetic discipline combining elements of the geography of global development, topical country studies and the study of globalization. He studied Russia's transition to a market economy and conducted multiple research projects analyzing the border regions of the Russian Federation.

Olga Medvedkov, Professor Emeritus in Geography, graduated from Moscow State University, Geography department in 1972, and then defended her PhD in the Institute of Geography, Soviet Academy of Science in 1975.

After leaving the Soviet Union in 1986, she is residing in the United States with her husband, Yuri Medvedkov, and their two children. Starting from 1987, Dr. Olga Medvedkov dedicated her professional career to teaching and research during her 27 years of tenure at Wittenberg University (Springfield, Ohio).

Concurrently, she conducted research at the Ohio State University, where she was a senior research fellow. She published numerous books and articles in professional journals on the subject of urbanization.

Dr. Olga Medvedkov is twice a recipient of Fulbright award.

Pavel Polian is a Russian historian, geographer and philologist, as well as a published author writing under the pen name of Nerler. He graduated from the Geography faculty of the Moscow State University in 1974, obtaining his doctorate in geography in 1998. He is a senior researcher of the Institute of Geography of the Russian Academy of Sciences and a professor and a member of the academic council at several universities. Professor Polian serves as president of the Mandelstam

Center and is a member of the editorial staff at several magazines. He has authored multiple books focusing mostly on geography, demography and history and including several books on the Holocaust. He lives in Freiburg, Germany.

BLAIR A. RUBLE is currently a Distinguished Fellow at the Wilson Center. Previously, he served as the Center's Vice President for Programs, and earlier as the Director of the Kennan Institute while simultaneously coordinating the Center's programming in comparative urban studies. He received his MA and PhD degrees in Political Science from the University of Toronto (1973, 1977), and an AB degree with Highest Honors in Political Science from the University of North Carolina at Chapel Hill (1971). He has edited more than a dozen volumes, and is the author of seven monographic studies including *Washington's U Street: A Biography*.

TATYANA RUNOVA holds a Candidate of Sciences degree (1957) from the Leningrad State University. In 1960–1995 she worked for the Institute of Geography of the Soviet Academy of Sciences (now the Russian Academy of Sciences). In 1996–2009 she served as a docent at the Moscow Industrial University, and in 2010–2017 she worked as a consultant for the Cadaster Research and Design Institute in Yaroslavl, Russia. Ms. Runova is currently retired. Her research interests include the northern regions of Russia, the geography of natural resources, and regional impacts on the environment. She has published several books on these themes and has authored a number of textbooks and study guides.

Павел Ильин

Две жизни — один мир

Предисловие

Уроки Павла Ильина

Блэр Рубл

*ведущий научный сотрудник Центра им. Вудро Уилсона,
г. Вашингтон*

Не помню, как мы узнали друг о друге, но отлично помню, как мы познакомились с Павлом Ильиным. В восьмидесятые годы я работал в «Научном совете по социальным исследованиям» в Нью-Йорке. Совет располагался на 17-м этаже самого южного небоскрёба в Среднем Манхэттене на углу 39-й улицы и Третьей авеню. Перед моим окном простиралась вся центральная часть Манхэттена: от здания Эмпайр-стейт-билдинг до Всемирного торгового центра и дальше, и это был чарующий вид — особенно для того, кто является урбанистом по специальности.

Павел зашел во время одного из своих первых приездов в Нью-Йорк. Когда он вошел в мой кабинет, его глаза засверкали. Потом настала его очередь рассказывать, и он стал объяснять мне сущность открывавшегося перед нами урбанистического механизма. Павел был знаком с малейшими нюансами жизни в Нью-Йорке, хотя сам прежде никогда не видел того, что предстало нашим взорам. В этот момент я понял, что может быть больше никогда не познакомлюсь с человеком, который был бы большим знатоком-урбанистом, чем Павел.

Мы поддерживали тесный контакт, став коллегами после того, как я переехал в Вашингтон, чтобы возглавить Институт Кеннана, научным сотрудником которого был Павел, и тех пор стали близкими друзьями. Нам часто доводилось работать вместе и всегда удавалось делиться друг с другом своей любовью к городам и городской жизни. Иногда Павел редактировал мои статьи, и я знал, что из его откликов на написанное я всегда буду узнавать что-то новое о своей собственной работе.

Для меня Павел был идеалом ученого и интеллектуала. Всегда честный, не теряющий живого интереса к окружающему его миру, он придерживался высочайших принципов интеллектуальной порядочности и был не просто другом, он был образцом для подражания.

В конце 1990-х и в начале нулевых мне выпала большая часть стать соредактором тома, посвященного Москве начала 20-го века вместе с Павлом и Эллой. В результате в 2004 году увидел свет сборник «Москва рубежа XIX и XX столетий. Взгляд в прошлое издалека», в который вошли восемь глав, написанных шестью авторами. Я всегда считал, что этот проект позволил обоим исследователям, жизнь которых больше не была обременена институциональными узами, совершенно раскованно изложить свои мысли о Москве. Я с увлечением участвовал в этом проекте, потому что он давал мне свободу выполнять и публиковать сравнительный анализ Москвы и Нью-Йорка на рубеже веков — то есть делать то, к чему я стремился с той самой встречи с Павлом, когда мы вместе смотрели сверху на Манхэттен. Я всегда считал, что эта книга — и вклад, который в нее внес Павел — раскрыла в нем исследователя, которым он мог бы стать, если этому не воспрепятствовала жизнь.

Глава Павла о культурной географии Москвы на рубеже веков являет собой мастерски написанный новаторский труд, призывающий читателей полностью пересмотреть свое отношение к культуре этого города. Она начинается с мысли о том, что — как это бывает со всеми аспектами человеческого существования — культуре свойственно собственное пространственное распределение, отражающее индивидуальный характер города, который влияет на это распределение. Например, в Москве и в Нью-Йорке вопрос о том, где и каким образом будут размещаться театры решается по-разному — и он был столь же важен для Москвы сто лет тому назад, как и для Москвы, которую мы знаем сегодня. Осознание различий подобного рода помогает нам лучше понять Москву и ее искусство.

Павел отмечает, что Москва не всегда была центром театральной жизни. В середине девятнадцатого столетия в ней было только два профессиональных театра: Большой театр, в котором ставились оперы и балеты, и Малый драматический театр, в котором шли драматические спектакли. Всего несколько десятилетий спустя в городе появилось великое множество любительских и профессиональных сцен, существование которых было обусловлено невероятным разнообразием актеров и актрис. Эта трансформация отражала того, что по мнению Павла, было следствием глубинных изменений во всех аспектах городской жизни в Москве в момент, когда она стала одним из самых быстро растущих городов в мире.

В своем повествовании об истории московской театральной жизни, Павел глубоко и подробно раскрывает информацию о купцах, строивших и финансировавших театры, о театральных зрителях, которыми в основном были представители среднего класса, актерах, писателях и режиссерах, под чьим руководством осуществлялось все, что происходило на сцене, о рабочих сцены, без которых не могло обойтись ни одного спектакля, и так далее. Прочитав написанную Павлом главу, читатель получает полную картину того, что происходило в Москве того времени.

Таким же подробным образом Павел описывает развитие музыки и кинематографа, делясь важными соображениями о том, как технический прогресс отражался и на городе, и на его художественной жизни одновременно. Он противопоставляет культурную среду Москвы, в которой преобладало финансирование частными спонсорами, культурной жизни в Санкт-Петербурге, которая в основном поддерживалась государством, таким образом отмечая различие между этими столь непохожими друг на друга и столь российскими одновременно городами.

При подготовке этой главы Павел потратил много времени на то, что он называл «географией адресов». Именно в этот момент становится очевидным, как географ-урбанист возобладал над всем остальным таким же образом, как это произошло, когда мы стояли у окна, из которого открывался вид на Манхэттен. Его кропотливая работа, которая стала своего рода преддверием его последующих исследований в вашингтонском Музее Холокоста, посвященных названиям городов, позволяет нам по-новому увидеть, каким образом город Москва складывается из множества составляющих. Автор указывает на расширение московского культурного ареала, которое тоже является важной частью повествования о том, как развивался этот город в столь значимый исторический период. Завершающий раздел главы, посвященный московским пригородам, наглядно показывает постепенное слияние города и области в единый городской организм.

Написанная Павлом глава стала для меня открытием, также, как и другие материалы, подготовленные им для нашей книги. В дополнение к тщательно собранным данным, анализ Павла открывает совершенно новую Москву, которая непохожа на ту, о которой я узнал из других публикаций и благодаря моей собственной работе. Он продемонстрировал важность деталей, таких как конкретные уличные адреса, для понимания общей картины урбанистических процессов в Москве и Московской области.

После выхода этой книги Павел и я больше никогда официально не работали вместе. Тем не менее, сила его интеллектуального воздействия на мое понимание всего, связанного с городами, продолжала возрастать. Наблюдая за тем, как он осваивает новые области, и имея счастливую возможность обсуждать с ним как его работу, так и мои собственные изыскания, я продолжал испытывать его глубокое формирующее влияние на мое восприятие городов. Но главное — это то, что Павел научил меня ощущать слово «город» не как существительное, а как другую часть речи — некий глагол, ибо город постоянно меняется и эволюционирует, а это совсем не присуще статичным объектам.

Обращаясь мысленным взором к первой встрече с Павлом в Нью-Йорке, я всё лучше понимаю, что он обладал настоящим даром предвидения. Наше знакомство произошло на фоне эпидемии крэк-кокаина в городе, которому, как казалось, грозило неминуемое самоуничтожение. Чтобы встретиться со мной, Павлу приходилось ездить в уже давно отслуживших свой век вагонах метро — как и мне приходилось проделывать это по дороге на работу. Улицы требовали ремонта, по мере приближения к наземному уровню становилось все более очевидно, что никто ни за чем не ухаживает и ничего не работает так, как надо.

Когда-то с высоты семнадцатого этажа Павел показал мне, что, отстранившись на несколько мгновений от этих повседневных трудностей, можно разглядеть в Нью-Йорке комплексный городской механизм, преисполненный динамизма. Он заставил меня поверить в то, что Нью-Йорк сможет отвоевать свою прежнюю национальную и мировую известность. Через пару десятилетий этот город вновь оказался на вершине мировой славы — именно так, как это предсказывал Павел, глядя на сиявшее на солнце здание Эмпайр-стейт-билдинг.

Введение

Элла Каган

В книге «Павел Ильин: две жизни — один мир» собраны избранные работы моего покойного мужа, Павла Ильина (1936–2015). Я включила в эту книгу только те его тексты, которые сам Павел считал удачными. Среди них читатель найдет статьи и материалы не только разного времени, но и разного жанра.

Павел Ильин — географ, историк Холокоста, специалист по русской городской культуре и одновременно — многолетний автор популярных детских радиопередач. Он проработал в своей жизни без малого шестьдесят лет, первая половина которых прошла в России, а вторая — в Америке.

Павел закончил Московский Государственный Университет, Географический факультет; работал в Государственном институте проектирования городов; затем защитил кандидатскую диссертацию в Институте географии Академии Наук в Москве и остался там работать. Свою научную деятельность он совмещал с многолетним сотрудничеством с Детской редакцией Всесоюзного радио, где вел серию передач с географическими загадками. Статьи, содержавшие результаты научных исследований Павла, были опубликованы в СССР и в Америке, задолго до того, как он оказался в США

В 1982 году наша семья подала документы на эмиграцию. Когда нам было отказано в выезде, американские коллеги обратились к советскому правительству с письмом, в котором требовали немедленно отпустить Павла Ильина и его семью. Письмо было утверждено на конференции Американской Ассоциации Географов и подписано ведущими учеными. (см. полный текст этого документа в Приложении).

Наконец, в 1987 году Павел и его семья прибыли в Америку, и у нас началась вторая жизнь. Вскоре после приезда Павел получил грант в Кеннановском институте в Вашингтоне (*Kennan Insti-*

tute), крупнейшем международном центре восточно-европейских и русских исследований. Вслед за Павлом вся семья переехала в Вашингтон.

По приезде в Америку Павел стал заниматься топонимикой СССР и Российской империи, то есть изучением названий населенных мест, что включало историю, географию, языковедение, архитектуру и другие области знаний. Павла больше всего интересовал историко-географический подход, или историческая топонимика. Результаты его исследований были опубликованы в статье «О переименовании городов в Советском Союзе в честь «выдающихся личностей». Статья имела успех, была переведена на русский язык и напечатана в разных изданиях. В другой статье «Топонимический погром на Украине» он показал на примере Украины, как в разные периоды истории в СССР проводились кампании массового переименования городов по политическим соображениям. Обе эти работы включены в Часть I.

Бо́льшую часть своей американской жизни Павел работал в Мемориальном Музее Холокоста (Holocaust Memorial Museum), где он занимался изучением географических аспектов Холокоста европейского еврейства. Он считал эту работу одной из самых важных в своей жизни. Он изучал изменения в названиях стран, границ их территорий, названий городов и искажение информации об этих изменениях. Его исследования затрагивали территории всех европейских государств, которые были оккупированы Германией в годы Второй мировой войны. За годы работы в Музее Холокоста Павел собрал уникальную коллекцию исторических карт, которые отражают эти изменения; теперь эта коллекция находится в библиотеке Музея.

Павел считал работу в Музее святым еврейским делом и часто повторял: «Если бы я был богатым человеком, я бы платил за то, что мне дали эту работу». Результаты исследований географии Холокоста также представлены в Части I книги.

Павел был москвичом в третьем поколении и очень любил Москву — город, где он прожил первые пятьдесят лет своей жизни. Он знал этот город как линии своей ладони. Его знания включали историю, географию, фольклор и архитектуру города, а любимым занятием — было побродить по переулкам Старой Москвы, заходя в подворотни и проходные дворы. Павел бесконечно читал и собирал книги о Москве, среди которых были как исследования ученых, так и воспоминания москвичей разных профессий и социального статуса.

Результатом этого многолетнего увлечения, огромных личных знаний и систематических исследований стала книга «Москва рубежа Х1Х–ХХ столетий. Взгляд в прошлое издалека» (2004). У этой книги два редактора: Павел Ильин и Блэр Рубл. В Части II читатель найдет статью Павла «География культуры в Москве в конце XIX — начале XX века», а также написанные ими совместно Введение и Заключение к книге.

Отец Павла, Михаил Ильич Ильин (Мирон Ильич Туркельтауб, 1901–1967), был известным журналистом и популярным детским писателем. В апреле 1958 г. он начал серию детских передач на Всесоюзном радио, где главным героем был юнга по имени Захар Загадкин. (см. Часть III). Это были географические вопросы-загадки, которые юные радиослушатели должны были разгадать и прислать свои письма с ответами. В те докомпьютерные годы сбор материалов для передач и обработка почты требовали многих усилий и времени. Павел помогал отцу на всех этапах этой работы со своих студенческих лет. Передача стала очень популярной — бывало, что иногда авторы получали больше тысячи ответов. В Часть III включены рассказы о содержании передач; тексты выступлений Павла на конференциях об этом цикле передач; и письма бывших радиослушателей.

Когда отца не стало, Павел продолжал сам вести передачу, где бы он в то время ни работал. Ни отец, ни сын не позволяли объявлять по радио имена авторов, чтобы дети верили в существование своих героев — юнги Захара Загадкина и его друга корабельного кока. Передача просуществовала двадцать четыре года и была закрыта. Историю этих событий я рассказываю в своих воспоминаниях в Части III.

Павел был патриотом Америки в самом лучшем смысле этого слова. Он писал: «Я с момента приезда знал, что это моя страна... Я стал жителем США в ноябре1987-го, гражданином в мае 1993-го, и ощутил себя американцем в сентябре 2001-го... Я люблю Америку и ни разу не изменял этому чувству».

Павел был поражен, когда после взрыва башен World Trade Center 11 сентября 2001 г. в Нью-Йорке он увидел членов Конгресса, хором поющих «God bless America!» на ступенях Капитолия. Он ощутил себя человеком двух культур, которые ему захотелось соединить. Для этого Павел выбрал три самые популярные американские песни (This Land is my Land; America the Beautiful; God Bless America) и рассказал читателям об авторах их музыки и слов. Главное, что он сделал — это поэтический русский перевод текстов песен, слова которого прекрасно ложатся на музыку. Статья Павла, посвященная этим трем песням, тексты в русском переводе и его воспоминания об этой работе включены в Часть IV.

Часть V содержит личные воспоминания о Павле его друзей, коллег и членов его семьи.

* * *

Появление этой книги стало возможным благодаря помощи многих людей. Прежде всего хочу выразить свою искреннюю благодарность двум людям, которые давали мне бесценные советы и поддерживали словом и делом в течение всех лет работы над книгой — Игорю Крупнику (Igor Krupnik) и Блэру Рублу (Blair Ruble). Не думаю, что без них я смогла бы довести эту работу до конца.

Хочу также поблагодарить наших друзей и коллег, которые, живя в разных городах и странах, каждый по-своему помогли мне в работе. Это, прежде всего Владимир Фрумкин (Vladimir Frumkin), Роберт Гостанд (Robert Gohstand), Григорий Иоффе (Gregory Ioffe), Павел Полян (Pavel Polyan) и Светлана Васильева (Svetlana Vasilyeva).

Мои самые искренние слова благодарности обращены ко всем, кто написал свои воспоминания о Павле Ильине. На всем этом пути рядом со мной были моя дочь Надя Ильина Бартол и ее муж Тим Бартол (Timothy Bartol). В издание этой красивой и дорогой моему сердцу книги вложили свои силы переводчики Мэри Кокран (Marie Cochran), Юлия ЛаВилла-Носова (Julia LaVilla-Nossova), Ирина Холмс (Irina Holmes), Ирина Кузес (Irina Kuzes), Инна Лоринг (Inna Loring), Лиза Евсеева (Liza Evseeva).

Спасибо всем!

Элла Каган

Часть I

Города и их судьбы
(историческая топонимика)

О ПЕРЕИМЕНОВАНИИ ГОРОДОВ
в Советском Союзе
в честь «выдающихся личностей»

Павел Ильин

Постоянные переименования городов и других мест в Советском Союзе получили на Западе название «советской игры в имена» [1]. И это действительно была игра, причем игра политическая. Как и всякая игра, эта игра имела свои правила, которые, однако, постоянно менялись на протяжении всей истории советского государства.

Советская власть с первых дней своего существования рассматривала географические имена — имена городов, улиц, промышленных предприятий и других объектов, даже физико-географических, с политической точки зрения. Политизация топонимов была интегральной частью политизации советского общества. Но поскольку различные аспекты политики постоянно менялись, менялась и практика наименования и переименования мест в Советском Союзе.

Данная статья касается в основном наименований и переименований городов, сделанных в честь разных личностей. Другими словами, мы рассматриваем здесь данные в советское время названия городов, которые относятся к мемориальным, или коммеморативным именам, то есть названия, «возникшие в память выдающихся людей...» [2].

Здесь следует отметить, что «выдающийся человек», «выдающаяся личность» — суть понятия исторические. Многие имена в современных или бывших названиях городов, принадлежавшие широко известным в свое время людям, мало что говорят нынешнему поколению. Других мы и сейчас рассматриваем как «выдающихся», но со знаком минус, — например, некоторых коммунистических вождей. Однако они были «выдающимися» — причем без кавычек — с точки зрения деятелей авторитарного режима, решавших в тот момент судьбы имен городов. Поэтому здесь не рассматривается правомерность появления на карте того или иного имени, каким бы одиозным оно нам ни казалось, а лишь отмечается факт его появления (или исчезновения — при очередном витке «игры в имена»).

Основными целями переименования городов в советское время было увековечение памяти коммунистических руководителей и лиц, им угодных, и стирание с карты имен лиц, неугодных режиму. При этом в разные периоды времени существовала своя мода на имена. Эта мода могла отражать личные пристрастия деятелей авторитарного режима, отношение власти в данный момент времени к определенным политическим течениям (например, к терроризму, как форме революционной борьбы), к культуре народов Советского Союза, к тенденциям большей или меньшей децентрализации власти, и т.д.

К угодным-неугодным в разное время могли относиться те или иные политические деятели настоящего и прошлого, деятели культуры, науки, исторические персонажи и др. Предпочтения в оценках менялись в соответствии с тем, как менялись политические оценки настоящего и прошлого. Заметим, что за 75 лет несколько раз пересматривалась и переоценивалась история России и СССР и соответственно переписывались учебники истории.

Правила игры в имена постоянно менялись. Впрочем, одно из правил оставалось неизменным: делать вид, что некоторых событий и явлений в прошлом никогда не было. Но это было общее правило советской политики. Эта фигура умолчания затрудняла и ограничивала возможности обращения к советским источникам в процессе настоящего исследования. Работа порой напоминала своеобразный детектив, так как приходилось отыскивать скрытое, выискивать ложь, заполнять пустоты в информации, проверять одни источники другими, а главное — на каждом этапе этой игры нужно было понять мотивы поступков «игроков».

Известно, что в регулярно выходивших справочниках «СССР. Административно-территориальное деление союзных республик» [3] приводятся сведения о переименованиях городов (в подстрочных примечаниях с указанием года, а иногда даже числа, когда переименование было произведено), и, кроме того, содержатся специальные алфавитные списки переименований — «Алфавит вновь присвоенных наименований» и «Алфавит прежних наименований». На первый взгляд, они поражают своей подробностью. Так, в «Алфавите прежних наименований» есть даже переименованные еще при царе Санкт-Петербург и Новый Маргелан. Но в обоих «алфавитах», как и в основном корпусе справочников, нет очень многих переименований советского времени — частично по цензурно-политическим причинам, а частично, как мне представляется, по небрежности и недостаточной компетентности составителей.

Тем не менее, указанные справочники очень полезны как один из источников информации, особенно если обращаться к изданиям разных лет. Но основным источником, из которого я черпал сведения о переименованиях городов после 1917 года, был для меня Указатель советских городов, составленный американским географом Чонси Харрисом [4] — наиболее полный список городов СССР с указанием их сменявших друг друга имен и годов переименований.

В любом случае, однако, в указанных источниках не говорится о том, в честь кого назывались или переименовывались города. И здесь на помощь должны были бы прийти энциклопедические издания. И действительно, в статьях о городах, помещенных в советских энциклопедических изданиях, приводятся сведения о переименованиях городов с указанием дат и лиц, в честь которых города назывались. Но и данные энциклопедий далеко не полны, и в первую очередь по той же причине: замалчивании явлений, нежелательных для правящего режима, что приводило к искажению фактов и прямой лжи.

Вот, например, цитата из Географического энциклопедического словаря, вышедшего в 1983 году (с. 478): «Чапаевск, город в Куйбышевской области, до 1929 Иващенково». Нынешний Чапаевск действительно назывался Иващенково, но только до 1918 года, а затем, до 1929 года он носил имя Троцк — в честь Л. Д. Троцкого [5]. Искажение истории, практиковавшееся в Советском Союзе в течение десятилетий, затрудняет использование советских изданий при создании картины переименований. Тем не менее они, несомненно, могут быть во многих случаях полезны, особенно если знаешь, в какой степени какой информации можно доверять.

Узнать о переименовании города — только полдела. Надо еще установить, в честь кого он был переименован. Во многих случаях для меня это было ясно. Но не всегда. Вот один из примеров поиска ответа. В списке Ч. Харриса я нашел, что город Ленинск в Узбекистане (Андижанская обл.) назывался в материалах переписи населения 1926 года Ассаке, а позднее — до 1938 года — Зеленск [6]. Между тем в советских источниках о том, что Ассаке-Ленинск носил одно время имя Зеленск, ничего не говорится. Из этого я выдвинул предположение, что, во-первых, это название происходит от фамилии (скорее всего, Зеленский), а во-вторых, носитель этой фамилии был партийным функционером, работавшим в Средней Азии и занимавшим там высокое положение. Он, несомненно, был репрессирован в 1937–1938 году, скорее всего тогда же погиб, а впоследствии посмертно реабилитирован. Следовательно… И, обратившись к Советскому энциклопедическому словарю (1987), я нашел в нем на стр. 458 статью о И. А. Зеленском, который в 1924–1931 годах был секретарем Среднеазиатского бюро ЦК ВКП(б) и дата смерти которого — 1938 год (!). Гипотеза подтвердилась, и мой список лиц, в честь которых назывались города, пополнился еще одним человеком.

Естественно, тема «игры в имена» была запретной в Советском Союзе. Но в свободной русской прессе на Западе работы на эту тему были возможны. Мне известна одна такая работа: книга Андрея и Татьяны Фесенко «Русский язык при советах», вышедшая в Нью-Йорке в 1955 году, в которой одна глава посвящена этническим и географическим аспектам. Эта книга представляет большой интерес как, возможно, одна из первых попыток рассмотреть советский «новояз» в самых разных его проявлениях, в том числе и на географической карте. В Советском Союзе об этой проблеме стали широко писать только в период «перестройки» и «гласности».

Несколько слов о принятой мной системе ссылок. Чтобы не перегружать ими работу, я не делаю ссылок в случаях, когда приводимые мною данные содержатся в общедоступных советских энциклопедических изданиях — в Большой Советской энциклопедии (2-е и 3-е издания), Географическом и Советском энциклопедических словарях (ГЭС и СЭС). Даты в скобках означают, если не оговорено иное, год наименования или переименования города. Административное деление дается, как правило, для первых лет Советской власти «по-старому» (губернии), для остального периода — «по-новому» (как оно было накануне развала Советского Союза).

Работа посвящена поселениям, которые носят (или носили) имена, данные в честь людей, и имеют (или имели) статус города. Число таких городов увеличивалось также при преобразовании названых в честь кого-либо поселков в города. Я старался отмечать подобные явления, когда имел соответствующие данные.

Представленный здесь материал ни в коем случае нельзя считать исчерпывающим, — как в исторической части, так и в современной. Я уверен, что более глубокое знакомство с различными источниками, изданными за годы существования Советской власти, позволит сделать новые открытия. Что же касается современных переименований, то, к сожалению, не вся информация о событиях, происходящих в различных «новых независимых государствах», становится быстро доступной.

Наконец, я прошу простить меня за мельтешение имен и дат в этой статье — они объясняются масштабами советской игры в имена.

ПЕРВЫЕ ГОДЫ ПОСЛЕ РЕВОЛЮЦИИ

Увековечивание имен «вождей», революционеров, деятелей Коммунистической партии и Советского государства всегда составляло основу советской топонимической политики. Первые переименования городов были сделаны уже на следующий год после Октябрьской революции — в 1918 году. И весьма знаменательно, что среди них было переименование, призванное увековечить на карте имя руководителя большевистской революции — В. И. Ленина: его имя получило село Талдом Московской губернии, которое было объявлено городом и стало называться Ленинск [7]. А в 1923 году на карте появился город, названный в честь второго большевистского вождя, Л. Д. Троцкого: Гатчина под Петроградом была переименована в Троцк [8]. Эти переименования, как и другие, им подобные, проводились якобы по инициативе жителей самих населенных пунктов. Возможность подобного рода инициативы — во всяком случае, со стороны партийных руководителей в то революционное время не исключается, однако трудно представить, чтобы переименования могли быть проведены без одобрения самих Ленина и Троцкого.

Присвоение городам имен здравствующих людей было в то время исключением, хотя и достаточно показательным. Гораздо чаще в первые годы после Октябрьской революции города назывались именами погибших участников революции и гражданской войны. На карту попали имена как известных большевиков (таких, как М. С. Урицкий и В. Володарский) [9], так и мало кому известных [10]. Как правило, новые названия образовывались от фамилий, однако на Кавказе, в соответствии с местной традицией называть известных людей не по фамилии, а по имени, в основе нового названия могло лежать имя. Так, при образовании Нагорно-Карабахской автономной области в 1923 году ее центр село Ханкенды было преобразовано в город и переименовано в Степанакерт в память большевика Степана Шаумяна [11].

Одно переименование этого периода носило откровенно политический характер. В 1922 году был убит руководитель коммунистической партии Эстонии В. Кингисепп, и тут же его имя было присвоено старинному русскому городу Ямбургу, стоявшему тогда у границы с независимой Эстонской республикой. Главный путь из капиталистической Эстонии в Советскую Россию лежал теперь через город, названный именем главного эстонского коммуниста [12].

В 1921 году село Романовский Хутор на Северном Кавказе было переименовано в Кропоткин (с одновременным преобразованием его в город). Это переименование было сделано в память скончавшегося в этом году знаменитого анархиста П. А. Кропоткина. Анархизм в революционном движении был течением, отличным от большевизма, однако в те годы большевики еще признавали заслуги других революционных партий в борьбе с царизмом. Впоследствии, когда при Сталине лишь марксисты были провозглашены носителями истины, а все остальные революционные движения и партии были объявлены враждебными рабочему классу, соответствующие правила топонимических игр изменились, и подобное переименование было бы невозможным. Это же относится и к переименованию в 1923 году города Орлова Вятской губернии в город Халтурин — в память Степана Халтурина, революционера-террориста XIX века. [13]

В 1918 году на карте появилось имя большевистского «бога» — Карла Маркса. Город Екатериненштадт (известный также под именем Баронск, Саратовская губерния) был переименован в Марксштадт [14]. Для полноты картины надо назвать еще одно переименование: в 1918 году город Николаевск Саратовской губернии был переименован в Пугачев — в память вождя крестьянского восстания XVIII века Емельяна Пугачева. Всего, таким образом, в 1918–1923 годах 14 городов получили имена разных лиц (в том числе двух живых). Но в это же время с карты стираются имена других лиц — переименовываются многие города, названные в свое время в честь лиц императорской фамилии, а также царских генералов.

Первыми в этой группе городов был уже упомянутые Николаевск и Екатериненштат Саратовской губернии, а также Елизаветполь, которому власти тогда независимого Азербайджана вернули его древнее имя Ганджа, или Гянджа (1918) [15]. Затем исчезают имена Екатеринодар (Краснодар с 1920), Константиноград (Красноград с 1922). Чуть позднее переименовываются Екатеринбург (Свердловск с 1924), Александрополь (Ленинакан с 1924), Екатеринослав (Днепропетровск с 1926) [16], Новониколаевск (Новосибирск с 1926) [17].

Когда наступила Октябрьская революция, на карте было три города, названных в честь генералов царской армии, и все три были переименованы. Первой «жертвой» стал Пржевальск на озере Иссык-Куль в Киргизии, названный так в память выдающегося путешественника Н. М. Пржевальского. Но Пржевальский имел генеральское звание, и только по одной этой причине рассматривался новыми «хозяевами» как враг; его заслуги перед наукой в те годы никого не интересовали. И в 1921 году городу Пржевальску возвращается его старое имя Каракол [18]. Затем переименовываются города Скобелев (быв. Новый Маргелан) — в Фергану (1924) и Перовск (быв. Ак-Мечеть) — в Кзыл-Орду (1925) [19].

Как мы видим, если не считать получивших старые имена Каракола и Ганджи, только один город получил политически нейтральное, «безыдейное» имя: Фергана — по месту, где этот город расположен.

В эти же годы было сделано одно парадоксальное переименование, когда город был переименован из-за сходства своего имени с фамилией лица, нежелательного для советской власти. В Пензенской губернии при слиянии рек Керенки и Вада стоял город, названный по имени одной из них: Керенск. Это имя город носил с XVII века, но так как оно напоминало большевикам фамилию свергнутого ими председателя временного правительства А. Ф. Керенского, город был переименован и с тех пор называется по второй реке — Вадинск [20].

ПОСЛЕ ЛЕНИНА — ЖИВЫЕ

Смерть Ленина в 1924 году ознаменовала начало нового периода в процессе наименований городов. Сразу после смерти Ленина Петроград переименовывается в Ленинград. Вслед за этим появляются Ульяновск (быв. Симбирск), Ленинакан (быв. Александрополь), Ленинск в Туркмении (быв. Чарджуй, или Старый Чарджуй) — в 1924 году [21] и Ленинск-Кузнецкий (быв. Кольчугино, в Кузбассе) — в 1925. Но — вот он, еще один парадокс советской игры в имена — в 1927 году Ленинск в Туркмении снова становится Чарджуем [22], а в 1929 году на карте вместо подмосковного Ленинска снова появляется Талдом [23]. Никакого объяснения стирания в то время ленинских имен я найти не смог, и ничего рационального сказать по этому поводу не могу [24]. Тем более, что затем появляются Ленинабад (быв. Ходжент, 1935), Ленинск в Узбекистане (быв. Зеленск, до этого Ассаке, 1938), Лениногорск в Восточном Казахстане (быв Риддер, 1941) [25].

Но главная особенность нового периода — появление большого числа городов, названных именами живых людей. Первыми на карте появились имена генерального секретаря ЦК ВКП(б) И. В. Сталина, председателя Исполнительного комитета Коммунистического интернационала Г. Е. Зиновьева и председателя Совета народных комиссаров СССР А. И. Рыкова, а также председателя Центрального исполнительного комитета Украины Г. И. Петровского. «Лидером» сразу становится Сталин, как генеральный секретарь ЦК партии: его имя в течение пяти лет на карте появляется трижды — в названиях городов Сталино (1924, быв. Юзовка, ныне Донецк), Сталинград (1925, быв. Царицын, ныне Волгоград), Сталинабад (1929, быв. Дюшамбе, ныне Душанбе). Имена других названных деятелей получают города Зиновьевск (1924, быв. Елизаветград), Рыково (1928, быв. Енакиево в Донбассе) и уже названный выше Днепропетровск.

Сохранилась фотография, сделанная на праздновании пятидесятилетия И. В. Сталина в Кремле 21 декабря 1929 года. На ней вождь снялся вместе со своими ближайшими соратниками — Г. К. Орджоникидзе, К. Е. Ворошиловым, В. В. Куйбышевым, М. И. Калининым, Л. М. Кагановичем и С. М. Кировым. Эта «великолепная семерка» большевиков получила 29 городов — одни при жизни, другие после смерти.

После того, как в 1929 году Сталин установил свое единоначальное правление в партии и стране, он начал награждать городами (и не только городами, но о другом у нас речь сейчас не идет) своих приспешников, «получивших» города при жизни: К. Е. Ворошилов — четыре города [26], Л. М. Каганович — два города [27], М. И. Калинин — два города [28], Г. К. Орджоникидзе — два города [29]. А. И. Микоян — один город [30], В. М. Молотов — три города [31]. Один город «получил» С. М. Буденный, провозглашенный героем гражданской войны [32]. При этом Сталин не забывал и себя: на карте появились еще три города, названные его именем [33].

Не занимая в то время формально никаких государственных постов, Сталин сам не мог подписывать правительственных постановлений. И временами советская игра в имена доходила до абсурда: постановление Центрального исполнительного комитета СССР о переименовании города Тверь в город Калинин подписал... председатель Центрального исполнительного комитета СССР М. Калинин! [34]

Люди, узурпировавшие в 1917 году власть в стране, как будто чувствовали всю незаконность их притязаний. Имя на карте казалось им оправданием их действий, методом укрепления власти. Оно удовлетворяло их тщеславие, с его помощью они надеялись остаться в истории. Тем более, что многие переименования производились «по желанию трудящихся», во что руководители часто верили, и преподносились как награды (каковыми, по-существу, и были — за верную службу режиму). Появились даже города, названные в честь местных партийных руководителей: Кабаковск, быв. Надеждинск на Северном Урале — в честь первого секретаря Уральского комитета партии И.Д. Кабакова (1935); Мирзоян, быв. Аулие-Ата на юге Казахстана — в честь казахстанского партийного лидера Л.И. Мирзояна, (1936); Махарадзе, быв. Озургети (1934) и Миха Цхакая, быв. Сенаки в Грузии (1935, с 1977 Цхакая) — в честь местных руководящих большевиков Ф.И. Махарадзе и М.Г. Цхакая [35].

Особенно массовым было желание увековечить свои имена у партийных деятелей Украины. Вслед за Днепропетровском появились Постышево в Донбассе, быв. Гришино [36], Чубаровка в Запорожской области, быв. Пологи [37], поселок имени товарища Хатаевича, быв. Синельниково [38], и Косиорово [39], названные в честь руководителей Украины П.П. Постышева, В.Я. Чубаря, М.М. Хатаевича, С.В. Косиора. Эти населенные пункты (кроме Косиорово) стали в 1938 годах городами, но я не могу сказать под какими именами — под только что названными или под теми, под которыми мы их сейчас знаем: Красноармейск, Пологи, Синельниково. Это же относится и к упомянутому в начале статьи поселку Зеленск в Узбекистане (быв. Ассаке), известному позднее как город Ленинск. Но о причине очередной смены имен этими поселениями — чуть ниже.

Были «награждены» городами четыре писателя — за их верную службу режиму. Широко известен факт переименования в 1932 году города Нижнего Новгорода в город Горький, но не «великий пролетарский писатель» был первым литератором, получившим город. Первым был придворный кремлевский поэт Демьян Бедный, с которым дружил Сталин: еще в 1925 году город Спасск Пензенской области был переименован в Беднодемьяновск [40]. Демьян Бедный был слабым поэтом, но не критерии мастерства были решающими при награждении деятелей литературы и искусства в сталинское время (как, впрочем, и в более поздние времена): Демьян Бедный верно служил своим хозяевам. По тем же причинам станица Усть-Медведицкая на Дону (Ростовская область) была переименована в город Серафимович — в честь писателя А. С. Серафимовича (1933), а позднее появилось на карте имя казахского акына (народного поэта) Джамбула. Нелишне заметить, что произведения Демьяна Бедного, Серафимовича и Джамбула сейчас заслуженно почти забыты.

Чести попасть на карту удостоился в те годы также селекционер-садовод И. В. Мичурин, чьи работы были провозглашены официальной биологией образцом «материалистической» науки: в 1932 году город Козлов Тамбовской области был переименован в Мичуринск [41].

Всего в 1918–1940 годах в названиях поселений, которые были городами или стали ими, можно было увидеть имена 29 деятелей, «получивших» городские поселения при жизни [42]. Но советская игра в имена порой приобретала кровавый оттенок, и имена двенадцати из них исчезли с карты вскоре после появления, что в 1930-е годы стало знаком их ареста, а затем и физического уничтожения. Первым в 1929 году было стерто с карты имя Троцкого [43]: быв. Гатчина была переименована в Красногвардейск [44]. В 1934 году были переименованы Зиновьевск, получивший имя Кирово (с 1939 — Кировоград) и Рыково, которому вернули имя Енакиево.

Затем, в 1937–1939 годах исчезают имена Кабакова, Мирзояна, Постышева, Чубаря, Хатаевича, Косиора, Зеленского [45]. Имя Баталпашинска, в то время центра Черкесской автономной области, меняется трижды на протяжении 1936–1938 годов: сначала Баталпашинск получил имя Сулимов — в честь председателя Совнаркома РСФСР Д. Е. Сулимова, затем, после ареста Сулимова, был переименован в Ежово-Черкесск — в честь народного комиссара внутренних дел Н. И. Ежова, чьими руками Сталин осуществлял кровавый террор 1937–1938 годов, и наконец, после того, как всесильного главу НКВД постигла судьба его жертв, стал просто Черкесском...

ПОСЛЕ ЛЕНИНА – МЕРТВЫЕ

Умершие и погибшие революционеры также не были забыты в переименованиях. Условно переименования, сделанные в их честь, можно разделить на две группы: сделанные через годы после их гибели или естественной смерти и сделанные сразу после их ухода из жизни. К числу первых относятся переименования в память умершего в 1918 году Я. М. Свердлова (в 1924 году Екатеринбург стал Свердловском) [46] и умершего в 1926 году Ф. Э. Дзержинского (первый город в честь первого чекиста появился в 1929 году, когда пос. Растяпино под Нижним Новгородом был переименован в Дзержинск) [47].

Шесть городов на карте быв. Советского Союза названы в честь большевика Артема, умершего в 1921 году. Все они расположены в районах горной промышленности: Артем (Ф. А. Сергеев) был на руководящей работе в Донбассе, затем возглавлял профсоюз горнорабочих. Первый город в его честь появился в 1924 году, когда Бахмут в Донбассе был переименован в Артемовск. Еще четыре города в память этого большевика, чье имя сейчас мало кто помнит, появились в 1938–39 годах и один — после войны [48].

В 1930 году в Подмосковье были переименованы три города, носившие религиозно-церковные имена. Два из них получили имена покойных большевиков. Город Сергиев стал называться Загорск, в память В. М. Загорского [49], Богородск стал Ногинском — в память В. П. Ногина [50].

Ряд городов был назван именами погибших героев гражданской войны. Почти все видные участники гражданской войны впоследствии попали в число «врагов народа», но некоторые, в основном из тех, кто успел погибнуть раньше (своеобразное «везение»), были «канонизированы». Первым появилось на карте имя Чапаева, заменившее имя Троцкого в названии быв. Иващенкова, затем — имена Г. И. Котовского [51] и... героя, которого не было — Н. А. Щорса. То есть человек по имени Щорс существовал и участвовал в гражданской войне на стороне красных, но его действительные заслуги были несущественны. Героическая биография Щорса была придумана по заданию Сталина, провозгласившего Щорса «украинским Чапаевым» [52]. В 1935 году город Сновск (Черниговская область) был переименован в Щорс.

Известности этих трех канонизированных героев способствовали созданные о них художественные фильмы. Особенно был популярен фильм «Чапаев», обладавший несомненными художественными достоинствами. Фильм был снят по одноименному роману писателя Д. А. Фурманова, бывшего комиссара Чапаевской дивизии. В 1941 году город Середа в Ивановской области был переименован в Фурманов.

Имена умерших революционеров получили некоторые другие малые города [53]. В 1941 году город Мысовск в Забайкалье был переименован в Бабушкин, в память большевика И. В. Бабушкина, расстрелянного в здесь в 1906 году.

Наконец, в 1930 году появился город, названный в честь второго «основоположника марксизма» — Фридриха Энгельса: столица АССР Немцев Поволжья город Покровск была переименована в город Энгельс.

В 1920-е годы города получали имена в память умерших партийных и государственных руководителей, так сказать, «по свежим следам», после смерти Ленина, М. В. Фрунзе [54], и А. Д. Цюрупы [55], в 1930-е годы — после смерти Кирова, Куйбышева и Орджоникидзе. По поводу переименований городов в честь этих последних, хотелось бы заметить следующее: по моему мнению, массовое переименование городов и других объектов в память этих руководителей после их смерти может служить косвенным подтверждением причастности Сталина к их уходу из жизни: Сталин был великий лицемер, и жестом переименования в их честь городов, поселков, предприятий и прочих мест и организаций он демонстрировал свою якобы великую скорбь и уважение к их памяти.

Киров был убит 1 декабря 1934 года, и тут же его имя получили Зиновьевск [56] — ныне Кировоград, Вятка, переименованная в Киров, и Хибиногорк на Кольском полуострове, ставший Кировском. В 1935 году Караклис в Армении становится Кироваканом, Ганджа в Азербайджане — Кировабадом [57], Калата в Свердловской области — Кировградом. Еще через год на карте появляется второй Киров: это имя получает преобразованный в город бывший поселок Песочня в Калужской области [58].

После смерти Куйбышева в 1935 году три города получают имя Куйбышев: два на Волге — Самара и Спасск-Татарский и один в Западной Сибири — Каинск. Еще один город его имени появляется в Амурской области: Куйбышевка-Восточная (быв. Александровка) [59].

В 1937 году умер Орджоникидзе [60]. В дополнение к двум городам, уже носившим его имя [61], появляются еще два: Орджоникидзе в Донбассе (быв. Енакиево, одно время Рыково) и Серго (быв. Кадиевка), названный по партийному псевдониму Орджоникидзе.

Другую группу переименований «по свежим следам» составили в те годы переименования в память погибших летчиков. Успехи советских летчиков в дальних перелетах, в исследованиях Арктики, а также в гражданской войне в Испании широко рекламировались в 1930-е годы. Они помогали создать видимость выдающихся достижений социализма и отвлечь внимание от действительной ситуации в стране. Летчики возводились в ранг национальных героев, а в случае их гибели в их память назывались города. В 1938 году Оренбург получает имя Чкалов — в честь трагически погибшего Валерия Чкалова, командира экипажа самолета, совершившего первый перелет из Москвы через Северный полюс в Америку. Еще три города получают имена погибших летчиков в 1939 году: Осипенко (быв. Бердянск на Азовском море) — в честь участницы перелета из Москвы на Дальний Восток Полины Осипенко, Бабушкин (быв. Лосиноостровское под Москвой) — в честь полярного летчика Михаила Бабушкина и Серов (вновь сменивший свое имя Надеждинск) — в честь участника войны в Испании Анатолия Серова [62].

Мне удалось найти только четыре имени, полученные городами до войны, которые бы не были прямо связаны с политикой, во всяком случае, на первый взгляд. Это Пушкин под Ленинградом, названный в честь русского поэта А. С. Пушкина [63], Форт-Шевченко на полуострове Мангышлак — в честь украинского поэта Т. Г. Шевченко [64], Карпинск на Северном Урале — в честь президента Академии наук СССР геолога А. Н. Карпинского [65] и Сабирабад в Азербайджане — в честь азербайджанского поэта Сабира.

[1930]-е годы были в Советском Союзе временем наиболее массовых переименований городов в честь разных деятелей. Но было одно несостоявшееся переименование, о котором, тем не менее, я хочу рассказать. В 1937–1938 годах на основании писем трудящихся (скорее всего, инспирированных) обсуждался вопрос о переименовании Москвы в... Сталинодар (Сталинодар означает дар, подарок Сталина, как Екатеринодар — подарок Екатерины). В одном из сохранившихся писем говорится: «...Я глубоко убежден в том, что все человечество земного шара нашей эпохи и все человечество многих будущих веков с удовлетворением и радостью воспримет переименование Москвы в Сталинодар». Этот вопрос обсуждался на Чрезвычайном XVII Всероссийском съезде Советов, на Политбюро ЦК ВКП(б), на Президиуме Верховного Совета СССР и РСФСР. Однако Сталин, по-видимому, высказался против этого предложения, и Москва осталась Москвой. [66]

ВОЙНА И ПОСЛЕ

В июне 1941 года нацистская Германия напала на Советский Союз, и в игре в города наступил перерыв. Но он был недолгим: уже в 1942 году город Джаркент в Казахстане (Талды-Курганская обл.) был переименован в Панфилов, в память генерала И. В. Панфилова, погибшего в битве под Москвой. Игра в города возобновилась, хотя и в значительно меньших масштабах: было сделано всего 12 переименований, связанных с личностями. Причем, как и прежде, имена людей городам как давались, так и отнимались. В 1943–1944 годах были переименованы все города, названные в честь Орджоникидзе: Орджоникидзеград опять стал Бежицей [67], городу Серго было возвращено имя Кадиевка, столица Северной Осетии получила нейтральное имя Дзауджикау [68]. Что же касается города Орджоникидзе в Донецкой области (которая тогда называлась Сталинской), то «большевики предпочли вернуться к старому названию Енакиево, по имени одного из крупнейших шахтовладельцев, чем оставить за ним имя члена Политбюро» [69], так сильно ненавидел Сталин своего бывшего соратника, которому он не мог простить самоубийства [70].

Кроме того, в 1943 году по непонятным причинам «потеряли» по одному городу Ворошилов и Каганович: на карте Северного Кавказа снова появился Ставрополь, а в Донбассе — Попасная. А вот причина потери «своего» города Микояном совершенно ясна: в 1944 году была упразднена Карачаевская автономная область, карачаевцы выселены с их родной земли, и все имена карачаевского происхождения были переименованы. К тому же часть территории быв. автономной области была передана в состав Грузии. И бывший областной центр Микоян-Шахар, оказавшийся в Грузии, стал называться Клухори [71]. Наконец, городу Слуцку под Ленинградом было возвращено его историческое имя Павловск (1944) [72].

Таким образом, имена большевиков были, по разным причинам, отобраны у восьми городов. Новые же имена в память личностей получили всего четыре города. Два переименования городов на Украине носили политический и патриотический характер. Они были сделаны путем прибавления к старому имени города новой части: Переяслав-Хмельницкий (1943, в честь украинского гетмана XVI века Богдана Хмельницкого) [73] и Корсунь-Шевченковский (1944, в честь Тараса Шевченко).

Два города во время войны были переименованы в честь погибших героев. Это уже упомянутый Джаркент-Панфилов и город Лихвин в Тульской области, получивший имя Чекалин в честь партизана Александра Чекалина (1944). После войны в ходе проводившейся в 1946 году кампании по переименованию городов на территории аннексированной Советами Восточной Пруссии шесть городов были названы в честь Героев Советского Союза, погибших в боях на этой земле. Это города Черняховск (быв. Инстербург), Гусев (быв. Гумбиннен), Гурьевск (быв. Нойхаузен), Ладушкин (быв. Людвигсорт), Мамоново (быв. Хайлигенбайль), и Нестеров (быв. Шталлупёнен) [74].

В ходе другой кампании—по переименованию населенных мест на захваченном у Финляндии Карельском перешейке—город Уурас был переименован в Высоцк (1948) [75]. В целом число городов, названных в честь участников войны 1941–1945 годов удивительно мало, если учесть, то пропагандистское значение, которое придавалось этой войне, получившей официальной название Великой Отечественной [76].

С началом войны прервалась практика наименования городов и других поселений именами здравствующих людей. Теперь надо было умереть, прежде чем «получить» город. Представители же более молодого поколения руководителей, такие, как Н. С. Хрущев, Г. М. Маленков, Л. П. Берия при Сталине получить города не успели [77]. Но при тоталитарном режиме возможны исключения из любых правил,—и на карте городских поселений появилось имя Хрущева. Правда, произошло это несколько позднее, при Хрущеве... [78]

После войны городам по-прежнему давались имена руководящих деятелей. На карте появились второй Калининград—после смерти Калинина (1946, быв. Кенигсберг), города Щербаков—после смерти А. С. Щербакова (1946, быв. Рыбинск, Ярославская область), Жданов—после смерти А. А. Жданова (1948, быв. Мариуполь, Донецкая область), Мир-Башир—после смерти азербайджанского государственного деятеля Мир Башира Касумова (до 1949 пос. Тертер).

После второй мировой войны к Советскому Союзу были присоединены Южный Сахалин и Курильские острова, и в 1946 году производилась замена японских географических названий на русские. Четыре города на Южном Сахалине получили имена в честь российских деятелей прошлого: на карте появились Чехов (быв. Нода)—в честь писателя А. П. Чехова, побывавшего в конце XIX века на Сахалине [79], Невельск (быв. Хонто)—в честь мореплавателя Г. И. Невельского, открывшего пролив между материком и Сахалином, Макаров (быв. Сиритору) — в честь адмирала С. О. Макарова, погибшего в русско-японской войне в 1904 году, и Корсаков (быв. Отомари) — в честь гидрографа В. А. Римского-Корсакова [80].

Иногда наименования приурочивались к юбилейным датам. Так, к столетию со дня рождения литературного критика В. Г. Белинского его родной город Чембар Пензенской области был переименован в Белинский (1948); годом раньше, к столетию со дня рождения «отца русской авиации» Н. Г. Жуковского поселок, в котором находился созданный им Центральный аэро-гидродинамический институт (ЦАГИ) был преобразован в город и получил имя Жуковский (Московская область). Появились города, названные именами двух других русских ученых, однако эти переименования, сделанные в 1948 году — переименование Ораниенбаума под Ленинградом в Ломоносов [81] и Раненбурга в Липецкой области в Чаплыгин [82] нельзя отнести к чисто коммеморативным: это была откровенная замена старых германизированных названий русскими именами. Этими переименованиями было завершено стирание с карты Советского Союза «немецких» имен, начатое в России еще в начале первой мировой войны в 1914 году, когда Санкт-Петербург был переименован в Петроград [83]. «Советы оказались более истыми руссификаторами, чем царское правительство...» [84]

В первые послевоенные годы на карте появились также имена двух деятелей прошлого: героя войн с Наполеоном генерала Багратиона (город Прейсиш-Эйлау в бывшей Восточной Пруссии был переименован в Багратионовск, 1946) [85] и военного летчика, одного из основоположников высшего пилотажа П. Н. Нестерова (город Жолква в Львовской области был переименован в Нестеров, 1951) [86].

ПРИ ХРУЩЕВЕ

В 1953 году умер Сталин, и уже на следующий год было сделано первое политическое переименование: городу Дзауджикау было возвращено его имя [87]. Этот акт носил явно антисталинский характер и был одним из предвестников предстоявшего вскоре хрущевского разоблачения культа Сталина.

В 1957 году игра в имена совершила неожиданный поворот. Н. С. Хрущев вышел победителем в борьбе со своими противниками в Политбюро ЦК КПСС — так наз. «антипартийной группой Молотова, Маленкова, Кагановича». Имена некоторых членов этой группы — Молотова, Кагановича и Ворошилова (который тоже входил в эту группу, о чем тогда не сообщалось), были на карте СССР. Понятно, что Хрущев не мог дальше это терпеть. И был принят специальный указ Президиума Верховного Совета СССР, в соответствии с которым запрещалось называть города и другие объекты именами каких-либо деятелей при их жизни [88]. И имена членов «антипартийной группы» были стерты с карты «на законном основании». Город Молотов опять стал Пермью, одному Молотовску было возвращено имя Нолинск, а другой, более молодой, получил имя Северодвинск. Ворошиловград опять стал Луганском. Город Ворошилов был переименован в Уссурийск [89]. Город Каганович — в Ново-Каширск [90].

Были переименованы и все другие поселения, носившие имена Молотова, Ворошилова, Кагановича, а также Микояна и Буденного. На карте СССР не осталось поселений, носивших имена живых людей, кроме... поселка Хрущев. Можно ли представить человека, который без указания сверху подписал бы указ или постановление о переименовании поселения, носившего имя Первого секретаря ЦК КПСС? А указание, видимо, последовало не сразу. Более того, в 1961 году этот поселок даже был преобразован в город! [91] Но на следующий год указание, по-видимому, наконец-то пришло, имя Хрущева с карты исчезло, и появился город Кремгэс (аббревиатура Кременчугкой ГЭС) [92].

В 1957 году еще трем городам (кроме Луганска, Перми и Нолинска) были возвращены их исторические имена: Чкалов снова стал Оренбургом, Щербаков — Рыбинском и Осипенко — Бердянском. К сожалению, этот процесс не получил в то время развития.

Разоблачение преступлений Сталина, начатое Хрущевым на XX съезде КПСС в 1956 году, достигло в то время своего апогея на XXI съезде в 1961 году. Этот съезд имел прямое влияние на топонимию: после него были переименованы все географические объекты, носившие имя Сталина, в том числе и города. Были возвращены старые имена Сталинску — Новокузнецк, Сталинири — Цхинвали и, с небольшим различием в написании, Сталинабаду — Душанбе (до 1929 года Дюшамбе). Новые имена получили Сталинград — Волгоград, Сталино — Донецк и Сталиногорск — Новомосковск [93].

Таким образом, при Хрущеве были переименованы 17 городов, названных при Сталине в честь разных личностей. Но в то время, как одни города теряли свои новые имена, другие теряли старые: практика переименований городов в честь различных деятелей продолжалась. Однако круг этих лиц, по сравнению с предшествовавшими периодами изменился: уменьшилась доля ре-

315

волюционеров и деятелей коммунистического режима в СССР. Среди немногих переименований этого рода — переименование в 1955 году поселка Новая Письмянка в Татарии в город Лениногорск и города Мариямполе в Литве в Капсукас (в память одного из руководителей компартии Литвы В. С. Мицкявичюса-Капсукаса); переименование в 1959 году города Нор-Баязет в Армении в Камо (в честь армянского большевика С. А. Тер-Петросяна, известного под партийной кличкой Камо); переименование в 1962 году поселка Баланда Саратовской области в город Калининск. Но на карте появляется новый топонимический слой: имена руководителей зарубежных коммунистических партий.

До этого времени зарубежные деятели были представлены на карте СССР весьма скромно: по городу в честь Маркса и Энгельса, и… всё. Новые переименования отражали политику ЦК КПСС укреплять так называемые «дружбу и единство международного коммунистического движения»: городам стали давать имена умерших коммунистических лидеров. Первым, в июле 1964 года, попал на карту лидер французских коммунистов Морис Торез [94], месяц спустя — его итальянский коллега Пальмиро Тольятти: имя Тольятти получает город Ставрополь на Волге, где в это время строился завод легковых автомобилей. Завод проектировали итальянские капиталисты (фирма «Фиат»), а город был переименован в честь коммуниста!

В 1963 году стал городом поселок Вахрушево в Луганской области [95], названный в память министра угольной промышленности В. В. Вахрушева — единственный случай среди всех наименований и переименований городов в СССР, когда город получил имя хозяйственного руководителя.

Восемь новых наименований было присвоено в честь писателей, из которых два были сделаны в России в честь русских писателей (переименование к 50-летию со дня смерти А. П. Чехова в 1954 году поселка Лопасня в Московской области в город Чехов и присвоение новому городу в Ставропольском крае имени Лермонтовский в честь М. Ю. Лермонтова [96]), остальные — в других союзных республиках и — за одним, но характерным для советской игры в города исключением — в честь местных писателей. На карте появились Навои в Узбекистане (быв. пос. Кермине, 1958), Физули в Азербайджане (быв. Карягино, 1959), Абай в Казахстане (Карагандинская область, быв. пос. Чурубай-Нура, 1961), Ивано-Франковск на Украине (быв. Станислав, 1962), Абовян в Армении (быв. село Элар, 1963) [97], Шевченко в Казахстане (быв. Актау, 1964).

На последнем переименовании стоит остановиться подробнее. Тарас Шевченко, как известно, украинский поэт, но часть его жизни прошла на полуострове Мангышлак в Казахстане, куда он был сослан царским правительством. И когда в 1960-е годы началось освоение природных ресурсов этого полуострова, было решено назвать главный город полуострова именем поэта: город в Казахстане, носящий имя украинского поэта, должен был символизировать и прославлять дружбу народов СССР. При этом упустили из виду, что на Мангышлаке уже был город, носящий имя ссыльного поэта — Форт-Шевченко. А скорее всего не упустили, а просто проигнорировали, ведь городу Шевченко, в отличие от мало кому известного Форта-Шевченко, предстояло стать большим городом! И в течение четверти века на одном полуострове было два города, носивших имя одного человека... Как теперь стало ясно, «дружба народов СССР» была одним из коммунистических мифов. Нет сейчас и города Шевченко: ему возвращено имя, данное при рождении — Актау.

Несомненно, что решение о переименовании Актау в Шевченко принималось, как говорят в России, «на самом верху». Так же, как и решение о переименовании города Станислава, принятое по указанию Хрущева [98].

В 1962 году на карте появился первый город, названный в память композитора — поселок строителей Воткинской ГЭС в Пермской области получил имя Чайковский [99].

Физическая карта мира полна именами данными в честь открывателей и исследователей Земли, но городов в их честь сравнительно немного. В этом отношении карта бывшего Советского Союза не представляет исключения. До революции два города были названы именами первооткрывателей: уже упомянутый Пржевальск и Хабаровск [100]. Немного появилось их и в советское время: кроме уже названных сахалинских Макарова и Корсакова, лишь Арсеньев в Приморском крае (1953, быв. пос. Семеновка), названный в честь путешественника и исследователя Дальнего Востока В. К. Арсеньева, Докучаевск в Донецкой области (1954, быв. пос. Еленовские Карьеры) — в честь выдающегося почвоведа В. В. Докучаева, Шелехов (Шелихов) в Иркутской области (город с 1962), названный в честь русского купца XVIII века Г. И. Шелихова (Шелехова), который основал первые русские поселения в Северной Америке, да еще два города в честь геологов: единственный город, получивший имя ученого до войны, — Карпинск (см. выше) и Губкин в Белгородской области [101].

Ряд городов был назван именами исторических персонажей. В 1954 году, когда отмечалось 300-летие воссоединения Украины с Россией, в дополнение к Переяславу-Хмельницкому появился просто Хмельницкий (быв. Проскуров). Другие появившиеся в этот период на карте имена: Салават, Бируни, Ермак [102]. В целом, как мы видим, число городов, названных в честь писателей, ученых, исследователей Земли и других «неполитических» фигур возросло.

ПРИ БРЕЖНЕВЕ

В октябре 1964 года Хрущев был отстранен от власти и Первым (в дальнейшем Генеральным) секретарем ЦК КПСС стал Л. И. Брежнев. Время, когда он и его наследники на этом посту А. В. Андропов и К. У. Черненко стояли во главе партии, получило при М. С. Горбачеве имя «застойного». В игре в имена его можно назвать «спокойным»: массовых кампаний по переименованию городов не проводилось, да и вообще переименований было сравнительно не много. Однако в «правилах игры» произошли изменения. Вновь изменилась общая тенденция, и имена политических фигур снова стали появляться в названиях городов чаще, чем писателей, ученых и других неполитических деятелей.

Брежневское руководство явно вело линию на сглаживание последствий хрущевской критики Сталина. Впрочем, на прямую реабилитацию Сталина оно не решилось, и Волгоград не стал снова Сталинградом [103], но эта политика, тем не менее, отразилась на игре в имена: появилась тенденция возвращать городам отнятые у них при Хрущеве имена сталинских помощников — после их смерти. Так, после смерти Ворошилова (1970) Луганск вновь стал Ворошиловградом, а после смерти Буденного (1973) Прикумск был вторично переименован в Буденновск. Кто знает, умри Молотов раньше — не в 1987 году, при Горбачеве, а года на три-четыре до этого, его имя снова засияло бы на карте, и Пермь опять стала бы Молотовым [104].

В то же время в стране продолжал нагнетаться культ Ленина, что отразилось и на топонимике: на карте появились несколько новых городов, названных в его честь. Почему-то в их названиях не традиционно для ленинских имен городов использовалось его отчество — Ильич, а также настоящая фамилия Ульянов. Появились город Ульяново в Узбекистане (1974, Джизакская обл., быв. пос. Обручево) и три Ильичевска — под Одессой (1973), в Узбекистане (Андижанская область, 1980) [105] и в Азербайджане (Нахичеванская АССР, 1981; до 1964 Норашен). Кроме того, стал городом поселок Порт-Ильич в Азербайджане (1971).

Впрочем, появился и новый город Ленинск — в дополнение к двум, существовавшим в это время [106]. Но мало кто в стране знал о его существовании: этот Ленинск вырос возле главного советского космодрома Байконур в Казахстане и был до самых последних лет секретным городом [107].

Как и в предыдущий период, много новых имен городов появилось в союзных республиках. Но если в хрущевское время на карте нередко появлялись имена писателей и других деятелей культуры, то при Брежневе города чаще переименовывались в честь местных партийных и государственных деятелей: появились города Стучка в Латвии (1967), Ахунбабаев в Узбекистане, (до 1975 пос. Суфикишлак), Гафуров в Таджикистане (Ленинабадская обл., до 1978 Советабад); в 1982 году стал городом пос. Гегечкори в Грузии (быв. Мартвили) [108]. Два города получили имя Нариманов — в честь революционера и государственного деятеля Наримана Нариманова: в Узбекистане (Ташкентская обл., до 1981 Бахтемир) и в Астраханской области (до 1984 пос. Нижневолжский) [109].

Продолжается переименование городов в честь зарубежных коммунистов. В 1965 году умирает румынский руководитель Георге Георгиу-Деж, и город Лиски Воронежской области переименовывают в Георгиу-Деж [110] — казалось, продолжается начавшаяся годом раньше традиция переименования городов в честь этой категории людей сразу после их смерти. Но потом вершители советской топонимии вспомнили, что были и другие весьма достойные (с точки зрения этих самых вершителей) лица, которые умерли тогда, когда присваивать городам имена зарубежных лидеров было еще не модно. И город Мелекесс в Ульяновской области получает имя Димитровград — в честь болгарского вождя Георгия Димитрова (1972) [111], а город Змиев Харьковской области переименовывается в Готвальд (1976) — в честь руководителя коммунистической Чехословакии Климента Готвальда [112].

В 1965 году на карте появляется «топонимический монстр» — Карлолибкнехтовск (Донецкая обл.), выросший из поселка имени Карла Либкнехта, немецкого революционера, погибшего в 1918 году [113].

В этот период на карте появилось всего лишь четыре города, названных в честь писателей. Одно из наименований городов следует отметить особо: в 1967 году город Лусаван в Армении был переименован в Чаренцаван — в честь армянского поэта Егише

Чаренца, погибшего в годы «большого террора» и посмертно реабилитированного — игра в имена сделала очередной зигзаг [114].

В 1981 году стал городом Маяковский в Грузии. Имя русского советского поэта В. В. Маяковского было присвоено селу Багдади, в котором он родился, еще в 1940 году. Это переименование можно понять: уроженец Багдади Маяковский, став знаменитым поэтом, неоднократно приезжал в Грузию и посвящал ей стихи. А вот появление в 1966 году города Пушкино в Азербайджане — «проявление» все той же мифологической дружбы народов СССР: Пушкин в Азербайджане никогда не был и стихов о нем не писал...

В 1978 году умер официозный таджикский поэт Мирзо Турсун-Заде, и тут же город Регар в Таджикистане был переименован в Турсунзаде.

Три города получили имена в честь ученых. В 1967 году поселок Биндюжный в Татарии был переименован в город Менделеевск — в честь выдающегося русского химика Д. И. Менделеева. В 1983 году стал городом поселок Курчатов при Курской атомной электростанции, названный в честь академика И. В. Курчатова, первого научного руководителя советского атомного проекта. При Горбачеве стало известно о существовании еще одного Курчатова, как и байконурский Ленинск, секретного — города при Семипалатинском атомном полигоне в Казахстане.

В 1968 году во время полета на самолете разбился первый в мире космонавт Юрий Гагарин. Первые космонавты, особенно Гагарин, пользовались несомненной любовью народа, а для правящего режима успехи Советского Союза в космических полетах играли примерно ту же роль, что и успехи летчиков в 1930-е годы, — они помогали камуфлировать провалы социализма. И когда Гагарин погиб, его родной город Гжатск в Смоленской области был переименован в Гагарин [115].

В памятном Указе Президиума Верховного Совета СССР от 11 сентября 1957 года, среди разного рода деятелей, чьи имена могли присваиваться городам и другим географическим объектам, были названы и «герои труда». Однако ни до этого указа, ни позже — за одним исключением, к которому мы сейчас переходим, — имена «героев труда» — рабочих — городам не давались. Пожалуй, самым знаменитым рабочим в стране был в 1930-е годы шахтер Алексей Стаханов, установивший в 1935 году рекорд по добыче угля [116]. Стаханова превозносили как героя, его именем было названо движение передовиков производства («стахановское движение»), но городов в его честь не было: города при жизни могли иметь, как правило, только высшие партийные и государственные руководители. Правда, в 1938 году поселок Отдых под Москвой был в его честь назван Стаханово [117], но когда этому поселку пришло время становиться городом, он был переименован в Жуковский. Стаханов «получил» город только после смерти — в 1978 году, когда Кадиевка в Луганской области была переименована в Стаханов.

Последние «громкие» переименования в «период стагнации» были сделаны после смерти Л. И. Брежнева, Ю. В. Андропова, Д. А. Устинова и К. У. Черненко: их имена получили Набережные Челны в Татарии (с 1982 город Брежнев), вновь переименованный Рыбинск (с 1984 город Андропов), столица Удмуртии Ижевск (с 1984 город Устинов) и Шарыпово в Красноярском крае (с 1985 город Черненко). Решения об этих переименованиях принимались в Политбюро ЦК КПСС и оформлялись как постановления ЦК КПСС, Президиума Верховного Совета и Совета Министров СССР.

ПРИ ГОРБАЧЕВЕ И ПОСЛЕ

В 1985 году, после смерти Черненко, Генеральным секретарем ЦК КПСС стал М. С. Горбачев. И вскоре подул ветер перемен: началась «перестройка». Конечно, она не могла не затронуть и географические имена: в стране развернулось движение за возвращение городам их исторических имен. И процесс пошел в обратную сторону. Деятели «периода застоя», которые «получили» города последними, первыми их «потеряли»: в 1987 году с карты было стерто имя Устинова, на следующий год — Брежнева и Черненко [118]. Желание жителей этих городов, носивших имена названных деятелей, вернуть городам старые имена, совпало с нелюбовью к этим деятелям нового руководства страны. Но игра осталась игрой, и на вопросе возвращения городу Андропову его исторического названия Рыбинск произошла заминка: ведь Андропов был «крестным отцом» Горбачева. Однако выход и здесь был найден: в отличие от других правительственных постановлений об «обратных переименованиях» [119], постановление о переименовании города Андропова в Рыбинск было составлено без упоминания имени переименовываемого города! [120]

Вместе с «перестройкой», как известно, развивалась «гласность». По мере ее развития, наряду с движением за возвращение городам их исторических имен, развивалось движение за стирание с карты имен коммунистических вождей. Первые прямые требования «убрать этого деятеля с карты» были направлены против одной из наиболее одиозных фигур сталинского времени Жданова [121]. И вот в январе 1989 года советское руководство, наконец, принимает решение о переименовании городов и всех других объектов, носивших имя этого деятеля [122].

Затем, постепенно подошла очередь и других коммунистических «святых». В 1989 году исчезает имя Кировабад (ныне, как и в старину Гянджа), на следующий год переименовываются Ворошиловград (ему вновь возвращается имя Луганск), Калинин (Тверь), Орджоникидзе в Северной Осетии (Владикавказ), Горький (Нижний Новгород) [123].

Впервые за всю историю страны Советов власти вынуждены считаться с мнением населения. Но пока еще не тронуто на карте имя коммунистического «бога» — Ленина. Наконец, в ноябре 1990 году появляется, казалось бы, первая «ласточка»: в одной из статей в газете «Труд» говорится, что городу Ленинакану возвращено его «старое имя Гюмри» [124]. Однако не проходит и двух недель, как «Труд» публикует опровержение [125]. Тем не менее, Ленинакан оказывается первым городом, потерявшим в ходе перестройки свое ленинское имя [126].

В начале 1991 года Куйбышев снова становится Самарой [127]. Затем переименовываются Фрунзе [128] и Ленинабад [129]. Ряд других городов теряет имена коммунистических вождей, но главная борьба разгорается вокруг имени «колыбели революции» — Ленинграда.

С самого начала перестройки партийная бюрократия выступала против переименований городов и часто блокировала предложения о возвращении им старых имен. Иногда постановления о переименовании сопровождались заявлениями, что память о лице, имя которого носил город, сохраняется в названиях улиц и других объектов. Но ни одно предложение не встретило такого сопротивления со стороны сторонников коммунистической системы, как предложение о переименовании Ленинграда в Санкт-Петербург (или Петроград) [130]. Борьба вокруг имени этого города широко освещалась в печати, и достаточно хорошо известна. Против изменения имени города выступил даже сам президент СССР Горбачев. Однако на состоявшемся 11 июня 1991 года референдуме 54 процента избирателей Ленинграда проголосовали за возвращение их городу имени, которое дал ему его основатель Петр Великий: Санкт-Петербург. Но мнение населения города не являлось окончательным, и только в сентябре — после провала августовского путча — был принят Указ Президиума Верховного Совета РСФСР о восстановлении исторического имени города.

В этом же сентябре 1991 года были возвращены исторические имена Свердловску — Екатеринбург и Загорску — Сергиев Посад. Был переименован и город Шевченко в Казахстане, ему вернули его первое имя Актау [131].

Всего, по имеющимся у меня сведениям, в 1987–1991 годах 39 городов на территории быв. СССР, названные в советское время в честь различных деятелей, переименованы, причем им, как правило, возвращены их старые имена [132]. Возможно, были и другие переименования, но сведениями о них я не располагаю.

В декабре 1991 года Советский Союз прекратил свое существование. Но новым независимым государствам досталось тяжелое коммунистическое наследие. В том числе и на картах: многие города, в основном в России и на Украине, продолжают носить навязанные им коммунистическими правителями имена. Так что картографам еще остается немало работы. И не всегда понятно, какими путями пойдут законодатели... Игра в имена, теперь уже «пост-советская», продолжается.

ЗАКЛЮЧЕНИЕ

В заключение я хотел бы назвать города, чаще других менявших свои названия. Это:

Енакиево — Рыково — Енакиево — Орджоникидзе — Енакиево;
Рыбинск — Щербаков — Рыбинск — Андропов — Рыбинск;
Луганск — Ворошиловград — Луганск — Ворошиловград —
    Луганск;
Владикавказ — Орджоникидзе — Дзауджикау — Орджоникидзе —
    Владикавказ;
Лиски — Свобода — Лиски — Георгиу-Деж — Лиски.

И могу предсказать абсолютного рекордсмена: город, названный в честь сталинского маршала Буденного. Его первое имя было Святой Крест, затем он назывался Прикумск, потом Буденновск, снова Прикумск и снова Буденновск. Нет сомнения, что он будет переименован, вопрос лишь в том, когда и как. Впрочем, может быть сейчас, когда я дописываю эту статью, российские картографы наносят на карту его новое имя...

Литература

Асанкулова С. «Имя для города». «Известия», 17.10.1989.

Большая Советская энциклопедия, изд. 3-е, в 50 тт. М., «Советская энциклопедия», 1970–1978.

Большой энциклопедический словарь, т. 1–2. М., «Советская энциклопедия», 1991.

Географический энциклопедический словарь. Географические названия. М., «Советская энциклопедия», 1983.

Горбаневский М. «Топонимический беспредел». «Посев», 1991, № 5, с. 100–108.

Ивина Наталья. «"Зачем нам отреченья?" Размышления над письмами». «Литературная газета», 28.09.1988.

«Имя на карте». Интервью с В. П. Нерознаком и М. Горбаневским, «Коммунист», 1989, № 5, с. 82–85.

Карякин Юрий. ««Ждановская жидкость» или против очернительства». «Огонек», 1988, № 19, с. 25–27.

Кисловский С. В. *Знаете ли вы? Словарь географических названий Ленинградской области.* Ленинград, Лениздат, 1974.

Лушин Юрий. «Космодром и его люди», «Огонек», 1991, № 13, с. 3–5.

Масленников Б. *Морская карта рассказывает.* Изд. 2-е, М., Воениздат, 1986.

Мурзаев Е. М. *Очерки топонимики.* М, «Мысль», 1974.

Никонов В. А. *Введение в топонимику.* М., «Наука», 1965.

Никонов В. А. *Краткий топонимический словарь.* М., «Мысль», 1966.

Санкт-Петербург. Петроград. Ленинград. Энциклопедический справочник. М., Большая Российская энциклопедия, 1992.

Советский энциклопедический словарь. Изд. 4-е, М., «Советская энциклопедия», 1987.

СССР. Административно-территориальное деление союзных республик на 1 апреля 1960 года. М., 1960.

СССР. Административно-территориальное деление союзных республик. Дополнение к справочнику выпуска 1960 года. М., 1961.

СССР. Административно-территориальное деление союзных республик. Январь 1965 года. М., 1965.

СССР. Административно-территориальное деление союзных республик на 1 января 1983 года. М., 1983.

СССР. Административно-территориальное деление союзных республик на 1 января 1967 года. М., 1987.

Фесенко А. П. «Щорса вы знаете?». *Вопросы истории,* 1989, № 12, с. 169–173.

Фесенко Андрей и Татьяна. *Русский язык при советах.* Нью-Йорк, 1955.

Чернов А. «Город под псевдонимом. Пока». *Московские новости,* 12.05.1991.

Dobbs, Michael. «Andropov Succumbs Again, by Popular Demand», *Washington Post,* March 4, 1989.

«The Game of the Name», *The Economist,* June 8, 1991.

Harris, Chauncy D. «Index and Gazetteer», *Soviet Geography: Review and Translation* (special issue), v. 11, No. 5, May, 1970.

Tarkhov, S. A. «From Karlo-Libknekhtovsk and New York to Propoysk and Rastyapino? How Place Names are Changing in the Former USSR», *Post-Soviet Geography*, 33, 7: 454–462.

Tumarkin, Nina. «The End of the Soviet Name Game?» *Boston Globe*, November 16, 1988.

Примечания:

[1] См. например: Nina Tumarkin, «The End of the Soviet name Game?» («Конец советской игры в имена?»), *The Boston Globe*, November 16, 1988; Michael Dobbs, «Andropov Succumbs Again, by Popular Demand», The Washington Post, March 4, 1989 — в этой статье автор говорит о «великой советской игре в перемену имен»; «The Game of the Name» («Игра в имена»), The Economist, June 8, 1991.

[2] Е.М.Мурзаев, Очерки топонимики. М, «Мысль», 1974, с. 22.

[3] В ссылках на это издание — АДТ с прибавлением года выпуска. Последний справочник вышел в 1987 году (АДТ-87).

[4] Harris, Chauncy D., «Index and Gazetteer», *Soviet Geography: Review and Translation* (special issue), v. 11, No. 5, May, 1970.

[5] Эта же, мягко говоря, «неполная» информация содержится и в других изданиях, например, в Советском энциклопедическом словаре (СЭС). Она даже не исправлена в последнем издании этого словаря, вышедшем в 1991 г. под новым названием — Большой энциклопедический словарь (БЭС) — если не считать того, что Чапаевск теперь «город в Самарской области»...

[6] Harris, Cit. op., р. 104.

[7] Годом позже появился еще один Ленинск — быв. село Пришиб (ныне в Волгоградской области). Но этот Ленинск приобрел статус города только в 1963 году.

[8] К этому времени на карте уже был один Троцк — быв. слобода Иващенково (Самарская губерния). Но он тогда не был городом.

[9] В 1918 году на карте появились Пошехонье-Володарск, быв. Пошехонье (Ярославская губерния) и Урицк, быв. Лигово в Петроградской губернии (город с 1925, с 1935 в черте Ленинграда, см. Санкт-Петербург, Петроград, Ленинград, Энциклопедический справочник, М., 1992, с. 631).

[10] В 1918 году были переименованы Павловск под Петроградом — в Слуцк в память революционерки В. К. Слуцкой, Поречье

(Смоленская губерния) в Демидов — в память председателя местного комитета коммунистической партии Я. Е. Демидова, Романово-Борисоглебск (Ярославская губерния) в Тутаев — в память красноармейца И. П. Тутаева; в 1919 году Асхабад получил имя Полторацк — в память одного из руководителей Советской власти в Туркестане П. Г. Полторацкого (в 1927 году ему было возвращено его старое имя в несколько ином, привычном для нас написании Ашхабад).

[11] Личное имя С. Шаумяна еще раз появилось на карте в 1924 году на территории Армении, когда село Джалал-Оглы было переименовано в Степанаван; город с 1938). Еще одно название города на Кавказе, образованное от личного имени — Махачкала (быв. Петровск-Порт), или «крепость Махача», данное в 1922 году в память дагестанского революционера Магомеда Али Дахадаева (Махач — сокращенная форма имени Магомед). Другой город в Дагестане, переименованный в то время (1921) — Буйнакск, быв. Темир-Хан-Шура, получил имя по фамилии другого местного большевика — У. Буйнакского.

[12] После присоединения Эстонии к Советскому Союзу имя первого руководителя эстонских коммунистов появилось и на карте этой республики: в 1952 году город Курессааре на острове Сааремаа (в Российской империи этот город назывался Аренсбург) был переименован в Кингисепп. В годы «перестройки» он стал одним из первых, вернувших себе свое досоветское имя. А вот сообщений о переименовании российского Кингисеппа пока не поступало.

[13] Впрочем, уже данные имена в таких случаях не отнимались. Использовался другой путь: «редактировались» биографии. В Кратком топонимическом словаре В. А. Никонова (М., «Мысль», 1966) сказано, что Романовский Хутор «переименован в память революционера и ученого-географа П. А. Кропоткина» (с. 217). Здесь тот случай, когда за правдой скрыта неправда, или когда неправда облачена в правдивые одеяния: кн. Петр Кропоткин действительно был выдающимся географом (он оставил научную деятельность, чтобы целиком посвятить себя делу революции), однако не за заслуги в изучении четвертичного периода Земли в его честь был назван город. (Примечание к примечанию. В подобного рода неточностях, или недоговоренностях, которых в словаре не мало, нельзя винить его автора, известного ученого в области ономастики — науки об именах: он, как и все авторы, публиковавшиеся в Советском Союзе, имел негласного соавтора-цензора).

Приведу еще один пример «правдивой неправды». Сразу после смерти Кропоткина его именем были названы и другие географические объекты, в том числе улица в Москве. Лет двадцать назад на углу этой улицы висела табличка, в которой говорилось, что улица названа в честь выдающегося русского географа и путешественника П. А. Кропоткина; о том, что Кропоткин был революционером, тем более анархистом, не было ни слова. Правда, табличку потом сняли (или она сама случайно разбилась), но новую, кажется, так и не повесили. (Сейчас улице возвращено ее прежнее имя — Пречистенская).

О Ст. Халтурине в том же словаре сказано, что он был «рабочим-революционером» (с. 450). И здесь неправда скрыта за правдой. Халтурин действительно был рабочим и одним из первых в России революционеров из рабочих. Однако в историю русского революционного движения он вошел благодаря организованному им покушению на Александра II и другим террористическим актам. Впоследствии сталинская историография отвергла терроризм как метод революционной борьбы. В частности, биография Халтурина делилась на две части: «правильную», когда он еще не был террористом, и «неправильную», когда он им стал.

[14]   Этот город возник в XVIII веке, когда Екатерина II заселяла Нижнее Поволжье немецкими колонистами. После революции он оказался на территории АССР Немцев Поволжья. В начале войны с нацистской Германией все немцы из Поволжья были депортированы, их республика упразднена и все немецкие географические имена заменены русскими. Город Марксштадт потерял тогда вторую половину своего имени и с тех пор называется просто Маркс.

[15]   В дальнейшем городу предстояло снова терять и приобретать это имя.

[16]   Екатеринослав, нареченный так при рождении в честь Екатерины II, трижды терял свое «царственное» имя. Первый раз — при Павле I, когда он был переименован в Новороссийск; второй раз — при С. Петлюре, когда городу было дано имя Січеслав — в честь запорожских казаков (Фесенко, Русский язык при советах, с. 74); и третий раз — при большевиках. Последнее название города образовано от фамилии Г. И. Петровского и названия реки Днепр, на которой этот город расположен.

[17]   На этом переименование городов, названных в честь лиц императорской фамилии закончилось, и ряд городов свои имена сохранил, — например, Павлоград, Александрия, Николаевск-на-Амуре. Правда, еще один город был переименован в 1948 году, когда Мариуполь стал Ждановым, но это было связано с тем, что А. А. Жданов родился в этом городе.

[18]   Имя Пржевальск было возвращено этому городу в 1939 году, когда произошел очередной поворот в советской политике и историографии по отношению к прошлому России. Ныне в Киргизии

вновь говорят о возможности переименования Пржевальска «обратно» в Каракол (Tarkhov, 1992, с. 461).

[19] Кзыл-Орда, по-казахски, «красная столица» — город был в это время столицей Казахстана.

[20] Этот любопытный факт приводит М. Горбаневский (1991, с. 105) со ссылкой на Е. Орловского и К. Янкова. В 1920-е годы Керенск-Вадинск был переведен из городских поселений в сельские в числе других городов, потерявших всякое экономическое значение.

[21] В некоторых источниках — Ленинск-Туркменский.

[22] С 1940 года — Чарджоу.

[23] То, что имя Ленина не только давалось городам, но и отнималось, было до последнего времени одной из запретных тем в Советском Союзе.

[24] Короткое время в 1930-е годы имя Ленинск носил также Петергоф под Ленинградом (см. Ch. Harris, Index and Gazetter, p. 419).

[25] Еще один Лениногорск появился в 1955 году в Татарии.

[26] Ворошиловск — в Донбассе (1931, ранее Алчевск, ныне Коммунарск), Ворошиловград (1935, ранее и ныне Луганск), Ворошилов (1935, быв. Никольск-Уссурийский, ныне Уссурийск) и еще один Ворошиловск — на Северном Кавказе (1935, ранее и ныне Ставрополь). Можно ли из того, что Ворошилов «получил» больше всех городов, сделать вывод, что Сталин любил его больше других?

[27] В честь Кагановича был переименован один город — Терновск в Московской области (город Каганович, 1935, с 1957 — Новокаширск, позднее вошел в состав Каширы). Но в честь этого деятеля, так же как и в честь других здесь упомянутых, были названы также поселки городского типа и другие поселения, промышленные и сельскохозяйственные предприятия, учебные заведения, улицы, площади и другие объекты. В частности, железнодорожная станция Попасная в Донбассе была переименована в «станцию имени Л. М. Кагановича». В 1938 г. носивший это же имя поселок при станции был преобразован в город, который стал называться «город имени Л. М. Кагановича»! Нелепые советские названия типа «поселок имени...» не так уж редки, например, поселки городского типа имени В. И. Ленина, имени М. И. Калинина, имени Кирова (АТД-87; понять, почему Ленин и Калинин — с инициалами, а Киров — без, невозможно), или еще «красивее»: поселок городского типа имени 26 Бакинских Комиссаров (там же). Но «г. им Л. М. Кагановича» (так он писался в сокращенном виде, причем без кавычек, все кавычки в этон примечании мои — П.И.) представляет венец советского топонимического творчества. (Впоследствии на карты вернулось имя Попасная.) Попутно заметим, что с «городом имени...» может по нелепости словосочетания соперничать только «село имени...» Но были и такие, например, «с. им Свердлова» на

Украине — так назывался Свердловск Луганской области до того, как он стал городом (см. АДТ-83, с.).

[28] Калинин (1931, до этого и ныне Тверь) и образованный в 1938 году под Москвой город Калининград, до этого — пос. Калининский, быв. Подлипки. Еще один Калининград — быв. Кёнигсберг — появился уже после смерти Калинина. Позднее появились также Калининабад в Таджикистане (1956), Калининск в Саратовской области (1962) и Калинино в Армении (город с 1983, ныне Ташир).

[29] Орджоникидзе (1931, до этого и ныне Владикавказ) и Орджоникидзеград (1935, до этого и после Бежица, ныне в черте города Брянска).

[30] Именем Микояна в 1929 году был назван центр Карачаевской автономной области город Микоян-Шахар (по-карачаевски, «город Микояна», ныне Карачаевск).

[31] Молотов «получил» свой первый город позднее других — в 1938 году, когда поселок Судострой в дельте Северной Двины был преобразован в город, названный Молотовск (ныне Северодвинск). Но зато в 1940 году ему было «даровано» сразу два города: Молотов (до этого и ныне Пермь) и второй Молотовск — в Кировской области (до этого и ныне Нолинск).

[32] Буденновск (1935, быв. Прикумск, до 1920 Святой Крест).

[33] Сталинск (1932, до этого и ныне Новокузнецк), Сталиногорск (1934, быв. Бобрики, ныне Новомосковск в Тульской области) и центр Юго-Осетинской автономной области Сталинири (1934, до этого и ныне Цхинвали).

[34] Текст постановления был опубликован в «Известиях» 23 ноября 1931 г. (См. Н. Ивина, ««Зачем нам отреченья»? Размышления над письмами». Литературная газета, 28 сентября 1988 г.)

[35] Сейчас этим грузинским городам возвращены старые названия.

[36] А. и Т. Фесенко, Русский язык при советах, с. 75.

[37] Ch. Harris, *Index and Gazetter*, p. 420.

[38] Ch. Harris, *Index and Gazetter*, p. 393.

[39] Ch. Harris, *Index and Gazetter*, p. 429.

[40] Всякий ли человек, даже свободно владеющий русским языком, сумеет без запинки произнести это название? Но это не единственный продукт «имятворчества» знатоков русского языка в правительстве: позднее появились такие имена, как Ивано-Франковск и Карлолибкнехтовск...

[41] Мичурин жил и работал в Козлове.

[42] Не одновременно; иногда они даже сменяли друг друга в названии одного и того же города.

[43] В 1929 году Троцкий был выслан из СССР, и его имя было стерто с карты. Но уничтожен он был не сразу: «рука Сталина» дотянулась до него в 1940 году.

[44] В это же время поселок Троцк Самарской области (быв. Иващенково) был преобразован в город, получивший, однако, другое имя — Чапаевск (в память героя гражданской войны В. И. Чапаева).

[45] Кабаковск на короткое время снова стал Надеждинском; Мирзоян, быв. Аулие-Ата, получил имя Джамбул — в честь казахского поэта, прославлявшего в своих стихах партию, Сталина и «батыра» Ежова; Постышев, быв. Гришино, — ныне Красноармейск; Чубаровка и поселок имени товарища Хатаевича получили свои старые имена — Пологи и Синельниково; Косиорово сейчас называется Станично-Луганское. Зеленск был переименован в Ленинск.

[46] В 1991 году Свердловск вновь стал Екатеринбургом. Но на карте сохраняется другой Свердловск, в Луганской области (город с 1938).

[47] Позднее появились второй Дзержинск — в Минской области (1932, быв. Койданово), Днепродзержинск (1935, быв. Каменское), еще один Дзержинск — в Донецкой области (1938, до этого — поселок Щербиновка) и Дзержинский в Московской области (город с 1981). Все они «с гордостью» продолжают носить свои имена.

[48] В 1938 — Артем в Приморском крае, Артемовский (быв. пос. Егоршино) в Свердловской обл. и Артемово в Донецкой (таким образом, в этой области есть города Артемовск и Артемово); в 1939 — Артемовск в Красноярском крае; в 1961 — еще один Артемовск, в Луганской области. По числу названных в его честь городов Артем мог соперничать с самим Сталиным! Предпочтения законодателей не всегда объяснимы... Добавлю, что городАртемово первое время сохранял название поселка, из которого он развился, и назывался город имени Артема.

[49] До переименования город носил имя св. Сергия Радонежского, основателя Троице-Сергиевского монастыря — сначала Сергиев Посад, затем, с 1917 года, город Сергиев. В 1991 году ему возвращено имя Сергиев Посад.

[50] Третий переименованный город — Воскресенск, ныне Истра.

[51] Котовск, быв. Бирзула в Молдавской АССР (1935, город с 1938). После присоединения Бессарабии в 1940 году бывшая Молдавская АССР была разделена на две части: вошедшую во вновь образованную Молдавскую ССР и переданную в состав Одесской области. Котовск оказался на «одесской» территории, и Молдавия на четверть века осталась без города Котовска: хотя в том же году поселку Ганчешты на бессарабской территории Молдавии было присвоено имя Котовское, но только в 1965 году Котовское было преобразовано в город Котовск. Сейчас молдавскому Котовску возвращено прежнее имя, но в его молдавском написании — Хынчешть.

В 1940 году появился Котовск и в России: это имя было дано вновь образованному городу, который был выделен из городской черты Тамбова.

[52] Историю посмертного возвеличивания Щорса см. в статье А. П. Фесенко «Щорса вы знаете?», Вопросы истории, 1989, № 12, с. 169–173.

[53] Конаково в Тверской области, — в память местного рабочего-революционера (1930, город с 1937, быв. Кузнецово); Цулукидзе в Грузии — в память грузинского революционера А. Г. Цулукидзе (1936, до этого и теперь Хони); Ханлар в Азербайджане — в память азербайджанского революционера Ханлара Сафаралиева (1938, быв. Еленендорф); еще один город в Азербайджане, Кази-Магомед — в память другого местного революционера, Кази Магомеда Агасиева (до 1938 пос. Аджикабул); Сковородино в Амурской области — в память первого председателя местного Совета (1938, быв. Рухлово, см. Никонов, с. 385); Рошаль в Московской области — в память участника Октябрьской революции С. Г. Рошаля (город с 1940).

[54] Столица Киргизии Пишпек получила имя Фрунзе в 1925 году. Вот еще один пародокс советской игры в имена: в киргизском языке нет звука «ф», а согласные звуки, как правило, строго чередуются с гласными. И коренные жители Киргизии произносили придуманное в Москве имя их столицы как «Боронсо» или «Пурунзе» (С. Асанкулова, «Имя для города», Известия, 17.10.1989). Сейчас городу возвращено его старое имя, но в несколько ином написании: Бишкек.

[55] Город Алёшки Херсонской области был переименован в Цюрупинск в 1928 году.

[56] Зиновьев обвинялся в организации убийства Кирова.

[57] В 1936 году у азербайджанского Кировабада появился «тезка» — поселок Кировабад в Таджикистане, который в 1953 году стал городом, но в 1963 году был переименован в Пяндж. Азербайджанский Кировабад потерял свое «кировское» имя уже при «перестройке»: в 1989 году ему было возвращено его древнее имя в однозначном написании: Гянджа.

[58] Позднее появились еще четыре города, названные в честь Кирова: Кировск в Ленинградской области (1953, быв, пос. Невдубстрой, затем *имени Кирова*), Кирово-Чепецк в Кировской области, названный по фамилии Кирова и реке Чепце, на которой он расположен (1955), Кировское в Донецкой области (1958) и еще один (третий) Кировск — в Луганской области (1962).

[59] Городов, носящих имя Куйбышев, на Волге больше нет — они переименованы в 1991 году (Куйбышевка-Восточная была переименована еще в 1967 году, вероятно, из-за некоторой необычности имени. Сейчас она называется Белогорск.)

[60] Орджоникидзе покончил с собой, — факт, который был в то время скрыт и стал известен только после смерти Сталина. Таким трагическим способом один из ближайших помощников Сталина выразил протест против его политики в этот период, что в дальнейшем отразилось на судьбе имен городов, названных в честь Орджоникидзе (см. ниже).

[61] Орджоникидзе (Владикавказ) и Орджоникидзеград (Бежица).

[62] Сейчас на карте осталось только одно из названных имен — Серов. Оренбургу и Бердянску были возвращены их исторические имена в 1957 году, а Бабушкин в 1960 году вошел в черту г. Москвы. Впрочем, города, названные в честь Чкалова, на карте есть. Еще при его жизни, в 1937 году, село Василево на Волге, где он родился, было переименовано в Чкаловск (город с 1955). А в 1956 году появился еще один Чкаловск — в Таджикистане.

[63] Город Детское Село (до 1918 Царское Село) был переименован в Пушкин в 1937 году к столетию со дня смерти поэта.

[64] Быв. Форт-Александровский (при Шевченко — Новопетровское укрепление). Переименован в Форт-Шевченко в 1939 году. В 1930-е годы назывался также Форт Урицкого (Ch. Harris, *Index and Gazetter,* p. 390).

[65] Образован в 1941 г. из поселков Богословского и Угольного.

[66] «Как Москва чуть не стала Сталинодаром», Известия ЦК КПСС, 1990, № 12, с. 126–127.

[67] В 1956 г. Бежица вошла в черту Брянска.

[68] Происходит от личного имени и «кау», деревня (Никонов, 1966, с. 311).

[69] А. и Т. Фесенко, Русский язык при советах, с. 75–76. Енакиево переименовывали четырежды на протяжении 16 лет.

[70] Имя Орджоникидзе в названиях поселков тогда уцелело. Два из них впоследствии стали городами: Орджоникидзе в Днепропетровской области (1956, до 1939 Александровка) и Орджоникидзеабад в Таджикистане (1965, до 1936 Янгибазар).

[71] В 1957 году автономия карачаевцев была восстановлена, Черкесская автономная область была преобразована в Карачаево-Черкесскую, и в ее состав были переданы карачаевские земли, находившиеся на территории Грузии. Тогда же город Клухори (быв. Микоян-Шахар) был переименован в Карачаевск.

[72] Тогда же было возвращено историческое имя Гатчина и городу Красногвардейску — быв. Троцку.

[73] В 1654 году Богдан Хмельницкий провозгласил в Переяславе воссоединение Украины с Россией и принес присягу на верность московскому царю. После того, как Украина стала независимым государством, собравшиеся в июне 1992 года в Переяславе-Хмельницком украинские казаки во главе со своим гетманом Вячеславом Черновилом от этой присяги отреклись («Черновил

поправил Богдана Хмельницкого», Московские новости, 28.06.1992). Однако имя города пока не изменено. Более того, именем гетмана назвали улицу в столице Украины. Игры продолжаются...

[74] Названы в память генерала армии И. Д. Черняховского, И. С. Гусева, С. С Гурьева, И. М. Ладушкина, Н. В. Мамонова, С. Н. Нестерова.

[75] В память погибшего в 1940 году во время Советско-Финской войны Героя Советского Союза пулеметчика К. Д. Высоцкого (Кисловский, 1974, с. 31).

[76] За все последующие годы имена героев войны получили еще всего лишь четыре города — Ватутино в Черкасской области (1952), названный в честь генерала армии И. Ф. Ватутина, Городовиковск в Калмыкии (1971, быв. пос. Башанта) — в честь генерал-полковника О. И. Городовикова, Кузнецовск в Ровенской области (1984), названный в честь разведчика Н. И. Кузнецова и Шопоков в Киргизии (1985) — в честь бойца Панфиловской дивизии Д. Шопокова. Заслуживает внимания вопрос, по какому принципу отбирались участники войны для «награждения» их городами? Дивизия генерал-майора Панфилова отличилась в битве под Москвой; генералы армии Ватутин и Черняховский командовали фронтами и погибли в боях. Имена этих трех военачальников пользовались широкой известностью в годы войны. Имя разведчика Кузнецова стало известно и приобрело широкую популярность после войны. Что касается генерал-полковника Городовикова, то он оказался выделен из множества не менее заслуженных военачальников по одной причине: город в Калмыкии был назван его именем потому, что генерал Городовиков был калмыком. Аналогично, Шопоков попал на карту Киргизии потому, что был киргизом. Остальные попали на карту по-существу случайно.

[77] Существовал только поселок Берия в Армении.

[78] Имя Хрущев первоначально получил поселок строителей Кременчугской гидроэлектростанции на Днепре (Кировоградская обл.). О дальнейшей истории этого названия см. ниже.

[79] Впрочем, на Южном Сахалине Чехов не был.

[80] Переименование Отомари в Корсаков было, по-существу, восстановлением старого названия, существовавшего до захвата Южного Сахалина Японией в войне 1904–1905 годов. На месте города тогда находился пост Корсаковский. Японцы, присоединив Южный Сахалин, переименовали все русские названия. Вообще, переименования на свой лад географических имен на завоеванных территориях — обычная практика на протяжении всей истории человечества. Советы, как мы видим, делали то же самое.

[81] В честь русского ученого XVIII века М. В. Ломоносова.

[82] В честь советского ученого-механика в области аэродинамики С. А. Чаплыгина.

[83] Это стирание приобрело характер кампании в годы второй мировой войны, когда была отброшена вторая часть названия Марксштадт и переименованы города Петергоф — в Петродворец, Шлиссельбург — в Петрокрепость, а также Бальцер в быв. АССР Немцев Поволжья в Красноармейск (тотальное переименование других населенных мест, носивших немецкие названия, выходит за рамки данной статьи).

[84] А. и Т. Фесенко, Русский язык при советах, с. 77.

[85] Генерал Багратион отличился в сражении под Прейсиш-Эйлау в 1807 году.

[86] П.Н.Нестеров погиб во время первой мировой войны в воздушном бою над этим районом, впервые применив таран.

[87] Как всегда в таких случаях, создавалась либо видимость народной инициативы, либо видимость одобрения принимаемых решений. Вот например, что писали газеты Северной Осетии о перемене названия столицы республики: 1931 год — «Трудящиеся одобряют постановление правительства о переименовании Владикавказа в Орджоникидзе. Продолжительные аплодисменты, перешедшие в овацию... говорят об этом». 1944 год — «Переименование города Орджоникидзе в город Дзауджикау... отвечает культурным и экономическим интересам осетинского народа. В этом акте видна личная забота Сталина об осетинском народе, его настоящем и будущем». 1954 год — «Трудящиеся Северной Осетии с глубокой радостью, удовлетворением встретили указ о переименовании города Дзауджикау в город Орджоникидзе, отвечающем их воле и чаяниям». («Имя на карте». Интервью с В. П. Нерознаком и М. В. Горбаневским, «Коммунист», 1989, № 5, с. 83.)

[88] «Установить, что впредь присвоение имен... может производиться только посмертно...» (из Указа Президиума Верховного Совета СССР от 11 сентября 1957 года. Цит. по: Никонов, 1965, с. 175).

[89] По непонятным причинам, один из городов, носивших имя Ворошилова — Ворошиловск в Луганской области (быв. Алчевск) сохранил свое имя до 1961 года, когда был переименован в Коммунарск.

[90] Позднее вошел в черту Каширы. Интересно, если бы Каганович оставался в фаворе, не было бы Указа 1957 года и пришло бы время этим двум городам объединяться, кто был бы к кому «присоединен»?

Тогда же город Буденновск был переименован в Прикумск. Его самое первое имя — Святой Крест — было, конечно, абсолютно неприемлемо для Советов.

[91] В моем сообщении на тему этой статьи на ежегодной конференции Ассоциации американских географов в Майами в 1991 году в этом месте было одно из наиболее эффектных мест моего выступления. На основе источников, которыми я к тому времени

располагал, я считал, что для удаления с карты имени Хрущева был найден остроумный прием, такой, что это имя исчезло с карты без переименования: в 1961 году поселок городского типа Хрущев был объединен с соседним городом Новогеоргиевском в один город, получивший третье имя — Кремгэс. Но в Дополнении к АДТ-60 я неожиданно обнаружил, что 17 марта 1961 года город Новогеоргиевск был действительно объединен с поселком городского типа Хрущев, который был преобразован в город Хрущев! (с. 25, 61, 62).

Это редкое издание — *СССР. Административно-территориальное деление союзных республик. Дополнение к справочнику выпуска 1960 года. М., 1961* — я обнаружил на полке у моего друга и коллеги проф. Боба Гостанда, у которого гостил в Лос-Анжелесе. Я хотел бы выразить Бобу свою особую признательность за то, что он предоставил мне возможность изучить этот источник. Правда, пропало эффектное место статьи, зато мы теперь знаем, что, пусть короткое время, но на карте был город Хрущев.

[92] Позднее имя Кремгэс было заменено на более благозвучное: Светловодск.

[93] Старые названия этих городов были неприемлемы для советской топонимики. Юзовка (Сталино) называлась по фамилии английского предпринимателя Джона Юза, владевшего заводами, при которых развился город. Бобрики (Сталиногорск) были раньше селом, названным по фамилии его владельца графа Бобринского. Прежнее имя Сталинграда — Царицын — ассоциировалось с некоей царицей, хотя происходило от тюркского сары-су «желтая вода» или сарыгшин «желтоватый», переделанного русскими поселенцами в более понятное им Царицын (Никонов, 1966, с. 127, 296, 88).

[94] Имя Торез получил город Чистяково в Донецкой области.

[95] Быв. поселок Шахты №5-бис (Ch. Harris, Index and Gazetter, p. 131).

[96] Город Лермонтовский позднее был переименован в Лермонтов.

[97] Эти города были названы в честь узбекского поэта Алишера Навои, азербайджанского поэта Мухаммеда Физули, казахского поэта Абая Кунанбаева, украинского писателя Ивана Франко, армянского поэта и просветителя Хачатура Абовяна.

[98] См. «Имя на карте», интервью с В. П. Нерознаком и М. Горбаневским, «Коммунист», 1989, № 5, с. 83. Решение решением, но придумать имя города в честь Ивана Франко оказалось не таким уж и прстым делом, поскольку был жив однофамилец украинского писателя испанский диктатор Франко. Для этого одного ученого заперли в аудитории вместе с термосом и горой бутербродов. Так «родилось» имя Ивано-Франковск. (там же. с. 83–84).

[99] Я сказал «первый город, названный в память композитора» и... ошибся. Ибо за «первым» должен идти «второй». Но «второго» не последовало: город Чайковский остался единственным в своем роде.

[100]   Хабаровск был назван в честь русского казака XVII века Ерофея Хабарова, совершившего ряд походов в Приамурье.

[101]   Поселок Губкин в Белгородской области, центр добычи железной руды на месторождениях Курской магнитной аномалии, был преобразован в город в 1955 году Он был назван в честь исследователя этих месторождений геолога И. М. Губкина (до 1939 Коробково).

[102]   Эти города были названы: Салават в Башкирии (1954) — в честь башкира Салавата Юлаева, сподвижника Пугачева; Бируни (Беруни) в Каракалпакии (до 1957 пос. Шаббаз, см. Harris, 1970, p. 383) — в честь среднеазиатского ученого X–XI веков Бируни (Беруни); Ермак в Казахстане (Павлодарская область, 1961) — в честь Ермака Тимофеевича, с походов которого в XVI веке началось присоединение Сибири к России.

[103]   Разговоры о том, что готовится такое решение, время от времени возникали в брежневское время.

[104]   Мне кажется, что это предположение не лишено оснований: в 1984 году Молотов был восстановлен в партии, причем сообщил ему об этом лично Черненко («Московские новости», 5.5.1991). Хотя сейчас, надо полагать, его имя все равно было бы стерто с карты городов, как это в конце концов произошло с именем Ворошилова — хочется думать, навсегда.

[105]   Таким образом, в этой области Узбекистана стало два города, названных в честь Ленина — Ленинск и Ильичевск.

[106]   В Волгоградской и Андижанской областях.

[107]   Город находится в Кзыл-Ординской области возле станции Тюра-Там. Существование секретных городов — характерная особенность советской географии. Принципы их номинации были разные. Одни назывались по близлежащему большому городу с прибавлением номера почтового ящика (например, Арзамас-16, Томск-7, Челябинск-65, Красноярск-26 и др.), другие принимали имя мест, близ которых они располагались (Плесецк в Архангельской области), третьи получали новые имена (например, Степногорск в Казахстане). Ленинск прошел разные стадии. Его называли Ташкент-50, потом Звездоград и, наконец, Ленинск (Б. Коновалов, «Как поделим Байконур», Известия, 3.10.1991).

Что касается секретности, то любопытен рассказ, опубликованный в «Огоньке». Работавший на Байконуре специалист вспоминает, как еще в начале шестидесятых годов увидел в американском военном журнале карту Казахстана, на которой по-английски значилось Тюра-Там, а в скобках — Russian Kanaveral… (Ю. Лушин. Космодром и люди. «Огонек», 1991, № 13).

[108]   Названы в память одного из основателей компартии Латвии П. Стучки, узбекского государственного деятеля Ю. Ахунбабаева, таджикского партийного руководителя Б. Г. Гафурова, грузинского большевика А. А. Гегечкори. Кроме того, в 1976 году в

Казахстане появился город Баутино на полуострове Мангышлак, названный в честь председателя местного Совета А. Г. Баутина, погибшего во время гражданской войны (Масленников, 1986, с. 34).

[109] Интересно заметить, что хотя почти вся деятельность Наримана Нариманова прошла в Азербайджане, города его имени в этой республике не было, был лишь поселок городского типа Нариманабад. Но руководство этой республики меньше всего можно обвинить в пренебрежении памятью коммунистов: в 1966 году стал городом Ждановск (второй в СССР город в честь Жданова) и появился город Касум-Измаилов — в честь еще одного местного революционера. Кроме того, в 1978 году в Нахичеванской АССР появился город Бабек — в честь предводителя народного восстания в Азербайджане и Западном Иране в X веке.

[110] С 1991 года город снова называется Лиски.

[111] Но на несколько лет раньше — в 1965 году поселок имени Димитрова в Донецкой области был преобразован в город. Знали ли об этом законодатели в Москве? Или надо было в тот момент еще раз громкогласно напомнить о советско-болгарской дружбе?

[112] С 1990 года снова Змиев.

[113] Карл Либкнехт был убит вместе с другим руководителем немецких социалистов Розой Люксембург. Поселок, названный в честь Розы Люксембург, тоже был на карте — бывший Екатеринофельд в Грузии. Но он был переименован в Болниси и стал городом уже под этим, чисто грузинским именем: Роза Люксембург так и осталась без города. А интересно, если бы появился город в ее честь, какое бы имя ему дали? Розалюксембургск?

[114] Впрочем, это оказался не «зигзаг», а скорее, «зигзажек», так как Чаренц так и остался единственным реабилитированным, «получившим» город. Больше никто из тех, кто был репрессирован при Сталине, на карту городов не попал, даже те, чьи имена были на этой карте в 1930-е годы, после реабилитации на нее не вернулись. Улицы в их честь назывались, но город — слишком заметный объект. Иное дело Ворошилов и Буденный — их «обидел» Хрущев, которого новые правители ненавидели, а не Сталин, которого они боготворили...

[115] Еще один город Гагарин появился в 1974 году в Узбекистане (быв. поселок Ержар, Джизакская область). Какое отношение этот город имел к первому космонавту, или первый космонавт к этому городу, остается неизвестным. Хотя можно посмотреть на эти два наименования (как и на другие, им подобные) с другой стороны: новые города могут получать любые имена, в том числе и в честь знаменитых людей; в таких случаях они становятся своего рода топонимическими памятниками. Переименование же старых городов — разрушение культурного и исторического наследия.

[116] Рекорд Стаханова был подготовлен, но мы сейчас говорим о его славе, а не о том, как она была достигнута.

[117] Ch. Harris, *Index and Gazetter*, p. 444.

[118] В результате получили свои старые имена города Ижевск (Устинов), Набережные Челны (Брежнев), Шарыпово (Черненко).

[119] Вот, например, текст сообщения ТАСС, переданного в декабре 1988 года: «ЦК КПСС, Президиум Верховного Совета СССР и Совет Министров СССР решили *удалить* (курсив мой — *П.И.*) имена Леонида Брежнева и Константина Черненко из названий всех предприятий, административных районов, учебных заведений и любых организаций».

[120] В опубликованном «Правдой» официальном сообщении об этом переименовании сказано так: «Пункт 2 постановления ЦК КПСС, Президиума Верховного Совета СССР и Совета Министров СССР № 204 от 23 февраля 1984 года в части переименования города Рыбинска Ярославской области отменен» («Правда», 4.3.1989).

[121] Особенно большой общественный резонанс вызвала опубликованная в мае 1988 г. статья Юрия Карякина ««Ждановская жидкость» или против очернительства» («Огонек», № 19).

[122] Были переименованы, в частности, оба города, носившие его имя, и вместо Жданова и Ждановска (в Азербайджане) на карте теперь вновь Мариуполь и Бейланган.

[123] Судьба имен этих городов привлекала всеобщее внимание, и на их фоне менее заметными были переименования в республиках Прибалтики, в Молдавии и в Грузии, где были переименованы все города, названные в честь коммунистов: в 1988 году Кингисепп в Эстонии снова стал Куресааре; в 1989 году Капсукас в Литве получил свое старое имя Мариямполе, а в Грузии одним указом были переименованы четыре города, носившие имена большевиков (имя города Маяковский тогда уцелело, но через год и он получил свое старое имя — Багдади); в 1990 году Стучка в Латвии был переименован в Айзкраукле, Котовск в Молдавии — в Хынчешть. Кроме того, Готвальдов на Украине опять стал Змиевым.

[124] «Труд», 11.11.1990. До своего переименования в Александрополь в 1837 году этот город назывался Гумри (Никонов, 1966, с. 231).

[125] «Труд», 24.11.1990.

[126] Сейчас можно встретить два написания его нового имени: Кумайри и Гюмри. Но точный год преименования я указать не берусь: в этом не всегда уверены даже люди, в чьи служебные обязанности входит фиксировать все текущие перемены на географической карте. Например, в первом томе Большого энциклопедического словаря сказано, что Ленинакан переименован в 1990 году в Кумайри (с. 863), а во втором — что он переименован в 1991 году в Гюмри (с. 764).

[127] Был переименован и другой Куйбышев — в Татарии. Но если раньше действовали единые для всей страны правила игры в имена, то с ослаблением центральной власти каждая бывшая союзная республика, и даже некоторые национальные образования в Российской Федерации стали устанавливать свои правила. Раньше этот Куйбышев назывался Спасск-Татарский, но не могло правительство Татарии, которое проводит сугубо националистическую политику, вернуть городу старое имя: он был переименован в Булгар — в память о предках татар волжских болгарах (булгарах).

[128] Городу Фрунзе (быв. Пишпек) возвращается его киргизское имя, но в несколько другом написании: Бишкек.

[129] Ленинабаду также возвращается его старое имя, но, судя по прессе, оно (как и в случае с Гюмри-Кумайри) употребляется сейчас в двух формах: Ходжент (так город официально назывался раньше) и Худжанд (имя, под которым город был известен еще с VII века, см. Никонов, 1966, с. 231)

[130] А.С.Солженицын предлагал для города другие имена: Невоград («город на Неве») и Свято-Петроград (русская форма имени Санкт-Петербург, т.е. «город святого Петра»). См. Андрей Чернов, «Город под псевдонимом. Пока», «Московские новости», 12.5.1991.

[131] В течение 1991 года были переименованы также города Георгиу-Деж в Воронежской области (ныне снова Лиски), Ильичевск, Касум-Исмаилов, Мир-Башир и Пушкино в Азербайджане (ныне они называются Шерур, Геренбой, Тертер и Билясувар), Калинино в Армении (ныне Ташир), Ленинск и Ильичевск в Узбекистане (ныне Асаке и Карасу).

[132] На фоне «обратных» переименований незамеченным оказалось сделанное в процессе дерусификации имен в Казахстане переименование города Никольский (Джезказганская область) в Сатпаев — в память известного казахского ученого-геолога К. И. Сатпаева (1990).

Топонимические игры на постсоветском пространстве

Павел Ильин

Это первоапрельское утреннее заседание весьма уместно открывается выступлением о «топонимических играх». Трудно вообразить себе более несуразное словосочетание, чем «город Санкт-Петербург Ленинградской области»...

В 1988 году в газете Boston Globe появилась статья историка Нины Тамаркиной под названием *The End of the Soviet Name Game?* («Конец советской игры в названия?»). Сегодня, шесть лет спустя, я могу сказать, что хотя советские игры, может быть, и закончились, на постсоветском пространстве они не прекращаются. Перестройка в бывшем СССР и образование новых государств на постсоветском пространстве привели к изменению огромного количества топонимов — от названий стран до названий городов. Это мотивировалось прежде всего стремлением избавиться от коммунистической атрибутики, возрождением национализма и тенденцией к восстановлению прежних исторических названий. В различных уголках бывшего Советского Союза использовались разные подходы к присвоению названий, тем не менее, повсеместно большую роль играла политика. В качестве примеров можно привести сохранение названий Ленинградской, Свердловской и Ленинабадской областей, административным центрам которых были возвращены их прежние имена: Санкт-Петербург, Екатеринбург и Худжент.

А начались эти топонимические игры еще до распада Советского Союза в 1989 году. Всем известно, что столица Эстонии — город Таллин. В эстонском написании этого названия конечная буква «n» удваивается, а по-русски оно пишется с одной «н». В 1989 году эстонское правительство стало настаивать на том, чтобы русское написание названия столицы Эстонии было изменено, и чтобы в нем, точно также как и в эстонском эквиваленте, удваивалась конечная согласная. Это произошло в период, когда народы Эстонии и ее соседей Латвии и Литвы добивались своей независимости. Правительство Горбачева предоставлять ее не намеревалось, тем не менее, согласившись удовлетворить требование об изменении написания названий. Основная мысль была ясна: «Бог с вами — пишите названия своих столиц как вам угодно, но независимости вам не видать». Однако сопротивление оказалось напрасным: Эстония все равно стала независимым государством, а русское написание названия ее столицы исчезло. (В настоящее время оно снова восстановлено — по-русски название эстонской столицы пишется с одной буквой «н» — *прим. пер.*)

За этим периодом последовало то, что впоследствии стали называть «парадом суверенитетов»: одна за другой бывшие союзные и автономные республики СССР стали провозглашать независимость, и некоторые из них стали назваться по-новому. Если говорить более точно, эти названия и раньше существовали в языках народов, населяющих эти республики. Белоруссия по-белорусски всегда называлась Беларусью; Молдавия всегда по-молдавски называлась Молдовой; Киргизия называлась по-киргизски Кыргызстаном. Однако теперь, наивно пытаясь самоутвердиться, правительства этих стран стали требовать, чтобы весь мир использовал именно эти названия, не учитывая исторических и лингвистических традиций других народов. Россия официально удовлетворила это требование по политическим соображениям.

Теперь представьте себе карту со странами под названием Polska, Deutschland, Ellas, Magyarorsag, Chzhun-Go, Nippon. И это лишь немногие из примеров. Страна, которую ее собственные жители называют Deutschland, по-разному называется на разных языках: Allemagne по-французски, Niemcye по-польски, Германия по-русски, Німеччина по-украински, Germany по-английски, Saksa по-фински, Vokietuja по-литовски — практически существует столько же вариантов ее названий сколько есть языков на белом свете. Однако сама Германия этим нисколько не оскорблена. Даже в бывшем Советском Союзе жителей საქართველო (Сакартвело) нисколько не задевало то, что по-русски их республику называют Грузией, а по-английски Georgia. Тоже самое можно сказать и о Республике Lietuva, которую по-русски называют Литвой и Lithuania по-английски, и об Армении, «родным» названием которой является Аястан.

Вовсе неудивительно, что многие деятели российской культуры высказывались против использования новых наименований. В одной из своих речей, посвященных А. С. Пушкину, академик

Д. С. Лихачев, упоминая Молдавию, подчеркивал, что не хочет использовать слово Молдова, так как выступает по-русски. Слово «Кыргызстан» звучит действительно не самым удобным образом, так как подобное сочетание букв и звуков органически не присуще русскому языку. Тем не менее, новые названия получили официальное добро и стали распространяться в русской разговорной речи.

Вслед за требованиями об изменении названий стран появились новые требования: изменить фонетику и орфографию в названиях городов. В Туркмении, Казахстане и Молдавии были приняты специальные законы, предписывающие написание и произношение названий городов на русском языке: Ашгабат (вместо Ашхабада), Алматы (вместо Алма-Ата) и т.д.

Необходимо отметить, что некоторые люди все-таки понимают, насколько смехотворны требования руководства их стран. Один из моих друзей отправился в командировку в Львов, где должен был встретиться с местными экономистами. Они общались по-русски, но из чувства уважения к собеседникам мой друг продолжал называть этот город Львивом. И каждый раз они пытались его исправить: «Не Львив, Львов. Мы же по-русски говорим». Я вернусь к вопросу Украины позднее, а сейчас мне хотелось бы более подробно остановиться на переименовании названий городов в других бывших республиках Советского Союза.

До сих пор я в своем выступлении говорил только об изменениях в написании названий городов и стран. В своем законодательстве Верховный Совет Казахстана назвал этот процесс «реорганизацией написания названий городов на русском языке». Нам не следует приравнивать элементарные изменения в написании и произношении (Ашхабад/Ашгабад) к переименованию. Например, в период избавления от русского написания названий в Казахстане написание некоторых городов было изменено (Алма-Ата стала писаться как Алматы, Чимкент как Шымкент), в то время как другие населенные пункты были переименованы. Например, городу Шевченко вернули его прежнее название Актау. Однако переименование города Гурьев в Атырау вовсе не способствует восстановлению исторической справедливости — наоборот, оно ее нарушает и носит сугубо националистический характер. Гурьев был назван в честь его основателя рыбака Михаила Гурьева. Одновременно с этим, на карте Казахстана по-прежнему можно найти город Лениногорск (В 2002 году город переименован в Риддер — *прим. пер.*), второй Лениногорск находится в Татарии.

В Киргизии есть город, который раньше назывался Рыбачьим. Местные жители называли его Балыкчи, переведя это русское название на киргизский язык. В 1989 году город был переименован в Иссык-Куль в честь одноименного озера. Однако это название используется только в официальных целях. Население по-прежнему зовет его либо Рыбачье, либо Балыкчи. (С 1993 года город официально называется Балыкчи— *прим. пер.*) Второму городу на озере Иссык-Куль Пржевальску в 1992 году вторично было возвращено его прежнее название Каракол. Одновременно с этим многие улицы по-прежнему носят имена коммунистов. Только часть улицы Дзержинского вблизи Посольства США в Бишкеке была переименована в Бульвар Эркиндик. (В настоящее время Посольство США в Кыргызстане находится на улице Мира— *прим. пер.*) Кстати, слово «эркиндик» по-русски означает «свобода»!

Топонимическая обстановка в Закавказье еще сложнее. Армяно-азербайджанской борьбе за Нагорный Карабах уже шесть лет. На протяжении этих лет все географические названия в Армении с тюркскими лингвистическими корнями были переименованы. В Азербайджане произошло обратное: были изменены все названия с армянскими корнями. Например, Варташен превратился в Огус, а Гетакшен теперь называется Габелна. Кроме того, были переименованы все города Армении, названные в честь коммунистов, за исключением города Степанаван. Этот город назван в память о большевике Степане Шаумяне. Еще одним городом, названным в честь Шаумяна, является город Степанакерт в Нагорном Карабахе. Азербайджанские власти объявили о восстановлении его прежнего названия Ханкеди, однако это переименование не признали ни в Нагорном Карабахе, ни в Армении.

У армян возникли некоторые трудности с названием Кировокан. Старое название Караклис нельзя было использовать из-за его тюркских корней. В течение двух лет ломали голову над новым названием и наконец в прошлом году переименовали этот город в Ванадзор.

У меня до сих пор хранится экземпляр газеты «Известия» от 16 июня 1992 года с двумя статьями о Южной Осетии. В статье, представляющей ситуацию с грузинской точки зрения, столица Южной Осетии именуется Цхинвали, а в статье, отражающей взгляды осетинской стороны, ее называют Цхинвал. Один и тот же город по-разному называют на одной и той же газетной странице.

Конечно, это свидетельствует о том, что в разных регионах бывшего Советского Союза происходит очень сложный, зачастую трагический процесс. Вполне понятно, что многими правительствами проводится политика дерусификации. Однако действия правительств новых независимых государств во многих случаях лишь повторяют прежние поступки Москвы, хотя и несколько в ином преломлении. И это неудивительно. Во-первых, лидеры этих государств выросли при коммунистическом режиме. Во-вторых, многие из них ранее занимали видные руководящие посты в местных органах коммунистической партии. Всех превзошел бывший первый секретарь ЦК КП Туркменистана Сапармурад Ниязов, ныне ставший президентом независимого Туркменистана. В честь него названы: Каракумский канал (ранее носивший имя Ленина), бывший Ленинский район и улица Ленина в столице, центральные улицы областных центров, Академия сельскохозяйственных наук, несколько промышленных предприятий, колхозов, совхозов и многое другое. Три региона (по-туркменски этрапа) также названы в честь президента: Ниязовский, имени С. Ниязова и имени Сапармурада Туркменбаши.

На этой фамилии следует остановиться более подробно. «Сапармурад Туркменбаши» означает «вождь всех туркменов». Это имя было официально присвоено Ниязову. Было также внесено предложение построить новый, современный город в Туркменистане и назвать его «Сапармурад Туркменбаши». Однако, как известно, строительство городов занимает много времени, поэтому в декабре 1993 года город Красноводск переименовали в город Туркменбаши. В газете «Новое русское слово» появилась статья под заголовком «Страна, названная в честь президента».

Между антикоммунистическими и националистическими интересами возникают весьма поучительные противоречия. Лидеры большевиков по-прежнему прославляются в таких названиях как Днепропетровск (ранее Екатеринославль) и Кировоград (ранее Елизаветград) на Украине. Возвращение им прежних имен означало бы дань российским царицам Екатерине второй и Елизавете, что вряд ли приемлемо для украинских националистов.

В бывшем Советском Союзе в ходе топонимических игр создавались не только новые названия стран, но и новые названия географических регионов. При просмотре российских газет всем бросается в глаза слово Балтия, заменившее собой слово Прибалтика. Может ли кто-нибудь объяснить, чем Балтия лучше Прибалтики? У меня есть только одно объяснение этого феномена: в настоящее время русский язык подвергается сильнейшему воздействию со стороны американского английского. Согласно американской географической и геополитической традиции, Литва, Латвия и Эстония называются балтийскими странами, то есть странами Балтии.

А вот еще один пример американского влияния. В русской географической традиции существует два термина: Центральная Азия и Средняя Азия. Согласно статье в «Энциклопедическом словаре географических названий», Средняя Азия — это «часть территории Центральной Азии, простирающаяся от Каспийского моря на запад до Китая на восток и от Арало-Иртышского водораздела на север до Ирана и Афганистана на юг. Очень часто этот термин используется исключительно для обозначения территории, включающие Узбекистан, Киргизию, Таджикистан и Туркмению». В противоположность этому Центральная Азия — это природный регион, который охватывает континентальные части Китая и Монголии. Однако по американской географической традиции, Центральная Азия состоит из территорий, которые в Советском Союзе обозначались как Средняя Азия и Казахстан. В настоящее время страны этого региона относят себя к Центральной Азии по-русски, и это название вслед за ними повторяется в российских газетах. Вынужден признаться, что в этом ни в коей мере нельзя винить английский язык или Соединенные Штаты Америки.

К сожалению, у меня недостаточно времени для того, чтобы рассказать вам о других проявлениях игры в названия. Поэтому я ограничусь ссылками на последние новости. Две недели назад агентство Associated Press сообщило из Москвы о том, что «российская игра в названия, на протяжении десятилетий представляющая собой практику изменения географических названий в начале каждого политического сезона, делает новый виток. В программах, транслируемых по телевидению и радио на русском языке, опускается произношение, которое использовалось со времен распада Советского Союза в 1991 году. Согласно новым правилам, бывшая советская республика Беларусь вновь называется Белоруссией, Молдова становится Молдавией, а Кыргызстан превращается в Киргизию. Столица Казахстана будет снова называться Алма-Атой, а не Алматы, а республики Татарстан и Башкортостан Российской Федерации снова станут называться Татария и Башкирия».

И как следует реагировать на это решение?

Associated Press цитирует высказывание представителя Академии русского языка: «Ни один язык не может навязывать произношение и написание имен собственных, соответствующие его собственным правилам, русскому языку...» Иными словами, российские чиновники пользуются лингвистической аргументацией, чтобы поддержать изменение политического курса. Совершенно очевидно, что у этих лингвистических перемен будут политические последствия. У меня есть подозрения, что по своему обыкновению российские политики не до конца продумали все детали. Названия Башкортостан и Татарстан закреплены в принятой три месяца назад Конституции Российской Федерации.

У меня есть все основания закончить теми же словами, которыми я завершил свое выступление в Майами три года назад: игра в названия продолжается. Вот еще одна свежая новость: одной из улиц города Барановичи в Брестской области вернули уже утраченное ей коммунистическое название «Улица 50-летия ВЛКСМ». Всё возможно в так называемых «новых независимых государствах».

Политические карты времён
Второй мировой войны: обзор

Павел Ильин

В этом докладе я сделаю обзор нескольких карт, опубликованных в Германии, Италии, СССР, США и других странах во время Второй мировой войны, останавливаясь на вопросах точности и степени надежности этих карт с точки зрения их пригодности для исследовательской работы. Его можно рассматривать как введение в масштабную тему: хотелось бы продемонстрировать важность исследований подобного рода — во-первых, для изучения того, как военные события отображались на картах, а во-вторых, для понимания различных подходов к политической географии Европы в военное время (иными словами, к политике и картографии).

Представленный анализ карт, в основном, базируется на собрании Библиотеки Конгресса (БК). В архиве лиц, переживших Холокост, в Американском Музее Холокоста находится большая коллекция карт, большинство из которых являются фотокопиями карт из БК. Она включает карты из 26 стран на 18 языках. Кроме того, мною использовались карты на цифровых дисках, выпущенных Национальным географическим обществом, а также атласы из моей собственной скромной коллекции старых американских изданий. Старейшая карта в моем собрании опубликована в 1830 г. — однако, это произошло задолго до войн, разразившихся в XX веке.

Теперь мне хотелось бы поднять вопрос о том, когда же наступил конец Первой мировой войны для картографов. Это не случилось 11 ноября 1918 г. в День перемирия, отмечаемый теперь в качестве Дня ветеранов. Это не произошло ни после подписания Версальского договора в 1919 г., ни после того, как в последующие несколько лет изменился картографический облик Европы. Для картографов Первая мировая война завершилась лишь 13 января 1935 года. В этот день небольшой кусочек довоенной Германии, позднее получивший известность как Саар и находившийся под управлением Франции в течение пятнадцати послевоенных лет, отошёл к Германии после референдума о том, какой стране принадлежит эта провинция.

Соответственно, Вторая мировая война для картографов началась почти за полтора года до первого сентября 1939 г. — а именно, 13 марта 1938 г., когда в Линце Гитлером было объявлено о законодательстве, учреждавшем присоединение Австрии к германскому рейху.

За этим последовало Мюнхенское соглашение: Германия, а затем Венгрия и Польша присоединили к своей территории различные части Чехословакии — некоторые из них побольше, а некоторые поменьше. И это было только начало — за время войны границы в Европе менялись 40 раз!

Еще несколько вопросов. В какой стране находился главный концентрационный лагерь нацистов Освенцим? В Польше? Нет, он находился в прусской провинции Верхняя Силезия на территории Германии. А в какой стране находился город Białystok, к примеру, в 1940 году? Тогда он принадлежал Советскому Союзу и назывался Белостоком.

При изучении политической географии Европы приходится пользоваться картами, которые были опубликованы в разных странах, ибо очень трудно понять, какие события произошли в действительности, когда разные карты противоречат друг другу. Давайте остановимся на некоторых из повествуемых ими историй, которые представляют наибольший интерес.

Венское издательство Freytag & Berndt уже более ста лет занимается публикацией карт, с помощью которых очень интересно отслеживать изменения, происходившие в стране или на континенте на протяжении нескольких десятилетий.

Здесь вы видите карту Европы, основанную на карте, опубликованной Freytag & Berndt в 1942 г. (см. *Приложение III, Карта 1*)

Война в полном разгаре. Исчезают восемь стран довоенного времени: Чехословакия, Польша, Вольный город Данциг, три балтийских государства (Эстония, Латвия и Литва), Югославия и Люксембург. Появляются два новых государства: Словакия и Хорватия. У Германии новые границы — теперь это Великая Германия. У десяти других стран тоже появляются новые очертания. Мы видим шесть административных округов: Протекторат Богемия и Моравия и Округ Белосток в составе Великой Германии; Рейхскомиссариат Остланд и Украина на территории Советского Союза под гражданским управлением Германии; Сербия под военным управлением Германии; и Монтенегро под управлением Италии. Только у трёх стран-участниц сохранились те же границы, что и в 1937 г. — у Нидерландов, Дании и Норвегии. Многие изменения на картах с точки зрения агрессоров были вполне оправданы: Германии и Венгрии были возвращены земли, утраченные после Первой мировой войны; Болгария вновь получила земли, уступленные соседним государствам после Второй балканской войны. Албания расширилась, поглотив земли с албанским населением.

Изменения происходили с такой скоростью, что за ними не могли за угнаться издатели. В результате им приходилось заниматься допечатыванием карт и изображать примерные границы вместо настоящих. Иногда в качестве источника приходилось использовать газеты, о чем говорится на полях карты Германии, изданной Генеральным штабом Красной армии.

Сначала мне хотелось бы продемонстрировать фрагменты карты Германии (Немецкого Рейха), опубликованной накануне войны. *(Карты 2 и 3 — Германия перед войной)*

Здесь вы видите за пределами территории Германии границы территорий, которые она утратила после Первой мировой войны — это своего рода картографическое возмездие.

Вот два отрывка карт Германии, напечатанных издательством Ravenstein. *(Карта 4 — Германия после Мюнхенского соглашения)*.

Первый из них опубликован в 1938 г., второй — после Мюнхенского соглашения.

На карте изображена Австрия. Мы видим старые австрийские названия, такие как Österreich и названия провинций Ober- и Nieder-Österreich (Верхняя и Нижняя Австрия). Одновременно с этим, мы видим допечатанное на карте название Ostmark; нацисты переименовали Österreich (Восточное государство) в Ostmark (Восточная марка). Еще одной особенностью этой карты является допечатывание новых границ Чехословакии поверх названия страны, а также названия аннексированной территории: рейхсгау Судетенланд.

Вторая карта была опубликована годом позже — после окончательного раздела Чехословакии.

Обратите внимание на допечатку новых границ Чехословакии. Первая часть в прежнем названии страны вычеркнута, а название новоиспеченной Словакии начинается с черточки.

Второе: Ober и Nieder Österreich (Верхняя и Нижняя Австрия) исчезают: у этих провинций появляются названия Ober и Nieder Donau (Верхний и Нижний Дунай), они становятся «рейхсгау».

Таким образом, бывшая Австрия теперь называется Остмарк. Однако это продлится недолго. В 1942 г. этот термин официально заменили на «рейхсгау Альпы-Дунай» или «Альпийский и Дунайский рейхсгау» (Альпийские и Дунайские земли). (*Карта 5 — Новые названияоккупированных стран*)

Раздел Чехословакии начался с отделения Судет. Это фрагмент того, что, по всей вероятности, было первой немецкой картой с новыми германо-чехословацкими границами рейхсгау Судетенланд в 1938 г. (*Карта 6 — Чехословакия в 1938–1939*).

Радость нацистских картографов была столь велика, что они выделили новую пограничную линию в таблице условных обозначений больше, чем на самой карте.

Здесь вы видите фрагмент еще одной немецкой карты, отображающей разными цветами раздел Чехословакии между Германией, Венгрией, Польшей и Словакией в 1938–1939 гг.

В марте 1939 г. Богемия и Моравия вошли в состав Германии на правах протектората. Было объявлено об образовании независимого государства Словакия, которое в настоящее время называется Словацкой Республикой. Однако эта независимость была столь ограниченной, что на первых картах — в том числе на немецких — Словакия считается частью Германии (тоже в качестве протектората).

Давайте сравним две немецкие карты Германии 1940 г.:
Франция, 1940. Эльзас и Лотарингия во Франции *(Карта 7)*.
Франция, 1942. Эльзас и Лотарингия в Германии *(Карта 8)*.
А на французской карте того же периода — 1942 г.Эльзас и Лотарингия во Франции! Это явно не ошибка: прочие территории, аннексированные Германией — Эйпен-Мальмеди и Люксембург — показаны в пределах Великой Германии. Мы уже говорили о картографическом возмездии, а здесь, как мне кажется, можно говорить о картографическом сопротивлении!

На территории довоенной Украины 1939 г. нацисты учредили так называемый Рейхскомиссариат Украина под гражданским управлением Германии *(Карта 9 — Украина, оккупированная Германией)*.

Это схематическая карта Рейхскомиссариата, отображающая его деление на общие или административные округа. Эта карта, озаглавленная «Рейхскомиссариат Украина» была издана Freytag & Berndt.

Эта карта (*Карта 10 — Транснистрия, 1941*) имеет особую ценность, потому что на ней отмечены границы Приднестровья. В 1941 г. Румыния вернула себе земли, отошедшие к Советскому Союзу в 1940 г. (Бессарабия и Северная Буковина), и получила территорию между реками Днестр и Южный Буг, называемую Приднестровьем со столицей в Одессе. Интересно отметить, что хотя эти земли были присоединены к Румынии, на большинстве немецких карт они изображены как советская территория, оккупированная Румынией. Для меня это продолжает оставаться загадкой.

КАРТЫ, ОПУБЛИКОВАННЫЕ В РАЗНЫХ СТРАНАХ

Насколько исследователь может доверять картам? Давайте посмотрим!

До 1 сентября1939 г., когда Польша была захвачена Германией и Советским Союзом, картам доверять можно.

После 1 сентября 1939 г. на картах, опубликованных в Германии, Италии и их странах-союзницах, по-прежнему отражается действительное положение дел в Европе. Это вполне понятно, так как границы европейских стран изменялись с благословения Германии и Италии. Однако следует отметить, что Германия использовала карты в пропагандистских целях, о чем свидетельствует название этой обычной карты: «Новый Порядок на востоке» (*Карта 11 — Италия и Албания, 1941*). И еще один комментарий: нулевой меридиан на итальянских картах проходит не через Гринвич, а через Рим!

Советский Союз

Мы также можем доверять картам СССР, бывшего в то время союзником Германии (*Карта 12 — Белоруссия, 1938*).

Следует отметить, что польская территория, оккупированная Германией, на советских картах помечается как «сфера государственных интересов Германии». Всё меняется после начала войны между Германией и Советским Союзом 22 июня 1941 г. Все границы на картах, опубликованных в СССР, вернулись к своему состоянию до заключения Мюнхенского соглашения за исключением одной страны — Советского Союза!

Обратимся к карте, опубликованной в Советском Союзе после 22 июня 1941 г. *(Карта 13 — Польша после 1942)*. Здесь можно увидеть границы, указанные по состоянию после сентября 1939 г., в то время как всё остальное соответствует периоду до заключения Мюнхенского соглашения. Я помню, что, когда во время войны мне было семь или восемь лет, я не мог понять, почему у Польши был небольшой и странный анклав к северу от Белостока. Я не знал, что тогда эта территория в районе города Сувалки была частью Восточной Пруссии.

США

А как насчет американских карт? Интереснейший вопрос! Должен вам честно признаться, что я ничего не понимаю. Давайте рассмотрим следующие примеры.

Атлас Collier's 1941 г. открывается картой Европы, составленной Rand McNally. Польша изображена как поделенная между Германией и СССР.

Атлас Collier's 1943 г. Польша не поделена между Германией и СССР!

Стандартная карта Европы Александра Гросса, опубликованная Geographia Map Co.

Здесь границы Румынии с Венгрией и Болгарией указаны по состоянию после августа 1940 г., однако румыно-советская граница отражает положение до июня 1940 г. А Польша не показана как поделенная Германией и СССР! Не показано и разделение Югославии.

А теперь посмотрим на карты географического гуру Америки — Национального географического общества.

Май 1940 г. Все в порядке. Польша поделена, Вильно находится в Литве.

Сентябрь 1941 г. Дальнейшие карты Европы выходили в 1942 и 1943 гг. — и снова на них не было некоторых из существовавших тогда границ.

Здесь можно увидеть карты Германии (опубликована Национальным географическим обществом в июле 1944 г.) и СССР (опубликована им же в декабре 1944 г.). Европа на этих картах выглядит по-разному. *(Карта 14 — Германия, 1944)*. На карте Германии все границы отражают положение 1 сентября 1939 г. На карте СССР советские границы помечены «в соответствии с российскими договорами и претензиями на 1 октября 1944 г.» *(Карта 15—Германия, 1944)*.

Иногда политкорректность того периода кажется даже странной. Издательство Hammond опубликовало три небольшие карты на одной странице. *(Карта 16—Польша, республики Прибалтики, Венгрия и Словакия)*. На двух из них указаны довоенные границы советских республик Прибалтики и Польши! На карте советских прибалтийских республик Вильно (Вильнюс) указан в качестве столицы Литовской Советской Социалистической Республики; на карте Польши он является столицей польского Виленского воеводства! Географический вымысел!

А вот еще несколько примеров, свидетельствующих о том, что нам следует критично относиться к картам, опубликованным в разных странах.

Давайте сравним две карты **Литвы**, опубликованные до войны. На этих картах контуры Литвы выглядят по-разному.

На карте, вышедшей в Литве *(Карта 17—Литва перед войной)*, мы видим литовские границы по состоянию на 1918 г. после провозглашения независимости этой страны. В 1920 г. Польша оккупировала, а в 1922 г. официально присоединила значительную часть литовского государства — что никогда не было признано Литвой. В результате этого появилась новая действительная граница, так называемая «административная линия» («демаркационная линия» на некоторых других картах). Соответственно, утраченные земли обозначены как «оккупированные Польшей», причем используются литовские названия населенных пунктов.

На карте, опубликованной в Польше *(Карта 18—Литва перед войной)*, «демаркационная линия» показана как настоящая государственная граница.

Еще один пример. Весь мир считал **Бессарабию** частью Румынии. Советский Союз считал Бессарабию своей территорией, незаконно оккупированной Румынией — поэтому на всех советских картах, опубликованных до 1940 г., эта территория заштрихована *(Карта 19—Украина и Бессарабия до 1940 г.)*

ЗАКЛЮЧЕНИЕ

В заключение хотелось бы сказать несколько слов о практическом значении понимания подлинных границ государств для изучения Холокоста. В 1941 г. Югославия была поделена между шестью администрациями: Албании, Болгарии, Венгрии, Германии, Италии и Хорватии. В каждой из них «еврейский вопрос» решался по-разному. Под управлением Германии местные власти Сербии первыми в оккупированной Европе объявили свою территорию свободной от евреев («Judenfrei»). Политика правительства Болгарии в отношении евреев была весьма противоречивой. Можно сказать, что болгарские власти пожертвовали евреями Македонии и Тракии ради спасения болгарских евреев. В Хорватии уже через несколько дней после провозглашения независимости появились концлагеря для евреев, сербов и цыган. Италия не только пыталась спасти собственных евреев, но и предоставляла убежище хорватским евреям, бежавшим из оккупированной немцами северной Хорватии на оккупированный Италией юг. Албания оказалась единственной страной в Европе, где еврейское население после войны превышало довоенный уровень. Конечно, Албания находилась под управлением Италии, однако сами албанцы и их правительство не были врагами евреев. В Венгрии правительство называло евреев Vačka, а также евреев Приднестровья, на юге Словакии и в Рутении «венгерскими евреями», и они чувствовали себя в относительной безопасности — вплоть до немецкой оккупации страны в 1944 г.

И еще несколько слов о послевоенной Европе. После 1945 некоторые из довоенных границ были восстановлены, однако к 1947 г. контуры 11 стран отличались от довоенных, а четыре независимых государства совсем исчезли. Но это уже другая история...

Там, где родился И. М. Маергойз, или топонимический погром на Украине

Павел Ильин

МЕСТЕЧКО РОЖДЕНИЯ

Мне не довелось слушать И. М. Маергойза учась на геофаке — нам, студентам кафедры экономической географии СССР, лекций он не читал. Но я всегда обращал на него внимание, когда встречал в университетских рекреациях (коридорах Главного здания МГУ). Небольшого роста, плотного сложения, с большой головой и гривой седых волос, он обладал внешностью, которую нельзя было не запомнить. Эти встречи случались редко: наши кафедры находились на разных этажах. И впервые я услышал его уже после того, как в 1960 году окончил университет.

В те годы у МФГО своего помещения не было, и его приютило Московское общество испытателей природы, квартировавшее в старом здании университета на Моховой. Вот там, в знаменитой Коммунистической аудитории, главной в МГУ до постройки нового здания, я впервые попал на выступление Маергойза. И тогда, и потом, встречая И. М. в официальной или неофициальной обстановке, я всегда восхищался его мыслями, талантом лектора, манерой общаться с другими людьми. Он был окружен молодыми, у него не было и тени менторства, он был мягок и терпелив. Его всегда хотелось слушать.

И. М. умер в 1975 г. А через десять лет после его кончины у меня случилась новая встреча с ним. Его ученики задумали издание трудов своего учителя. Для перепечатки текста им нужна была машинистка.[1] А моя семья, подавшая в 1982 г. заявление на выезд в Израиль, пребывала, казалось бы, в безнадежном отказе. И, как

---

[1] Имеется в виду пишущая машинка, так как компьютеры в то время были недоступны советским гражданам для персонального пользования.

это следовало в те годы, лишилась почти всех источников существования. К счастью, у нас были друзья, которые находили для нас возможности заработать. И среди них — Павел Полян, который предложил нам перепечатать текст книги И.М. Большую часть работы проделала моя жена, но и я принял в перепечатке участие.

Затем Павел принес вторую готовившуюся тогда книгу И.М. — о географических проблемах городов. Но тут настали новые времена, мы получили выездные визы и в июле 1987 года покинули Советский Союз. Говорить кому-нибудь о нашей «левой» работе и работодателях тогда было рискованно. И я рад, что могу сейчас публично поблагодарить Павла Марковича Поляна за искреннюю и небезопасную помощь в наши нелегкие годы. Как и за предложение участвовать в этом сборнике.

Размышляя о том, чему посвятить свою статью, я стал просматривать книги, где было написано что-нибудь об И. М. Меня заинтересовало место его рождения: местечко Янов[2] Винницкой области по одним источникам, Янов в Подолии — по другим. Собственно, тут нет противоречия, современная Винницкая область раньше была частью Подольской губернии. Уже работая над статьей, я обнаружил третью версию: местечко Янов в Подолии, ныне Иванполь Житомирской области. Но его прежнее имя — не Янов, а Янушполь. Кроме того, Житомир никогда не был в Подолии, это город на Волыни. По-видимому, поводом для ошибки послужило то, что И.М. окончил педагогический техникум в Житомире и учительствовал в Овруче.

Итак, Янов под Винницей. А где он на карте? Тут меня подстерегала неожиданность: населенного пункта с таким названием не оказалось... во всей Украине! Не помог и справочник административно-территориального устройства Украинской ССР 1987 года из моей библиотеки. Скорей всего, Янов переименован. Но как он теперь называется? Понадобились более ранние издания. И вот в Библиотеке Конгресса в Вашингтоне нашелся справочник 1946 года. Как я и подозревал, Янов переименовали: теперь он Иванов.

Мне повезло, что интрига поиска вывела меня на этот «древний» источник. Дело в том, что украинские справочники АТД, в отличие от российских, приводили имена *всех* населенных пунктов, в том числе *старые для всех переименованных после издания преды-*

---

[2] По-украински, был Янів, стал Іванів. Поскольку эта статья публикуется на русском языке, все географические названия в ней даются по-русски.

дущего справочника, в данной книге — за 1941–1946 гг. Среди них и Янов-Иванов в Калиновском районе Винницкой области, и все другие украинские Яновы. Всего за этот период там переименовали, если я правильно посчитал, около трех тысяч населенных пунктов. Надо полагать, что во время нацистской оккупации советской власти было не до переименований. А с ее возвращением на Украину возобновилась и смена географических имен, ставшая массовой в 1944 и особенно в 1946 гг.

Так родился замысел написать о переименованиях в Украинской ССР в конце Второй мировой войны и сразу после нее. Добавлю, что этот процесс затронул не только родное местечко И.М., но и его лично: в 1950 г., в разгар борьбы с так называемым космополитизмом, то есть развязанной Сталиным антисемитской истерии, в Географгизе вышла написанная Маергойзом книжка «Киев». Вместо его имени на обложке и титульном листе стоит: «И. М. Марченко».[3]

Но сначала — об истории местечка Янова, оно же село Иванов.

ЯНОВ ДО РЕВОЛЮЦИИ

Старые люди помнят и знают ЯНОВ, а не Иванов. Тот самый ЯНОВ, который славился своими ярмарками и шумными базарами, пьяными корчмами и многочисленными крамницами.

Леонид Резник, уроженец местечка Янов[4]

Когда знаешь, где расположен населенный пункт, то указать его на карте нетрудно, даже если у него уже другое имя. В 30 километрах выше Винницы по Южному Бугу река меняет свое направление, уклоняясь (если следовать от истока) круче на юг, а слева в Буг впадает река Снивода. Вот там — в ее устье и на излучине Бу-

---

[3] Это одна из реликвий моей библиотеки. В Москве у меня были еще две столь же уникальные книжки, изданные Географгизом в начале 1950-х гг. в серии «Страны мира»: В.М. Венин «Гватемала» и его же «Панама и Панамский канал», авторами которых на самом деле был другой замечательный географ и человек Вениамин Максович Гохман, которого – увы! – тоже давно нет среди нас.

[4] Л. Резник. Воспоминания по дорогам моей жизни. Я родом из местечка Янов. — **http://leonid-70.narod.ru /text/Doc12.htm.**

га — стояла «городня Яновская», упомянутая в описании Винницкого замка в 1552 г. Этимология названия прозрачна: его основателем или первым владельцем был поляк по имени Ян. В то время Янов относился к Подольскому воеводству Великого княжества Литовского, но уже в 1566 г. оказался в Брацлавском воеводстве, выделенном из Подольского. Этот административный акт привел к появлению нового географического понятия: Брацлавщина. Причем современники твердо знали: Брацлавщина — это не Подолье. Еще через три года Польша и Литва объединяются по Люблинской унии, но с разделом подчиненных каждой территорий. Подолье и Брацлавщина переходят под власть Польской Короны. Янов (по-польски Janów — Янув) в Брацлавском воеводстве относился к Пиковской гмине (волости) Винницкого повета (уезда).

По местным легендам, Янов первоначально располагался на правом берегу Буга, а затем перебрался на левый, к устью Сниводы. Здесь, под защитой рек и лесов, яновцы чувствовали себя в большей безопасности. Но, главное, рядом проходил оживленный торговый путь из Винницы в Хмельник. Если в упомянутом 1552 г. в Янове было 16 домов, то через четверть века их стало, как минимум, втрое больше. И 1 марта 1578 г. польский король Стефан Баторий даровал ему статус местечка. Согласно королевской Грамоте, направленной тогдашнему владельцу Янова Гневошу Стрижевскому, ему предоставлялось право «основания города в имении его Янев Брацлавского воеводства». Было разрешено строить замки для защиты жителей окрестных селений от нападений и проводить дважды в год ярмарки, а населению предписывалось «выпивать, торговать, покупать, платить налог от товаров своих» и «иметь в домах своих корчмы разные, медовые, пивные, водочные и иное всякое питье», а «торговлю каждую неделю в пятницу». Главными занятиями первых обитателей Янова были скотоводство, рыболовство, землепашество и лесные промыслы. Статус местечка дал толчок его развитию как торгового и ремесленного центра (раньше говорили: промышленного — от слова промысел). По-видимому, в это время в местечке появились евреи.

Небольшое отступление о местечке вообще. Мы знаем, что это нечто среднее между селом и городом (вроде поселка городского типа), что оно было населено преимущественно евреями, отличаясь от окружения характером быта и культуры. И что это понятие стало синонимом своеобразного образа жизни и мировоззрения евреев в черте оседлости. Почему они жили в местечках? Ответ лежит в социально-экономической и юридической плоскости: местечки (как и города) привлекали еврейских купцов и ремесленников тем, что в них разрешались ярмарки и базары, без которых была невозможна регулярная коммерческая деятельность. А владельцы местечек, заинтересованные в их экономическом развитии, предоставляли евреям некоторые привилегии: право застраивать определенную территорию, иметь свое кладбище, синагогу, самоуправление и ряд других.

Известно, что в старину и реки были полноводнее, и леса погуще. Но ни те, ни другие не могли защитить Янов от крымских татар, постоянно разорявших Подолье и Брацлавщину. Янов оказался между двумя дорогами, по которым двигалась татарская конница при набегах на Правобережную Украину и Польшу: по левобережью Буга, а точнее, по его водоразделу с Днепром, проходил Черный шлях, по правобережью — водоразделу с Днестром — Кучманский. Прибавьте к этому антифеодальные выступления крестьян и горожан, и станет понятно, почему Гневош Стрижевский затеял строительство замка. Но был он, судя по тому, что современники называли его «замочек», невелик.

В начале XVII века Пиковская и соседние волости стали ареной борьбы между двумя магнатами: Яном Тышкевичем и князем Яном (Иваном) Острожским, вошедшим в историю под уменьшительным именем Януш. Конфликт закончился разграничением их владений, причем Пиковская волость досталась Янушу Острожскому. Завладев, среди прочих мест, Яновом, новый владелец перекрестил его в Янушполь — город Януша (первое официальное переименование). Но это название не прижилось; к тому же местечко вообще исчезло на время из письменных документов — наверное, было разрушено татарами. Во всяком случае, на знаменитой Генеральной карте Украины Боплана, изданной в 1648 г., оно подписано как «новый град Иоанов», а в других документах того времени встречается под именем Новый Янов. В 1672 г. Подольем и Брацлавщиной завладела Турция, но в 1699 г. они вернулись в состав Речи Посполитой.

Янов относился к категории частных («владельческих») местечек и не раз менял хозяев, пока не перешел во владение Холоневских — будущих графов Австрийской и Российской империй, родственников короля Яна Собеского. В конце XVII века Холоневским принадлежало в Янове 300 с лишним крестьянских дворов и до 2 тысяч крепостных. В начале следующего века Холоневские делают Янов своей резиденцией. В 1750 г. король Август III подтверждает за Яновым права местечка. На средства Холоневских

359

возводится новый замок, основывается монастырь бернардинцев, строятся костел Непорочного зачатия и ратуша с часами на башне. Янов бурно растет как торгово-ремесленный центр. Особенным спросом пользовались яновские ткани и продукция цеха сапожников; сапожники даже наряжались по-особому — носили одежду зеленого цвета.

Ремесленники и торговцы жили в центре, недалеко от замка. Надо полагать, что это были в основном (если не исключительно) евреи. Их число в Янове и окрестных деревнях в 1765 г. составляло 795 человек. Остальные жители местечка были украинцы, и, в меньшем числе, поляки. За Сниводой, вверх по течению Буга, возникает «пригород» Янова — Яновская Слободка.

В 1793 г. при втором разделе Польши Янов со всей Брацлавщиной отходит к Российской империи. На землях воеводств создаются Подольское и Брацлавское наместничества, а в 1797 г.— Подольская губерния с центром в Каменец-Подольске. Брацлавщина уходит в небытие, и сам Брацлав навсегда теряет какое-либо серьезное значение. «Подолье» постепенно превращается в «Подолию». Янов включают в состав Литинского уезда, но в 1882 году переводят в Винницкий.

В начале XIX века в местечке работали, хотя и не одновременно, две типографии: хасидская и «христианская», где печатались польские и раскольнические книги. В 1864 г. в Янове были две церкви: православная церковь Св. Николая с 1617 прихожанами (приход стал православным после присоединения к России; до этого он был униатским) и римско-католическая — уже знакомый нам костел Непорочного зачатья — с 1010 прихожанами. Синагоги и их прихожан источник не упоминает, приводя лишь общее число евреев в губернии и отмечая места их обитания (точнее, наличие в них «еврейских обществ»), подчеркиванием названий населенных пунктов. Среди них и наш Янов: по ревизии 1847 г., в Яновском «еврейском обществе» состояли 1798 душ.

После 1861 г. в Янове установили памятник Александру II. Устроили две школы, одну из них — для девочек. А вот данные 1882 года: *«Жителей до 2000, из коих половина евреи, домов 410. Костел... 2 каменных церкви, 2 синагоги, пивоваренный и винокуренный заводы, 4 мельницы, 26 базаров, 44 лавки; 362 ремесленника, из которых выделяются сапожники. 1372 десятины обрабатываемых земель...».*

В XIX веке Янов И. М. Маергойза был далеко не последним среди одноименных местечек западных губерний. По крайней мере, в трех изданиях авторитетного географического словаря Липпинкота о нем сказано: *«Янов (Yanov, Ianov, or Janov, Ya'nov), название нескольких торговых поселений (market-towns) в России, знатнейшее (the principal) из которых находится в Подольской губернии на реке Буг в 14 милях к северо-востоку от Литина».* Л. Резник, ссылаясь на «архивные материалы», рисует такой портрет:

«Через все местечко проходит почтовая дорога. Центральная часть... занята еврейскими жилищами. Посредине находится базарная площадь, на которой, в качестве гостиничного ряда, сохраняются остатки четырехугольной ратуши. На краю этой площади, при въезде в местечко с западной стороны, помещается усадьба Холоневского с дворцом в виде замка и примыкающим к нему римско-католическим костелом. Часть местечка, расположенная на возвышенном берегу реки Сниводы, носит название «Царской горы»... как говорит народное предание, некогда, во время польско-турецкой войны, здесь стоял лагерем один из польских королей...

Цеховое деление среди ремесленников местечка Янов сохранилось и до сих пор: делятся они на три главные категории — сапожников, горшечников и свинобоев. Эти цехи составляют особого рода касты, которые стараются не смешиваться с людьми других званий и сохраняют известные особенности в одежде... Кроме указанных промышленников, большинство православных прихожан состоит из крестьян, которые занимаются преимущественно земледелием...

Всех православных в приходе насчитывается... около 3000 душ; католиков около 400 душ; больше всего здесь евреев... в 1887 году в местечке было 2220 евреев, одна синагога и два еврейских молитвенных дома».

По переписи 1897 г. в Янове было 5545 жителей, в т.ч. 2088 евреев. В начале XX века здесь появились сельский банк и почта. По-прежнему пользовалась большим спросом продукция ремесленников. Одних только вышитых рубашек из Янова вывозилось и сбывалось на местных ярмарках тысячи на три — немалые деньги по тем временам. В 1900 году через Янов провели узкоколейную железную дорогу Бердичев — Калиновка. Один из ее участков должен был пройти по земле графа Холоневского, который разрешил строить дорогу при условии, что его именем будет названа станция. Условие было принято, и с тех пор здешняя станция называется Холоневская.

А вот картинка Янова в годы, когда И. М. Маергойз появился на свет:

> «Два раза в месяц по пятницам на Яновский рынок съезжались торговцы и покупатели из ближних и не очень ближних сел и местечек. На Базарной и Конной площадях скапливалось до четырехсот подвод, на продажу стояло 150 голов крупного рогатого скота и несчетное число более мелкой живности. Два дня шел оживленный торг, корчмы были полны народу. Особенно славился знаменитый на всю округу «Голубой Дунай». Затем жизнь затихала до следующего базарного дня».

ЯНОВ ПОСЛЕ РЕВОЛЮЦИИ

Фронт Первой мировой войны до Янова не дошел. В 1917 г. была провозглашена Украинская Народная республика. Реальная власть там, и в Янове тоже, часто менялась: приходили и уходили войска разных украинских правительств, махновцы, всякие банды. Происходили еврейские погромы — И. М. Маергойз должен был их помнить. Самый страшный погром длился три дня, с 15 по 17 июля 1919 г., когда были убиты 300 евреев. В местечке был создан еврейский отряд самообороны, но защитить яновцев от громил ему не удалось. Современник называет Янов в числе мест, наиболее пострадавших от погромов. В 1920 г. в Янов вошли поляки; через несколько недель — Красная армия.

Губернское деление на Украине в 1922–1923 гг. заменили окружным, а уездное — районным. Янов вошел в состав Пиковского района Винницкого округа Украинской ССР. Категория местечек была упразднена, и официально Янов стал селом, хотя все продолжали называть его местечком, даже в документах. Так, справки, выдаваемые Яновским сельсоветом, сопровождались подписью: «Предсельсовета м. [местечка] Янова» на русском языке, или «Голова сельради м. [містечка] Янева — на украинском.

Годы НЭПа для Янова были относительно благополучными. Его жители, как и прежде, занимались кустарными промыслами, торговлей, сельским хозяйством. Появились машинно-тракторная станция и первые сельхозартели — украинская, затем польская (просуществовала недолго). Евреев тоже призывали обратиться к земле, была организована еврейская артель «Хлебороб». Документы Пиковского райисполкома за 1922–1925 гг. дают представление о небезынтересных сторонах жизни Янова. Самым большим из «промышленных предприятий» там была водяная мельница, в прошлом принадлежавшая Холоневскому, с «двигательной силой» 12 л.с. и тремя работниками; два кожевенных и сахарный завод были того же масштаба. Он типичен для местечек, как и тот факт, что эту деятельность, да и коммерческую, вели исключительно евреи: в списках ремесленников и торговцев я не нашел ни одной нееврейской фамилии.

В 1929 г. здесь проживал 6481 человек, в том числе 4570 украинцев, 240 поляков, 47 русских, 5 белорусов и 1619 евреев. В Янове был организован второй сельсовет — еврейский национальный. В нем в 1931 г. числился 2301 житель. Несмотря на антирелигиозную пропаганду, еще действовали церкви, молитвенные дома и синагога, еврейские дети учились в своей школе.

В те годы И. М. Маергойз, как многие его земляки, покинул родное местечко навсегда. Оставшиеся стали жертвами «великого перелома»: раскулачивания и насильственной коллективизации. В Янове организовали еще один колхоз — им. Ворошилова. Крестьяне, как повсюду на Украине и в других зерновых, скотоводческих районах, пытались сопротивляться. Чтобы не отдавать в колхозы свой скот, они стали его забивать. Катастрофа пришла в 1932 г., когда не осталось ни еды, ни посевного зерна, конфискованного подчистую. Самой страшной была зима 1933 года. Началось людоедство. По некоторым данным, в Янове от голода умерли триста человек. Голодомор сломил сопротивление, и в 1935 г. уровень коллективизации в Янове достиг желаемых властями 100%.

В 1932 г. Винницкий округ вошел в состав вновь образованной Винницкой области. Произошло укрупнение районов, и Янов попал в Калиновский, где пребывает по сей день. Жизнь в местечке постепенно наладилась. В 1936 г. через Янов прошла новая железная дорога Киев — Каменец-Подольский. Материально жить стало легче, но были закрыты все культовые учреждения, еврейский национальный сельсовет и школа. Не миновал местечко «большой террор». А вскоре пришел год 1941-й.

Немцы заняли Янов ровно через месяц после начала войны, 22 июля 1941 г. Мало кому удалось эвакуироваться. Вначале местечко находилось под управлением военной комендатуры, а в конце октября было передано под начало германской гражданской администрации и получило следующий «адрес»: *Janow, Rayon und Kreisgebiet Kalinowka, Generalbezirk Shitomir, Reichskommissariat Ukraine*. Для яновских евреев настали самые черные дни. Им предписали носить шестиконечную звезду, к которой позднее добавили желтый круг; запретили покидать местечко; посылали на тяжелые работы, часто без всякой оплаты. Как повсюду на Украине, их грабили и избивали украинские полицаи и антисемиты-добровольцы. А в начале 1942 года для них было создано гетто. В марте в него пригнали группу молодых мужчин и женщин из Пикова. Работали они на лесозаготовках в ближнем лесу, в мае их перегнали в Калиновку. Яновское гетто просуществовало недолго: 30 мая там расстреляли 814 евреев. Не все обреченные покорно встретили свою смерть. Портной Лейб Яновский, пожилой и немощный человек, подозвал жандарма и, выхватив из кармана бритву, полоснул врага по затылку: одним фашистом стало меньше. Еще 194 еврея были убиты в акциях 6 и 11 июня. Таким образом, число жертв среди яновских евреев составило 1008 человек.

Вот фрагмент из воспоминаний Леонида Резника:

«Дедушка, бабушка и еще 7 членов нашей семьи, которые не смогли уехать..., были заключены в гетто вместе со всеми евреями местечка и 30 мая 1942 года расстреляны во рву в центре поселка... В 1945 году, сразу после окончания войны, моя сестра... приезжала в Винницу и была в местечке Янов на могиле родных и близких. На братской могиле евреев местечка стоял скромный памятник. Местечко было как вымерший пустырь».

Янов освободили 9 марта 1944 года войска 1-го Украинского фронта. Евреи были уничтожены, но село, уже и по-существу не местечко, осталось. Переименование в Иванов только подчеркнуло разрыв с его прошлым.

В современном Иванове живут 5,4 тыс. человек. Население в основном занимается земледелием (главные культуры — пшеница и сахарная свекла) и животноводством. Имеются мельницы, предприятия по ремонту сельскохозяйственной техники, учреждения бытового обслуживания — обычный для большого села набор. Разве что гранитный карьер и щебеночный завод выделяются из этого стандартного ряда.

Интересна судьба приметных зданий села. В замке в 1920 г. разместили заготконтору, через три года — детскую колонию, а незадолго до войны — детский дом для детей репрессированных родителей. С 1963 г. это школа-интернат. Ратуша разрушена во время войны. Продолжает действовать по назначению вокзал станции Холоневская. Церковь св. Николая разобрали в 1935 г. на кирпичи, пустив их на строительство школы. Через 70 лет построили новую церковь. Костел использовался как клуб, потом был передан спортивной школе. Сейчас в нем снова проводятся богослужения, но красная звезда с его фасада еще не удалена. А вот синагоги в Иванове нет: после Второй мировой войны евреев здесь не осталось. Они появляются в бывшем местечке раз в году — 30 мая, когда родственники расстрелянных фашистами евреев собираются у памятника, установленного на месте их массовой гибели.

ТОПОНИМИЧЕСКИЙ ПОГРОМ

— Кто же жил раньше на Владимирской земле? — спрашивал писатель Солоухин карту во «Владимирских проселках». И карта ему отвечала… — А кто жил раньше на Украинской земле? — спросим мы карту. Скудный будет ее ответ…

В 1918 г. Украинская Центральная Рада переименовала Екатеринослав в Сечеслав (Катеринослав — в Січеслав) в честь Запорожской сечи, по-украински, січи. В Советской Украине переименования расцвели пышным цветом — как всюду «под солнцем Октября». Исторические названия городов, поселков, сел, хуторов теснили имена типа Советское и Комсомольское, Октябрьское и Жовтневое, Красно- и Червоноармейское, Перво- и Першемайское. Немалую группу новых имен составили те, что давались в честь партийных и советских руководителей. Но переименования 1943–1946 гг. отличаются, во-первых, массовостью, и, во-вторых, украинизацией топонимии Украины — своего рода «пролетарским национализмом». Напомню, что справочник АТД Украины, которым я пользовался, зафиксировал более трех тысяч случаев принудительной смены имен населенных пунктов в те годы. Эта «топонимическая реформа» может служить темой отдельного исследования. Сейчас я хочу вкратце осветить только изменения имен, имеющих отношение к вопросу «кто жил раньше на Украинской земле?».

Советизацию географических названий называют теперь на Украине топонимическим геноцидом. Но пройдитесь по любой карте, и вы увидите, что плотность «советских» названий, на самом деле, не столь высока, просто они сразу бросаются в глаза. К тому же, при советизации топонимии не ставилась задача уничтожить украинское. А вот явление, обсуждаемое в этой статье, правомерно назвать *топонимическим погромом*, направленным на искоренение имен немецкого, польского, еврейского, венгерского, румынского, татарского и другого «чуждого» происхождения.

До топонимического погрома на Украине было 9 Яновых и 33 Яновки, плюс еще 69 населенных пунктов, названия которых происходили от корня Ян. Находились они не только на аннексированных в 1939 г. польских территориях, но и в «старосоветских» областях, унаследовавших названия от дораздельной Польши и затем царской России. Пример тому — родина И. М. Маергойза.

Возможно, не все эти названия восходили к польскому имени Ян или уменьшительному Януш, но 107 из них явно переименованы из-за первых двух букв. Место Янов и Янушей на карте заняли, как правило, Иваны: половину этих селений назвали Ивановка, остальные — Иванов, Иванковка, Иванковичи, Иваничи, Иванинцы, Рудня-Ивановская и др. А поселок Янов Львовской области получил имя «п.г.т. Ивана Франка», столь же нелепое, как «город (село) имени…». Уцелели тогда Янишевка в Одесской области, Янушевка в Харьковской и «поселок ж.д. станции Янов» в Киевской области. Но судьба этого Янова еще трагичнее: рядом построили Чернобыльскую АЭС и при ней город Припять, поэтому ныне поселение захоронено и «снято с учета в связи с отсутствием жителей». Нет и харьковской Янушевки. Одесская Янишевка осталась в одиночестве, одна из ста десяти.

Вторым после Янова популярным топообразующим польским именем на карте Украины был Юзеф: 20 сел Юзефовка, 5 Юзефполей, Юзефин и Юзефины, Юзефов и Юзефово, Юзефка, Юзина, Юзини и другие, всего 48 населенных пунктов, чьи имена начинались на «Юз». И ни одного не осталось, причем 43 получили имя Осиповка.

Та же участь постигла и другие иноязычные имена людей на карте. Всего было 60 таких имен, и они легко распознавались на старой карте. Большинство имен польские и немецкие, но есть чешские, венгерские, румынские, болгарские и даже имена представителей народов, обитающих далеко от украинских земель и занесенных сюда каким-то ветром: французское Андре, шведское Густав, грузинское Ираклий. Личные имена входили в географические в разных формах, например, просто Герман, Германов, Германовка, Германовская Слободка и хутор Германа. Всего я насчитал 220 населенных пунктов, чьи названия произошли от названных (кроме Яна и Юзефа) имен. И все они исчезли.

Я не упомянул еще имена, которые для законодателей того времени звучали хуже иноземных: имена еврейские. А ведь были

Мееровка, Таубовка, Лейбовка, Герцево, Берков и просто Беня, без всяких прикрас. Уж они-то уцелеть никак не могли. К еврейским топонимам я еще вернусь. А к числу неугодных добавлю имя Аристарх: хотя и есть оно в святцах, но тоже какое-то «не нашенское»: Аристарховка не уцелела.

Перейдем к рубрике «Страны, народы, города». Были на Украине тезки зарубежных земель: хутор Америка в Львовской области и Ново-Америка в Николаевской, Китай и две Манчжурии, две Швейцарии, Эльзас, Баден и Альт-Насау (Старый Насау), Боснячина. Все — переименованы. Правителей Советской Украины не устроили даже названия «братских» республик у хуторов Литва, Молдова и Новая Молдавия.

Стерто с карты и большинство названий, производных от этнонимов. А на Украине, через которую проходили и в которой селились разные племена и народы, их было много. Первое место занимали поляки, по-украински ляхи. Первые четко просматривались в именах лишь двух хуторов — Поляки и Польский, а ляхи — в сорока с лишним: Ляхи, Ляхов, Ляховцы, Ляцкое, Ляшки Шляхетские, Ляшки Королевские и др. Ни одного из них теперь нет. За ляхами-поляками шли татары — 29 имен: Татары, Татаринцы, Татаровка, Татарка, Татарский Брод и др. Были село Немецкое, хутор Немцев-Колонистов и Хатки Немца, Прусы и Швабы, был хутор Еврейская Долина (в Станиславской, ныне Ивано-Франковской области). Были хутор Литовский, Чехоград, Болгарка, Угорцы (венгры), Турки, Турчанка и Турецкая Гора, Французы, Британы, Греки, Киргиз, Итальянка, Цыганы, Персияновка. Плюс производные от этих и других этнонимов. Были, да сплыли. Несколько лет еще продержался Ногайск — ныне Приморск.

Особую, и немалую, группу топонимов составляли пары типа Долина Украинская и Долина Чешская, Лани Немецкие и Лани Польские, Новоселки Русские и Чешские, Слободзея Молдавская и Украинская, Ульяники Польские и Украинские и т.д. Определения в этих названиях говорили о народах, живших, по-существу, в одном поселении или в соседних. Все они удалены, отброшены даже такие определения, как «Украинская» и «Русская». А как же иначе: если оставить, например, Крошню Украинскую, а Чешскую переименовать, то, глядишь, и возникнет у кого-нибудь мысль, что раз есть Крошня Украинская, значит, была какая-то другая. И стала Крошня Украинская просто Крошней, а Чешская — Крошней Второй. Украинский топонимист А. П. Коваль рассказывает о происхождении нескольких уцелевших названий, например Чехи, но из этнонимов, полностью стертых с карты, говорит только о ляшско-польских и прусских (но не немецких!), а об остальных даже не упоминает.

Теперь о весях, то есть сельских поселениях, названных по дальним градам. Весей много — поселенцы часто давали им имена родных мест. Особенно много было тезок немецких городов: немцы-колонисты играли большую роль в освоении украинских земель, особенно новороссийских. Карту Украины украшали Лесные Берлинцы и Воробьево-Берлин, Галле и Гейдельберг, Старый Данциг и Новоданцевка, Кассель и утративший второе «с» Касель, Мюнхен и Ново-Мюнхен, Мангейм и Ново-Мангейм, Карлсруэ, Дармштадт и целых три Страсбурга. А еще Далекий Рим, Цюрихталь (Цюрихская Долина), Варшава, Варшавка и т.д. И все они – жертвы 1946 года. Уцелевший тогда Нью-Йорк, поселок в Донбассе, та же участь постигла через несколько лет.

Может быть, дело в переизбытке чуждых топонимов? Давайте ненадолго покинем Украину и перенесемся на Южный Урал, в Челябинскую область. Я помню, как на студенческой практике 1957 г. мы проезжали Варну и на следующий день въехали в Фершампенуаз — центр Нагайбакского района. Сколько лет прошло, давно позабылись имена других селений края, но Варну и Фершампенуаз помню. А есть там еще села и поселки Париж, Кассель, Арси, Берлин, Лейпциг, Бородино, Тарутино, Березинский, Чесма и другие, названные при освоении этих земель в честь побед российской армии и флота.

Бородино, Тарутино и Березино есть и на карте Украины — в Южной Бессарабии, бывшей Измаильской области. Они тоже названы в честь памятных сражений. И там же были свои Лейпциг, Берлин, Париж и Новый Париж, Старый и Новый Фершампенуаз да еще Кульм, которого нет на Урале. Эти имена в память битв союзников с Наполеоном селения Южной Бессарабии получили при ее колонизации в начале XIX века, но найти их можно только на старых картах. С Уралом Украину топонимически связывало и название Оренбург. Уральский город перекрестили за три года до войны; теперь та же участь постигла его украинскую тезку — хутор в Днепропетровской области. Когда же в 1957 г. российскому Оренбургу вернули его историческое имя, об украинском Оренбурге вряд ли кто-нибудь вспомнил.

Коротко о других иноземных названиях. Начну с немецких. На Украине было много мест, имена которых оканчивалось (в скобках значения и примеры) на -*берг* (*гора*: Гайберг); -*бург* (*город*: Ямбург); -*штадт* и -*штедт* (тоже *город*: Либенштадт, Гохштедт); -*таль* (*долина*: Кляйнлибенталь); -*вальд* и -*вальден* (тоже *долина*: Гринвальд, Унтервальден); -*фельд* (*поле*: Дорнфельд); -*штейн* (*камень*: Блюменштейн); -*гейм* (*дом*: Гнагенгейм); -*дорф* (*село, деревня*: знаменитый одесский Люстдорф, ставший Черноморкой). Или начинались на *ней-, най-, ной-* (*новый*: Найдорф). И еще масса других. Ничего не осталось! Наряду с такими категориями сельских населенных мест, как село, хутор, поселок, на Украине были колонии — напоминание о немецких колонистах. Это слово входило в названия села Колония Дубровка, хутора Колония Мельница и т.п. И с ними покончили: колонию как тип поселения упразднили, имена изменили.

У польских названий своя специфика. Если немецкие, обычно занесенные колонизацией XIX века, были все же «пришлыми», то польские можно рассматривать как «коренные», поскольку украинские земли входили в разные — и весьма длительные — периоды своей истории в польское государство. Отсюда исторические особенности этой топонимики. Так, я насчитал 24 названия, связанные со словом войт: Войтов, Войтовка, Войтовцы и др. и шесть производных от слова солтыс: Солтысы, Солтыство и др. Кроме того, на карте были две Шляхты и четыре Ксендзовки, Панка и Панская, Жеребки Королевские, Жеребки Шляхетские и т.д. Все они сгинули.

Тюркские названия, тоже ведь коренные! Перед войной десять имен начинались на ак — «белый» (Акмангит и др.); были Юртук, Урзуф, Хаджи-Хурда; Черемурза; Кайраклия; Калга Саръяры, Аджиголь и другие — не осталось ничего.

Неугодными стали названия, напоминавшие о чуждых православному уху верованиях: Скопцы и хутор Молоканский, Баптисты и Масонов, Мечет и Мечеть. Или о ненавистной унии — Унев и Униев. Их не стало, как и всяких Карузо, Орианда, Ландскроне, Камбурлиевка, Гегелевка, и еще 19 населенных мест с чуждыми названиями.

По сравнению с весями, переименованных городов было немного, а в «чужеземном» аспекте вообще только два: Севлюш в Закарпатье, ныне Виноградов (калька с венгерского названия), и Каменка-Струмиловская в Львовской области, с 1944 г. Каменка-Бугская.

Теперь о судьбе еврейских имен. Хотя, возможно, с них надо было начинать: еврейские названия стали стирать с карты сразу после освобождения от нацистской оккупации (благо евреев не осталось физически). Как известно, в языке идиш много слов, совпадающих с немецкими. Например, в обоих языках *дорф* означает село, а *фельд* — поле. Понять, еврейскими были, скажем, Найдорф и Найфельд или же немецкими, можно только зная, когда и при каких обстоятельствах эти имена получены. Наибольший материал для определения именно бывших еврейских «дорфов», «фельдов» и других подобных названий на Украине мне дали исследования Якова Пасика.

В первой половине XIX века правительство России инициировало и поощряло колонизацию недавно присоединенных причерноморских земель, в том числе еврейскую. Всего с 1807 по1860 гг. в Новороссии — Херсонской и Екатеринославской губерниях — было создано 38 еврейских колоний. Но только четыре, из числа самых первых, получили названия на иврите: Сейдеменуха, Ефингар, Нагартав и Израилевка. С этой практикой власти быстро покончили.

Следующий этап создания еврейских земледельческий поселений в Южной Украине пришелся на советское время: в 1924–1938 гг. возникли более 120 таких поселков, и многие из них получили имена на идише: Ленин-, Войков-, Ратн-, Фрай- и другие *дорфы*; Блюмен-, Ройт, Фрунзен- и прочие *фельды*; Гроссер, Найвельт, Фрайланд и Фрайлебен, Эмес, Эрштмай, Шолом Алейхем... Тогда же Большую Сейдеминуху переименовали в Калининдорф, Малую — в Штерндорф. Новообразованный поселок Чемеринск получил имя Сталиндорф. Топонимы оказались недолговечными. Еще немецкие оккупанты, уничтожив не успевших уйти евреев, дали их поселениям свои названия: Калининдорфу — Большой Ингулец (Gross Ingulez), Сталиндорфу — Фризендорф (Friesendorf). Не исключено, что из-за имен советских вождей. К сожалению, у меня нет сведений о переименовании других поселков, но мыслимо ли, чтобы на территории Рейхскомиссариата Украина сохранялись, например, Юдендорф и Нитгедайгид?

Они не сохранились и на территории Украинской Советской Социлистической Республики: еврейский вопрос на карте Украины был окончательно решен после освобождения. Большую часть еврейских имен стерли (или, употребляя терминологию современных антисемитов, смыли) в 1944 году, остальные — в 1946-м. Переименовали и поселок Озетовку — чтоб не напоминала о ликвидированном перед войной Обществе по земельному устройству трудящихся евреев (ОЗЕТ). Остались — по недосмотру или другой неведомой причине — только названия села Малая Сейдеминуха (его вернули в 1944 г.) и станции Калининдорф Одесской железной дороги.

Вот так прошелся каток топонимических репрессий по земле Украины.

* * *

Нынешний Иванов — бывший Янов — гордится своими уроженцами. Среди них писатели Стефан Витвицкий, Олег Черногуз и Виталий Березинский, другие замечательные люди.

К их числу по праву должен быть причислен профессор Московского университета географ И. М. Маергойз.

Смена ведущих функций города и ее влияние на динамику городского расселения

П. М. Ильин

Д инамика расселения в СССР характеризуется постоянным ростом удельного веса больших городов (людностью более 100 тыс. жителей) в городском населении и населении страны в целом. Но развитие отдельных городов неравномерно — в разные периоды высокой динамичностью отличаются города с разными функциями. При этом среди множества функций, присущих городам, имеются ведущие, которые привлекают к городу другие функции, ведут их за собой и соответственно стимулируют развитие, рост городов, оказывая влияние на всю картину городского расселения. Смена ведущих функций связана с закономерностями развития всего общества.

Исследование динамики населения больших городов СССР по межпереписным периодам показало, что можно выделить два этапа развития сети больших городов: первый, на котором ведущей была промышленная функция, и второй (современный), на котором ведущая роль перешла к административной функции (имеется в виду функция столицы союзной и автономной республики, областного и краевого центра).

В качестве исходного был принят 1926 г. — прошедшая в декабре этого года первая Всесоюзная перепись населения зафиксировала людность городов к концу восстановительного периода. Начавшаяся индустриализация СССР сопровождалась громадным ростом городского населения. Число больших городов с 1926 по 1939 г. увеличилось с 31 до 84, причем 28 из них выросли в 3 и более раза. В том числе 5 возникли фактически на пустом месте (Новокузнецк, Караганда, Магнитогорск, Мурманск, Дзержинск) и 7 выросли в 5 и более раз (Прокопьевск — в 10 раз, Горловка, Кривой Рог, Кемерово, Запорожье, Жданов, Брянск.

Ни один из этих 12 городов не был в начале своего развития административным центром, да и среди остальных они немногочисленны. Индустриализация требовала в первую очередь развития угольно-металлургических баз, поэтому именно угольно-добывающие и металлургические города растут наиболее интенсивно — таких городов оказалось 16 из 28.

Административное деление СССР в этот период проходит две стадии. Сначала — укрупнение, когда во главе крупных краев и областей становятся города, которые в силу своего промышленного потенциала и экономико-географического положения были способны управлять обширными территориями; затем начинается разукрупнение, продолжавшееся и в первые послевоенные годы. Кроме того, возникает большое число центров национальных образований. Однако административный статус еще не играет, как правило, значительной роли как движущей силы развития городов (за исключением некоторых национальных центров). Более того, именно промышленное развитие приводит к тому, что многие из динамичных городов этого периода становятся областными центрами (Караганда, Донецк, Мурманск, Ворошиловград, Запорожье, Кемерово, Брянск и др.).

1959 г. можно условно принять за год перелома в механизмах, движущих развитием городов, — перелома, связанного с научно-технической революцией. Резко возрастает динамичность административных центров, а рост чисто промышленных, особенно угольных и металлургических городов замедляется; в ряде случаев он даже останавливается. Так, среди больших городов 1970 г., выросших по сравнению с 1959 г. незначительно — менее, чем на 20% (таких городов 18, не считая Москвы и Ленинграда.занимавших по абсолютному приросту населения первое и второе места среди всех городов страны), нет ни одного административного центра, а семь стотысячников 1959 г. (все — угледобывающие) сократили свое население.[1] Таких случаев раньше в мирное время не было. Причем 11 из этих 25 городов, население которых уменьшилось или выросло незначительно, были в период индустриализации и войны в числе наиболее динамичных.

Эти же тенденции сохраняются и в 70-е годы. Среди 17 больших городов, учтенных переписью 1979 г., чье население выросло по сравнению с 1970 г. менее чем на 10%,[2] числится всего лишь один областной центр (Караганда). Нет административных центров и среди 5 стотысячников, сокративших свое население; все

---

[1] *Итоги Всесоюзной переписи населения 1970 г.* т. 1, М., 1972.

[2] В связи с общим снижением прироста городского населения снижается и критерий отнесения городов к пунктам с «высокой» и «низкой» динамичностью.

они — чисто промышленные города. Самый крупный из «неадминистративных» городов — Кривой Рог — занимает по размеру населения 31-е место в списке городов страны.

Преимущественное развитие административных центров припало к резко выраженному моноцентризму в системах городского населения СССР: людность почти 2/3 «вторых» городов составляет менее 30% людности соответствующих административных центров.[3] По данным переписи 1979 г. остались только две области — Вологодская и Кемеровская, в которых население «вторых» городов (Череповца и Новокузнецка) превышает население областных центров.

Конечно, развиваются и порой весьма быстрыми темпами не только административные города. Более того, 6 самых динамичных больших городов, выросших в период 1970–79 гг. в 2 и более раза — неадминистративные. Это Набережные Челны, Тольятти, Нижнекамск и Старый Оскол — центры размещения крупнейших предприятий общесоюзного значения, Сургут и Нижневартовск — центры освоения новых районов на базе добывающей промышленности (в данном случае — нефтяной в Западной Сибири; развитие подобных центров может даже привести к их преобразованию в областные центры, как это произошло с Шевченко на Мангышлаке). Но уже среди 14 городов, выросших в полтора и более раза, мы находим 10 областных центров (в том числе упомянутый Шевченко) и 4 спутника городов-миллионеров.[4]

Неадминистративные города растут, если можно так сказать, «штучно», «выборочно», административные же — почти «поголовно». Если в 1959 г. 33 административных центра из 118 в РСФСР, на Украине, в Белоруссии и в Казахстане (или 28%) имели людность менее 100 тыс. жителей, то сейчас большими городами еще не стали только 6 из нынешних 121 административного центра этих республик (или всего 5%).

Несколько отвлекаясь в сторону, заметим, что, видимо, не для всякого времени в качестве «больших» следует рассматривать города людностью более 100 тыс. жителей. Если в понятие «большие города» вкладывать не только количественное, но и качественное содержание в зависимости от роли городов в территориальной организации жизни общества, от их места в иерархии городов, то для более ранних периодов правомерно принимать за

---

[3] См. В. В. Покшишевский. Проблема «второго» города. В кн. Проблемы урбанизации и расселения. М., 1976.

[4] Зеленоград и Одинцово (спутники Москвы), Колпино (спутник Ленинграда) и Сумгаит (спутник Баку).

таковые города с меньшей людностью, а для текущего это могут быть города от 200 тыс. жителей. В этом плане любопытны такие данные: из 34 городов, имевших в 1970 г. население 151–200 тыс. чел., 20 — административные центры, и все они к 1979 г. превысили 200 тыс.; из остальных 14 это удалось только восьми.

Можно привести и другие статистические данные, свидетельствующие о явной тенденции преимущественного роста административных центров в сети больших городов СССР за последнее двадцатилетие. Однако уже сказанного достаточно для демонстрации этого факта. Важнее попытаться ответить на вопрос — какие причины способствовали и способствуют тому, что административные функции стали ведущими, стимулирующими развитие других функций и привлечение населения?

Ответ на этот вопрос, по-видимому, лежит в двух плоскостях. С одной стороны — в общих закономерностях развития урбанизации, с другой — во внутренних свойствах самих городов. В период индустриализации урбанизация в значительной степени зависела от развития материального производства,[5] соответственно ведущей для развития сети больших городов была промышленная функция. В условиях НТР положение коренным образом меняется. Так, снижается роль ресурсных факторов в размещении народного хозяйства,[6] увеличивается значимость управления, информации, науки, культуры, социальной инфраструктуры и т.п. Соответственно требованиям и условиям научно-технической революции меняются критерии оценки территории как организациями, занимающимися планированием размещения народного хозяйства, так и населением.[7] Непосредственная роль материального производства в развитии урбанизации в условиях НТР снижается, что, в частности, проявляется в утрате промышленной функцией ведущей роли в развитии сети больших городов (для отдельных городов это ее значение, как показано выше, может и сохраниться).

Это — как бы внешняя по отношению к самим городам сторона. Внутренняя же заключается в том, что административные центры оказались наиболее подготовленными к современному

---

[5] См. А. С. Ахиезер, А. В. Кочетков. *Урбанизация и интенсификация производства в СССР.* В кн.: Проблемы современной урбанизации. М., 1972.

[6] См. А. А. Минц. *Прогнозная гипотеза развития народного хозяйства Европейской части СССР.* В кн. Ресурсы, среда, расселение. М., 1974, с. 30–33.

[7] См. А. С. Ахиезер, П. М. Ильин. *Задачи разработки социальных оценок территории в условиях научно-технической революции.* Известия АН СССР, сер. геогр., 1975, № 1.

перевороту в производственных силах, «который характеризуется интеллектуализацией труда и возрастанием масштабов и значимости духовного производства»,[8] к требованиям, выдвигаемым НТР к местам локализации многих важнейших сфер деятельности, включая размещение передовых отраслей промышленности.

Какие же внутренние свойства способствовали этому? Е. Е. Лейзерович называет среди преимуществ областных, краевых и республиканских (АССР) центров сосредоточение в них крупных учреждений культурно-бытового обслуживания; высших учебных и научных учреждений; общественных, государственных и хозяйственных учреждений.[9] Еще в большей мере этими преимуществами обладают столицы союзных республик. Первичным фактором здесь является последний — концентрация общественных, государственных и хозяйственных учреждений, вызываемая статусом этих городов. Административные центры представляют из себя комплексные многофункциональные города, в которых обеспечивается наибольшее разнообразие городской среды, важное для развития личности.[10]

В условиях НТР процесс урбанизации и интенсификации производства «приводит к существенным сдвигам, которые заключаются прежде всего в опережающем развитии центров производства, хранения, переработки, трансляции информации, в развитии центров управления... Чем выше темпы развития общества, тем выше роль центров управления и производства информации».[11] Такими центрами в СССР и являются административные центры.[12]

Следует ожидать, что ведущая роль административной функции для развития сети больших городов СССР на современном этапе урбанизации будет и дальше возрастать.

---

[8] А. С. Ахиезер. *Научно-техническая революция и некоторые социальные проблемы производства и управления*, М., 1974, с. 102.

[9] См. Е. Е. Лейзерович. *Особенности развития областных, краевых и республиканских (АССР) центров в СССР*. Вестник МГУ. География, 1971, № 2.

[10] См. О. Н. Яницкий, *Урбанизация и некоторые проблемы общественного развития*. В кн. Урбанизация и формирование систем расселения. М., 1978

[11] А. С. Ахиезер, А. В. Кочетков. Урбанизация и интенсификация производства в СССР. В кн. *Проблемы современной урбанизации*. М., 1972, с. 82.

[12] В других странах административная функция может и не играть столь существенной роли. О различиях в этом отношении между СССР и США см. В. М. Гохман, П. М. Ильин, Ю. Г. Липец. Значение фокусов роста в региональном развитии. *Известия АН СССР, серия геогр.*, 1979, № 6.

Значение фокусов роста в региональном развитии

В. М. Гохман, П. М. Ильин, Ю. Г. Липец

(Институт географии АН СССР, ЦЭМИ АН СССР)

В статье рассматриваются некоторые закономерности социально-экономических аспектов поляризованного развития территории и дается сжатый критический обзор ряда концепций поляризованного роста. На примере СССР и США показываются социально обусловленные различия значимости административного статуса городов в формировании фокусов роста.

Проблемы экономического роста и тесно связанные с ними более общие вопросы социально-экономического развития приобрели важное значение для всех стран. Поскольку в большинстве из них имеются территории с отчетливо выраженной пространственной дифференциацией природных и социально-экономических условий, территориальные аспекты развития приобретают не меньшее значение, чем общеэкономические и отраслевые. Особую роль они играют в крупнейших государствах мира, таких, как СССР, США, Индия, но этими аспектами нельзя пренебрегать в любой стране, независимо от ее размера.

Региональная сбалансированность, преодоление региональных диспропорций, подъем ранее отсталых и освоение новых районов — таков далеко не полный перечень территориальных проблем социально-экономического развития. В этой связи все большее значение приобретают поиски закономерности пространственного развития на основе анализа соответствующего опыта различных стран. Они приводят нас к пониманию механизмов отраслевой и территориальной концентрации производства и населения как неотъемлемого фактора индустриализации и урбанизации.

Механизм концентрации экономической активности наиболее ярко выступает не в континуальном, а в дискретном пространстве — в виде локализованных очагов и фокусов (полюсов, центров) роста. Важность пространственных аспектов концентрации и ее выражения в поляризованном, а не в равномерном развитии территории уже в XIX в. признавалась многими географами и экономистами (например, Тюненом, Колем, Лалланом и др.).

В СССР с первых лет существования Советского государства пространственные аспекты развития привлекали самое пристальное внимание научных и планово-административных кругов. Уже в первых работах по районированию СССР отмечалось, что «районирование не есть прием децентрализации, а, наоборот, один из важных методов концентрации сил, внимания, воли, руководства и организации в советском строительстве» (Районирование СССР, 1962, с. 11).

В плане ГОЭЛРО и первых пятилетних планах наряду со значением старых (опорных) центров и промышленных районов учитывалась роль новых центров и очагов роста, что нашло практическое воплощение в создании Урало-Кузнецкого комбината, целого ряда заводов-гигантов, в переходе к созданию территориально-производственных комплексов (ТПК). Эта хозяйственная практика позволила активному участнику плановых разработок Н. Н. Колосовскому уже в 40-х годах создать стройную теорию ТПК (Колосовский, 1947).

Экономическая практика в СССР убедительно показывала принципиальное значение *поляризованного экономического роста* и его важность для регулирования регионального развития с целью его оптимизации. Но для этого требовалось его теоретическое осмысливание.

КОНЦЕПЦИИ ПОЛЯРИЗОВАННОГО РОСТА

Широкое использование новых математических методов, линейной алгебры и программирования в сочетании с применением ЭВМ позволило по-новому сформулировать ряд важных положений теории пространственного и регионального развития. В СССР это нашло отражение главным образом в дальнейшем совершенствовании теории ТПК и ее приложения к практическим задачам хозяйственного строительства, особенно в районах нового освоения. В западной пространственной экономике стремление учесть возросшую роль пространственных и региональных аспектов развития, обострившиеся противоречия между отдельными районами в эпоху НТР и общего кризиса капитализма привели, в частности, к созданию теории полюсов роста, которая послужила ядром концентрации целого ряда методологических и методических подходов к проблемам пространственной экономики и экономической географии. Предложенная первоначально Ф. Перру (Perroux, 1950, 1955), взявшим в качестве исходной основы модели статического межотраслевого баланса, разработанные В. Леонтьевым и его учениками, теория полюсов роста формализовала мультипликационные эффекты, которые сопровождают рост производства в определенных отраслях. Принцип полного учета межотраслевых связей при расчетах коэффициентов полных затрат в леонтьевской модели позволил ввести теоретическое предположение, что рост определенных отраслей в данном центре (полюсе роста) может способствовать росту всей региональный экономики. В аспектах принятия решений теорию полюсов роста предлагалось использовать для выбора центров при планировании инвестиционной деятельности, особенно при распределении государственных и иных общественных фондов, предназначенных для подъема отсталых, слаборазвитых или депрессивных районов, т.е. для хотя бы частичного решения важных социальных задач, стоящих перед правительствами капиталистических стран. Выбор центров роста мог способствовать также косвенным экономическим мерам — налоговым и иным льготам для привлечения частного капитала.

В течение следующих десятилетий теория полюсов роста неоднократно обсуждалось в научной печати; уже накопилась целая библиотека статей и книг по ее критике, развитию, возможностям практического приложения. Наиболее серьезные критические замечания в ее адрес, на наш взгляд, связаны с тем, что сама методологическая основа теории — модель межотраслевого баланса — статична и мало пригодна для концепции, претендующей на объяснение экономической динамики (Lausen, 1969). Кроме того, нет и необходимых для анализа динамики данных о происхождении пропульсивных отраслей в первом из полюсов роста. Указывалось также, что трудно выразить количественно понятие доминации центра роста (Blaug, 1964) на недооценку роли диффузии нововведений и чаще всего на слабую связь с другими теориями в географии и пространственной экономике. Чтобы отразить систему взаимосвязей и исследований пространственного развития,

Д. Тодд предложил схему, в которой региональные проблемы и их исследования группировались по трем основным направлениям (Todd, 1973).

Первое из них было связано с *эмпирическими* региональными работами, типологией районов, использованием описательных моделей (типа коэффициентов локализации и метода «сдвиг и доля»), анализом региональной дифференциации (например, в понятиях теории центральных мест) и построением схем районирования (например, выделением поляризованных районов по Будвиллю; Boudeville, 1966).

Два других направления, выделяемых Тоддом, — *теоретического характера*. Одно из них чисто экономическое; оно связано с попытками использования моделей экономической динамики типа моделей сбалансированности роста Харрода–Домара и Хартмана–Шеклера или модели несбалансированного роста Хиршмана.

Концепция поляризации Перру была отнесена Тоддом к третьему направлению наряду с теориями экспортной базы, распространения нововведений, анализа производственного комплекса. Ближе всего этот круг идеи связан с экономическим районированием, теорией несбалансированного роста и анализом размещения и комплексирования производства.

На наш взгляд, общая теория поляризованного развития, хотя она несовершенна и отчасти противоречива, в принципе может служить важным методологическим инструментом при прогнозировании и планировании регионального развития. Однако во избежание разочарования в не практической приложимости (см., например, Darkoh, 1977) следует придать этой теории более широкий историко-географический и пространственно-экономический аспект. При этом её следует связать с углублением моделей межотраслевого баланса и территориально производственного комплекса (ТПК).

Для детализации и количественной оценки пропульсивных отраслей и мультипликативных эффектов необходимо разделение отраслей по масштабам их пространственного воздействия по крайней мере на четыре основные группы — локальные, региональные, национальные, международные (Tinbergen, 1963). Дальнейшая детализация должна вестись в рамках системы модели ТПК, где учитываются взаимосвязанные эффекты развития отраслей на всю территорию (Моделирование..., 1976). Подобные системы моделей были первоначально разработаны для социалистической экономики с учетом вероятного дефицита рабочей силы, но уже созданы их модификации и для специфических условий развивающихся стран, учитывающие наличие избыточных рабочих рук и необходимость согласованного развития крупного и мелкого производства (Кузьмин, Липец, 1974). В рамках подобных моделей роль отдельных полюсов роста и их систем можно проследить более обоснованно, особенно в районах нового освоения.

Однако подобное развитие теории поляризованного роста, заметно усиливая ее операциональность и экономическую обоснованность, не избавляет ее (как, впрочем, и многие другие современные экономические теории) от существенного методологического недостатка. Полюса роста рассматриваются в них только в рамках производственно-экономических категорий; при этом недостаточно учитывается их социальная сущность и обусловленность; не анализируются общие тенденции развития системы центров и факторы, определившие рост этих центров в прошлом (а это необходимо ввиду «ультра-стабильности» городских систем; см., например, Steiss, 1975).

В традиционной терминологии теория полюсов роста — важная сфера приложения историко-географического анализа, без которого, по нашему мнению, она (и прежде всего ее практическое применение) будет базироваться на весьма непрочном фундаменте.

Наш сжатый анализ исходит из необходимости дифференцированного функционально-генетического подхода к поведению полюсов роста в общей системе городских центров. Мы не согласны с теми критиками, которые вместе с недостатками и ограничениями, присущими работам Ф. Перру и его последователей, начисто отвергают и сам факт существования закономерности поляризованного развития, проявляющихся по-разному в социалистических, развитых капиталистических и развивающихся странах. Изучение исторических закономерностей поляризованного развития, как нам представляется, необходимо и для общего экономического и социального прогнозирования, и для более рационального размещения производительных сил, и для прогноза систем расселения.

Поляризация роста (развития) — это отражение двуединого характера процессов общественного развития. «Развитие ведущих центров и периферии — не два взаимодействующих процесса, а две стороны одного процесса. Ведущие центры нуждаются в развитии периферии, точно также, как периферия нуждается в развитии ведущих центров... Следует, однако иметь ввиду, что эти стороны развития общества далеко не равноправны, не симметричны. Определяющим является развитие ведущих центров, их организующая, направляющая роль, так как именно там находятся точки роста» (Ахиезер, 1974, с. 178–179). Из этого следует объективная неизбежность поляризации в ходе развития и возникновения полюсов роста, в том числе географических.

РОЛЬ АДМИНИСТРАТИВНОГО СТАТУСА КАК ФАКТОРА ПОЛЯРИЗОВАННОГО РОСТА В СССР

При всеобщности поляризации весьма интересно проследить относительность факторов, способствующих превращению данного центра в фокус развития. Структура подобных факторов обычно отражается в генетических классификациях городских центров. В данной работе за основу взята исходная типология, в который выделены административные, транспортно-распределительные, горнодобывающие, промышленные центры и малые центры с выгодным транспортно-географическим положением (потенциальные фокусы роста, особенно во вновь осваиваемых или бурно развивающихся районах).

Изучение динамики фокусов роста должно основываться на количественных показателях. Наиболее простой и доступный из них — изменение численности населения народов или (или агломераций), которые фактически и выступают в качестве центров роста.

Сочетая функциональную типологию и количественный анализ людности всех центров в системе городов, мы можем подойти к изучению динамики фокусов роста в ретроспективе. При этом мы берём за основу относительный рост людности, который при всей показательности абсолютного прироста лучше отражает тенденции развития.

В связи с тем, что «вес» одного процента роста зависит от масштаба рассматриваемой величины, следует ввести нижний предел людности учитываемых фокусов роста. Во многих работах в качестве такого предела берется людность 20 тыс. человек (или близкая к ней); однако для макросистемы в целом мы сошли более верным рубеж 100 тыс. жителей (отметим, что для более ранних стадий развития нами был принят более низкий предел).

При анализе того, каким городам присуща повышенная вероятность превращения в фокусы развития и, в частности для каких из них характерны наиболее высокие темпы роста населения и расширения зон влияния, важное значение имеет учет их **административно-политического статуса**. Изучение этого вопроса показывает, что роль административных центров так фокусов роста очень сильно зависит от степени сосредоточения в руках государственного аппарата не только политико-административных, но и хозяйственно-управленческих функций, т.е. от того, в какой мере государство влияет на экономическую жизнь страны.

Проследим на примерах СССР и США, насколько велики различия в роли административных центров как фокусов роста и как они проявляются в темпах роста городов с различным административным статусом и выполняемыми функциями в разных странах, проанализировав эти различия как во временном, так и в территориальном разрезе.

В разные периоды развития в качестве фокусов роста в СССР выдвигались города разных типов, поэтому важна периодизация рассматриваемого явления. Наиболее удобно использовать для этой цели данные переписи населения, группируя межпереписные периоды по исторически значимым эпохам. Но в России дело осложняется тем, что между первыми переписями — 1897 и 1926 гг. — произошли первая мировая и гражданская войны. Поэтому за начальный рассматриваемый период мы принимаем время между переписью 1897 г. и первый мировой войной.

Этот период может рассматриваться как период ускоренного развития капитализма в России. Нами рассмотрены города, имевшие к началу войны не менее 50 тыс. жителей. Промышленное развитие страны опиралось на уже сложившиеся к тому времени крупные города. Однако капитализм нуждался и в новых центрах, что было особенно важно ввиду обширности слабо освоенных пространств России. И в десятке самых динамичных городов оказались восемь городов Сибири и Дальнего Востока, то есть города, которые можно отнести к двум типам центров роста: «транспортно-распределительным» и «потенциальным, с выгодным транспортно-географическим положением». Несомненно, на их развитие повлияло проведение Транссибирской магистрали, резко облегчавшие их экономические связи с Европейской Россией.

К центрам этой группы примыкает и Новороссийск — порт на Черном море с его выгодным транспортно-географическим положением.

Все эти города выросли в три и более раза. Такой же рост наблюдается и в Иванове, выросшем в центре старого района распределения кустарных промыслов и мануфактур; столь бурное развитие этого центра в старопромышленном районе объясняется тем, что ведущее производство обосновалось там на старой технологии (текстильная промышленность). В традиционных районах древесноугольной металлургии такой центр вырасти не мог, так как прогрессивная для этого времени металлургия уже основывалась на коксе. В то же время 3 центра роста в Южном угольно-металлургическом районе выросли в два и более раза.

В целом в это время административный статус не играл значительной роли (за исключением центров густонаселенных окраинных регионов — Закавказья и Средней Азии). В Европейской России весьма динамичными были центры, находившиеся в благоприятных транспортно-географических условиях независимо от их статуса.

Великая Октябрьская социалистическая революция привела к смене социально-экономического строя, к коренной перестройки всей системы народного хозяйства. После восстановления разрушенного в период первой мировой и гражданской войны народного хозяйства начинается эпоха индустриализации, сопровождающаяся громадным ростом городского населения. Сильно растут города — старые промышленные центры; в то же время возникает большое число новых центров роста. Так, 28 городов из числа стотысячников 1939 г. выросли по сравнению с 1926 г. в три и более раза, из них 5 возникли практически на «пустом месте» и еще семь выросли в пять и более раз. Среди этих 12 городов не было ни одного административного центра, да и среди остальных они немногочисленны. Индустриализация требовала в первую очередь развития угольно-металлургических баз, поэтому именно угледобывающее и металлургические города растут наиболее интенсивно: таких городов оказалось 16 из 28. Соответственно большинство из наиболее динамичных центров роста концентрировалось в трех районах; Юг (10 городов), Урал (5 городов), Кузбасс (4 города с Новосибирском).

Административное деление СССР в этот период проходит две стадии. Сначала — укрупнение, когда во главе крупных краев и областей становится города, которые в силу своего промышленного потенциала и экономико-географического положения были способны управлять обширными территориями; затем начинается разукрупнение, продолжавшееся и в военные, и в первые послевоенные годы. Кроме того, возникает большое число центров национальных образований. Однако административный статус, хотя роль его как движущей силы развития градов и возрастает, еще не играет, как правило, значительной роли (за исключением некоторых национальных центров). Более того, именно промышленное развитие привело к тому, что многие из динамичных фокусов роста этого периода стали областными центрами.

Великая Отечественная война 1941–1945 гг. привела к замедлению развития районов на западе и к еще более сильному росту городов в восточных районах, чему способствовало эвакуация промышленности из районов, подвергавшихся вражескому нашествию. О динамики городов в военные и первые послевоенные годы можно судить по материалам переписи 1959 г.: среди 25 наиболее динамичных стотысячников 1939–1959 гг. нет ни одного, временно находившегося на оккупированной территории, а 15 расположены на Урале и в Сибири.

1959 год можно условно принять за год перелома в механизмах, движущих центры роста, — перелома, связанного с *научно-технической революцией*. Резко снижается роль чисто промышленных, особенно угольных и металлургических городов, и возрастает значение административного статуса. Так, среди стотысячников 1970 гг., выросших менее чем на 20% (таких городов 18), нет ни одного областного центра; а 7 стотысячников 1959 г. (все угледобывающие) даже сократили свое население. Причем 11 из этих 25 городов, сокративших или не значительно увеличивших свое население, были в период индустриализации и войны в числе наиболее динамичных.

Эти же тенденции сохраняются и в семидесятые годы. Среди 17 больших городов, учтенных переписью 1979 г., чье население выросло по сравнению с 1970 г. менее чем на 10%, числится всего лишь один областной центр (Караганда). Нет и административных центров среди 5 стотысячников, сокративших свое население; все они чисто промышленные города. Самый крупный из «неадминистративных» городов — Кривой Рог занимает по размеру населения 31-е место в списке городов страны.

В современный период наибольший рост населения имеют, как правило, города следующих типов: административные центры (столицы союзных и автономных республик, центры краев и областей); вновь создаваемые на основе выполнения больших государственных программ центры передовых отраслей промышленности (Тольятти, Набережные Челны, Волгодонск и др.); города при крупнейших гидроэлектростанциях, где наличие дешевой энергии и мощных строительных баз способствует развитию крупной промышленности; города — плацдармы освоения новых районов. Развитие этих последних может привести к преобразованию их в областные центры (как это произошло с Шевченко). Но *неадминистративные города* растут, если можно так сказать, «штучно», «выборочно», *административные* же — почти «поголовно». Если в 1959 г. 33 административных центра из 118 в РСФСР, на Украине, в Белоруссии и в Казахстане (или 28%) имели людность менее 100 тыс. жителей, то к 1979 г. большими городами еще не стали только 6 из нынешнего 121 административного центра этих республик (или всего 5%).

Преимущественное развитие административных центров привело к резко выраженному моноцентризму в системах городского расселения СССР: людность почти ⅔ «вторых» городов составляет менее 30% людности соответствующих административных центров (Покшишевский, 1976). Только в двух областях — Вологодской и Кемеровской — население «вторых» городов (Череповца и Новокузнецка) превышает население областных центров.

Какие же факторы способствовали тому, что административные центры стали столь привлекательными для развития самых разных сфер деятельности, в том числе производственной? Е. Е. Лайзерович (1971) называет в качестве преимуществ областных, краевых и республиканских (АССР) центров сосредоточение в них крупных учреждений культурно-бытового обслуживания, высших учебных и научных учреждений, общественных, государственных и хозяйственных учреждений. Первичным фактором, определяющим остальные, здесь является, по нашему мнению, последний — концентрация общественных, государственных и хозяйственных учреждений.

Можно считать, что любое центральное место представляет из себя потенциальный центр роста. Однако для его реального превращения в центр роста нужны соответствующие условия. В условиях НТР, когда ослабляется влияние ресурсного фактора на размещение промышленности (Приваловская, 1974) и увеличивается значимость управления, информации, науки, образования, социальной инфраструктуры и т.п. практически все административные центры в СССР становятся фокусами роста. Именно в них обеспечивается наибольшее разнообразие городской среды, важное для развития личности (Яницкий, 1978), от уровня которого зависит прогресс всех видов деятельности, в том числе и производственной. Территориальном плане наблюдаемые процесс ведет к совершенствованию сети больших Городов СССР.

МАЛАЯ РОЛЬ АДМИНИСТРАТИВНОГО СТАТУСА В США

Иную картину мы наблюдаем США. Прежде всего отметим, что в число 25 крупнейших городских агломерации страны, помимо ее столицы Вашингтон, входят лишь 3 административных центра штатов (из 50) — Бостон, Атланта и Денвер, причем последние 2 находится в самом конце списка. Уже одно это показывает, что *административный статус не играет сейчас существенной роли как фактор роста американских городов и мало способствует их роли как фокусов развития*. О том же говорит и то обстоятельство, что лишь в 13 штатах столица является самым большим городом и ведущим экономическим центром. При этом в большинстве случаев это можно объяснить выгодным экономико-географическим положением города, независимо от его политико-административных функций.

Рассмотрим теперь данные о наиболее быстро развивающихся городах США в различные периоды с 1900 по 1970 г. Эти периоды выбраны с таким расчётом, чтобы их рубежами служили годы переписей и в тоже время чтобы они примерно соответствовали периодам, рассматриваемым для СССР.

За период 1900–1930 гг. из 25 городов США, население которых показало наибольший рост — увеличилось в три и более раза, лишь 2 были административными центрами штатов; в число наиболее быстро растущих городов не входила тогда и столица страны Вашингтон. Анализ ведущих функций этих фокусов роста показал, что для 10 из них это была горнодобывающая промышленность вместе с переработкой ее продукции, главным образом нефти; в 9 случаях — выгодное приморское положение и важные портовые функций; в 7 — развитие пропульсивных для того времени отраслей обрабатывающей промышленности (в первую очередь автомобильной и связанной с ней).

В 1930–1940 гг., которые были ознаменованы сильнейшим в истории капитализма экономическим кризисом и резким усилением государственного вмешательства в экономическую жизнь («Новый курс» президента Ф. Рузвельта), в число 25 агломераций, росших быстрее других, вошли Вашингтон и 5 административных центров штатов (все на юге и западе). Промышленные центры из этого списка исчезли, резко сократились число и темпы роста горнодобывающих центров.

В 1940–1960 гг., когда темпы экономического развития и роста населения США несколько повысились в результате военного «бума» и послевоенной разрухи в других воевавших странах, среди 25 наиболее быстрорастущих агломераций было 6 административных центров штатов, причем лишь два из них (Феникс и Сакраменто) входили и в предыдущий список. По меньшей мере в 3 из этих центров быстрый рост, как показал проведенный нами анализ не имел главной причиной административные функции города.

Наконец, в 1960–1970 гг. в число 25 наиболее активных фокусов роста вошли Вашингтон и еще 4 административных центра штатов, в том числе один (Финикс) третий раз подряд. В этом списке резко преобладают комплексные экономические центры различного ранга и крупные «пригородные» и курортные агломерации. Роль административного фактора по-прежнему невелика.

Таким образом, в течение по меньшей мере 20-го века роль «столичного» фактора в США становится заметной лишь на общенациональном уровне (Вашингтон) тогда, когда даже в наиболее крупных и экономических мощных штатах она практически не ощущается.

Наиболее активные фокусы роста во все рассматриваемые периоды были расположены в более молодых и энергично осваивавшихся районах запада и юго-запада, а в последние периоды все больше из них на до недавнего времени экономически социально резко отставшим Юго-востоке. В 1900–1930 гг., из 25 таких фокусов на севере находилось 5, на юго-востоке — 6, на юго-западе — 8 и на западе — 6. В 1930–1940 гг. их было соответственно: на юго-востоке — 9, на юго-западе 7 и на западе — 8 (остается Вашингтон, которые мы не включаем ни в состав севера, ни юго-востока). Мало отличается от указанных и картина 1940–1960 гг.: 1 — на севере, 6 — на юго-востоке, 11 — на юго-западе и 7 — на западе.

Наконец, в 1960–1970 гг. таких центров было: на севере — 2, юго-востоке — 9, на юго-западе — 3 и на западе — 10.

Необходимо отметить, что неполные данные, имеющиеся за последние годы (после 1970 г.), свидетельствуют о резком усилении появившейся несколько ранее *тенденции к частичному «размазыванию»* роста, замедлению развития большинства более крупных центров и ускорению развития ряда территорий, лежащих вне городских агломераций. При этом развивается рассредоточенное расселение без формирования крупных «точечных» ядер. Примером его могут служить некоторые агломерации Калифорнии (особенно Анахайм–Санта-Ана–Гарден Гров) и Флориды.

Сопоставление динамики фокусов роста и смены ее факторов в России — СССР и США показывает определенные различия, обусловленные прежде всего сменой социально-политического строя в СССР после Октябрьской революции, все большим значением централизованного планирования и возрастанием роли административных функций. Последний фактор типичен не только для СССР, но и для других европейских социалистических стран, например Польши. Наряду с этим обширные территории СССР и США, пространственно-временная дифференциация в освоении территории позволяют выделить и некоторое сходство в факторах роста центров, прежде всего обладающих выгодами транспортно-географического положения, и горнодобывающих центров. Но это сходство имеет ограниченный характер: так, новые центры Сибири растут не на освоенной ранее территории, а центра юго-востока США — на «старом рабовладельческом Юге».

ФАКТОРЫ ДИНАМИКИ ЦЕНТРОВ РОСТА В РАЗВИВАЮЩЕЙСЯ СТРАНЕ (ПРИМЕР ИНДИИ)

При использовании функционально-генетического подхода к анализу динамики центров роста в развивающихся странах следует уже на предварительной стадии учитывать время зарождения и историю развития городских поселений, традиции городской жизни, размеры и природно-экономическую дифференциацию страны. Очевидно, что факторы динамики будут различны для государств, где города сформировались лишь в XVIII–XIX, а то и в начале XX в., и для такой страны, как Индия.

В ряде работ уже было показано, что центры с преимущественным развитием функций обслуживания составляют самую многочисленную группу городов Индии (Сдасюк, 1975), но ¾ из них — небольшие, медленнорастущее города. Наряду с этим все столицы штатов, сконцентрировавшие административные функции, отличаются заметно повышенными темпами роста. Однако наиболее высокие темпы были типичны для индустриальных центров с преобладанием обрабатывающей промышленности (подробнее см. Mitra, 1967).

Наметившаяся с начала XX в. в Индии тенденция опережающего роста крупных городов привела к тому, что там сложилась система таких городов (Sdasyuk, 1971). Для ее изучения информация о городах была обработана методом компонентного анализа. По данным переписи 1961 г., для 103 городов и городских агломераций был отобран 41 показатель, который отразил 9 основных групп: численность и темпы общего прироста населения (3), миграции (3), естественный прирост (4), отраслевую структуру занятости (10), плотность (3), степень скученности и обеспеченности жильем (6), благоустроенность арены жизни (6), уровень модернизации промышленности (2), доступность города или относительное положение (4).

В результате расчетов было получено 13 факторов-компонент, объяснивших 80% общей дисперсии показателей. Степень отражения каждой из 41 переменной высока: она колеблется в пределах от 64 (показатель прироста городского населения с 1905 по 1961 г.) до 93% (6 показателей отражены более чем на 90%).

Сопоставление с аналогичными по методике исследованиями стран Европы (Медведкова, 1976) показало большую многоаспектность динамики индийских городов. Число независимых факторов, отражающих предпосылки роста в Индии, оказалось значительно выше (13 против 3–4 для Польши и ГДР), что явилось следствием тысячелетней истории страны, давних традиций городской жизни, высокой плотности заселения в основных очагах расселения.

Полученные обобщенные факторы можно интерпретировать как инерционность процессов роста в старых промышленных центрах, рост новых центров, модернизацию производства, заполнения пустых мест в сети городов, рост непроизводственной сферы и усиление миграционных потоков из перенаселенной сельской местности (при разной привлекательности городов для переселенцев из сел и других городов), благоустройство и жилищное строительство и др. Факторный анализ выявил относительно малую роль чисто транспортной специализации и сочетание высокой степени занятости в сельском хозяйстве с горнорудной специализацией.

Историко-географический анализ позволяет выявить изменение форм поляризации экономико-географического пространства. Точечные фокусы роста — отдельные города сменяются (особенно быстро в крупных горнопромышленных бассейнах и хинтерландах городов-миллионеров) *агломерированными формами*, при которых группы смежных городов тесно связаны ежедневными трудовыми, технологическими и информационными потоками. В свою очередь наиболее бурно растущие агломерации образуют «ленточные формы» в виде мегалополисов, коридоров, поясов. При этом не всегда просто в рамках подобных объединений выделить конкретный фокус роста ввиду неравномерности развития, присущей отдельным частям этих образований, а также сложной функциональной взаимозависимости внутри их.

Характерным примером «ареалов роста» в СССР служат ТПК Западной и Восточной Сибири, где пропульсивные отрасли размещаются в плановом порядке по многим центрам разных рангов, в том числе во вновь создаваемых поселениях, выгодно расположенных по отношению к используемым ресурсам, источникам гидроэнергии и транспортным путям. В этих случаях очевиден прямой *переход проблемы фокусов роста в более общую проблему регионального развития*, которая и должна стать методологической основой при переходе от общенациональных планов к их территориальным аспектам вплоть до уровня отдельных городов.

В процессе планирования на достаточно продолжительный период времени следует использовать стратегию *смены приоритетов при выборе и использовании фокусов роста*. Новые и новейшее производства, в принципе обладающие пропульсивными свойствами, желательно размещать в новых фокусах роста, чтобы предотвратить возможные отрицательные последствия поляризованного роста.

Такими последствиями могут быть: 1) инерция роста ранее возникших центров; 2) усиление диспропорций в экономическом региональном развитии; 3) возникновение социальных проблем, особенно в национальных и окраинных районах. При этом надо детерминированность населения будет все больше сменяться социальной» (стр. 83).

Именно смена приоритетов и продуманное направление инвестиций на различных этапах развития фокусов роста и региональных систем расселения может служить наиболее эффективный политикой, направленной на ограничение роста сверхкрупных урбанизированных ареалов. Смена пространственных акцентов поляризованного роста необходима для сохранения равновесия в эколого-экономических системах, нарушение которого трудно избежать при неизменном росте одних и тех же центров.

Подобная смена обусловлена целым рядом объективных факторов, таких, как научно-технический прогресс, проявлениями которого является возникновение новых отраслей и сокращение издержек на транспорт, различия в инерционности отраслевых и территориальных структур, изменения в структуре и объемах потребления.

В территориальном аспекте это находит отражение в изменение такой интегральной характеристики, как *экономико-географическое положение фокусов роста различных масштабов*. Экономико-географическое положение и его динамиком во многом определяют формы развития фокусов роста на различных исторических этапах социально-экономического развития.

ЛИТЕРАТУРА:

Ахиезер А. С. *Научно-техническая революция и некоторые социальные проблемы производства и управления*. М., «Наука», 1974.

Ахиезер А. С., Кочетков А. В. *Организация интенсификации производства СССР.* —

Горячева А. М. Анализ факторов роста крупнейших городов Индии и дифференциации их хозяйственных функций. *Изв. АН СССР. Сер. географ.* 1976, #3.

Ильин П. М. О значимости административных функций для роста городов СССР.—*В кн.: Урбанизация и формирование систем расселения*. М., МФГО 1978.

Колосовский Н. Н. Производственно-территориальные сочетания (комплекс) в советской экономической географии. *Вопросы географии, сб. 6.* М., Географгиз, 1947.

Кузьмин С. А., Липец Ю. Г. Использование моделей ТПК в выборе оптимального варианта кооперации крупный и мелкой промышленности в развивающихся странах. — В сб.: *Экономико-географические проблемы ТПК Сибири, вып. 6.* Новосибирск, 1974.

Лайзерович Е. Е. Особенности развития областных, краевых и республиканских (АССР) центров в СССР. *Вестн. МГУ. География*, 1971, #2.

Медведкова О. Л. Параметризация макросистем городов на основе процедур геоинформационной системы. *Международная география, 76.* XXIII Междунар. геогр. конгр., т. 7. М., 1976.

Моделирование формирования территориально-производственных комплексов. Новосибирск, 1976.

Покшишевский В. В. Проблема второго города. В сб.: *Проблемы организации и расселения*. М., «Мысль», 1976.

Покшишевский В. В. *Население и география. Теоретически очерки*. М., «Мысль», 1978.

Приваловская Г. А. Природный фактор в системе условий размещения промышленного производства в СССР. *Вопросы географии, сб. 95.* М., «Мысль», 1974.

Районирование СССР. Сб. материалов по районированию с 1917 по 1925 г. Под ред. К. Д. Егорова. М.—Л., «Плановое хозяйство», 1926.

Сдасюк Г. В. *Индия. География хозяйства*. М., «Мысль» 1975.

Яницкий О. Н. Урбанизация и некоторые проблемы общественного развития. — В кн. *Урбанизация и формирование систем расселения.* М., МФГО, 1978.

Blaug, M. *A case of the emperor's clothes: Perroux's theories of economic domination.* «Kyklos», 1964.

Boudeville J. P. *Problems of regional economic planning.* Edinborough, 1966.

Darkoh M. Growth Poles and growth centers with special reference to developing countries. A critique. *The Journal of Tropical Geography* (Malaysia), v. 44, 1977.

Goryacheva A. M., Lipets Yu. G. Interrelation of factors of growth in the system of Indian cities. In: *Urbanization in Developing Countries.* Eds S. Manzoor Alam, V. V. Pokshishevsky. Hyderabad, 1976.

Lausen J. R. On growth poles. *Urban studies, v. 4.* 1969.

Mitra A. *Internal Migration and Urbanization. Office of Registrar General.* India, Delhi, 1967.

Perroux F. Economic space, theory and application. *Quarterly J. of Economics, v. 64,* 1950.

Perroux F. Note sur la notion des poles de croissance *Economie Appliquée, 1955,* 1 et 2 (Paris).

Sdasyuk G. Urbanization and Spatial Structure of Indian Economy. In: *Economic and Socio-Cultural Dimensions of Regionalization. Census Cent.* Monograph, #7, 1971.

Steiss P. Models for the analysis and planning of urban systems. *Lexington Books.* Lex. 1975.

Tinbergen J. The spatial dispersion of production: a hypothesis. *Schweiz. Zeit. fur Volkswirt. And Statistik.,* v. 97, 1963, #4.

Todd D. The Development Pole Concept and its Application to Regional Analysis. An Appraisal of the State of Art. *London Sch. of Econ. and Polit. Science. Discuss. Paper,* 1973, #47.

О значимости административных функций для роста городов СССР

П. М. Ильин

Сеть больших городов и городских агломераций может быть принята, в первом приближении, в качестве опорного каркаса территориальной структуры народного хозяйства страны (Лаппо, 1978). Ее формирование и развитие неравномерны как по территории, так и во времени: каждая историческая эпоха выдвигает свои центры роста. Эта неравномерность связана, в частности, с тем, что для каждого периода характерны свои ведущие функции города; они «ведут за собой» другие функции, стимулируют их развитие.

Одной из функций города, которые при определенных условиях выступают как ведущие, является административная функция. Она была присуща городам всегда — начиная с самого возникновения городов. Но ее значимость для развития городов менялась. Не останавливаясь на более ранних этапах, попытаемся проследить влияние административного статуса[1] на динамику людности больших городов — центров роста в сравнении с другими факторами по межпереписным периодам за последние 80 лет.[2]

В связи с тем, что между первыми переписями населения 1897 и 1926 гг. произошли первая мировая и гражданская войны, за начальный период примем время между переписью 1897 г. и первой мировой войной. Этот период может рассматриваться как период ускоренного развития капитализма в России. Промышленное развитие опиралось на уже сложившиеся к тому времени центры.

---

[1] Имеется в виду статус губернского и областного города до революции и статус столицы союзной и автономной республики и областного и краевого центра после 1926 г.

[2] Под большими городами понимаются для дореволюционного периода города с населением более 50 тыс. жителей, для последующего, как это общепринято, более 100 тыс. жит. Рассматривается относительный прирост населения как лучше отражающий тенденции развития (сравнительно с абсолютным). Возможны и другие пути, например, сравнение географии крупнейших городов на разные годы (Harris, 1970)

Однако капитализм нуждался в новых центрах, что было особенно важно ввиду обширности слабо освоенных пространств России. И в десятке самых динамичных городов, достигших к началу войны 50 тыс. жителей, оказались 8 городов Сибири и Дальнего Востока (Челябинск, Омск, Новониколаевск, Барнаул, Красноярск, Чита, Хабаровск, Владивосток). В их развитии несомненна роль Транссибирской железнодорожной магистрали.

Все эти города выросли в 3 раза и более. Такой же рост наблюдался в Новороссийске, обладавшем выгодным транспортно-географическим положением, и в Иванове, выросшем в центре старого района распространения кустарных промыслов и мануфактур; столь бурное развитие этого центра в старопромышленном районе объясняется тем, что ведущее производство основывалось на старой технологии (текстильная промышленность). В традиционных районах древесноугольной металлургии такой город вырасти не мог, так как прогрессивная для того времени технология основывалась на коксовой металлургии; в то же время три центра роста в Южном угольно-металлургическом районе выросли в два и более раза (Екатеринослав, Луганск, Александровск). Хотя многие из названных (и следующие вслед за ними в списке самых динамичных центров) городов предреволюционного периода — центры губерний или областей, можно утверждать, что административный статус в то время, как правило, не играл ведущей роли в развитии городов. Среди исключений — центры густонаселенных окраинных регионов, такие как Тифлис и Ташкент.

После восстановления разрушенного в годы первой мировой и гражданской войн народного хозяйства начинается индустриализация СССР, сопровождающаяся громадным ростом городского населения. Сильно растут города — старые промышленные центры; возникает большое число новых центров роста, несравнимое с дореволюционным временем ни по количеству, ни по темпам роста. Так, 28 городов из числа «стотысячников» в 1939 г. выросли по сравнению с 1926 г. в 3 и более раза, из них 5 возникли фактически на пустом месте (Новокузнецк, Караганда, Магнитогорск, Мурманск, Дзержинск) и еще 7 выросли в 5 и более раз (Прокопьевск — в 10 раз, Горловка, Кривой Рог, Кемерово, Запорожье, Жданов, Брянск).

Ни один из этих 12 городов не был в начале своего развития административным центром, да и среди остальных они немногочисленны. Индустриализация требовала в первую очередь развития угольно-металлургических баз, поэтому именно угольно-добывающие и металлургические города растут наиболее интенсивно —

таких городов оказалось 16 из 28. Соответствено большинство из наиболее динамичных центров роста концентрировались в трех районах: Юг (10 городов), Урал (5 городов), Кузбасс (4 города — с Новосибирском).

Административное деление СССР в этот период проходит две стадии. Сначала — укрупнение, когда во главе крупных краев и областей становятся города, которые в силу своего промышленного потенциала и экономико-географического положения были способны управлять обширными территориями; затем начинается разукрупнение, продолжавшееся в военные и первые послевоенные годы. Однако административный статус еще не играет, как правило, значительной роли как движущей силы развития городов (за исключением некоторых национальных центров).

Более того, именно промышленное развитие приводит к тому, что многие из динамичных центров роста этого периода становятся областными центрами (например, Караганда, Донецк — в 1932 г., Мурманск, Ворошиловоград, Запорожье — в 1938–39 гг., Кемерово, Брянск — в 1943–44 гг.). Таким образом, ведущими функциями города в это время являются промышленные.

Великая Отечественная война 1941–1945 гг. привела к замедлению развития городов на западе и еще более сильному росту городов в восточных районах, чему способствовала эвакуация промышленности из районов, подвергнувшихся вражескому нашествию. Среди 25 наиболее динамичных больших городов 1939–1959 гг. нет ни одного, находившегося на оккупированной территории, а 15 расположены на Урале и в Сибири.[3] 1959 г. можно условно принять за переломный в механизмах, движущих развитием центров роста. Резко снижается роль чисто промышленных, особенно угольных и металлургических городов и возрастает значение административных центров. Так, среди больших городов 1970 г., выросших незначительно, менее, чем на 20% (таких городов 18[4]) нет ни одного административного центра; а семь «стотысячников» 1959 г. (все — угледобывающие) даже сократили свое население. Таких случаев раньше в мирное время не было. Причем 11 из этих 25 городов, население которых уменьшилось или выросло незначительно,

---

[3] 7 городов в западных районах, чье население накануне войны превышало 100 тыс. жит. или было близко к этой цифре, даже не успели к 1959 г. восстановить свое население (Ленинград, Витебск, Смоленск, Керчь, Новороссийск, Константиновка, Кременчуг).

[4] Не считая Москвы и Ленинграда, занимавших по абсолютному приросту населения первое и второе места среди всех городов страны.

были в период индустриализации и войны среди «лидеров» (в том числе среди уменьшивших население — Прокопьевск, Киселевск, Копейск, Черемхово). В то же время только 5 административных центров с населением менее 800 тыс. жит. выросли меньше чем на 30%. Эта же тенденция преимущественного роста административных центров сохраняется и в 70-е годы (СССР. Административно-территориальное деление... 1977).

Какие же факторы способствуют тому, что административные функции становятся столь важными, стимулируя развитие других, в том числе и промышленных функций? Е. Е. Лейзерович (1971) выделяет следующие преимущества областных, краевых и республиканских (АССР) центров: сосредоточение крупных учреждений культурно-бытового обслуживания; концентрацию высших учебных, а также научных учреждений; концентрацию общественных, государственных, хозяйственных учреждений.[5]

Оставляя в стороне вопрос о порядке значимости этих факторов, отметим, что с развитием НТР их роль в формировании опорного каркаса территориальной структуры народного хозяйства будет все больше возрастать.

А. С. Ахиезер и А. В. Кочетков (1972, стр. 82) отмечают, что процесс урбанизации и интенсификации производства «приводит к существенным сдвигам, которые заключаются прежде всего в опережающем развитии центров производства, хранения, переработки, трансляции информации, в развитии центров управления... Чем выше темпы развития общества, тем выше роль центров управления и производства информации» (подчеркнуто мною — *П. И.*). Таковыми в СССР и являются административные центры.

В условиях НТР, когда ослабляется влияние естественных ресурсов на размещение промышленности (Приваловская, 1974) и увеличивается значимость управления, информации, науки, трудовых ресурсов, социальной инфраструктуры и т.п., практически все административные центры становятся центрами роста.

Конечно, развиваются, и порой весьма быстрыми темпами, и другие города. В первую очередь это города, в которых создаются крупнейшие предприятия общесоюзного значения (например, Тольятти, Набережные Челны, Волгодонск и др.); города при крупнейших гидроэлектростанциях, где наличие дешевой энергии и мощных строительных баз способствует развитию крупной промышленно-

---

[5] Еще в большей мере этими преимуществами обладают столицы союзных республик.

сти; города-«плацдармы» освоения новых районов.[6]Но «неадминистративные» города развиваются, если можно так сказать, «выборочно»; административные же центры растут почти «поголовно». Если в 1959 г. 31 административный центр (области, края, АССР) из 112 в РСФСР, на Украине и в Казахстане (или 29%) имел людность менее 100 тыс. жителей, то сейчас большими городами еще не стали только 6 из нынешних 115 административных центров этих республик (или всего 5%). Причем три из них уверенно продвигаются к стотысячному рубежу (Ужгород, Талды-Курган, Джезказган).[7]

Заметим, что, видимо, не для всякого времени в качестве больших следует рассматривать города людностью не менее 100 тыс. жителей. И так же, как представляется правомерным принимать за таковые для начала ХХ века города людностью от 50 тыс. жителей, то для текущего периода это могут быть города от 200 тыс. жителей. В этой связи любопытны такие данные: из 33 городов, имевших в 1970 г. население 151–200 тыс. чел., 19 были административными центрами, и все они к 1977 г. превысили 200 тыс.; из остальных четырнадцати это удалось только шести.

Преимущественное развитие административных центров привело к резко выраженному моноцентризму в системах городского расселения СССР (Покшишевский, 1976). Обращает внимание, что в трех из тех четырех областей, где людность второго города выше, чем первого, абсолютный прирост населения центра (не говоря уж об относительном) последние годы выше, чем второго города: Кемерово постепенно догоняет Новокузнецк, Фергана — Коканд, Джезказган — Балхаш.[8] Лишь Череповец пока (абсолютно и относительно) продолжает обгонять Вологду. «Пока» потому, что можно, основываясь на опыте других городов, рассматривать это явление как временное (если только Череповец не вернет себе свой административный статус 1918–1927 гг., когда существовала череповецкая губерния!).[9]

---

[6] Некоторык центры роста относятся к смешанному типу. Например, Братск, один из самых динамичных современных городов, развивающийся у крупнейшей ГЭС на Ангаре, одновременно служит базой для дальнейшего освоения районов Восточной Сибири.

[7] Остальные три — Кызыл, Элиста и совсем еще юный Аркалык.

[8] Аркалык обогнал Державинск ещё несколько лет назад (СССР. Административно-территориальное деление…, 1974).

[9] Еще в четырех случаях второй город обгонял в 1970–1976 гг. первый по абсолютному приросту населения. Это — Тольятти, Набережные Челны, Севастополь и Кременчуг. Что касается первых двух, то в отношении их временность этого явления еще более очевидна, чем в случае с Череповцом: вряд ли есть

Подведем некоторые итоги. В современных условиях НТР, когда возрастает роль центров управления и производства информации, когда прогресс всех сфер деятельности, в том числе и производственной во все большей степени зависит от уровня развития личности, меняются критерии оценки разных мест как организациями, занимающимися планированием размещения народного хозяйства, так и населением (Ахиезер, Ильин, 1975).

Следствием этих процессов является преимущественный (по сравнению с другими типами поселений) и повсеместный рост городов — административных центров (и их агломераций) в СССР.

Литература

Ахиезер А.С., Ильин П.М. Задачи разработки социальных оценок территории в условиях научно-технической революции. — *Известия АН СССР, сер. геогр.*, 1975, № 1.

Ахиезер А.С., Кочетков А.В. Урбанизация и интенсификация производства в СССР. — В сб.: *Проблемы современной урбанизации.* М.,1972.

Лаппо Г.М. Опорный каркас территориальной структуры народного хозяйства. — В сб.: *Территориальная организация производительных сил СССР.* М., 1978.

Лейзерович Е.Е. Особенности развития областных, краевых и республиканских (АССР) центров в СССР. — *Вестник МГУ. География*, 1971, № 2.

Покшишевский В.В. Проблема «второго» города. — В сб.: *Проблемы урбанизации и расселения.* М., 1976.

Приваловская Г.А. Природный фактор и система условий размещения промышленного производства в СССР. *Вопросы географии, сб. 95*, М., 1974.

СССР. Административно-территориальное деление союзных республик на 1 января 1974 года. М., 1974.

СССР. Административно-территориальное деление союзных республик на 1 января 1977 года. М., 1977.

Harris Ch.D. *Cities of the Soviet Union.* Chicago, 1970.

какие-нибудь основания предполагать, что они обгонят по людности Куйбышев и Казань.

Задачи разработки социальных оценок территории в условиях научно-технической революции

*А. С. Ахиезер, Институт международного
рабочего движения АН СССР*
П. М. Ильин, Институт географии АН СССР

Оценочная проблематика занимает в последние годы все большее место в географических исследованиях. Проводятся работы по экономической оценке природных ресурсов, природных условий жизни населения, технологической оценке природных комплексов, территориальных различий потребностей населения в услугах и т.д. (Лопатина, Минц и др., 1970; Минц, 1972; Лопатина, Назаревский, 1972; Мухина, 1973; Ковалев, 1973, и др.).

Увеличение количества и разнообразия оценок неизбежно ставит перед географической наукой проблему их упорядочения, выявления их внутренней связи. Важность решения этой проблемы определяется, в частности, тем, что при увеличении разнообразия оценок возрастает возможность противоречий между вариантами решения любой территориальной проблемы, опирающимися на разные виды оценок территории. Чтобы избежать этой опасности, необходимо выявить логику соотношения различных оценок, их иерархию, закономерности их последовательности. Это даст научную основу для адекватного выбора оценок в конкретных ситуациях, что крайне важно для развития оценочного подхода в географии.

В данной статье рассматриваются некоторые вопросы развития социальных оценок территории при социализме и их специфика в условиях научно-технической революции (анализ понятия «территория» дан Минцем, Петряковой, 1973). Эти оценки неразрывно связаны с динамикой функций места (Минц, Преображенский, 1970).

Всякая человеческая деятельность всегда включает в себя предпочтение одних пунктов территории другим. Ценностное отношение к любому месту определяется тем, что с различными точками территории люди связывают различные потребности, возможности, различную эффективность своей деятельности. «Ценность возникает на основе противоречивого характера практической деятельности человека как нереализованная, но уже требующая своей реализации возможность» (Дробницкий, 1966). Оценка территории складывается как оценка людьми их собственной практической возможности достижения своих целей в соответствующих точках пространства. Многообразие форм деятельности человека определяет многообразие форм оценок территории.

Объективные потребности общества, их соотношение с объективными территориально локализованными условиями производства, всех видов человеческой деятельности преломляются в форме системы социальной ориентации людей в пространстве. Вся территория видится людьми как своеобразное поляризованное культурное поле с фокусами притяжения и отталкивания (Ахиезер, 1972). Это оценочное отношение к территории носит социальный характер, так как оно есть аспект человеческой деятельности. Любая оценка территории содержит, во-первых, фиксацию некоторого предметного содержания территории, исторически сложившихся функций места, определенной совокупности локализованных в данной точке территории условий, существенных для целей деятельности. Во-вторых, социальная оценка территории включает цель, потребность, пространственную задачу, которую ставит перед собой человек. И наконец, она включает средства, реальную возможность, практический путь достижения цели в данном месте. Необходимость достижения практических целей требует снятия возникающих противоречий между оценками, что возможно при критическом отношении к самим оценкам, их переосмысливании. Это делает оценки динамичными и стимулирует их усложнение в процессе развития производства, в процессе усложнения социальных целей и потребностей.

Конкретно-исторические ведущие оценки территории определяются общим развитием ведущих целей общества. В нашей стране важнейшей задачей всей производственно-практической деятельности является развитие человека. В условиях коммунистической формации всестороннее развитие «творческих дарований человека» становится самоцелью.[1] Достижение этой главной социальной цели общества требует в качестве своего условия раз-

---

[1] См. К. Маркс и Ф. Энгельс. Соч., т. 46, я. 1, стр. 476.

решения различных непосредственных задач, каждая из которых связана с определенным типом оценки территории. Кратко рассмотрим иерархические уровни этих типов.

Для удовлетворения любой общественной потребности, связанной с необходимостью выбора места, должна быть проделана оценка территории с точки зрения наличия Предметных условий решения данной задачи в каждом из некоторого множества мест. Оценка территории по этому критерию фиксирует как природные условия и ресурсы, так и наличие инженерных сооружений, весь опредмеченный прошлый труд, т.е. весь комплекс природных и техногенных свойств, от которых зависит возможность, степень эффективности строительства и функционирования необходимых человеку объектов. Этот тип оценок, поскольку он нацелен на любые важные для человека элементы природы, в единстве с любыми результатами предшествующей человеческой деятельности, может быть условно назван натурально-технологическим, хотя и он имеет принципиально социальный характер. В географической науке значение такого рода оценок выразилось в стремлении вскрыть и зафиксировать на карте все бесконечное многообразие природных ресурсов страны, а также предметные результаты творческого труда людей. К этому типу оценок относятся технологическая оценка природных комплексов, агро-производственная оценка, медико-биологическая оценка и т.п.

Однако оценка территории не может ограничиваться натуральными предпосылками возможности решения тех или иных хозяйственных задач. Общество всегда располагает ограниченными ресурсами, поэтому оценка территории с точки зрения натуральных возможностей должна быть дополнена оценкой по критерию минимума совокупных затрат, необходимых для реализации этих возможностей.[2] Натурально-технологическая оценка при этом сохраняется как необходимое условие, методологическая ступень для более высокой оценки, учитывающей социально-экономическую потребность в общей экономии ресурсов, экономию совокупных затрат общественного труда при достижении того же уровня удовлетворения всего комплекса общественно необходимых потребностей. Ориентация на минимизацию затрат для удо-

---

[2] А. А. Минц (1972) обращал внимание на устойчивость среди части географов воззрений, заключающихся в преимущественно натуралистическом и техническом истолковании проблемы использования естественных ресурсов и природных условий при недоучете ее социально-экономического аспекта.

влетворения необходимых потребностей получила, например, свое отражение в известном «законе добывающей промышленности» А. Е. Пробста (1962) и в ряде других исследований по размещению производства.

С ростом и обогащением структуры народного хозяйства задачи экономической оценки намного усложняются, и Она приобретает новые формы. Примером может служить разработанный ЦЭМИ АН СССР с привлечением специалистов других ведомств, в том числе Института географии АН СССР (А. А. Минц), проект методики экономической оценки природных ресурсов в массовых планово–проектных расчетах. В соответствии с этой методикой критерием оценки любого вида природных ресурсов выступает «...совокупный народно–хозяйственный эффект, приносимый этим ресурсом... Наиболее полным выражением совокупного народно–хозяйственного эффекта является вклад в критерий оптимальности народно–хозяйственного плана, приносимый данным ресурсом» (Экономические проблемы..., 1973).

Таким образом, задача минимизации затрат превращается в подчиненную задачу максимизации эффекта затрат, что достигается не при минимальных, а при оптимальных затратах; так возникает задача оценки территории с точки зрения возможности достижения максимальной эффективности народного хозяйства.

Однако экономическая оценка, как и все предшествующие уровни иерархии оценок, оставаясь необходимой, оказывается тем не менее недостаточной в условиях развитого социализма, в условиях научно–технической революции, когда функционирование производства все в большей степени зависит от способности работника принимать эффективные решения, от уровня развития его личности, его образования и квалификации. XXIV съезд КПСС указал на необходимость создания условий, благоприятствующих всестороннему развитию способностей и творческой активности советских людей, всех трудящихся, т.е. развития, главной производительной силы общества.[3] В этих условиях критерий оценки деятельности каждой отрасли, каждого предприятия должен полнее отражать самые широкие культурные и социальные потребности человека, общества. Таким образом, важнейшее значение приобретает социальная оценка территории в собственном смысле слова. В соответствии с основными методологическими положениями исторического материализма существенным мо-

---

[3] Материалы XXIV съезда КПСС. М., 1971, стр. 41.

ментом такой оценки остаются экономические отношения, взятые во всем многообразии их взаимосвязей и взаимодействий.

Анализ территории по критерию степени благоприятности условий для развития личности показывает, что каждая сфера человеческой деятельности, будь то производство станков, балет, летний отдых и т.д., имеет свою географию, которая фиксирует существенные различия, достигнутые ею в каждой точке пространства, и, следовательно, значимость этой точки для развития личности. В любой сфере деятельности имеются локализованные центры, дающие наивысшие творческие результаты, объективно приобщающие людей к этим высшим, наиболее эффективным результатам, путям и методам их достижения. Более того, различные сферы деятельности не независимы друг от друга. На территории складываются зоны, в которых творческий потенциал множества форм деятельности достигает максимального интегрального эффекта. Высшую оценку по этому критерию получают наиболее урбанизированные территории, где сконцентрирован основной творческий потенциал общества.

Ведущая оценка территории всегда подчиняет себе все предшествующие. Чем выше значение территории для целостного развития личности, тем в принципе в большей степени она является источником и условием большего экономического эффекта, более высокого мастерства, более производительного труда. На этой территории возрастает значение экономии ресурсов, которая, однако, расценивается не абсолютно, а в рамках общей задачи развития личности. Одновременно здесь усиливается необходимость мобилизации всех натуральных ресурсов для той же цепи. Сдвиги в социальных потребностях общества могут перекроить иерархию оценок, т.е. превратить ранее скрытую, подчиненную оценку в ведущую, превратить опосредованную перспективную оценку в элемент повседневного труда людей и т.д. Этот процесс фиксируется в директивных партийных и государственных документах, в научных исследованиях, в массовом сознании людей. Он отражает дальнейшее развитие социальных потребностей социалистического общества, совершенствование его способностей разрешать свои все более сложные проблемы, в том числе и территориальные.

Любая оценка территории не может быть одновременно содержанием мотива деятельности всех слоев общества, каждой социальной группы, каждой личности. Оценки территории, складывающиеся в головах миллионов работников, от которых в конечном итоге зависит социально–экономическое развитие общества, могут отличаться, и подчас существенно, от оценок, формируемых плановыми органами и проектными организациями. Примеров таких рассогласований более чем достаточно.

Например, для миграции сельского населения СССР характерна особенность, оказывающая отрицательное влияние на сельское хозяйство: люди уходят в города как раз из тех сельских районов, где они больше всего нужны, где их не хватает (Переведенцев, 1974). Много пишется в литературе о несоответствии потоков стихийно складывающейся миграции, нацеленных преимущественно на юг, задачам освоения природных ресурсов восточных районов. Налицо противоречия между стремлением людей жить и работать в одних местах, т.е. сложившейся системой оценок территории значительными слоями населения, и некоторыми оценками территории, заложенными в народно–хозяйственном плане. Такие противоречия возникают, когда игнорируется ста чрезвычайная множественность мотивов и способов поведения, которая определяет конечный результат миграционного перераспределения населения» (Покшишевский, 1973).

Игнорирование сложившейся мотивации приводит подчас к невозможности реально управлять процессами перемещений людей и к результатам, противоположным задуманным. Так, например, не всегда удачны попытки обречь определенные поселения–спутники на постепенное «выморачивание» (по выражению проектировщиков) с переселением их жителей в более крупные центры: их население иногда не только не сокращается, но даже продолжает расти (Пути развития..., 1967). Стягивание сельского населения горных районов Алтая в немногие населенные Пункты нередко приводит к снижению эффективности использования угодий и к усилению оттока населения (Гинзбург, 1968). Подобные примеры можно продолжить.

Реальная оценка мест широкими массами имеет самые разнообразные последствия. Она, например, включает отношение населения к жилью. Так, А. Томсеном (1970) установлено, что жилье в Москве, расположенное далее 15 мин. от станций метро, обесценивается в глазах людей на 17%. Система ценностей горожан в принципе является исходной для всей системы обслуживания города; «Широкий круг разнообразных производственных, общественных и индивидуальных интересов человека определяет и систему размещения, и типы зданий культурно– бытового обслуживания населения» (Орлов, 1973).

В то же время не соответствует потребностям социально-экономического прогресса стремление сохранить устаревшую мотивацию, не ориентированную на прогресс. Например, выдвигается мысль, что «соразмерный человеку масштаб» присущ такому городу, в котором преобладает малоэтажная застройка и основным видом передвижений являются пешеходные (Жемчужникова, 1969). Тенденция, к «локализованному микрокосму», которая связывалась Марксом с земледельческой общиной,[4] противоречит необходимости социалистического общества стимулировать стремление каждого человека ю высшим ценностям, где бы они ни были локализованы.

Таким образом, в условиях научно-технической революции, когда эффективность внешнего воздействия на поступки человека снижается (Файнбург, 1969), различия в оценках одной и той же территории оказывают особенно сильное отрицательное влияние на решение народно-хозяйственных задач. Для ликвидации этой негативной тенденции должны быть разрешены две тесно связанные задачи. Во-первых, возникает необходимость разработки научно обоснованной иерархии оценок территории, отражающих назревшие потребности общества, выявления ведущей оценки и поисков путей гармонизации всей иерархии оценок на основе выявления этой ведущей оценки. Во-вторых, возникает практическая потребность превращения прогрессивной иерархии оценок территорий в содержании мотивации широких масс. Это требует изучения путей формирования мотивации и совершенствования методов управления ее развитием.

Располагая научно обоснованной системой оценок территории, социалистическое общество приобретает теоретическую предпосылку для снятия противоречий в оценках, что может быть достигнуто в процессе освоения научно обоснованных оценок всем обществом, всеми его слоями и институтами. Но это не может быть воплощено в жизнь лишь просветительной пропагандой результатов науки. Необходимо совершенствовать условия, стимулирующие более высокую оценку человеком самой территории. Те места, которые плановые органы, проектные организации на основе выводов науки считают ценными для общества, необходимо, практически сделать ценными, привлекательными и для населения. Это достигается не только чисто экономическими методами (введением различных надбавок к заработной плате и т.п.).

---

4   К. Маркс и Ф. Энгельс. Соч., т, 19, стр. 405.

С развитием нашего общества повышается значимость для населения комфортных условий жизни. И – что исключительно важно – в условиях научно-технической революции возрастает ценность мест с высоким культурным потенциалом.

Социальная оценка территории повышается в процессе снижения социальной гомогенности множества ранее однородных мест, в процессе увеличения территориального разнообразия форм деятельности. Оценка того или иного места определенными группами населения возрастает, если локализованное там предприятие или учреждение становится ведущим в своей сфере, например в данной отрасли народного хозяйства. Наиболее передовые предприятия, открывающие перспективу роста квалификации, лучшие вузы и школы, лучшие театры и т.п. расширяют возможности освоения личностью разных видов деятельности, их высших форм. В результате, создаются предпосылки для развития самых различных способностей, для развития личности во всем многообразии ее проявлений, что повышает объективную значимость для человека соответствующих мест. Эти процессы приводят к прогрессивным сдвигам в оценке территории широкими массами. Развитие уникальной творческой деятельности, будучи мощной притягательной силой для людей, является все более важной предпосылкой для решения любых сложных народно-хозяйственных проблем. «На первый план выступает повышение общественной значимости места, увеличение его «отдачи», т.е. переход от менее насущных и эффективных для общества в данный момент функций к более насущным и эффективным» (Минц, Преображенский, 1970).

Вторым важнейшим аспектом повышения ценности территории является повышение доступности данного места. Очевидно, что каждый человек располагает ограниченными возможностями посещений различных мест, а также получения из них необходимой информации. Затраты времени и средств на приобщение к одной точке пространства ограничивают возможности приобщения к другим точкам, поэтому каждый акт развития транспорта и связи есть результат стремления увеличить возможности общества освоить места, имеющие наибольшую общественную значимость, их сложившиеся и вновь складывающиеся функции – и вместе с тем, результат стремления к дальнейшему повышению ценности территории.

Таким образом, реальная общественная значимость территории определяется, во-первых, уникальностью и уровнем локализованного на ней творческого процесса и, во-вторых, ее доступностью для периферийной территории. Между этими двумя сторонами существует сложная связь. Развитие одной из них создает условия, стимулирующие развитие другой. Но их совместный рост может сопровождаться нарастанием несоответствия между ними. Например, несмотря на сильный абсолютный рост городского транспорта в г. Горьком, время доступности центра города с 1914 до 1964 г. увеличилось и возможности его посещения горожанами снизились (Каган, 1970). Иначе говоря, наблюдается неравномерность роста двух упомянутых выше сторон, составляющих ценность такого важного места, как центр города.

Социалистическое общество, управляя развитием поселений, центров производства, науки и культуры, распределением и размещением капиталовложений, обладает рычагами воздействия на оценки территории широкими массами, на структуру мотивации в интересах всего общества через изменение функций мест, повышение их разнообразия и уровня, повышение доступности наиболее значимых с позиций человека и общества мест.

Для дальнейшего углубления представлений о закономерности формирования ценностной иерархии территории требуется разработка количественных показателей. Можно наметить некоторые пути количественного измерения социальной оценки территории. Например, при определении общественной значимости каждого места должно учитываться количество людей, стремящихся приобщиться, опосредованно или непосредственно, к данному месту. Опосредованное приобщение к месту связано, прежде всего, со стремлением получить отсюда информацию, используя все возможные каналы связи. Стремление к непосредственному приобщению проявляется в реализации желания попасть в это место, вступить в осязаемый контакт с людьми, занятыми в этом месте какой– то специфической формой деятельности. Такого рода оценки могут быть в принципе рассчитаны через фиксацию в каждой точке территории, во-первых, потока исходящей из нее информации, зафиксированной в документах или идущей по радиотелефонным каналам и т.д., во-вторых, реального прибытия в нее людей в единицу времени. Дальнейшее совершенствование подобных оценок может идти по пути учета различными косвенными методами неудовлетворенной (в силу ограниченности каналов связи, рабочих мест, мест в вузах, ограничений административного характера и по другим причинам) потребности к непосредственному или опосредованному общению с изучаемым местом. Дальнейшее изучение системы показателей социальных оценок территории позволит перейти к составлению специальных оценочных карт.

В данной статье сделана попытка лишь первого, подхода к вопросам социальной оценки территорий в условиях научно–технической революции. Это сложная и многогранная проблема, которая находится «на стыке» социологии и географии, проблема социальной географии. Сейчас еще трудно провести четкую линию разграничения между задачами этих наук в ее исследовании, да и вряд ли это нужно делать. Но можно определенно указать, что выявление, общественной значимости территории на разных иерархических уровнях, исследование доступности территории с точки зрения ее социально важных параметров, изучение использования территории в социальном аспекте, поиск путей измерения социальных оценок территории, картографирование оценок, относятся к сфере интересов географических наук.

ЛИТЕРАТУРА:

Ахиеэер А. С. Рабочий класс и урбанизация в условиях научно-технической революции. В сб.: *Урбанизация, научно-техническая революций и рабочий класс.* М., 1972.

Гинзбург Н. С. Выступление. В сб.: *Материалы Второго междуведомственного совещания по географии населения,* вып. 1. М., 1968.

Дробницкий О, Г. Некоторые аспекты проблемы ценностей. В сб.: *Проблема ценностей в философии.* Л., 1966.

Жемчужникова Н. И. Будущее малых городов в районах Интенсивного промышленного развития. В сб.: *Научные прогнозы развития и формирования советских городов на базе социального и научно-технического прогресса,* вып. 3. М., 1969.

Минц А. А., Петрякова Т. И. Использование территории как экономико-географическая проблема. *Изв. АН СССР. Сер. геогр.,* 1973, № 4.

Минц А. А., Преображенский В. С. Функция места и ее изменение. *Изв. АН СССР. Сер. геогр.,* 1970, № 6.

Мухина Л. И. *Принципы и методы технологической оценки природных комплексов.* М., «Наука», 1973.

Орлов М. О. Прогнозы развития сети и типов зданий торговли и бытового обслуживания, В сб.: *Перспективы развития советского градостроительства.* М., 1973.

Переведенцев В. *Для всех и для каждого. Заметки социолога.* Наш современник, 1974, № 1.

Покшишевский В. В. Миграции населения как общественное явление и задачи статистического их изучения. В сб.: *Статистика миграции населения.* М., «Статистика», 1973.

Пробст А. Е. *Размещение социалистической промышленности (теоретические очерки).* М., Экономиздат, 1962,

Пути развития малых и средних городов центральных экономических районов СССР. М., «Наука», 1967.

Томсен А. Проблемы эффективности капитальных вложений в градостроительстве. *Плановое хозяйство,* 1970, № 1.

Файнбург З. И. Перспективы научно-технической революции и развитие личности. *Вопросы философии,* 1969, № 2.

Экономические проблемы оптимизации природопользования. М., «Наука», 1973.

Часть II

Москва: география культуры

Введение

Россия всегда интересовала американцев — и в периоды «потеплений», и в периоды «похолоданий» российско-американских отношений. И в фокусе разнообразных интересов американского читателя и исследователя была, есть и будет Москва — центр и символ России. В США написано и опубликовано множество работ, посвященных Москве, и среди них заметное место занимают работы о Москве конца XIX — начала XX в. Интерес к этому периоду истории России особенно усилился в последнее десятилетие, когда страна начала возвращаться к рыночной экономике. И нам хотелось бы, предваряя эту книгу, сказать, хотя бы кратко, чем же так привлекает Москва столетней давности.

Но сначала — несколько слов об истории российско-американских отношений. На редкость лаконично о них сказал американский историк Норман Соул, опубликовавший два тома (из трех намеченных) под общим заглавием «Соединенные Штаты и Россия», но с разными подзаголовками: «1763–1867. Друзья на расстоянии» и «1767–1914. Согласие и конфликт». [1] Вот в этих подзаголовках и отражена в наиболее краткой форме вся сущность отношений России с Северо-Американскими Соединенными Штатами (так долгое время страна называлась в России).

Как писал американский путешественник, посетивший Россию в 1880-е гг., у американцев, в отличие, например, от англичан, в то время не было никаких поводов для разногласий с русскими. [2] «Часто говорят, что американцы и русские являются естественными друзьями. Мы являемся таковыми потому, что так мало знаем друг о друге. Между нами практически нет ничего общего, наши интересы не вступают между собой в конфликт», — писала газета «Нью-Йорк таймс» в мае 1878 г. [3] Но дело не только в этом: в Америке не забывали, что во время гражданской войны Россия поддерживала Север, и что именно это, возможно, предотвратило вмешательство Англии в войну на стороне южных штатов. [4]

Конфликты между США и Россией начались позднее, на рубеже веков. Наиболее серьезных было два: на первых этапах русско-японской войны 1904–1905 гг., когда президент США Теодор Рузвельт открыто занял прояпонскую позицию, [5] и так называемый «паспортный конфликт». [6] Но все же не случайно в подзаголовке книги Соула об этом периоде российско-американских отношений «согласие» стоит впереди «конфликта».

Конечно, американцам нравилось далеко не все, с чем они сталкивались при поездках в Россию. «Очень многое трудно понять здесь путешественнику, приехавшему из страны свободных школ и свободной прессы, страны, где каждый может свободно высказываться», — писал главный редактор журнала «Нэшэнл джеографик мэгэзин» Гилберт Х. Гровенор, посетивший Россию накануне Первой мировой войны. И далее он называет то, что, по-видимому, произвело на него наибольшее впечатление: «Обескураживающая нехватка хороших школ... американская газета, целые куски которой вымараны цензором, причем зачернены так, что нельзя разобрать ни единой буквы; боязнь, если не сказать страх, быть подслушанным при откровенных разговорах на политические темы; наконец, непомерная власть, сосредоточенная в руках одного человека». [7] Но Гровенор увидел в России и другие стороны жизни, давшие ему основание назвать свою статью «Молодая Россия — страна неограниченных возможностей».

Забежим немного вперед и вспомним, что интерес в Америке к России (под которой стал подразумеваться весь Советский Союз) значительно возрос во время Второй мировой войны, когда США и СССР были союзниками, и особенно во время холодной войны, когда они стали врагами. И как следствие этого интереса, в Америке появилась масса работ, посвященных самым разным сторонам современной жизни и истории России — Советского Союза. Основные кадры современных американских ученых-москвоведов сформировались в этот период.

Вернемся, однако, к теме книги. Период конца XIX — начала XX в. занимает особое место в истории России. «На заре двадцатого века Россия предстала перед Западом как одна из самых выдающихся стран современного мира». [8] Свободная экономика развивалась. [9] Страна, с остановками и отступлениями, но двигалась по пути демократизации. Искусство переживало «серебряный век». В 1900 г. Россия была единственной в мире страной, кроме США, два города которой входили в десятку самых больших на Земле. [10] И выдающуюся роль в жизни страны играла Москва — «вторая столица» России. «Москва во всех отношениях главный город (metropolis) России... город-мать русского народа», — так начинает свой очерк о Москве американский путешественник начала XX века. [11]

Интерес именно к этому периоду развития Москвы не случаен еще и потому, что большая часть ткани городской застройки старой Москвы осталась от этого времени. Город бурно рос вширь — захватывая новые территории, и ввысь — новая техника и строительные материалы позволили перейти от малоэтажной к многоэтажной застройке. Возникали новые промышленные предприятия, учебные заведения, культурные учреждения, транспортные сооружения.

Однако большевики, захватившие власть в октябре 1917 г., отказались признавать какие-либо успехи дореволюционной России, они акцентировали внимание на ее слабостях и пороках. Экономические успехи замалчивались, социальный прогресс отвергался. Искусство начала XX в. было объявлено «упадническим», «декадентским». Признавались «передовыми» лишь те писатели, чье творчество устраивало официальную критику. Архитектурные стили этого времени оценивались отрицательно. [12]

Замалчивание и искажение истинной значимости изменений, происходивших в стране на рубеже веков, не было случайным, оно вытекало из определенной идеологической концепции. Официальная доктрина состояла в следующем: Россия была в полном упадке, когда произошла революция. Большевики вывели страну из упадка, и новое общество обеспечило развитие России — экономическое, социальное, культурное и т.д. Что же касается Москвы, то, как подчеркивалось в правительственном постановлении о Генеральном плане реконструкции Москвы, принятом в 1935 г., «стихийно развивавшаяся на протяжении многих веков Москва отражала даже в лучшие годы своего развития характер варварского российского капитализма».

Реабилитация эпохи конца XIX — начала XX в. началась в конце 1960 — начале 1970-х гг., когда начали появляться объективные исследования, посвященные деятелям искусства того времени, литературным течениям, архитектурным стилям и т.п. [13] Однако писать об успехах России в экономическом и социальном развитии, как и о роли буржуазии в этом процессе, по-прежнему не допускалось. Весьма «модным», например, было напоминать о нереализованных планах Московской городской думы, «забывая» о том, что деятельность этой думы — самой прогрессивной в России — была насильственно прекращена с приходом к власти большевиков.

Одновременно к изучению дореволюционной Москвы обратились многие западные ученые. Они не подвергались цензурным ограничениям, и поэтому могли свободнее выражать свои мысли и свободнее пользоваться любыми материалами. Один из редакторов и авторов этой книги [14] был свидетелем того, какой фурор произвело выступление едва ли ни первого американского географа—москвоведа Роберта Гохстанда (Robert Gohstand) на XXIII Международном географическом конгрессе в Москве в 1976 г., [15] и особенно его карты, на которых, среди прочего, были показаны индустриальные зоны Москвы, причем не только столетней давности, но и современные! [16] Карты Гохстанда были широко распространены среди советских географов, однако случаи упоминания этих карт в советской печати нам не известны — цензура никогда бы этого не допустила. Географические карты и планы городов в СССР были засекречены, а для широкого пользования издавались некие подобия карт и планов, выполненные с большими искажениями масштаба. [17]

Вот далеко не полный список западных ученых—авторов книг и капитальных статей о различных аспектах жизни Москвы на переломе веков: Джеймс Бейтер (James Bater), Уильям «Билл» Брумфилд (William «Bill» Brumfield), Джозеф Брэдли (Joseph Bradley), Уильям «Билл» Глисон (William «Bill» Gleason), Роберт Джонсон (Robert Johnson), Даян Конкер (Diane Koenker), Тимоти Колтон (Timothy Colton), Томас Оуэн (Thomas Owen), Джо Энн Ракман (Jo Ann Ruckman), Алфред Рибер (Alfred Rieber), Блэр Рубл (Blair Ruble), Роберт Терстон (Robert Thurston), Дэйвид Хофман (David Hoffman), Уильям Чейс (William Chase), Алберт Шмидт (Albert Schmidt), Лора Энгелстейн (Laura Engelstein). [18]

Ситуация в России изменилась во время «перестройки» и «гласности». Ученые получили такую свободу выражения своих идей и публикации результатов научных исследований, о которой не могли даже и мечтать. Стали доступными многие материалы по истории России, в том числе архивные и мемуарные. И особенно возрос интерес к истории России конца XIX — начала XX в., что напрямую связано с возвращением страны на путь капиталистического развития.

Предлагаемая вниманию читателей книга является результатом коллективного труда нескольких авторов. Среди авторов книги представители разных общественных наук: географии, политологии, истории градостроительства и архитектуры, литературо- и искусствоведения. Их объединил интерес к одному из величайших городов нашей планеты, к изучению различных сторон жизни Москвы. Авторы книги рассматривают Москву в разных аспектах, их интересует облик города и его история, сопоставление с другими мировыми городами такого же масштаба, его экономика, культура, другие стороны жизни вечно меняющегося и вечно развивающегося живого городского организма.

Авторы книги стремятся рассказывать о Москве, акцентируя внимание на пространственных аспектах жизни города. Этот географический подход проявляется, уже с первой главы (Павел Ильин и Микаэлла Каган), представляющей собой краткий историко-географический очерк Москвы, дающий общее представление о Москве того времени. Авторы рассматривают роль Москвы в экономике и культуре России (особое внимание уделяется сравнению двух столиц — Москвы и Петербурга), динамику населения и пространственного развития, территориальную структуру города, внутригородские различия. В целом в этой главе делается попытка подготовить читателя к лучшему пониманию последующих глав.

Сравнение разных мест — излюбленное занятие ученых и путешественников с античных времен. И вторая глава, написанная Блэром А. Рублом, посвящена сопоставительному анализу развития Москвы и Нью-Йорка на рубеже XIX—XX вв. В судьбах этих городов оказалось много схожего. Не будучи столицами своих стран, они, тем не менее, играли выдающуюся роль в их жизни и были в это время наиболее быстро развивающимися городами мира. Конечно, различия в уровне экономического и социального развития России и США были огромными, что и определило наиболее существенные различия между городами.

Очевидно, что сравнение разных городов требует наибольшего внимания к их макрочертам. В то же время, исследование неоднородности конкретного города предполагает изучение внутригородских пространственных характеристик. Роберт Гохстанд в третьей главе анализирует одну из наиболее существенных характеристик неоднородности городского пространства — цену на землю. Главу завершает составленная автором и впервые публикуемая уникальная карта ценности земли в Москве в начале XX века.

Четвертая глава (Павел Ильин) посвящена географии культуры Москвы того времени. В ней показывается размещение в плане города театров, музеев, кинотеатров, цирков, концертных залов. Учреждения культуры в целом явно тяготели к центру города, однако специфика их видов диктовала особенности размещения. Кроме того, автора интересует размещение не только учреждений культуры, то есть мест, где культура реализуется, но и мест, где она создается — мест жительства и встреч деятелей культуры.

В конце XIX — начале XX в. в Москве шел активный процесс создания новой среды большого города. Этот процесс охватывал все стороны его жизни и внешне проявлялся в появлении новых типов зданий и сооружений. Доходные дома и особняки буржуазии, конторские и торговые здания, гостиницы и вокзалы росли в разных районах города. Их строительство, которое велось в новых архитектурных стилях, среди которых доминировал модерн, отражало новые веяния в экономике. Размещение и архитектурно-инженерные решения этих зданий, которые и поныне выделяются в застройке Москвы, рассматривает в пятой главе Уильям К. Брумфилд.

Не счесть произведений литературы и искусства, в которых присутствует Москва. В книге этой теме посвящены две главы. Роберт Виттакер пишет о месте, которое Москва занимает в произведениях А. Чехова, в мыслях и действиях его персонажей. Чеховская Москва часто конкретна и реальна, а иногда выступает как некий идеал («Три сестры»). Катя Короткина-Розенцвейг рассматривает образ Москвы в работах живописцев русского авангарда — К. Малевича, В. Кандинского, А. Лентулова, — художников, которые почти полностью оторвались от воспроизведения реальной среды города и сосредоточили свои усилия на передаче его атмосферы, настроения, духа.

Октябрьская революция 1917 г. привела к слому социальной системы в России. Микаэлла Каган в своей главе исследует динамику функции места в Москве после смены режима. Новая власть приложила усилия к смещению или разрушению старых идеологических доминант в городе и замене их новыми, либо построив новые здания, либо переоборудовав старые здания под новые нужды. Хотя внешне, казалось бы, произошли большие перемены, однако парадокс заключается в том, что сама функция места — идеологическая — оказалась весьма устойчивой. То же самое произошло с культурными, жилыми и другими функциями места в городе.

В Заключении, написанном ответственными редакторами книги, читатель переносится в современную Москву, которая сравнивается с Москвой столетней давности. Это сравнение помогает лучше понять как прошлое, так и настоящее главного города России.

Авторы книги считают своей приятной обязанностью поблагодарить коллег и друзей, чьей помощью они пользовались в работе. При этом мы хотели бы особенно отметить видного американского историко-географа, профессора Мерилэндского университета Роберта Митчела (Robert D. Mitchell), чья поддержка была важна для нас в течение работы над книгой.

На разных стадиях работы рукопись книги прочитали Реваз Гачечиладзе и Игорь Крупник. От имени авторов книги мы выражаем им искреннюю признательность за их доброжелательную критику и предложения.

Б. Рубл хотел бы поблагодарить Тэда Бестора (Ted Bester), Элизабет Вуд (Elizabeth Wood), Игоря Жевелева, Григория Каганова, Питера Маркусе (Peter Marcuse), Рут О'Браен Миллер (Ruth O'Brien Miller), Дэйвида У. Плата (David W. Plath), Леонарда Плотникова, Стефана Танака (Stefan Tanaka), Джозефа Талчина (Joseph Tulchin), Роберта Терстона (Robert Thurston), Елену Хоссило (Helena Goscilo), и Уильяма Чейса (William Chase) за их весьма полезные комментарии, сделанные после прочтения разных вариантов его главы. Аналогичную помощь получили П. Ильин и М. Каган от Александра Кириллова, Ирины Кузес, Александра Синкова, Виктории Фельдман и Вадима Щеглова.

К. Розенцвейг-Короткина благодарит Майкла Миценмакера (Michael Mitzenmacher) за его помощь в работе над ее главой.

П. Ильин и М. Каган считают своим долгом поблагодарить всех, кто помогал им в поиске необходимой литературы по обе стороны океана: их «книжного агента» в Москве Бориса Иванова, Беллу Дижур, Николая Петрова, Салли Рубл, Леонида Седова, Александра Синельникова, Наю Смородинскую, Людмилу Смыковскую, Владимира Фрумкина, Виктора Штейна, а также работниц быв. магазина Виктора Камкина в Вашингтоне и особенно Наташу Никитину.

Книга о городе выглядит бедной, если в ней нет карт и иллюстраций. Поэтому с самого начала была поставлена задача избежать этого недостатка. Карты сопровождают три главы, и их авторы — Р. Гохстанд, П. Ильин и М. Каган — глубоко признательны Дэйвиду Фуллеру (David Fuller) и Дэйвиду Дейсу (David Deis) из картографической лаборатории Университета штата Калифорния в Нортридже (Лос-Анджелес) за их участие в разработке этих карт. Что же касается иллюстраций, то было решено помещать в книгу оригинальные фотографии, репродукции подлинных почтовых открыток и фотоснимки из книг, изданных в интересующее нас время, — так, чтобы их можно было «предъявить». И мы весьма благодарны всем, кто помог нам справиться с этой задачей: москвичам Борису Иванову и Григорию Каганову, Ингрид Хёнш (Ingrid Hoencsh) из Лейпцига (Германия), жителям Нового Света Вадиму Алцкану, Александру Кириллову, Ирине Кузес, Эдуарду Раснеру, Брюсу Тапперу (Bruce Tapper). Мы также признательны Аллисон Абрамс (Allison Abrams), Кристоферу Гейту (Christopher Gait) и Ирине Хомутовой за помощь в работе над рукописью.

Особо мы хотели бы отметить поддержку, оказанную нам Юрием Александровичем Айхенвальдом, замечательным человеком, ученым, поэтом и публицистом. Запомнились длинные разговоры, которые мы вели с ним в Вашингтоне, обсуждая планы будущей книги и его участия в ней. Неожиданная смерть Юрия Александровича прервала наше сотрудничество.

Отдельные главы книги были представлены их авторами на съездах Американской ассоциации славистов и Ассоциации американских географов. Замечания и предложения, высказанные в дискуссиях на съездах, несомненно, помогли нам в работе.

На рубеже XIX и XX вв. человечество еще не имело представления об электронно-вычислительных машинах, что не мешало, однако, совершать великие научные открытия, изобретать замечательные машины, создавать бессмертные произведения литературы и искусства. Теперь же мы не мыслим жизни без компьютера, а он иногда требует особого умения. И мы в высшей степени благодарны Владимиру Котлеру и Виктору Прудовскому, без которых мы не справились бы с возникавшими трудностями.

Наконец, мы выражаем сердечную благодарность Наде и Тиму Бартолам (Bartol), без поддержки которых эта книга никогда бы не дошла до издательства. Мы также искренне признательны Тамаре Рожковской из Новосибирска и Владимиру Штерну из Москвы за их помощь в издании этой книги в России.

Москва удивительный город. Ее можно любить или не любить, но вряд ли возможно относиться к ней равнодушно. Один из крупнейших городов мира, по праву относящийся к категории мировых, Москва — как нынешняя, так и ушедшая, — неизменно привлекает к себе внимание. И мы надеемся, что взгляд на Москву столетней давности, излагаемый в этой книге, покажется читателю, особенно московскому, интересным.

Примечания:

[1] Saul N. E. Distant Friends: The United States and Russia, 1763–1867. University Press of Kansas, 1991; Saul N. E. Concord and Conflict: The United States and Russia, 1763–1867. University Press of Kansas, 1996.

[2] Bouton J. B. Roundabout to Moscow. An Epicurean Journey. N.Y.: D. Appleton and Company, 1887. P. vi.

[3] Цит. по: Иванян Э. А. Энциклопедия российско-американских отношений. XVIII–XX века. М.: «Международные отношения», 2001. С. 19.

[4] Grosvenor G. H. Young Russia — The Land of Unlimited Possibilities // National Geographic Magazine. 1914. November. P. 309–310.

[5] В дальнейшем Т. Рузвельт, опасаясь усиления Японии за счет России, выступил за скорейшеее прекращение войны и стал посредником при мирных переговорах. За заслуги в деле инициирования и заключения мира между Россией и Японией Т. Рузвельт был первым среди американских президентов удостоен Нобелевской премии мира. См.: Иванян Э. А. Энциклопедия российско-американских отношений. С. 459–460.

[6] Так называемый «паспортный конфликт» возник в последнее десятилетие XIX в. вследствие отказа российских властей признавать право американских евреев — выходцев из России, а позднее и всех других евреев, включая американских граждан, на свободный въезд в Россию. «Паспортный конфликт» не находил разрешения вплоть до Февральской революции 1917 г., отменившей все ограничения, касавшиеся евреев. См.: Иванян Э. А. Энциклопедия российско-американских отношений. С. 386–388

[7] Grosvenor G. H. Young Russia P. 310.

[8] Holmes B. Travelogues. With Illustrations and Photographs by the Author. Volume 8. Chicago — N.Y.: The Travelogues Bureau, 1914. P. 5.

[9] Бывший американский посол в России Чарлз Эмори Смит отмечал промышленный прогресс в России как «весьма знаменательный». См.: Smith Ch. E. Russia // National Geographic Magazine. 1905. February. P. 59.

[10] Bradley J. Muzhik and Muscovite: Urbanization in Late Imperial Russia. Berkeley: University of California Press, 1985. P. 9. Российскими «представителями» в первой десятке мировых городов, были, естественно, Москва и Петербург, американскими — Нью-Йорк и Чикаго.

[11] Holmes B. Travelogues. P. 115.

[12] Иллюстрацией такого замалчивания может служить второе издание Большой Советской Энциклопедии. Например, из пятидесяти иллюстраций к статье «Москва» только на одной изображено здание, построенное в конце XIX — начале XX в., и то только потому, что в нем размещался Центральный музей В. И. Ленина.

См.: Большая Советская Энциклопедия. 2-е изд. Т. 28. М., 1954. С. 361–386.

[13] Среди первых безусловно правдивых и объективных работ об искусстве этого периода следует назвать книги: Стернин Г. Художественная жизнь России на рубеже XIX–XX веков. М.: Искусство, 1970; Борисова Е., Каждая Т. Русская архитектура конца XIX — начала XX века. М.: Наука, 1971; Сарабьянов Д. Русская живопись конца 1900-х — начала 1910-х годов. Очерки. М., 1971; Кириченко Е. Федор Шехтель. М.: Стройиздат, 1973.

[14] П. Ильин.

[15] Гостанд (Гохстанд) Р. Эволюция московской розничной торговли с XIX века // Историческая география. Международная география — 76. М.: XXIII Международный географический конгресс, 1976. С. 47–50 (опубликовано также на англ, языке). См. также: Gohstand R. The Internal Geography of Trade in Moscow from the Mid-nineteenth Century to the First World War. Ph. D. Dissertation (Department of Geography, University of California, Berkeley, 1973).

[16] Gohstand R. Moscow: Aspects of Urban Morphology. Maps. Design and Graphics: David L. Fuller. Washington, D.C.: Association of American Geographers, 1976.

[17] Другой автор этой книги, Микаэлла Каган, любит вспоминать, как директору института, в котором она работала, группа зарубежных ученых — гостей института преподнесла изданный на Западе подробный план Москвы, выполненный без искажений. Не успела закрыться дверь за гостями, как этот план был «захвачен» начальником секретного отдела и похоронен в его сейфах.

[18] Bater James H. «The Industrialization of Moscow and St. Petersburg», and «Modernization and the Municipality: Moscow and St. Petersburg on the Eve of the Great War». Studies in Russian Historical Geography / Eds. James H. Bater and R. A. French. London — N.Y.: Academic Press, 1983. Vol. 2. P. 279–303 and 305–327; Bradley J. Muzhik and Muscovite: Urbanization in Late Imperial Russia. Berkeley: University of California Press, 1985; Brumfield W. C. The Origins of Modernism in Russian Architecture. Berkeley: University of California Press, 1991; Chase W. J. Workers, Society, and the Soviet State. Labor and Life in Moscow, 1918–1929. Urbana — Chicago: University of Illinois Press, 1987; Gleason W. Public Health, Politics, and Cities in Late Imperial Russia // Journal of Urban History. 16, no. 4. August 1990. P. 341–365; Colton T. J. Moscow. Governing the Socialist Metropolis. Cambridge: Harvard University Press, 1995; Engelstein L. Moscow, 1905. Working-Class Organization and Political Conflict. Stanford, Cal.: Stanford University Press, 1982; Hoffman D. L. Peasant Metropolis: Social Identities in Moscow, 1929–1941. Ithaca, N.Y.: Cornell University Press, 1994; Johnson R. E. Peasant and Proletarian: The Working Class of Moscow in the Late-Nineteenth Century.

New Brunswick, N.J.: Rutgers University Press, 1979; Koenke D. Moscow Workers and the 1917 Revolution. Princeton, N.J.: Princeton University Press, 1981; Owen T.C. Capitalism and Politics in Russia: A Social History of the Moscow Merchants. 1855–1905. N.Y.: Cambridge University Press, 1981; Rieber A.J. Merchants and Entrepreneurs in Imperial Russia. Chapel Hill: University of North Carolina Press, 1982; Ruckman J.A. The Moscow Business Elite: A Social and Cultural Portrait of Two Generations. 1840–1905. DeKalb, Ill.: Northern Illinois University Press, 1984; Schmidt A.J. The Architecture and Planning of Classical Moscow: A Cultural History. Philadelphia: American Philosophical Society Press, 1989; Thurston R.W. Liberal City, Conservative State: Moscow and Russia's Urban Crisis, 1906–1914. N.Y.: Oxford University Press, 1987. Последней по времени в этом ряду стоит книга: Ruble B.A. Second Metropolis. Pragmatic Pluralism in Gilded Age Chicago, Silver Age Moscow, and Meiji Osaka. Washington and N.Y.: Woodrow Wilson Center Press and Cambridge University Press, 2001.

География культуры Москвы в конце XIX — начале XX века

Москва дала начало новому русскому искусству — искусству большого города, молодому, современному, свежему.

Борис Пастернак [1]

Под географией культуры в контексте данной статьи я понимаю географию человеческой деятельности в области искусства, литературы и тому подобной деятельности по созданию и распространению творческих, или, если можно так сказать, нетехнических достижений человеческого интеллекта.

Как и любой вид человеческой деятельности, культура имеет свою территориальную дифференциацию, или, иначе говоря, свою географию. Если мы обратимся к карте любой страны, то увидим, что культурная деятельность в ней не распределяется равномерно по всей обитаемой поверхности, и четко выделяются отдельные культурные очаги. В пределах каждого такого очага существует свое размещение деятельности. Когда говорят «театр на Бродвее», то имеют в виду не почтовый адрес некоего театра, а то, что этот театр расположен в совершенно определенной части Нью-Йорка, характеризуемой совершенно определенными особенностями.

Однако география культуры не должна ограничиваться изучением размещения учреждений культуры и их влияния на окружающее их пространство. В ее сферу, по моему мнению, входит изучение мест, где культура производится и реализуется, где люди культуры: а) создают произведения культуры; б) распространяют культуру; в) обмениваются информацией. Иначе говоря, география культуры изучает места с точки зрения их культурной функции. При этом несомненный интерес представляют места наибольшей творческой активности.

Культурная дифференциация городского пространства является таким же объектом исследования, как социальная дифференциация, этническая и т.д. В качестве примера хочу сослаться на заметки Д. С. Лихачева «Об интеллектуальной топографии Петербурга первой четверти двадцатого века» [2], в которых он размышляет о наличии в городе районов различной творческой активности. Однако то, что я называю «культурной географией», Лихачев называет «интеллектуальной топографией». Я предпочитаю термин «география», поскольку топография ограничивается лишь описанием места, а география включает в себя также изучение взаимосвязей между явлениями. Кроме того, вряд ли можно говорить о «топографии страны» [3].

Следует также отметить весьма существенную особенность географии культуры, которая заключается в большей свободе интеллектуальной деятельности от материальных форм. Например, география промышленности — это, по существу, география заводов, шахт и т.д., география сельского хозяйства — география ферм, полей, плантаций, география транспорта — это география дорог и транспортных терминалов. А география культуры, как она понимается в этой работе, — это география деятельности отдельных творческих личностей, коллективов и групп.

В соответствии с этим нас интересуют как театры, клубы, картинные галереи, библиотеки, книжные магазины, редакции журналов и другие культурные учреждения, так и места, где писатели, художники, актеры и прочие «производители культуры» жили, работали, собирались, общались, проводили свой досуг, т.е. занимались деятельностью, в результате которой происходило создание произведений культуры и взаимообогащение, способствовавшее ее развитию.

Ни поэту, ни писателю, ни художнику или композитору для того, чтобы творить, коллектив, как правило, не нужен, они работают в одиночку. Но им требуется творческая атмосфера. Эта атмосфера возникает в процессе общения людей, живущих творческой жизнью, это общение стимулирует его участников. Им важно общаться друг с другом, общаться с почитателями их таланта, общаться с публикой — «потребителем» продукции их творчества. Это же относится и к представителям «коллективных» искусств, например, к актерам, которым мало чисто профессионального общения с коллегами по театру. Людям искусства важно обитать в пределах некоторого культурного поля: возникают своего рода «кусты», зоны концентрации мест общения, в которые «собираются «места деятельности», куда тянет собираться, обсуждать работы, беседовать, где обстановка располагает к творческой откровенности» [4].

В этом смысле представляет также интерес география мест общения деятелей культуры и мест их жительства — «география адресов». Заметим, что пространство «адресов культуры» уже пространства города. Это можно объяснить двумя факторами. Первый: в пространстве города существует социальная дифференциация; деятели культуры принадлежат к определенным социальным слоям, которые расселяются в определенных районах города. Второй: деятели культуры должны жить в доступности от учреждений культуры и других мест общения. Обоим этим условиям удовлетворяла центральная часть Москвы в пределах Садового кольца, та, что сейчас зовется «Старой Москвой».

Рассматриваемое нами время развития московской культуры пришлось на краткий период «нормального» капиталистического развития города, который закончился крушением российского общества в 1917 г. Развитие культуры в этот период опиралось на богатые духовные традиции дворянской Москвы. Так называемый «серебряный век» в русском искусстве связан, в основном, с двумя городами — Москвой и Петербургом. Естественно, что география культуры «серебряного века» базировалась на географии предшествовавшего периода. И, в свою очередь, послужила основой культурной географии последующего, советского периода. Достаточно сказать, что более половины профессиональных театров Москвы размещались в конце 1980-х гг. на месте зрелищных учреждений начала века, и чаще всего — в зданиях и помещениях тех лет.

Давайте бросим беглый взгляд на культурную карту Москвы конца XIX — начала XX в. (*приложение 4, карта 1*).

К середине XIX в. в городе сложился мощный культурный центр, который развился по оси Театральная площадь (с двумя императорскими театрами — Большим и Малым) — Охотный ряд (Благородное, или Дворянское собрание) — Моховая (Университет, Манеж [5] и Румянцевский музей). Большинство культурных учреждений Москвы конца XIX — начала XX в. размещались в секторе, развивавшемся от этой оси, между Большой Никитской и Петровкой и со «стержнем» на Тверской: театры, концертные залы, клубы, кафе, где собирались актеры, поэты, писатели и другие представители интеллектуальной элиты Москвы.

Почти вся культурная жизнь замыкалась в пределах Белого города, выходя за Бульварное кольцо, за редкими исключениями, только на Тверской. Но развитие шло не только по радиусам от оси Театральная площадь — Охотный ряд — Моховая. Эта ось получила продолжение по Волхонке, в начале которой возник Музей изящных искусств, и развивалась далее в большой степени как линия изобразительных искусств.

Вне этой зоны, которую я называю «главной культурной зоной города», плотность культурных учреждений снижалась. Тем не менее, некоторые «анклавы культуры» достойны быть отмеченными, как, например, Строгановское училище на Рождественке, Немецкий клуб на Софийке (ныне Пушечной) [6], Политехнический музей у Ильинских ворот Китай-города, Лазаревский институт в Армянском переулке, Школа живописи, ваяния и зодчества и Тургеневская библиотека около Мясницких ворот Белого города. Примечательна культурная пустыня купеческого Замоскворечья. Первый театр здесь возник только в 1916 г. Но, как и в естественных пустынях, здесь были оазисы. В них находились, по меньшей мере, две жемчужины Москвы: Галерея братьев Третьяковых и Театральный музей Бахрушина.

Здесь же, в Замоскворечье находилась типография издательства И. Д. Сытина. Но редакция его газеты «Русское слово», так же как рабочий кабинет и квартира самого Сытина находились в центре города — на Тверской!

Обращает на себя внимание также почти полное отсутствие учреждений культуры в московском «сити» — Китай-городе. Авторы путеводителя «По Москве» называют Никольскую улицу «улицей просвещения старой Москвы» и даже посвящают ей отдельную экскурсию [7], но это, скорее, дань ее прошлому [8].

Культурная деятельность москвичей выходила за пределы города, но и здесь она концентрировалась в определенных зонах. Так, в начале XX в. в этом отношении явно выделялись дачные поселки у станций Северной и особенно Рязанской железных дорог.

Несколько слов об оценке расстояний в Москве того времени, то есть о том, что тогда считалось «далеко», — это может пригодиться в дальнейшем для лучшего понимания некоторых рассуждений в тексте. «Сезон 1909/10 года я встретил... в Москве и с любопытством стал знакомиться с ее театральной картой... — вспоминал замечательный театровед П. А. Марков. — Немногочисленные театры находились рядом друг с другом, в самом центре. Добираться туда даже от Красных ворот, где я жил, было довольно трудно» [9].

И еще один пример. А. А. Бахрушин мечтал показать свой театральный музей (о нем — ниже) Г. Н. Федотовой, одной из великих актрис Малого театра, на сцене в это время уже не игравшей. Но, как вспоминал его сын, было неделикатно приглашать ее к себе *«на край Москвы»* (курсив мой. — *П.И.*). А этот «край» был у Садового кольца, но... в Замоскворечье, напротив Павелецкого вокзала. Неловкость удалось преодолеть, привезя Федотову в дом к Бахрушину на автомобиле [10].

Ниже делается попытка рассмотреть распространение разных видов творческой деятельности в городском пространстве Москвы на переломе веков. Конечно, охватить в кратком очерке все, что происходило в это время в Москве, невозможно. И пусть читатель понимает, что адресов культурной жизни в городе было во сто крат больше. Так же как и то, что если о каком-нибудь месте говорится, что там бывали, скажем, И. Бунин и С. Рахманинов, то это означает, что данное место привлекало и массу других посетителей: я старался называть, в основном, имена, которые «у всех на слуху». Но если читатель увидит богатство интеллектуальной жизни в Москве в это время и почувствует различия в культурной ткани города — автор будет считать свою задачу выполненной.

ТЕАТР

Зрелища всегда были популярны в России, а в то время, о котором мы говорим, одним из самых популярных зрелищ был театр. Американский исследователь и поклонник русского театра писал, что для русских театр — это «не уход от жизни... это, скорее, особый микрокосмос, в котором жизнь концентрируется и объясняется». «Если же жизнь не поддается объяснению, то с этой ее необъяснимостью можно, по крайней мере, примириться...» [11]

В середине XIX в. в Москве было только два профессиональных театра — Большой театр — театр оперы и балета, и Малый — драматический. В это время в столицах существовала государственная монополия на театральное искусство — театры могли быть только императорскими. Но потребность в театральном искусстве среди образованной части населения Москвы не могла быть удовлетворена двумя театрами, каким бы высоким ни был их профессиональный уровень. Тем более, что с ростом населения города увеличивалось и число потенциальных потребителей театрального искусства. И дело не только в ограниченности репертуара: труппы двух театров не могли вместить всех желающих попробовать себя на театральных подмостках. К тому же не всякий, даже хороший актер, подходит к уже сложившейся театральной труппе.

Естественно, что любители театрального искусства искали различные пути для создания не подвластных правительственному контролю театральных коллективов и организации театральных представлений. Одним из таких путей был домашний театр. В истории русского театра широко известны крепостные театры графов Шереметевых в подмосковных имениях Останкине и Кускове и князя Юсупова в Архангельском, существовавшие в XVIII — начале XIX в. Им на смену пришли театры в домах богатых дворян уже в пределах самой Москвы. География этих театров определялась географией городских имений, владельцы которых организовывали у себя театры. Поскольку ареал размещения московских дворянских усадеб был довольно большой, то и разброс театров в плане города был существенным. Так, среди театров, пользовавшихся наибольшей известностью, один — театр графа Апраксина — находился на Знаменке, а другой — театр князя Юсупова — в Большом Харитоньевском переулке.

Домашний театр в таком виде прекратил свое существование с наступлением капиталистической эпохи. Ему на смену пришли любительские спектакли в частных домах. Собственно говоря, театральное представление, карнавал и тому подобные «легкие действа», приуроченные к семейным праздникам, к Рождеству или иным событиям, были обычным развлечением во многих дворянских домах начиная с XVIII в. В XIX в. с развитием класса буржуазии они проникли и в купеческие дома. Основатели многих московских купеческих фамилий сами были людьми малообразованными, будучи, однако, часто самородками в области финансовой и хозяйственной деятельности. Но их наследники, воспитанные в более культурной среде, начинали интересоваться не только делами своей фабрики или торговой конторы. Не случайно столько выдающихся меценатов выросло среди представителей этого сословия во второй половине XIX в. — на переломе общественных отношений в России.

«Москва, — вспоминал знаменитый московский журналист Влас Дорошевич, — была полна любительскими кружками. Публики не было. Все были актерами» [12]. Зачастую эти спектакли так и оставались лишь приятными воспоминаниями в памяти их участников. Но вот, например, один из корифеев русского и мирового театра Константин Сергеевич Станиславский впервые вышел на сцену в домашнем любительском спектакле [13].

Популярность домашних любительских спектаклей, стремление любителей театрального искусства к более широкому творческому общению, привели к наиболее продуктивному для развития московской сцены в это время пути: любители театрального искусства стали создавать постоянные театральные коллективы под видом любительских. Одной из форм таких коллективов были различные театральные общества, носившие обычно название «кружков». Эти кружки ставили свои спектакли в частных домах, и их география оказалась намного уже географии домашних театров крепостнической эпохи. Там актер принадлежал владельцу театра, был его собственностью, и соответственно жил здесь же, в доме или при нем; зритель же принадлежал к тому же богатому сословию, что и владелец театра, и для него не было проблем посетить представление в любом месте Москвы.

Иное дело новые театральные коллективы,— под каким бы видом они не появлялись. И их участники, и зрители принадлежали в основном к среднему классу, точнее к московской интеллигенции — студенты, профессора, учителя, чиновники, врачи, юристы и т.д. Эта группа населения сильно возросла в период бурного капиталистического развития города и сосредоточивалась, в основном, в Белом и Земляном городе, в секторе между Волхонкой — Остоженкой и Маросейкой — Покровкой [14].

Один из таких театральных коллективов существовал в 1860–1880-е гг. под именем Московского артистического кружка Общества русских актеров. Этот кружок снял бельэтаж дома купца Бронникова, стоявшего на Театральной площади напротив Малого театра, и переоборудовал его в театральное помещение с большим зрительным залом [15]. Так вся северная часть Театральной площади, первоначально создававшейся как площадь двух императорских театров — Малого и Большого, стала окружена театрами.

Как правило, театральные артистические кружки были действительно общественными организациями, но иногда служили только прикрытием для частных трупп. Актрисе Анне Бренко удалось создать на Тверской театр, который фактически стал первым профессиональным частным театром Москвы. Этот театр известен под именем Пушкинского, поскольку находился поблизости от памятника Пушкину на Тверском бульваре [16].

Парадоксально, что театр Бренко прекратил свое существование (хозяйка разорилась) в 1882 г.— историческом для театрального искусства Москвы. В этом году была отменена государственная монополия на театральное дело. И сразу стали официально возникать частные театры и появляться новые театральные помещения — начался своего рода «театральный бум».

Тут самое время сказать о социально-пространственной роли Театральной площади. Эта площадь была спланирована архитектором О. И. Бовэ в 1817–1824 гг. именно как *театральная* площадь, и официально получила это имя в 1829 г. [17] Вместе с расположенным буквально «за углом» — на углу Охотного ряда и Большой Дмитровки — Благородным собранием с его великолепным Колонным залом она послужила мощным культурно-градостроительным узлом, на который в дальнейшем ориентировалось территориальное развитие московского театра.

Уже в 1882 г., сразу после отмены государственной монополии на театральное дело, дом Бронникова на Театральной площади был перестроен, уже открыто, под театр, который стали называть Новым [18] — по-видимому, по сравнению со «старыми» Большим и Малым театрами. Новый театр стал сдаваться различным антрепренерам; в 1909 г. его занял драматический Театр К. Н. Незлобина.

В 1880–1890-е гг. создается театр в доме купца Т. М. Лианозова в Камергерском переулке [19], строят свои театры антрепренеры Ф. А. Корш и Г. Парадиз, открывается театр Г. Г. Солодовникова на Большой Дмитровке (лучшие годы его сцены связаны с выступлениями Частной русской оперы С. И. Мамонтова и пришедшей ей на смену Оперы С. И. Зимина). Наконец, в 1902 г. благодаря меценатству Саввы Тимофеевича Морозова перестраивается для Московского художественного театра (МХТ) здание театра Лианозова.

Все эти театры размещены на небольшой части городского пространства вблизи главной культурной оси города и его главной улицы — Тверской. Но характерным для Москвы было то, что Большой театр остался единственным театром в Москве, который стал композиционным центром городского пространства, в данном случае, Театральной площади.

Другой особенностью театральной Москвы было то, что многие профессиональные театры размещались в переоборудованных зданиях, первоначально для этого не предназначавшихся. Так, Солодовниковский театр с улицы нельзя было отличить от доходного дома. В Художественном театре только спроектированный архитектором Ф. О. Шехтелем вход с горельефом скульптора А. С. Голубкиной, говорит о «театральности» здания (проекты реконструкции всего фасада остались неосуществленными). Заметим, что даже более старый Малый (императорский!) театр имел со стороны Неглинного проезда (ныне Неглинная ул.) фасад, ничем не отличавшийся от многих других фасадов рядовой застройки города. Его помещение было переоборудовано под театр из частного дома купца В.В. Варгина, который, хотя и имел концертный зал (Варгин был большим любителем музыки), но не был предназначен для общественных собраний [20]. Не имело театрального вида и здание Нового (Незлобинского) театра.

В конце XIX в. были построены только два здания, с самого начала создававшиеся как театральные: в 1885 г. в Богословском переулке на Петровке — для театра Корша и в 1887 г. на углу Большой Никитской и Калашного переулка — для театра Парадиза. Оба здания, несомненно, являются характерными архитектурными памятниками эпохи, но какой-либо роли в организации городского пространства они не сыграли: они строились там, где удалось найти для них место в условиях уже существовавшей плотной застройки центра Москвы. В дальнейшем новых театральных зданий больше не строилось [21]. Открывшиеся незадолго до революции первый театр в Замоскворечье (театр П.П. Стрыйского на Большой Ордынке) и ставший впоследствии знаменитым Камерный театр А.Я. Таирова на Тверском бульваре также расположились в перестроенных для них зданиях [22].

В 1913 г. появились две новые серьезные театральные труппы: Первая студия МХТ, игравшая в старом особняке на Скобелевской (ныне Тверской) площади, и Свободный театр К. Марджанова (Марджанишвили) в саду «Эрмитаж». Через год Свободный театр распался на три коллектива: Московский драматический театр, оставшийся в «Эрмитаже», театр имени Комиссаржевской, расположившийся в Настасьинском переулке на Тверской, и Камерный театр.

Почти во всех названных театральных помещениях основной театральной зоны Москвы играли, как правило, профессиональные труппы серьезного жанра, на представления которых ходила соответствующая публика. От них до опереточного Никитского театра, как заметил Дон-Аминадо, «дистанция огромного размера» [23]. Но население большого города требует разнообразия жанров зрелищного искусства. Основная театральная зона имела по Тверской продолжение — в районе Триумфальной площади, на пересечении с Садовым кольцом, размещался узел театров легкого жанра — опереточный театр «Буфф» (позднее театр И.С. Зона), театр-варьете «Альказар», Европейский театр. Одним из популярных мест отдыха москвичей был сад, который первоначально назывался «Чикаго» [24], а после реконструкции в 1897–1898 гг.— «Аквариум». В этом саду также существовало театральное здание, в котором давались, в основном, представления легкого жанра.

Этот развлекательный театральный узел, рассчитанный на более широкий круг зрителей, сформировался на контакте зон с различным социальным составом жителей: более интеллигентной среды внутри Садового кольца и более мещанской за его пределами. Достойно внимания, однако, что интеллигентная публика все эти «европейские» и «альказары» театрами не считала. Так, знаменитая актриса и режиссер М. О. Кнебель, родившаяся накануне XX в., пишет, что в годы ее детства было всего шесть театров «на всю Москву»: Большой театр и Опера Зимина, Малый и Художественный театры, театр Корша и театр Незлобина [25].

Среди названных Кнебель театров нет театра, построенного Парадизом: этот театр отошел от серьезного жанра. Он стал называться Интернациональным — его сцену обычно занимали легковесные гастролеры из-за рубежа, потом Никитским — по улице, на которой он был расположен. В Интернациональном театре одно время подвизался «Фарс» Сабурова — «явление чрезвычайное по цинизму и пошлости» [26]. Об этом можно было бы сейчас и не вспоминать, если бы не одно обстоятельство: его спектакли посещались «настоящей», то есть интеллигентной театральной публикой. В других драматических театрах — в Малом, Художественном, Коршевском и Незлобинском с их серьезным репертуаром было много «звезд», и зритель ходил туда на спектакли, К Сабурову же тот же зритель ходил исключительно «из-за одной из самых изумительных актрис — Е. М. Грановской» [27].

Я задержался на этом случае, чтобы показать, как даже одинокий талант может определять ценность места на культурной карте города.

С началом войны в 1914 г. театральная и вообще светская жизнь Москвы отнюдь не замерла, как можно было бы ожидать. Как вспоминает П. А. Марков, 1914 год «был началом войны и одновременно страшно разнузданной театральной жизни, распространения большого количества театров миниатюр, баров с запрещенными спиртными напитками…» [28] «Кутежи, роскошь, бриллианты, блестящие благотворительные концерты, переполненные рестораны… Бесчисленные театры миниатюр, две оперетты, рестораны, фарсы совершенно изменили прежде строгое в целом лицо театральной Москвы…» [29]

П. А. Марков называет только четыре театра миниатюр, популярных во время войны, остальные, как можно понять из текста его воспоминаний, даже недостойны упоминания, он их скопом называет «театриками». Эти же четыре размещались — все смешалось во время войны — в главной театральной зоне: в Мамоновском переулке на Тверской, на Большой Дмитровке, в Петровских линиях, а также на Никольской [30]. На Тверскую — в Большой Гнездниковский переулок — переехал и самый старый и знаменитый театр миниатюр, «Летучая мышь» Н. Ф. Валиева [31]. Весьма популярным у всех слоев населения во второй половине XIX — начале XX в. видом искусства был цирк. Первое капитальное (каменное) цирковое здание в Москве было построено в 1868 г. на Воздвиженке — но там цирк не мог удержаться долго, население окрестных кварталов в массе предпочитало более серьезные театральный и музыкальный жанры. И не случайно появившиеся позднее стационарные цирки были построены также «на контакте» социальных зон: цирк Саламонского (в 1880 г.) на Цветном бульваре и цирк братьев Никитиных (в 1911 г.) на Садовом кольце у той же Триумфальной площади — центра развлечений «легкого жанра».

За пределами основной театральной зоны находились театры садов «Эрмитаж» — старого и нового. Сначала, в 1878–1893 гг., сад под этим названием находился за Садовым кольцом на Божедомке. Во главе этого «Эрмитажа» стоял выдающийся театральный деятель того времени Михаил Лентовский — «маг и волшебник», как его звали москвичи [32]. Проводившиеся там феерические представления, развлекательные обозрения, постановки оперетты, карнавалы пользовались среди москвичей большой популярностью, но сад, тем не менее, закрылся, его деревянные постройки оказались недолговечны. Почему же его хозяева не стали поддерживать сад? Может быть, на их решении сказалась, наряду с другими причинами, и отдаленность от основной культурной зоны Москвы? Во всяком случае, когда в 1894 г. предприниматель Я. В. Щукин открыл сад под тем же названием «Эрмитаж», но гораздо ближе к центру — в Каретном ряду, то ему вместе с его театральными зданиями уже не грозила судьба «Старого Эрмитажа». Новый «Эрмитаж», который, будучи общественным садом, был призван быть местом отдыха и развлечения публики, стал, однако, местом рождения двух серьезных театров — Художественного и Свободного.

Явным доказательством стремления театрального искусства к концентрации и приближению к основному культурному ядру является так же такой факт. Вновь возникавшие серьезные коллективы часто начинали работу там, где удавалось снять помещение. Так, Частная опера Мамонтова выступала одно время в зале на Пречистенском бульваре, Опера Зимина начинала в театре сада «Аквариум», Художественный театр первые четыре сезона играл в саду «Эрмитаж» в Каретном ряду. Но при первой же возможности они перебирались в «ядро» театральной Москвы: Мамонтов снял театр Солодовникова, Зимин — Новый театр на Театральной площади [33]. Художественный театр занял помещение бывшего театра Лианозова в Камергерском переулке.

Возвращаясь к роли актера в привлечении публики, показанной выше на примере Сабуровского театра, напомним, однако, что в основном зритель ходит «на театр» или «на спектакль». При этом каждый театр имел, как правило, свою собственную публику. Вот как, несколько иронически, преподносит Дон-Аминадо публику Малого театра, явно противопоставляя ее более демократической публике других драматических театров, и в первую очередь, Художественного: «...Не выскочки, не декаденты... а вся первая [купеческая] гильдия, московская и замоскворецкая, именитое купечество и чиновный мир, и уезд и губерния, и лицеист...— в мундирах, при шпагах, и из институтов для благородных девиц розовые барышни во всем крахмальном... И даже в четвертом ярусе, и на галереях, и на балконах,— не жужжат, не галдят, а в четверть голоса разговаривают...» [34]

Но великие актеры собирали публику не только в зрительных залах. Тот же Дон-Аминадо рассказывает, как «толпой выходила молодежь, по преимуществу, женская, в одиннадцатом часу утра на Кузнецкий мост и терпеливо ждала...» Ибо знали обожательницы Василия Ивановича Качалова, что направляясь в Камергерский на репетицию, совершает он свою утреннюю прогулку по Кузнецкому. «И дождавшись, шли за ним... За полубогом...» [35]

А теперь читатель, уже встречавшийся в этой книге с описанием московского «дна» — Хитрова рынка будет удивлен, прочитав, что это место входило в географию театральной жизни Москвы. Тем не менее, это так. В те времена в Москве почти не было печатных пьес, они либо переписывались, либо литографировались. Этим занималась театральная библиотека на Тверской, откуда театры получали нужные им пьесы с расписанными ролями. Но вся переписка велась в грязнейшей ночлежке Хитрова рынка, где переписчики, волею судьбы оказавшиеся выброшенными из жизни, делили пополам с нищими большую комнату. Это была каторжная работа, за которую платили гроши [36].

Если театр был зрелищем для образованной публики, то другие слои населения удовлетворялись более доступными им видами зрелищ, которые, однако, в социальном плане выполняли ту же роль, что и театры, но на другом уровне. Это были, например, балаганы, которые также имели свою географию. Балаганы, в которых устраивались развлекательные театрализованные представления, рассчитанные на более простую публику, располагались вне пределов основной культурной зоны Москвы, преимущественно в местах народных гуляний, главным из которых было на рубеже веков Девичье поле.

МУЗЫКА

Музыкальная жизнь Москвы издавна была очень богатой. В ней, может быть более, чем в других искусствах, проявились социально-географические различия. Серьезная музыка, как наиболее абстрактный из всех видов искусств, требует большей подготовки, чем другие искусства, как для исполнения, так и для восприятия. В разных частях города музыкальные события происходили в разных по характеру помещениях, исполнялась разная музыка, и эта музыка собирала разную аудиторию.

Центром музыкальной жизни Москвы долгое время, — до создания Московской консерватории, — было Благородное собрание с его замечательным Колонным залом. Инициатива открытия Московской консерватории принадлежала превосходному музыканту, пианисту и дирижеру Николаю Григорьевичу Рубинштейну, который стал ее первым директором и дирижером симфонических вечеров [37]. Основанная в 1866 г. на Воздвиженке, консерватория затем переехала в собственное просторное здание на Большой Никитской, которое было капитально перестроено для нее в 1890-х гг. [38] С этого времени консерватория с ее двумя зрительными залами — Большим и Малым — стала центром классической музыки в Москве. Здесь исполнялась как западноевропейская симфоническая, так и русская музыка, ставились оперные спектакли.

Основными слушателями в залах консерватории были интеллигентные представители высших и средних классов общества. Но помимо этих платных концертов, музыканты, входившие в Московское отделение Русского музыкального общества, проводили общедоступные концерты для широкой публики в Колонном зале и в Манеже. Концерты устраивали также Московское филармоническое общество, Московское хоровое общество, Кружок любителей русской музыки, Артистический кружок и другие объединения музыкантов. Концерты русской и зарубежной музыки — «Музыкальные выставки» — проводились в Синодальном училище хорового пения, находившемся на Большой Никитской по соседству с консерваторией.

Концертная деятельность явно тяготела к основной культурной зоне Москвы. Добавим, что частные оперы — сначала опера Мамонтова, затем опера Зимина (не говоря уже о Большом театре) давали представления все в том же секторе города. Очень богата была музыкальными традициями Поварская с окружающими ее переулками [39]. Заметной культурной точкой в этих местах было училище сестер Гнесиных. Сначала сестры организовали училище в своей квартире в Гагаринском переулке на Арбате, а через несколько лет они сняли для себя и для училища небольшой особняк между Арбатом и Поварской — на Собачьей площадке [40]. Неподалеку, на самой Поварской, находились женские музыкальные курсы Н. А. Муромцевой, а в Мерзляковском переулке — музыкальная школа В. Ю. Зограф-Плаксиной. В этой школе состоялось первое публичное выступление Марины Цветаевой — она играла в ученическом концерте [41].

Музыка составляла неотъемлемую часть жизни всех социальных групп, неотъемлемую часть многих событий — как больших праздничных, так и повседневной жизни. Но обычные музыкальные формы в мещанской городской среде были иные. В конце XIX в. стали популярны хоры — хоры русской народной песни, цыганские хоры. Эти музыкальные формы были доступны весьма широком слоям населения. Хоровые концерты собирали обширную аудиторию.

Широкое распространение получил жанр городского романса. В домах среднего достатка романсы исполняли в домашних концертах под аккомпанемент фортепиано, а в более бедных — под гитару. На рабочих окраинах жила своя музыка — здесь пели русские песни под гитару и гармошку.

КИНО

Накануне XX в. в Москву пришел новый вид зрелищного искусства — синематограф: первые киносеансы состоялись в мае 1896 г. в театре Солодовникова и в саду «Эрмитаж», затем кинопрограммы показывались во временных помещениях на Девичьем поле [42]. На исходе 1897 г. открылся первый в Москве кинотеатр — «Электрический театр» в здании Верхних торговых рядов, просуществовавший около полугода [43]. Первые же более или менее постоянные кинотеатры появились в 1903–1904 гг. В 1913 г. в Москве было 67 кинотеатров [44]. Их расположение в городе отличалось от расположения театров, и эти различия в выборе места объяснялись отличиями кино от театрального искусства.

В театре процессы создания спектакля и его представления пространственно совмещены. В каждый момент времени спектакль может быть показан только в одном месте — как правило, это происходит в месте его создания (в данном театре). В кино процессы создания фильма и его демонстрации оторваны друг от друга. Однажды созданный на любой кинофабрике фильм тиражируется и может быть показан в любом месте, где есть киноустановка.

Театральные представления рассчитаны на публику, подготовленную к восприятию сценического искусства, в этом смысле — на элитарную публику (не случайно существует понятие «театральная публика»). Кино, как вид искусства, рассчитано на массового зрителя. Кроме того, кинотеатр не требует столь сложного и дорогостоящего оборудования, как театр. Поэтому размещение кинотеатров в плане города намного шире, чем размещение театров. Конечно, больше всего их было в центре и самой «кинематографической» улицей слыла Тверская, на которой — от центра до нынешнего Белорусского вокзала [45] — в 1916–1917 гг. можно было встретить более десяти «синематографов», но посмотреть кино можно было и во многих других местах, в том числе периферийных, — на Нижней Масловке и в Марьиной роще, на Палихе и Новослободской, в Сокольниках и на Преображенке, на Таганке и на Яузской, на Пятницкой и Шаболовке, в Дорогомилове и на Сущевском валу [46]. Но и здесь есть свои закономерности: устроители стремились размещать кинотеатры на главных магистралях города, отдавая при этом предпочтение транспортным узлам, каковыми являлись места пересечения главных улиц Москвы с Бульварным и Садовым кольцами.

Первые кинотеатры размещались в жилых домах, часть помещений которых приспосабливалась под кинозалы [47]. Затем стали строить специальные здания: «Художественный» на Арбатской площади, «Колизей» на Чистопрудном бульваре, «Форум» на Садово-Сухаревской улице [48], «Великан» на Серпуховской площади. В только что построенной гостинице «Метрополь» был оборудован трехзальный кинотеатр «Модерн». Капитально, подобно многим театральным помещениям, были переоборудованы под кинотеатры старые дома на Триумфальной площади — для кинотеатра А. А. Ханжонкова, основателя первой московской кинофабрики, и на Сретенке — для кинотеатра «Уран» [49].

В кинотеатрах перед экраном устраивалась сцена, на которой сидел тапер, сопровождавший своей игрой действие на немом в те времена экране. В обширных фойе играл оркестр, под который танцевали зрители, ожидавшие своего сеанса. Устраивались даже симфонические концерты. Стало традицией прийти в кинотеатр пораньше и закусить или выпить чего-нибудь легкого в буфете. Верхнюю одежду можно было оставить в гардеробе.

Интересно отметить, что сама архитектура зданий кинотеатров была как бы продолжением архитектуры театров. В качестве типичного примера можно привести кинотеатр «Колизей», построенный в 1912–1914 гг. архитектором Р. И. Клейном. Вход в «Колизей» был выполнен в классическом стиле, который казался более подходящим для театральных зданий, в зале были балкон и ложи. Здания кинотеатров, их залы и фойе стремились украшать мрамором, хрустальными люстрами. Эти элементы декора также напоминали стиль украшения театральных зданий [50].

МУЗЕИ

Согласно последнему дореволюционному московскому путеводителю издательства братьев Сабашниковых, который неоднократно здесь цитируется, в Москве накануне революции насчитывалось около пятидесяти музеев и галерей, как публичных, так и частных [51]. Среди них были музеи исторические, технические, художественные, медицинские, естественно-научные, сельскохозяйственные, педагогические, мемориальные... Их размещение в плане города зависело, в первую очередь, от того, кому принадлежал тот или иной музей. И, конечно, не удивительно, что большинство из них находились в пределах главной культурной зоны города [52]. К сожалению, здесь нет возможности рассказать о всех московских музеях, и я остановлюсь лишь на немногих, наиболее выдающихся.

В самом центре Москвы, в ее культурном ядре, размещались государственные музеи — Румянцевский и Исторический. Румянцевский музей, первоначально представлявший собрание графа Н. П. Румянцева, перевезенное в 1861 г. из Петербурга, располагался в одном из самых замечательных зданий Москвы — в доме Пашкова на Моховой [53]. В его состав входили этнографический музей, картинная галерея и библиотека, которые постоянно пополнялись благодаря частным пожертвованиям.

Возникновение Исторического музея иное. Он был задуман как главный музей, отражающий историю России, и его непосредственными создателями были историки и археологи граф А. С. Уваров и И. Е. Забелин [54]. Это происходило на волне подъема интереса русского общества к своей истории, и место для Российского Исторического музея было выбрано, что называется, самое центральное из всех центральных в России — Красная площадь. Здание музея спроектировал в «русском» стиле архитектор В. О. Шервуд.

Идея устройства Исторического музея зародилась во время московской Политехнической выставки 1872 г., проходившей у Варварских ворот Китай-города. Как наследство этой выставки появился еще один музей — Политехнический, или Музей прикладных знаний. Интересно, что если для Исторического музея был выбран исторический центр города — Красная площадь, то для Политехнического — место вблизи ее делового центра, у Ильинских ворот Китай-города. Этот музей был построен архитектором И. А. Монигетти тоже в «русском» стиле, и впоследствии расширен, причем в архитектуре его новых зданий также можно видеть русские мотивы.

Еще один общественный музей в центре города появился в 1880-х гг. — и тоже на волне интереса к истории России. В 1882 г. на Ходынском поле проходила Всероссийская художественно-промышленная выставка, на которой были широко представлены народные промыслы Московской губернии. На их экспозиции был создан Торгово-промышленный музей кустарных изделий Московского губернского земства, или, попросту, Кустарный музей, который временно разместился в приспособленных для него помещениях сначала на Знаменке, а потом у Никитских ворот [55]. Постоянное место музей обрел в первые годы XX в., когда архитектор С. У. Соловьев переделал для него старые палаты в Леонтьевском переулке [56]. Но, в отличие от домов перестраивавшихся под театры, фасад Кустарного музея был сделан заново, причем тоже в «русском» стиле.

Совсем по-иному был задуман и выполнен облик Музея изящных искусств имени императора Александра III, созданного по инициативе и под руководством профессора Московского университета И. В. Цветаева как учебный музей университета: он был построен на месте бывшего Колымажного двора на Волхонке [57] в классическом стиле. Этот стиль был выбран архитектором Клейном в соответствии с назначением здания и в русле традиционно принятого в Европе направления в музейном строительстве (Лондон, Будапешт и др.) [58].

Справил новоселье и еще один, но уже естественный музей Университета — Зоологический. Этот музей, существовавший к этому времени уже более ста лет, перестал, наконец, ютиться в своем старом тесном помещении и переехал в специально построенное для него здание в составе университетского комплекса на Большой Никитской (архитектор К. М. Бычковский).

Как мы видим, для общественных музеев Москвы было принято в это время строить новые индивидуальные здания. В результате центральная часть Москвы оказалась местом сосредоточения ряда публичных музеев, представлявших большую культурную ценность. К названным музеям надо прибавить еще один, самый старый музей в Москве — Оружейную палату в Кремле [59].

Но среди экспозиций всех этих музеев почти отсутствовало изобразительное искусство, ему целиком была посвящена одна лишь картинная галерея Румянцевского музея [60]. Дело, по-видимому, в том, что организаторы названных музеев ставили перед собой, в основном, либо идеологические, либо практические задачи, либо научные и учебные цели. Коллекционирование предметов искусства было в Москве почти исключительно делом частных лиц. Этим Москва отличалась от Петербурга, где уже давно существовал императорский «Эрмитаж».

В то же время неудивительно, что в Москве — древней столице России — раньше, чем в Петербурге проявился интерес к русскому искусству. Скачок в развитии коллекционирования произведений искусства произошел с ростом купеческого сословия. У многих его представителей развивался дух московского патриотизма, и они начинали собирать предметы искусства и старины. Конечно, для одних это было лишь стремлением тянуться за дворянством, для других — способом «благородно» украсить свои дома. Но иногда коллекционирование превращалось едва ли не в главное дело жизни, и в таких случаях возникали музеи национального и даже мирового значения.

Естественно, что говоря о Москве, мы в первую очередь вспоминаем текстильного фабриканта Павла Михайловича Третьякова, собравшего крупнейшую коллекцию русской живописи. Известными собирателями предметов русского искусства были Мамонтовы, Морозовы, Рябушинские, В. И. Гиршман, художник Илья Остроухов, К. Т. Солдатенков, И. Е. Цветков — я назвал только наиболее значительные фигуры. Были среди московских купцов и любители западной живописи, ее коллекционировали брат П. М. Третьякова Сергей Михайлович, М. А. Морозов, Д. П. Боткин и другие. У богатого промышленника Ивана Щукина было шесть сыновей, и пять из них стали собирателями. Наибольшую известность получили Петр и Сергей: Петр Иванович Щукин собирал произведения древнерусского искусства и изделия народных промыслов, а Сергей Иванович Щукин отличался от многих других собирателей тем, что коллекционировал произведения современной европейской живописи и был одним из немногих — не только в России, но в то время и во Франции! — кто сразу распознал значение импрессионистов, постимпрессионистов и их последователей. Другим выдающимся собирателем нового искусства был Иван Абрамович Морозов — «тонкий знаток и ценитель французской и отечественной живописи» [61].

Многие московские коллекционеры были не только собирателями, — они были меценатами: поддерживали художников и покупали их произведения, что, в свою очередь, способствовало пополнению самих коллекций.

Частные собрания начинались в собственных домах. Со временем, понимая общественную значимость своих коллекций, некоторые меценаты открывали их для публики, фактически превращая их в музеи. Первым сделал свое собрание общедоступным П. М. Третьяков [62]. А в 1892 г. он преподнес свою коллекцию, вместе с собранием покойного к тому времени С. М. Третьякова, своему городу — Москве. Вслед за ним подарил свое собрание Москве И. Е. Цветков, Собрание П. И. Щукина стало филиалом Исторического музея и получило официальное имя «Музей П. И. Щукина». Открыли свои собрания для публики Боткины, жившие на Покровке, Гиршман — у Красных ворот, Остроухов — в Трубниковском переулке на Поварской, С. И. Щукин — в Большом Знаменском переулке на Волхонке.

Собиратели перестраивали свои дома, чтобы они лучше подходили для музейных экспозиций, или строили для них специальные здания, приглашая для этого выдающихся художников и архитекторов. Главный вход в Третьяковскую галерею оформил художник Виктор Васнецов, по его же проекту построено здание Цветковской галереи на Пречистенской набережной. Здание музея прикладного искусства П. И. Щукина построил архитектор Б. В. Фрейденберг; для этого музея Щукин купил участок земли на Малой Грузинской улице. Все три названных проекта выполнены в том же «русском стиле». Дом С. И. Щукина в Большом Знаменском переделывал архитектор Л. Н. Кекушев.

Таким образом, география частных музеев (или начинавшихся как частные) зависела от того, где жили их владельцы. А жили они нередко, в силу своего социального происхождения, вне пределов основной культурной зоны Москвы, как например, уже названные Третьяковы, Боткины, Гиршман. Исключения были, и одно из них — это галерея С. И. Щукина, которая оказалась сначала по соседству, а затем, после строительства буквально рядом с ней Музея изящных искусств, непосредственно в «культурном центре» Москвы. Конечно, это можно считать случайным, — Щукин разместил галерею в собственном доме, который мог оказаться и в другом месте. Но дело в том, что дом этот — бывший дворец князей Трубецких — приобрел отец С. И. Щукина, богатый промышленник И. В. Щукин, и в этом видится проявление двух тенденций, работавших в одном направлении: стремление верхушки московского купечества вытеснить дворянство не только из верхних эшелонов политической и экономической власти, но и из наиболее престижных мест города, и, в тоже время, «переход через реку» и внедрение в дворянские кварталы способствовали изменению широко бытовавшего представления о купцах как исключительно людях «темного царства» [63].

Открытый для посетителей Щукинский дом, на стенах которого висели полотна Клода Моне, Сезанна, Гогена, Матисса, Пикассо, Андре Дерена стал центром, в котором художественная молодежь приобщалась к новому авангардному искусству. Представители же старшего, «передвижнического» поколения русских живописцев сходились на том, что со Знаменки шла «зараза» [64].

Второй знаменитый собиратель новой французской живописи, И. А. Морозов, разместил свою коллекцию в своем доме на самой, может быть, «дворянской» улице «дворянского гнезда», — на Пречистенке. Покупал он и новую русскую живопись. Но Морозовскую галерею, в отличие от Щукинской, могли посещать лишь немногие избранные лица.

Особое место среди созданных московским купечеством музеев занимает Театральный музей Алексея Александровича Бахрушина. Этот представитель одной из богатейших московских купеческих фамилий был страстно влюблен в театр и всю жизнь собирал различные предметы, связанные с театральным искусством: программы спектаклей, портреты деятелей театра, театральные костюмы и эскизы декораций, документы и вещи, принадлежавшие выдающимся актерам, различные театральные реликвии. И в 1894 г. основал в своем доме на Лужнецкой, или Лужниковской улице в Замоскворечье Театральный музей, который впоследствии передал в ведение Академии наук [65].

Передача коллекций в пользование широкой публике не была делом лишь отдельных филантропов. Одни собиратели предпочитали дарить или завещать свои коллекции уже существующим музеям, например, К. Т. Солдатенков отказал свою коллекцию живописи картинной галерее Румянцевского музея, а М. А. Морозов — Третьяковской галерее, где она пополнила и продолжила собрание С. М. Третьякова. Другие, как мы видели, превращали свои собрания в музеи. Было известно, что Москве предстояло приобрести еще несколько замечательных коллекций. Во-первых, согласно завещанию С. И. Щукина, его собрание, уже открытое для публики, должно было после его смерти перейти к Третьяковской галерее, где ей было предназначено присоединиться к картинам, собранным С. М. Третьяковым и М. А. Морозовым [66]. Следуя его примеру, собирался подарить свое собрание Москве И. А. Морозов, так тщательно оберегавший своих французских и русских авангардистов от «нежелательного» глаза.

Современные москвичи знают ампирный особняк в Колымажном (быв. Антипьевском) переулке по соседству с бывшим Музеем изящных, а ныне изобразительных искусств, в котором размещается отдел гравюр этого музея, переехавший туда сравнительно недавно. Но музей в этом доме должен был открыться еще много десятилетий назад: владелец дома П. А. Бурышкин собрал великолепную коллекцию предметов московской старины, которую он намеревался подарить городу вместе с домом для организации музея «Старая Москва» [67]. Готовились передать свои собрания городу и его музеям Степан и Михаил Рябушинские, другие коллекционеры...

Рассказывая о московских собирателях и меценатах конца XIX — начала XX в., я пока называл имена только представителей третьего сословия. Но вот имя дворянина, относившегося к высшей аристократии России, которое вошло в историю художественной Москвы: князь Сергей Александрович Щербатов [68]. В 1911–1913 гг. архитектор А. И. Туманов [69] построил для него дом на Новинском бульваре — дом, который его владелец назвал «вкладом в московскую архитектурную сокровищницу» [70]. Этот дом вместе со своими замечательными коллекциями живописи, фарфора и других предметов искусства Щербатов намеревался завещать

Москве с тем, чтобы в нем был устроен городской музей частных собраний [71]. Впрочем, рассказывая о домах, которые хранили несметные художественные ценности, но так и не успели в то время стать музеями, я, кажется, вторгся в предмет следующего раздела — «географии адресов».

«ГЕОГРАФИЯ АДРЕСОВ»

Культурная жизнь Москвы протекала не только в рамках культурных институтов — театров, концертных залов, музеев и т.д., но и в домах, где жили и собирались писатели, художники, артисты, музыканты, в салонах, где проходили художественные выставки, в излюбленных московской богемой кафе и ресторанах, и т.п. География этих мест — «география адресов» — шире, чем география культурных учреждений, однако, тесно с ней связана. И здесь наблюдалась концентрация — концентрация мест, где жили деятели искусства, и мест, где они собирались.

В качестве первой иллюстрации приведем конкретный адрес одного из таких культурных гнезд: Мясницкая 21, напротив Почтамта. Здесь в бывшем доме генерала Юшкова [72], помещалось Московское училище живописи, ваяния и зодчества. Там преподавали или учились (или сначала учились, а потом преподавали) многие выдающиеся художники: Алексей Саврасов, Абрам Архипов, Исаак Левитан, Константин Коровин, Михаил Нестеров, Валентин Серов, Роберт Фальк и многие другие. Но здесь же были и квартиры преподавателей. А в начале XX в. на принадлежавшей училищу земле были построены доходные дома, где также поселились многие преподаватели и были созданы общежития студентов. В училище постоянно устраивались художественные выставки, а дискуссии часто продолжались (или начинались) в квартирах художников. И не только художников можно было встретить в домах по этому адресу. Будущий великий поэт Борис Пастернак провел детские годы в доме училища, где имел квартиру его отец, художник Леонид Пастернак, преподававший в училище. В своих воспоминаниях поэт рассказывает о том богатом духовном общении, которое посчастливилось ему испытать в те годы [73].

Другим заметным культурным центром притяжения на рубеже веков на Мясницкой был особняк, стоявший на углу Фуркасовского переулка. Один из его прошлых владельцев, археолог и нумизмат А. Д. Чертков собрал в нем знаменитую библиотеку, вошедшую в историю книжной Москвы под именем «Чертковской». На исходе века в доме помещалось Московское архитектурное общество, организовавшее там Архитектурно-художественно-техническую выставку, работавшую в течение двух лет. Затем один год в особняке собирался Литературно-художественный кружок [74].

И архитектурное общество, и кружок были, по существу, клубами, объединявшими представителей творческой интеллигенции Москвы. Таких объединений — кружков, обществ, товариществ — было много. Например, Артистический кружок объединял деятелей искусства, придерживавшихся общих взглядов. Кто входил в состав Московского товарищества художников и Московского общества любителей искусств, — понятно из их названий. Но эти объединения не только предоставляли профессионалам и любителям возможность общаться в творческой атмосфере, но и устраивали выставки: Товарищество — в стенах Строгановского училища на Рождественке, а Общество — в своем помещении на углу Малой Дмитровки и Страстного бульвара [75].

Творческие клубы не раз меняли свои адреса, но все их «миграции» почти не выходили за пределы главной культурной зоны Москвы. Так, Литературно-художественный кружок начинал на Воздвиженке, затем перебрался на Мясницкую, потом переехал на Тверскую, пока, наконец, не обосновался на Большой Дмитровке, 15, — в особняке купцов Востряковых [76]. Большая Дмитровка вообще была одной из центральных в культурной жизни Москвы. В ее начале находились Благородное собрание и театр Солодовникова, на ней до переезда на Малую Дмитровку размещался Купеческий клуб, в художественных салонах выставлялись картины, проходили выставки.

Литературно-художественный кружок может служить хорошей иллюстрацией широты интеллектуальных интересов московской интеллигенции: директорами правления этого кружка одно время были поэт Валерий Брюсов, актер и драматург Александр Сумбатов-Южин [77] и певец Леонид Собинов [78]. Как вспоминала современница, «...хотя были разные кружки... причастные к интересам театральным, литературным; профессорские и другие, — но все они соприкасались близко, и везде можно было встречать одних и тех же людей...» [79]

География литературной (впрочем, также, как музыкальной, театральной и т.д.) жизни Москвы в конце XIX — начале XX в. могла бы составить тему отдельного исследования. Отметим здесь только, что представители различных литературных направлений имели свои излюбленные места. Например, символисты группировались вокруг издательства «Скорпион» и редакции журнала «Весы», которые находились в здании гостиницы «Метрополь» на Театральной площади, а посидеть «за рюмкой ликера» любили в кафе на Тверском бульваре [80]. Футуристы открыли свое кафе-кабаре «Розовый фонарь» в Мамоновском переулке на Тверской [81]. И, конечно, литераторы всех школ и направлений, так же как и их почитатели и враги, были хорошо знакомы с Большой аудиторией Политехнического музея, где часто проводились литературные вечера и дискуссии, собиравшие перед входом толпы желающих попасть на вечер, пахнущий скандалом [82].

Излюбленным местом встреч у артистов был трактир Щербакова («Щербаки») в Кузнецком переулке между Неглинным проездом и Петровкой (ныне часть улицы Кузнецкий мост), а после его закрытия — ресторан «Ливорно» или немецкий ресторанчик Вельде за Большим театром [83]. Один из финансовых покровителей Художественного театра Николай Тарасов и актер Никита Балиев создали в доме Перцова у храма Христа Спасителя нечто вроде клуба Художественного театра. Впоследствии этот клуб развился в театр-кабаре «Летучая мышь» [84].

Постоянными местами встреч московской богемы были заведения, расположенные либо в самом центре Москвы — ресторан «Славянский базар» на Никольской, трактир «Большой Московский» на Воскресенской площади (ныне Площадь Революции), кабаре «Максим» на Большой Дмитровке, трактиры Тестова и Соловьева в Охотном ряду [85] и другие, либо за городом — ресторан Крынкина на Воробьевых горах, откуда вся Москва была как на ладони, и рестораны Петровского парка, включая знаменитый «Яр», этот «дворец веселья», который славился своими цыганами — и хорами, и сольными исполнителями [86]. Один раз в году богемным становился ресторан «Эрмитаж» на углу Неглинного и Петровского бульваров. Обычно этот шикарный ресторан был местом встреч богатого купечества, но в день основания Московского университета (в день св. Татьяны — 12 января по принятому тогда в России юлианскому календарю) он становился центром празднеств после торжественного заседания в Университете. Как эти празднества протекали, можно судить по фразе Чехова: «В этом году было выпито все, кроме Москвы-реки, которая избегла злой участи только благодаря тому обстоятельству, что она замерзла» [87].

Центральные улицы привлекали и любителей спорта. Шахматисты проводили турниры в своем клубе на Большой Дмитровке, известном под именем Московского шахматного кружка [88], а теннисисты играли на кортах Московского общества любителей лаун-тенниса (МОЛЛТ) на Петровке [89]. Зимой на месте кортов заливался каток.

Говоря о местах общения москвичей, их времяпрепровождении, было бы непростительным забыть о банях. Баня для москвича всегда представляла нечто большее, чем просто место, где можно помыться. Бани предоставляли посетителям целый комплекс обслуживания: в них были парикмахерские, косметические и медицинские кабинеты, бассейны, буфеты. А главное — подобно древнеримским термам, это были своеобразные места встреч и общения духовно близких людей.

В Москве было шестьдесят бань, и «все они имели постоянное население, свое собственное, сознававшее себя настоящими москвичами» [90]. Бани находились во всех районах города, некоторые старые бани существуют до сих пор. Большинство банных зданий были построены в конце XIX в.— часто на месте старых. Причина этого «банного бума» на рубеже веков — технический прогресс, связанный с широким использованием водопровода и электричества. Современное здание самых знаменитых московских бань — Сандуновских [91] (на языке москвичей — Сандунов) построено в 1896 г. (архитектор Б. В. Фрейденберг). Здесь были даже устроены собственные электростанция (вторая в городе!) и водопровод [92]. Над оформлением помещений работали лучшие художники, в отделке использовался каррарский мрамор, привозимый из Италии. Раздевальный зал Сандуновских бань был «клубом, где встречалось самое разнообразное общество,— каждый находил свой кружок знакомых, и притом буфет со всевозможными напитками, от кваса до шампанского...» [93] Предприниматели, актеры, писатели приходили купаться в бассейн Сандунов. Издатель нотной литературы П. И. Юргенсон даже открыл в здании бань музыкальный магазин — и не прогадал!

Часть здания Сандуновских бань занимали комфортабельные квартиры. Квартиру на первом этаже с окнами, обращенными в Звонарный переулок, снял после женитьбы А. П. Чехов, большой любитель Сандунов [94]. География мест жительства представителей московской творческой интеллигенции представляет особый интерес, и, чтобы показать его более наглядно, я воспользовался материалом, представленным Н. А. Шестаковой. В своей книге, посвященной театральной Москве, она приводит все адреса (кроме временных прибежищ в гостиницах), по которым жили в Москве четыре представителя московской театральной элиты: драматург и писатель Антон Павлович Чехов, один из основателей и руководителей Художественного театра Владимир Иванович Немирович-Данченко, актер этого театра Василий Иванович Качалов, и актер и драматург, а позднее руководитель Малого театра Александр Иванович Сумбатов-Южин [95] (*приложение 4, карта 2*). Как мы видим, большая часть мест жительства этих замечательных людей находится в центре города и в северо-западном секторе Садового кольца, то есть в неоднократно упомянутой в этой книге зоне расселения московской интеллигенции.

Несколько адресов замечательной четверки оказываются однако, за пределами этой зоны. Все они родились не в Москве и приехали в Москву молодыми людьми, поэтому первые их адреса были в известной степени случайными, хотя полностью случайными назвать их нельзя. Так, Чехов, ставши москвичом, жил вначале на заслуженно пользовавшейся дурной славой Грачевке (Трубной улице), на Сретенке и в Замоскворечье на Большой Якиманке (точки на карте с 41 до 46). В эти годы начинающий писатель был беден и вынужден был часто менять квартиру и жить там, где позволяли ему средства. При этом в первые годы он старался не удаляться от центра города, где он изучал медицину в Московском университете, проходил практику в университетских клиниках на Рождественке [96] и в Екатерининской больнице у Петровских ворот, сотрудничал в различных редакциях. А на Якиманке к его двери уже была прикреплена табличка «Доктор А. П. Чехов».

Обратим внимание,—с точки зрения пространственной оценки районов Москвы,—как Чехов отозвался о своем жилище на Большой Якиманке: «Квартира моя за Москвой-рекой, а здесь настоящая провинция: чисто, тихо, дешево и... *глуповато* (курсив мой.—*П.И.*)» [97].

Жить так далеко от театров и вообще от центра города писателю было скучно—ему не доставало общения. И, как рассказывает его брат Михаил, «наш доктор» завел у себя по вторникам приемы, которые назвал журфиксами [98], на них собирались, в основном, молодые музыканты—друзья его другого брата, Николая, приезжавшие с Большой Никитской». Тем не менее, Чехов выдержал в «провинции» всего несколько месяцев—с осени до весны. А следующей осенью, вернувшись с дачи, он сразу въехал в «домкомод» на Садовой-Кудринской—в особняк, принадлежавший его коллеге, тоже доктору Я. А. Корнееву.[99]. Об этом своем жилище Чехов отозвался уже по-другому: «...место чистое, тихое и *отовсюду близкое...* (курсив мой.—*П.И.*)» [100].

«Отовсюду близкое» можно понимать и как «от всех близкое» и «для всех близкое». И «дом Корнеева... мог бы гордиться тем, что в нем побывало столько знаменитых людей» [101]. Вот лишь некоторые имена: Д. В. Григорович, Н. С. Лесков, П. И. Чайковский, В. Г. Короленко... И в дальнейшем Чехов снимал квартиры только в местах, «отовсюду близких». Даже в годы, когда писатель постоянно жил в своем подмосковном имении Мелихово, он, наезжая в Москву, обычно останавливался в Большой Московской гостинице на Воскресенской площади — в самом сердце города.

Находящиеся также не в лучших районах Москвы первые адреса А. И. Сумбатова-Южина и В. И. Качалова, возможно, тоже объясняются скромными средствами молодых актеров, но обращает на себя внимание близость первых московских квартир Качалова к саду «Эрмитаж» в Каретном ряду, где давал в это время спектакли Художественный театр, и первых московских квартир Сумбатова-Южина к Малому театру. А последняя квартира Южина на углу Большого Палашевского и Трехпрудного переулков оказалась в центре «зоны расселения» замечательных актеров — его коллег по Малому театру: как вспоминает бывавшая у Южина Кнебель, в Трехпрудном «жили тогда и А. П. Ленский и А. А. Остужев». «А на углу Мамоновского переулка стоял старенький особняк Садовских» [102].

Вл. И. Немирович-Данченко прожил всю жизнь в центре Москвы, где находились и места его деятельности, главными из которых были Филармоническое училище на углу Большой Никитской и Леонтьевского переулка и Художественный театр.

Большая часть московской творческой (артистической, художественной, научной) интеллигенции жили в одном секторе города, и читатель уже знает, о каком секторе идет речь, — о местах, что звались в Москве «дворянским царством» или «гнездом». «Смутно... чуялось, — вспоминал мир своего детства сын профессора Московского университета писатель Андрей Белый, — там океан опоясывает, ограничивая ‚’нашу» площадь: Арбат, Поварскую, Собачью площадку, Толстовский, Новинский, Смоленский, Пречистенку...» [103].

«Мы все жили в тех краях», — вспоминал писатель Борис Зайцев [104]. Это, конечно, так, но и не так. Так — как символ, а не так потому, что было и немало исключений. О некоторых мы уже упоминали, о других — чуть позже.

А пока хотелось бы назвать еще несколько замечательных точек на карте мест жительства москвичей. К ним, несомненно, относятся дом на Спиридоновке, хозяйкой которого числилась Зинаида Морозова, но фактическим владельцем был ее муж, выдающийся меценат Савва Морозов, а после его смерти дом купил известный собиратель картин Михаил Рябушинский; и дом на той же Спиридоновке, но на углу с Малой Никитской, принадлежавший Степану Рябушинскому, который собрал у себя уникальную коллекцию икон. Но дело, конечно, не только в ценности художественных сокровищ, но и в культурной атмосфере этих домов, которую поддерживали хозяева и их гости.

Оба дома на Спиридоновке принадлежат к числу гениальных творений Федора Шехтеля. Но архитектурные и художественные достоинства дома не обязательно должны совпадать с его значимостью на карте культуры. Так, например, третий построенный Шехтелем замечательный особняк — дом купчихи А. И. Дерожинской в Штатном (ныне Кропоткинском) переулке — никак не может быть отнесен к местам высокой культуры. То же можно сказать и об особняке купца Н. В. Игумнова на Большой Якиманке (архитектор Н. И. Поздеев). Дом этот и сейчас приводит в восторг «москвичей и гостей столицы», а когда он был построен, то один «гость из Америки» снабдил его фотографию в своей книге такой подписью: «Самый прекрасный частный дом в Москве» [105]. Но сколько-нибудь заметного следа в истории культуры его хозяева не оставили. В то же время ничем не приметный дом в Столешниковом переулке был в течение почти полувека местом скрещения путей московских литераторов, журналистов, издателей, актеров, художников: здесь, в квартире на третьем этаже, жил «дядя Гиляй» — Владимир Алексеевич Гиляровский. «Все пути к московским театрам и циркам проходили через Столешники», — шутили современники [106], и эта шутка хорошо отражала значимость места на карте Москвы.

Одним из мест собраний писателей были «литературные среды» писателя Николая Дмитриевича Телешова, на которых бывали Леонид Андреев, Иван Бунин, Максим Горький, Борис Зайцев, Владимир Короленко, Александр Куприн, другие писатели, а также артисты, музыканты, художники [107]. Телешов за свою долгую жизнь несколько раз менял место жительства — Чистые пруды, Земляной вал, снова Чистые пруды, наконец, Покровский бульвар, — вместе с ним переезжали и его «среды». Ни один из домов, где жил Телешов, не обладал заметными архитектурными достоинствами, но на культурной карте города был несомненно значимой точкой.

Надо сказать, что среда вообще была популярным днем в Москве [108]. Чем это объяснить — не знаю, может быть тем, что это средний день недели? Так, кроме «литературных сред» у Телешова проводились «среды» на Большой Молчановке у коллекционера В. Е. Шмаровина, на них собирались до ста художников и любителей живописи [109], а также «среды» поэтов у Валерия Брюсова на Цветном бульваре [110]. На этих «средах», по замечанию Владислава Ходасевича, «творились судьбы если не всероссийского, то во всяком случае московского модернизма» [111]. Собрания Литературно-художественного кружка проводились по вторникам, но среда там тоже не пустовала — в этот день в столовой Кружка встречалось Общество свободной эстетики. Более ста музыкальных «сред» провел обитатель Трубниковского переулка адвокат А. М. Керзин, большой любитель музыки [112]. Так что устроителей собраний по другим дням недели можно считать своего рода «оригиналами». Одним из них был актер театра Корша А. И. Чарин, живший со своей женой, тоже актрисой Корша, в Сытинском переулке на Тверской. Супруги «любили принимать, устраивали «четверги», и народу у них перебывало немало» [113]. «Четверги» одно время проводил у себя и художник Виктор Васнецов [114]. А по воскресеньям в два часа дня художники собирались на «завтраки» у Михаила Абрамовича Морозова на Смоленском бульваре — угол Глазовского переулка [115].

Были, однако, в Москве и другие адреса встреч и собраний, которые совсем не обязательно привязывались к определенным дням недели. У В. А. Морозовой (матери Ивана и Михаила Абрамовичей) на Воздвиженке собирался литературный салон, среди посетителей которого были Чехов, Короленко, Боборыкин, Глеб Успенский, Брюсов [116]. Дон-Аминадо рассказывает о «небольшом, но шумном» кружке литературной богемы, собиравшемся «за стаканом вина и филипповской сайкой с изюмом» [117] у Брониславы («Бронички») Рунт, свояченицы Брюсова, когда она жила в Дегтярном переулке между Малой Дмитровкой и Тверской [118]. Музыкальные вечера проводились у скрипача А. А. Сулержицкого в 1-м Зачатьевском (тогда просто Зачатьевском) переулке на Остоженке [119], у пианиста А. Б. Гольденвейзера в Борисоглебском на Поварской [120], у основателя «Музыкальных выставок» пианиста Б. Л. Яворского в Леонтьевском переулке [121], у того же С. И. Щукина в Большом Знаменском. Масса интересных людей перебывала у композитора А. Скрябина в его доме в Большом Николопесковском (ныне ул. Вахтангова). У М. К. Морозовой, вдовы рано умершего М. А. Морозова, собиралось Религиозно-философское общество памяти Владимира Соловьева [122]. И так далее…

(Здесь я должен сделать небольшое отступление: я надеюсь, что читатель понимает, что все эти «среды», «четверги» и другие собрания, о которых я рассказываю, не всегда совпадали во времени: в этой книге вспоминаются события, которые происходили на протяжении примерно сорока лет.)

Мы неоднократно подчеркивали, что почти вся культурная жизнь Москвы протекала на сравнительно ограниченной части территории города. Однако отмечали, что и за ее пределами были отдельные культурные анклавы и оазисы. Были они и в «географии адресов». На карте мест жительства выделяются дома, хозяева которых сыграли выдающуюся роль в развитии культуры. Такими домами в конце XIX в. были, например, находящиеся неподалеку друг от друга два дома на Садовом кольце близ Красных ворот: дом Саввы Ивановича Мамонтова, который был «приютом для молодых талантливых художников, скульпторов, артистов, музыкантов, певцов, танцоров» [123], и дом фабрикантов Алексеевых, где проходили спектакли Алексеевского драматического кружка, которым руководил сын хозяев — К. С. Станиславский [124]. А в начале XX в.— дом купцов Носовых на на Малой Семеновской. Хозяйка дома Евфимия Павловна (урожденная Рябушинская) превратила его в художественный салон [125]. Или вилла «Черный лебедь» в Петровском парке, которую построил для себя издатель журнала «Золотое руно» меценат Николай Рябушинский, известный своей экстравагантностью.

Один из популярных салонов собирался в довольно странном, казалось бы, месте,— в казенной квартире полицейского врача (Д. П. Кувшинникова), под пожарной каланчей в доме Мясницкой полицейской части в Хитровском переулке близ Покровского бульвара. Фактической хозяйкой салона была жена Кувшинникова, Софья Петровна,— «интересная по своим дарованиям женщина», которая, к тому же, сама увлекалась живописью [126].

Большинство художников имели мастерские (которые чаще всего совмещались с жильем) во все той же зоне проживания интеллигенции, но некоторые селились и работали за Садовым кольцом. Возможно, это объясняется тем, что для художника важен размер помещения, которое может служить мастерской, а недвижимость там стоила меньше. Мастерские Валентина Серова и Константина Коровина одно время находились в одном доме на Долгоруковской; скульпторы Сергей Коненков и Степан Эрзя имели мастерские близ Бутырской заставы; позднее Коненков снял мастерскую на Пресне. Виктор Васнецов выстроил себе дом в тихом месте в районе Мещанских улиц [127]. Михаил Нестеров, который перебрался в Москву, чтобы работать над росписью храма в Покрово-Марфинской обители на Большой Ордынке, стал искать такую квартиру, которая могла бы служить ему одновременно мастерской, чтобы она была и недалеко от места работы, и вместительной, и недорогой. После долгих поисков он нашел устроившее его жилье на Донской улице [128].

В стороне от зоны расселения московской интеллигенции жил с 1892 г. Исаак Левитан, но это случай особый: большой почитатель его таланта С. Т. Морозов, с которым вы уже встречались на этих страницах в рассказе о Кустарном музее, предоставил в его пользование двухэтажный дом во дворе своего имения в Большом Трехсвятительском переулке на Покровском бульваре. На втором этаже этого дома находилась мастерская, на первом — жилые комнаты [129].

Деятели искусства экспериментировали в поисках лучшего для себя места. Петр Ильич Чайковский, чья жизнь в значительной степени связана с Москвой, облюбовал для себя живописные окрестности города Клина по Петербургской дороге. Однажды, в конце жизни, он попытался поселиться на зиму в Москве, но, как оказалось, неудачно. Чайковский снял квартиру на Остоженке, но ему скоро стали мешать посещения посторонних лиц, и он вывесил на входной двери надпись: «Дома нет. Просят не звонить». Композитор, однако, не учел некоторых особенностей московской городской среды: каждый мимоидущий школьник, прочитав эту надпись, считал своей непременной обязанностью позвонить посильнее и немедленно скрыться [130]. Кончилось тем, что Чайковский «сбежал» за границу, а вернувшись, вновь поселился под Клином.

Но не все могли себе позволить такую роскошь. Например, композитор Н. К. Метнер предпочитал жить и работать круглый год за городом, но в конце концов, как вспоминает его племянница, вынужден был снять квартиру в Москве: частные уроки, дававшие средства к существованию, и работа в музыкальном издательстве требовали его постоянного присутствия в городе. Поселился он, однако, на окраине тогдашней Москвы, в тихом переулке близ Новодевичьего монастыря [131].

Студентам в выборе мест приходилось быть менее разборчивыми. Композитор Р. М. Глиэр вспоминает, как его товарищ по консерватории — в будущем композитор и музыкальный критик Ю. С. Сахновский — попросил его помочь ему в занятиях по гармонии, а в качестве платы предложил поселиться в его доме на Петербургском шоссе за Тверской заставой Камер-Коллежского вала. Обладавший тогда стесненными средствами Глиэр с радостью ухватился за это предложение. Его поселили в комнате, в которой незадолго до этого жил С. В. Рахманинов, как предполагает Глиэр, на тех же условиях. Вряд ли этот дом был лучшим местом для проживания музыкантов — по соседству с ипподромом и у дороги, ведшей в «злачные места» Петровского парка. Однако Глиэр вспоминает проведенные у Сосновского полгода с благодарностью, они принесли ему «много интересного и полезного», так как Сосновского навещали отличные музыканты, включая его бывшего постояльца Рахманинова [132].

РАСШИРЕНИЕ КУЛЬТУРНОЙ ЗОНЫ МОСКВЫ

Передовые представители московской интеллигенции искали пути распространения культуры среди широких масс населения города. Так, К. С. Станиславский организовал на фабрике, одним из владельцев которой он был, выездные спектакли Художественного театра. А когда помещение, в котором давались спектакли, понадобилось для расширения производственных площадей, театр стал часть билетов на свои спектакли распределять среди работников фабрики.

Демократические деятели Московской городской думы нашли другой путь расширения культурного пространства: создание народных домов — культурно-просветительских учреждений, своего рода клубов в районах, населенных рабочими и другими малообразованными слоями населения. Развитию этой инициативы способствовали щедрые пожертвования московского купечества.

В начале XX в. в Москве было девять казенных народных домов; они находились в ведении Московского столичного попечительства о народной трезвости [133]. Обычно в таком доме были библиотека, театрально-лекционный зал, иногда воскресная школа. При Введенском народном доме на Введенской площади работал драматический, а при Алексеевском (Грузинском) доме на Васильевской улице [134] — оперный театр. В их работе принимали участие видные деятели русской культуры. Так, создатель Театрального музея А. А. Бахрушин был попечителем Введенского народного дома [135].

Очагами культуры на периферии городского пространства были также высшие учебные заведения. Некоторые из них размещались в зданиях, которые город откупал у представителей старой дворянской знати. Константиновский межевой институт, готовивший специалистов по землеустройству, геодезистов и топографов, занял бывший дом Демидова в Гороховском переулке на Старой Басманной, Императорское техническое училище разместилось в Слободском дворце в Лефортове, а для сельскохозяйственной и лесной академии было передано загородное имение Петровско-Разумовское [136].

XX в. принес новые потребности в специалистах высшей квалификации для развивающейся экономики страны. Возникли два новых института: Институт инженеров путей сообщения и Коммерческий институт. Институт инженеров путей сообщения разместился близ Сущевского Камер-Коллежского вала на севере Москвы, а Коммерческий институт стал первым высшим учебным заведениям в Замоскворечье [137]. К этому времени для новых и расширяющихся учебных заведений стали строить специальные здания.

В 1880-х гг. на Девичьем поле (Большая Царицынская, ныне Большая Пироговская улица) в юго-западной части Москвы были построены здания клиник медицинского факультета Московского университета, а в начале XX в. в этом же районе сооружены здания Высших женских курсов — первого высшего женского учебного заведения в России.

Наконец, в 1912 г. появился, видимо, последний на территории дореволюционной Москвы значительный культурный анклав: на Миусской площади было сооружено здание Московского городского народного университета. Это учебное заведение для лиц, не имевших систематического образования, было создано по идее и на средства московского филантропа генерала А. Л. Шанявского. Сам Шанявский не дожил до открытия университета. Университет, получивший его имя, был открыт в 1908 г. и первоначально ютился в разных помещениях в центре Москвы.

Освоение Миусской площади представляет пример планировочной деятельности Московской городской думы. Существовавший здесь большой пустырь был в конце века распланирован, созданы площадь со сквером посредине, улицы и проезды. Миусская площадь застраивалась, в основном, зданиями учебных заведений [138]. На ней были построены, кроме университета имени Шанявского, Промышленное училище и два так называемых городских училищных дома, в которых размещалось несколько начальных технических училищ. Кроме того, здесь были построены Физический институт Общества Московского научного института и Московский археологический институт. Миусская площадь стала одной из весомых точек на культурной карте Москвы, являясь еще одним подтверждением концентрации деятельности в отдельных «кустах».

За пределами городской застройки Москвы были места отдыха москвичей и народных гуляний. В конце XIX — первые годы XX в. местом гуляния простого люда было Девичье поле. Гулянья на Девичьем поле продолжались до 1911 г., когда они были вынесены за Пресненскую заставу. На прежнем месте они были прекращены по настоянию медицинских учреждений, которые к этому времени заняли уже большую часть Девичьего поля: построенные здесь клиники не могли ужиться с шумом и пылью, которые сопутствовали гуляньям [139].

Другим местом массовых гуляний и увеселений москвичей служило Ходынское поле. В начале Ходынского поля был построен ипподром, а далее по Петербургскому шоссе [140] было место, на котором проводились различные выставки [141]. Два массовых мероприятия конца XIX в., проводившиеся на Ходынском поле, остались в истории России, хотя и с противоположными знаками: Всероссийская торгово-промышленная выставка 1882 г. и катастрофа на празднествах по случаю коронации последнего русского императора Николая II [142].

Места отдыха и гуляний более благородной и интеллигентной публики в это время — Сокольники, Воробьевы горы, Серебряный Бор, Петровский парк.

Петровский парк славился своими ресторанами «Яр», «Стрельна», «Эльдорадо». В теплое время года в парке давались спектакли на сцене летнего театра [143]. Парк был разбит в начале XIX в. при Петровском путевом дворце, пример которого показывает, как своеобразно порой изменение средств сообщения приводит к изменению ценности места. Дворец был построен в конце XVIII в. М. Ф. Казаковым для императрицы Екатерины II: здесь она делала последнюю остановку перед въездом в древнюю столицу [144]. Торжественное сооружение не могло не привлекать внимания всех путешественников, въезжавших в Москву по Петербургскому тракту. Оно могло нравиться или не нравиться, но никого не оставляло равнодушным. В этом смысле поразительно единодушие французского аристократа маркиза де Кюстина, путешествовавшего по России в 1839 г. («неуклюжее дурного вкуса здание»), и пожелавшего остаться анонимным американца, въезжавшего в Москву из Петербурга на пятнадцать лет позднее («неуклюжий замок, построенный в весьма странном вкусе») [145]. Тем не менее, как мы видим, оба уделили Петровскому дворцу место в своих путевых заметках. Те же, кто позднее въезжал в Москву из Петербурга по железной дороге, как правило, вообще не видели этого дворца. О нем, не упоминают ни американский журналист Джон Бутон, ни датский литературовед и историк Георг Брандес, хотя последний рассказывает в своей книге о ресторане «Яр» и тамошних цыганах [146]. Но он ехал в «Яр» по Петербургскому шоссе с юга — из Москвы и, оказавшись в ресторане, до дворца не доехал. (Да и что ему там после цыган было делать?)

Любопытно, что заложенную Екатериной традицию — делать остановку в Петровском дворце перед торжественным въездом в Москву — российские монархи сохранили и в эпоху железных дорог: была построена специальная ветка для передачи царских поездов с Николаевской железной дороги на ближайший к Петровскому дворцу Брестский вокзал. Ветка так и называлась — Царская ветка [147].

Было за Петровским парком еще одно место, которое, вопреки своему предназначению, оказалось на время местом высокой культуры. Это психиатрическая лечебница доктора Ф. А. Усольцева, куда был помещен безнадежно больной художник Михаил Врубель. Здесь, по заказу издателя журнала «Золотое руно» Николая Рябушинского, он работал над портретом поэта Валерия Брюсова, который остался неоконченным… [148]

ПОДМОСКОВЬЕ

Московская культурная жизнь не ограничивалась территорией города, она выходила за пределы Москвы. Это объясняется как минимум двумя причинами. Первая заключается в том, что в течение эпохи, которая предшествует рассматриваемому нами времени, носителем культуры в России было просвещенное дворянство, владевшее землями и поместьями. Поэтому вполне естественно, что те деятели культуры, которые происходили из этих кругов или были связаны с ними, наследовали загородные владения, жили и творили в этих местах. Но таких «дедовских» имений к XX в. осталось немного. Как правило, поместья разделяли судьбу барских домов в московском «дворянском гнезде»: их покупали у прежних владельцев новые богачи — коммерсанты, фабриканты, банкиры. Но поскольку имения были разные, то иной раз такую покупку могли себе позволить и не очень богатые люди, как например, университетские профессора. Несколько лет владел «подмосковной» А. П. Чехов, который к этому времени из бедности вышел, но богатым ему так и не довелось стать.

Одни усадьбы служили их владельцам круглый год, другие — только в летнее время. И многие из них были местом, где творилась культура, где встречались писатели, художники, музыканты, актеры и почитатели их талантов. Некоторые «помещики» сдавали дачи людям сходных с ними интересов.

Вторая причина выхода «культурных анклавов» за пределы города заключалась в сезонности московской жизни вообще и культурной жизни в частности. География культурной жизни летом была несколько иная, чем зимой. Учебный год в высших и средних учебных заведениях заканчивался, театрально-концертный сезон закрывался. В летнее время светская жизнь в Москве замирала. Москвичи уезжали в свои имения, а тот, кто их не имел, снимали дачи [149].

Это, однако, не означало, что культурная жизнь в городе вообще прекращалась — она переносилась в другие места. Во время летнего сезона устраивались спектакли в летних театрах — в Петровском парке и др. Проводились также концерты в парках и садах, например, большой популярностью пользовались летние симфонические концерты в Сокольниках. Однако основная часть культурной жизни перемещалась в Подмосковье [150] (*приложение 4, карта 3*).

Одним из самых приметных артистических мест Подмосковья была усадьба Абрамцево, которой в конце XIX в. владел Савва Мамонтов. В Абрамцеве собирались художники — братья Васнецовы, Репин, Левитан, Нестеров, Врубель, Поленов, Серов, певец Шаляпин, актриса Ермолова и др. Здесь были столярная и гончарная мастерские, ставились драматические и оперные спектакли, обсуждались литературные произведения. Группировавшиеся вокруг Мамонтова художники и артисты составили кружок, известный под названием Мамонтовского, или Абрамцевского художественного кружка. Пожалуй, никто не сказал об атмосфере Абрамцева лучше, чем И. Е. Репин: «В Абрамцеве у С. И. Мамонтова жилось интересно: жизненно-весело (курсив мой. — П.И.)» [151]. Абрамцево утратило свою роль в 1900 г., когда Мамонтов разорился [152].

Мелихово, к югу от Москвы, в истории русской культуры навсегда связано с именем Чехова. В этот дом к писателю приезжали Гиляровский, Левитан, Немирович-Данченко и многие другие — небольшой усадебный дом всегда был полон гостей [153].

Целый куст усадеб, обитатели которых оставили яркий след в истории русской культуры, был в районе Клина к северо-западу от Москвы по Петербургской дороге. В усадьбе Демьяново, принадлежавшей социологу и философу В. И. Танееву, бывали многие деятели московской и петербургской науки и культуры. Одни, как например, брат владельца усадьбы композитор С. И. Танеев и химик И. Д. Каблуков, приезжали навестить хозяев, другие, среди них биолог К. А. Тимирязев, сестры Гнесины, художник Аполлинарий Васнецов, снимали в усадьбе дачи и жили там не один сезон [154]. Много лет жил в этих краях П. И. Чайковский: сначала в Майданове, потом во Фроловском, а в конце жизни — в усадьбе на окраине Клина, где впоследствии был организован музей.

В Клинском уезде, неподалеку друг от друга, находились два имения: Шахматово, которое приобрел ректор Петербургского университета А. Н. Бекетов, и где прошли детские и юношеские годы его внука — поэта Александра Блока, и Боблово, принадлежавшее другому петербургскому профессору — Д. И. Менделееву [155]. Многократные посещения поэтом Боблова кончились тем, что он женился на дочери хозяина усадьбы [156].

Недалеко от станции Тарасовская Северной дороги находилась Любимовка — имение фабрикантов Алексеевых. На домашней сцене в Любимовке состоялся дебют сына хозяев Константина, в будущем великого Станиславского [157], здесь через много лет он обсуждал с В. И. Немировичем-Данченко идею создания нового театра, и это место со временем стало своего рода филиалом МХТ.

В начале XX в. в России проявился интерес к усадьбоведению. Некоторые владельцы превращали свои усадьбы в музеи, как, например, владельцы тесно связанных с русской культурой усадеб Остафьево и Мураново. Но некоторые усадьбы зажили новой жизнью при новых хозяевах. Так, например, заново расцвела старая усадьба Середниково, связанная с жизнью М. Ю. Лермонтова, при своей последней хозяйке — В. И. Фирсановой [158]. В Середниково часто наезжали Шаляпин, Рахманинов, многие другие деятели культуры, а его окрестности сделались популярным среди интеллигенции дачным местом [159].

Москвичи начали массово снимать дачи с развитием слоя капиталистической городской интеллигенции, не имевшей своих имений. Первые дачи были в местах самых ближайших к Москве, таких, как Сокольники, Петровский парк, Петровско-Разумовское, Покровско-Стрешнево, Люблино, Богородское и др. Появились местные жители, для которых сдавать дома горожанам на лето стало существенным, а иногда и главным источником дохода. Стали сдавать дачи и владельцы некоторых имений, — как правило, людям, близким к ним по духу и интересам. Затем предприимчивые дельцы стали строить у железных дорог специальные дачные участки и продавать их [160]. Дачи строились на всех направлениях выходящих из Москвы железных дорог, но наиболее освоенными были территории вдоль самых старых — Николаевской (Петербургской), Северной (Ярославской), Рязанской, Брестской железных дорог, а наименее — вдоль Савеловской и Павелецкой, построенных позднее других. Впрочем, большая или меньшая освоенность территорий под дачи зависела не только от времени постройки дороги, но и от того, по каким местам она была проведена: по пустым и живописным или по уже застроенным. Так, например, Нижегородская линия — одна из первых, выходивших из Москвы, — прошла через уже существовавшие промышленные поселения [161].

Художник Константин Коровин, находясь после революции в эмиграции, так вспоминал подмосковные дачи начала века:

> «Окрестности Москвы были прекрасны. Они постепенно обстраивались дачами, и эти деревянные дачи были летом поэтичны... Понравилось Томилино по Рязанской железной дороге, и там, на приволье, в лесу, близ реки, строили дачи. И какие дачи! Из сосны, с резьбой, финтифлюшками... Терраса спускалась в сад, полный сирени и жасмина. Эти дачи были, как новые игрушки, выглядывающие из леса. В даче пахло сосной, из лесу и из сада неслись ароматы цветов и сена...» [162]

В эти поселки и перемещалась на лето творческая жизнь москвичей. Дачные поселки обычно имели свой центр, прилегающий к железнодорожной станции: общественный парк с открытой эстрадой для танцев, небольшие магазины и лавки, нередко ресторан и... театр! [163] (Потом появились и кинотеатры.) Летом в дачных театрах гастролировали московские и петербургские труппы, выступали маститые актеры, дебютировали молодые. Наибольшей известностью пользовался театр в Малаховке по Рязанской дороге [164].

Упомянем несколько других мест, важных для истории культуры.

В Пушкине по Северной железной дороге летом 1898 г. готовился к открытию своего первого сезона Московский Художественный театр. Репетиции проводились в сарае, приспособленном для этой цели, а артисты жили в снятых для них дачах [165]. А в 1905 г. этот опыт был повторен при создании студии театра, которой руководил Всеволод Мейерхольд. «Пушкино еще раз стало очагом нового искусства» [166].

В Краснове по Рязанской дороге жил на даче Владимир Гиляровский, которого навещали Чехов, Куприн, Шаляпин. Позднее Гиляровский купил себе дом в Малеевке близ Звенигорода. Эти края к западу от Москвы, прозванные за свою живописность «русской, или подмосковной Швейцарией», давно уже привлекали москвичей своей красотой. В разные годы здесь проводили лето композиторы Чайковский и Танеев, художники Саврасов, Коровин, Левитан, Борисов-Мусатов и другие. Особенно любили художники ездить на этюды в Саввинскую слободу, что под боком у Саввино-Сторожевского монастыря [167]. Бабкино в пяти километрах от Воскресенска (ныне Истра) сыграло выдающуюся роль в творчестве писателя Чехова и художника Левитана.

В Кунцеве была дача архитектора Федора Шехтеля, на которой провел лето 1913 г. Владимир Маяковский [168]. Гостями на даче были многие художники, архитекторы, литераторы.

Часто московские интеллигенты оказывались соседями по дачам. Тогда составлялись как бы культурные сообщества на лето. Борис Пастернак вспоминает, какую важную роль в его жизни сыграло общение с композитором А. Скрябиным, когда их семьи жили по соседству летом 1903 г. в Оболенском близ Малого Ярославца по Киевской дороге [169].

И так далее, и так далее, и так далее... Одним словом, тем или иным образом, творческая жизнь и общение деятелей культуры продолжались и за пределами города в Подмосковье.

География московской культуры выходила в ряде мест за пределы Московской губернии. Известны своей красотой берега Оки у города Тарусы. «Первооткрывателем» этих мест был художник Василий Поленов, который поселился на противоположном от Тарусы берегу в начале 1890-х гг. В своей усадьбе, названной им «Поленово», он организовал музей и художественный центр, в гостях у него постоянно бывали художники, музыканты, писатели, ученые. Таруса, город Калужской губернии, стал на рубеже веков популярным дачным местом московской интеллигенции. Здесь много лет жил на даче основатель Музея изящных искусств И. В. Цветаев; его дочери, поэтесса Марина и писательница Анастасия, проводили в Тарусе летние месяцы в свои детские и юношеские годы [170]. Особенно полюбились Таруса и ее окрестности художникам.

Другим популярным среди москвичей дачным местом на Оке были окрестности города Алексина Тульской губернии. Здесь провел одно лето А. П. Чехов, его навещали «прекрасная Лика» — Л. С. Мизинова и Исаак Левитан [171].

Сходную с Абрамцевым роль в развитии русской культуры сыграла усадьба княгини М. К. Тенишевой в Талашкине. И хотя эта усадьба находилась в Смоленской губернии, ее несомненно можно отнести к анклавам московской культуры (впрочем, также как и петербургской). В Талашкине собирались многие художники, в том числе и участники Абрамцевского кружка — М. Врубель, К. Коровин, С. Малютин, М. Нестеров, И. Репин, другие деятели московской и петербургской культуры.

И, наконец, география московской культуры за пределами самой Москвы и Московской губернии была бы не полна, если не упомянуть о Ясной Поляне, где провел многие годы своей жизни Лев Толстой. Ясная Поляна была очагом притяжения не только москвичей, но и культурных людей всего образованного мира.

ЗАКЛЮЧЕНИЕ

Мы совершили культурно-географическую прогулку по Москве рубежа XIX и XX вв., и я хотел бы принести вам свои извинения за то, что эта прогулка получилась несколько сбивчивой, и мы не раз отклонялись от курса. Некоторым оправданием мне может служить то, что культурная жизнь в Москве была настолько богата, разнообразна и интересна, что удержаться от экскурсов в сюжеты, порой весьма далекие от пространственных, иногда было просто невозможно. Кроме того, объем главы не позволил уделить достаточно внимания библиотекам, издательствам, редакциям газет и журналов, книжным магазинам и развалам, в том числе букинистическим, мастерским художников, гостиницам, в которых останавливались, а иногда и подолгу жили деятели искусства. Напомню также сказанные в начале главы слова о том, что адресов культурной жизни в городе было во сто крат больше, чем возможно охватить в столь кратком очерке. И все же я надеюсь, что представление о географии культуры в Москве в те, теперь уже далекие времена, вы получили. Тем не менее, мне представляется нелишним сформулировать некоторые выводы.

- География культуры включает в себя как географию учреждений культуры, так и географию мест общения и мест жительства деятелей культуры и наиболее активных потребителей их творчества — интеллигентной московской публики («географию адресов»).

- Схематически городское пространство можно представить в виде четырех концентрических кругов: первая — культурное ядро, или главная культурная зона города — зона концентрации культурных учреждений и «институциональных» мест творческого общения (клубов, ресторанов, кафе и т.п.); вторая — зона преимущественного расселения интеллектуальной элиты и, соответственно, высокой плотности адресов общения творческой интеллигенции — производителя и главного потребителя культуры; третья — зона преимущественного расселения массового потребителя культуры — средней интеллигенции и, соответственно, пониженной плотности адресов общения; четвертая — зона преимущественного расселения более низких и малообразованных слоев общества, почти не приобщенных, а иногда и совсем не приобщенных к культуре.

- В конкретном городе эти зоны имеют свои особенности конфигурации, которые зависят от пространственной организации города и в большей или меньшей степени связаны с культурным зонированием предшествующего исторического периода. Естественно, что в Москве они накладываются на радиально-кольцевую транспортно-планировочную и социальную структуру территории города. Понимая, что границы этих зон могут быть проведены весьма условно, попробую, тем не менее, их очертить. Напомню, что главная культурная зона Москвы на рубеже веков находилась, в основном, в пределах Белого города в секторе между Большой Никитской и Петровкой. Другие зоны, это зона расселения интеллектуальной и творческой элиты — Белый и Земляной город между Волхонкой — Остоженкой и Тверской, она частично накладывалась на главную культурную зону; зона расселения средней московской интеллигенции захватывала все пространство внутри Садового кольца от набережных Христа Спасителя и Пречистенской [172] на север и затем на восток до Маросейки-Покровки, включая предыдущие две зоны; большую часть остальной территории города занимала четвертая зона. В пределах названных зон были ареалы (подзоны), характеризовавшиеся какими-либо специфическими социальными и культурными особенностями — «дворянское гнездо» во второй зоне, Замоскворечье в четвертой и др.

- В культуре, как и во всех видах человеческой деятельности, проявляются две пространственных тенденции: первая — концентрация деятельности в немногих ареалах, где существуют наилучшие условия ее развития, причем чем выше концентрация, тем лучше условия; и вторая — привлекательность мест, уникальных с точки зрения данной деятельности — независимо от их расположения. Таковы, например, упомянутые в этой главе анклавы высокой культуры внутри зон более низкого уровня, такие как дома П. М. Третьякова и А. А. Бахрушина в Замоскворечье, Музей П. И. Щукина на Грузинах, Народный дом на Введенской площади и находившийся по соседству дом Носовых и др. [173]
- Масштабы развития культуры на рубеже XIX и XX столетий были настолько велики, что, несмотря на все социальные катаклизмы минувшего столетия, основные очаги культуры в начале XXI в. в Москве те же, что были сто лет назад, и большая часть из них концентрируется в тех же частях центра Москвы.

Примечания:

[1] Пастернак Б. Л. Люди и положения. Избранное в двух томах. Т. 2. М.: Художественная литература, 1985. С. 230.

[2] Лихачев Д. С. Заметки и наблюдения. Из записных книжек разных лет. Л.: Советский писатель, 1989. С. 39–48.

[3] Как известно, вопрос понятий и терминов один из самых сложных в науке. Традиционно география культуры, или культурная география (cultural geography), будучи разделом географии человеческого общества (human geography), «фокусировалась на изучении явлений и их взаимодействия в области человеческой культуры (как материальной, так и нематериальной) в ее взаимосвязи с естественной средой» (The Dictionary of Human Geography / Eds. R. J. Johnston, D. Gregory and D. M. Smith. Third

edition. Oxford, UK, and Cambridge, Mass.: Blackwell Publishers, 1994. P. 111. Все переводы с английского в этой главе принадлежат ее автору). Близкое по смыслу определение содержится в Географическом энциклопедическом словаре (М.: Советская энциклопедия, 1988. С. 58); согласно этому определению, география культуры, или культурная география, «изучает территориальную дифференциацию культуры и отдельных ее компонентов...», и ее «следует отличать от географии учреждений культуры». Однако «сегодня этот термин (cultural geography) применяется к самым разным сферам исследования, иногда лишь отдаленно связанным с традиционными» (The Dictionary of Human Geography). Этому, несомненно, способствует сама многозначность понятия «культура» в языке.

[4] Лихачев Д. С. Заметки и наблюдения. С. 48.

[5] Грандиозное здание манежа использовалось для проведения народных гуляний, симфонических концертов, выставок.

[6] С началом Первой мировой войны Немецкий клуб был переименован в Славянский. См.: Москва. Энциклопедия. М.: Советская энциклопедия, 1980. С. 454.

[7] По Москве. Прогулки по Москве и ее художественным и просветительским учреждениям / Под ред. Н. А. Гейнике, Н. С. Елагина, Е. А. Ефимовой, И. И. Штица. М.: Издание М. и С. Сабашниковых, 1917 (репринт, М.: Изобразительное искусство, 1991). С. 192–208.

[8] В рассматриваемое нами время на Никольской остались Синодальная типография с ее ценной библиотекой, музей в здании Старого печатного двора, книжные магазины и лавки букинистов у Китайгородской стены. И еще ресторан «Славянский Базар» — одно из излюбленных мест московской богемы. Впрочем, не так уж и мало для одной не очень длинной улицы.

[9] Марков П. А. Книга воспоминаний. М.: Искусство, 1983. С. 14.

[10] Бахрушин Ю. А. Воспоминания. М.: Художественная литература, 1994. С. 404–405.

[11] Sayler O. M. The Russian Theatre. N.Y.: Brentano's Publishers, 1922. P. 7–8.

[12] Дорошевич В. М. Избранные страницы. М.: Московский рабочий, С. 267.

[13] Псевдоним Станиславский, под которым московский купец К. С. Алексеев стал впоследствии известен всему культурному миру, впервые был использован им также на сцене любительского театра — театра Секретарева, см.: Шестакова Н. А. Прогулки по театральной Москве. М.: Союз театральных деятелей РСФСР, С. 151. Этот театр, популярный среди московской публики во 2-й половине XIX в., находился в Нижнем Кисловском переулке на Воздвиженке. Другим популярным любительским театром в Москве был театр Немчинова на Поварской.

[14] Я предлагаю читателю проделать такой опыт: взять в руки книгу С. К. Романюка «Из истории московских переулков» (М.: Сварог и К0, 1998) и хотя бы бегло просмотреть ее. Этого будет достаточно, чтобы убедиться в том, как резко сокращается число упомянутых автором деятелей культуры и науки, живших или работавших в конце XIX — начале XX в. в восточной части Белого и Земляного города и в Замоскворечье — по сравнению, скажем, с переулками районов Пречистенки, Поварской, даже Мясницкой. Причем чаще всего это были либо «временные жильцы», как, например, Чехов, либо уроженцы этих мест. Один из них — писатель И. С. Шмелев, родившийся в Замоскворечье, жил одно время, как я узнал из книги Романюка (с. 628), в нынешнем доме 27 по Старомонетному переулку. В 1970-е гг. в этом доме помещался отдел экономической географии Института географии Академии наук, в котором я тогда работал. Мы даже представления не имели о том, что здесь жил замечательный московский писатель, да и вряд ли кто из нас читал его произведения: имя Шмелева, противника большевиков и эмигранта, советской властью замалчивалось.

[15] Анисимов А. В. Театры Москвы. Время и архитектура. М.: Московский рабочий, 1984. С. 37.

[16] Описание этого театра см.: Айхенвальд Ю. А. Александр Иванович Сумбатов-Южин. М.: Искусство, 1987. С. 65–78. Владимир Гиляровский посвятил Анне Бренко очень сочувственный очерк, см.: Гиляровский В. А. Яркая жизнь. Сочинения в четырех томах. Т. 1. М.: Изд-во «Правда», 1989. С. 316–324.

[17] Москва. Энциклопедия. С. 556.

[18] Анисимов А. В. Театры Москвы. С. 38.

[19] В лианозовском театре дебютировали театр Корша (в 1882 г.) и Частная опера Мамонтова (в 1885 г.). См.: Шестакова Н. А. Прогулки по театральной Москве. С. 189–190.

[20] Напротив Малого театра в Неглинном проезде, угол Софийки, находилось Императорское театральное училище (по существу школа Малого театра), также занимавшее бывший жилой дом (Шестакова Н. А. Прогулки по театральной Москве. С. 53–62).

[21] Если не считать ряда облегченных и некапитальных театральных помещений в летних садах и парках.

[22] Первое после театров Корша и Парадиза капитальное театральное здание в Москве было построено в 1934–1940 гг. для Центрального театра Красной Армии (Анисимов А. В. Театры Москвы. С. 173–174).

[23] Дон-Аминадо. Поезд на третьем пути. М.: ВАГРИУС, 2000. С. 116.

[24] Название Чикаго было очень популярно в это время в связи с проходившей там в 1893 г. Всемирной Колумбовой выставкой.

[25] Кнебель М. О. Вся жизнь. М.: ВТО, 1967. С. 28.

[26] Марков П. А. Книга воспоминаний. С. 15.

[27] Там же. Известный в начале века театральный критик А. Р. Кугель назвал Грановскую «жемчужиной в навозной куче» (Дон-Аминадо. Поезд на третьем пути. С. 179).

[28] С началом Первой мировой войны продажа спиртных напитков была официально запрещена.

[29] Марков П. А. Книга воспоминаний. С. 77–78.

[30] Там же. С. 81.

[31] О театрах миниатюр в Москве этого времени подробно рассказано в книге: Тихвинская Л. И. Кабаре и театры миниатюр в России. 1908–1917. М.: РИК «Культура», 1995. С. 19–36, 293–376.

[32] О Лентовском и его «Эрмитаже» см.: Гиляровский В. Сочинения. Т. 1. С. 330–334.

[33] С 1908 г. опера Зимина играла в тетре Солодовникова.

[34] Дон-Аминадо. Поезд на третьем пути. С. 109.

[35] Там же. С. 121.

[36] См.: Гиляровский В. Сочинения. Т. 1. С. 344–359. Там же рассказывается о том, как Гиляровский привел в дом, где работали переписчики, актеров Художественного театра, которые готовили к постановке пьесу Максима Горького «На дне». Выполненные участником этого «похода» художником В. А. Симовым декорации к спектаклю в точности соответствовали тому, что он увидел в тот день.

[37] Любопытно, что брат Николая Рубинштейна, Антон Рубинштейн, был основателем и первым директором Петербургской консерватории. Братья были выходцами из московской купеческой семьи.

[38] Как и многие театральные здания, здание консерватории первоначально было жилым домом.

[39] См.: Александровская О. Музыкально-театральные традиции Поварской слободы // Дом Остроухова в Трубниках. М.—СПб.: Златоуст, 1998. С. 7–40.

[40] Этот исторический для московской культуры особняк был уничтожен вместе со всей Собачьей площадкой при строительстве Нового Арбата в 1960-е годы.

[41] Цветаева А. И. Воспоминания. М.: Изограф, 1995. С. 11–12.

[42] Москва. Энциклопедия. С. 301.

[43] Михайлов В. П. Рассказы о кинематографе старой Москвы. М.: Материк, 1998. С. 18–21.

[44] Москва. Энциклопедия. С. 302.

[45] Белорусский вокзал до революции назывался в разные годы Смоленским, Брестским и с 1912 г. Александровским.

[46] Михайлов В. П. Рассказы о кинематографе старой Москвы. С. 41, 52 и др.

[47] Описание одного из первых московских кинотеатров на Елоховской улице см. в воспоминаниях ветерана московского кино Николая Анощенко: Анощенко Н. Из воспоминаний // Минувшее. Исторический альманах. 10. М. — СПб.: Athenium — Феникс. С. 343–393.

[48] В те времена, о которых рассказывается в этой книге, названия Садовых улиц было принято писать так: Сухаревская-Садовая, Кудринская-Садовая и т.д. Мы придерживаемся в данном случае современного написания.

[49] Интересно проследить дальнейшую судьбу этих старых московских кинотеатров. Лишь один из них — «Художественный» — сохранился в малоизмененном виде. Кинотеатр Ханженкова сменил и имя (теперь он называется «Москва»), и внешний вид, став частью нового большого дома. «Великан» (позднее «Спорт») был разбомблен во время войны; на его месте построен новый кинотеатр — «Буревестник». (Немецкая бомба попала также в стоявший рядом с «Художественным» дом, в котором некогда зародилась Московская консерватория, но кинотеатр уцелел). Долго держался «Форум», но недавно и он, подобно многим другим старым кинотеатром, получил к своему имени добавку «бывший». «Колизей» сменил свои функции, о чем чуть ниже, а как выглядел давно закрытый «Уран», правда, не в начале века, а в мои школьные годы после войны, можно увидеть в кинофильме моего покойного друга и ровесника Саввы Кулиша «Железный занавес».

[50] Не случайно здание «Колизея» в дальнейшем неоднократно использовалось как театральное. С 1974 г. в нем располагается театр «Современник».

[51] По Москве. С. 648, 651–655.

[52] Так, например, Анатомический, Антропологический, Геологический, Географический, Зоологический и другие музеи Московского университета размещались в университетских зданиях на Моховой.

[53] Официальное название музея в начале XX в. было Императорский Московский и Румянцевский музей (По Москве. С. 533).

[54] Об истории создания и строительства музея см.: Кириченко Е.И. Исторический музей. М.: Московский рабочий, 1984. С. 22.

[55] Дом на Знаменке, где родился Кустарный музей, не сохранился, а второе его «жилище» хорошо известно москвичам как здание Кинотеатра повторного фильма. Этот внешне неприметный дом на углу Большой Никитской и Никитского бульвара является замечательным памятником истории и культуры. Не касаясь более ранней истории дома, назову лишь три учреждения, которым он дал приют после того, как из него выехал Кустарный музей, и

которым не нашлось места в основном тексте главы: Высшие женские курсы В. А. Полторацкой, художественно-промышленная школа И. М. Галкина и Н. С. Богданова и хоровые классы Народной консерватории. А в 1913 г. дом был перестроен для кинотеатра «Унион». См.: Синютин М. М. и Ястржембский Л. А. Дом большой судьбы. М.: Московский рабочий, 1982. С. 8–9.

[56] Эти палаты XVII в. были куплены Сергеем Тимофеевичем Морозовым и после перестройки подарены им Кустарному музею. См.: Романюк С. К. Из истории московских переулков. С. 155.

[57] Дочь художника Валентина Серова, снимавшего накануне нового столетия квартиру в Малом Знаменском переулке по соседству с Колымажным двором, вспоминает, что «там, где теперь Музей... находился плац, на котором проезжали лошадей, и мы детьми залезали на деревья и часами наблюдали это зрелище...» (Серова О. В. Воспоминания о моем отце Валентине Александровиче Серове. Л.: Искусство, 1986. С. 18). Серовы жили на первом этаже, и в памяти автора воспоминаний сохранился забавный случай, как как-то во время завтрака к ним в столовую въехал на велосипеде скульптор Паоло Трубецкой (Там же). Этот курьезный эпизод мог бы послужить иллюстрацией на тему «Роль этажности в жилище художника».

[58] Эта традиция сохранилась и позже: пример тому, здание Национальной галереи в Вашингтоне, построенное в 1941 г. также в классическом стиле.

[59] Оружейная палата была фамильным музеем династии Романовых (По Москве. С 390).

[60] Залы для художественных выставок предоставлял также Исторический музей.

[61] Журавлев В. В., Сорокин А. К. К читателю // Предпринимательство и предприниматели России от истоков до начала XX века. М.: РОССПЭН, 1997. С. 5.

[62] П. М. Третьяков открыл свою галерею в собственном доме в Лаврушинском переулке. И, поскольку мы изучаем географию культуры в Москве, то нельзя не сказать о неудачности расположения галереи: дом Третьякова было не так просто найти среди замоскворецких переулков. На это еще в начале века жаловался американский путешественник Невин О. Уинтер, см.: Winter N. O. The Russian Empire of On-Day and Yesterday. Boston: L. C. Page & Company, 1913. P. 67. Я сам хорошо помню, как вопросы «Как пройти к Третьяковке?» и «Где здесь Лаврушинский переулок?» можно было часто услышать на Кадашевской набережной.

[63] См.: Clowes Edith W. Merchant on Stage and in Life: Theatricality and Public Consciousness // Merchant Moscow: Images of Russia's

Vanished Bourgeosie / Ed. J. L. West and Iu. A. Petrov. Princeton, New Jersey: Princeton University Press, 1998. P. 156–157.

[64] См.: Демская А. А., Семенова Н. Ю. У Щукина на Знаменке... М.: Банкъ Столичный, 1993. С. 133–135.

[65] О том, как создавался этот музей, подробно рассказано в книге сына его основателя Юрия Бахрушина: Бахрушин Ю. А. Воспоминания. М.: Художественная литература, 1994.

[66] См.: Демская А. А., Семенова Н. Ю. У Щукина на Знаменке... С. 66.

[67] Бурышкин П. Москва купеческая. С. 223.

[68] Предшественником князя Щербатова в собирательском деле среди московской аристократии можно считать князя Михаила Александровича Голицына, который создал в своем доме в Малом Знаменском переулке, по соседству с Колымажным двором, первый в Москве частный художественный музей. Этот музей, известный как Голицынский, открыл в 1865 г. сын собирателя кн. С. М. Голицын, и он же его закрыл в 1886 г. Впоследствии в голицынском доме находились классы Московской консерватории (во время перестройки дома на Большой Никитской), Русское хоровое общество, женская гимназия, лаборатории университета Шанявского и другие культурные учреждения (см.: Романюк С. К. Из истории московских переулков. С. 66–68). После революции в голицынском доме разместились различные научные учреждения, и среди них — Институт философии Академии наук СССР, главной задачей которого было «научное обоснование» того, что творила советская власть, в том числе и в области культуры. Дом, бывший в старой Москве одним из рассадников культуры превратился в рассадник «анти-культуры».

[69] Туманов — русифицированная форма фамилии архитектора-армянина, под которой он получил известность до революции.

Позднее он прославился как строитель столицы Армении Еревана, но уже под своей армянской фамилией Туманян.

[70] Щербатов С. А. Художник в ушедшей России. М.: «Согласие», 2000. С. 321.

[71] Там же. С. 355.

[72] Строительство этого дома, как и Пашкова дома на Моховой, приписывается архитектору Василию Баженову.

[73] Пастернак Б. Л. Люди и положения. С. 226–229.

[74] Об истории Чертковского дома см.: Шикман А. П. Улица Кирова, 7. М.: Московский рабочий, 1989.

[75] Стернин Г. Ю. Художественная жизнь России на рубеже XIX–XX веков. М.: Искусство, 1970. С. 237.

[76] «Из песни слова не выкинешь»: на верхнем этаже особняка был большой зал, где играли в карты, — как подверженные этой страсти представители литературного, театрального и музыкального мира, так и московские фабриканты, банкиры, адвокаты, врачи.

Благодаря доходам от этого зала, кружок мог снимать раскошное помещение, пополнять свою великолепную библиотеку, украшать стены картинами первоклассных художников, проводить разного рода заседания, вечера, диспуты, на которые приходили «все сливки литературно-художественной Москвы» (Вересаев В. В. Воспоминания. М. — Л.: Гослитиздат, 1946. С. 434–438).

[77] Настоящая фамилия этого замечательного деятеля русского театра была Сумбатов; Южин — его театральный и литературный псевдоним. Поэтому его имя можно встретить в разных вариантах: Южин, Южин-Сумбатов и Сумбатов-Южин (наиболее частое в последние десятилетия). Добавлю, что в дореволюционной литературе и на афишах перед его фамилией (любой) часто добавлялось слово «князь» — этот «лицедей» носил аристократический титул. В советское время об этом старались не вспоминать: Народный артист Республики — и на тебе — князь!

[78] «Кружком управлял совет старшин, скорее напоминавший директорию. Из недр этой директории и вышел первый консул, Валерий Брюсов» (Дон-Аминадо. Поезд на третьем пути. С. 130).

[79] Ельцова К. М. Сны нездешние // Книга о Владимире Соловьеве. М.: Советский писатель, 1991. С. 120–121.

[80] Точеный О. Валерий Яковлевич Брюсов // Русские писатели в Москве. М.: Московский рабочий, 1973. С. 766. Пастернак писал: «Хотя у летней кофейни на Тверском бульваре не было своего названия, звали ее все Café Grec», см.: Пастернак Б. Л. Охранная грамота // Избранное в двух томах. Т. 2. М.: Художественная литература, 1985. С. 153. Добавим, что посидеть в Café Grec любили не только символисты.

[81] Это кафе просуществовало совсем недолго. Оно было закрыто полицией после скандала, вызванного чтением своих стихов Владимиром Маяковским, который любил эпатировать публику.

[82] Один из таких вечеров футуристов, на котором выступали Давид Бурлюк, Василий Каменский и Владимир Маяковский, красочно описан одним из его участников в книге: Каменский В. Путь энтузиаста. Автобиографическая книга. Н.-Й.: «Орфей», 1986. С. 140–147.

[83] Гиляровский В. Сочинения. Т. 4. С. 342–345.

[84] Клуб-кабаре Художественного театра открылся в 1908 г. в подвале дома Перцова. Но в этом же году весеннее половодье на Москва-реке, самое знаменитое в истории города, затопило помещение клуба, и «Летучей мыши» пришлось перебраться в другой подвал — в Милютинском переулке на Мясницкой. Наконец, в 1915 г., «Летучая мышь», которая к этому времени стала открытым для публики театром-кабаре, переехала в свой третий и последний подвал в доме Нирнзее в Большом Гнездиковском переулке близ Тверской.

[85] Дон-Аминадо приводит рассказ И. Д. Сытина о том, как за чаем с бубликами в трактире Соловьева Влас Дорошевич, будущий великий газетчик, продал ему, своему будущему патрону и великому издателю, святочный рассказ Гоголя, выдав его за свой. Дорошевич был тогда начинающим журналистом, вечно нуждающимся в деньгах, а Сытин торговал книгами («держал ларь») на толкучем рынке у Китайгородской стены и был, по его собственным словам, «тогда (в конце девяностых годов. — П.И.) совсем сырой и, правду сказать, еще по складам читал...» (Дон-Аминадо. Поезд на третьем пути. С. 65–67).

[86] О местах встреч московской богемы см.: Абарбарчук С. Где собиралась богема. Часть вторая. Москва // Новое русское слово. 13.11.1992.

[87] Чехов А. П. Полное собрание сочинений и писем. В 30-ти томах. Т. 16. М.: Наука, 1979. С. 141. Празднование татьянина дня стало проходить более пристойно с конца XIX в. — после призыва Льва Толстого не делать из праздника просвещения подобия того, что творится в праздники в глухих деревнях, см.: Телешов Н. Записки писателя. Воспоминания и рассказы о прошлом. М.: Московский рабочий, 1980. С. 242. О дне Татьяны в Москве см. также в книге: Муравьев В. Московские слова и словечки. М.: Изограф, 1999. С. 198–295. В начале 1920-х гг. празднование Татьянина дня было советской властью прекращено и возобновилось только во времена «перестойки», в 1990-е гг. Хочу добавить, однако, что на одном из факультетов МГУ его отмечали в послевоенные годы: к этому дню был приурочены вечера встречи выпускников географического факультета. Они проводились в первую субботу студенчесхих каникул, попадавшую обычно на ту же неделю, что и 25-е число — Татьянин день по новому стилю. Мне еще посчастливилось участвовать в них — в начале 1960-х гг. их проведение было запрещено.

[88] В этом клубе начал играть в турнирах будущий чемпион мира А. А. Алехин, см.: Линдер В. И., Линдер И. М. Алехин. М.: Academia, 1992. С. 9, 13.

[89] Фоменко Б. И. История лаун-тенниса в России. М.: Большая Российская энциклопедия, 2000. С. 14.

[90] Гиляровский В. Сочинения. Т. 4. С. 283.

[91] Сандуновские бани названы по имени актера Силы Сандунова, построившего на этом месте — на берегу реки Неглинной — первые бани в середине XVIII в.

[92] Рубинов А. Бильярд в Турецком зале // Новое русское слово. 15.02.1996. Водопровод, подававший воду из Москва-реки в Санду ны, начинался на Пречистенской набережной (Романюк С. К. Из истории московских переулков. С. 316).

[93] Гиляровский В. Сочинения. Т. 4. С. 291–292.

[94] Федосюк Ю. А. Москва в кольце Садовых. 2-е изд., перераб. и доп. М.: Московский рабочий, 1991. С. 205.

[95] Шестакова Н. А. Прогулки по театральной Москве. С. 232–233.

[96] Позднее университетские клиники переехали в специально построенные для них здания на Девичьем поле, и их место на Рождественке заняло в 1890 г. Строгановское художественнопромышленное училище. См.: Федосюк Ю. А. Москва в кольце Садовых. С. 212.

[97] Чехов А. П. Письма. В 12-ти томах. Т. 1. Письма 1875–1886 гг. М.: Наука, 1974. С. 165.

[98] Это слово означает прием гостей в определенный день недели и происходит от французского jour-fixe, определенный день.

[99] Чехов М. П. Вокруг Чехова. Встречи и впечатления // Чехов М. П. Вокруг Чехова. Чехова Е. М. Воспоминания. М.: Художественная литература, 1981. С. 188–189.

[100] Чехов А. П. Письма. Т. 1. С. 259.

[101] Чехов М. П. Вокруг Чехова. С. 132.

[102] Кнебель М. О. Вся жизнь. С. 37.

[103] Белый А. Старый Арбат (Из книги «Начало века») // Белый А. Старый Арбат. Повести. М.: Московский рабочий, 1989. С. 43. Собачья площадка и Толстовский (Большой Толстовский, ныне Карманицкий) — переулки на Арбате, Новинский и Смоленский — бульвары на Садовом кольце. Ту же территороию, то есть ограниченную Пречистенкой, Садовыми, Спиридоновкой и бульварами, понимает под арбатским районом современный «арбатовед». См.: Кнабе Г. С. Арбатская цивилизация и арбатский миф // Москва и московский текст русской культуры. Сборник статей / Отв. ред. Г. С. Кнабе. М.: РГГУ, 1998. С. 137.

[104] Зайцев Б. К. Далекое // Сочинения: В 3 томах. Т. 3. М.: Художественная литература; ТЕРРА, 1993. С. 362.

[105] Holmes B. Travelogues. Volume 8. Chicago — N.Y.: The Travelogue Bureau, 1914. P. 158.

[106] Лобанов В. М. Столешники дяди Гиляя. М.: Московский рабочий, 1972. С. 149. Автор книги искусствовед В. М. Лобанов, зять Гиляровского, называет более ста имен посетителей своего свекра, причем, естественно, он отобрал имена наиболее, с его точки зрения, достойные упоминания. Среди них — Лев Толстой, Чехов и Горький; Леонид Андреев, Глеб Успенский и Бунин; Короленко и Брюсов; Шаляпин, Собинов и Рахманинов; Константин Коровин и Архипов; братья Васнецовы и Серов; Нестеров и Суриков; Сумбатов-Южин и Владимир Немирович-Данченко; Качалов и Москвин; Мейерхольд и актер Михаил Чехов; газетные «киты» Влас Дорошевич и Амфитеатров...

[107] Телешов Н. Д. Записки писателя. Воспоминания и рассказы о прошлом. М., 1966. С. 32–58.

[108] И не только в Москве. Центром притяжения литературного мира Петербурга в 1900-е гг. были «среды» на «Башне», проходившие на квартире поэта Вячеслава Иванова и его жены, писательницы Лидии Зиновьевой-Аннибал (Санкт-Петербург — Петроград — Ленинград. Энциклопедический справочник. М.: Большая Российская энциклопедия, 1992. С. 229–230). Московские литераторы были частыми гостями на ивановских средах.

[109] См. очерк Гиляровского ««Среды» художников» (Сочинения. Т. 4. С. 127–132).

[110] Выходец из среды среднего московского купечества, В. Брюсов провел первые 32 года своей жизни в доме своего отца на Цветном бульваре. Когда же пришло время его покинуть, он остался в привычном для него районе, обретя свое новое жилье на 1-й Мещанской улице. Описание «сред» у Брюсова см. в воспоминаниях Б. Погореловой «Валерий Брюсов и его окружение» (Воспоминания о серебряном веке / Сост. Вадим Крейд. М.: Республика, С. 34–35).

[111] Ходасевич В. Ф. Некрополь. Воспоминания. Paris: YMCA-PRESS, 1976. С. 31.

[112] Александровская О. Музыкально-театральные традиции Поварской слободы. С. 24–25.

[113] Дон-Аминадо. Поезд на третьем пути. С. 115.

[114] Стернин Г. Ю. Художественная жизнь России на рубеже XIX–XX веков. М.: Искусство, 1970. С. 145.

[115] Семенова Н. Русские меценаты. Морозовы // Огонек. 1991. № 7. С. 15.

[116] Думова Н. Московские меценаты. М.: Молодая гвардия, 1992. С. 74–75.

[117] Предвосхищая вопрос молодых читателей «А что это такое?», поясню: филипповская сайка с изюмом — одно из хлебных изделий, которыми славилась булочная Филиппова на Тверской.

[118] Дон-Аминадо. Поезд на третьем пути. С. 144–150. На этих страницах автор вспоминает завсегдатаев броничкиной «полуподвальной квартирки» — Владимира Маяковского, Вячеслава Ходасевича, Вадима Шершеневича, художника Георгия Якулова и еще многих других интересных людей, чьи имена, казалось бы, навсегда канули в Лету, а сейчас выплывают в потоке воспоминаний, ставших доступными читающему люду России. И среди них — сама хозяйка салона Б. М. Рунт, в замужестве Погорелова, оставившая воспоминания о литературной жизни Москвы начала века (см., например, прим. 47–1).

[119] Глиэр Р. М. Статьи и воспоминания. М.: Музыка, 1975. С. 134–135.

[120] Александровская О. Музыкально-театральные традиции Поварской слободы. С. 20.

[121] Глиэр Р. М. Статьи и воспоминания. С. 93.

[122] Думова Н. Московские меценаты. С. 103

[123] Станиславский К. С. Моя жизнь в искусстве. М.: Искусство, 1962. С. 118.

[124] О доме Алексеевых на Садовой см.: Шестакова Н. А. Садовая-Черногрязская улица, 8. Первый театр Станиславского. М.: Московский рабочий, 1984.

[125] Е.П.Носова намеревалась подарить свое собрание русской живописи вместе с особняком Москве для организации там музея, но, как и многие другие собиратели, не успела. См.: Романюк С. К. По землям московских сел и слобод. Часть I. М.: Сварог и К°, 1998. С. 319–320.

[126] Об этом салоне и его хозяйке, которая вошла в историю литературы как прототип рассказа А. П. Чехова «Попрыгунья», рассказывает М. П. Чехов, см. его воспоминания «Вокруг Чехова» (С. 103–105). Он, однако, ошибается в адресе салона, который здесь приводится по кн.: Романюк С. К. Из истории московских переулков. С. 281.

[127] Описание этого дома, выстроенного в русском стиле, см. в кн.: Васнецов В. А. Страницы прошлого. Воспоминания о художниках братьях Васнецовых. Л.: Художник РСФСР, 1976. С. 91–102.

[128] Нестеров М. В. Воспоминания. Изд. 2-е. М.: Советский художник, 1989. С. 340.

[129] Романюк С. К. Из истории московских переулков. С. 284.

[130] Кашкин Н. Д. Воспоминания о П. И. Чайковском. М.: Музгиз, 1954. С. 176.

[131] Тарасова В. К. Страницы из жизни Н. К. Метнера // Н. К. Метнер. Воспоминания. Статьи. Материалы. М.: Советский композитор, 1981. С. 46.

[132] Глиэр Р. М. Статьи и воспоминания. С. 80, 162; Рахманинов С. В. Воспоминания, записанные О. фон Риземаном / Пер. с англ. В. Н. Чемберджи. М.: «Радуга», 1992. С. 55.

[133] Москва. Энциклопедия. С. 450.

[134] Алексеевский—по его официальному названию Народный дом имени цесаревича Алексея Николаевича (Романюк С. К. По землям московских сел и слобод. Часть I. С. 167), Грузинский—по-видимому, из-за его расположения по соседству с районом Грузин.

[135] Ю.А.Бахрушин рассказывает, что из всей общественной деятельности его отца наибольшее количество времени отнимал у него Введенский народный дом. «Дела в нем шли настолько хорошо, что даже был открыт летний филиал театра этого дома в Сокольниках» (Бахрушин Ю. А. Воспоминания. С. 536).

[136] В бывших аристократических домах размещались не только высшие, но и средние учебные заведения. Например, вторая

московская гимназия занимала дворец Мусиных-Пушкиных у Разгуляя, четвертая гимназия — бывший дом Апраксина у Покровских ворот, и т.д. В бывшем городском дворянском имении на Пречистенке помещалась также лучшая в Москве частная гимназия Л.И. Поливанова. Другими общественными учреждениями, под которые отводились бывшие дворцы московской знати, были больницы.

[137] Размещение Коммерческого института в этом районе Москвы не случайно: в Замоскворечье жил основной «потребитель» его «продукции».

[138] Рогачев А.В. Окраины Старой Москвы. Экскурсии для москвичей. М.: МИРОС, 1993. С. 34–47.

[139] Там же. С. 78.

[140] С переименованием в 1914 г. Петербурга в Петроград Петербургское шоссе было переименовано в Петроградское. Затем оно стало Ленинградским, каким и осталось поныне, несмотря на возвращение Ленинграду его старого имени. Впрочем, обсуждать загадки современной России не входит в задачи этой книги.

[141] На планах Москвы того времени оно так и называлось: «Место выставок».

[142] Во время народных гуляний по поводу коронации Николая II на поле произошла давка, при которой погибло около 1400 человек и было ранено около 1300. После этого москвичи стали презрительно именовать ответственного за «мероприятие» великого князя Сергея Александровича «князем Ходынским», а само слово «Ходынка» стало в русском языке нарицательным.

[143] Театра давно нет, но память о нем осталась в названии Театральной аллеи.

[144] В России свойственно все «петровское» связывать с именем Петра I. Но этот дворец получил имя по селу Петровскому, рядом с которым он был построен. Село же тоже не имеет отношения к первому российскому императору: оно принадлежало московскому Высоко-Петровскому монастырю, в имени которого хранится память о Петре — первом московском митрополите.

[145] См.: Кюстин Астольф де. Россия в 1839 году // Россия первой половины XIX в. глазами иностранцев. СПб: Лениздат, 1991. С. 82; и A Trip from St. Petersburg to Constantinople // National Magazine. 5, no. 3. September 1854. P. 214. Восхищаясь тем, как много Кюстин сумел увидеть и понять в России, я в данном случае ни с ним, ни с анонимным американцем, согласиться не могу. Мне гораздо ближе отзыв Константина Коровина, любившего в молодости «пошататься» с дузьями в предместьях Москвы: «Мы подходили к Петровскому дворцу. Я любовался архитектурой. Такие формы бывают на старых фарфоровых

вазах, где пейзажи и все дышит радостью, обещанием чего-то восхитительного, фантастического...» (Коровин К. Воспоминания. Минск: Современный литератор, 1999. С. 202.)

[146] Brandes G. Impressions of Russia. N.Y.: Thomas Y. Crowell Company, 1966 (reprinted from the edition of 1889). P. 123.

[147] Рогачев Д. В. Окраины старой Москвы. С. 145.

[148] Брюсов рассказал о своих посещениях больного художника в очерке «Последняя работа Врубеля», см.: Брюсов В. Я. Из моей жизни: Автобиографическая и мемуарная проза. М.: ТЕРРА, С. 16–25.

[149] Мой отец рассказывал, что в годы, предшествовавшие Первой мировой войне, его семья с наступлением лета отказывалась от снимаемой в городе квартиры и переезжала на дачу, а осенью вновь снимала квартиру на зимний сезон. Такая практика была распространена среди москвичей среднего достатка.

[150] Усадьбы и дачные места, в которых москвичи проводили лето, служили, в известном смысле, продолжением города. Как пишет современный английский исследователь, «дачи были уникальным, с точки зрения развития культуры, местом, потому что они, находясь вне пределов города, оставались целиком урбанистическим явлением; потому, что они собирали вместе людей, которые, будучи обитателями одного города, могли, тем не менее, принадлежать к различным мирам; и потому, что они, как изолированные анклавы культуры «среднего класса» в поляризованном обществе, давали возможность этому самому среднему классу глубже осознать себя» (Lovell S. Between Arcadia i Suburbia: Dachas in Late Imperial Russia // Slavic Review. V. 61. no. 1. Spring 2002. P. 87).

[151] Репин И. Е. Далекое близкое. Л.: Художник РСФСР, 1982. С. 368.

[152] Абрамцево давно стало музеем, но одна вещь, созданная в усадьбе, живет живой жизнью до сих пор: художник Сергей Малютин нарисовал там эскиз первой куклы «матрешка», созданной по образцу японской игрушки.

[153] Как вспоминал брат писателя, «несмотря на... отвратительную дорогу от станции... и на недостаток помещений, наезжало столько гостей, что их негде было разместить, и приходилось иной раз устраивать постели в прихожей и даже в сенях» (Чехов М. П. Вокруг Чехова. С. 156).

[154] Очень тепло написал о Демьянове и его постоянных и временных жителях сын А. Васнецова Всеволод, см.: Васнецов В. А. Страницы прошлого. С. 45–76.

[155] О Шахматове см. в воспоминаниях тетки поэта Марии Андреевны Бекетовой: Бекетова М. А. Воспоминания об Александре Блоке. М.: Изд-во «Правда», 1990. С. 36–37, 408–427 и др. О Боблове — там же. С. 48–53.

[156] В Боблове ставились любительские спектакли, на которые собиралось до двухсот человек. В одном из них, в «Гамлете», главного героя играл Саша Блок, а Офелию — его будущая жена Люба Менделеева. Они составляли «прекрасную гармоническую пару» (Бекетова М. А. Воспоминания об Александре Блоке. С. 51).

[157] Станиславский К. Моя жизнь в искусстве. С. 75–77.

[158] Об одном из московских владений Фирсановой уже рассказывалось в этой главе, она была хозяйкой Сандуновских бань.

[159] Была даже устроена специальная остановка дачных поездов, получившая название Фирсановка.

[160] Некоторые подмосковные станции — Перловская, Загорянская, Немчиновка — до сих пор хранят в своих названиях имена предпринимателей, освоивших прилегающие к ним земли под дачи.

[161] Для меня долго оставалось загадкой, почему была бедна дачами Брянская (Киевская) дорога. Разгадку я нашел в воспоминаниях Ю. А. Бахрушина, где он описывает поездку по этой дороге в Апрелевку: поезда ходили медленно и с большим опозданием, вагоны были «грязные и зашарпанные», станции имели захудалый вид. Мемуарист объясняет это тем, что «Брянская дорога... была частной, и акционеры совершенно не были заинтересованы в пассажирском движении» (Бахрушин Ю. А. Воспоминания. С. 550).

[162] Коровин К. Шаляпин. Встречи и совместная жизнь. М.: Московский рабочий, 1993. С. 186. Однако не все подмосковные дачные места заслуживали столь поэтического описания. Например, Новогиреево (тогда говорили Новое Гиреево) с началом дачного строительства: «...Девственный лес начал беспардонно оскверняться клочками грязной газетной бумаги, пустыми консервными банками, яичной скорлупой, битыми бутылками и прочими следами человеческой «культуры». Огромные задумчивые пруды... были разбужены беспрерывным визгом купающихся и пьяными песнями катающихся на лодках» (Бахрушин Ю. А. Воспоминания. С. 238). Вид дачных мест зависел от социального состава дачников и отдыхающих.

[163] В очерке о дачах Подмосковья (Нащокина М. Гости съезжались на дачу... // Подмосковье. Памятники отечества. № 31. 1994. С. 80) названо 12 поселков, в которых в начале XX в. были театры, причем их перечень заканчивается словами «и др.».

[164] Фасад театра в Малаховке, построенного в 1912 г. на месте сгоревшего, был спроектирован по рисунку Шаляпина, см.: Белицкий Я. М. Окрест Москвы. М.: Легпромбытиздат, 1960. С. 108.

[165] Станиславский К. Моя жизнь в искусстве. С. 237–238.

[166] Вергина В. По дорогам исканий // Встречи с Мейерхольдом. Сборник воспоминаний. М.: ВТО, 1967. С. 32. Эта студия, известная

по ее московскому адресу как «Студия на Поварской», просуществовала, к сожалению, недолго, — ее жизнь была прервана революционными событиями 1905 года.

[167] «Место... дивное» (Коровин К. Воспоминания. С. 147).

[168] Рахманова Л. Владимир Владимирович Маяковский // Русские писатели в Москве. М.: Московский рабочий, 1973. С. 791.

[169] Пастернак Б. Л. Люди и положения. С. 231–233.

[170] Об этих столь полюбившихся сестрам местах и об их жизни на тарусской даче много и подробно рассказывает А. И. Цветаева в своей книге «Воспоминания» (М.: Изограф, 1995).

[171] Чехов М. П. Вокруг Чехова. С. 150–153.

[172] Сейчас это одна Пречистенская набережная.

[173] Противоположным примером — примером «отталкивающего» анклава внутри зоны более высокого уровня может служить бывшая Грачевка.

Москва тогда и сегодня

Город как человек: если с ним не установить подлинных взаимоотношений, то со временем в памяти остается только его имя, а образ постепенно блекнет и увядает. Для того, чтобы установить эти взаимоотношения, нужно научиться наблюдать и понимать его особенности, его «личность», его «Я», его подлинное лицо, те обстоятельства жизни города, которые развертывались в его пространстве и времени.

Иван Клима [1]

Что составляет «Я» Москвы, ее дух, ее индивидуальность? Что из наиболее значительного, характерного для Москвы рубежа XIX–XX вв., повторяется, как эхо, в сегодняшней Москве несмотря на то, что этот город во многих отношениях совершенно другое место? Как старая, так и новая Москва — это город контрастов, город колоссальных богатств и глубокой нищеты; это выдающийся центр науки и культуры, место создания великих произведений искусства; это внешне беспорядочное место, лишенное поверхностной элегантности более «аристократических» городов вроде Петербурга; это сердце России.

Эта книга о Москве рубежа XIX–XX вв. выходит в начале XXI. С тех пор произошло множество событий, оказавших влияние на все стороны жизни России и ее столицы: революция и развязанный Лениным большевистский террор, Гражданская война и нэп, индустриализация и коллективизация, сталинский большой террор и Вторая мировая война, хрущевская оттепель и брежневский застой, горбачевская перестройка, развал и падение коммунистической империи...[2] Менялись политический и экономический режимы. Изменялся город, его население, материальная среда. Изменялось содержание жизни. Добавим, что для Москвы важнейшее значение имело возвращение ей статуса столицы государства.

Во Введении к книге мы заметили, что сравнение разных мест — это излюбленное занятие ученых и путешественников. Но не менее увлекательным может быть сравнение одного и того же места, но в разное время. И сейчас мы попытаемся, хотя бы крупными мазками, сравнить Москву сегодняшнюю с Москвой, описанной в этой книге. При этом, сопоставляя Москву «тогда» и «сегодня», мы постараемся не забывать, что было «посредине», чтобы было яснее, почему стало так, как есть сейчас. И попытаемся ответить на такие вопросы: стала ли Москва другим городом? И какое сугубо московское качество характера города руководило и руководит ее развитием? Впрочем, читатель уже сам, наверное, сделал для себя вывод: главная черта характера Москвы, ее «Я» — быть лидером [3].

ТЕРРИТОРИЯ И НАСЕЛЕНИЕ

В начале XX столетия — в 1913 г. — территория Москвы была 177 кв. км. Начиная с 1917 г., официальные границы Москвы неоднократно раздвигались, и современная площадь Москвы после последнего расширения в 1985 г. составляет 998 кв. км — в 5,6 раза больше, чем в начале века. Любопытно, что население города в официальных границах выросло за это время почти в такой же пропорции — с 1,8 до 10 млн. чел. Однако в наше время цифры населения и территории большого города в его официальных границах недостаточны для его характеристики: Москва, сама по себе крупнейший город России и всего бывшего Советского Союза, возглавляет самую большую в стране городскую агломерацию. По мнению разных экспертов, ее население превышает 20 млн. человек, а территория покрывает значительную часть Московской области, и местами выходит за ее пределы.

Поскольку численность населения Москвы выросла в 5 с лишним раз, то число коренных москвичей (то есть потомков дореволюционных жителей Москвы) при нормальном развитии должно быть, как минимум, около одной пятой общего числа жителей. Но население Москвы понесло колоссальный урон в советское время. И дело не только в количестве — численность населения Москвы, сильно уменьшившаяся после 1917 г., восстановилась через 9 лет. В результате Гражданской войны и большевистского террора погибли многие тысячи представителей московского дворянства, купечества, буржуазии, духовенства, интеллигенции, а многие, к счастью для них, эмигрировали сами или были высланы за границу.

И это было только начало: впереди были страшные годы сталинского террора. Далеко обогнав все другие города СССР по численности населения, Москва «обогнала» всех и по числу жертв коммунистического режима. Население Москвы восстанавливалось и росло за счет мигрантов из других городов и сельской местности; эти люди в массе своей должны были заново осваивать быт и культуру большого города. В результате сейчас в Москве коренных москвичей всего 200–300 тыс. — не более 3% населения города [4].

Москва давно уже многонациональный город. Но всегда подавляющую часть ее населения составляли русские — 95% в начале XX в. и около 90% в конце.

Считается, что на рубеже веков москвичи отличались большой терпимостью к «иноверцам» и «иноземцам». Но именно в это время, в 1891–1893 гг., из Москвы выселяли евреев. И еще одна страница. Когда в 1914 г. после начала войны с Германией в России поднялась волна шовинизма, в Москве были разгромлены многие заведения, принадлежавшие немцам.

Ксенофобия, качество, всегда распространенное в России, усилилась в советские времена, особенно во время железного занавеса, опущенного при Сталине, когда недозволенное общение с иностранцами влекло за собой репрессии. Этот занавес приоткрылся при Хрущеве: Москва стала местом проведения международных кино- и музыкальных фестивалей, научных конгрессов и т.д., но неофициальное общение с иностранцами оставалось опасным. Сейчас железного занавеса нет, и массовое чувство страха при общении с иностранцами сильно ослабло. Ныне Москва самый интернациональный город России. Однако традиционное чувство ксенофобии ведет к тому, что многие москвичи винят в своих бедах «чужаков» и плохо относятся к представителям других стран и нерусских народов, к заимствованию идей, традиций, методов ведения хозяйства и т.д.

ПРОМЫШЛЕННОСТЬ

Сто лет назад Москва, наряду с Петербургом, была крупнейшим промышленным центром России, причем была бесспорным лидером в текстильной промышленности. Но во главе индустриализации в Москве уже тогда шло машиностроение, опережавшее по темпам развития старые отрасли московской индустрии.

Начиная с конца 1920-х гг., в годы так называемой «социалистической» индустриализации, ни один город в стране не развивался (в абсолютных показателях) так, как Москва. И первое место по объемам производства и занятости в промышленности прочно заняло машиностроение. Среди его отраслей наиболее развитыми в столице стали автомобильная промышленность, станкостроение, электротехника, оборонная промышленность.

Но дело, как известно, не только в количественных показателях развития. Самые передовые для данного времени производства и отрасли промышленности появлялись в Москве и других городах Московской агломерации, откуда их достижения распространялись по другим городам и предприятиям страны. В то же время унаследованные от прошлого заводы и фабрики нередко по-прежнему располагались в старых постройках и в течение долгого времени продолжали использовать устаревшее оборудование. Самая передовая в стародавние времена текстильная промышленность давно уже потеряла свою эффективность и превратилась в самую отсталую отрасль, но продолжала искусственно поддерживаться государством.

Московская промышленность, которая могла безбедно существовать при социализме, оказалась не готова к переходу к капиталистическим методам ведения хозяйства. В новых условиях, когда государственные вложения в производство резко сократились и появилась необходимость конкурировать с другими предприятиями, многие московские заводы и фабрики оказались в критическом положении. Лишь накануне нового столетия наметились некоторые положительные сдвиги, в первую очередь в отраслях, производящих товары широкого потребления.

НЕПРОИЗВОДСТВЕННАЯ СФЕРА

Долгое время в советской Москве занятость в промышленности превалировала над другими отраслями. Однако общемировые законы социального развития работали, хотя и со скрипом, и в Советском Союзе. И в Москве, первой из городов СССР, началось снижение доли рабочего класса в населении и возрастание доли занятых в непроизводственной сфере, особенно в науке, образовании и обслуживании населения.

В начале XX в. Москва была главным, наряду с Петербургом, торговым и финансовым центром России, а по объемам банковских бумаг даже превосходила столицу [5]. В советское время она сохранила и преумножила эту функцию, превратившись в главный центр распределения финансов и других ресурсов страны, но в другой «упаковке»: Москва стала центром административно-командной системы тоталитарного государства. С падением этой системы Москва продолжает быть ведущим административным и финансовым центром России. В столице находится одна треть коммерческих банков [6] и производится до 80% всех финансовых операций страны [7]. В Москве также совершается большая часть международных финансовых операций России.

Значимость «столичности», и ранее оказывавшей решающее влияние на развитие Москвы, в новых условиях становится еще более существенной.

НАУКА И ОБРАЗОВАНИЕ

Москва была вторым в Российской империи центром науки и образования. Ведущее место занимал Московский университет, который был не только великолепным учебным заведением, но и местом, где концентрировалась большая часть научной деятельности в Москве. В целом, однако, Петербург, где было два главных центра науки — университет и Академия наук, опережал Москву. В 1930-е гг. Академия наук СССР была переведена из бывшей столицы в Москву. В Москве также был образован ряд отраслевых академий — Академия медицинских наук, Академия педагогических наук, Академия сельскохозяйственных наук и другие. Москва стала крупнейшим в стране научным центром — по числу научных учреждений, числу работающих в науке, по уровню научной квалификации работников.

Особенно значительно место Москвы в науке, связанной с военно-промышленным комплексом: в столице находится около 40% всех научных и проектных организаций, работающих в России на оборону; ВПК принадлежит более половины научно-исследовательских институтов Москвы [8].

Москва — по-прежнему крупнейший научный центр, но структура научных исследований изменилось. Резкое сокращение государственного финансирования привело к тому, что большое число научных работников оказались не востребованными. Научные учреждения стали в значительной степени зависеть от спонсоров, а те, как правило, больше заинтересованы в прикладных исследованиях. Поэтому больше всего пострадали фундаментальные научные направления, не имеющие непосредственного выхода в практику.

Исключительно высока значимость Москвы в высшем образовании России. Научные учреждения высокого уровня есть и в других местах. Но мало найдется высших учебных заведений вне Москвы, которые могут сравниться по своей престижности с московскими. Это в наибольшей степени относится к гуманитарному и естественно-научному образованию и в меньшей мере — к техническому.

Москва всегда отличалась многообразием высших учебных заведений, а теперь их круг еще более расширился. Появились частные университеты, которые иногда включают в свои названия слова «свободный» или «независимый».

КУЛЬТУРА

Вместе с Петербургом, Москва была центром «серебряного века» в русском искусстве. Но нам кажется уместным повторить здесь в несколько расширенном виде слова Бориса Пастернака, с которыми читатель уже встречался в этой книге, что именно Москва, «обгоняя Петербург... дала начало новому русскому искусству — искусству большого города, молодому, современному, свежему» [9].

После революции в стране настало время «демонизации культуры и духовности», и «серебряный век эмигрировал» [10]. Эта демонизация нанесла колоссальный ущерб московской культуре. Но вряд ли правомерно говорить о полном упадке культуры в Москве. Во-первых, какое-то время действовала инерция «серебряного века»; во-вторых, вопреки всей идеологизации культуры, цензуре, давлению и репрессиям, мыслящие, творческие люди всегда появлялись, и если где-нибудь они пробивались, то больше всего в Москве. Здесь была более благоприятная творческая атмосфера, чем где бы то ни было в стране, и выросло не одно поколение творческой интеллигенции.

Партийно-государственное давление на культуру несколько ослабло в 1960-е гг., чтобы затем вновь возрасти. Однако не случайно именно в Москве была наиболее распространена неподцензурная неофициальная культура: по рукам ходили неопубликованные рукописи; художники-авангардисты устраивали выставки, против которых власти пускали бульдозеры; в домах устраивались просмотры западных фильмов, не допущенных к широкому прокату, проходили свободные научные семинары. Здесь началась и расцвела авторская песня, которая для многих стала откровением. Большинство интеллигентов-диссидентов дала Москва.

Интенсивная интеллектуальная жизнь была всегда характерна для этого города более, чем для других, в силу особой атмосферы, царившей здесь, и высокого статуса в обществе творческих людей, независимо от их социального или финансового состояния. Многие начинающие писатели, поэты, художники, музыканты, актеры были замечены и поддержаны московской публикой. Иногда срабатывал эффект «от противного»: именно авторы, подвергавшиеся официальной критике, получали неофициальную поддержку со стороны интеллигенции, которая таким образом выражала свое противостояние режиму.

На рубеже нового столетия Москва, как и прежде, остается самым передовым культурным центром России.

ПЛАНИРОВКА И ЗАСТРОЙКА

Как известно, наиболее устойчивой из всех градостроительных компонентов является пространственно-планировочная структура города. Сложившаяся еще в средние века радиально-кольцевая система улиц Москвы остается самым старым наследием прошлого в современной столице. Но ткань городской застройки неизбежно претерпевает изменения, поскольку у города, как у всякого живого организма, появляются в течение жизни новые нужды и потребности. Между этими потребностями и исторической ценностью существующей застройки постоянно возникают противоречия, — явление, хорошо знакомое старым городам мира.

В Москве многоэтажное строительство началось в конце XIX в. Тогда же историческая застройка центра понесла первые жертвы — освобождалось место для доходных домов. В советское время Москва почти повсеместно стала многоэтажной, новые здания в историческом центре возводились на месте сносимых старых домов. Если бы был осуществлен «Сталинский» план реконструкции Москвы, от старой застройки вообще почти ничего бы не осталось, но его выполнение остановила война [11]. Позднее принималось много решений о сохранении исторической застройки города, однако наступление на нее, по-существу, никогда не останавливалось [12].

Неузнаваемо изменился силуэт города. В старом силуэте доминировали шпили колоколен и маковки церквей, возвышавшиеся над крышами домов. Москва с тех пор стала выше, и теперь они закрыты многоэтажными зданиями. В новом силуэте Москвы доминируют высотные дома — как построенные в первое послевоенное десятилетие (со шпилями), так и современной архитектуры. Сейчас лишь Кремль и Пашков дом напоминают о прежней живописности силуэта города.

Разумеется, за сто прошедших лет изменились и формы организации городского пространства, и формы жилья, и техническое обеспечение городских территорий. Не рассматривая содержания этих перемен, отметим главное — Москва и здесь оказалась лидером, здесь смелее, чем где-нибудь еще, совершались градостроительные эксперименты. В Москве опробовались новые планировочные и инженерно-строительные приемы: микрорайон, свободная планировка, повышенная этажность застройки и др. Впоследствии они тиражировались во многих городах страны — как удачно, так и неудачно.

Знакомство с пост-советской Москвой вызывает противоречивые чувства. Центр города выглядит обновленным; восстановлены многие старые здания, культовые постройки; приведены в порядок улицы и переулки, незатронутые реконструкцией. Москва внутри Садового кольца становится более похожей на Запад, чем вся остальная Россия по мере того, как международный и национальный капитал приспосабливает исторический центр города для своих нужд. При этом часто бросается в глаза сочетание уверенности и агрессивной безвкусицы, своеобразный вызов традиционным эстетическим нормам.

Зона за пределами Садового кольца, включая районы, которые еще не так давно считались новыми, явно пользуется меньшим вниманием московских властей. Современное строительство перешагнуло их и ведется у внешних границ города.

В капиталистических странах Запада маловероятно увидеть стоящие по соседству особняк миллионера и лачугу бедняка — разные социальные и имущественные слои, как правило, территориально не смешиваются. В Москве партийно-государственная элита советских времен селилась в специально отведенных для нее старых и новых домах внутри рядовой застройки центра города. Пришедшая ей на смену новая элита — верхушка московского делового мира — продолжает ту же практику. Современные хозяева переоборудуют старые и строят новые дома в центре в соответствии со своими потребностями и вкусами. Но началось и территориальное обособление элиты: в лучших в экологическом отношении окраинных районах на западе города появились элитные кварталы.

Меняется и ближнее Подмосковье, где появились и продолжают возникать жилые поселки московской элиты с благоустройством, о котором традиционные дачники и владельцы садовых участков не могли даже и мечтать.

МОСКВА – ЛИДЕР

Стала ли Москва другим городом за прошедшие сто лет? И да, и нет. Да — потому что за это время произошли колоссальные изменения в материальной среде города и в образе жизни москвичей. Нет — потому, что «Я» Москвы, ее дух, ее индивидуальность не изменились: Москва была и остается лидером.

Это свойство характера присуще Москве с «незапамятных времен», и она сохраняет его независимо от политического и экономического режима. Даже когда столицей был Петербург, «в некоторых отношениях Москва продолжала играть основную роль». «Так, Москва служила по-прежнему регулятором общественного мнения. С этим считались даже Петр Великий и все последующие русские цари» [13].

Москва вступила в XX в. как лидер капиталистического развития России. Затем Москва возглавила коммунистический мир. Огромную роль в ее жизни играл фактор столичности. Москва — «столица первого в мире социалистического государства», витрина страны — получала от правительства большие ассигнования на любые нужды, чем любой другой город страны.

Москва оказалась магнитом огромной притягательной силы для людей самых разных интересов: здесь было престижно учиться и работать, здесь были лучшие условия жизни, здесь была более свободная атмосфера в творческих кругах.

Магнетическая привлекательность Москвы побуждала многих к активным действиям. Показательным примером тому могут служить провинциальные лидеры, которые стремились сделать карьеру и получить место в Москве. Для того, чтобы продемонстрировать, что они способны продвинуться в высшие круги власти, эти лидеры должны были показать свою пригодность, добившись улучшений в подвластных им городах и других местах действия [14].

Но вот пришли новые времена, и Россия, спустя семьдесят лет коммунистического господства, вновь вступила на путь капиталистического развития. И Москва очень быстро стала главным экономическим и финансовым центром изменившейся России, она снова — лидер. «Москва, урча, поглощает денежные потоки, на девять десятых порождаемые одним ее столичным статусом» [15].

В Москве существовало и существует колоссальное поле привлекательности, создаваемое разнообразием видов деятельности, их доступностью и возможностью приобщиться к их уникальным образцам [16]. Ни один другой город в стране не дает людям такого широкого выбора, как Москва.

Лидерство — главная черта характера Москвы. Но есть весьма распространенная ошибка — идеализировать лидера. Как и лидер-человек, лидер-город обязательно имеет не только светлые, но и темные стороны. Лидер и притягивает, и отталкивает. Москва притягивает культурной средой, возможностью выбора, праздничностью обновленного центра. Но Москва многим и отталкивает: запущенностью некоторых районов города, ксенофобией, длинными и долгими поездками на работу. В результате поляризации общества, произошедшей в последние годы, в Москве сегодня можно наблюдать демонстративную роскошь, соседствующую с вопиющей нищетой.

Но для массы людей и сейчас актуальна мечта чеховских героинь: «В Москву! В Москву! В Москву».

Примечания:

[1] Klima I. The Spirit of Prague // The Spirit of Prague and Other Essays. N.Y.: Granta Books, 1994. P. 39.

[2] «Вчера была Империя, / А нынче ты — Московия». (Городницкий А. Праздник 850-летия Москвы // Когда судьба поставлена на карту. М.: ЭКСМО-пресс, 2001. С. 349.)

[3] Этим свойством Москвы объясняется, в частности, неослабевающий интерес западных ученых к Москве. Однако единственным капитальным исследованием о Москве двадцатого столетия, вышедшем на английском языке, остается монография Тимоти Колтона (Colton T. Moscow: Governing the Socialist Metropolis. Cambridge, Mass.: Harvard University Press, 1995). Большинство же посвященных Москве работ, опубликованых за океаном в последнее десятилетие, разбросаны в виде статей по различным изданиям. См., например, статьи, помещенные в специальном «московском» выпуске журнала Eurasian Geography and Economics. 2002, no. 3 / Edited by John O'Loughlin and Vladimir Kolossov,

а также отдельные статьи: Alden J, Crow S., and Beigulenko Y. Moscow: Planning for a Word Capital City Toward 2000 // Cities. 1998, no. 5. P. 363–374; Argenbrigt R. Remaking Moscow: New Places, New Selves // Geographical Review. 1999, no. 1. P. 1–22; Bater J. H. Housing Development in Moscow in 1990s // Post-Soviet Geography. 1994, no. 9. P. 557–574; Bater J. H. Adjusting to Change: Privilege and Place in Post-Soviet Central Moscow // The Canadian Geographer. 2001, no. 2. P. 237–251; Bater J. H., Amelin V.M, and Degtyarev A. «Politics in Moscow: Local Issues, Areas, and Governance // Political Geography. 1995, no. 8. P. 665–687; Alexander J., Degtyarev A. A., and Gel'man V. Democratization Challenged: The Role of the Regional Elites // Fragmented Space in the Russian Federation / Eds. Blair A. Ruble, Jodi Koehn, and Nancy E. Popson. Washington, D.C. and Baltimore: The Woodrow Wilson Center Press and Johns Hopkins University Press, 2001. P. 157–217. Многие работы написаны западными учеными в соавторстве с их российскими коллегами — еще совсем недавно это было практически невозможно.

[4]   Алексеев А.И. и др. Москвоведение. География Москвы и Московской области. М.: Экопрос, 1994. С. 79.

[5]   См.: Ананьич Б. В. Банкирские дома в России 1860–1914 гг. Очерки истории частного предпринимательства. Л.: Наука, 1991. С. 153–154.

[6]   Алексеев А.И. и др. Москвоведение. С. 125.

[7]   Там же. С. 123.

[8]   Там же. С. 131.

[9]   Пастернак Б. Люди и положения // Избранное в двух томах. Т. 2. М.: Художественная литература, 1985. С. 230.

[10]   Крейд В. Встречи с серебряным веком // Воспоминания о серебряном веке / Сост. Вадим Крейд. М.: Республика, 1993. С. 6–7.

[11]   Один из пародоксов истории: война спасла Москву.

[12]   «Я часто с ужасом думаю: а что стало бы с Римом, Прагой или Вильнюсом, попади они в руки, определяющие судьбу Москвы». (Комеч А. «Реконструкция» Москвы продолжается // Новый мир. 1997. № 1. С. 247.)

[13]   Бахрушин С. В. Труды по источниковедению, историографии и истории России эпохи феодализма. М.: Наука, 1987. С. 165.

[14]   Это хорошо продемонстрировано на примере ленинградских вождей послевоенного времени в книге: Ruble B. A. Leningrad. Shaping a Soviet City. Berkeley: University of California Press, 1990.

[15]   Глазычев В. Рим № 3 и его окрестности // Москва — территория 2000. М.: GIF, 1999. С. 5.

[16]   См.: Ахиезер А. С. и Ильин П. М. Социальная оценка территории в условиях научно-технической революции // Известия АН СССР. Серия географическая. 1975. № 1. С. 11–23. Американский ученый

Ричард Флорида в своей блестящей книге «Рост созидательного класса» показывает, что ведущими в обществе являются места, которые характеризуются разнообразием, толерантностью и возможностью развития всех видов творчества, поскольку «люди всех слоев и групп хотят там жить» (курсив автора). См.: Florida R. The Rise of the Creative Class, And How It's Transforming Work, Leisure, Community and Everyday Life. N.Y.: Basic Books, 2002. Р. х. Не подлежит сомнению, что Москва, оцененная по методике Флориды, получила бы среди городов России наивысшую оценку.

Часть III

Кто такой Захар Загадкин?

В ОДНОЙ РУБКЕ С ЗАХАРОМ ЗАГАДКИНЫМ

Павел Полян

«ПУТЕШЕСТВИЕ ПО ЛЮБИМОЙ РОДИНЕ»

Наверное, самым первым советским радиосериалом — к тому же необычайно популярным и любимым — стал «Клуб знаменитых капитанов», впервые вышедший в эфир 31 декабря 1945 года. Вторым чем-то подобным была наша любимая географическая радиоигра — «Путешествие по любимой Родине», стартовавшая в апреле 1958 года. Третьим и последним представителем этого радиотеатрального жанра, — но с акцентом на вопросах экологии и бионики, — стал знаменитый «КОАПП» («Комитет Охраны Авторских Прав Природы»), стартовавший в декабре 1963 года.

Героями географической передачи — и ее ведущими — был дуэт бывшего юнги Захара Загадкина и его друга кока Антона Камбузова (с попугаем Жако). Придумал их всех Пашин отец — Михаил Ильич Ильин (1901–1967), талантливый журналист и стихийный географ, большой знаток Советского Союза и мира. Его первые географические книжки — авторская «От Черного до Каспийского моря» и авторско-составительская «Земля Советская: очерки и рассказы о новом в географии СССР» — вышли в 1948 и 1950 годах.

В эти мрачные годы как нельзя более кстати пришлась вторая фамилия — «Ильин». Это у Владимира Ильича Ульянова-Ленина тот же самый «Ильин» — классический псевдоним, а у Михаила Ильича Тиркельтауба (коренная его фамилия) вторая фамилия приклеилась к нему несколько иначе.

Вот семейная легенда об этом, и в ней — несомненная толика правды.

Дело было в Гражданскую, на которой Михаил Ильич воевал за красных в санитарном поезде. Начальник поезда все никак не мог выговорить слово «Тиркельтауб», отчего звал его, ориентируясь на отчество, «Ильиным». В 1928 году, при получении паспорта, «Тиркельтауб» уже сам записался Ильиным, так что дети — и Павлик, и Юля — Ильиными и родились.[1]

В апреле 1958 года, в хрущевскую оттепель, трио «Загадкин, Камбузов и Ильин» возникло на радио. Первые два года оно охватывало внимание весь земной шар, но, начиная с 1960 года, подопечный им окоем вшестеро сузился — до территории СССР.

В 1959 году в издательстве «Детская литература» вышли «Воспоминания юнги Захара Загадкина», а в 1963 «Необыкновенные путешествия или удивительные, но совершенно правдивые географические приключения Захара Загадкина на 1/6 земной суши, рассказанные им самим и дополненные примечаниями будущего ученого Фомы Отгадкина». В 1965 году обе книги были изданы вместе под названием «Воспоминания и необыкновенные путешествия Захара Загадкина» (художник Анатолий Иткин). И т.д., и т.п. Всего книги о Захаре Загадкине издавались в СССР, Польше, Чехословакии и Китае в общей сложности 14 раз, на восьми языках и общим тиражом более 600 тысяч экземпляров.

У передачи была еще и третья жанровая ипостась. Московский планетарий подготовил и размножил по ее материалам популярную лекцию с диапозитивами о Захаре Загадкине.

Что касается самих передач, то они выходили в эфир раз в две недели, каждый второй четверг, в 16.00, и длились 20 минут. Музыкальной заставкой верой и правдой служил припев из песни «Веселый ветер» Исаака Дунаевского на слова Василия Лебедева-Кумача: «Кто весел, тот смеется, кто хочет, тот добьется, кто ищет, тот всегда найдет!». Промурлыкав концовку припев, слово первым брал кок: «Здравствуйте, други мои!..». После чего вступал Захар Загадкин — со своими байками, они же загадки.

Вот одна из таких новелл — под названием: «Почему я не стал владельцем попугая Жако»:

> «На рассвете я выбежал на палубу и был поражен видом моря. Насколько хватало глаз, оно было покрыто оливково-зеленой травой. Легкий ветерок колыхал травяные заросли, местами перемежавшиеся густо-синими полосами воды. Не было сомнения, мы плыли по огромному лугу! Я любовался редким зрелищем, когда внезапно

---

[1] Однако фамилия претерпела трансформацию еще раз. 1 ноября 1950 г. на хвосте компании по «борьбе с безродными космополитами» Михаил Ильич был арестован и провел в лагере шесть лет. При выходе из лагеря в 1956 году он получил паспорт, где черным по белому стояло: «Тиркельтауб, он же Ильин». Дети еще долго дразнили отца этим «он же»!

душу мою обуял страх не запутается ли киль корабля в бесчисленных растениях? Ведь тогда мы надолго застрянем в диковинном море-луге...

Я спустился в камбуз, где кок готовил у плиты оладьи к утреннему кофе, и высказал свои опасения.

Кок ухмыльнулся. — Не ты первый, Захар, кого смущает это море, — произнес он, протягивая мне кружку дымящегося кофе. — В тысяча четыреста девяносто втором году один знаменитый мореплаватель был удивлен не менее тебя, когда впервые увидел эти изумрудные луга. Странный звук, с которым корабли разрывали зеленый ковер травы, напугал матросов, и, как ты, они боялись, что суда будут опутаны плавающими растениями. Однако все обошлось благополучно.

Знаменитый мореплаватель выбрался из этих мест, а будущее показало, что растения нисколько не мешают судоходству. Бесспорно, не застрянем и мы. Поэтому выпей горячего кофейку, Захар, и забудь о своих опасениях. Нам грозит иная, более серьезная неприятность: у моря, по которому мы плывем, нет берегов!

— Как — нет берегов? У всех морей есть берега...

— У всех есть, а у этого нет. История не знает мореплавателя, который хотя бы раз высаживался на его берегах. Если юнге Загадкину удастся увидеть их, пусть даже на горизонте, это будет величайшим географическим событием! Тогда я, скромный корабельный кок, тоже ознаменую твое открытие — подарю тебе своего попугая!

Кто-бы отказался от возможности сделать величайшее открытие, да еще получить в подарок серого Жако — любимца всей команды? Только не юнга Загадкин! И все свободное время я торчал на палубе, терпеливо ожидая минуты, когда на горизонте покажутся берега луга-моря. Мне было все равно, какими предстанут они глазам первооткрывателя — скалистыми или песчаными, высокими или низменными, обитаемыми или безлюдными, — но я должен был увидеть их во что бы то ни стало, ведь моря без берегов не может быть!

Увы, дежурства на палубе оказались напрасными! Мы пересекли море с востока на запад, и я с огорчением убедился, что ни на востоке, ни на западе оно действительно не имело берегов. На обратном пути мы прошли это море с севера на юг, но на севере и юге у него тоже не было берегов!

Я так и не стал владельцем серого попугая Жако»

Поскольку я не умею писать текст отгадки вниз головой, то напишу головою вверх: «САРГАССОВО МОРЕ».

...Сформулировав свою загадку, Захар (его голосом был Лев Дуров) прощался и весело звал *кока Антона Камбузова*: «*Антон Антонович, принимай вахту!..*». Тогда слово снова брал Леонид Броневой — пардон, Антон Камбузов. Задав слушателям пару своих фирменных загадок, попроще, он переходил к гвоздю своему программы — оглашению свежего «географического диктанта», то есть фразы, составленной из слов, которые вместе с тем можно составить из топонимов на карте СССР. Он же, кок, сообщал ответы на загадки и называл по имени лучших отгадчиков предпоследней передачи. Звучала музыкальная заставка, и передача кончалась.

Итак, между двумя ведущими было своеобразное разделение по сложности их загадок, а значит — и по возрастам слушателей: Захар адресовался к школьникам постарше, а кок — к тем, что помладше. Вот образчик его загадки:

> «Антон Камбузов предложил юным географам найти кратчайшую дорогу от Амура до Днепра. Но многие, зная «характер» кока, догадались, что в вопросе есть хитрость. И нашли в Днепропетровске, чуть ли не на берегу Днепра, железнодорожную станцию Амур — тезку дальневосточной реки».

Другим камбузовским «жанром» были географический диктант. Вот его образчик, сохраненный Галиной Копытовой (о ней мы еще скажем) и содержащий в себе 32(!) географических названия:

> «Красивый дом на берегу реки. Тут юнга, я и кок жили. Утро. Захар пошёл по лесу ягоды искать. Мы с коком шли на глухое озеро. Там Антон и я поймали шесть зайцев».

Они представляли собой осмысленные фразы, полностью составленные из географических названий, причём границы имён не обязательно совпадали с границами слов текста. Поэтому приходилось самому как бы заново разбивать его на топонимы и искать их на картах и атласах. Свидетельство Галины Копытовой: *«Но были два великолепных Атласа СССР, были походы в читальный зал библиотек, где доступна была Большая советская энциклопедия и много иной литературы. Приходилось потрудиться основательно, но это потом помогло в студенчестве — работа с источниками была освоена ещё в школе. Составляла попутно свой справочник географических объектов нашей страны».*

Тем самым в слушавших передачу школьниках и школьницах пробуждался и рос интерес к более глубокому и занимательному, нежели в школе, изучению географии, зарождались и развивались навыки работы с книгой, картой и атласом и вообще — навыки целенаправленного и систематического труда. Ведь для того, чтобы достойно ответить на загадки и диктант, школьных знаний было недостаточно, и в поисках ответов играющим приходилось много и разнообразно трудиться. И без лучших атласов и книг, то есть без визитов в библиотеки, диктант не разгадаешь.

ПАВЛИК ПОЛЯН ИЗ ВОСЬМОГО «А»

Сам я был в восторге от «Большого Советского Атласа Мира», а высшим пилотажем считал «Морской атлас»: в конце обоих были перечни географических названий, встречающихся внутри на картах!

В радиоигре участвовали школьники всех классов, но около половины играющих приходилось на седьмой и восьмой, в которых проходилась география СССР. Кстати, слушали эти передачи и школьные учителя географии, а некоторые даже использовали элементы радиоигры на своих уроках.

Как писал П. Ильин, «...многие школьники включаются в радиоигру благодаря спортивному интересу, возникающему при разборе диктантов, затем они пытаются разгадывать загадки Захара, развивая свой географический кругозор». <...> М.И. Ильин прекрасно знал психологию детей, знал, что для поддержания интереса им нужно общение с героями передачи и друг с другом. Поэтому он придумал и форму игры, и дипломы победителям, и путевые журналы. Дети легко и охотно воспринимают и поддерживают игру. Многие верят в реальность Захара и кока» приглашают в гости, делятся с ними мыслями о жизни, мечтами о будущем».[2]

После каждой передачи приходило до 1000 и более писем с отгадками, не считая коллективных писем от примерно 150 школьных географических кружков и обществ. Примерно две трети «радиопутешественников» жили на селе или в небольших городах и поселках. Но общее число слушателей передачи «Путешествия

---

[2] Ильин П. М. «Путешествие по любимой Родине» — географическая радиоигра для советских школьников // Географическое образование, географическая литература и распространение географических знаний. *Международная география*, 1976. М.: XXIII Международный географический конгресс, 1976. С. 114–115.

по любимой Родине» было, по-видимому, гораздо больше: ведь далеко не каждый преодолевал робость и вступал в переписку с Захаром и Антоном.

На тех же, кто вступал в такую переписку, то есть включался в участники радиоигры как таковой, заводилась карточка, в которой записывались оценки его ответов в очках (баллах). Периодически,— как правило, раз в месяц,— ребята получали индивидуальные «путевые журналы», напечатанные на фирменных, формата А-5, бланках с цветной эмблемой передачи и неизменной подписью: «С морским приветом, Захар Загадкин». В журналах сообщалось о текущих «дорожных» успехах каждого.

Пишу об этом не только как участник радиоигры, но и как бы с другой ее стороны, поскольку Паша вскоре предложил мне помогать ему с рутинным просмотром корреспонденции и проставлением баллов. Сами ответы школьникам он тюкал на машинке сам. Делал я это с сентиментальным удовольствием, радио платило за это небольшую денежку, что тоже не было лишним при стажерской-то зарплате.

По окончании каждого «тура» (так назывались годичные циклы радиоигры, каждый тур имел свой порядковый номер) около 500–600 наиболее знающих «радиопутешественников» награждались фирменными именными дипломами на плотной бумаге, а самые лучшие — еще и премиями — подписанными Антоном и Захаром книгами по географии, Общее число школьников, отмечавшихся наградами за успехи в радиоигре, можно оценить в 13–14 тысяч. Формой поощрения было и называние коком имен тех, кто лучше всех отвечал на вопросы той или другой передачи.

В летнее время передач не было, но Захар и кок проводили на каникулах специальные конкурсы (типа «Мой родной край», «Реки моего края», «Географические названия в нашем краю», «Как я провел лето» и т.п.). Ребята присылали целые тетради и альбомы с описаниями летних путешествий, картами, рисунками и фотографиями, лучшие, разумеется, тоже премировались.

Немало школьников, впервые заинтересовавшихся географией благодаря Захару Загадкину, поступали потом на геофаки университетов и педвузов. Иные, став учителями географии, создавали в своих школах географические кружки, вместе с которыми снова «включались» в любимую игру. А некоторые бывшие «радиопутешественники» защищали кандидатские и докторские по географии, становились профессорами и завкафедрами. Таких ветеранов иногда приглашали в эфир: помню передачу, в которой участвовал и сам вместе с Нико Беручишвили, впоследствии заведующим кафедрой физической географии Тбилисского университета.

ГАЛЯ КОПЫТОВА ИЗ ИРКУТСКА

Конечно, не все юные любители географии, даже очень сильные в формате передачи или помешанные на путешествиях, становились потом профессионалами-географами. Но все — и это видно из писем ставших взрослыми друзей Захара и кока — сохранили самую лучшую память об этой, по их словам, познавательной и чудесной «сказке-игре».

Вот одна такая история, отыскавшаяся в сетевом интернете. Прошу любить и жаловать — Галина Германовна Копытова[3] из Иркутска, одна из верных слушательниц и успешных участниц радиоигры. Свой связный, да еще с картинками, рассказ она озаглавила... ***«Путешествие по любимой Родине»***

Цитирую:

«Моё приобщение к передаче произошло в 1971 году и сначала имело «внутреннее потребление» — разгадывала диктанты, поскольку атласы были одними из любимейших книг, но робость не позволяла отправлять письма на передачу, и как уж так случилось, что однажды удалось преодолеть эту робость — не знаю... Но в ответ получила письмо от самого Захара Загадкина!!!!

Это случилось в начале 1972 года... И с тех пор я уже не пропускала ни одной передачи. Когда мы учились во вторую смену, приходилось просить кого-то записать задания на бумаге (в то время не было магнитофонов и, тем более, иных современных способов записи). Задания всегда были интересными и увлекательными. Чтобы найти ответы, приходилось подолгу засиживаться в читальных залах библиотек, но оно того стоило — результат всегда радовал и воодушевлял. Познания в географии расширялись и сама география становилась объектом вожделения... К слову сказать, у нас был ещё и замечательный преподаватель географии! Увлечение в дальнейшем сказалось на выборе профессии... Но сейчас о передаче... <...>

Ответы на вопросы Захара Загадкина и расшифрованный диктант надо было отправлять на радио. В ответ периодически присылались страницы путевого журнала с сообщением о заработанных

---

[3] Девичья фамилия.

баллах и информацией о предстоящих передачах. Бывало имя твое произносили в самой передаче — приятно!

Цикл передач одного учебного года назывался туром. По итогам тура присылался Диплом. Получение Диплома было даже волнительнее, чем получение грамоты в школе на общешкольном собрании... Принимала участие в пяти турах и получила пять Дипломов.

В летние каникулы последних двух лет проводились конкурсы Лето-74 и Лето-75, где надо было тоже выполнить определенные географические задания. По их итогам вручались призы — замечательные книги.

В 1976 году прозвучал последний школьный звонок... После зачисления на географический факультет Ленинградского университета, написала письмо своим радиодрузьям Захару Загадкину и Антону Камбузову... и в ответ получила последний листок своего путевого журнала.

А вот и Пашин (пардон, Захаров!) ответ:

«Здравствуй, дорогая Галочка! Поздравляю тебя с поступлением на геофак университета. Кок поздравил тебя по радио, а я это делаю в пуевом журнале...Спасибо за теплые слова в наш адрес.

Посылаю диплом, заслуженный тобой в XVII туре нашей радиоигры- твой пятый и последний диплом. А премии за Лето-75 и Лето-74 еще за мной: я помню о них и скоро пришлю. Желаю и дальше больших успехов.

С морским приветом,
Захар Загадкин».

А чуть позже Галочка получила и те книги, что ей «задолжал» Захар.

Всего передача просуществовала в эфире около четверти века, из которых 9 лет пришлись на Ильина-отца и 16 — на Ильина-сына. Общее число эфиров за 1958–1982 гг. превысило 400!

P.S.

...Однажды в путешествие — подальше от любимой родины! — собрался и сам Павел Ильин с женой и дочкой Надей, тогда юным музыкантом. В июне 1982 года они подали документы, после чего радиопередачу тотчас же, на излете жизни Брежнева, закрыли.

«Путешествие по любимой Родине» — географическая радиоигра для советских школьников

Ильин П. М. (СССР, Москва)

Начиная с апреля 1958 года школьники Советского Союза слушают по Московскому радио географические передачи с участием Захара Загадкина и его друге кока Антона Камбузова. За прошедшие 18 лет состоялось около 300 таких передач. Этих персонажей придумал писатель Михаил Ильич Ильин (1901–1967). Он был автором всех передач о Захаре Загадкнне первые девять лет. С конца 1967 года тексты передач пишет автор настоящего сообщения.

Захар Загадкин сразу полюбился ребятам. Молодой человек, любитель приключений и любознательный, он часто попадает в разные «истории», которые записывает в дорожную тетрадь. Каждая такая «история» — географическая загадка, поданная в занимательной форме.

Вначале Захар Загадкин рассказывал по радио о своих приключениях на всех материках и океанах Земли: он в те годы «служил юнгой» на одном из судов торгового флота. А в 1960 году началось «Путешествие по любимой Родине», радиоигра-соревнование школьников на лучшее знание географии Советского Союза. В течение учебного года проводится один тур радиоигры. «Путешествуя» раз в две недели с героями передачи, юные радиослушатели знакомятся с политической, экономической и физической географией СССР.

Каждая передача длится 20 минут. Обычно она состоит из географичесгого рассказа-загадки Захара Загадкина и одной-двух загадок кока. Через одну передачу кок сообщает ответы на загадки и называет лучших отгадчиков. Рассказы-загадки Захара рассчитаны на школьников постарше, загадки кока- на учеников младших классов. Чтобы дать представление о приемах подачи материала, приведу сюжеты трех загадок.

Захар Загадкин и кок едет поездом из Крыма на Кавказ. Юнга уверен, что поезд пойдет по суше вокруг Азовского моря и даже заключает с коком пари. Но к его удивлению, поезд плывет по волнам! Это — в двух словах, а весь рассказ о споре Захара с коком и об их необычном путешествия длится около 10 минут. В нем даются сведения, необходимые для того, чтобы загадку можно было отгадать, но не сообщается, что через Керченский пролив ходит железнодорожный паром (юнга об этом не знал).

Действие другой загадки происходит на севере Европейской части СССР. Захар рассказывает о разговоре со встреченным в поезде гидрологом. Тот вспоминает, как потерял в экспедиции товарища. Шли они вдаль небольшой речки, он — по правому берегу, товарищ — по левому. Река раздвоилась на два рукава, которые не сошлись! Потом каждый гидролог вышел к большой реке, но не к одной и той же. И эта загадка минут на десять, в ней на примере раздвоения реки Пижмы на Мезенскую Пижму и Печорскую Пижму школьники знакомятся с бифуркацией рек.

Антон Камбузов предложил юным географам найти кратчайшую дорогу от Амура до Днепра. Но многие, зная «характер» кока, догадались, что в вопросе есть хитрость. И нашли в Днепропетровске, чуть ли не на берегу Днепра, железнодорожную станцию Амур — тезку дальневосточной реки.

Регулярно кок диктует фразы, все слова которых состоят из географических названий, взятых с карты СССР. Расшифровка таких географических диктантов требует меньшей подготовки, чем разгадывание загадок Захара. Многие школьники включаются в радиоигру благодаря спортивному интересу, возникающему при разборе диктантов; затем они пытаются разгадывать загадки Захара, развивая свой географический кругозор.

После каждой передачи приходит до 1000 и более писем с отгадками. В радиоигре участвуют школьники всех классов — от первого до десятого; около половины играющих — ученики седьмого и восьмого классов, в которых изучается география СССР. Кроме того, письма с отгадками регулярно присылают свыше 150 школьных географических кружков и обществ, в которых занимаются тысячи ребят. Примерно две трети «радио-путешественников» живут в сельской местности и небольших городах и поселках. Общее же число школьников, которые слушают передачи «Путешествия по любимой Родине» и таким образом получают новые знания по географии, по-видимому, намного больше.

Участникам игры приходится немало трудиться: знаний, полученных на уроках, недостаточно для того, чтобы хорошо ответить на загадки Захара и кока. По многу часов проводят школьники за картами, роются в географических картах, справочниках, энциклопедиях. Свидетельство тому — выписки из книг, ссылки на источники, откуда взят материал для ответа. Многие ответы снабжены самоцельными картами, рисунками, чертежами. Ребята и сами придумывают задания: почти все диктанты кока полностью составлены «радиопутешественниками»; по темам, подсказанным школьниками, сделаны большинство загадок кока и некоторые рассказы Захара.

На каждого участника игры заведена карточка, в которой записываются оценки его ответов в очках (баллах). Периодически ребята получают «путевые журналы», напечатанные на бланках с эмблемой и подписью «Захар Загадкин»; из них они узнают о своих «дорожных» успехах. По окончании каждого тура 500–600 наиболее знающих «радиопутешественников» награждаются дипломами, которые тоже специально напечатаны для этой передачи, а самые лучшие — премиями (книгами по географии). Общее число школьников, отмечавшихся наградами за успехи в радиоигре, приближается к 10 тысячам.

Захар и кок проводят также специальные конкурсы, обычно во время летних каникул, например, «Мой родного край», «Реки моего края», «Географические названия в нашем краю», «Как я провел лето» и др. На конкурсы приходят целые тетради и альбомы с описаниями летних путешествий, рисунками, фотографиями. Лучшие работы также премируются.

М. И. Ильин прекрасно знал психологию детей, знал, что для поддержания интереса им нужно общение с героями передачи и друг с другом. Поэтому он придумал и форму игры, и дипломы победителям, и путевые журналы. Дети легко и охотно воспринимают и поддерживают игру. Многие верят в реальность Захара и кока, приглашают в гости, делятся с ними мыслями о жизни, мечтами о будущем.

В многочисленных письмах учителей, родителей школьников и самих ребят отмечается, что передачи «Путешествие по любимой Родине» помогают в учебе, вызывают у школьников интерес к географии СССР, воспитывают желание лучше узнать свою Родину, учат ребят работать с книгой и картой, приучают к систематическому труду. Многие учителя используют материалы передач на уроках. Немало школьников, впервые заинтересовавшихся географией благодаря Захару Загадкину, поступили на географические факультеты университетов и педагогических институтов. Среди бывших «радиопутешественников» есть кандидаты географических наук. Некоторые, став учителями географии, создали в своих школах географические кружки, вместе с которыми снова «включились» в игру.

Конечно, не все юные любители географии, даже очень сильные, становятся потом профессионалами-географами. Но все — это видно из писем ставших взрослыми друзей Захара и кока — сохранили самую лучшую память об этой, по их словам, «чудесной сказке-игре». Как написала бывшая школьница из города Мирный в Якутии, выбравшая себе другую профессию, — «Я унесу эти встречи детства как лучшие воспоминания во взрослую жизнь».

Около 100 рассказов-загадок, переданных по радио в 1958–1965 годах, опубликованы. Книги М. И. Ильина о Захаре Загадкине издавались в СССР, Польше, Чехословакии и Китае 14 раз на 8-ми языках общим тиражом более 600 тысяч экземпляров. Но материалам книг в Московском планетарии была подготовлена и размножена популярная лекция с диапозитивами о Захаре Загадкине.

Письма участников передачи

Воспоминания Александра Гаврилова

В конце 60-х годов я учился в Железнодорожной школе № 2 в подмосковном поселке Кратово. Казалось бы, до столицы рукой подать. Но разница в качестве образования была кардинальной. Я это ощутил в полной мере, когда с родителями переехал в «саму» Москву. Пришлось тянуться изо всех сил, догоняя одноклассников почти по всем дисциплинам. Говорю «почти», потому что был один предмет, в котором я оказался вполне на уровне. Это — география. А успевал я в ней благодаря «Путешествию по любимой Родине», радиоигре, к которой нас приучила «географичка» В. Б. Гаттенберг.

Она записывала передачи Захара Загадкина и кока Антона Камбузова на магнитофон, а потом дважды в неделю после уроков собирала учеников разных классов для увлекательной сессии разгадок и догадок. Загадки были не простые. Приходилось копаться в библиотеке, и тут нам повезло, потому что в соседнем городе авиаконструкторов Жуковский была хорошая библиотека. До сих пор помню громадный Атлас СССР на отдельном столике. Радиопутешествия,открыли ребятам Кратовской железнодорожной школы № 2 двери в большой мир. А это трудно переоценить.

Маша Гусева о Захаре Загадкине

Я очень много читала, когда была маленькой. Скорее, больше читала, чем жила на самом деле. Поэтому большая часть моих детских познаний о географии была почерпнута из рассказов и загадок Захара Загадкина. Тени сомнения не возникало, что это — реальный человек, наблюдательный и пытливый, с хорошим морским юморком. И все его рассказы были на редкость емкими, задорными и провоцировали изучать планету — насколько в то время это было возможно, в рамках существующего мира СССР.

Что такое Гольфстрим и цунами, как понять, как нужно плавать в Саргассовом море, и почему Луна вызывает приливы и отливы — я, прочитав и прослушав, была потенциально готова к путешествиям по всему земному шару.

Последнее зеленое 1964 года (мое личное, из детства) издание Захара Загадкина с удовольствием читали и мои дети.

Что сказать? Такого рода книги сейчас не делаются.

ЛЕРА ФРЕЙДЛИН О ЗАХАРЕ ЗАГАДКИНЕ

У меня двое детей, и я уже бабушка. До сих пор помню радиопередачу о путешествиях и приключениях Захара Загадкина. Я слушала эту передачу вместе с детьми, и мы все получали большое удовольствие. Это была наша любимая радиоигра. У нас на стене висела большая географическая карта. Дети пользовались ей, когда разгадывали загадки Захара и писали ответы на передачу. Мы все научились читать карту. В Америке мне это помогло водить машину, когда еще не было GPS (навигатор). Мои дети полюбили науки о природе и, ставши взрослыми, выбрали специальности, связанные с природой. Они любят путешествовать по Америке и другим странам и приучили к этому своих детей.

КРЮКОВ О ЗАХАРЕ ЗАГАДКИНЕ

В семье, в которой я вырос, родители все время работали. Моим воспитанием занималась бабушка, у которой все время было включено радио. Невольно я слушал все передачи, одну из которых особенно полюбил. Это были незабываемые путешествия с Захаром Загадкиным! Мы с бабушкой прибавляли громкость радиоприемника, усаживались поудобней и отправлялись в путь! Я очень полюбил географию и до сих пор помню многие географические названия и т.п. В школе по предмету проблем не было, были легко заработанные пятерки и все благодаря З.З. мы с моим другом — одноклассником Владимиром и на других предметах загадывали друг другу географические загадки, что было очень увлекательно!

Уже будучи отцом, я, вспоминая свои школьные годы и Захара, постарался привить любовь к географии и к нашей необъятной Родине своим детям.

Часть IV

Слово

Эта земля моя, она прекрасна, Боже, храни ее!
Три патриотические песни Америки[1]

Павел Ильин

Последние годы жизни в России, еще до того, как моя семья подала заявление на эмиграцию, я перестал говорить о Советском Союзе «мы». Но когда после пятилетнего отказа моя семья приехала в Америку, я о ней тоже не мог говорить «мы». Причины этого «там» и «здесь» были разные. В Союзе я отказывался отождествлять себя с режимом, под которым вынужден был жить, а здесь... Я с момента приезда знал, что это — моя страна, но что-то меня останавливало. Наверное, то, что я еще недостаточно чувствовал себя американцем.

И вот — то самое 11 сентября, день величайшей трагедии и величайшего сплочения американского народа. «United we stand», «Вместе мы выстоим», — вот лозунг тех дней. И я неожиданно для себя заметил, что говорю об Америке: «мы». Я стал жителем США в ноябре 1987-го, гражданином в мае 1993-го, и ощутил себя американцем в сентябре 2001-го.

Я люблю Америку и ни разу не изменял этому чувству. В моей голове постоянно звучали мелодии трех американских патриотических песен. Я сжился с ними и захотел перевести их слова на русский язык. И еще мне захотелось узнать, когда и почему эти песни написаны, узнать больше об авторах их слов и музыки, о биографии песен. Так появились переводы и сопровождающие их очерки, которые я предлагаю читателю. Но сначала я хотел бы выразить мою признательность Семену Резнику, Александру Синельникову, Инне Тальми и Владимиру Фрумкину, которые прочитали эти очерки и сделали замечания, которые помогли мне улучшить текст, и Ирине Хомутовой, чьими консультациями я пользовался, работая над переводами.

---

[1] Опубликовано в русскоязычном литературном журнале «Время и место». См. Павел Ильин. Три песни. *Время и место, №3 (20)*. Нью-Йорк, 2011: 113–136.

GOD BLESS AMERICA

11 сентября 2001 года, когда на глазах всего мира рушились башни Всемирного Торгового центра, телезрители увидели и оптимистические кадры: члены Конгресса, стоя на ступенях Капитолия, хором пели песню! И нужно ли напоминать какую, ибо ее первая строчка уже назавтра появилась буквально повсюду — на бамперах автомобилей, в витринах магазинов, на стенах домов, на заборах: «God Bless America!» Величайшая в истории страны катастрофа сплотила американцев, и символом этого единства, наряду с американским флагом, стала песня, написанная евреем — эмигрантом из белорусского местечка Толочин.

Израиль (Изя) Исидор Бейлин прошел Эллис-Айленд в 1893 году, будучи пяти лет от роду. В памяти мальчика сохранилось только одно воспоминание о предыдущей жизни — как он, завернутый в одеяло, лежит на обочине дороги и смотрит, как горит их дом, подожженный погромщиками. В Америке Бейлины поселились в Нью-Йорке — на Нижнем Ист-Сайде, где селились тогда еврейские иммигранты из России. Изя начал зарабатывать деньги с восьми лет — нормальная доля эмигрантского мальчика в то время. Он брался за все: продавал газеты, служил матросом, был поводырем у слепого певца и пел сам. Сначала — на улице, а потом в музыкальном кафе в Чайна-тауне, куда его взяли «поющим официантом». И здесь, в 1907 году, он написал слова песни, музыку к которой сочинил игравший в кафе пианист. Песня была напечатана, но наборщик ошибся. Автором ее слов был назван не И. Бейлин (I. Beilin), а И. Берлин (I. Berlin). А получив новую фамилию, он, заодно, решил сменить и имя.

Вскоре Ирвинг Берлин (правильное ударение на втором слоге, как у столицы Германии) стал сочинять не только слова песен, но и музыку. И, спустя какое-то время, знаменитый в Америке композитор Джером Керн (Jerome Kern, 1885–1945) сказал, что у Ирвинга Берлина нет своего «места» в американской музыке, потому что «он сам и есть американская музыка».

В 1938 году, когда над Европой нависла угроза новой большой войны, Ирвинг Берлин ощутил себя обязанным создать мирную — не военную — патриотическую песню. Но работа над ней не заладилась: «положить на музыку патриотизм оказалось сложнее, чем любовь и страстное желание».[2] И тут к Берлину обратилась

---

[2] Nancy Furstinger. *Say it with Music. The Story of Irving Berlin* (2003), p. 63.

популярнейшая в то время певица Кэт Смит (Kate Smith, 1909–1986) — «певчая птица Америки». Она готовилась к выступлению по радио в день двадцатилетия окончания Первой мировой войны (Armistice Day — День Перемирия, как до 1954 года назывался День Ветерана), и песня ей была нужна «завтра». И Берлин вспомнил о песне, которую он написал в 1918 году для финала одного мюзикла, но отложил, найдя ее для того шоу излишне патетической. Это была «God Bless America». (Слова, ставшие названием песни, Изя часто слышал от мамы — жительницы квартала бедняков на Манхаттане. Не напоминает ли это наших стариков, которые могут жаловаться на здоровье, работу социальных служб, вообще на жизнь, но затроньте их чувства, и услышите: «God bless America!»). Он взял эту песню, заменил несколько строк, приведя текст в соответствие со временем, и отдал певице.[3] Песня дождалась своего часа.

Берлин написал два куплета, но мы («мы» — это мы, американцы, которые любят свою страну, независимо от того, «старые» мы американцы или «новые»), поем один. Я, как и очень многие (о специалистах не говорю), даже не предполагал, что у песни есть второй, а вернее, первый куплет, пока не обнаружил его в «Справочнике патриота» Каролины Кеннеди.[4] И это помогло мне понять значение слова bless и, соответственно, название песни в контексте замысла автора.

Все мы (здесь я уже говорю о *нас* — «новых» американцах) знаем значение слова bless — благословлять. Поэтому общепринятый перевод названия песни — «Боже, *благослови* Америку». Но ведь слово может иметь и другие значения, и несоответствие привычного перевода смыслу песни я почувствовал еще сразу после 11 сентября, когда эти слова были у всех на слуху и на глазах: меня смущало несоответствие между bless — благослови, и следующими дальше словами «Stand behind her and guide her...». Окончательно же эта строка, а, следовательно, и название песни стали понятными мне

---

[3] Одна из поправок в тексте отражает изменения, произошедшие в языке американцев за годы, истекшие со времени написания песни. Как вспоминал сам Берлин, первоначально в песне было: «Stand behind her and guide her to the right (то есть в правильном направлении) with a light from above». В 1918 году слова «to the right» еще не носили политической окраски, а к 1938 году она появилась; и Берлин заменил эти слова на «Through the night». См. Philip Furia. *Irving Berlin: A life in Song* (1998), p. 193. Иногда можно видеть эти слова, напечатанные в упрощенном виде: «Thru the night».

[4] *A Patriot's Handbook: Songs, Poems, Stories, and Speeches Celebrating the Land We Love.* Selected and introduced by Caroline Kennedy (2003), p. 577.

после того, как я прочитал первый куплет (напомню, что Берлин выпустил песню в свет в предчувствии мировой катастрофы):

> While the storm clouds gather
> Far across the sea,
> Let us swear allegiance
> To a land that's free;
> Let us all be grateful
> For a land so fair,
> As we raise our voices
> In a solemn prayer.

Вот прозаический перевод этого куплета: «В то время, как за морем сгущаются грозовые облака, давайте присягнем на преданность земле, которая свободна, и поблагодарим (Бога) за эту прекрасную землю, возвышая, свои голоса в торжественной молитве.»[5]

И вот теперь, уловив тревожную ноту в первом, незнакомом мне ранее куплете, я прояснил для себя значение главной строки песни: «Боже, *храни* Америку!».[6]

God Bless America	**Боже, храни Америку**
God bless America,	God bless America,
Land that I love.	Мою любовь.
Stand behind her and guide her	Поддержи ее, и веди ее,
Through the night with a light	Освещая ей путь вновь
from above.	и вновь, —
From the mountains	Через горы,
To the prairies,	Через прерии,
To the oceans	Под небесным
White with foam.	Шатром.
God bless America,	God bless America,
My home, sweet home,	Мой дом, милый дом,
God bless America,	God bless America,
My home, sweet home.	Мой дом, милый дом.
Irving Berlin	*© 2011 Pavel Ilyin (transl.)*

---

[5] Мой друг Владимир Фрумкин помог мне с переводом этого куплета.

[6] Я искренне благодарен моим друзьям Блэру Рублу, Ирине Хомутовой и Вадиму Щеглову, беседы с которыми помогли мне понять значение слова *bless* в названии песни И. Берлина.

Как видит читатель, я сохранил строку «God bless America» по-английски. Эти три слова знают все, иногда относясь к ним с безразличием, порой с ненавистью, но чаще произносят как молитву. Тот самый случай, когда слово из песни не выкинешь и не заменишь, даже переводя ее на другой язык. God bless America!

Кэт Смит представила «God Bless America» на радио как одно из самых прекрасных когда-либо созданных сочинений и как песню, которая никогда не умрет. И, как сказано в одной из бесчисленных книг о Берлине, исполненная ею песня распространилась по стране «подобно лесному пожару»: ее пели в школах и церквах, в театрах и на стадионах, — везде. Обе партии — как Демократическая, так и Республиканская, сделали ее своей официальной песней в президентских кампаниях 1940 года. Всерьез обсуждался вопрос о провозглашении этой песни государственным гимном США: утвержденная в 1931 году в качестве официального гимна песня на стихи Фрэнсиса Скотта Ки «Знамя, усеянное звездами» («The Star-Spangled Banner») многим казалась громоздкой и трудной для исполнения и потому не совсем подходящей для гимна страны. Сам Берлин был против этого, в частности потому, что его песня — это песня-молитва.[7]

Но не всем «God bless America» пришлась по вкусу. Церковные проповедники находили ее религиозный дух и патриотизм показными, многих раздражало, что песня написана эмигрантом, а куклуксклановцы призывали к бойкоту песни просто потому, что ее автор Ирвинг Берлин — еврей.

«God bless America» — это не только песня, которая вдохновляет живых; это еще и одна из тех великих песен, которые помогают достойно умереть. 8 июля 2002 года Президент Соединенных Штатов Америки Джордж Буш-младший передал семье капитана Хэмберта «Рокки» Версаче Медаль Славы (Medal of Honor). Капитан Версаче стал первым американским военнопленным, удостоенным этой высшей награды. В 1963 году он попал в плен во Вьетнаме, пережил два года жестоких пыток и был расстрелян 26 сентября 1965 года. Когда товарищи Рокки по заключению слышали его голос последний раз, он пел «God Bless America» во всю силу своих легких.[8]

---

[7] *New Grove Dictionary of American Music.* Volume 3, 1986, p. 488.

[8] Ellen Sorokin. «Bush awards Medal of Honor to POW». *Washington Times*, 9 July 2002, p. A3.

...Шло время, и когда на смену музыкальным стилям, в которых работал Берлин — рэгтайм, свинг, пришли новые ритмы, популярность Ирвинга Берлина, как и других его современников, пошла на убыль. Но в день Великой Трагедии оказались нужны именно эта музыка и эти слова. Американцы воспряли с «God Bless America», впервые прозвучавшей за шестьдесят три года до этого. Сбылись слова Кэт Смит: эта песня будет жить вечно.

Остается добавить, что в знак благодарности стране, которая его приняла, Ирвинг Берлин пожертвовал весь гонорар от исполнения «God Bless America» бой- и герл-скаутам Америки. Эти деньги продолжают поступать на счета скаутских организаций США.

THIS LAND IS YOUR LAND

В июле 1912 года, в разгар очередной предвыборной кампании в Соединенных Штатах Америки, в семье жителя городка Окема (Okemah) в Оклахоме Чарльза Гатри появился на свет мальчик, которого назвали Вудро Вильсоном — в честь одного из претендентов на пост президента США. Этот претендент потом стал президентом, а мальчик — великим американским музыкантом и народным певцом Вуди Гатри (Woodrow Wilson «Woody» Guthrie, 1912–1967).

Окема, «раньше и теперь» неприметный городок на Среднем Западе, в то время оказался втянутым в нефтяной бум и переживал недолгий период расцвета. В своей автобиографии Вуди назвал его одним из самых поющих, танцующих, орущих, болтливых, смеющихся, пьянствующих, драчливых и набитых проповедниками городов.[9] Но жизнь в этом городе не баловала мальчика: он пережил трагическую смерть любимой сестры, разорение отца, тяжелую болезнь матери, пожар, уничтоживший их дом. Чтобы поддержать семью, Вуди был готов на любую работу, лишь бы платили. Он даже играл на губной гармонике,— это тоже приносило кое-какие гроши. В шестнадцать лет он бросил школу, а в девятнадцать, покинув приходящую снова в упадок Окему, направился в соседний Техас. Он научился играть на гитаре и начал сочинять песни. Он пел и играл всюду, где можно было заработать — в салунах, на праздниках, вечеринках, просто на улицах, но жизнь его оставалась тяжелой. А тут еще Великие равнины Среднего Запада постигло стихийное бедствие, одно из самых больших в истории США: страшная засу-

---

[9] См. Joe Klein. *Woody Guthrie: A Life* (1981), p. 160.

ха, превратившая главную пшеничную зону страны в «dust bowl» — «котел пыли».[10] Засуха высушивала верхний слой распаханной почвы, ее частицы при малейшем ветре поднимались в воздух, и черные тучи пыли покрывали землю и затмевали небосвод. Засуха длилась все тридцатые годы, она пришлась на время Великой депрессии, и обнищавшее население бежало с давно насиженных земель: Великие равнины покинули два с половиной миллиона человек.[11] И одним из них был Вуди Гатри.[12] Передвигаясь на товарных поездах, попутных машинах, пешком, пробиваясь случайными заработками, Вуди, как и многие беженцы, двинулся в Калифорнию. Обосновался он в Лос-Анжелесе, где получил работу на радио. Его песни имели успех, жизнь стала налаживаться, но, как отмечает его биограф, Вуди никогда не чувствовал себя комфортно, никогда не пользовался успехом, никогда долго не засиживался в одном месте.[13] И в 1940 году он направляется через всю страну с западного берега на восточный — в Нью-Йорк.

В Нью-Йорке Вуди примыкает к крайне левым, сближается с радикальной интеллигенцией, сотрудничает в газете Компартии «Дейли Уоркер». Он — активный участник антивоенного движения и борьбы за гражданские права, среди его близких друзей и партнеров по выступлениям — Пит Сигер (Peter «Pete» Seeger, род. в 1919 г.), другой выдающийся народный певец, бывший одно время членом Коммунистической партии США. «Я был красным всю мою жизнь», — говорил о себе Вуди.

---

[10] Обычно «dust bowl» переводится на русский язык как «пыльный котел» или, реже, как «пыльная чаша». Предлагаемый здесь перевод — «котел пыли» — принадлежит моему близкому родственнику Александру Синельникову. Мне он кажется удачнее, хотя бы потому, что грамотнее. Ср. «котел каши», «чашка кофе».

[11] Такое грандиозное явление, как «котел пыли» не могло не найти отклика в литературе, музыке, изобразительном искусстве, кинематографе. Среди множества посвященных ему произведений — роман Джона Стейнбека «Гроздья гнева» и «Баллады «котла пыли»» самого Вуди Гатри.

[12] Засуха, как природное, метеорологическое явление, человеку не подвластна. Но в катастрофе 1930-х годов виноват именно он. Земледельцы обрабатывали плодородные прерии, высасывая из них все, что можно было высосать, нисколько не заботясь о том, что будет завтра. А «завтра» обернулось «котлом пыли». Советская пропаганда приводила пыльные бури в США как результат «хищнического использования земель при капитализме», умалчивая о том, что после наиболее катастрофического 1935 года Америка проснулась, и в результате совершенствования правил землепользования и введения новых методов обработки земли подобное стихийное бедствие больше не повторялось. Хотя жестокие засухи не раз с тех пор посещали Великие равнины.

[13] Jorge Arevalo. *Woody Guthrie's Biography*. **http://www.woodyguthrie.org/biography/ biography4.htm.**

This Land Is Your Land

This land is your land,
    this land is my land,
From California
    to New York Island,
From the redwood forest
    to the Gulf Stream Waters,
This land was made for you and me.

As I was walking
    that ribbon of highway,
I saw above me
    that endless skyway,
I saw below me
    that golden valley
This land was made for you and me.

I've roamed and rambled,
    and followed my foot steps
To the sparkling sands of
    her diamond desert,
While all around me
    a voice was chanting:
This land was made for you and me.

When the sun came shining,
    and I was strolling
And the wheat fields waving
    and the dust clouds rolling.
As the fog was lifting,
    a voice was chanting:
This land was made for you and me.

Nobody living
    can ever stop me,
As I go walking
    that freedom highway.
Nobody living
    can make me turn back.
This land was made for you and me.

Woody Guthrie

Эта земля — твоя

Эта земля твоя,
    эта земля моя,
От Калифорнии
    и до Нью-Йорка,
От рощ секвойи
    до струй Гольфстрима, —
Здесь все вокруг для нас с тобой.

Люблю шагать я,
    направив стопы
По уходящим
    Ввысь горным склонам,
По уходящим
    вниз каньонам, —
Здесь все вокруг для нас с тобой.

Когда брожу я
    под небом синим
Среди алмазных
    песков пустыни,
То где б я ни был,
    я слышу голос:
«Здесь все вокруг для нас с тобой».

Восходит солнце,
    и свежий ветер
Листву колышет,
    день будет светел,
Туман уходит,
    и слышен голос:
«Здесь все вокруг для нас с тобой».

Остановить нас
    никто не сможет,
Преодолеем
    мы все невзгоды,
И не свернуть нас
    с пути свободы, —
Здесь все вокруг для нас с тобой.

© 2011 Pavel Ilyin (transl.)

Вуди Гатри поселяется на Манхаттане — на 43-й улице возле 6-й авеню. Здесь, 23 февраля 1940 года, он заканчивает свою самую знаменитую песню: «This Land Is Your Land».[14] В основу ее мелодии Вуди положил музыку старой религиозной песни «Oh, My Loving Brother» («О, мой любящий брат»).[15] Вуди часто писал свои песни на уже известную музыку, и никогда не возражал, если кто-нибудь использовал его мелодии.

Вуди написал «This Land Is Your Land» в ответ на «God Bless America» Ирвинга Берлина: ему надоела эта песня, постоянно звучавшая по радио в исполнении Кэт Смит, его раздражало ее пение; он находил текст песни слишком благодушным. Об этом свидетельствуют зачеркнутые слова, которыми заканчивался каждый куплет в первом варианте песни: «God blessed America for us». Слово bless имеет разные значения, и мой перевод в данном случае будет: «Бог освятил Америку для нас.» Но чем же его песня менее «благодушна», чем «God Bless...»?

Пять куплетов, которые я перевел, это те, которые массово поются, особенно первые четыре. Но немногие знают, что в песне есть еще два куплета. Это:

> As I was walking, I saw a sign there,
> And on the sign, it said «No Trespassing».
> But on the other side it didn't say anything:
> That side was made for you and me.

«Я шел и увидел надпись, и эта надпись говорила: «No Trespassing» («Прохода нет»), а на другой стороне ничего не было сказано. Эта сторона — для нас с тобой!» В первых вариантах песни на месте «No Trespassing» стояло: «Private Property» — «Частная собственность».

И:

> In the shadow of the steeple, I saw my people,
> By the relief office I seen my people;
> As they stood there hungry, and I stood there asking,
> Is this land made for you and me?

---

[14] Эти адрес и число стоят на сохранившемся рукописном автографе песни. Факсимиле автографа приведено на веб-сайте **http://web.archive.org/web/19970814121656/http://www.artsci.wustl.edu/~davida/pics/woody/this_land.gif**

[15] Эта песня под названием «When The World's On Fire» («Когда мир в огне») стала популярной после ее исполнения группой «Carter Family» («Семья Картер»).

«Я видел мой народ в тени здания со шпилем (в тени церкви), видел его около бюро по безработице; люди там стояли голодные, а я стоял там, спрашивая: «Для нас ли с тобой эта земля?».[16]

Этими куплетами Вуди противопоставляет неравенство жителей Америки красоте ее земли. С ними песня становится песней протеста против несправедливостей жизни, но куплеты эти вспоминают редко, да и сам Вуди их исполнял не всегда. И «This Land Is Your Land» стала одной из самых патриотических американских песен, претендовавших на то, чтобы стать гимном США.

Вуди не раз меняет место своего обитания. Он переезжает в Гринвич-Виллидж—«гнездо» радикалов в Нью-Йорке, уезжает в Орегон, возвращается в Калифорнию и снова в Нью-Йорк, на этот раз на Кони-Айленд. Душа бродяги не дает ему покоя, но его настигает тяжелая болезнь,—та, что много лет назад свела в могилу его мать. Последние годы жизни он проводит в больнице...

Вуди Гатри писал не только «песни протеста», он писал также детские песни, романы, биографические произведения, эссе. Но «Эта земля—твоя» осталась в его наследии самой знаменитой. Она распространилась по всей планете и во многих странах приняла местное обличие. Так, в Канаде поют: «От Полярного круга до Великих озер», в Великобритании: «От Корнуолла до гор Шотландии». Свои варианты есть на Американских Виргинских и на Багамских островах, в Ирландии, Израиле и Намибии. Ее поют не только на английском, но и на валлийском и шведском языках, на иврите и даже на эсперанто.[17]

Звучит эта песня и во многих кинофильмах, телевизионных передачах и по радио,—часто с измененными словами, как, например, «Put your hand in my hand...» («Положи свою руку в мою...») или «This song is my song» («Эта песня моя...»).[18] А в 2004 году на развлекательном веб-сайте Джиб-Джаб (JibJab) появилась пародия на нее, изображавшая претендентов на пост президента США Джоржа Буша и Джона Керри. Оба согласны, что «This land is your

---

[16] Оба куплета существуют в разных, хотя и близких по смыслу вариантах; сам Вуди пел их по-разному. Я выбрал вариант из «Справочника патриота» Каролины Кеннеди, стр. 646–647. (См. прим. 3,)

[17] http://en.wikipedia.org/wiki/This_Land_Is_Your_Land

[18] «This song is my song» поет Арло Гатри (Arlo Guthrie, род. в 1967 г.), сын Вуди, в одной из популярных радиопередач. Арло также стал известным народным певцом. (См. о нем *New Grove Dictionary of American Music*, Volume 2, 1986, p. 299). Музыкантами и певцами стали и дети Арло — сын и три дочери. Их «музыкальную линию» продолжает внук Арло и правнук Вуди,— четвертое поколение поющих Гатри.

land, this land is my land», но каждый из них утверждает, что «This land will surely vote for me!» («Эта земля будет, без сомнения, голосовать за меня!»).[19]

В заключение — слово трем современникам Вуди Гатри:

Джон Стейнбек: *«Вуди — это просто Вуди. Тысячи людей не знают, что у него есть какое-то другое имя… Он поет народные песни, и, как мне кажется, в известном смысле он и есть этот народ… Но в его песнях есть нечто еще более важное… Это — готовность все вынести и бороться против угнетения. Я думаю, что это и есть то, что мы называем американским духом».*

Боб Дилан: *«Вуди Гатри был мой последний кумир. Последний и одновременно первый».*

Пит Сигер: *«Сказать вам, что я думаю о Вуди? Он — гений».*

Можно разделять или не разделять политические пристрастия Вуди Гатри, но нельзя не согласиться с Питом Сигером.

AMERICA THE BEAUTIFUL

Как возникает песня? Либо композитор сочиняет музыку на уже написанные стихи, либо поэт пишет слова под уже готовую музыку… А бывает, что композитор и поэт объединяются в творческом дуэте и работают вместе. Эта песня другая: поэтесса — автор слов — не знала, что музыка для песни давно написана; композитор умер, не успев познакомиться со стихами, создавшими славу его музыке.

Начну издалека. В 1805 году экспедиция под началом капитана Зебулона Пайка (Zebulon Pike, 1779–1813) открыла в Передовом хребте Скалистых гор на краю Великих равнин в Колорадо вершину, которая получила имя в честь руководителя экспедиции: Pike's Peak (пик Пайка).[20] Позднее апостроф в названии горы исчез, и с тех пор она известна как Pikes Peak (по-русски принято писать Пайкс-Пик).[21] Пайк не смог подняться на вершину горы,—

---

[19] http://sendables.jibjab.com/originals/this_land (видео).

[20] Высота горы 4302 м.

[21] Апостроф с буквой s ('s) в английском языке означает принадлежность, и его первоначально имели в своих названиях многие географичские объекты. Так, например, городок Harpers Ferry (Харперс-Ферри) на Потомаке назывался Harper's Ferry: здесь некогда держал паром (ferry) основатель

помешала непогода; это удалось сделать только через пятнадцать лет. А в 1859 году в районе горы было обнаружено золото, и началась золотая лихорадка. Золотоискатели шли на поиски желтого металла под лозунгом «Pike's Peak or Bust» (в моем вольном переводе: «Возьмем Пайкс-Пик — или конец!». И хотя в самой горе золота не нашли, ее имя попало на первые страницы крупнейших американских газет. Но не золотая лихорадка прославила Пайкс-Пик.[22] Его прославила профессор английской литературы Катарина Ли Бейтс (Gatharine Lee Bates, 1859–1929).

Катарина Ли Бейтс всю жизнь прожила в Массачусеттсе. Она родилась в городке Фалмут (Falmouth) на южном берегу полуострова Кейп-Код (Cape Cod — Тресковый Мыс) в семье, хранившей пуританские традиции.[23] Когда ей было двенадцать лет, семья переехала в Гранвилл (Granville) около Уэлсли (Wellesley) поблизости от Бостона;[24] в семнадцать Катарина поступила в колледж Уэлсли,[25] который окончила в 21 год — в 1881 году. Потом она работала школьным учителем, а с 1885 года стала преподавать литературу в Уэлсли.[26] И всегда и везде писала стихи.

И вот, в июне 1893 года, профессор колледжа Уэлсли поэтесса Катарина Ли Бейтс, 33-х лет от роду, отправилась поездом из Бостона в Колорадо. В то лето президент колледжа Колорадо в городе Колорадо-Спрингс пригласил группу ведущих специалистов Востока, чтобы познакомить студентов Запада «с ярчайшими умами страны и ее наиболее прогрессивным духом».[27] Катарина Ли Бейтс

города по фамилии Харпер; а смущающие многих пенсильванские названия Pottsville и Pottstown (Поттсвилл и Поттстаун) когда-то писались как Pott's Ville и Pott's Town: их основал предприниматель John Pott (Джон Потт), происходивший из немецких поселенцев. Все такие места свой апостроф отбросили: без него удобнее.

[22] Колорадская золотая лихорадка оставила следы в других местах: города Денвер и Боулдер выросли из поселков старателей

[23] Отца Катарина (Кити) не знала, он умер через месяц после ее рождения. См. Lynn Sherr. *America the Beautiful: The Stirring True Story Behind Our Nation's Favorite Song* (2001), p. 15. Я знаю еще только одну «книгу о песне»: Judy Rosen. White Christmas: The Story of an American Song (2002), посвященную песне Ирвинга Берлина «Белое Рождество».

[24] Гранвилл, ныне Уэлсли Хилл (Wellesley Hill) — часть города Уэлсли. Сам Уэлсли, когда Катарина училась в нем, был частью города Нидэма (Needham). Оба они входит сейчас в состав Большого Бостона.

[25] Колледж Уэлсли (Wellesley College) — женский колледж свободных искусств, самый известный среди женских колледжей США, основан в 1875 году — за год до поступления туда Бейтс.

[26] Катарина Ли Бейтс проработала в Уэлсли более 40 лет, — до своего выхода на пенсию в 1926 году.

[27] Lynn Sherr, p. 30.

была включена в эту группу; ей предстояло в течение трех недель читать лекции в летней школе колледжа.

Бейтс уже довелось побывать в дальнем путешествии, но на восток, через океан. На запад она отправилась впервые. И, благодаря этой поездке, мы имеем «America the Beautiful». В пути Бейтс сделала знаменательную, как потом оказалось, остановку в Чикаго, где проходила Всемирная выставка, посвященная 400-летию открытия Америки Христофором Колумбом. Это была выставка достижений и возможностей человеческого разума. Достижений современности и возможностей будущего. Фантастическая иллюминация, восьмидесятиметровое колесо обозрения (чертово колесо) американского инженера Ферриса,[28] другие технические чудеса... Но наибольшее впечатление на Бейтс произвел «Белый город» — сама выставка со всеми ее павильонами, бассейнами, каналами, и особенно ее центральная часть: воздвигнутые ведущими американскими архитекторами неоклассические здания, покрытые специальной штукатуркой, как бы светились белым («алебастровым») светом, создавая незабываемый эффект. «Образец красоты», — так Бейтс охарактеризовала «Белый город» в своем дневнике.[29]

Дальнейший путь Катарины Ли Бейтс лежал через Канзас; мимо проплывали поля пшеницы. Было 4 июля, праздник независимости США, и, глядя на картины за окном, Бейтс все больше проникалась чувством любви к Америке...

Поезд привез Катарину Ли Бейтс в Колорадо-Спрингс, город, основанный за двадцать два года до этого у подножья горы Пайкс-Пик. Приезжие профессора вели занятия в летней школе, а в свободное время осматривали окрестности города. До отъезда оставалось совсем немного, когда, наконец, пришла очередь Пайкс-Пика: Катарина Ли Бейтс и ее коллеги отправились на вершину горы.

К этому времени уже была проложена зубчатая железная дорога, по которой туристы могли без труда подниматься на вершину Пайкс-Пика. Но в этот день она не работала. И путешественники наняли фургон, — из тех, на которых пионеры преодолевали просторы Дикого Запада, с традиционным девизом «Возьмем Пайкс-Пик — или конец!», вполне уместным для данного случая. Сначала фургон тащили лошади, в середине пути их сменили более крепкие мулы. Подъем потребовал нескольких часов, и Бейтс очень

---

[28] По-английски колесо обозрения так и называется: Ferris Wheel (колесо Ферриса).

[29] Lynn Sherr, p. 29.

устала. Но когда перед ней открылась панорама Великих равнин, безбрежных, как море, ее наполнил безграничный восторг. Казалось, перед ней лежит вся великая страна, где сияют белые города, ветер колышет колосья пшеницы, и счастливо живут люди...[30] И возникла первая стихотворная строчка: «O, beautiful...» («Ты прекрасна...»)

Вернувшись в гостиницу, Бейтс записала эту строчку. И следующие, написанные тут же. В этот день — 22 июля 1893 года — родилось стихотворение, ставшее потом словами великой песни.

Стихотворение, названное автором «Америка», впервые было напечатано 4 июля 1895 года в популярном бостонском еженедельнике «Конгрегешионалист» («Congregationalist»): редакция держала «Америку» в своем портфеле несколько месяцев, чтобы приурочить ее публикацию к Дню Независимости. Второй раз оно появилось в ноябре 1904 года в ежедневной газете «Бостон ивнинг транскрипт» («Boston Evening Transcript»), в то время самой влиятельной в Новой Англии; Катарина Ли Бейтс отдала в газету новую редакцию «Америки». Но поэтесса продолжала работать над стихотворением, и в 1911 году опубликовала его окончательную редакцию под новым, тоже окончательным, названием в своей книге, на обложке которой стояло: «America the Beautiful and other poems (и другие стихи)».

В тексте «America the Beautiful» явно прослеживаются эмоциональные и зрительные впечатления автора от поездки в Колорадо. Здесь и «сияние алебастровых городов» («Белый город»), и «янтарные волны хлебов» (прерии Канзаса), и «величие пурпурных гор» (Скалистые горы), и вид с вершины Пайкс-Пика на необъятные просторы Америки — «From sea to shining sea», то есть «от океана до океана», или, что то же, «от берега до берега», иначе говоря, вся страна.[31] К сожалению, при поэтическом переводе не всегда удается буквально передать слова автора, особенно когда стремишься сохранить ритмический строй оригинала, а для песни это важно. Так, в предлагаемый перевод не вместилось слово «алеба-

---

[30] На следующий день мать Катарины получила от нее телеграмму: «Привет с Пайкс-Пика восхитительно ошеломляюще хочу ты была здесь.» См. Lynn Sherr, p. 38–39.

[31] Фраза «From sea to shining sea» стала идиомой, и несчетное число раз с тех пор использовалась в литературе, искусстве и средствах массовой информации. См. **http://www.phrases.org.uk/meanings/from%20sea%20to%20shining%20 sea.html.** Shining, по-английски, — сияющий, но значене отдельных слов (и их сочетаний) в идиомах, как известно, может не иметь никакого отношения к смыслу идиомы..

America the Beautiful

O beautiful for spacious skies,
For amber waves of grain,
For purple mountain majesties
Above the fruited plain!
America! America!
God shed His grace on thee,
And crown thy good with brotherhood,
From sea to shining sea!

O beautiful for pilgrim feet
Whose stern, impassion'd stress
A thoroughfare for freedom beat
Across the wilderness!
America! America!
God mend thine ev'ry flaw,
Confirm thy soul in self-control,
Thy liberty in law!

O beautiful for heroes proved
In liberating strife,
Who more than self their country loved,
And mercy more than life!
America! America!
May God thy gold refine
Till all success be nobleness,
And ev'ry gain divine!

O beautiful for patriot dream
That sees beyond the years
Thine alabaster cities gleam
Undimmed by human tears!
America! America!
God shed His grace on thee
And crown thy good with brotherhood
From sea to shining sea!

Katharine Lee Bates

Ты прекрасна, Америка!

Прекрасна небесами ты
И золотом хлебов;
Величьем гор прекрасна ты
Над зеленью садов!
Америка! Америка!
Бог милостив к тебе,
И братства свет здесь светит всем
На всей твоей земле!

Прекрасна пилигримов ты
Наследством на земле
Пути свободы – их следы –
Проложены везде!
Америка! Америка!
Тебя Бог укрепит,
Свободы ниспошлет закон,
И душу закалит!

Прекрасна героизмом тех,
Кто жизни не щадя,
Боролся за свободу всех,
Страну свою любя!
Америка! Америка!
Тебя Бог вдохновит,
Он благородство даст тебе,
Со славой породнит!

Прекрасна ты мечтами тех,
Кто видел сквозь года,
Как будет счастлив человек
В лазурных городах!
Америка! Америка!
Бог милостив к тебе,
И братства свет здесь светит всем
На всей твоей земле!

© 2011 Pavel Ilyin (transl.)

525

стровый» — очень важное для поэтессы, которая видит свои города именно такими. Я заменил «алебастровые города» на «лазурные», которые представляются мне столь же прекрасными.

Но более серьезного объяснения, как мне кажется, требует мой вариант русского названия стиха, поскольку публика бывает недовольна, когда отходят от привычного ей. Произнесите с требуемой по смыслу экспрессией: «America the Beautiful». А теперь произнесите эти же слова в буквальном переводе: «Америка Прекрасная», — и что получилось? Нечто размазанное, без нужного пафоса и экспрессии. Не многим лучше и «Прекрасная Америка». А теперь, мое: «Ты прекрасна, Америка». Чувствуете? Два ударных слова и сокращение числа безударных слогов, — и русское заглавие адекватно оригиналу.[32]

И еще одно замечание. Обращение к Америке в переводе на «ты» полностью соответствует оригиналу: Катарина Ли Бейтс использует по отношению к любимой стране малоупотребительные уже в то время формы местоимения второго лица единственного числа. [33]

Но вернемся к биографии песни. Едва стихи Катарины Ли Бейтс появились в печати, их стали петь. Петь на любой подходящий мотив. Композитор Сайлас Дж. Пратт (Silas G. Pratt, 1846–1916) был первым, кто положил стихи на музыку. Но никто не знал, что Музыка для «America the Beautiful», Музыка с большой буквы, уже написана, что написал ее композитор Сэм Уорд, и называется она «Матерна» («Materna»).

Самуэль Аугустус Уорд (Samuel Augustus Ward, 1848–1903) служил органистом и руководителем хора в епископальной церкви в Ньюарке, штат Нью-Джерси. И в один прекрасный летний день 1882 года (прекрасный как в прямом, так и в переносном смысле) он отправился со своим другом хормейстером Генри Мартиным в парк развлечений на Кони-Айленд. Попасть на Кони-Айленд можно было экипажем, можно было поездом, но друзья выбрали пароход. Мы не знаем, как они провели день в этом замечательном парке и на его великолепном пляже, но можно не сомневаться, что они отплыли домой в чудесном настроении.

— Генри, — неожиданно обратился Сэм к своему спутнику, — ко мне только что пришла мелодия, но не на чем ее записать. Не найдется ли у тебя листка бумаги?

---

[32] Лингвисты найдут мое объяснение наивным, но я так чувствую.
[33] Thou (ты), thee (тебе, тебя), thy, thine (твой, твоя, твое).

Генри пошарил по карманам, но там не было ни клочка. И тогда он оторвал рукав своей накрахмаленной рубашки и протянул его Сэму. И Сэм тут же начертил на нем нотные линейки и записал мелодию, которая крутилась у него в голове. Мелодию песни «America the Beautiful».

Возможно, это легенда. Но кто сказал, замечает Линн Шер, что парк развлечений и океан могут вдохновить художника меньше, чем всемирная выставка и гора?[34] Я с этим полностью согласен. А было Сэму Уорду тогда тридцать три, — столько же, сколько Катарине Ли Бейтс, когда она поднялась на Пайкс-Пик.

Конечно, никакой «Америки» еще не было, до ее написания оставалось одиннадцать лет. «Мелодия на рукаве» предназначалась для религиозного гимна «О, мать, родной Иерусалим» («O Mother Dear Jerusalem»). Этот старинный гимн, по мнению композитора, нуждался в новой музыке. Уорд назвал ее «Матерна».[35] В 1888 году «Матерна» вышла за стены церкви в Ньюарке, — ее напечатал еженедельник «Приходской хор» («Parish Chorus»), и она оказалась лучшей и самой долговечной из всего, созданного композитором.

Самуэль Уорд умер в 1903 году.[36] Ему не довелось встретиться с Катариной Ли Бейтс, и он не дожил до триумфа своей «Матерны». Слова и музыка встретились через год после смерти композитора, в ноябре 1904 года. Их свели вместе д-р Кларенс Барбур (Clarence Barbour, 1869–1937), пастор баптистской церкви на Лейк-авеню в Рочестере, штат Нью-Йорк, и его жена, опытный музыкант. «Матерна» Уорда была им знакома, она регулярно входила в сборники религиозных гимнов, а стихотворение Бейтс пастор прочитал в «Бостон ивнинг транскрипт». И супруги нашли, что эти стихи и эта музыка идеально подходят друг к другу.[37]

Церковь на Лейк-авеню стала первым местом в стране, где песню «America the Beautiful» спели на музыку «Матерны». Позднее, в 1910 году, Барбур опубликовал слова и музыку песни в состав-

---

[34] Lynn Sherr, p. 48.

[35] Materna — материнская (исп.).

[36] В некрологе, помещенном в ньюаркской газете «Дейли адвертайзер» («Daily Advertiser»), Уорд был назван «одним из самых известных музыкальных деятелей штата». (Lynn Sherr, p. 59).

[37] Lynn Sherr, p. 58. В конце своей жизни д-р Кларенс Барбур был избран президентом одного из университетов Лиги плюща (Ivy League) — Брауновского университета в Провиденсе, штат Род-Айленд. См. http://en.wikipedia.org/wiki/Clarence_Barbour.

ленном им сборнике религиозных гимнов. «America the Beautiful» широко распространилась по стране. Ее включали в поэтические сборники, школьные учебники и книги для чтения. Солдаты, отправлявшиеся на европейский театр военных действий в 1918 году, уносили с собой эту песню, напечатанную в изданном для них песеннике, и пели ее на марше и в день окончания войны. «America the Beautiful», писал «отец американской музыкальной комедии» Джордж М. Коэн (George M. Kohan, 1878–1942),— это было то, за что они воевали, и то, с чем они вернулись домой. [38]

Но не все признавали «Матерну» наиболее подходящей для «America the Beautiful», ей пришлось соперничать с мелодиями других композиторов.[39] Апофеоза это соперничество достигло в конце 1926-начале 1927 года, когда американская Национальная федерация музыкальных клубов проводила конкурс на новую — лучшую! — музыку для песни. На конкурс пришла 961 мелодия, авторы которых жаждали славы и денег. Но приз в 500 долларов [40] остался не врученным: авторитетное жюри не сочло ни одну из присланных мелодий достойной быть музыкой для «America the Beautiful». «Матерна» одержала безусловную победу.

Катарина Ли Бейтс никогда не высказывала предпочтения той или иной музыке. И воздерживалась от какой-либо критики. Выбор музыки — это дело певцов, а не поэта, объясняла она. Но она не колеблясь отвергала — вежливо, но решительно, все попытки и предложения внести поправки в стихотворный текст. У песни, подчёркивала поэтесса, должен быть один текст, а не много, как это случилось с музыкой. [41]

В то же время Бейтс не имела ничего против перевода текста песни на другие языки и не возражала против его изменения в других странах: свои варианты пелись в Австралии, Бирме, Германии, Индии, Канаде, Мексике, и на Филиппинах. [42] «Если им это нравится, то почему бы нет?»,— говорила Бейтс.

Профессор Катарина Ли Бейтс заведовала кафедрой английской литературы, писала книги и статьи по своей специальности, публиковала сборники стихов, рассказы о своих путешестви-

---

[38] Lynn Sherr, p. 66.

[39] Линн Шерр поместила в своей книге факсимиле некоторых вариантов музыки песни. См. Lynn Sherr, p.64, 65 и 67.

[40] Более 6000 долл. на современные деньги. См. **http://www.dollartimes.com/calculators/inflation.htm.**

[41] Там же.

[42] Там же.

ях, писала для детей, редактировала.[43] И — отвечала на письма. Ее корреспонденты слали ей отклики и поправки к тексту песни, многие просили совета и, конечно, обращались за автографом. Она никому не отказывала в их просьбах. «Я работала как бобер», — говорила Бейтс о себе.[44] А писем было столько, что под них пришлось выделить в ее доме особое помещение.

...Мне представляется курьезом, что еще в начале XX века Соединенные Штаты Америки жили без государственного гимна.[45] Вопрос о гимне возникал неоднократно, и в 1912 году был вынесен на обсуждение Конгресса: было предложено объявить гимном страны песню на стихи Фрэнсиса Скотта Ки (Francis Scott Key, 1779–1843) «The Star-Spangled Banner» («Знамя, усыпанное звездами»). Но решение тогда принято не было, а за стенами Капитолия все громче раздавались голоса, призывающие провозгласить гимном США песню «America the Beautiful»: это было время расцвета ее популярности. Еще в 1904 году «Бостон ивнинг транскрипт» представил стихотворение Катарины Ли Бейтс как «американский гимн»,[46] а в 1908 году один чикагский юрист написал президенту Теодору Рузвельту, что стихи такой потрясающей красоты и силы, как «America the Beautiful», должны стать нашей национальной песней. Количество таких голосов множилось, и в 1926 году Общество национального гимна (National Hymn Society) официально призвало Конгресс провозгласить «America the Beautiful» государственным гимном США. Песня «вышла в финал», став единственным соперником «The Star-Spangled Banner».

Спортивные болельщики знают, что, команда, казавшаяся им фаворитом, побеждает далеко не всегда. Дебаты в Конгрессе вспыхнули с новой силой в 1930 году, и в апреле следующего года президент Герберт Гувер подписал закон, в соответствии с которым Государственным гимном США стало «Знамя, усыпанное звездами».

Но сторонники песни Бейтс и Уорда считают, что они проиграли сражение, а не войну. В 1985 году в Конгресс поступил законо-

---

[43] Список книг, которые вышли под пера Катарины Ли Бейтс или были ею отредактированы, содержит около пятидесяти названий. См. **http://en.wikipedia. org/wiki/Katharine_Lee_Bates**.

[44] Lynn Sherr, p. 66.

[45] В США государственный гимн называется *national anthem*. *Anthem* и *hymn* в английском языке синонимы, но для официального гимна предпочтение отдано слову *anthem*.

[46] Факсимиле газетной публикации см. в Lynn Sherr, p. 58.

проект, внесенный бывшим морским пехотинцем-членом конгресса об объявлении «America the Beautiful» гимном страны вместо «The Star-Spangled Banner». Аналогичные предложения вносились и позднее. Пока никакого движения в этом направлении не наблюдается, но — продолжение следует. [47]

Имя Катарины Ли Бейтс носит улица в ее родном Фалмуте; извещение на въезде в город сообщает, что здесь родилась автор «America the Beautiful»; бережно сохраняется дом ее детства. В Уэлсли и Колорадо-Спрингс есть школы имени Бейтс. Слова ее великой песни сияют золотом на мемориальной доске, установленной на вершине Пайкс-Пика.[48] Имя Самуэля Уорда увековечено на стене церкви в Ньюарке, в которой служил композитор. Один из парков в Колорадо-Спрингс называется «America the Beautiful Park». Есть ли в еще в Америке парки, носящие имя песни?

2001–2011
Вашингтон

---

[47] Подробный рассказ об обсуждения вопроса о гимне в Конгрессе см. в книге Lynn Sherr, p. 85–89.

[48] Пайк погиб в войну 1812 года с англичанами в битве под Йорком. Его имя носят полтора десятка городов и других географических объектов. Я много раз проезжал по Балтиморской кольцевой дороге не подозревая, что город Пайксвилл, на который ведет пересекающая ее 140-я дорога, и гора Пайкс-Пик — тезки.

«Я ЗНАЮ: ВЕК УЖ МОЙ ИЗМЕРЕН…»

Павел Ильин

> *Я знаю, век уж мой измерен;*
> *Но чтоб продлилась жизнь моя,*
> *Я утром должен быть уверен,*
> *Что с вами днем увижусь я…*

Пушкин. Письмо Онегина к Татьяне. Волшебные строчки, может быть, самые волшебные в русской поэзии, или, может быть, одни из самых волшебных. Во всяком случае, ничего более волшебного быть не может. Мы произносим их вслух, читаем про себя, схватываем глазами — музыка: «Я знаю: век уж мой измерен… Но чтоб продлилась жизнь моя… Я утром должен быть уверен… Что с вами днем увижусь я…»

А между тем эти строчки потрясающе не логичны! Схваченный этой неожиданной, нежданной мыслью, останавливаешься, не веря сам себе, и начинаешь снова: « Я знаю: век уж мой измерен… Но чтоб продлилась жизнь моя… Я утром должен быть уверен… Что с вами днем увижусь я…»

Да, правда… Судите сами. «Я знаю: век уж мой измерен…» То есть знаю, мне известно, то где-то там уже отмерен срок моей жизни и известно, сколько мне предстоит прожить, а то, что знать этот срок мне не дано, не меняет самого факта. Но следующая строка опровергает первую: «Но чтоб продлилась жизнь моя…» То есть существует что-то, что может продлить мою жизнь, но если это что-то существует и жизнь может быть продлена, то как же быть с тем, что «век уж мой измерен»?

Но, допустим, воля Провидения может быть изменена. Для этого, для того, «чтоб продлилась жизнь моя», — «я утром должен быть уверен, что с вами днем увижусь я». Снова противоречие, и не одно.

Если я уверен, что увижусь с вами днем, — это продлит мою жизнь, и я уверен, вы подали мне знак, и эта уверенность продлит мою жизнь, то,.. простите... что продлит жизнь — уверенность, что увижусь, или то, что увижусь? А если увереннось есть, а не увижусь, тогда что будет?

Логично? Логично. То есть логичны мои рассуждения, а не строки поэта. Но —

> Я знаю: век уж мой измерен;
> Но чтоб продлилась жизнь моя,
> Я утром должен быть уверен,
> Что с вами днем увижусь я...

И чего стоят мои рассуждения по сравнению с этим волшебством? Волшебство, оно и потому и есть волшебство, что не поддается никакой логике... Волшебство!

Мэрилэнд

Фрагменты воспоминаний
Отрывки моей памяти

Павел Ильин

Много лет назад, собирая в Библиотеке Конгресса материал для книги о Москве на рубеже XIX и XX веков, я встретил в одной из работ ссылку на изданные в Петербурге в 1800-х годах мемуары Анненкова, сына знаменитого пушкиниста, озаглавленные «Отрывки памяти». Книгу эту я найти не смог, но ее название запомнилось, я решил, что если когда-нибудь надумаю писать воспоминания, то я их так и назову: моя очень хорошая (не хвалюсь, а констатирую факт) память с годами не стала еще лучше, а повела себя совсем наоборот. И сейчас она в значительной мере состоит из лакун. Это говоря по-научному, я, в какой-то степени, считаю себя причастным к науке. Ну а если по-простому, то в моей памяти сейчас полно дыр, которые расширяются и вместе с новыми дырами поглощают ее куски. Память уже давно стала подобной шагреневой коже. Но, не желая буквально следовать старому мемуаристу, я отредактировал название моих воспоминаний так: «Отрывки моей памяти». Этим я также хотел подчеркнуть, что речь пойдет именно о моей, а не о чьей-нибудь еще памяти. Хотя, как увидит читатель, я часто ссылаюсь на воспоминания других людей, как правило, друзей и родственников.

Но когда я приступил к воспоминаниям, меня озадачил вопрос: а насколько оригинально их название? Ответ я нашел в Гугле: ой, не оригинально... Менять его, однако не стал: пусть уж так будет.

Среди родственников, на которых я ссылаюсь, я сразу должен назвать мою сестру Юлю. Юлия Михайловна Ильина, в замужестве Кеда, младше меня на целых три года и, как положено более молодым, шустрее: свои воспоминания она уже написала! И в них, естественно, много сюжетов, общих с моими, тех, что касаются, в основном, нашей семьи. Юля дала мне первому прочитать написанное ею, я внес в текст несколько поправок и дал кое-какие советы, но и узнал много для себя нового. А некоторые места меня просто поразили: как я мог такое забыть? И в своих воспоминаниях я буду ссылаться на ее мемуары, а иногда их просто цитировать: они ведь уже написаны!

Еще два слова о том, почему «Отрывки». Мне, как и любому другому человеку, не хочется выносить на публику все события и случаи жизни, даже если они четко запечатлелись в памяти. Либо, чтобы кого-нибудь не задеть, либо что бы не нарушить данное когда-то слово (даже если оно дано «по умолчанию»), либо, если его освещению может быть придан противоположный смысл. А также… старая интеллигенция помнит слово «раздеться» еще в одном, переносном смысле: раскрыть о себе всю подноготную, что отнюдь не считалось comme il faut. Например, «Вошел гость и сразу начал раздеваться»,— скорее всего, имело именно этот смысл. Это свойство мне не свойственно (извините за каламбур). Я предпочитаю раздеваться исключительно в прямом смысле, и исключительно там, где это уместно.

А теперь — вперед! Мое введение и так затянулось… Начну, как и полагается, с рождения.

САМЫЕ РАННИЕ ГОДЫ

Эта главка грозит быть самой короткой: много ли может рассказать человек о своих первых годах на земле? Тем не менее…
Я родился 24 августа 1936 года…

* * *

В мае 1980 года я перешел на работу в издательство «Советская энциклопедия», которое было более известно под своим старым именем «Большой Советской энциклопедии». И вскоре с удивлением обнаружил. что там хранятся полные комплекты «Правды» и «Известий» начиная с 1935 года! Довоенные газеты, которые повсеместно были или уничтожены или, в лучшем случае, сданы в спецхран, здесь были доступны сотрудникам издательства без каких-либо сложностей или затруднений. И я, вспомнив популярные газетные и журнальные рубрики типа «О чем писали русские газеты сто лет назад», захотел посмотреть, о чем писала газета «Правда» в день моего рождения — 24 августа 1936 года. И, взяв подшивку, открыл этот номер: на первой полосе был опубликован приговор по делу Зиновьева и Каменева и сообщение о том, что приговор приведен в исполнение. У меня нет симпатии к этим большевикам, особенно к Зиновьеву, одному из самых страшных большевистских вождей, однако — под какой звездой я родился?

* * *

10 сентября этого года исполнилось 60 лет моего трудового стажа. В этот день, 10 сентября 1952 года, я вышел на работу — рабочим на завод. А лет мне тогда было шестнадцать, столько, сколько сейчас Сашеньке.

Я рос в интеллигентной московской семье, мои родители были журналисты. Папа был литературным редактором газеты «Труд», входившей в первую пятерку крупнейших газет СССР. Мама многие годы работала в сельскохозяйственной печати, была корреспондентом Совинформбюро –Информационного агентства Советского Союза. Но последние годы она нигде не служила: нас, детей, в семье было трое, и родители решили, что она посвятит свое время нашему воспитанию. Наша семья была вполне благополучной. В «Труде» едва ли не каждую неделю появлялась папина статья; у него вышли две книги очерков; еще одна книга была уже почти готова к печати, ее толстая рукопись лежала на его письменном столе, и я хорошо помню, как она выглядела. И вдруг все сломалось…

Это случилось поздно вечером 1 ноября 1950 года. В дверь позвонили, вошли, предъявили ордер на арест и увели папу. Уходя, он сказал маме: «Соня, не волнуйтесь, за мной ничего нет. Я скоро вернусь…» Он вернулся — через пять с половиной лет.

После того, как папу увели, в квартире остались три сотрудника МГБ — Министерства государственной безопасности, как тогда называлась нынешняя ФСБ …

* * *

Начало МГУ — из воспоминаний сестры Юли

Наступил 1954 год, четвертый год папиного пребывания в лагере. Павел заканчивал 10-й класс вечерней школы, встал вопрос о поступлении в институт. С детства отец увлек его географией. В старших классах, продолжая работать на заводе, он участвовал в географических олимпиадах, проводимых МГУ (Московским государственным университетом), каждый раз занимая призовые места. Это было настолько необычно, чтобы рабочий выигрывал университетские олимпиады, что его даже пригласили выступить по радио в «Клубе юных географов» — была тогда такая детская передача. А на церемонии закрытия последней олимпиады к Павлу обратился профессор... Хотя об этом, пожалуй, лучше расскажет он сам:

«Премию — книги по географии и диплом мне вручал завкафедрой экономгеографии СССР Юлиан Глебович Саушкин. И, пожимая мне руку, спросил: «Ну, теперь, конечно, к нам?» — «Да-а-а, — протянул я. — но мне хотелось бы с вами поговорить...»

— Ну, что ж, подойдите, когда все закончится, — очень дружелюбно ответил Саушкин. И вот я снова на сцене у стола, за которым сидят еще не успевшие разойтись профессора и доценты. И рассказываю Саушкину, что я мечтаю стать студентом геофака, но я еврей, и у меня отец в лагере.

Саушкин, естественно, начал с конституции, но я его прервал, сказав, что все это так, но на практике мы видим совсем другое. И мой собеседник сменил тон.

— На нашем факультете это не имеет значения. И наш декан так думает. Не правда ли, Анатолий Георгиевич? — обратился он к сидящему рядом профессору, который подтвердил эти слова. (Это был, как я узнал позже, завкафедрой биогеографии Воронов.)

— А что касается того, что ваш отец в лагере, то ведь вы работаете на заводе, вы человек самостоятельный. Поступайте к нам».

Павел последовал его совету, сдал вступительные экзамены на географический факультет МГУ и набрал полупроходной балл. Среди всех абитуриентов с таким баллом приемной комиссии следовало выбрать всего несколько человек. Мой брат попал в число избранных, почему именно он, мы не задумывались. А спустя какое-то время, когда вступительные страсти еще не утихли, он с мамой был в гостях у маминой двоюродной сестры Евы Синельниковой, актрисы кукольного театра Образцова, благодаря которой мы просмотрели много спектаклей этого замечательного театра. За столом собралась небольшая компания, и одна дама, оказавшаяся членом приемной комиссии геофака, стала с сожалением рассказывать, как на заседании приемной комиссии, решавшей, кого из получивших полупроходной балл зачислить в студенты, она не сумела отстоять одну талантливую девочку, прекрасно сдавшую ей экзамен.

— Я так старалась, убеждала, — сетовала она, — но профессор Воронов настаивал на каком-то Ильине, а он председатель приемной комиссии, его слово решающее.

— А вот он сидит этот Ильин со своей мамой, — с улыбкой сказали ей.

— Откуда вы знаете профессора Воронова?! — воскликнула она. — Кем он вам приходится?

— В глаза его не видала, — ответила мама и рассказала всю историю.

— Тогда все было сделано правильно, — облегченно вздохнула дама.

Вот такие случались коллизии.

Часть V

Воспоминания друзей и коллег о Павле

Мой Павел

Элла Каган

Мы прожили вместе сорок девять лет...
Будучи очень разными по темпераменту, мы прожили жизнь как pavella — наш электронный адрес. Хотя мы оба были достаточно независимыми личностями, мы, в то же время, были тесно связаны и влияли друг на друга.

Павел очень любил жизнь, любил семью, любил путешествовать и собирать книги. Друзья вспоминают его как доброго, веселого, легкого человека. Он любил застолье и был гостеприимным хозяином дома

Павел всю жизнь кому-то помогал, причем это могло быть как по мелочи, так и по-крупному, а иногда даже с опасностью для себя. Он легко раздавал сюжеты для размышления: это могли быть соображения о структуре дорожной сети или суждения по поводу недавно написанной книги. Это было той стороной его личности, которая была обращена к миру людей.

Но была и другая сторона, не столь открытая и легко доступная окружающим— это была его работа (не служба, а работа), его идеи и принципы. Здесь он жестко стоял на своем, ни о какой гибкости или уступчивости не могло быть и речи.

Работал Павел всегда мучительно трудно. Он предъявлял к себе высокие требования и боялся им не соответствовать. Всю жизнь над ним витала тень отца, которого он боготворил. Он постоянно сравнивал себя с ним и никак не хотел «огорчить» отца плохим письмом. Михаил Ильич Ильин был популярным детским писателем, человеком необычайно талантливым, и выдержать сравнение с ним было отнюдь нелегко. Видя и чувствуя эти сложности, я пыталась помочь Павлу с ними справиться. Но все мои аргументы о разности тематики и стиля большого успеха не имели.

Чтобы понять, как сложился такой тип личности, нужно, как минимум, знать ключевые события его жизни и среду, в которой происходила его социализация.

СЕМЬЯ ИЛЬИНЫХ

Семья Ильиных казалась всем нам необычной: родители были на ВЫ...При первом взгляде они казались старомодно-аристократичными, но в дальнейшем оба оказались очень теплыми людьми..

Они жили на Пушечной улице позади Детского мира и вблизи ЦДРИ (Центральный дом работников искусств) в доходном доме, построенном перед революцией. Дом принадлежал церкви, которая, говорят, сохранилась до сих пор. Никто не помнит, когда церковь превратилась в нечто за высоким забором с колючей проволокой по верху забора. Влияние церкви, однако, проявилось в том, что в доме не было квартиры за номером тринадцать, а за двенадцатым следовал сразу четырнадцатый. Этого дома больше нет, его снесли, и на этом месте построили очередной корпус КГБ — организация расширяет свои владения от Лубянки к Бульварному кольцу как метастазы рака по живому телу.

Их было пятеро: Михаил Ильич, Софья Ильинична, Павел, Юля и Вова. Последний был племянником Софьи Ильиничны, которого она взяла, потому что его родители погибли от репрессий. В квартире жила еще одна семья и Верочка — так все звали Веру Ильиничну, сестру Михаила Ильича.

У семьи из пяти человек были две крошечные проходные комнаты. В первой комнате происходила вся жизнь, вторая принадлежала родителям. Там стоял большой письменный стол, за которым работал Михаил Ильич. Он происходил из интеллигентной семьи. Его отец, дед Павла, закончил Краковский университет. В те годы в Москве евреи могли жить только, если они были купцами первой гильдии, врачами или имели диплом о высшем образовании. Благодаря университетскому диплому дед Павла получил право жительства в Москве, и отец Павла родился в Москве.

Михаил Ильич очень много работал, практически всегда, когда не спал, но его стол был повернут лицом в сторону первой комнаты, и он мог наблюдать все, что происходило в доме. Будучи малоразговорчивым, замкнутым, очень проницательным человеком, он обладал великолепным чувством юмора. Иногда делал весьма меткие замечания. При внешней сдержанности он был фантазером и мистификатором. Иногда Павел был его партнером в домашних розыгрышах. Сын унаследовал от отца любовь к неожиданностям, к загадочным затеям, к новым местам. Отец звал сына «босяком», потому что они были разного склада. Михаил Ильич был любезен в старом стиле. Например, он приподнимал шляпу, проходя мимо кумушек, сидевших у входа в дом, хотя не помнил ни одного имени. Стиль поведения Павла был совсем другой. Он всем говорил ТЫ, даже моим коллегам, с которыми я была на ВЫ. Он всегда был прямолинеен, даже когда выражал свою отрицательную точку зрения, не пытаясь облечь свои слова в какую-то обтекаемую форму. Иногда это очень дорого ему стоило, но он не менял своего поведения. Софья Ильинична была совсем другого склада, чем ее муж. Она происходила из купеческой среды. Будучи совсем молодой, она приехала одна из Суража в Москву. Она была разговорчивой и гостеприимной хозяйкой дома.

Семья жила большой в тесноте. Хотя платяной шкаф был выселен в коридор, но и это все равно не решало проблемы: негде было уложить всех спать, поэтому один из мальчиков спал в комнате у Верочки. Несмотря на эту тесноту, нас всегда были рады принять.

В доме у Ильиных все курили. Хотя форточка всегда была открыта, в доме стоял неистребимый запах табака: пахла мебель, шторы, одежда обитателей. Этот запах был одним из моих первых впечатлений при входе в дом.

Родители были журналистами. Михаил Ильич в молодости писал стихи, входил в несколько литературных ассоциаций. Однако все они просуществовали недолгое время — в 30-е годы свобода кончилась. Он ушел в журналистику, писал театральные рецензии, работал в газетах, много писал о стране для детей и взрослых. Работа требовала путешествий, и он любил это сам и пристрастил Павла.

Софья Ильинична принадлежала к тому поколению журналистов, которые ходили брать интервью с портативными машинками. Она печатала со скоростью речи, не прекращая курить и не делая опечаток.

Жили благополучно и спокойно, но все нарушилось с началом войны. Семья была эвакуирована сначала в Омск, потом в Алма-Ату. Они пробыли в эвакуации полтора года и вернулись в Москву в 1943 году.

ИСПЫТАНИЯ ЮНОСТИ

Жизнь постепенно налаживалась, пока не произошло событие, которое перевернуло жизнь семьи. Павел вспоминает:

«Наша семья была вполне благополучной. В «Труде» едва ли не каждую неделю появлялась папина статья; у него вышли две книги

очерков; еще одна книга была уже почти готова к печати, ее толстая рукопись лежала на его письменном столе, и я хорошо помню, как она выглядела. И вдруг все сломалось...

Это случилось поздно вечером 1 ноября 1950 года. В дверь позвонили, вошли, предъявили ордер на арест и увели папу. Уходя, он сказал маме: «Соня, не волнуйтесь, за мной ничего нет. Я скоро вернусь...» Он вернулся — через пять с половиной лет».

Отца арестовали по нелепому обвинению. Его «вина» заключалась в том, что в юношеские годы он состоял в анархистской организации. В момент ареста ему было сорок девять лет.

Семья жила впроголодь. Софью Ильиничну не брали на работу нигде, потому что она была женой «врага народа». Она научилась шить и этим кормила семью. Она выносила из дома на продажу все, что можно было продать, включая книги. Если это были стихи, то их сначала читали и учили наизусть. С тех пор поэзия серебряного века стала любимой поэзией Павла на всю оставшуюся жизнь.

В момент ареста отца Павлу было четырнадцать лет. В августе 1952 года Павлу исполнилось шестнадцать лет и в сентябре того же года он пошел работать на завод рабочим — моложе этого возраста на работу не брали. Он перешел учиться в вечернюю школу рабочей молодежи. Интеллигентный юноша со стихами в голове погрузился в другую среду и на работе, и в школе. Володю отдали в ремесленное училище, и только Юля — младшая из троих детей — осталась в обычной школе.

Как это часто бывает, беда сплотила семью. За годы отсутствия отца Павел стал взрослым человеком, мужчиной в доме. Он зарабатывал деньги, кормил семью. В семье все поддерживали друг друга. Павел ходил вместе с матерью по всем инстанциям подавать прошения в защиту отца и посылать посылки в лагерь. В эти труднейшие годы Павел сумел остаться тем же добрым, теплым человеком в семье.

Однако другая сторона его личности претерпела принципиальные изменения. Он довольно быстро нашел общий язык с рабочими на заводе и познакомился с жизнью и проблемами незнакомого ему прежде другого мира. Именно здесь у него сложилась привычка разговаривать со всеми на ТЫ, но постепенно стали меняться не только манеры и стиль поведения. В круге общения Павла появились ребята из вечерней школы. У каждого из них была в жизни своя история и своя драма, иначе они бы не оказались в вечерней школе. Он стал иначе видеть и воспринимать мир, и в этом новом для него мире Павла все больше привлекали люди с жесткими социальными оценками. В эти юные годы происходила социализация личности Павла. Оставались святыми СЛОВО и верность СЛОВУ.

В это трудное время была как никогда важна поддержка друзей. Первым оказался школьный друг — Саша Кириллов. Эта дружба продолжалась всю жизнь независимо от того, как поворачивались судьбы друзей. Александр Александрович Кирилов стал всемирно известным математиком, живет в Филадельфии.

В вечерней школе жизнь свела Павла с двумя замечательными людьми — Вадимом Щегловым и Женей Кокориным. Вадим стал членом Комитета по защите прав верующих. Он был неудобен властям, посадить его, конечно, могли, но видимо предпочли «выдавить» из страны. Ему «помогли» уехать в Америку. К сожалению, ни Вадима, ни Жени уже нет в живых.

Наступил 1954 год. Пора было думать о продолжении учебы. Любовь к географии, привитая папой, в его отсутствие еще больше укрепилась. Каждый год Павел получал награды на географических олимпиадах МГУ. Это было очень необычно: рабочий получает награду на олимпиаде. Вопрос о выборе учебного заведения упирался в то, что отец сидел по 58 статье — «измена Родине».

Дальше слово Павлу:

> *«Премию — книги по географии и диплом мне вручал завкафедрой экономгеографии СССР Юлиан Глебович Саушкин. И, пожимая мне руку, спросил: «Ну, теперь, конечно, к нам?» — «Да-а-а, — протянул я. — но мне хотелось бы с вами поговорить...»*
>
> *— Ну, что ж, подойдите, когда все закончится, — очень дружелюбно ответил Саушкин. И вот я снова на сцене у стола, за которым сидят еще не успевшие разойтись профессора и доценты. И рассказываю Саушкину, что я мечтаю стать студентом геофака, но я еврей, и у меня отец в лагере.*
>
> *Саушкин, естественно, начал с конституции, но я его прервал, сказав, что все это так, но на практике мы видим совсем другое. И мой собеседник сменил тон.*
>
> *— На нашем факультете это не имеет значения. И наш декан так думает. Не правда ли, Анатолий Георгиевич? — обратился он к сидящему рядом профессору, который подтвердил эти слова. (Это был, как я узнал позже, завкафедрой биогеографии Воронов.)*
>
> *— А что касается того, что ваш отец в лагере, то ведь вы работаете на заводе, вы человек самостоятельный. Поступайте к нам».*

Павла приняли на Географический факультет университета, и началась счастливая студенческая жизнь.

Михаил Ильич вернулся домой в 1956 году. Странно звучит, но в лагере Михаил Ильич выжил, потому что у него нашли опухоль, которую вырезал хирург-заключённый. Этот же хирург выписал справку, освобождающую М.И. от тяжелых работ. М.И. дали работу в конторе, где он заслужил любовь начальника по двум причинам: М.И. хорошо работал, но что еще важнее — он отдавал начальнику свой паек махорки.

В семейном архиве сохранились две фотографии — после лагеря и через десять лет. На второй он выглядел гораздо моложе. После лагеря в новом паспорте паспортная серия значилась ЗК, т.е. заключенный В графе имя и фамилия было написано: «Ильин, Михаил Ильич, он же Тиркельтауб, Мирон Ильич». Семейная кличка «он же» жила довольно долго.

В эти послелагерные годы Михаил Ильич сотворил Юнгу Захара Загадкина и Кока Антона Камбузова. Только человек с безграничной фантазией мог создать такие образы, которые прожили двадцать четыре года на радио и продолжают жить в книгах и на интернете.

Когда Михаила Ильича не стало, то Павел продолжал этот цикл радиопередач до лета 1982 года. Передача была закрыта немедленно после того, как к нам пришли КГБшники с обыском. Но это уже другая история.

КОГДА МЫ БЫЛИ МОЛОДЫМИ...

В 1960 году Павел и я — тогда недавно закончившие учебу — волею судеб оказались в Государственном институте проектирования городов (Гипрогор). Мы попали в одну мастерскую и иногда были заняты на одних и тех же проектах. Это были светлые годы нашей жизни, мы были молоды и полны надежд. Через несколько лет мы поженились.

1967 год был сложным в нашей семье. В июне родилась наша дочь, Надя, наша Надежда. В октябре того же года умер отец Павла. У старых евреев есть поверье, что в семье один уходит, другой приходит. Не знаю, насколько это верно, но в нашей семье так и произошло.

Павел был очень трогательным отцом — слова «нет» в его отношениях с Надей не было. Главную свою задачу он видел в том, чтобы научить девочку тому, что он знает сам. Когда Наде было три года, Павел повесил на стену огромную карту страны, и это было началом «домашнего университета». Дальше пошли рассказы об истории, работа с картой и многое другое. Дочь унаследовала от папы «ген путешественника».

Та же история повторилась, когда у нас родились внучки. Павел их обожал и, конечно, учил, причем учил весело, играючи, всему, чему мог. Например, когда пришло время старшей, Саше, разбираться в структуре вселенной, дедушка явился в дом с глобусом. Чтобы Саше все было понятно, он стал ходить вокруг стола с глобусом в руках, вращая его вокруг оси. Однако главное, чему он их учил, это искусству путешествовать: читать заранее доступную литературу, готовить карты, вести путевые записи и зарисовки. Они получили для работы красивые альбомы.

После каждого путешествия мы получали бесценную информацию. Например, в Италии Моргоша, младшая, каждый день методично записывала, какое мороженое он ела. А в Новой Зеландии Саша, старшая, рисовала экзотических птиц, которые не живут в наших краях. Дедушкин «ген путешественника» был передан следующему поколению.

Однако вернемся в Гипрогор. Время шло, и прелесть новизны проектных работ растаяла. Павел поступил в аспирантуру Института Географии Академии Наук (ИГАН), защитил диссертацию и остался работать в ИГАНе. Отделом тогда руководил Алексей Александрович Минц — молодой талантливый ученый, который переориентировал исследования в отделе с районоведения на проблемную тематику.

Диапазон интересов Павла в этот период жизни был довольно широким: от теоретической географии, до географических загадок на радио и поэзии.. Коллеги в Гипрогоре относились к этой «двойной жизни» с симпатией и пониманием, потому что многие из них были разносторонне одаренными людьми и сами имели какие-то увлечения помимо основной работы. Его академические коллеги в большинстве придерживались других взглядов: наука требует полной отдачи, полного посвящения. Многие из них считали несерьезными какие-то занятия помимо науки.

Но Павла мало интересовали чьи-то мнения. Он всегда, помимо обязательных работ, делал что-то, что считал для себя интересным. Он сначала писал, а потом искал, кому еще, кроме него самого, это может быть интересным.

Сам процесс написания текста всегда был трудным, и начало любого письма, статьи, рукописи было для него тяжелым. Вспоминаю, как много раз он проговаривал со мной свои соображения по поводу предполагаемой работы, мы обсуждали, иногда спорили. Но у нас был разный склад ума: если Павел всегда начинал с «вот например,...», то я просила сначала сформулировать идею. Тем не менее, мы всегда договаривались до какого-то разумного решения. Мы помогали друг другу, печатались вместе и часто участвовали в одних и тех же конференциях.

Из ИГАНа Павел перешел работать в издательство «Советская энциклопедия» в Географический отдел. Он любил работать со СЛОВОМ, и редакторская работа давала такую возможность. Павел сочетал работу в издательстве со своими научными занятиями: продолжал писать, печататься, выступать на конференциях. Его интересы все больше сдвигались к социальным проблемам и в науке, и в обществе.

ТУЧИ ...

В учреждениях, где Павлу пришлось работать, атмосфера была относительно приличная, но вокруг было настроение полной бесконечной беспросветности. Сам Павел никогда не был активным диссидентом, но он дружил с этими людьми. Как позже сказал ему сотрудник КГБ: Вы, Пал Михалыч, хороший человек, а друзья у вас плохие. Не помню среди его друзей ни одного верноподданного гражданина, у каждого из них была своя ниша: у кого религия, у кого диссидентство.

Люди стали уезжать, и мы понимали, что и нам пора двигаться. Мы не хотели жить в этой системе и не хотели растить там дочь.

Как раз в это время, летом 1982 года, к нам пришли с обыском КГБшники. В этот день обыск был проведен в восьми семьях наших друзей. Мы понимали, что к нам пришли именно потому, что мы дружили с «плохими людьми».

Это была мерзейшая процедура, которая укрепила нас в правильности нашего решения уехать. Обшарили весь дом, допросили всех, включая дочь, которой за месяц до этого исполнилось пятнадцать лет, забрали несколько мешков с бумагами и пишущую машинку. Павла увезли в Лефортовскую тюрьму.. Его отпустили, но не оставили в покое.

В истории семьи произошли мистические повторы: когда арестовали Михаила Ильича, Павлу было 14 лет, а нашей дочери было 15, когда арестовали Павла.

Вскоре после обыска, преодолев кучу бюрократических препятствий, мы подали документы на отъезд. Это дало нам моральное облегчение — чувство, которое трудно объяснить. Мы обрели некую степень внутренней свободы, что, конечно, было наивно, так как наша внешняя свобода, наоборот, сократилась — мы знали, что за нами идет слежка.

Павел продолжал работать, но его перевели в другой отдел и понизили в должности. Мы ничуть не удивились, когда нам отказали в выезде. Мы вполне органично влились в толпу отказников, где уже было много друзей.

Павел опять продолжал писать, только тематика сменилась. Друзья знали, что он не только пишет, но и хорошо редактирует. Пошли письма в защиту кого- то или протеста против чего-то. Павла стали увозить с работы «побеседовать», грозили, давили, хотели сделать из него стукача. Но не вышло...

Мы с друзьями не сидели без дела: мы писали письма, устраивали демонстрации и голодовки, собирали посылки тем, кого посадили.

По инициативе Роберта Гостанда, коллеги и друга Павла, в марте 1987 года Американская Ассоциация Географов (AAG) приняла Резолюцию[1] в поддержку семьи Павла Ильина:

> *В то время как Павел Михайлович Ильин и Микаэлла Исааковна Каган, коллеги и члены Ассоциации, желают эмигрировать с их семьей, им было неоднократно отказано в разрешении,... Члены Ассоциации Американских Географов... настаивают на том, чтобы семье Ильина было предоставлено право эмигрировать без дальнейших промедлений.*

Наконец, после пяти лет ожидания, в мае 1987 года мы получили разрешение на отъезд и в июле улетели из Москвы.

МЕЖДУ МОСКВОЙ И БОСТОНОМ

Первая посадка самолета была в Вене, где нас встречали вежливые служащие аэропорта и улыбающиеся представители ХИАСа. Нас привели в зал, где мы увидели Ксерокс, к которому можно было свободно подойти и сделать копию любой бумажки. Несколько часов назад мы покинули страну, где все копировальные маши-

---

[1] См. Приложение IV

ны были под семью замками и нужно было письменное разрешение начальства на любую копию. Это была первая ошеломляющая неожиданность, потом они продолжились.

Вена — это город истинной красоты. Гулять по нему было большим удовольствием. Однако в процессе прогулок мы увидели, что не все так розово в этом раю. При входе в синагогу стояла вооружённая охрана.: При входе в ХИАС тоже стояла вооруженная охрана, а кроме того, там были какие-то специальные защитные устройства в тамбуре при входе. У ХИАСа были основания для опасений: нам объяснили, что накануне нашего приезда в городе были нападения на евреев. На знаменитом Центральном Венском Кладбище, где похоронены главы правительства Австрии и знаменитые деятели культуры, имеется также еврейская часть. Мы застали эту часть настолько заросшей, что пройти между могилами можно было только с большим трудом. Памятники заросли, так что надо было раздирать кусты, чтобы прочитать имена похороненных.

В Вене у нас произошел конфликт с ХИАСом, который отказался оплатить перевозку одного ящика нашего весьма скромного багажа. В этот ящик Павел положил коллекцию морячков, которых он собирал почти всю жизнь. Дело в том, что герои его радиопередачи — юнга Захар Загадкин и кок Антон Камбузов — были моряками. В их честь и было собрано больше трёхсот фигурок. Павел собирался подарить эту коллекцию Роберту Гостанду, который в молодости служил во флоте и которому нравилась эта коллекция. С помощью Роберта коллекция попала в Америку и оказалась на полках кабинета Роберта в университете, где он работал (California State University, Northridge). К сожалению, во время сильнейшего землетрясения 1994 года вместе со зданием университета пострадали и морячки. Роберт потом собирал руки-ноги-головы.

ВТОРАЯ ЖИЗНЬ

Это был прыжок с парашютом в неизвестность. Два кандидата наук в возрасте пятидесяти лет со специальностями, не очень популярными в Америке, начинали новую жизнь, имея в кармане по девяносто долларов и одному чемодану на человека. Это то, что нам разрешили взять с собой. С нами были наша дочь и моя мама.

Мы были поражены и растроганы приемом, который Еврейская община устраивала эмигрантам Нас обеспечили всем необходимым на первое время. Нам также помогали наши спонсоры — Валерий и Этя Годяк, наши друзья-отказники, которых отпустили раньше нас. Мы принимали это с благодарностью, но понимали, что это скоро кончится, и нужно срочно искать работу. Спустя несколько лет мы узнали, что в Еврейском агентстве, принимавшем нас, мы считались самой безнадежной парой этого года.

Павел тем временем рассылал повсюду свои бумаги, но реакция была почти никакая. Пришло приглашение выступить в Русском центре в Гарварде. Он предложил свою тогдашнюю тему «Урбанизация в СССР». Приняли с удовольствием, потому что в ту пору всех интересовала эта страна, но, что там происходило, было непонятно. Поехал, выступил, стали задавать вопросы: Скажите, а что происходит с урбанизацией в период перестройки? Ответ: Ничего не происходит.(Заметим, что перемены начали происходить в 1991 после принятия закона о приватизации) Левая профессура была разочарована: вместо розовой картинки они получили честный ответ. Даже если бы Павел знал, что они хотят услышать, он все равно ответил бы то же самое. Больше его туда не приглашали.

В это время произошло некое событие, которое имело большие последствия в нашей жизни. В газете (не помню ни названия газеты, ни имени автора) была напечатана статья о переименованиях в России. Павел давно интересовался этой темой. Он любил собирать информацию по ходу событий, так что он имел представление о предмете. Статья была написана бойко, но автор явно не владел материалом. Павел не терпел халтуры, он ответил автору, подробно объяснив его ошибки. Автор статьи не ответил. Но главный результат состоял в том, что это событие дало Павлу толчок, и он снова начал работать.

Возникла идея обратиться в Институт русских исследований имени Кеннана. Павел поехал в Нью-Йорк на интервью с Блэром Рублом, тогда директором Института. Блэр принял его очень дружелюбно и предложил подать документы на грант. Новая волна эмиграции только началась, и Павел был ее первым экзотическим представителем. Возникла неожиданная проблема: нужно было представить публикации за последние несколько лет. Естественно, в отказе их не было и не могло быть. В конце концов, Блэр каким-то образом уладил эту проблему, и Павел получил грант. Это был прекрасный год в его жизни.

Через год снова нужно было искать работу. Павлу повезло — в это время набирали людей вWashington Processing Center (WPC). Организация занималась обработкой документов, поданных на эмиграцию из бывшего Советского Союза в Соединенные Штаты.

Павла приняли, за что мы были благодарны Елене Рабен, которая принесла его резюме начальству. Его обязанности состояли в проверке географической информации, которая содержалась в эмиграционных документах. В это время в бывшем Союзе происходили бесконечные изменения в названиях городов и стран — бывших союзных республик. Работа давала нам средства к существованию. в течение нескольких лет.

КНИГА

Время шло и делало свое дело. Павел задумал участвовать в ежегодной конференции American Association of Geographers (AAG,1998). Идея была собрать людей, которые могли бы участвовать в сессии, посвященной Москве. Сложилась пестрая группа панелистов и тех, кто их рецензировал. Все они оказались представителями разных отраслей исследований, соответственно каждый представлял свой взгляд и понимание проблем. Это создавало интересную мозаичную картину сложнейшего города.

На этом заседании присутствовал Блэр Рубл. После заседания он сказал Павлу, что из этих материалов нужно делать книгу. Павел сначала не поверил ушам своим, решив, что Блэр просто хочет сказать ему что-то приятное. Но Блэр был вполне серьезен. Книга состоялась: «Москва рубежа XIX и XX столетий. Взгляд в прошлое издалека». Ответственные редакторы Павел Ильин и Блэр А. Рубл.

В книге есть как совместные статьи редакторов, так и отдельные каждого из них. В создании книги принимали участие следующие авторы: Роберт Гостанд, Уильям К. Брумфилд, Роберт Виттакер, Катя Короткина-Розенцвейг, Микаэлла Каган.

Работа над книгой длилась много лет. По разным причинам происходили длинные перерывы. Но тогда, когда Павел работал, он никогда не торопился. Это была работа для души, и он наслаждался самим процессом. На первом этапе он бесконечно искал новые источники информации. Когда уже было ясно, что писать и о чем писать, он продолжал свою бесконечную работу над СЛОВОМ... Потом возникла проблема подбора иллюстраций. Павел ни в коем случае не хотел иметь дело с Россией по поводу авторских прав на иллюстрации, поэтому решил ограничиться дореволюционными открытками. Он ездил по открыточным ярмаркам, писал коллегам в Москву и в Германию. Всего на подбор иллюстраций ушло около двух лет. Эта книга была детищем Павла. Он любил Москву и прекрасно знал город со всеми подробностями, включая дворы и подворотни. Иногда мне казалось, что ему жалко расстаться с рукописью, как ребенку с любимой игрушкой.

Павел любил и собирал книги всю жизнь, покупая их даже тогда, когда было туго с деньгами. В конце концов, он собрал уникальную библиотеку, посвященную Москве, в которой больше тысячи томов.

У Павла была предварительная договоренность с весьма престижным издательством в Чикаго. Но за несколько лет интерес к России упал, и издательство решило, что книга о Москве им не нужна. Теперь нужно было всю книгу, приготовленную для издания на английском языке, переделывать на русский. Тут в Павле взыграл редакторский энтузиазм, и он пошел «гулять по всем статьям.»

В 2001 году мы были в Москве. Павел, наконец, заключил контракт на издание книги в России, и она вышла в 2004 году в издательстве Росспэн.

ПОЛИТИЧЕСКИЕ ИГРЫ

Разумеется, все эти годы Павел занимался не только Москвой. В России шла эпидемия переименований городов, улиц, объектов природы. Павел развлекался, наблюдая издали эти политические игры, и, как обычно, не торопясь собирал в свою копилку информацию об этой «гульбе» по картам. Наконец, он подготовил доклад о переименованиях городов и выступил с ним на очередной ежегодной конференции AAG. Доклад вызвал большой интерес, однако сами по себе топонимические политические игры представлялись настолько нелепыми, что вызвали неожиданную реакцию. Никогда за мою долгую жизнь ни до, ни после этого события мне не пришлось присутствовать на ученом собрании, где ученые мужи так искренне смеялись

Когда мы вернулись домой, Павел обнаружил у себя на столе письмо из редакции Post-Soviet Geography с предложением опубликовать у них статью на тему представленного доклада. В 1993 году вышла статья Renaming of Soviet Cities after Exceptional People: A Historical Perspective on Toponymy.

Статья была потом перепечатана несколько раз и добралась даже до Японии. Некоторые работы Павла были переведены на французский, польский, финский и другие языки, но мысль о публикации в Японии никогда не приходила ему в голову.

СВЯТАЯ РАБОТА

В 1995 году Павел ушел из WPC и в 1996 начал работать в Музее Холокоста (United States Holocaust Memorial Museum). Помогла статья о переименованиях. Коллега Павла, Вадим Алцкан, отнес в Музей эту статью очень вовремя: там в это время начиналась работа над созданием базы данных населенных мест, где происходил Холокост. Для такого проекта нужен был специалист, занимающийся топонимикой.

Павел считал свою работу святым делом для еврейского человека. Он много раз повторял одну и ту же фразу: «Если бы я был богатым, я бы платил за то, чтобы мне дали делать эту работу».

Помимо базы данных, Павел был занят в нескольких проектах, которые были в работе в Музее. Он редактировал географическую часть музейных изданий. Особую часть работы Павла составляли бесконечные ответы на вопросы коллег и людей, разыскивающих родных и друзей. В работе над этими поисками часто возникали трудности в нахождении населенных мест. Каждый раз, когда удавалось кому-то помочь, Павел искренне радовался — соединились разлученные души.

Появились публикации, затрагивающие тему Холокоста: Там, где родился И.М. Маергойз, или топонимический погром на Украине. К сожалению, работы по топонимике, представленные на конференциях в Новом Орлеане (2003), Бостоне (2008), (Бад Аролсен, Германия, Вильнюс, Тбилиси, 2013) так и не были опубликованы.

Для работы, которую выполнял Павел, нужны были карты стран Центральной и Восточной Европы. Павел любил карты и собирал старые карты. В его домашней коллекции есть знаменитая Madaba map. Это самая старая в мире мозаичная карта на полу Византийского храма, построенного в начале н.э. на территории современного Иордана.

Работа над картами происходила, в основном, в Картографическом отделе Библиотеки Конгресса. Когда Павел начал работать, ему пришлось разбирать ящики некаталогизированных карт. Он устанавливал дату, страну-издателя и другие показатели, необходимые для описания карты. Когда Павла не стало, его коллеги передали в Библиотеку музея Холокоста коллекцию из 39 карт, которые он собрал за годы работы: *Pavel Ilyin collection of published road and tourist maps.*

СЛОВО

Трепетное отношение к СЛОВУ Павел сохранял всю жизнь, независимо от того, чем он занимался — детскими передачами или наукой. Павел очень любил стихи и мог читать их наизусть часами. Интерес к поэзии культивировали в семье всю жизнь. Отец в молодые годы начинал как поэт, мать читала детям стихи перед тем, как пришлось продавать книги в голодные годы.

Единственный раз, когда Павел решился написать о стихах, было эссе о пушкинской строфе из письма Онегина Татьяне:

> Я знаю: век уж мой измерен,
> Но чтоб продлилась жизнь моя,
> Я утром должен быть уверен,
> Что с вами днем увижусь я...

Да, логики в этом четверостишии нет, но Пушкин есть Пушкин, и эту строфу повторяют уже триста лет.

Павел долго привыкал к Америке, но ощутил ее своей только после взрывов в Нью-Йорке 11 сентября. Как человек, живущий в двух культурах, двух языках, он по-своему пытался их соединить. Он выбрал три самые популярные американские песни и перевел их на русский язык так, что они ложатся на музыку. Это была очень долгая и тонкая работа. Каждое слово он выверял в разных источниках, терзал друзей-переводчиков бесконечными вопросами, пока ему удавалось найти вариант перевода, который бы его устраивал. Он рассказал о создателях этих песен — поэтах и композиторах, а также о самых популярных их исполнителях. Он посетил многие места, связанные с этими людьми. Он хотел почувствовать, кто эти люди, которым удалось создать песни, ставшие столь популярными и живущие так долго. Это была последняя большая работа Павла. «Эта земля моя, она прекрасна, Боже, храни ее! Три патриотические песни Америки».

В последние годы своей жизни Павел продолжал выступать с докладами на конференциях, посвященных Холокосту, делал переводы статей по тематике, которая его интересовала, написал несколько рецензий на книги.

Игорь Крупник, близкий друг Павла, нашел самые точные и теплые слова о Павле — ТРУЖЕНИК СЛОВА.

Мы прожили вместе сорок девять лет.

Павла не стало 12 марта 2015 года.

Мой отец

Надя Ильин-Бартол

Как мы говорим по-русски, мой отец «родился в рубашке». Он пережил 5 раков, несколько переломов костей, вывих плеча, потенциально смертельные автомобильные аварии и КГБ. Другими словами, у него был ангел-хранитель. Мой отец родился в 1936 году. Ему было 5 лет, когда в России началась Вторая мировая война, 14 лет, когда его отца посадили, и 20 лет, когда его отец вернулся. Ему было 42 года, когда мы подали заявку на эмиграцию — и в этот раз из КГБ пришли за ним. Вскоре они его вернули, только чтобы потом опять забрать. Они думали, что он слабый человек и поэтому будет стучать на своих друзей. Как человек вежливый, он не посылал их в соответствующем направлении, а пытался объяснить, что доносчиком не будет. По-видимому, с их точки зрения отец не был недостаточно интересен, и не стоил трудов, необходимых для посадки в тюрьму. Поэтому он всегда возвращался — но эти визиты ему дорого обошлись.

Когда его отца арестовали, ему пришлось бросить обычную школу, устроиться на работу на завод и пойти в вечернюю школу. Несмотря на его обстоятельства и еврейство, его приняли в Московский университет, как работающего на заводе пролетария. — Каким-то образом приемная комиссия упустила тот факт, что он сын врага народа. С учебой он справлялся хорошо. Я думаю, что у него была прекрасная слуховая память, потому что он закончил университет практически не учась, со средними оценками.

Его отец был журналистом, который писал о разных географических местах и театре. Когда мой отец был маленьким, его отец брал его с собой, когда он путешествовал. Они объездили весь Советский Союз. Много лет спустя мой отец стал географом и продолжил путешествия, которые он начал со своим отцом. Приехав в Штаты, он, когда мог, продолжал путешествовать, и начал собирать магниты на холодильник изо всех мест, где побывал. Куда бы я ни ездила, он просил привезти ему всегда только одну вещь — магнит, по которому можно было узнать откуда он привезен.

От своего отца он унаследовал не только любовь к путешествиям. Мой дедушка был автором известной радиопередачи, которая популяризовала географию для детей используя географические загадки. После смерти моего деда, мой отец много лет продолжал работу над этой передачей. Передача была остановлена, когда мы подали документы на эмиграцию.

Когда я ездила на другой конец земного шара, я говорила ему, что чувствую себя героем его передачи — прилетаю через два часа после отлета или до вылета, невзирая на продолжительность полета.

Я научилась читать карты почти одновременно с тем, как читать. Я знала наизусть все об Огромной карте Советского Союза, которая висела над диваном моих родителей. Когда мы путешествовали, папа рассказывал мне о тех местах, где мы были, а мама о том, как были спроектированы города и здания. Они оба передали мне их страсть к путешествиям, и я передала ее своим дочерям, отчасти к огорчению моего мужа. В конце каждого отпуска дети задавали один и тот же вопрос «куда мы поедем в следующий раз».

Он унаследовал любовь к путешествиям и книгам от своего отца и к театру и искусству от своей матери. Он знал так много, что коллеги называли его Дидро Деламбертович по имени создателей первой французской энциклопедии. У него действительно был энциклопедический ум. Он учил меня русской средневековой истории — с 9 по 16 век со всеми именами, генеалогией и датами — рассказывая истории пока мы собирали грибы. Надо заметить, что это была феодальная Россия, где, прежде чем она стала абсолютной монархией, было много княжеств, которые он все знал.

Мои родители подали документы на эмиграцию в 1982 году. Уехали мы в 1987 году, одними из первых в последней волне советской еврейской эмиграции. Пока мы сидели в отказе, нас очень поддерживали американская еврейская община и американские политики, которые были неуклонны в своей решимости вывезти нас всех оттуда. Коллеги родителей сумели включить их в список ученых, к которому американцы обращались каждый раз, когда Советам нужна была помощь Запада. В конце концов это сработало.

В Линне, штат Массачусетс, куда приехала наша семья, нас считали самыми безнадежными иммигрантами года. Два 51-летних кандидата наук по географии и градостроительству, и дочь с музыкальным образованием. Мы их всех удивили, хотя это было нелегко. Первой работой моего отца стал грант в Институте русских исследований им. Кеннана. Когда закончился срок его гранта, отец начал работать по контракту, предоставляя географические консультации Государственному департаменту, где в то время (начало 90-х годов) занимались обработкой документов советских иммигрантов. А потом папин друг принес его статью о переименовании географических мест в СССР в Музей Холокоста.

В течение следующих 20 лет отец стал одним из ведущих мировых экспертов по географии Холокоста. Он научился фонетическому чтению и транскрипции всех восточноевропейских языков, включая венгерский. Он проводил много времени в Библиотеке Конгресса в поисках старых карт, чтобы понять какие изменения произошли на территориях стран Западной и Восточной Европы, оккупированных Германией. Эти источники помогли ему создать карты этих изменений. Когда он приехал в Иерусалим и пришел в Яд Вашем, к нему отнеслись как к знаменитости. В Картографическом отделе Библиотеки Конгресса он каталогизировал многие карты, с которыми работал. Он говорил, что если бы он был богатым, то платил бы музею, чтобы ему позволили делать эту работу — так он ее любил.

В нашем доме в Москве всегда было много гостей. Мама готовила целый поднос еды, потому что «кто знает, кто зайдет». Она готовила, а он делал водку. Точнее, он настаивал водку на сверхсекретной смеси специй, которую он унаследовал от своего отца. За прошедшие годы он усовершенствовал этот процесс и передал мне свой рецепт. Должна сознаться, что я использовала его только несколько раз, и я предупреждаю, что вы будете подвергнуты многолетним экспериментам. Моя цель — добиться качества продукта, который делал он.

Когда родились его внучки, он стал «Диди». По-русски Деда, дедушка, но это звучит почти как Дэдди (папа по-английски). Поэтому Саша звала его Диди. Когда появилась Маргоша, она тоже стала его так звать. Он говорил, что ему все равно, как его называют, лишь бы они его любили. Дедушка стал любимым конем/ослом, партнером в настольных играх и учителем всего на свете. Когда Саша начала изучать Солнечную систему, он принес глобус и начал ходить вокруг стола и крутить глобус, чтобы продемонстрировать солнечную систему. И он показал известный трюк со светом, чтобы объяснить, как происходит затмение. Он учил

Марго о созвездиях — то, чему я сама так никогда от него и не научилась по какой-то непонятной причине.

Диди научил нас удивляться, привил любовь к разным странам и культурам, и любовь к книгам. Его библиотека потрясающе обширна и разнообразна. У него всегда было много друзей, что мы видим сегодня. И мы все будем скучать по его заразительному смеху ...

15 марта 2015 г.

Саша и Паша

Александр Кириллов

ДЕТСТВО

Жили-были в городе Москве два мальчика: Саша и Паша. Они оба родились в 1936 году, были в эвакуации и вернулись в Москву в конце войны.

Саша пошёл в первый класс осенью 1944 года. Тогда в России мальчики и девочки учились в разных школах. Во время войны многие школы были закрыты и ближайшая к его дому мужская школа 239 была в Колокольниковом переулке близ Трубной площади. Школа была переполнена и в ней было 10 первых классов.

Паша был слаб здоровьем и пошёл в школу только в 1947 году сразу в третий класс, тот самый, где учился Саша. Там они и встретились, но подружились не сразу.

К четвертому классу выяснилось, что в классе есть три отличника: Саша, Паша и Камиль Абъянов. Этот Камиль, проживавший в татарских трущобах на Трубной, пользовался большим авторитетом в классе, поскольку был на три года старше всех остальных (он попал под трамвай и лишился обеих ног) и намного сильнее. Он почему-то проникся уважением к Паше и тот до конца средней школы был под его покровительством.

Класса с 6-го у Саши и Паши, помимо обычных мальчишеских занятий, появились свои увлечения. У Саши это была математика, у Паши — география. Кроме того, они решили по примеру Льва Кассиля придумать себе свою собственную страну, разместив ее в Антарктиде с посольствами в ближнем зарубежье.

Школа была семилетняя. В 1951 году мальчики кончили последний седьмой класс и детство кончилось. К этому времени они уже крепко подружились и много времени проводили вместе.

Паша жил с родителями, сестрой Юлькой и приемным братом Вовкой (оба на 3 года моложе) и тетей Верой в отдельной квартире из трех маленьких комнат, а Саша — в одной 20-метровой комнате коммунальной квартиры вместе с родителями и сестрой Юлькой. Поэтому мальчики проводили время или в прогулках по Москве, или у Паши дома.

ОТРОЧЕСТВО

Война была позади, в Москву стали возвращаться люди из эвакуации (хотя далеко не все). Школу решили постепенно сделать десятилетней и набрали два восьмых класса: А и Б.

Саша оказался в 8-А, а у Паши судьба оказалась сложнее. Его отца, журналиста и детского писателя Мих. Ильина (это его псевдоним, взятый, чтобы отличаться от другого писателя М. Ильина), арестовали органы КГБ. Формальной причиной ареста был назван факт сотрудничества Мих. Ильина в газете, которая позже была закрыта как эсеровская. Но все понимали, что это было частью начинавшейся тогда антиеврейской кампании.

Павел вынужден был бросить школу, поступить работать на завод «Серп и молот» и перейти учиться в школу рабочей молодежи на улице Мархлевского. Но дружба Саши и Паши на этом не кончилась.

Тогда отношение людей к родственникам арестованных было очень разным. Одни прекращали всякое общение и смотрели волком, другие делали вид, что ничего не произошло, но на всякий случай сторонились, третьи искренне сочувствовали и старались помочь. Семья Саши была среди последних несмотря на то, что его отец работал в КГБ.

Жизнь продолжалась, и наши герои достигли первых заметных успехов. Оба в десятом классе получили первые премии на городских Олимпиадах: Павел на географической, а Саша на математической. Тогда только что получили распространение авторучки (в школах писали перьевыми). У Паши и Саши оказалась одна авторучка на двоих, которой они и писали свои работы, благо Олимпиады проходили в разные дни. Потом они долго хранили эту ручку, но в конце концов она сломалась и потерялась.

Еще в девятом классе, в ноябре 1952 года ребята ходили смотреть на строящееся здание Университета на Ленинских горах. Но погода была плохая, стоял густой туман и от забора, окружавшего стройку, ничего не было видно.

Оба решили после окончания школы идти в МГУ, соответственно на географический и механико-математический факультеты. И оба поступили!

Для Саши это было сравнительно легко: он кончил школу с золотой медалью и должен был только пройти собеседование.

Для Паши проблема была сложнее. Но шел уже 1954 год, наступила оттепель и его первая премия на олимпиаде и поддержка одного из профессоров факультета преодолели, казалось, непроходимый барьер — Пашу зачислили в студенты.

Началась веселая и напряженная студенческая жизнь. У Саши образовался большой круг друзей-студентов, в который вошел и Паша. Конечно, теперь у каждого было много своих дел и занятий. Но общение продолжалось и летом после третьего курса Павел приехал навестить Сашу на целину в Кустанайскую область. Он легко вписался в математическую среду и даже вошел в мех-матский фольклор, став одним из персонажей «Целинной Азбуки», опубликованной в книге «Мы математики с Ленинских гор», Москва, 2003.

ВЗРОСЛАЯ ЖИЗНЬ.

Быстро пролетели студенческие годы, и наши друзья поступили в аспирантуру: Павел в Институт Географии, а Саша на мех-мат. Оба защитили диссертации, обзавелись семьями; встречались реже, но регулярно и с взаимным удовольствием.

Два–три раза в год они устраивали «экспедиции» — совместные поездки по городам и деревням. Сначала пешком по Москве и окрестностям, потом на разном транспорте, а когда Саша из командировки во Францию в 1967 году привез машину, то и на ней.

Обычно географическое обоснование и обеспечение маршрута предлагал Павел, он же был и штурманом, а бессменным водителем был Саша.

Летом 1986 года друзья отметили совместное столетие: сумма возрастов достигла 100 лет. По этому поводу состоялась многодневная поездка по северу Московской области.

Но российская жизнь шла своим чередом и не совсем к лучшему. Политика разрядки в 70-е годы ненадолго смягчила внутреннее напряжение. Началась, но вскоре закончилась еврейская эмиграция. В 1980 году в Москве вместо ранее объявленного коммунизма состоялись олимпийские игры, омраченные бойкотом многих стран. Вместо обещанного изобилия была объявлена продовольственная программа. Увеличилось идеологическое давление на научную, техническую и культурную интеллигенцию (как бы ее ни поносили сейчас, но в те годы этот слой населения старался как мог сохранить немногие оставшиеся идеалы).

Саша долго не представлял себе жизни вне России. Тем более, что в 50-х и начале 60-х годов МГУ был сильнейшим математическим центром в мире по степени концентрации первоклассных математиков. (Позже это время было названо «золотыми годами советской математики»).

К тому же под крылом ректора Петровского и на фоне успехов оборонной техники, основанной на современной физике, математики избежали участи генетики и кибернетики. Однако, научная изоляция стала усиливаться.

После двух поездок — в 1962 году в Швецию на Международный Конгресс математиков (в составе делегации) и в 1968 году во Францию по приглашению Института Анри Пуанкаре (на семестр, из которого пробыл только 4 месяца), Саша понял, что за границей живут тоже люди и страх перед «капиталистическим окружением» в основном навеян нашей пропагандой.

Друзья вели длинные разговоры о взаимоотношениях человека и государства, во многом соглашались (например, что человек важнее государства), но по вопросу о том, где жить, так и не пришли к согласию.

«Ведь ты — советский еврей», — говорил Саша Паше. Ты прожил полвека в России, ты знаешь и любишь русский язык и русскую культуру. Мы с тобой и все наши друзья всегда различали страну и ее правителей. И ты еще многого можешь добиться, не уезжая из страны. Но Пашу эти аргументы не убедили. Он начал склоняться к возможности эмиграции и в конце концов подал документы на выезд в Израиль.

1987 ГОД

Пять лет Паша был «отказником». В таком же статусе был другой Сашин однокурсник и друг Марк Фрейдлин, вместе с многими другими, кто подал документы на выезд в 1980 году. Друзья не переставали общаться, хотя жизнь отказников сильно изменилась.

Наконец, в 1987 году влияние начавшейся перестройки дошло до выездной политики. И Паша, и Марк получили разрешение на выезд. Это было и радостное и печальное событие. Впереди ждала свобода (а у Марка еще и гарантированная интересная работа), а позади — вся прошлая жизнь и друзья. Никто не знал, когда расстающиеся увидятся вновь, но все были уверены, что не скоро (и, может быть, не в этой жизни).

В том же году Саша получил разрешение поехать на конференцию в Болгарию. В первый же свободный день, взяв бутылку красного вина, он забрался на гору Витоши, чтобы в свободной и приятной обстановке подумать о жизни, как они с Пашей неоднократно делали во время их экспедиций в России. Ему вдруг пришла в голову идея, что Болгария вообще, и Витоша в частности,— это прекрасное место, куда можно приехать и из Москвы, и из Америки.

Идея была настолько хороша, что захотелось немедленно выпить. Поскольку штопора в наличии не было, Саша решил применить старинный народный метод вышибания пробки, постучав дном бутылки о березу. То ли у него не было достаточно сноровки, то ли болгарская пробка сидела в бутылке слишком прочно, но кончилось тем, что горлышко бутылки отвалилось, а оставшаяся часть чуть не отрезала Саше большой палец на правой руке. Как ни странно, это его нисколько не огорчило, а напротив внушило уверенность, что они с Павлом скоро увидятся. За это говорил и тот факт, что в бутылке осталось больше половины вина. Уняв кровь и перевязав палец, Саша не спеша допил бутылку, не забывая символически чокаться с Павлом и обсуждать с ним случившееся. Спустившись с горы и вернувшись в гостиницу, он сочинил и отправил Павлу письмо с описанием приключения. Павел ответил несколькими письмами, в которых он с юмором описывал свои первые впечатления о Европе и Америке. Только много позже Саша узнал, что это время для Паши было чрезвычайно трудным и адаптация к американской жизни далась ему нелегко.

1988–1990 ГОДЫ

Для внешнего мира перестройка в России началась в 1985 году. В МГУ она не торопилась. Все начальство, включая иностранный отдел оставалось прежним и вело себя по-прежнему.

В 1988 году в Дании была организована конференция по методу орбит в теории представлений, который был предложен в Сашиной диссертации. Его пригласили на конференцию и предложили прочитать курс лекций в Университете Копенгагена.

Когда Саша пошел за разрешением в иностранный отдел, его начальник сказал, что на конференцию можно подавать документы, а насчет курса лекций в приглашении ничего не сказано. Хотя приглашение у Саши лежало в кармане, он благоразумно не стал об этом говорить и получил разрешение на поездку.

Уже в Дании он спросил датского чиновника, нельзя ли ему продлить пребывание в Дании для прочтения курса лекций. Разумеется можно, ответил чиновник и дал соответствующую бумагу. Но когда Саша принес ее в Советское посольство, чиновник очень строго спросил, откуда эта бумага, а потом закричал:

— Кто вам разрешил обращаться к датчанам! Вы должны немедленно покинуть Данию и вернуться в Москву.

Саша показал официальное приглашение, объяснил, что его лекции объявлены в университетском расписании, а обратный билет действителен только на рейс через две недели. В ответ чиновник сказал, что он пошлет в Москву телекс (предшественник современного факса) за инструкциями, а Саша обязан наутро явиться в посольство. Так и было в течение 5 или 6 дней, и каждый раз тот же чиновник встречал его сердитым окриком: — Как? Вы все еще здесь?! На седьмой день (видимо, пришел этот таинственный телекс) он хмуро сказал — можете оставаться.

Через год перестройка сделала еще один шаг: Саше разрешили поездку во Францию.

Но в этом же году запретили поехать на конференцию в Израиль, мотивируя это тем, что Московский Университет — это идеологическое заведение, а Израиль — очень реакционная страна.

Наконец, в 1990 году наступили реальные перемены. Весной Саше разрешили поехать в Израиль (правда, как частному лицу, а не как профессору МГУ), а осенью, ко всеобщему удивлению, не возражали против поездки на семестр (!) в университет штата Мериленд, где работал Марк Фрейдлин и где жил Паша, который работал в музее Холокоста в Вашингтоне.

Так друзья оказались в одном городе всего через 3 года после расставания в Москве.

В день приезда Саша позвонил Паше, однако встретиться немедленно не удалось: между ними было около 20 миль расстояния, ни у одного из них не было машины, а городской транспорт отсутствовал.

ЖИЗНЬ В АМЕРИКЕ

Я думаю, что о характере наших отношений лучше всего говорит наш обмен письмами после лета 2013 года:

On 08/07/2013 08:40 PM, Pavel Ilyin wrote:

Привет, синьор!

Сначала ты мне не писал, потом я тебе не писал, потом я тебе написал, точнее еще не написал, но пишу.

В конце мая – начале июня я побывал в Германии, а оттуда – в Грузии. Я был в Тбилиси несколько раз, последний весной 1982 года накануне подачи. И очень приятно было встретиться со старыми знакомыми (включая город Тбилиси) и узнать, что меня многие помнят. Мы с Эллой отправились туда для участия в конференции в честь семидесятилетия нашего хорошего друга Резо Гачечиладзе. Ты его видел — он был тамадой на моем шестидесятилетии. За первые четыре дня я, кроме доклада на конференции, выступил на презентации книги Резо, сказал пять тостов, (один по-английски) и дал два интервью: для телевидения и для вечерней газеты.

Потом нашим хозяином стал наш другой старый друг, он когда-то был аспирантом в Москве. Несколько лет назад он купил домик с виноградником в Кахетии, и в этом домике угощал нас замечательным вином. В общем, путешествие было замечательным. Но зато по приезде я оказался плотно занятым до самого отъезда в Мэн. Где сейчас и пребываю в полной нирване. Как твое выступление у Гельфанда? Я прочитал в Википедии о нем (там ты упоминаешься среди его учеников до слова «и другие») и о тебе (впечатляет). Жду твоих рассказов о московских настроениях. Про Академию, конечно, знаю. Удастся ли что-нибудь изменить от более худшего, к менее? Передай большой привет Шурику А. Скажи ему, что я не нахожу для себя адекватных слов ни на каком языке. Встретился ли ты на этот раз с моими родственниками? В общем, нам есть чем поделиться. Домой вернусь 20-го. А празднование состоится день-в-день — 24-го. Луизе, при случае, привет.

П.И.

P. S. Будет время – взгляни на http://www.youtube.com/watch?v=yZTgv29lXbY –П.

Привет, Синьор!

Рад, что ты хорошо поездил и достойно выступил. У меня в лаптопе нет звука, и я твоё выступление не прослушал, а проглядел. Если бы ты ещё не смотрел всё время себе под нос — выглядел бы блестяще. Но и так хорошо. Первая половина Гельфандовского Столетия прошла неплохо. Много первоклассных математиков, почти никого из академического начальства. Моё краткое резюме: Российский парламент – не место для дискуссий (по словам его спикера), а Президентский зал РАН (где проходила конференция) – не место для научных докладов. Немного погулял по Москве; ноги быстро устают и всё время хочется спать. От Чистых прудов, где мы живём, до Большого Каретного, где мой институт, дохожу пешком с некоторой усталостью. Но уже дважды ходил туда и обратно разными путями.

День рождения твоей Юльки в этом году я пропустил и с Женькой тоже не виделся. Ездил на дачу к Бобу Минлосу по Горьковской ветке Курской дороги.

Был в Независимом Университете на конференции молодых математиков. Были у Ковалёвых. Сергей Адамович чувствует себя неважно (ему уже 84). Сейчас опять поедем на Юго-Западную, но не в гости, а в сберкассу за пенсией. Москва по-прежнему город дорогой. Метро стоит 30 рублей (а доллар 33). Мою зарплату повысили и теперь она 24000 плюс 7000 за степень. Обед в МУМУ стоит 250–300 рублей. (А пиво в отеле «Корстон»- бывшая гостиница «Орлёнок»- стоит 400 рублей за 0.5 л). Но люди как-то живут, приспособились. Пока кончаю, до встречи (24 августа?).

Саша.

Каким я знал и помню

Вадим Алцкан

Я друг и коллега Павла. Я познакомился с Павлом и Эллой в середине 1990-х годов, работая в Центре еврейской общины Большого Вашингтона, который расположен в Роквилле. Меня поразила сложность их долгой и богатой событиями жизни, которую они оставили позади, и в то же время их энтузиазм по отношению к новой главе своей жизни. Павел и Элла представляют печально известную группу советских евреев, которых называют «отказниками». Они были среди тех людей, которые осмелились выразить желание покинуть Советский Союз. В этом праве им было отказано, и при этом им больше не было позволено продолжать нормально жить и работать в СССР.

Надо отметить, что история персонального «исхода» Эллы и Павла стала частью недавно открытого Еврейского музея в Москве, в котором экспонируется уникальный исторический документ из семейного архива Эллы и Павла — так называемая «выездная виза», которую они, наконец, получили в 1987.

Приехав в Америку, Павел и Элла столкнулись еще с одной проблемой — найти свое собственное место в новой стране. В это самое время я познакомился с Павлом и был поражен его энциклопедическими знаниями географии.

По счастливому стечению обстоятельств, я в то время работал в Отделе регистрации евреев, переживших Холокост, который был создан Музеем и нуждался в специалисте, знающем географические названия. Таким образом, в жизни иногда случаются и хорошие вещи: вскоре мы с Павлом стали коллегами. Сотрудники музея приветствовали Павла с большой благодарностью за его мастерство.

В течение следующих двадцати лет Павел был единственным специалистом Музея по историческим картам и названиям мест, а также уникальным ресурсом для сотрудников, стажеров, ученых, исследователей, людей, переживших Холокост и их семей, и вообще для любого, кто приходил к нему с вопросом по географии.

В жизни не так много вещей, столь же запутанных, как политическая география Восточной Европы с ее постоянно меняющимися границами, топонимами и вариациями их написания на десятках языков. Павел был одним из тех немногих людей на свете, кого никогда не смущали подобные вещи. На самом деле, он был настоящим авторитетом в этой области. Он знал не только все места по их названиям и нынешним географическим границам, но также и почему, когда и как долго эти границы и названия существовали до того, как они были снова изменены.

Павел мог ответить на любой из этих вопросов. Тем не менее, он был очень скромным и щедрым в своем мастерстве. Неважно, кто задал ему вопрос — старшеклассник, стажер или выдающийся ученый, если этот человек нуждался в помощи Павла. Фраза «я не знаю» никогда не была вариантом ответа для Павла. Если он не мог предоставить информацию на месте, он давал ответ на следующее утро, проштудировав бесчисленные книги и карты. Имея дело с потоком географических запросов, поступающих в музей, я привык отсылать их Павлу, часто с замечанием: «Спросите Павла. Если Павел этого места не знает, то этого места, вероятно, никогда не существовало».

В последние два дня в память и в честь Павла Ильина флаги Мемориального музея Холокоста были наполовину приспущены. Для меня большая честь выступить здесь от имени Музея Холокоста, передать семье Павла соболезнования сотрудников музея и флаг, подаренный музеем.

Все коллеги по музею, с которыми я общался последние два дня, упоминали об особой открытой улыбке Павла, и так его и запомнят.

15 марта 2015 г.

Вспоминая Павла Ильина

Татьяна Рунова

Я знала Павла с середины 1960-х гг. ушедшего века, когда он, как уже поработавший в Институте Гипрогор экономико-географ, пришёл в Институт Географии АН СССР на стандартную для научной молодёжи должность младшего научного сотрудника. Это было время, когда наш отдел экономической географии переходил на новое для него направление работ — от традиционного географического страноведения к проблемно-географическим исследованиям. Этот кардинальный сдвиг инициировал и продвигал талантливый молодой заведующий отделом Алексей Александрович Минц, тогда ещё только набиравший авторитет в учёном мире. Как всякое кардинальное изменение, оно встретило объяснимое сопротивление сложившегося в 1940–1950 гг. коллектива маститых экономико-географов, на авторитет которых работал завершающийся в те годы выход «Синей серии» — более 20 томов самых полных на тот момент (да и до сих пор тоже) экономико-географических характеристик всех экономических районов и республик страны.

Для усиления своих позиций и, пользуясь уходом некоторых несогласных, А. А. Минц принял меры по укреплению молодёжной группы отдела, сделав ставку на сотрудников, уже поработавших в научных и проектных организациях, в чём-то проявивших себя и двигавшихся к защите диссертаций. Я, только что защитившая кандидатскую, оказалась в числе первых среди них. Затем в отделе появилась И. В. Канцебовская, Ю. Л. Пивоваров, Ю. А. Веденин, И. А. Зорин, А. Левинтов и др. Все они позже стали известными учёными, в большинстве — докторами наук и даже зачинателями новых направлений исследований.

В составе этого «призыва» был и Паша Ильин. Он вошёл в группу, разрабатывающую проблематику оценки природных условий и ресурсов как приоритетное и поисковое исследование, нацеленное на сближение географических работ с запросами практики. Как имеющий опыт проектной работы в Институте Гипрогор, он взялся за разработку оценки природных условий для целей градостроительства. Работа была очень актуальной и нужной для того времени, когда в стране, особенно в Сибири, шло активное освоение ресурсов, а около них росли новые города и посёлки. Помню его выступления по этой тематике в Географическом обществе, на ряде конференций, вызывавшие общий интерес. Этот интерес был определён, в частности тем, что в отличие от других, более маститых географов, работавших в сфере методик бальных, сравнительных, относительных оценок, Павел взялся за методику экономической, стоимостной оценки природных условий. Учитывая, что такая оценка была прерогативой учёных-экономистов, да и они к этой проблеме только подходили, и то в границах «ресурсных» оценок, хочу подчеркнуть его научную смелость, новаторство поисков, заявку на освоение новых нестандартных подходов.

Важно, что Павел довёл свои теоретико-методические построения до разработки подробной карты нашей страны с выявлением ареалов с разной степенью влияния этих условий на стоимость работ. Насколько я знаю, его карта широко использовалась в проектных разработках Гипрогора. Эта работа послужила ему основой кандидатской диссертацию, которую Павел успешно защитил, кажется, к 1970 г. и положила начало следующим его исследованиям. Очень жаль, что его научная стезя прервалась с отъездом из страны, где он стал уже авторитетным специалистом в своей области и где мог бы добиться вскоре более значимых результатов.

Это всё о науке. Но наше бытие в ней имело «много гитик», а Павел был всегда сторонником разностороннего подхода к жизни. Вспоминаю празднование первых успехов нашего резко помолодевшего отдела, наверное, в 1970 или в 1971 гг., когда, получив премию ИГ АН за научные достижения, мы всем коллективом, многие с детьми, отправились в трёхдневный тур на теплоходе по Волге в г. Углич. Веселье било через край и во главе его был Павел Ильин, как организатор (кажется, он был профоргом, кто помнит этот чин) нашего действа. Элла, его жена, выполняла роль общей мамы, сооружая бесконечные бутерброды и протягивая их из окна своей каюты всем страждущим, тусующимся (говоря современным языком) на палубе около этого общего центра притяжения.

Общая работа и наша молодость сближали и наши семьи. Мне не забыть поездку на Новогодние школьные каникулы в Пушкинские Горы, в жестоко морозную зиму 1978 г., в которую поехали вместе с детьми Г. А. Приваловская, В. Н. Аванесова, я и Павел с Эллой, человек с десяток. Не забыть замёрзшего вагона до

Пскова, в котором все спали в пальто и обуви, пробежек рысцой по Пскову — осмотр памятников, обед в ресторане вокзала, где я и Г.А. дали своим сыновьям (9–10 классы) по рюмке вина «для сугреву». А автобусы всё не шли в Пушгоры, — моторы замёрзли. Вопрос решился надёжным способом — собрали деньги и моторы завелись. В Пушгорах нас ждали номера с отключёнными батареями, но электричество работало и горячий чай (конечно, в номере Ильиных — общей гостиной), всегда был готов стараниями нашей хозяйки — Эллы. После путешествий между Михайловским-Тригорским-Петровским, то пробежкой, то на лыжах, а то в конных санях-розвальнях приветливых тогда местных обитателей, этот общий чай был особенно ценен, дружен и весел.

А в ночь встречи Нового 1978 года к нам пришёл настоящий Дед Мороз, младшие дети визжали от восторга и бегали с топотом по коридорам гостиницы, а старшие с недоверием приглядывались к домашним тапочкам, выглядывающим из-под его вывернутой шубы. Этот подарок (конечно и с персональными подарками из мешка) устроил дорогой Паша, признанный глава нашего детско-женского кагала! А как повысился авторитет этой нашей общей поездки, когда дети узнали, что в ней участвует давно им известный по радио сам Захар Загодкин! А после поездки мы всем составом были приглашены в Консерваторию, на выступление его музыкальной дочки Нади с последующим приёмом в радушном доме Ильиных-Каганов, как и полагается после премьеры дебютантки.

Вот так и жили. Время шло, многое изменилось. Пришли новые сотрудники, а из коллектива того времени, которое вспомнилось, осталось уже мало людей. Одних уж нет, а те далече. Так было, так всегда и будет. Надо сказать спасибо тому хорошему и доброму, что было. Спасибо и тебе, Павел.

Алаверды к Паше Ильину

Павел Полян

В АВГУСТЕ СЕМЬДЕСЯТ ЧЕТВЕРТОГО: МОЛОДОЙ И НАИВНЫЙ

В августе 1974 года я, по университетскому распределению, пришел в ИГАН — Институт географии Академии наук СССР, в отдел экономической географии, стажером-исследователем с окладом в 95 рублей. Начальником отдела был Георгий Михайлович Лаппо — единственный сотрудник, с которым я хотя бы виделся до этого. Виделся же я с ним у Исаака Моисеевича Маергойза — моего университетского профессора и нашего общего учителя, раз или два приглашавшего нас и еще несколько человек для «мозговых атак» на какую-то общеинтересную тему.

Я распределился в ИГАН явно не будучи в состоянии реально оценить невероятную степень своего везения и своей удачи!

Конечно же, я бывал не во всех, а лишь в нескольких десятках академических институтов плюс отзывы сотрудников еще нескольких десятков других. И на основании этой субъективной эмпирики беру на себя смелость утверждать: наш Институт географии был самым либеральным институтом в Академии наук, самым толерантным по отношению к своим научным сотрудникам и их естественным свободам. И дело не только в нашем вольготном режиме как таковом, а в самой атмосфере, постепенно установившейся в институте и бережно в нем поддерживавшейся. Предоставленная свобода порождала не анархию, а ответственность, и научная отдача была в разы выше той, что была бы при коллективном ежедневном радении.

Я проработал в институте 43 (sic!) года — при трех директорах: Иннокентии Петровиче Герасимове, Владимире Михайловиче Котлякове и Ольге Николаевне Соломиной. И могу засвидетельствовать, что каждый из них уважал и, поелику возможно, охранял этот режим, отдавая себе полный отчет в его не только в его справедливости и привлекательности для сотрудников, но и в эффективности для института и для науки.

573

Встреч в режиме один раз в неделю, — существовало даже понятие «отдельский день», — было совершенно достаточно для решения текущих вопросов, обсуждения научных докладов и общения сотрудников друг с другом. Разумеется, общеинститутские собрания, защиты, тематически близкие заседания ученых советов, а также 5-е и 19-е числа каждого месяца (дни выдачи зарплаты), — тоже исправно посещались.

Столь умеренное присутствие на службе создавало важный психологический фон: за единственный в неделю раз сотрудники просто не могли успеть надоесть друг другу или друг друга раздражить, что неминуемо происходило бы, сходись они на службе каждый божий день. Более того, многие друг другу даже радовались: дорогого стоит!

ОТДЕЛЬСКОЕ

Когда я пришел в ИГАН стажером-исследователем, за спиной у меня было уже лет 10–11 «географического стажа», — это если к пяти счастливым годам университетской учебы (у Маергойза!) прибавить еще лет 5–6 участия в географических олимпиадах и, особенно, в радиоигре «Путешествие по любимой родине». И тут, и там я бывал в победителях и призерах, так что профессионально я сразу же почувствовал себя в ИГАНе, как в своей тарелке.

С того августа утекло много времени, многое уже вытеснено позднейшими впечатлениями и благополучно стерлось, но кое-что устояло и все-таки не вытравилось из памяти.

Первыми меня встретило трио наших лаборанток — Вера Аванесова, Люба Оболонкина и Надя (Надежда Павловна) Мерзликина. Как научный сотрудник и координатор населенческой темы лично я на протяжении долгих лет и даже десятилетий с удовольствием и благодарностью работал и взаимодействовал именно с Надей, которой были даны надежность, тщательность и еще добрая душа.

Но вернемся к научному коллективу, в который я тогда пришел и погрузился. Была там мощная группа специалистов по природопользованию, которую, собственно, Алексей Минц и возглавлял, а после его смерти в 1973 году — Генриетта Алексеевна Приваловская и Татьяна Григорьевна Рунова; входили в нее еще и Инга Вениаминовна Канцебовская и Танечка Петрякова.

К этой же группе примыкали Таня Нефедова и Ира Волкова, но обе пришли в институт позднее. Как и Андрей Трейвиш (мой ближайший о ту пору друг): вместе с Нефедовой он трудился в МГУ.

Довольно скоро и закономерно Андрей вырос в самого сильного и яркого ученого в нашем экономгеографическом цеху.

В целом очень бережно отнесясь к проблемно-географическому направлению, ассоциирующемуся с именем А. А. Минца, Лаппо вместе с тем сознательно и осторожно стал продвигать и свой профиль — «географию населения» в широком смысле этого слова. При этом он нисколечко не боялся приглашать в отдел ярких ученых, таких как Григорий Абрамович Гольц или Жанна Антоновна Зайончковская!

ПАША ИЛЬИН

Как бы в обе группы — и «природников», и «населенцев» — входил и Паша (Павел Михайлович) Ильин, ученый секретарь отдела. В сентябре он вернулся из отпуска и сразу же пошел на меня с обезоруживающе-близорукой своей улыбкой и протянутой для рукопожатия рукой — знакомиться. Вот с кем было легко с первой же секунды знакомства!

В первые же пять минут первого в жизни разговора выяснилось, что собеседник — это просто материализовавшийся миф — «Захар Загадкин и Антон Камбузов» в одном лице и собственной персоной! Что, достойный сын своего отца и к тому же дипломированный и остепененный географ, он буквально подхватил из отцовых рук радиоэстафету и взял в свои.

И чуть ли не через неделю я был уже на Карла Маркса, 20 — у Паши в гостях, впервые ощутив на себе все радушие их дома, ведомого не им, а Эллой Каган. В начале 1960-х гг. Павел и Элла встретились и сошлись в «Гипрогоре»...

Пока Элла собирала на кухне на стол, Паша показывал мне свой домашний «уголок Захара Загадкина» — отцовские книги, коллекцию тельняшчатых моряцких статуэток из всевозможных материялов, ну и конечно — каталожный ящик (или два?) с картотекой адресов и баллов, заработанных корреспондентами Захара. Тут же и старинная пишущая машинка с круглыми, если не ошибаюсь, рычажками, на которой лично Захар Загадкин вытюкивал свои письма мне, Павлику Поляну, ученику таковского класса, причем сначала ему помогал в этом Михаил Ильин, а теперь вот другой Ильин — Павел, смотрящий на меня сейчас сбоку и молодо улыбающийся.

Легкомысленность (иногда даже в опасной для него самого) легко сочеталась в нем с перманентной готовностью к товарищескому застолью, но не усуглялась этим. Выпивохой Паша не был, но «веселие пити» испытывал и всегда был готов отложить «дела» заради «пиров». Оттого так и млел он, так и таял от Грузии, где застолье, в отличие от России, не безделье и не потеха, а тоже «дело», причем требующее от занятых им мужей не просто красноречия, но и тонкости выражения мысли, а значит и определенной — по возможности вековой — речевой культуры.

Паша и дома пытался завести свой собственный ритуал! Он делал какую-то особенную свою водку, держал ее в каком-то особенном штофе и подавал ее с какой-то ворожбой и как-то по-особенному охлажденной.

Но главным в нем было безусловно другое: интеллигентность, порядочность, дар товарищества и сильнейшее желание — и готовность! — помочь нуждающемуся, причем не дожидаясь момента, когда тебя об этом попросят. И еще удивление (всегда отдельное от осуждения!) — удивление на чье-то очередное неблагородство: мол, ну как же это можно?!

А еще он много читал (о, непередаваемая сладость самиздатская!) и, обожая поэзию и географию, полагал их состоящими в сестринских отношениях.

Это же сочетание не чуждо и мне, так что мы сблизились и на этой почве, или, вернее, почвах.

ПАШИНА ПОЧВА

Он родился 24 августа 1936 года, так что в момент нашего знакомства ему было 38 лет. Родительский дом — это две крошечные, насквозь прокуренные проходные комнаты в коммуналке в дореволюционном доходном доме на Пушечной улице. Первая была детской и общей, а вторая — родительской. И отец, Михаил Ильич (чьи предки — интеллигенты из Кракова), и мать, Софья Ильинична (чьи предки — купцы из Суража) были журналистами: отец, как сказали бы теперь, был колумнистом в «Труде». Были они, по слову их невестки, старомодно-аристократичны и даже обращались друг к другу на Вы! Дети же, — а это не только Павел и Юля, его младшая сестра, это еще и Вова — их двоюродный брат, чьи родители канули в репрессии. В той же квартире жила еще одна семья и еще Верочка, она же Вера Ильинична, — сестра Михаила Ильича: в ее комнате и спал Вова — больше было негде.

Сам Михаил Ильич работал всегда, когда не спал. Замкнутость и нелюдимость он как-то сочетал с шутками и фантазерством, и к веселым своим мистификациям он подключал и сына, которого вместе с тем упорно «натаскивал» по любви к географии и картам. Так что не удивительно, что на географических олимпиадах школьников в МГУ Павлик Ильин начал брать приз за призом.

Во время войны семья была эвакуирована — сначала в Омск, потом в Алма-Ату. Через полтора года, в 1943 году, они вернулись в Москву, и все, казалось бы, вернулось на круги своя...

В 1944 году Паша пошел учиться, и 1 ноября 1950 года — в день ареста отца –ему было 14 с небольшим лет. В августе 1952 года, когда ему стукнуло 16, Паша перевелся в вечернюю школу и пошел работать на завод: кормильца-то в семье не было! Но с географией не расставался — ни в душе, ни на олимпиадах, где его, вечерника (редчайший для олимпиад случай!), заметил и выделил профессор Саушкин. «Ну, молодой человек, теперь к нам?..» — спросил Павла Михайловича Юлиан Глебович. И тогда Паша честно рассказал ему о своих «дефектах»: во-первых, еврей, а во-вторых, сын врага народа. Отдадим должное собеседнику: Саушкин вчистую все это проигнорировал, и Пашу — о, счастье! — в 1954 году приняли на Геофак!

Отец вернулся в 1956 году. Закончив учебу в 1960 году, сын распределился в «Гипрогор», где проработал до 1965 года. Вот неполный перечень районных планировок и генпланов, в разработке которых он принял участие: области Свердловская, Горьковская и Рязанская, Мордовская АССР, промрайоны Орско-Халиловский Оренбургской области, Серово-Ивдельский Свердловской и Игрим-Берёзовский Тюменской, генпланы Ряжска в Рязанской, Киржача во Владимирской и Усть-Кута в Иркутской областях.

Благодаря «Гипрогору», как, впрочем, и Институту географии, Паша Ильин изрядно попутешествовал. Заграницу, правда, страна выпускала неохотно, особенно беспартийных: разве что по разу в Польшу и ГДР выпускали). А вот «коллекция» посещенных им за жизнь городов в СССР — перевалила за три сотни!

В 1965 году был объявлен прием в аспирантуру ИГАНа. Знакомые из института подсказали, что отдел экономгеографии переходит на новую тематику, и поэтому нужны будут как раз такие «практики», как Ильин. И, — о чудо — несмотря на Шестидневную войну, его, Павла Михайловича Ильина, приняли в аспирантуру!

Наступила совершенно другая жизнь: общество больших ученых, свобода расписания и свобода действий. Отдел тогда возглавлял Алексей Александрович Минц — молодой талантливый ученый, полный новых идей и энергии для их реализации. Географам, привычно занятым изучением районов страны, приходилось переключиться на анализ проблем.

Он же и был научным руководителем Павла Ильина. Тема: «Экономическая оценка природных условий градостроительства в СССР (опыт разработки методики на материале объектов массового строительства)». В 1971 году Павел ее успешно защитил.

Жизнь отдела был нарушена гибелью Минца в авиационной катастрофе в Праге в феврале 1973 года. Это была трагедия в науке для каждого, кто с ним был связан. В том числе и для Паши Ильина, ставшего к этому времени ученым секретарем отдела.

Тем не менее приход к руководству отделом Г. М. Лаппо — человека с таким же, как и у Ильина, биографическим заделом не в академической, а в практической сфере, серьезно улучшил Пашины стратегические позиции.

Развитие внешней ситуации в отделе счастливо совпало с его внутренней эволюцией — дрейфом в сторону социальной географии. Возможно, что дополнительно к этому же подталкивала и дружба с философом Александром Самойловичем Ахиезером, вместе с которым — и почти сразу после Пашиной защиты — они занялись проблемой социальной оценки территории.[1]

Параллельно и постепенно рос общенаучный вес Ильина, свидетельством чему стало и приглашение В. В. Покшишевского быть соредактором одного из изданий МФГО, посвященного миграциям населения в СССР.[2] Кстати, и по миграционной тематике соавтором Ильина выступил Ахиезер: их статья в этом сборнике была посвящена мотивационному механизму миграции населения.

1976 год был по-настоящему ярким в истории советской географии: в стране проводился XXIII Международный Географический Конгресс. Председателем Оргкомитета был наш директор, академик Иннокентий Петрович Герасимов, ученым секретарем — Юрий Владимирович Медведков. Все мы, сотрудники института были вдосталь нагружены обязанностями по организации и проведению конгресса. Так, Г. М. Лаппо отвечал за симпозиум по географии урбанизации, и я был его Санчой Пансой, то есть ученым секретарем симпозиума. Паше Ильину досталось секретарство по секции «Географическое образование, географическая литература и распространение географических знаний» при председателях

---

[1] Ахиезер А. С., Ильин П. М. Задачи разработки социальных оценок территории в условиях научно-технической революции. // Известия АН СССР. Сер. геогр. 1975. № 1. С. 86–92 (перевод на англ. язык: Soviet Geography: Review and Translation, December 1975, pp. 255–268).

[2] (Ред.) Покшишевский В. В., Ильин П. М. *Проблемы миграций населения в СССР.* М. Моск. филиал Геор. об-ва СССР, 1976, 69 с.

В. П. Максаковском и Л. С. Абрамове. Вместе с Пашей вдвоем мы отвечали за один из многочисленных постконгрессных симпозиумов — в Белоруссию, для которого он написал отличный маршрутный путеводитель.[3]

Между тем Паша продолжал нащупывать свое место в ландшафте социальной географии и геоурбанистики. Одной из таких тематических ниш явилась значимость административной функции для роста городов,[4] другой — фокусы роста в региональном развитии.[5]

ПУТЕШЕСТВИЕ ПО ЛЮБИМОЙ ВТОРОЙ РОДИНЕ

В июне 1982 года Павел Ильин с женой и дочкой Надей, тогда юным музыкантом, подали документы на путешествие — подальше от любимой родины — то есть на эмиграцию.

Пять лет — с 1982 по 1987 — Ильины провели в отказе, пережив в этом малоприятном состоянии еще двух генсеков — Черненко и Андропова. Из издательства («Большая российская энциклопедия», куда в свое время Пашу перетащили его тогдашние друзья — прежде всего Саша Горкин, заведовавший редакцией географии, а впоследствии и всем издательством) Пашу, правда, не уволили, но понизили в должности. А вот Эллу из ее ЦНИИПградостроительства — уволили.

Как бы то ни было жить стало особенно трудно, и я был рад тому, что находил для них тогда подработку — хотя бы в амплуа ма-

[3] П. М. Ильин. *Русская равнина Белорусская ССР*. Путеводитель для участников конгресса..

[4] Ильин П. М. О значимости административных функций для роста городов СССР. // *Урбанизация и формирование систем расселения*. М.: МФГО, 1978. С. 71–77; Ibid. Функции городов и развитие сети городских поселений СССР. М.— Киев: ИГАН СССР, СОПС УССР, 1979, 14 с.; Ibid. Смена ведущих функций города и ее влияние на динамику городского расселения // Некоторые проблемы урбанизации и градостроительства (социально-экономические аспекты). Под ред. А. С. Ахиезера, О. Н. Яницкого и др. М.: Секция социальных проблем Научного совета АН СССР по проблемам биосферы, 1980. С. 15–20.

[5] Гохман В. М., Ильин П. М., Липец Ю. Г. Значение фокусов роста в региональном развитии // Географические проблемы регионального развития и государственное планирование. Тезисы докладов советских участников Советско-Индийского симпозиума, Тбилиси — Баку, октябрь 1978 г. Тбилиси: ИГ АН СССР, ИГ им. Вахушти АН Груз. ССР, ИГ АН Азерб. ССР. С. 100–105; Ibid. Значение фокусов роста в региональном развитии // *Известия АН СССР. Сер. геогр. 1979*. № 6. С. 33–44 (англ. перевод: Soviet Geography: Review and Translation, April 1981. P. 255–268; нем. перевод: Geographische Berichte. Bd. 101. 1981. Nr. 4. S.209–224).

шинистки. Зато какую изысканную подработку! Статьи Маергойза и стихи Мандельштама!

Выехать из СССР им разрешили только при Горбачеве, в июне 1987 года.

Эмигрировали они в Штаты, обосновались сначала в Бостоне, а затем, более основательно, в Бетезде под Вашингтоном. Коллеги-географы, что начали тогда часто ездить в Америку, останавливались в их гостеприимном доме, рассказывали об их жизни, передавали приветы.

В 1991 году — на мандельштамовской конференции в Нью-Йорке — впервые оказался в Штатах и я.

А в 1999 году я поехал сразу на две американские стажировки: первая — в Вашингтоне, в Музее Холокоста, а другая — мандельштамовская — в Принстоне.

Именно Паша подобрал для меня приемлемую дешевую гостиничку с возможностью завтракать в определенные часы в больничной столовке — и всего в двух-трех остановках от Музея Холокоста. Паша в это время и сам работал в этом музее... ученым географом, разбираясь сам и помогая всем и каждому в вопросах непростой географии и топонимики Холокоста! Именно Паша был моим Вергилием по лабиринтам этого замечательного и очень американского учреждения, где познакомил со всеми «правильными» коллегами. Однажды он договорился и о моем интервью Фрумкину, своему приятелю из «Голоса Америки», — кажется, это было первое мое радиоинтервью.

Несколько раз выходные я проводил у Ильиных в Бетезде. Паша с Эллой подробно отвечали на мои старосветские вопросы и много возили по окрестностям, с гордостью показывая свои молодые еще американские «древности», в том числе и целый универмаг русской эмигрантской книги. Когда у меня сломался мой старый советский чемодан, они купили мне новый американский, которым я потом долго еще пользовался.

Сами Ильины, оказавшись в Америке, встретили пусть стандартное, но, самое главное, — человеческое к себе отношение, что весьма контрастировало с вытиранием о тебя ног в Союзе. Паша испытал тогда перед Америкой невероятный восторг, который только усиливался по мере того, как он узнавал особенности Америки и простых американцев — такие как внутренняя свобода, внутренняя ответственность, выстраиванье с государством равных отношений «на ты» и многое другое, в том числе и горизонтальный (т.е. не спущенный по вертикали) американский патриотизм.

Как только Паша осознал себя патриотом, его холодильник начал собирать на себе магнитки штатов, где он смог побывать.

Восьмидесятые годы почти полностью выпали из «библиографии» Павла Ильина. И это понятно: жизнь в отказе на родине, интеграция в жизнь на чужбине. Но все это время в нем вызревала новая и очень серьезная тема исследования — топонимическая, а точнее — анализ переименований географических названий в СССР и их логики. Эта тема, словно магма, накапливала втуне свой потенциал. В1993 и 1994 годах она разразилась двумя мощными публикациями на английском и русском языках, вобравшими в себя сильнейшие стороны Павла Ильина как географа-исследователя — пытливость и гуманитарность. Остается всего лишь упомянуть несколько других направлений Пашиных научных и человеческих интересов и публикаций в эмиграции. Это традиционное «градоведение», выплеснувшееся в очерки или рецензии на книги о Вашингтоне, Ленинграде и, главное, о Москве. Под редакцией Б. Рубла и П. Ильина в 2004 году в издательстве «РОССПЭН» вышла книга «Москва рубежа XIX и XX столетий. Взгляд в прошлое издалека»,[6] в которой Паша выступил в качестве автора или соавтора четырех текстов о Москве этого времени. Кроме того, это патриотические песни об Америке, ценителем и пропагандистом которых он стал.[7] Но, быть может, важнее остальных было еще одно направление — это географические, картографические и топонимические аспекты исследования Холокоста. Тут он со временем стал большим докой, полностью оправдывая всю торжественность именования своей должности в Мемориальном музее Холокоста в Вашингтоне: «Главный географ музея».

Умер он у себя в Бетезде 12 марта 2015 года...

---

[6] Ильин П., Рубл Б. (отв. Ред.). *Москва рубежа XIX и XX столетий. Взгляд в прошлое издалека*. М.: РОССПЭН, 2004, 302 с.

[7] Ильин П. «Эта земля моя, она прекрасна, Боже, храни ее!» Три патриотические песни Америки //*Время и место (Нью-Йорк)*. 2011. Вып. 4 (20). С. 116–137; Ibid. «Эта земля моя, она прекрасна, Боже, храни ее! Три патриотические песни Америки // *Панорама (Лос-Анжелес)*. 2012. № 6. 8–14 февраля. С. B10—B12.

Воспоминания Нэнси
и Тони Аллисон-Фишер

НЭНСИ:

В 1978 году мне было 23 года, и я училась в аспирантуре Лондонского университета под руководством Р. А. (Тони) Френча. В центре внимания моих научных исследований была Москва, точнее, ее транспортные сети и тенденции землепользования — сугубо географическая тематика. Когда университет выделил мне средства для исследовательской поездки на месяц в Москву, Тони Френч снабдил меня списком профессиональных контактов. Всего за два года до этого в Москве проводился Международный географический конгресс. Д-р Френч и многие другие английские и американские географы завязали контакты с советскими коллегами как в университетской среде, так и в Институте географии Академии наук СССР. В моем списке был и Павел Ильин, ученый из Института географии. Я прилежно ему позвонила. Павел сразу же предложил встретиться, чтобы обсудить мою работу и даже проконсультировать меня, если понадобится. Договариваясь о встрече, он дал мне первые указания, как доехать — потом подобных указаний будет множество — ехать на метро до такой-то станции, выйти на платформу, стоять у последнего вагона — там мы и найдем друг друга. Я описала свою внешность: длинные темные волосы, невысокая, «шотландское» пальто (я еще не знала, как по-русски сказать «в клетку»). В любом случае, я бы выделялась из толпы, как заморская птица, но эти опознавательные знаки пригодились при первой встрече. Мы прогулялись до элегантного ресторанчика в центре Москвы, где поговорили о своих научных интересах. Я очень скоро поняла, что передо мной человек с энциклопедическими (и к тому же глубоко личными) знаниями о Москве. Не могу вспомнить, когда начались наши систематические прогулки по городу, но очевидно это произошло очень скоро — ведь я в конце 1978 года провела в Москве всего месяц. Павел не просто хорошо ориентировался в городе. Он был сокровищницей знаний, знал каждый переулок, каждое здание и даже историю его жильцов. Из этих прогулок с Павлом выросло мое увлечение историей архитектуры. К моему большому удовольствию, к нам присоединилась Элла. Интересно, может кто-нибудь сразу не влюбиться в Эллу? В одно снежное воскресенье Павел с Эллой повели меня в действующую церковь у Бульварного кольца. Запах ладана, сияние свечей и голоса певчих откликнулись во мне духовным переживанием. Когда мы вышли из церкви, Павел тактично спросил, не принадлежу ли я к какой-нибудь религии, Павел с Эллой уже догадывались, что я еврейка (по моей фамилии и внешнему виду) в то время, как я наивно старалась это скрыть. «О, да, — ответила я, — я принадлежу к одной очень древней религии». «Значит, вы еврейка», — сказали Павел с Эллой, и добавили: «Мы тоже.» «Эта кровная связь, в дополнение к интеллектуальному родству, еще больше нас сблизила. Потом Павел с Эллой пригласили меня в гости, где я познакомилась с Надей, Мариам Абрамовной и отцом Эллы Исааком. Могла ли я тогда предположить, что мои отношения с этой необыкновенной семьей продлятся до сегодняшнего дня? Хотя Павла больше нет среди нас, он остается в моих мыслях — на узкой московской улочке или в залах Американского Музея памяти Холокоста, где Павел пользовался безусловной любовью коллег. Я глубоко благодарна судьбе за то, что знала Павла Ильина.

ЭНТОНИ:

Мои воспоминания начинаются позже по времени, и тоже в Москве, но в другую эпоху. Мы с Нэнси познакомились в аспирантуре Университета штата Вашингтон в Сиэтле, где она работала над диссертацией по географии. В январе 1986 года советско-американская рыболовецкая компания из Сиэтла послала меня открывать новое представительство в Москве.

Я свободно говорил по-русски и уже бывал в Советском Союзе. Мы с Нэнси обручились еще до моего отъезда в Москву, но она осталась в Сиэтле заканчивать диссертацию.

Через пару недель после приезда в Москву я позвонил по телефону, который мне дала Нэнси, ее друзьям Павлу и Элле. В Москве были снег и слякоть, мне было одиноко, я боролся с немыслимыми бюрократическими препонами и задержками на пути открытия нашей конторы. Я позвонил из телефонной будки на улице, что практиковалось во избежание прослушивания советскими силами безопасности. Горбачев пришел к власти за девять месяцев до этого, в воздухе пахло переменами, но известные мне правила жизни в Советском Союзе еще были в силе: нельзя было подвергать риску русских друзей контактами напрямую.

«Я хочу вас видеть!» сказала Элла, как только я объяснил, кто я такой и как связан с Нэнси. «Немедленно приезжайте!» Так началась традиция поездок на метро в запущенный, но очаровательный исторический район у станции метро «Бауманская» и семейных обедов. Для меня это стало убежищем от официального существования нового американского бизнесмена в Москве. Там была бабушка Мария Абрамовна, молчаливо ко мне благоволившая, и девочка-подросток Надя, удивительно смышлёная для своего возраста и очень похожая на мать. Еда, приготовленная Эллой, была потрясающей — не шла ни в какое сравнение с гостиничной, а разговоры — еще лучше. Часами разговаривали мы о русской литературе, науке и быстро меняющемся политическом смысле Перестройки. Разговорам способствовали рюмочки домашней водки-»ильинки», в превосходном сочетании с закуской из маринованных грибов, тоже приготовленной Павлом.

В воскресные дни мы втроем гуляли вокруг Бауманской или делали вылазки подальше — в монастыри или дворянские поместья царских времен. Вскоре я осознал, какая огромная, подробная и взаимосвязанная энциклопедия хранилась у Павла в голове. Он никогда ее не выставлял напоказ, просто отвечал на мои многочисленные вопросы спокойным изложением фактов, интересными отступлениями на цифры и места и юмористическими наблюдениями о русском и советском обществе. Я узнал, что его отец был создателем легендарного Захара Загадкина, обладавшего такой же всеобъемлющей эрудицией и добродушием героя детских радиоспектаклей, которые регулярно выходили в эфир. Когда я спрашивал об этом других московских друзей того же поколения, что и Павел, они с любовью вспоминали, как в детстве слушали радиопередачи про Захара Загадкина.

Когда Павлу исполнилось пятьдесят лет, Элла организовала веселое юбилейное торжество. Я приехал в их тесную, заставленную книгами квартиру и увидел шумную толпу. «Ильинка» текла рекой. Павел и другие ораторы декламировали остроумные неприличные стихи, хором, под гитару, пели песни запрещенных бардов. Это было полной радости данью любви к Павлу от его многочисленных друзей, представителей московской интеллигенции и, в некоторых случаях, таких же «отказников», как Павел и Элла. Тосты за его здоровье были красноречивыми, нежными, смешными и бесконечными.

Мы с Нэнси поженились в США летом 1986 года. К апрелю 1987 года мы с новорожденным сыном жили в собственной квартире на Октябрьской площади. Московское представительство моей компании процветало. Реформы Горбачева к тому времени уже давали себя знать, и жизнь в Москве быстро менялась. Мы продолжали ходить в гости к Элле и Павлу, но теперь и они могли приезжать к нам без особого страха. Они надеялись, что теперь им уже недолго оставалось сидеть в отказниках, как вдруг они получили разрешение на выезд и уехали в США. Теперь мы остались без них в Москве.

В последующие годы нам удалось несколько раз навестить их в Вашингтоне. Однажды, когда я по делам оказался в Вашингтоне, Павел устроил мне невыносимо наглядную «внутреннюю» экскурсию по Мемориальному музею Холокоста, где он в то время работал над определением малоизвестных географических мест проживания евреев в Восточной Европе и России, где они были полностью уничтожены. После этого, по моей просьбе, мы отправились в ближайший бар пропустить по нескольку необходимых рюмок водки.

За прошедшие годы Павел и Элла два раза приезжали к нам в Сиэтл и один раз — на нашу дачу на острове, где Павел умилялся нашему забавному деревенскому параду на Четвертое июля. Стоял 2011 год, и наши разговоры перешли, как всегда, к России — на этот раз к тому, как жаль, что она опять повернула к автократии. К тому времени здоровье у Павла пошатнулось, но острота ума, тепло души и чувство юмора остались неизменными. Это была наша последняя встреча: непроходящее счастливое воспоминание об отдыхе за рюмкой водки, хотя уже и не «ильинки», в летнюю погоду на острове в заливе Пьюджет-Саунд, на расстоянии в целый мир от зимней Москвы, где мы впервые повстречались.

Вспоминая встречи с Пашей Ильиным

Реваз Гачечиладзе

Я помню Пашу Ильина с середины 1970х годов. Высчитываю — это 40 с небольшим лет. Немало! А как будто было вчера.

Мы познакомились в 1975 году. Он приехал в Тбилиси то-ли на съезд географического общества, то-ли на какую-то Всесоюзную географическую конференцию за год до Конгресса Международного географического общества в Москве и мы, кажется, обсуждали какие-то детали экскурсии участников в Грузии после Конгресса.

Хотя Паша был лет на на 6–7 старше меня (сорок лет назад это еще что-то значило, с возрастом мы стали почти ровесниками!) мы сразу понравились друг-другу: почти одинаковое образование и похожий семейный бэкграунд — и отец Паши и мой были писателями. Художественная литература нам нравилась одинаковая! Помню, хорошо помню, отличный литературный стиль Паши: он буквально на глазах с легкостью обтесал мою статью, которую я написал на неродном мне русском языке.

В 1979 году в Москве проводился Советско-Индийский географический семинар с продолжением в Тбилиси, с экскурсией в грузинскую провинцию Кахети — край виноделия, и далее — в Баку. Москвичей из ИГАН было явно больше индийцев. Веселый, общительный Паша, как обычно, был одним из распорядителей семинара и неформальным лидером — душой общества. Это он с кем-то еще притащили в гостиницу «Интурист» в г. Телави (это центр Кахети) эмалированное ведро с вином и алюминиевую кружку и вся географическая компания (без индийцев, которые были исключительные трезвенники) укрепляла дружбу народов, черпая вдохновение в этом самом эмалированном ведре!

Через грузинский городок Лагодехи мы переехали в Азербайджан и заночевали в гостеприимном городе Нуха. Вместо вина там нас угощали отличным чаем и Паша Ильин подвел культурно-географический итог: «Теперь я знаю, где проходит граница между Европой и Азией — рядом с Лагодехи!»

Когда Паша с Эллой и дочкой, которую Паша боготворил, переехали в Америку, связь была потеряна, к счастью, временно. Грянул 1991 год. Настала свобода. Правда, сперва нелегкая. Но Железный Занавес рухнул. Не нужны стали партийные и профсоюзные рекомендации и решения где-то наверху и от «соседа» для поездок заграницу. Переписка стала свободной. Паша нашелся!

Когда 1990-е годы я ездил в США читать лекции и участвовать в конференциях, я не раз был дружески приглашен Пашей и Эллой в их уютный дом в Бетезде, рядом с Вашингтоном и оставлен там ночевать, что тогда было весьма кстати! Паша радовался, что в их кондоминиум забредают олени и всякая другая фауна и они мирно уживаются с людьми.

Тогда я не знал, что это за название такое — Бетезда? Но когда волей случая (у «случая» было конкретное имя — Эдуард Шеварднадзе!) в 1998 году я оказался первым послом Грузии в Израиле, в великом городе Иерусалиме я обнаружил исконную Бетезду!

В 2013 году я, наконец, смог заманить Пашу и Эллу в Тбилиси, где они давно не бывали. Как-то в 1980-е годы Элла приезжала в Тбилиси, и она ужаснулась из-за транспортных проблем в городе. Элла сказала своим коллегам-градостителям и мне, что если вовремя не принять должные меры, то город задохнется лет через 20–25.

Она оказалась провидцем! И увидела это воочию, хотя мы постарались поселить ее и Пашу поближе к Тбилисскому государственному университету, где должна была пройти международная конференция, которую молодые коллеги нашей кафедры (ныне именуемой департаментом) почему-то решили посвятить моему 70-летию. Поэтому тбилисские транспортные пробки для Ильиных были преодолимы!

Паша заявился в Тбилиси с палочкой. Но он по-прежнему блистал остроумием, а его выступление о границах в Европе во время Второй мировой войны вызвало бурный интерес у молодых географов.

Паша и я обменивались информацией о наших операциях. Тогда не все казалось фатальным. Но, оказалось, не нам судить!

Нет с нами человека большой души, прекрасного друга, мужа, отца, дедушки. Паши Ильина будет очень недоставать, нам, его старым друзьям.

Но будет память о Человеке, который умел дружить, писать, шутить и жить, как человек.

Идеал Географа Глазами Географа:
Воспоминания о Павле Ильине

Роберт Гостанд

Мы с моей женой Морин познакомились с Павлом и его семьей в 1984 году, когда я был в научной командировке в Советском союзе. Нас познакомил общий приятель, и я был сразу поражен его дружелюбием, теплотой и горячим интересом к окружающему миру и к географии. Его жена Элла Каган и дочь Надя были не менее дружелюбными и оживленными собеседниками. Я встретил в нем родственную душу в плане его интереса к исторической географии Москвы и исследованию карт. В наши последующие встречи Павел и Элла (по профессии городской планировщик) с энтузиазмом и изобилием фактов водили меня на экскурсии по московским районам. Нас к тому же сближало увлечение собирательством фактов и предметов, и оба мы любили возиться с мелкими починками; оба увлекались книгами и картами и не могли устоять перед новыми находками. Познания Павла в области географических фактов не знали границ, и мы провели много счастливых часов над картами Москвы. Он безусловно внес значительный вклад в мои знания обо всем, что касается России, но особенно — о Москве.

В то время, помнится, он был азартным собирателем грибов и их консервированием. Он очень гордился результатом своих трудов — грибами крутого посола. К грибам он выносил спиртовые настойки, приготовленные им самим по секретным рецептам. Иногда для их употребления требовалась известная смелость. У него была также чудная коллекция миниатюрных морячков-сувениров, собранных в разных портах по всему Советскому союзу. Поскольку мы оба имели слабость ко всему морскому (я был офицером запаса военно-морского флота США), на меня эта коллекция советских мореходов произвела сильное впечатление. Неизменно гостеприимные хозяева, Ильины познакомили меня, помимо домашних горючих смесей, с блюдами русской и грузинской кухни. Мы провели много приятных часов в их квартире.

Семья Ильиных была в числе так называемых «отказников» — еврейских семей, которые требовали права на эмиграцию, в котором им было отказано, и в результате теряли свой профессиональный статус и подвергались гонениям. Однако Ильины относились к трудностям с решительным оптимизмом и бодростью, невзирая на обстоятельства.

Мы расстались с ними с грустью и надеждой на лучшее будущее.

Вернувшись в Штаты, я приложил некоторые усилия, чтобы помочь их выезду из Советского союза: я заручился поддержкой Ассоциации американских географов, которая на своей ежегодной конференции приняла резолюцию, по составленному мной письму советским властям, в поддержку их выезда. Мы были рады узнать, что Ильины находятся на пути в Америку через Вену и Италию. Несмотря на трудности, с которыми встречаются новые иммигранты, Ильиным удалось с успехом начать новую профессиональную жизнь. Павел со временем стал уважаемым сотрудником Музея Холокоста, где он был признанным авторитетом в области карт и местностей, связанных с истреблением европейских евреев. Он написал ряд научных работ по теме географических названий и расположения населенных пунктов, которые помогли пережившим Холокост и их наследникам определить места своего происхождения. Его личная библиотека по самым разным вопросам, в частности, по России и Москве, продолжала расти, и мы по-прежнему имели много общего в наших библиографических интересах. Он стал горячим патриотом и гражданином, руководимым внутренней верой в идеалы справедливости и свободы в основании Американской мечты, как бы ни была несовершенна современная нам реальность. Он с любовью собрал материалы и написал статьи об американских патриотических песнях, отражающих его неизменно оптимистический взгляд на будущее Америки в качестве примера для всего мира.

Одним трогательным жестом Павла было его настойчивое желание подарить мне основную часть своей коллекции морячков. Хотя я вежливо отказывался, большинство этих маленьких мореходов переехали жить в мой университетский кабинет, где они годами улыбались посетителям с каждой полки. Теперь они окружают меня в моем домашнем кабинете, так что, когда я пишу эти строки, надо мной незримо парит присутствие Павла, моего товарища-моряка.

Поскольку мы жили на противоположных берегах Америки, мы встречались не так часто, как хотелось бы, но Павел с Эллой иногда выбирались в Калифорнию, а мы с Морин — в Вашингтон. Он часто звонил мне, чтобы поделиться новыми научными идеями или просто поболтать. Мы встречались на географических конференциях, где от него всегда можно было ожидать выступления с новым интересным докладом.

Отсутствие Павла остро ощущается всеми, кто его знал, но память о его радости созерцания жизни и уверенности, что мир будет продолжаться, служит примером для всех нас.

Павел-Павлик-Паша...

Владимир Фрумкин

Говорят, что чем мы старше, тем труднее заводить новых друзей. Так и есть — убедился в этом на собственном опыте. Мой узкий круг с некоторого времени перестал пополняться новыми лицами. Знакомых все еще становится больше, а вот настоящих друзей, родных, понимающих тебя с полуслова душ, не прибавилось. Точнее говоря, почти не прибавилось. Потому что одно знакомство переросло таки в тесную дружбу.

Произошло оно, это знакомство, вскоре после моего переезда из университетского городка Оберлин в штате Огайо в Вашингтон, где я получил работу в русской службе Голоса Америки. Снял комнату у коллеги, от дома которой до работы было минут десять хода. А в соседнем доме, принадлежавшем другому моему коллеге, снял комнату недавний эмигрант, бывший москвич, приехавший из Массачусетса по приглашению Института русских исследований имени Кеннана писать научный труд по географии. Лет за восемь до этого я тоже получил стипендию от Института, но для работы над темой, от географии весьма далекой. Занимался я тогда советской массовой песней и ее неофициальной, полуподпольной соперницей — «гитарной поэзией». Появление нового знакомого, человека симпатичного и общительного, как я предполагал, приятно пополнит мой «дальний круг». Не более того. Но случилось неожиданное, сработала какая-то таинственная центростремительная сила, которая быстро переместила Павла Ильина из дальнего в мой самый что ни на есть близкий дружеский круг. И вот он уже не Павел, а Павлик или Паша, с которым и поговорить одно удовольствие, и опрокинуть рюмку-другую так и тянет, особенно, если в рюмку будет налита живительная, ароматная «Ильинка», рецепта которой, кстати сказать, ее автор мне так и не открыл...

Однажды Павел явился ко мне не с «Ильинкой», а с «Манишевицем». Это было на заре нашего знакомства, весной, в день начала еврейской пасхи. Праздник избавления от рабства мне предстояло провести в одиночестве, никак его не отмечая: жена с дочкой были в Оберлине, а мои коллеги «еврейской национальности», которых на Голосе Америки было немало, позвать меня к себе не догадались. И вдруг — стук в дверь, на пороге появляется Павел с каким-то свертком в руках, из которого извлекает бутылку «Манишевица», мацу, яйцо, фруктовую смесь, овощи…

— Рюмки есть? Тарелки? — поинтересовался неожиданный гость. — Смотри, даже марор раздобыл, горькую зелень, ибо сказано: во все вечера мы едим разные овощи, а в эту ночь — марор. В память о том, что египтяне огорчали жизнь предков наших в Египте»…

«Ну и дела», — подумал я. Зря сомневался. Павел Ильин-то, оказывается — еврей, да еще какой! Знает, как надо пейсах справлять! Первую рюмку «Манишевица» мы выпили за исход наших предков из Египта. Вторую — за наш собственный, который тогда казался нам тоже своего рода чудесным избавлением из плена…

Вскоре Павел удивил меня опять — когда оказалось, что с ним интересно говорить не только о географии, о которой он знал массу занимательных историй, но и о литературе, музыке, поэзии, включая поэзию поющуюся: Павел был знатоком бардовской песни и тонким ценителем творчества лучших ее мастеров. Чувствовалось, что о музыке и песне он судит не извне, не издалека, что для него это не некий обязательный для столичного советского интеллигента «джентльменский набор», а свое, близкое, личное. Вскоре все разъяснилось: этой культурой жила его семья — дочка Надя окончила музыкальное училище как пианистка, а хобби у нее было гитарно-песенное. Исполняла Окуджаву, Галича… Павел на инструментах не играл и (при мне во всяком случае) песен не пел, но его эрудиция и вкус, плюс талант литературного редактора надоумили меня посылать ему до публикации свои новые статьи. Критиком он был строгим, замечания были всегда по делу и явно шли на пользу.

Я ничуть не удивился, что в Музее Холокоста Павел подружился с музыковедом Бретом Вербом, который иногда обращался к нему за помощью — скорее, правда, географически-этнографической, нежели чисто музыкальной. Как-то одна из Пашиных коллег по имени Эдна спросила его, не хочет ли он немного подработать, читая вслух русскую литературу для ее отца, видного американского слависта, который потерял зрение из-за диабета. По какой-то причине, которую я не помню, Павел за эту работу не взялся и предложил ее мне. — А как зовут профессора? — спрашиваю. — Фридберг. — Морис!? — Что-то вроде этого… Он заведовал кафедрой в университете штата Иллинойс в городе Урбана-Шампейн, недавно ушел в отставку из-за болезни и переезжает в Вашингтон поближе к дочке.

Надо же! Морис Фридберг, мой давний знакомый, родившийся в Кракове в том же году, что и я — 1929-м, в 1939-м бежавший с семьей в советскую Россию из оккупированной немцами Польши... В 80-е годы дважды приглашавший меня в свой университет с лекциями-концертами... Энергичный, остроумный, неутомимый... И вот — такой трагический излом судьбы. Павел, который, благодаря своим географическим познаниям, помогал воссоединению разметанных войной семей, помог, неожиданно для себя, воссоединению двух приятелей, один из которых попал в беду и остро нуждался в общении с русскоговорящим человеком и с русской литературой, которую он всю жизнь преподавал и о которой написал несколько книг. Наши регулярные — два раза в неделю — встречи-чтения продолжались целых четыре года, которые природа даровала моему тяжело больному другу...

Павел так и не вернулся в Массачусетс, чем сильно меня порадовал. Закончив свой годичный срок в Институте Кеннана, он нашел работу и перевез в Вашингтон Эллу и Надю. А потом и машину купил, хотя ни водительских прав у него не было, ни опыта вождения. Надо было все это приобретать. Так получилось, что водительскую практику он нарабатывал с моей помощью: я сидел справа и подсказывал, как удержаться в своей полосе, когда начать тормозить, как лучше сделать поворот, как научиться параллельной парковке... Не могу сказать, что Паша проявил в этом деле большие способности. Никак не давалось ему вначале это искусство, и Паше это явно не нравилось: он мрачнел и нервничал. Как видно, впервые в жизни столкнулся с навыком, которым не удавалось овладеть легко и просто...

* * *

Его имя подходило ему лишь отчасти. Оно гармонировало с его внешними габаритами: *paulus* по латыни — малый, небольшой. Во всем остальном его масштабы намного превосходили то, что принято называть средним уровнем. Он был большим ученым, крупной и яркой личностью. Человеком с большой буквы, которого те, кому посчастливилось близко его узнать, будут помнить с благодарностью и любовью.

Мои воспоминания о Павле Ильине

Григорий Иоффе

Паша — очень (не могу писать «был») весёлый, разудалый, добрый и благонамеренный человек. И ещё у него есть Элла. И это не отдельная история, хотя я раньше думал, что отдельная, т.к. познакомился с ними в разное время и при разных обстоятельствах, а потом удивился, узнав, что они муж и жена. На самом деле они идеально дополняют друг друга, ибо Элла — организатор и вдохновитель, а Паша — всех наших побед. В последние 25 лет эта удивительная семья была и есть для меня роднее самых близких родственников. Их квартира в Бетезде под Вашингтоном наполнена ностальгически родным, интеллигентским московско-русско-еврейским духом. Это такая единокровная среда, Пашина и Эллина среда, нечто намного большее, чем даже кухонные разговоры, коих значение я вовсе не умаляю. Но сами эти разговоры производны от духа, который в неволе не размножается, а тут ему так свободно, уютно и хорошо. Мне за всю жизнь удалось побывать не более, чем в двух домах с вот такой обволакивающе родной атмосферой, но тот второй дом сгинул уже давно, а Пашин и Эллин всегда со мной.

Сейчас смешно вспоминать, что у меня с Пашей были идеологические разногласия. Паша смотрел телеканал Фокс, казавшийся мне реакционным. А теперь так сложилось, что если я смотрю телевизор, то только Фокс и смотрю. Паша воспринял религиозные пищевые табу, он очень плохо относился к одному гражданскому советскому празднику, который я чту. Были и другие несовпадения. С возрастом, однако, а особенно с уходом близких людей, начинаешь проникаться ценностями, которые и словами-то не всегда можно выразить. Начинаешь понимать, что есть что. То, что Паша делал для Музея Холокоста по топонимике еврейских местечек Украины и Белоруссии, его статья о переименовании городов, книга о Москве и Питере, им отредактированная, приобрели для меня сейчас большее значение, чем когда Паша был (да, был!) с нами. Мало кому удаётся быть культуртрегером — учителем, миссионером, человеком, который денно и нощно работает для взаимопроникновения и взаимообогащения культур. Мы и детям-то своим не можем передать то, что сделало нас такими, как мы есть. Паша сумел и далеко не только Наде, их с Эллой дочке...

Всё время возвращаюсь мыслями к Пашиному жилищу. Дощатые книжные полки с разделяющими их кирпичами, книги, книги, книги, карта старой Москвы и космический снимок Израиля, и эта роскошная картина с изображением старого еврея в коридоре. Паша в переднике на кухне. Паша, вытаскивающий из шкафа и разливающий свою Ильинку (название водки, приготовленной по старому семейному рецепту). Паша, провозглашающий тост. Паша уснувший. И Паша, улыбающийся счастливо и радушно. Я тоже улыбаюсь, и на душе становится хорошо.

Павэлла

Ольга Медведкова

Почти полвека назад, летом 1972 года, я пришла в Институт географии Академии наук СССР (ИГАН) на собеседование для поступления в аспирантуру. Наверное, это было в обеденный перерыв, потому что помещение выглядело пустынным. Кроме профессора Минца, с которым у меня была назначена встреча, я заметила сидевшего в углу человека лет тридцати пяти, который смотрел на меня с любопытством и мягкой улыбкой. Время от времени в течение беседы с профессором Минцем этот человек мне подбадривающе кивал, и у меня было чувство, что мне здесь рады. Этим человеком был Павел Ильин (все звали его Пашей), и мы с тех пор стали близкими друзьями.

Я знаю, что многие коллеги уже написали о нем как об ученом, я же хочу отдать ему дань как другу. Мне очень трудно отделить Павла от Эллы, его жены — отсюда и прозвище ПавЭлла, которое до сих пор записано как адрес в моем мобильном телефоне, а также у меня в голове и в сердце. Они были не только партнерами по жизни, это были родственные души — пока их не разделила смерть.

Мы с мужем, Юрием Медведковым, провели много часов вместе с Павлом и Эллой на разных профессиональных конференциях, семинарах и симпозиумах, а также и в совместном слушании музыки, задушевных разговорах, путешествиях. В России дружба — это нечто святое: ты доверяешь друзьям свою жизнь. Мы убедились в этом на своей шкуре, когда нас объявили «персонами нон-грата» за вступление в независимое движение за мир после Советского вторжения в Афганистан.

Мы потеряли многих друзей в этот период своей жизни. Одни ругали нас открыто, другие отводили глаза, стоило нам с мужем появиться в поле зрения. Но только не ПавЭлла! Они стали даже ближе к нам перед лицом реальной опасности: мы в какой-то степени были защищены вниманием иностранных журналистов, а они — нет. И все же они часто приходили к нам в дом, который находился под наблюдением КГБ. Это требовало большого мужества.

Один случай я помню так отчетливо, как будто это было вчера: в самом начале нашей политической карьеры Юру арестовали, чтобы помешать его встрече со шведскими активистами движения за мир, под предлогом, что он якобы пьян, и бросили в камеру с компанией забулдыг. Это было летом 1982 года, и мои родители вместе с моим сыном отдыхали в деревне на Волге. Я была в ужасе от того, что родители узнают о Юрином аресте из «Голоса Америки» или «Свободы», и не избежать тогда сердечного приступа. Павел без колебаний вызвался к ним поехать.

В его отсутствие КГБ провело у него в квартире обыск, и Павел вернулся в измученное и поруганное жилище.

Действительно, в России дружба священна, и нам удивительно повезло на таких близких друзей как ПавЭлла.

Мой Сосед Павел Ильин

Игорь Крупник

С Павлом Ильиным (Пашей, или Панчиком, как мы скоро стали его называть) мы познакомились в июне 1991 г. на конференции о русских, тогда еще «советских» евреях, которую организовали в Стэнфорде Игорь Котлер и Виктор Рашковский. Помню, как Элла делала доклад по-русски; совсем молодая Надя переводила и смотрела на Эллу большими круглыми глазами, а рядом сидел Паша и улыбался. Через год мы встретились уже в Вашингтоне, где к тому времени все жили; но по-настоящему сблизились еще через три года, когда мы поселились в десяти минутах ходьбы друг от друга и стали, как мы смеялись, «зазаборными соседями». Значит, мы близко знали друг друга примерно двадцать лет.

Это было удивительно и даже несправедливо. У нас очень быстро обнаружилось такое количество общих друзей и знакомых, что было непонятно, как мы могли не знать друг друга в прошлой жизни. Мы закончили один факультет университета (правда Паша сделал это на 14 лет раньше) и имели близкий круг коллег, общих знакомых и даже бывших профессоров, притом, что некоторые Пашины однокашники были моими преподавателями. Многие из людей, с которыми Павел работал в Институте географии, потом в Энциклопедии, потом был в отказе, были мне хорошо знакомы. Мы, очевидно, ходили по близким, часто одним и тем же дорожкам, но почему-то не пересекались.

Все это изменилось, когда мы стали жить рядом. Жены наши работали в одном месте, мы ходили друг к другу в гости, любили справлять вместе шабат, и даже наша собака Финя могла рысцой привести нас с закрытыми глазами в дом к Элле с Павлом (и увести обратно), поскольку в их доме ее всегда ждала припасенная морковка. Но сейчас не об этом...

Вспоминая Пашу, наши разговоры, застолья, встречи в метро при поездках на работу, хочется сохранить главное, что было в нем в тот последний, относительно благополучный период его жизни. Не считая самых последних лет болезни, он все время работал, писал, любил общаться, вспоминать прошлое. У него была активная, по-настоящему творческая жизнь. Таким я его помню; при этом некоторые черты закрепились во времени и не связаны с конкретными событиями или воспоминаниями.

Павел Ильин был очень преданным человеком. У него были свои четкие моральные понятия, которые он не скрывал и не менял. Он был верен друзьям, старым и новым; не отрекался от своей прошлой жизни и сохранял романтические воспоминания о начале своей профессии; и глядел на свое совсем не легкое прошлое с неуловимым внутренним достоинством. В этом он был очень целен, как и в своей нескрываемой, откровенной преданности писанию, работе словом и над словом, в целом труду, который требуется для получения серьезного текста. Мы много говорили о необходимости такого «труда над словом», особенно когда он занимался, вместе с Блэром Рублом, составлением книги об исторической Москве (Ильин, Рубл 2004). Там были главы, сданные по-русски и по-английски; и Павел работал с какой-то исступленной тщательностью над переводами и оригиналами, а потом еще над иллюстрациями. Эта книга потребовала огромного труда, но она доставила ему огромную радость — от самого удовольствия преданности делу, а не от хвалебных отзывов и рецензий, о которых Павел никогда не упоминал.

Внешне сдержанный, даже молчаливый — особенно на людях и с незнакомыми — Павел был очень страстным человеком, тем, кто по-русски называется словом «истовый», а по-английски «intense». В нем было мало полутонов, а накал страстей часто был очевиден. Элла часто называла его «бешеным». Он мог встать и уйти или уклониться от разговора, если был не согласен или чувствовал, что беседа выходит за им самим отведенные рамки. На удивление, мы никогда не ссорились из-за политики (американской), хотя читали разные газеты, смотрели разные программы и голосовали в разных направлениях. Он был непреклонен, но умел прощать, особенно близким. В нем был очень сильный моральный компас, пусть даже иногда он полушутливо называл себя «сталинистом», что было странно при его семейной истории и собственной биографии.

Думаю, что это было связано с его внутренним стремлением к устойчивости, к твердой и справедливой традиции, с которой он очень сильно отождествлял Америку. Америку он любил опять же истово и никогда не позволял ее ругать и над ней иронизировать — замыкался и уходил в себя. Было видно, что такие разговоры ему неприятны. Так же истово он отождествлял себя с Израилем и еврейством, чего, полагаю, в его дальней московской жизни не было.

Эта истовость была как бы отдельной, эмоциональной стороной его преданности; но они жили вместе и составляли цельную личность. Мне было с ним легко — потому что многое у нас пересекалось, мы любили и ценили много общих знакомых и совпадали в главном, несмотря на свое разное склонение. Но не всем с ним было просто, и я понимаю почему.

С такой преданностью, твердостью и даже неуступчивостью на удивление сочеталась еще одна черта его характера — умение меняться и творчески преобразовывать себя, что свойственно редким людям. Я узнал Павла лишь в его «третьей», американской жизни, даже в последней части этой третьей жизни, когда он работал в Музее Холокоста, занимался историей топонимики и эмоционально тяжелой темой картографирования мест массовых уничтожений евреев в годы Второй мировой войны. Об этой последней теме мы тоже говорили, хотя было видно, что давалась она ему нелегко. Но было нетрудно представить, как в 1970-е годы он был веселым и общительным сотрудником Института географии и занимался городскими планировками и территориальными моделями. Так же было понятно, как далеко он внутренне от этого ушел и как приятно было ему, несмотря на его истовую (опять же!) приверженность географии и своему географическому образованию, заниматься гуманитарными делами: историей, городской культурной средой, а затем и поэзией. Поскольку я тоже ушел из географии в гораздо более гуманитарные области знания, мы хорошо чувствовали друг друга как два старых ренегата.

Его любовь к Америке и глубокая привязанность к американской истории и ее сегодняшней реальности были отражением той же способности творчески переделать, изменить себя. Ему пришлось сделать это в совсем не юном возрасте, уже сильно за пятьдесят, без какого-либо изначального знания английского и с минимальным запасом того, что могло пригодиться в новой жизни. При этом у него не было никакой горечи об оставленном прошлом. Он оставил в Москве свои любимые книги, но потом купил себе в Америке новые и дополнил их американскими энциклопедиями и трудами по истории евреев, а также старыми гравюрами и картами, которые с увлечением разыскивал по антикварным магазинам. Павел увлеченно возил своих гостей на экскурсии по Вашингтону и окрестным старэньким городкам, как будто провел здесь всю жизнь. Он нашел себя, сумел измениться, и в этом состоянии оказался очень гармоничным человеком. Хочется, чтобы таким он и остался в нашей памяти.

И в подтверждение этих воспоминаний, приведу в заключение его слова, написанные нам на его книге «Москва рубежа XIX и XX столетий» (2004):

«Дорогим Аллочке и Игорю Крупникам в знак огромной любви и дружбы и с искренней признательностью не только за то, что кое-что в этой книге вдохновлено ими, но и за то, что они живут в пешеходной доступности от нас, что позволяет выпивать с ними чаще, чем если бы они жили далеко. А также на память о городе, из которого мы и они вышли и ушли».

Спасибо, Панчик — за слова, за книгу и за добрую память о себе...

Об авторах Authors

Алекса́ндр С. Ахие́зер (1929–2007) — российский социальный философ и культуролог. Доктор философских наук. Известен своей социокультурной концепцией истории России. А. С. Ахиезер — автор более 500 научных статей и около 20 книг. Ввёл ряд новых культурологических и социологических терминов. Выдвинул концепцию социокультурной эволюции, осуществляющейся по спирали, и описал стадии развития нравственного идеала, преобладающего в обществе. На раннем этапе внёс значительный вклад в отечественную теорию урбанизации.

Тони Аллисон родился и вырос в Сиэтле. Основной областью его профессиональной деятельности было международное рыболовство, в связи с чем он долгое время жил и работал в Советском Союзе. В течение одиннадцати лет Тони был старшим исполнительным руководителем совместной американо-советской компании MRCI (Marine Resources Company International). Впоследствии он стал учителем истории в старших классах. В настоящее время Тони Аллисон живёт на острове Гуэмес в штате Вашингтон вместе с женой Нэнси.

Нэнси Фишер-Аллисон заинтересовалась Советским Союзом, читая журнал Soviet Life в своей школьной библиотеке. Она училась в Ленинграде и посвятила нескольких десятилетий глубокому изучению культуры и географии России. Благодаря этому ей посчастливилось познакомиться с Павлом и Эллой. В течение ряда лет она работала библиотекарем в школьной библиотеке. После выхода на пенсию Нэнси живёт на острове Гуэмес в штате Вашингтон вместе со своим мужем Тони Аллисоном.

Вадим Алцкан — историк, специализирующийся в восточноевропейской, балканской и еврейской истории. Вадим является директором международных архивных проектов в Институте документации Холокоста в Мемориальном музее Холокоста США в Вашингтоне, где он руководит архивными исследованиями на Балканах, в Прибалтике, Кавказе, Средней Азии и странах Восточной Европы, выполняя миссию музея по сохранению свидетельств Холокоста и предоставлению исторических материалов по изучению этой темы ученым и широкой общественности.

Надя Бартол, управляющий директор BCG Platinion, подразделения Boston Consulting Group. Надя имеет 25-летний опыт работы в сфере технологий кибербезопасности и управления в различных отраслях и государственных учреждениях. В BCG Надя консультирует клиентов во многих отраслях, включая финансовые услуги, технологии, энергетику, страхование, профессиональные услуги и потребительские товары, по вопросам стратегии и реализации кибербезопасности. Надя является соавтором ряда публикаций по кибербезопасности Национального института стандартов и технологий (NIST) и руководила разработкой нескольких стандартов ISO по различным темам кибербезопасности. От отца Надя унаследовала любовь к книгам, путешествиям и любопытство к тому, как устроен мир. Надя имеет степень магистра музыки по игре на фортепиано, магистра информационных систем и магистра делового администрирования. Она также является сертифицированным специалистом по системам информационной безопасности (CISSP) и сертифицирована в области управления корпоративными ИТ (CGEIT ™).

Владимир Фрумкин — музыковед, журналист, эссеист, выпускник теоретико-композиторского факультета и аспирантуры Ленинградской консерватории. Еще в советскую эпоху стал исследователем феномена независимой, неподцензурной «гитарной поэзии» и исполнителем песен Окуджавы, Галича и других поэтов-певцов. В 1974 эмигрировал в США, работал в Оберлин-колледже (штат Огайо) и Русской летней школе при Норвичском университете (штат Вермонт). С 1988 до 2006 года — сотрудник Русской службы «Голоса Америки» в Вашингтоне. Выпустил несколько книг, посвященных классической музыке и «гитарной поэзии».

Реваз Гачечиладзе — видный грузинский учёный и дипломат, выпускник факультета востоковедения Тбилисского Государственного Университета, где он также защитил кандидатскую и докторскую диссертации по экономической и социальной географии. Гачечиладзе работал директором института, исследующего проблемы соседних с Грузией стран, а также преподавал в Тбилисском университете, в Оксфорде и в Маунт Холиок Колледже в США. Гачечиладзе — автор множества книг и статей. Его самая известная книга на английском языке посвящена Грузии и выпущена издательством Университетского Колледжа в Англии в 1995 году. Гачечиладзе служил и служит своей стране в качестве Чрезвычайного и Полномочного Посла в Израиле, Армении, Великобритании и Словакии.

РОБЕРТ ГОСТАНД — Почетный профессор географии Университета штата Калифорния, Нортридж, где он преподавал географию и историческую географию России и Советского союза, интерпретацию карт и историю географии. Его исследования и публикации концентрировались на географии коммерческой деятельности в дореволюционной России. Родился в Китае, основатель и директор архива «Иностранных знатоков Китая» в университетской библиотеке. Многолетний пропагандист пользы и удовольствия от чтения, создал и финансирует «зал свободного чтения» в университетской библиотеке и цикл лекций о чтении, которые проводятся каждые два года. Он продолжает активно поддерживать библиотеку и собранные в ней коллекции. Женат, живет в Южной Калифорнии.

ВЕНИАМИ́Н М. ГО́ХМАН (1918–1986) — советский географ-американист. Внес большой вклад в развитие теории страноведения и теоретической географии. В. М. Гохман был одним из пионеров математизации географии в конце 1950-х годов. В 1960–1970-х года был одним из лидеров развития теоретической географии в СССР, вместе с коллегами предложил новую парадигму страноведческих исследований — проблемное страноведение. Выступал за усиление внимания к социальным аспектам экономической географии, был автором пионерных отечественных работ в области культурной географии и метагеографии. В. М. Гохман был одним из создателей школы географической американистики в СССР. Несмотря на то, что В. М. Гохман ни разу не был в США, его работы по экономической географии этой страны были хорошо известны в Америке, а сам Гохман пользовался большим авторитетом и среди американских географов. В. М. Гохман — автор более 150 научных работ, часть которых имеет закрытый характер, более 600 энциклопедических и около 80 обзорных статей и рецензий.

ГРИГОРИЙ ИОФФЕ родился и вырос в Москве, выпускник МГУ, где он специализировался по социально-экономической географии, работал в Институте географии Российской Академии Наук; в 1989 году эмигрировал в США; с 1990 непрерывно работал профессором в Рэдфордском университете в штате Вирджиния; автор и соавтор десяти книг, посвященных проблематике бывшего СССР.

ЭЛЛА (МИКАЭЛЛА) КАГАН родилась в Москве, Россия; закончила Инженерно-строительный институт; работала в Институте проектирования городов; в Институте городских исследований и защитила диссертацию о городском планировании. В 1982 году семья подала документы на эмиграцию и получила отказ. В 1987 году, во время горбачевской перестройки, семья получила разрешение на выезд и эмигрировала в Соединенные Штаты. Начиная с 1988 года Элла работала в разных еврейских организациях Большого Вашингтона. В 2003 году она открыла Учебный центр Шолом — воскресная школа для детей из еврейских семей иммигрантов из бывшего Советского Союза.

Александр Кириллов — советский и российский математик, известный работами в области представления теории и топологических групп. Работал в Московском государственном университете 1961–1994 гг. В настоящее время, профессор кафедры математики Университета Пенсильвании; Главный научный сотрудник Института проблем передачи информации Российской академии наук (Москва); Профессор Высшей школы экономики (2019 г., Москва); Член Американского математического общества; Доктор Honoris Causa (Почетный профессор) университета г. Реймс, Франция.

Игорь Крупник — этнограф-северовед, специалист по северным народам, куратор арктических коллекций в Национальном музее естественной истории Смитсоновского института (г. Вашингтон, США). Родился в Москве; закончил Географический факультет МГУ, после окончания аспирантуры работал в Институте этнографии АН СССР. Кандидат исторических наук, доктор биологических наук; автор многих книг, сборников и каталогов по культурам народов Арктики. В 1980-е гг. участвовал в еврейском культурническом движении в Москве; был ученым секретарем независимой Еврейской историко-этнографической комиссии (1980–1990).

Юлий Г. Липец (1931–2006) — советский и российский экономико-географ. Доктор географических наук. Специалист по географии мирового развития. Ю. Г. Липец — один из создателей проблемного страноведения. Известен как специалист в области географии мирового хозяйства. Занимался также вопросами теоретической географии и применения математических методов в географии, а также созданием тематических географических информационных систем для управления территориями. Ю. Г. Липец первым в СССР стал заниматься географией развития — синтетической областью на стыке географии мирового хозяйства, проблемного страноведения и глобалистики. Исследовал проблемы адаптации экономики России к рыночным условиям, занимался множеством прикладных работ по региональному анализу приграничных регионов Российской Федерации.

Ольга Медведкова — Заслуженный профессор географии в 1972 г. окончила географический факультет Московского государственного университета и защитила диссертацию в Институте географии РАН в 1975 г. После отъезда из СССР с 1986 г. она живет в Соединенных Штатах Америки со своим мужем Юрием Медведковым и двумя детьми. Начиная с 1987 г. доктор Ольга Медведкова 27 лет занималась преподаванием и исследовательской работой в Виттенберском университете (г. Спрингфилд, штат Огайо). Одновременно с этим она работала научным сотрудником Университета штата Огайо. Ей опубликовано множество книг и статей в научных журналах по теме урбанизации. Доктор наук Ольга Медведкова дважды удостаивалась гранта Фулбрайта.

ПАВЕЛ ПОЛЯН (литературный псевдоним Нерлер) — историк, географ и филолог. Выпускник Географического факультета Московского Государственного Университета (1974), доктор географических наук (1998); ведущий научный сотрудник Института географии Российской Академии наук; профессор и член ученого совета ряда университетов; председатель Мандельштамовского общества; член редакционной коллегии нескольких журналов. Автор многих книг, в основном, по географии, демографии, истории, включая несколько книг, посвященных Холокосту. Проживает во Фрайбурге, Германия.

БЛЭР А. РУБЛ — в настоящее время почетный член Центра Вилсона, где ранее работал Вице-президентом по программам. В прошлом, директор Института Кеннана и одновременно координатор научных работ по сравнительному анализу городов в Центре Вилсона. Выпускник Университета в Торонто, Канада, со званием магистра (1973 г.) и доктора (1977 г.) политических наук. Диплом бакалавра политических наук (с отличием) получил в Университете Северной Каролины, Чэпел Хилл, США (1971 г.). Редактор более десятка сборников и автор нескольких монографий, включая «Washington's U Street: A Biography».

ТАТЬЯНА РУНОВА — кандидат географических наук, закончила Ленинградский государственный Университет (1957); работала научным сотрудником в Институте географии АН СССР (ныне РАН) (1960–1995), доцентом Московского индустриального Университета (1996–2009), консультантом института «Кадастр» в Ярославле (2010–2017), сейчас на пенсии. Круг научных интересов — районы Севера России, география природных ресурсов и региональные проблемы экологии. Написала несколько книг, посвященных этой тематике; автор учебников и учебных пособий.

Appendices

Приложения

Appendix I / Приложение I

PHOTOGRAPHY / ФОТОГРАФИИ

Pavel: College years / Павел — студент

Before Leaving Moscow, July 1987

Семья в последний день перед отлетом из Москвы в Америку

Pavel at Annual Meeting of American Association of Geographers.
From left to right: Leonid Smirnyagvin, Olga Medvedkov,
Yuri Medvedkov, Pavel Ilyin. April 1988

Павел впервые на конференции Американской ассоциации
географов, Апрель 1988

Pavel and Ella at Capitol Hill Rotonda. National Conference of Soviet Jewry. 20th Anniversary of The 1987 March for Exodus of Soviet Jewry

Павел и Элла в ротонде на Капитолийском Холме. 20-я годовщина Марша 1987 года за свободный выезд советских евреев из страны

Pavel at Department of Cartography at the Library of Congress

Павел в Картографическом отделе Библиотеки Конгресса США

Pavel at US Holocaust Memorial Museum.
Павел в Мемориальном музее Холокоста.

Pavel at Museum Party
На банкете в Музее.

Pavel and Ella at their home
Павел и Элла дома

Pavel Ilyin. 2013
Павел Ильин. 2013 год

Pavel Ilyin. 2013
Павел Ильин. 2013 год

RESOLUTION ANNUAL MEETING OF THE ASSOCIATION OF AMERICAN GEOGRAPHERS, PORTLAND, 1987

РЕЗОЛЮЦИЯ ЕЖЕГОДНОГО СОБРАНИЯ АССОЦИАЦИИ АМЕРИКАНСКИХ ГЕОГРАФОВ, ПОРТЛАНД, 1987

RESOLUTION

ANNUAL MEETING OF THE ASSOCIATION OF AMERICAN
GEOGRAPHERS, PORTLAND, 1987.

"Whereas we, the members of the Association of American Geographers, are
encouraged by news of the recent actions of the Government of the Union of Soviet
Socialist Republics in releasing detainees of conscience, in the gradual
improvement in conditions relating to the right of emigration and reunification of
families, and in easing restrictions on cultural exchanges,

but

Whereas there are many individuals in the USSR who are still being denied the
right of emigration and who are experiencing social and economic sanctions as a
result of their applications to emigrate, circumstances which inhibit the further
development of international scholarly relations and undermines the basis of mutual
trust and respect upon which they depend,

and

Whereas Pavel Mikhailovich Il'in and *Mikhaella Isaakovna Kagan,* who
are professional colleagues of the members of this *Association,* desire to emigrate
with their family, but have been repeatedly refused permission to do so,

Be It Resolved, that the members of the *Association of American
Geographers,* while commending the Government of the USSR for the
liberalizing measures it has recently taken, strongly urges that these be fully
extended to the right of emigration, to free scholarly contacts, and to visits across
frontiers, *and that the Il'in family be granted the right of emigration
without further delay."*

This Resolution is introduced and sponsored by the following members:

James P. Allen	Chauncy D. Harris	Thomas M. Poulsen
William H. Berentsen	Gary J. Hausladen	Philip R. Pryde
William L. Biro	David J. M. Hooson	Joanna Regulska
Warren R. Bland	W. A. Douglas Jackson	William D. Romey
Barbara Borowiecki	Robert G. Jensen	Matthew J. Sagers
William A. Bowen	George Kish	Ihor Stebelsky
Kathleen Braden	Julie Laity	Michael F. Taugher
Branko Colakovic	Robert A. Lewis	Ronald Wixman
Arnold Court	Gordon R. Lewthwaite	
Darrick R. Danta	Gong-Yuh Lin	Also supporting:
George J. Demko	Gary Lobb	R. A. French
Leslie Dienes	Paul E. Lydolph	Judith Pallot
Dennis J. Dingemans	Carolyn G. McGovern-Bowen	Dennis J. B. Shaw
Kenneth Erickson	Elliot G. McIntire	(members, Institute of
Nancy A. Fisher	Abraham Melezin	British Geographers)
Robert Gohstand	Victor L. Mote	

Appendix III / Приложение III

POLITICAL MAPS ISSUED DURING WWII
ПОЛИТИЧЕСКИЕ КАРТЫ ЕВРОПЫ ВРЕМЕН
ВТОРОЙ МИРОВОЙ ВОЙНЫ

MAP 1. EUROPE IN 1942
КАРТА 1. ЕВРОПА В 1942 Г.

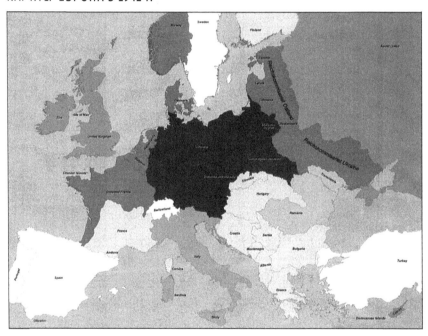

MAP 2. GERMANY BEFORE THE WAR (EASTBOUND)
КАРТА 2. ГЕРМАНИЯ ПЕРЕД ВОЙНОЙ (ВОСТОЧНАЯ ГРАНИЦА)

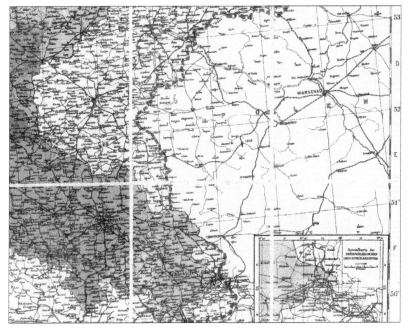

MAP 3. GERMANY BEFORE THE WAR (WESTBOUND)
КАРТА 3. ГЕРМАНИЯ ПЕРЕД ВОЙНОЙ (ЗАПАДНАЯ ГРАНИЦА)

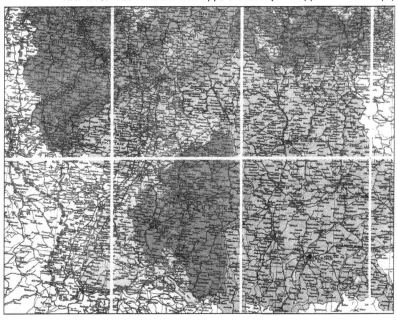

MAP 4. GERMANY AFTER MUNICH AGREEMENT, 1938
КАРТА 4. ГЕРМАНИЯ ПОСЛЕ МЮНХЕНСКОГО ДОГОВОРА. 1938 Г.

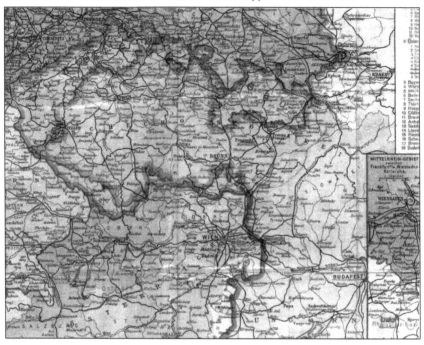

MAP 5. NEW NAMES OF COCUPIED COUNTRIES
КАРТА 5. НОВЫЕ ИМЕНА ОККУПИРОВАННЫХ СТРАН

MAP 6. **CZECHOSLOVAKIA IN 1939–1939**
КАРТА 6. **ЧЕХОСЛОВАКИЯ В 1938–1939 ГГ.**

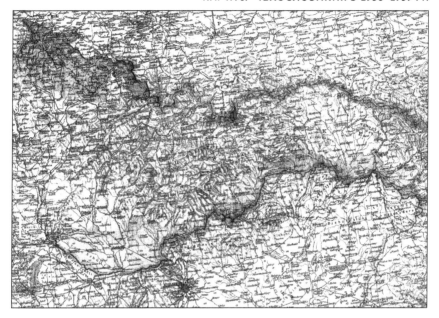

MAP 7. **FRANCE IN 1940** / КАРТА 7. **ФРАНЦИЯ В 1940 Г.**

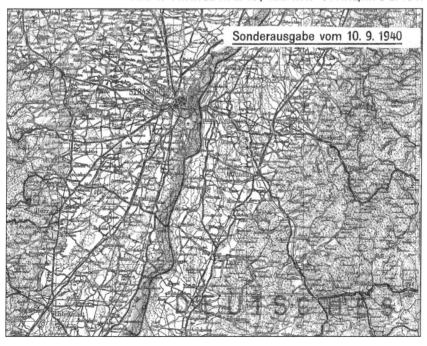

MAP 8. FRANCE IN 1942 / КАРТА 8. ФРАНЦИЯ В 1942 Г.

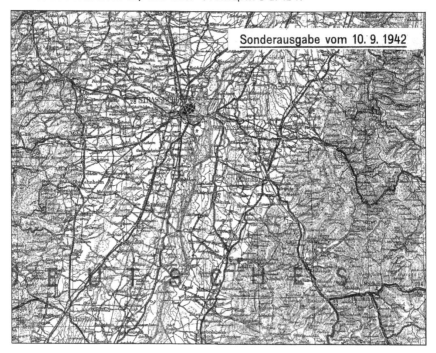

MAP 9. UKRAINE OCCUPIED BY GERMANY
КАРТА 9. УКРАИНА, ОККУПИРОВАННАЯ ГЕРМАНИЕЙ

MAP 10. **TRANSNISTRIA IN 1941** / КАРТА 10. **ТРАНСНИСТРИЯ В 1941 Г.**

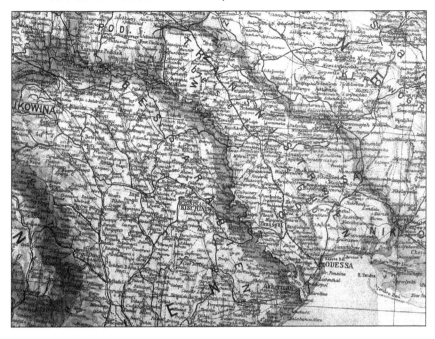

MAP 11. **ITALY AND ALBANIA IN 1941**
КАРТА 11. **ИТАЛИЯ И АЛБАНИЯ В 1941 Г.**

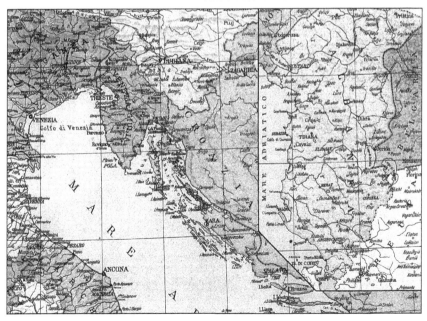

MAP 12. BELORUSSIA, 1938 / КАРТА 12. БЕЛОРУССИЯ, 1938 Г.

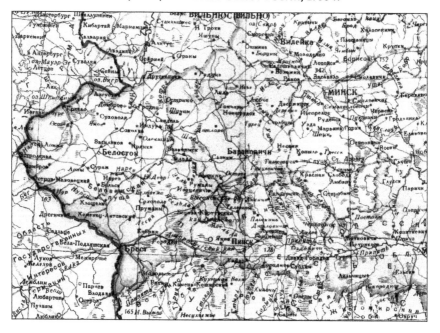

MAP 13. POLAND, AFTER 1942 / КАРТА 13. ПОЛЬША, ПОСЛЕ 1942 Г.

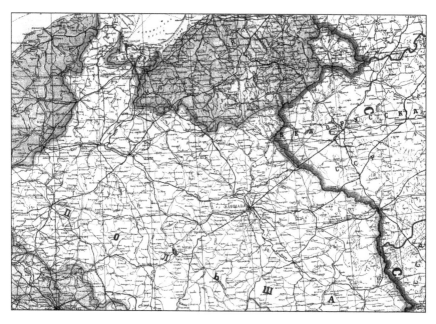

MAP 14. **GERMANY 1944** / KAPTA 14. **ГЕРМАНИЯ В 1944 Г.**

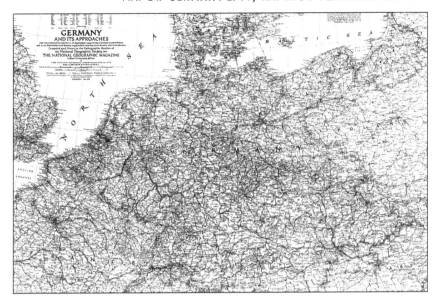

MAP 15. **GERMANY 1944** / KAPTA 15. **ГЕРМАНИЯ В 1944 Г.**

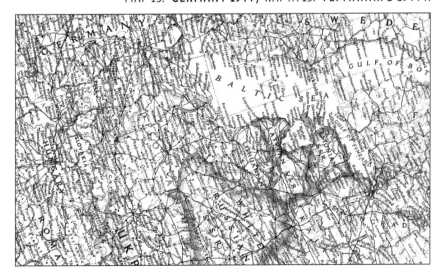

MAP 16. **POLAND, BALTIC REPUBLICS, HUNGARY AND SLOVAKIA**
КАРТА 16. **ПОЛЬША, ПРИБАЛТИКА, ВЕНГРИЯ И СЛОВАКИЯ**

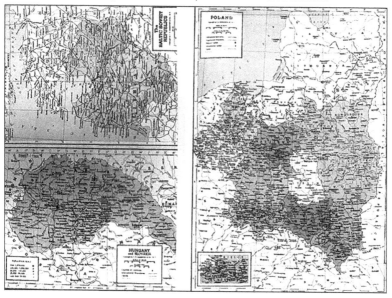

MAP 17. **LITHUANIA BEFORE WAR, PUBLISHED IN LITHUANIA**
КАРТА 17. **ЛИТВА ПЕРЕД ВОЙНОЙ (ИЗДАНА В ЛИТВЕ)**

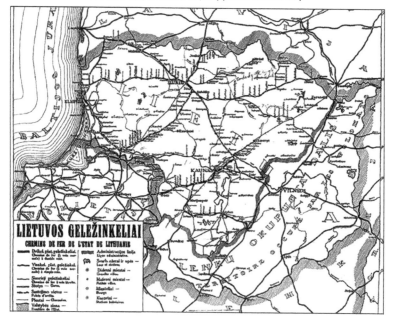

MAP 18. LITHUANIA BEFORE WAR, PUBLISHED IN POLAND
КАРТА 18. ЛИТВА ПЕРЕД ВОЙНОЙ (ИЗДАНА В ПОЛЬШЕ)

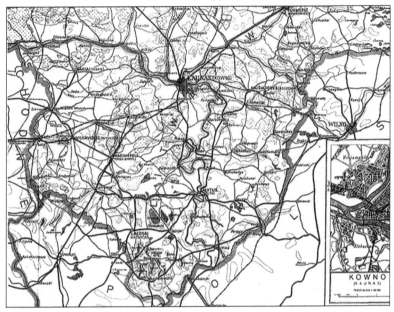

MAP 19. UKRAINE AND BESSARABIA BEFORE 1940, PUBLISHED IN USSR
КАРТА 19. УКРАИНА И БЕССАРАБИЯ (ДО 1940 Г. ИЗДАНА В СССР)

MAPS OF CULTURAL GEOGRAPHY OF MOSCOW
МОСКВА – ГЕОГРАФИЯ КУЛЬТУРЫ, КАРТЫ

CULTURAL MAP OF MOSCOW / КАРТА КУЛЬТУРНОЙ МОСКВЫ

● **Театры**
1. Большой театр
2. Малый театр
3. Новый театр (Незлобина)
4. Театр Солодовникова
5. Московский Художественный театр
6. Театр Корша
7. Театр-кабаре «Летучая мышь»
8. Любительский театр Секретарева
9. Театр Парадиза (Интернациональный)
10. Камерный театр
11. Любительский театр Немчинова
12. Театр Зона
13. Театр сада «Аквариум»
14. Театр-варьете «Альказар»
15. Европейский театр
16. «Старый Эрмитаж» (Лентовского)
17. Театр сада «Эрмитаж»
18. Театр Струйского

△ **Цирки**
1. Саламонского
2. братьев Никитиных

■ **Кино**
1. «Модерн» (в гостинице «Метрополь»)
2. «Художественный»
3. «Ампир»
4. «Унион»
5. «Палас»
6. Ханжонкова
7. «Экран жизни»
8. «Экспресс»
9. «Форум»
10. «Уран»
11. «Гранд-Электро»
12. «Колизей»
13. «Волшебные грезы»
14. «Вулкан»
15. «Таганский»
16. «Великан»
17. «Пятницкий»

▲ **Музеи**
1. Оружейная палата
2. Исторический музей
3. Румянцевский музей
4. Музей изящных искусств
5. Галерея С.И. Щукина
6. Цветковская галерея
7. Московский кустарный музей
8. Политехнический музей
9. Третьяковская галерея
10. Театральный музей Бахрушина
11. Музей прикладных искусств П.И. Щукина

▨ Концертный зал
▢ Музыкальное (театральное, художе-
ственное) училище
▧ Музыкальная школа и концертный зал

1. Благородное собрание
2. Консерватория
3. Синодальное хоровое училище
4. Филармоническое училище
5. Музыкальное училище сестер Гнесиных
6. Императорские драматические курсы
7. Строгановское художественно-
промышленное училище
8. Училище живописи, ваяния и зодчества

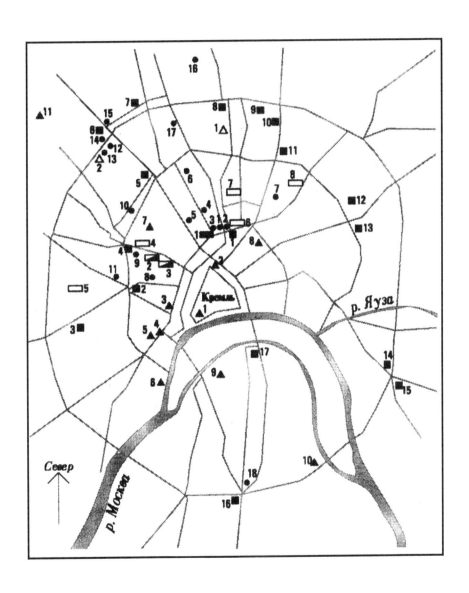

RESIDENCES OF CULTURAL FIGURES (BEFORE 1917)
АДРЕСА ДЕЯТЕЛЕЙ КУЛЬТУРЫ (ДО 1917 Г.)

А.П. Чехов

Ч1	1879	Грачевка (ныне Трубная), 36
Ч2	1879—1880	Грачевка (ныне Трубная), 23
Ч3	1880	Грачевка (ныне Трубная), 26—28
Ч4	1881—1885	Головин (ныне Малый Головин) пер., 3
Ч5	1885	Большая Якиманка, 50
Ч6	1885	Большая Якиманка, 45
Ч7	1886—1890	Садовая-Кудринская, 6
Ч8	1890—1892	Малая Дмитровка, 29
	(1892—1899)	(Мелихово)
Ч9	1899	Малая Дмитровка, 12
Ч10	1899	Малая Дмитровка, 11
Ч11	1901	Спиридоновка, 14—16
Ч12	1902	Звонарный пер., 2
Ч13	1903—1904	Петровка, 19
Ч14	1904	Леонтьевский пер., 24

В.И. Немирович-Данченко

Н1	1880—1885	Чудовский пер. (ныне пер. Огородной Слободы), 5
Н2	1895—1900	Гранатный пер., 11
Н3	1900—1902	Георгиевский (ныне Вспольный) пер., 9
Н4 с 1902		Большая Никитская, 50

А.И. Сумбатов-Южин

С1	1882—1884	Нижний Кисельный пер., 3
С2	1884—1886	Цветной бульвар, 19 или 21
С3	1886	Большой Ушаковский (ныне Коробейников) пер., 22
С4	1887	Неглинный проезд (ныне Неглинная улица), 4 гостиница «Европейская»
С5	1887—1892	Леонтьевский пер., 4
С6 с 1892		Большой Палашевский пер, 5/1

В.И. Качалов

К1	1900—1901	Семинарский тупик, 4
К2	1901—1902	Косой пер., 29
К3	1903—1912	Большая Дмитровка, 4
К4	1912—1915	Скатертный пер, 22
К5 с 1915		Малая Никитская, 20

1. Малый театр
2. Сад «Эрмитаж»
3. Московский Художественный театр
4. Московский университет
5. Клиники Московского университета (позже Строгановское художественно-промышленное училище)
6. Екатерининская больница
7. Большая Московская гостиница
8. Филармоническое училище

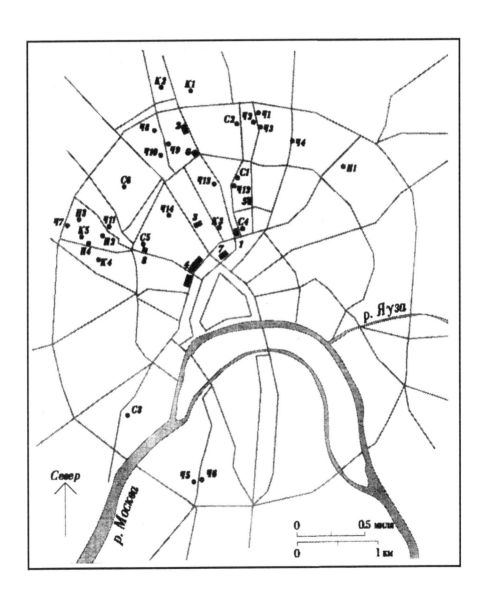

COUNTRY ESTATES AND DACHA SETTLEMENTS NEAR MOSCOW
ПОМЕСТЬЯ И ДАЧИ ДЕЯТЕЛЕЙ КУЛЬТУРЫ В ПОДМОСКОВЬЕ

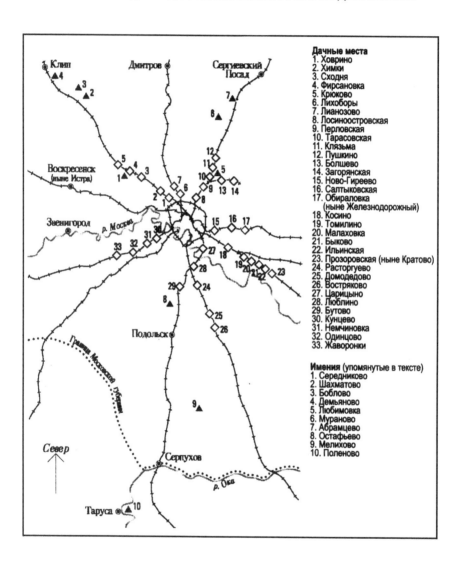

Дачные места
1. Ховрино
2. Химки
3. Сходня
4. Фирсановка
5. Крюково
6. Лихоборы
7. Лианозово
8. Лосиноостровская
9. Перловская
10. Тарасовская
11. Клязьма
12. Пушкино
13. Болшево
14. Загорянская
15. Ново-Гиреево
16. Салтыковская
17. Обираловка
    (ныне Железнодорожный)
18. Косино
19. Томилино
20. Малаховка
21. Быково
22. Ильинская
23. Прозоровская (ныне Кратово)
24. Расторгуево
25. Домодедово
26. Востряково
27. Царицыно
28. Люблино
29. Бутово
30. Кунцево
31. Немчиновка
32. Одинцово
33. Жаворонки

Имения (упомянутые в тексте)
1. Середниково
2. Шахматово
3. Боблово
4. Демьяново
5. Любимовка
6. Мураново
7. Абрамцево
8. Остафьево
9. Мелихово
10. Поленово

Appendix V / Приложение V

LIST OF PUBLICATION (COMPILED BY PAVEL ILYIN)
СПИСОК ПУБЛИКАЦИЙ (СОСТАВЛЕН П. ИЛЬИНЫМ)

2012

Павел Ильин. «Эта земля моя, она прекрасна, Боже, храни ее! Три патриотические песни Америки».—*Панорама* (Лос-Анжелес), № 6, 8–14 фев. 2012 г., с. B10—B12.

2011

Павел Ильин. «Эта земля моя, она прекрасна, Боже, храни ее! Три патриотические песни Америки».—*Время и место, вып. 4 (20), Нью-Йорк,* 2011, с. 116–137. (В тексты эссе включены переводы на русский язык: Ирвинг Берлин. «Боже, храни Америку» («Irving Berlin. God Bless America»), с. 120. Вуди Гатри. «Эта земля—твоя» («Woody Guthrie. This Land Is Your Land»), с. 123–124. Катарина Ли Бейтс. «Ты прекрасна, Америка!» (Katharine Lee Bates. «America the Beautiful»), с. 130–131.

2004

Павел Ильин, Блэр А. Рубл, отв. редакторы. *Москва рубежа XIX и XX столетий. Взгляд в прошлое издалека* [Moscow at the Turn of the XX Century. Glance into the Past from Afar. Pavel Ilyin and Blair A. Ruble, editors.] М.: РОССПЭН, 2004, 302 с. ***В книге:*** Павел Ильин, Блэр А. Рубл. «Введение», с. 7–18.

Павел Ильин, Микаэлла Каган. *«Москва на переломе столетий»,* с. 10–63.

Павел Ильин. *«География культуры в Москве в конце XIX—начале XX века»,* с. 131–194.

Павел Ильин, Блэр А. Рубл. *«Заключение. Москва тогда и сегодня»,* с. 272–284.

Перевод: Роберт Гохстанд. *«Стоимость земли в Москве в начале XX века»,* с. 89–130.

Reviews:

Galina Ulianova (Institute of Russian History, Moscow). *Russian Review,* Vol. 64, No. 3, July 2005, p. 526–527.

Gregory Ioffe. *Eurasian Geography and Economics.* Vol. 46, No. 5, July–August 2005, p. 399–401.

С. А. Арутюнов. *Этнографическое обозрение,* 2007, № 3, с. 167–169.

1998

Pavel Ilyine. «Èvolution des fonctions et des Systèmes Utbains». *La ville soviétique avant la Pérestroika, sous la direction de Galia at Guy Burgel, Villes an parallèle*, n° 26–27, Décembre 1998, p. 63–67.

1997

Павел Ильин. «Я знаю: век уж мой измерен…». — *Новый журнал*, Кн. 207, Нью-Йорк, 1997, с. 265–266,

1995

Pavel Ilyin. *«Renaming of Soviet Cities after Exceptional People: A Historical Perspective on Toponymy».]* In Japaneese, trans. Harumichi Yamada. — *Chizu (Map). Journal of the Japan Cartographers Associasion.* 1955, 33, p. 13–41. (Translation from *Post-Soviet Geography*, December 1993).

1994

Павел Ильин. «О переименовании городов в Советском Союзе в честь «выдающихся личностей»». — *Новый журнал*, Кн. 192–193, Нью-Йорк, 1993, с. 462–498. (Issued in 1994.)

П. Ильин, М. Каган. [Вступительная статья]. — *Столица и окрестности*, 1994, № 1, с. 1–2. [Без подписи].

П. Ильин, М. Каган. «Здесь мы живем». — *Столица и окрестности*, 1994, № 1, с. 3. [Без подписи].

П. Ильин, М. Каган. «Прогулки по Вашингтону и окрестностям. Бетесда». — *Столица и окрестности*, 1994, № 2, с. 3.

П. Ильин, М Каган. Еврейская эмиграция из бывшего СССР в США. — *Миграционная ситуация в России: Социально-политические аспекты*. Ред. Ж. А. Зайончковская. Программа по исследованию миграции, вып. IV. М.: Ин-т нар.-хоз. Планирования РАН; РЭНД, США, 1994, с. 95–105.

1993

Pavel Ilyin. «Renaming of Soviet Cities after Exceptional People: A Historical Perspective on Toponymy». — *Post-Soviet Geography*, December 1993, p. 631–660.

Pavel Ilyin. Book Review: William Craft Brumfield. The Origin of Modernism in Russian Architecture, 1991. — *Russian History*, vol. 20, Nos. 1–4, 1993, p. 303–305.

1992

Pavel Ilyin. «The Dolgan and Nganasan Peoples: Aborigines of Northern Siberia». — *Explorers Journal*, Spring 1992, p. 19–22.

Pavel Ilyin. [«My meetings with Theodor Shabad».] — *All the best, Ted. Memories of Theodore Shabad*. Robert Gohstand. ed. California State University, Northridge, 1992, p. 19–22. [Translated by Robert Gohstand]

Pavel Ilyin and Mikaella Kagan. «Soviet Émigré Organizations in American-Jewish Institutional life».— *New Voices: The Integration of Soviet Émigrés and Their Organizations into the Jewish Communal World. Papers presented at the 1991 General Assembly.* N.Y.: Council of Jewish Federations, 1992, p. 11–14.

1991

Pavel Ilyin. Book Review: Blair A. Ruble. Leningrad: Shaping a Soviet City. Berkley: University of California Press, 1990.— *Soviet Geography*, January 1991, p. 58–60.

1990

Pavel Ilyin. Review Article: «Research on Small and Dispersed Ethnic Groups in the Soviet Union».— *Slavic Review*, Winter 1990, p. 643–647.

1988

V. M. Gokhman, P. M. Ilyin, G. M. Lappo. «Problems of Formation of Regional Settlement Systems in the USSR».— *Regional Development and Planning in India and the Soviet Union*, Moonis Raza, editor. New Delhi: Satvahar Publications, 1988, pp. 173–184.

1981

V. M. Gokhman, P. M. Il'yin, Yu. G. Lipets. «The Significance of Growth Poles in Regional Development».— *Soviet Geography: Review and Translation*, April 1981, pp. 255–268. (Trans. Theodore Shabad. From: *Izvestiya Akademii Nauk SSSR, seriya geograficheskyia*, 1979, No. 6.)

Wenjamin M. Gochman, Pawel M. Iljin, Juri G. Lipez. «Wachstumspole in der Regionalentwicklung».— *Geographische Berichte*, 101, 4/1981, s. 209–224. (Перевод из *Известия Академии наук СССР, серия географическая*, 1979, № 6)

П. М. Ильин (с соавторами). *Maailman talousmaantiedon oppikirja.* Toimitattanut V. P. Mzksakovski. [Экономическая география мира]. Moskova: Kustannusliike Progress, 1981. Глава «Sosialististen Neuvostotasavaltojen Liitto», c. 67–102. (In Finnish.)

1980

А. С. Ахиезер, П. М. Ильин. «Географическая оценка территории и развитие городов».— *Географические основы фромирования народно-хозяйственных комлексов и систем расселения (Тезисы докладов секции I VII съезда Географического общества СССР).* Ленинград: Геогр. об-во СССР, 1980, с. 125–127.

П. М. Ильин. «Географическая радиоигра «Путешествие по любимой Родине»». В кн. *Пути повышения эффективности устной и печатной пропаганды географических знаний (Тезисы докладов секции*

VII VII съезда Географического общества СССР). Ленинград: Геогр. об-во СССР, 1980, с. 29–33.

П. М. Ильин. «Смена ведущих функций города и ее влияние на динамику городского расселения». В кн.: *Некоторые проблемы урбанизации и градостроительства (социально-экономические аспекты)*. Под ред. А. С. Ахиезера, О. Н. Яницкого и др. М.: Секция социальных проблем Научного совета АН СССР по проблемам биосферы, 1980, с. 15–20.

1979

П. М. Ильин. *Функции городов и развитие сети городских поселений СССР*. М. — Киев: ИГАН СССР, СОПС УССР, 1979, 14 с.

Обзор: Э. А. Миленина, К. И. Морозова. *Типы поселений в районах нового освоения. Архитектура, районная планировка, градостроительство. Обзорная информация. Вып. 14*. М.: Госгражданстрой СССР, Центр научно-техн. информации по гражданскому строительству и архитектуре, 1984, с. 8–11.

П. М. Ильин (Совместно с А. Г. Артемьевой, В. П. Максаковским, С. Н. Раковским, Н. Н. Смидович, М. Г. Соловьевой). *The Economic Geography of the World*, V. P. Maksakovskiy, editor. Moscow: Progress Publishers, 1979. Глава «The Union of Soviet Socialist Republics», p. 64–98.

То же — на франц. языке (P. Iline). *Géographie économique du monde*. Sous la direction de V. Maksakovski. Moscou: Editions du Progrès, 1979. Глава «L'Union des Républiques Socialistes Soviétiques», p. 75–111.

То же — на арабском языке. [*Экономическая география мира*. Ред. В. П. Максаковский. М.: Изд-во «Прогресс», 1979. Глава «Союз Советских Социалистических Республик», 43 с.]

В. М. Гохман, П. М. Ильин, Ю. Г. Липец. «Значение фокусов роста в региональном развитии». *Известия Академии наук СССР, серия географичвская*, 1979, № 6, с. 33–44.

П. М. Ильин, М. И. Каган. «Внутригиродские и межселенные связи в крупных городах и городских агломерациях».—*Моделирование городских систем. Труды I школы-семинара*. М.: ВНИИ системных исследований, 1979, с. 22–28.

1978

А. С. Ахиезер, П. М. Ильин. «Об экологических закономерностях деятельности».—*Проблены взаимодействия общества и природы (Тезисы I Всесоюзной научной конференции)*. М.: Изд-во Моск. ун-та, 1978, с. 7–8.

П. М. Ильин. «О значимости административных функций для роста городов СССР».— *Урбанизация и формирование систем расселения*. М.: Моск. филиал Геогр. об-ва СССР, 1978, с. 71–77.

П. М. Ильин, редактор (ученый секретарь редколлегии). *Географические проблемы регионального развития и государственное планирование. Тезисы докладов советских участников Советско-Индийского симпозиума, Тбилиси—Баку, октябрь 1978 г.* Тбилиси: ИГ АН СССР, ИГ им. Вахушти АН Груз. ССР, ИГ АН Азерб. ССР, 147 с. (**В книге**: В. М. Гохман, П. М. Ильин, Ю. Г. Липец. «Значение фокусов роста в региональном развитии», с. 100–105.

П. М. Ильин, Г. А. Приваловская и др., редакторы. *Советско-Индийский симпозиум «Региональное развитие в системе государственного планирования» (Тбилиси—Баку, октябрь 1978 г.). Маршруты полевых заседаний.* Баку: «Элм», 1978, 26 с.

A. S. Achiezer. P. M. Iljin. O mechanizmie motywacyjnym migracji.— *Problemy migracji wewnetrznych w Polsce i ZSRR.* Red. A. Kukliński i A. Lukaszewicz. Warszawa: Państwowe Wydawnictwo Ekonomiczne, 1978, s. 237–240.

P. M. Iljin, L. T. Litwinenko. Omówienie dyskusji.— [Там же], с. 248–252.

1976

P. M. Ilin, W. W. Pokszyszewski. Problemy naukowe badania migracji wewnetrznych ludnosci ZSRR. *Przeglad geograficzny.* XLVIII, 3, 1976, s. 401–415.

В. В. Покшишевский, П. М. Ильин, редакторы. *Проблемы миграций населения в СССР.* М.: Моск. филиал Геор. об-ва СССР, 1976, 69 с. (**В книге**: А. С. Ахиезер, П. М. Ильин. «О мотивационном механизме миграции населения», с. 52–55.

П. М. Ильин, Л. Т. Литвиненко. «Обзор дискуссии», с. 62–66.

P. M. Ilyin, Editor (Secretary; with eds. V. P. Maksakovsky and L. S, Abramov). *Geographical Education, Geographical Literature and Dissemination of Geographical Knowledge. International Geography, 1976.* Moscow: XXIII International Geographical Congress, 1976, 152 p. (**In the book** P. M. Ilyin. «Traveling Across the Beloved Homeland — Geographical Radio Game for Soviet Schoolchildren». In: *Geographical Education, Geographical Literature and Dissemination of Geographical Knowledge. International Geography, 1976.* Moscow: XXIII International Geographical Congress, 1976, pp. 127–131.

П. М. Ильин, редактор (секретарь; совместно с ред. В. П. Максаковским и Л. С. Абрамовым). *Географическое образование, географическая литература и распространение географических знаний. Международная география, 1976.* М.: XXIII Международный географический конгресс, 1976. In Russian. 135 с. (**В книге**: П. М. Ильин. «Путешествие по любимой Родине» — географическая радиоигра для советских школьников». В кн.: *Географическое образование, географическая литература и распространение географических знаний. Международная география, 1976.* М.: XXIII Международный географический конгресс, 1976. In Russian. С. 112–115.

П. М. Ильин. *Русская равнина Белорусская ССР. Путеводитель для участников конгресса.* P. M. Iljin. *Russian Plain. The Byelorussian SSR.*

A guide for congress participants. P. Iline. *La Plaine Russe. La RSS de Biélorussie. Guide les participants du congrés.* Moscow: 23rd International Geographical Congress, 1976, 52 с. (in Russian: 1–18; in English: 19–34; in French: 35–52).

1975

A. S. Akhieyezer and P. M. Il'yin. «The Social Evaluation of a Territory Under Conditions of the Scientific-Technical Revolution».— *Soviet Geography: Review and Translation,* December 1975, pp. 255–268. (Trans. Theodore Shabad. From: *Izvestiya Akademii Nauk SSSR, seriya geograficheskyia,* 1975, No. 1.)

А. С. Ахиезер, П. М. Ильин. «Задачи разработки социальных оценок территории в условиях научно-технической революции».— *Известия Академии наук СССР, серия географичвская,* 1975, № 1, с. 86–92.

П. М. Ильин. Рецензия: Территориальные проблемы в социологическом исследовании (А. С. Ахиезер. Научно-Техническая революция и некоторые социальные проблемы производства и управления. М.: Наука, 1974).— *Известия Академии наук СССР, серия географичвская,* 1975, № 3, с. 152–154.

1974

А. А. Гербурт-Гейбович, П. М. Ильин, ред. *Природно-климатическое районирование и проблемы градостроительства (Доклады к конференции «Климат–город–человек»).* М.: Гидрометеоиздат, Моск. Отд., 1974, 163 с. (*В книге*: П. М. Ильин. «О динамике городского расселения в зависимости от природно-географических условий.» С. 9–16.

А. А. Гербурт-Гейбович, П. М. Ильин. Климат — город — человек.— *Известия Академии наук СССР, серия географичвская,* 1974, № 4, с. 48–55.

P. M. Il'in. «Geographisches Aspects der Ökologie des Manachen» — *Fachsektion Physische Geographie, Mitteilungsblatt Nr.* 3. Leipzig: Geographische Gesellshaft der DDR, 1974, s. 24–28

1972

П. М. Ильин. «О географии жилищного хозяйства» — *География сферы обслуживания.* Ред. В. В. Покшишевский. Вопросы географии. Сб. 91. М.: Мысль. 1972, с. 164–175.

1971

П. М. Ильин. *Экономическая оценка природных условий градостроительства в СССР (опыт разработки методики на материале объектов массового строительства).* Автореферат диссертации на соискание ученой степени кандидата географических наук. М.: Институт географии Академии наук СССР, 1971, 24 с.

П. М. Ильин. *Экономическая оценка природных условий градостроительства в СССР (опыт разработки методики на материале объектов массового строительства).* Диссертация на соискание ученой степени кандидата географических наук. М.: Институт географии Академии наук СССР, 1971, 150 с.

1970

П. М. Ильин. «Опыт экономической оценки природных условий градостроительства».— *Известия Академии наук СССР, серия географичвская*, 1970, № 6, с. 44–54.

1969

П. М. Ильин, Г. С. Приваловская. «Проблемы формирования производственно-территориальной структуры Обь-Иртышского левобережья».— *Известия Академии наук СССР, серия географичвская*, 1970, № 1, с. 66–74.

Translations

Translation from the Russian. «Diary of Tanya Savicheva, Leningrad, Decemver 1941 to May 1942» In: Patricia Heberer, *Children During the Holocaust*. Lanham, MD: AltaMira Press in association with USHMM, 2011, p. 54. [Pavel Ilyin is among translators' names on the reverse side of title.]

Ред. перевода (совместно с В. Алцканом): *Мемориальный Музей Холокоста США. Путеводитель по музею.* Wash. D.C.: United States Holocaust Memorial Museum, [2005], 16 с. [Фамилии редакторов перевода не указаны.]

Перевод: Роберт Гохстанд. «Стоимость земли в Москве в начале XX века». В кн.: Павел Ильин и Блэр А. Рубл, отв. редакторы. *Москва рубежа XIX и XX столетий. Взгляд в прошлое издалека.* М.: РОССПЭН, 2004, с. 89–130.

Перевод (совместно с М. Каган.): Блэр Рубл. «Новый облик города: политика собственности в Ярославле». В кн.: *Международная научно-практическая конференция: «Представительные органы местного самоуправления в современном мире». Доклады, тезисы выступлений, материалы дискуссий. (27–28 апреля 1992 года).* Ярославль, 1992, с. 95–125.

Перевод: Блэр А. Рубл. «Москва — Нью-Йорк: Архитектурные традиции в развитии городов на рубеже столетий». *Московский журнал*, 1992, № 2, с. 12–15.

Проектные работы в Гипрогоре (1960–1965)

Районная планировка Свердловской области. Участие в экономических разделах.

Районная планировка Горьковской области. Раздел «Машиностроение».

Районная планировка Мордовской АССР. Разделы «Население и города», «Машиностроение».

Районная планировка Орско-Халиловского промышленного района Оренбургской области. Разделы «Население и города», «Машиностроение».

Районная планировка Рязанской области. Автор проекта-экономист (гл. экономист проекта Г. Кузьмина).

Районная планировка Серово-Ивдельского промышленного района Свердловской области. Главный экономист проекта (автор проекта-архитектор В. И. Ванчугов, гл. инженер проекта В. И. Кольбах).

Районная планировка Игрим-Березовского промышленного района Тюменской области. Главный экономист проекта (автор проекта-архитектор В. И. Ванчугов).

Генеральный план города Ряжска Рязанской области, Автор проекта-экономист.

Генеральный план города Киржача Владимирской области. Автор проекта-экономист (автор проекта-архитектор И. А. Поляк).

Генеральный план города Усть-Кута Иркутской области. Автор проекта-экономист (автор проекта-архитектор Л. И. Мартынова).

Экспериментальный проект Северного промышленного района города Новгорода. Автор проекта (совм. с арх. Ю. В. Кратюк, инж. С. П. Леви, Л. Л. Челганским, М. И. Каган и др.).

Основы освоения и развития нефте-газоносных районов Тюменской области. Передварительна записка. Автор работы (совм. с арх. П. П. Джишкариани и др.)

Основы освоения и развития нефте-газоносных районов Тюменской области. Автор проекта (совм. с арх. П. П. Джишкариани и др.)